W9-AMP-390

Inside Microsoft®
SharePoint® 2010

Ted Pattison

Andrew Connell

Scot Hillier

David Mann

Microsoft Press titles may be purchased for educational, business, or sales promotional use. Online editions are also available for most titles (*http://my.safaribooksonline.com*). For more information, contact our corporate/institutional sales department: (800) 998-9938 or *corporate@oreilly.com*. Visit our website at *microsoftpress.oreilly.com*. Send comments to *mspinput@microsoft.com*.

Microsoft, Microsoft Press, ActiveX, Excel, FrontPage, Internet Explorer, PowerPoint, SharePoint, Webdings, Windows, and Windows 7 are either registered trademarks or trademarks of Microsoft Corporation in the United States and/or other countries. Other product and company names mentioned herein may be the trademarks of their respective owners.

Unless otherwise noted, the example companies, organizations, products, domain names, email addresses, logos, people, places, and events depicted herein are fictitious, and no association with any real company, organization, product, domain name, email address, logo, person, place, or event is intended or should be inferred.

This book expresses the author's views and opinions. The information contained in this book is provided without any express, statutory, or implied warranties. Neither the author, O'Reilly Media, Inc., Microsoft Corporation, nor their respective resellers or distributors will be held liable for any damages caused or alleged to be caused either directly or indirectly by such information.

Acquisitions and Development Editors: Martin DelRe and Kenyon Brown
Production Editor: Holly Bauer
Editorial Production: Custom Editorial Productions
Technical Reviewer: David Mann
Indexing: Fred Brown
Cover: Karen Montgomery
Compositors: Octal Publishing, Inc., and Nellie McKesson
Illustrator: Robert Romano

978-0-735-62746-8

This book is dedicated to Patrick Tisseghem, our dear friend and colleague, who passed away at the beginning of this project. Those who were fortunate enough to know Patrick remember him and his outgoing sense of humor, his knowing smile, and his ability to completely explain complex topics using simple concepts and examples.

Patrick, we all learned so much from knowing you and working with you. Many of your keen insights and clear explanations of SharePoint that you shared with us live on in this book. We miss you, all your blog readers miss you, and the entire SharePoint platform misses you as well.

Contents at a Glance

Table of Contents

What do you think of this book? We want to hear from you!

Microsoft is interested in hearing your feedback so we can continually improve our
books and learning resources for you. To participate in a brief online survey, please visit:

microsoft.com/learning/booksurvey

Foreword

With the recent release of SharePoint 2010, one of Microsoft's fastest growing products has gotten even hotter. SharePoint 2010 has not only become more popular among end users and IT pros, but it's also doing extremely well with developers. This is in part due to the significant advances in the platform, but also because of the great tooling that Visual Studio 2010 has introduced.

Platform capabilities and tooling combined make SharePoint one of the most compelling collaborative platforms in the market today; a platform where many projects seek out custom development. Platform capabilities and tooling, though, are just the foundation; to truly build boundless solutions using SharePoint requires a solid understanding of how you can apply those capabilities. And as you embark on your custom development projects with SharePoint, it's important to get the right training and insight into the platform to ensure you not only understand what you can exploit in SharePoint 2010 but also how you can build and deploy compelling solutions.

If you're picking up this book, you've probably got more than a casual interest in SharePoint; you're likely ready to begin or are already actively engaged in SharePoint development. SharePoint 2010 offers so much for the developer, ranging from sandboxed solutions, new data modeling and management capabilities, improved user experience programmability, workflow, line-of-business integration, security, to enterprise content management, and much, much more. And to provide you with a clear, concise breakdown of each of these areas and to help you build the professional-grade solutions you need to build, I can't think of anybody better than Ted, Andrew, Scot, and David to deliver this to you. No matter where you are in your SharePoint development career, *Inside Microsoft SharePoint 2010* provides you with a technical understanding that cuts across new features and functionality, giving you invaluable insight into SharePoint 2010.

As you make your way through this book and beyond, I hope you'll see and experience the great potential that lies within SharePoint 2010. For the developer, it represents a significant shift enabling you to more easily build and deploy great solutions on what is one of the best collaborative platforms on the market today. And in the true spirit of the *Inside* series, with this book you'll get a deep look into the innards of SharePoint 2010; it's one of the core books you'll keep on your shelf as a reference that will eventually become dog-eared and tabbed from overuse.

Enjoy *Inside SharePoint 2010*, and best of luck in your SharePoint development!

Steve Fox
Director, Developer & Platform Evangelism
Microsoft

Acknowledgments

There are so many people we need to thank for helping us create this manuscript. First, we would like to thank the Microsoft folks on the Developer Platform Evangelism (DPE) team, including Steve Fox, Paul Stubbs, Donovan Follette, Bruno Nowak, Chris Mayo, Roger Doherty, and Neil Hutson. They gave us our first opportunity to work with SharePoint 2010 when they hired us to write content for a SharePoint developer's workshop back in July of 2008. We would also like to thank Wouter van Vugt, the flying Dutchman, who contributed significantly to this project with his ruthless code samples, his unorthodox presentation styles, and his timely comic relief.

There are many others at Microsoft who deserve our thanks for reviewing slides, code samples, and chapters, including Mike Ammerlann, Rob Howard, Brad Stevenson, Mike Morton, Reza Chitsaz, Chris (CJ) Johnson, Ryan Duguid, Paul Andrew, Richard Riley, Mike Gannotti, Arpan Shah, John Durant, Doug Mahugh, Mauricio Ordonez, Elisabeth Olson, Kirk Evans, Pej Javaheri, Steve Tullis, Matthew Burnett, Javier Dalzell, Harneet Sidhana, Eilene Hao, Umesh Unnikrishnan, Boris Scholl, Maxim Lukiyanov, Jie Li, Johanna White, and Jon Flanders. There are also folks on the MSDN team who helped in countless ways, including Randall Isenhour, Uma Subramanian, Beck Andros, and Jean Philippe Bagel.

We would like to thank our fellow colleagues at Critical Path Training for their valuable insight and feedback during the project, including Maurice Prather, Asif Rehmani, Matthew McDermott, Chris Predeek, and Karine Bosch. A special thanks also goes to Meredith Connell, Marshall Butler, and Maggie Smith for keeping our company afloat as the authors constantly disappeared into their SharePoint VMs for days at a time.

We would like to thank the SharePoint MVP community past and present, whose collective output has taught the industry so much about the SharePoint platform. Our special thanks goes out to Melissa Travers, April Dalke, Dan Larson, Spencer Harbar, Rob Foster, Todd (T-Bag) Baginski, Rob Bogue, Dan Holme, Ben Robb, Andrew Woodward, Reza Alirezaei, Eric Shupps, Gary Lapointe, Jan Tielens, Tony Bierman, Natalya Voskresenskaya, Carsten Keutmann, Shane Young, Darrin Bishop, Renaud Comte, Mirjam van Olst, Jeremy Sublett, Loke Kit Kai, Todd Bleeker, Sahil Malik, Bill English, Joris Poelmans, Nick Swan, Matt Ranlett, Dave McMahon, Adam Buenz, Steve Smith, Stephen Cummins, Todd Klindt, John F. Holliday, Ton Stegeman, Chandima Kulathilake, Penelope Coventry, Chris O'Brien, Tobias Zimmergren, Waldek Mastykarz, Randy Drisgill, Jeremy Thake, Liam Cleary, Ludovic Lefort, Martin Harwar, Debbie Ireland, Brendon Schwartz, Paul Schaeflein, Becky Bertram, Wictor Wilen, Heather Solomon, Dustin Miller, Cornelius J. van Dyk, Bob Fox, and even the infamous Ben "Can you believe I'm still talking" Curry.

We would also like to thank everyone on the publishing side who made this book possible. Thanks to everyone at Microsoft Press and O'Reilly. This includes Ben Ryan, who helped us put together the original contract, and the production staff made up of Dan Fauxsmith, Sumita Mukherji, Holly Bauer, and Linda Allen. Special thanks goes out to Ken Brown, who had the challenging task of getting us to ship our chapters on schedule. If not for Ken and his cattle prod, Ted would no doubt still be writing and rewriting Chapter 5 trying to get the explanation of page ghosting just a tad more clear and concise.

—*Ted Pattison*

So many people go into writing a book, but I'd like to specifically call out a few of them who made a significant impact in my contributions to this book. I'd first like to thank my colleagues Ted Pattison and Scot Hillier, who poured so much of their knowledge into this work. I also want to thank my wife Meredith and children Steven and Kathryn for their patience. No authoring experience can happen without the full buy-in from your family! I would also like to specifically thank Ryan Duguid and Chris Johnson at Microsoft, who shared many conversations around Enterprise Content Management and SharePoint Server 2010 over the last few years. Their insight into a lot of the "why" and reasoning behind certain decisions by the product team dramatically helped my understanding of Enterprise Content Management in SharePoint Server 2010.

—*Andrew Connell*

Introduction

The purpose of this book is to help you design and develop custom business solutions for SharePoint 2010, which includes the two products SharePoint Foundation and SharePoint Server 2010. Our goal is to teach you how to create, debug, and deploy the fundamental building blocks such as Features, Pages, Web Parts, Site Columns, Content Types, Event Handlers, and Workflow Templates. Once you apply yourself and become comfortable developing with these building blocks, there's no limit to the types of applications and solutions you can create on the SharePoint 2010 platform.

Who This Book Is For

This book is written for experienced Windows developers who are proficient with Visual Studio, the Microsoft .NET Framework, and ASP.NET. The code samples in this book are written in C# and have been created to provide a comprehensive overview of the projects you can create for SharePoint 2010. Our primary audience for this book is software developers and architects looking for expert guidance on designing and developing business applications on this platform. Developers who are new to the SharePoint platform as well as experienced SharePoint developers will benefit from this book.

System Requirements

- You'll need the following hardware and software to build and run the code samples for this book: Microsoft Windows Server 2008 or Microsoft Windows Server 2008 R2.
    - The operating system can be installed natively or on a Virtual Machine (VM)
    - For a native installation, we recommend at least 4 GB of RAM
    - For an installation on a VM, we recommend 8 GB of RAM on most machines
- Microsoft SharePoint Foundation or SharePoint Server 2010
- Microsoft Visual Studio 2010
- Microsoft SharePoint Designer 2010
- Microsoft Office Visio 2010

Code Samples

All the code samples discussed in this book have been added to a single .zip archive named InsideSharePoint2010.zip. This .zip archive can be downloaded from the support page for this book at the following address:

http://www.CriticalPathTraining.com/books/InsideSharePoint2010

This support page also provides a list of errata as well as a reference to step-by-step instructions that you can use to build a VM that is identical to the VM we used to write and test all our sample projects.

You can also download the companion code from this book's catalog page at:

http://oreilly.com/catalog/9780735627468/

Support for This Book

Every effort has been made to ensure the accuracy of this book and the companion content. Microsoft Press provides support for books and companion content at the following website:

http://www.microsoft.com/learning/support/books/

You can also find a list of errata at the following website:

http://oreilly.com/catalog/9780735627468/

Questions and Comments

If you have comments, questions, or ideas regarding the book or the companion content, or questions that are not answered by visiting the sites above, please send them to Microsoft Press via email to mspinput@microsoft.com.

Chapter 1
SharePoint 2010 Developer Roadmap

Unless you've been hiding under a rock or programming in the clouds, you've probably noticed that Microsoft SharePoint technologies have become popular. Over the last few years, IT professionals throughout the industry—including many people at Microsoft—have been surprised by the accelerated adoption rate of SharePoint and its impressive sales revenue, which is over a billion dollars.

It is safe to say that SharePoint technologies have made it into the mainstream of software products used by companies and organizations around the world. Today, millions of people work with SharePoint technologies every day, including business users, power users, executives, site administrators, farm administrators, and professional developers.

Microsoft has released four versions of SharePoint technologies, which are listed in Table 1-1. Each SharePoint release has included an underlying core infrastructure product and a second product that adds business value to the infrastructure. The core infrastructure product has always been free to customers who already have licenses for the underlying server-side operating system, Microsoft Windows Server. Microsoft makes money on SharePoint technologies by selling customers server-side licenses as well as client access licenses (CALs).

TABLE 1-1 A Brief History of SharePoint

Year	Core Infrastructure Product	Business Value Product
2001	SharePoint Team Services	SharePoint Portal Server 2001
2003	Windows SharePoint Services 2.0	Microsoft SharePoint Portal Server 2003
2007	Windows SharePoint Services 3.0	Microsoft Office SharePoint Server 2007
2010	Microsoft SharePoint Foundation	Microsoft SharePoint Server 2010

SharePoint 2001 introduced an environment that allowed users to create sites, lists, and document libraries on demand based on a data-driven design. The implementation was based on a Microsoft SQL Server database that tracked the creation of sites and lists by adding records to a static set of database tables. This initial version of SharePoint had a couple of noteworthy shortcomings. First, it was cumbersome to customize sites. Second, the files uploaded to a document library were stored on the local file system of the front-end Web server, which made it impossible to scale out SharePoint Team Services sites using a farm of front-end Web servers.

SharePoint 2003 was the first version to be implemented on top of the Microsoft .NET Framework and ASP.NET. This version began to open new opportunities for professional developers looking to extend the SharePoint environment with Web Parts and event handlers. Also in this version, Microsoft altered the implementation for document libraries to store files inside a back-end SQL Server database, which made it possible to scale out SharePoint sites using a standard farm of front-end Web servers.

SharePoint 2007 introduced many new concepts to the underlying SharePoint architecture, including site columns, content types, and features and solution packages. Microsoft also improved the integration of SharePoint with ASP.NET, which made it possible for .NET developers to extend SharePoint sites by creating familiar ASP.NET components such as master pages, user controls, navigation providers, authentication providers, and custom *HttpModule* components.

SharePoint 2010 is the fourth and most recent release of SharePoint technologies. It includes Microsoft SharePoint Foundation and Microsoft SharePoint Server 2010. The goal of this chapter is to build your high-level understanding of SharePoint Foundation from the viewpoint of a professional developer. Along the way, you will learn how SharePoint Server 2010 extends SharePoint Foundation to add extra functionality and business value.

SharePoint Foundation

SharePoint Foundation introduces many changes to the core platform from SharePoint 2007. The improved user experience in the browser constitutes the most obvious change for experienced SharePoint users moving to SharePoint 2010. The SharePoint 2007 user interface experience is outdated. It wasn't designed to today's HTML standards, nor does it embrace any of the principles of Web 2.0. These limitations negatively impact accessibility and cross-browser functionality. The user experience of SharePoint 2007 can also be criticized for triggering unnecessary server-side postbacks and confusing page transitions.

SharePoint 2010 introduces a new AJAX-powered user interface that significantly improves the user experience. The pages in a SharePoint 2010 site eliminate unnecessary postbacks by communicating with the Web server using asynchronous JavaScript calls. SharePoint Foundation also eliminates potentially confusing page transitions using inline editing and modal dialogs. Finally, SharePoint Foundation enhances the user experience by introducing the server-side Ribbon, which allows the user to locate and execute a larger number of contextual commands without having to navigate away from the current page.

SharePoint Foundation includes a wealth of enhancements beyond user interface changes. Table 1-2 lists some of the new enhancements that will be most interesting to developers moving from SharePoint 2007. These topics are covered throughout the course of this book.

TABLE 1-2 Enhancements for Developers in SharePoint Foundation

Enhancement	Benefit
Service application architecture	Redesigned infrastructure to facilitate sharing of resources across Web applications and farms.
Windows PowerShell support	New support and capabilities for writing administrative scripts.
Feature versioning and upgrade	New support for versioning and upgrading features.
SharePoint Developer Tools for Visual Studio 2010	A first-class development experience for SharePoint developers (finally).
Sandboxed solutions	New support for deploying solution packages at site collection scope in a sandboxed environment.
New features for throttling lists and controlling query execution	Enhanced support for stabilizing the farm by prohibiting large, inefficient queries.
New events for sites, lists, and workflows	Additional events for developers to hook up event handlers.
LINQ to SharePoint provider	New support for writing LINQ query statements to access SharePoint list data.
REST-based access to SharePoint list items	New support for accessing SharePoint list data from across the network using REST-based Web service calls.
Client-side object model	Ability to leverage the SharePoint object model from across the network when programming with .NET, Silverlight, and JavaScript.
Enhanced support for integrating Silverlight applications	Rich support for deploying and versioning Silverlight applications within a SharePoint environment.
Claims-based security	New authentication support for leveraging external identity management systems and extending access control in SharePoint sites using custom claims.
Business Connectivity Services (BCS) and external lists	New support for creating read-write connections to back-end databases and line-of-business systems and exposing their data as lists within SharePoint sites.
.NET Assembly Connectors for BCS	Support for creating a custom component to integrate any data source with the BCS.

SharePoint Foundation Architecture

At its core, SharePoint Foundation is a provisioning engine—that is, its fundamental design is based on the idea of using Web-based templates to create sites, lists, and libraries to store and organize content. Templates are used to create both new websites and various elements inside a website, such as lists, pages, and Web Parts.

SharePoint Foundation is particularly helpful to companies and organizations faced with the task of creating and administering a large number of websites because it dramatically reduces the amount of work required. Someone in the IT department or even an ordinary business user can *provision* (a fancy word for create) a site in SharePoint Foundation in less than a minute by filling in a browser-based form and clicking the OK button. Creating a new page or a new list inside a site is just as easy.

SharePoint Foundation takes care of all the provisioning details behind the scenes by adding and modifying records in a SQL Server database. The database administrator doesn't need to create a new database or any new tables. The ASP.NET developer doesn't need to create a new ASP.NET website to supply a user interface. And the system administrator doesn't need to copy any files on the front-end Web server or configure any Internet Information Services (IIS) settings. It all just works. That's the magic of SharePoint.

The architecture of SharePoint Foundation was specifically designed to operate in a Web farm environment. Figure 1-1 shows a basic diagram of a simple Web farm with two front-end Web servers and a database server. In scenarios that have multiple front-end Web servers, a network load balancer is used to take incoming HTTP requests and to determine which front-end Web server each request should be sent to.

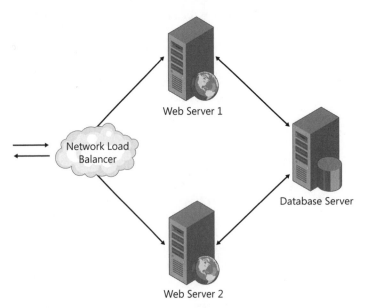

FIGURE 1-1 SharePoint Foundation is designed to scale out using a farm of front-end Web servers.

SharePoint Foundation and SharePoint Server 2010 are available only in 64-bit versions. They can be installed on a 64-bit version of Windows Server 2008 or Windows Server 2008 R2. When building a development environment, you also have the option of installing either SharePoint Foundation or SharePoint Server 2010 on a 64-bit version of a client operating system such as Windows 7 or Windows Vista.

SharePoint Foundation leverages IIS 7.0 on front-end Web servers to listen for incoming HTTP requests and to manage the server-side worker processes using the IIS application pool infrastructure. The runtime environment of SharePoint Foundation runs within a worker process launched from the IIS application pool executable, named w3wp.exe, as shown in Figure 1-2. You can see in Figure 1-2 that SharePoint Foundation is built on .NET Framework 3.5 and ASP.NET 3.5 with Service Pack 1.

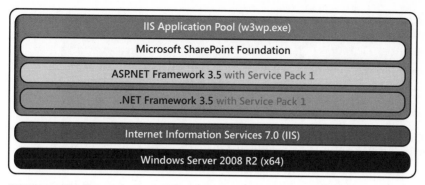

FIGURE 1-2 The SharePoint Foundation runtime loads into an IIS application pool running ASP.NET 3.5.

Recall that SharePoint 2007 was built on top of .NET 3.0. Although configuring front-end Web servers running SharePoint 2007 to support .NET 3.5 is possible, this task proved to be challenging for a number of reasons. Consequently, a large percentage of SharePoint 2007 development hasn't taken advantage of the programming techniques introduced in .NET 3.5. One nice aspect of moving to SharePoint 2010 is that this new version provides out-of-the-box support for valuable .NET 3.5 features such as AJAX, LINQ, and Silverlight. This book assumes that a healthy percentage of developers moving from SharePoint 2007 to SharePoint 2010 will be using these .NET 3.5 features for the first time.

You should also note that the initial release of SharePoint 2010 won't provide support for .NET 4.0. At the time of this writing, Microsoft has not yet made any announcements about when .NET 4.0 support will be integrated into either SharePoint Foundation or SharePoint Server 2010.

SharePoint Farms

Every deployment of SharePoint Foundation is based on the concept of a farm. Simply stated, a *SharePoint farm* is a set of one or more server computers working together to provide SharePoint Foundation functionality to clients. For simple scenarios, you can set up a SharePoint 2010 farm by installing and configuring everything you need on a single server computer. A SharePoint farm in a typical production environment runs SQL Server on a separate, dedicated database server and can have multiple front-end Web servers, as shown in Figure 1-3. As you will see later in this chapter, a farm can also run one or more application servers in addition to a database server and a set of Web servers.

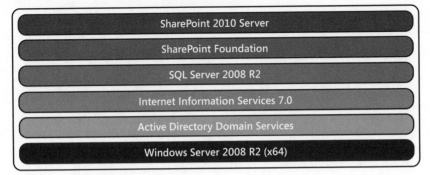

FIGURE 1-3 You can create a SharePoint development environment using a single server farm.

Each SharePoint farm runs a single SQL Server database known as the *configuration database*. SharePoint Foundation creates a configuration database whenever it creates a new farm in order to track important farm-wide information. For example, the configuration database tracks which front-end Web servers are associated with the farm as well as which users have been assigned administrative permissions within SharePoint Foundation at the farm level.

When creating a SharePoint development environment, it is best to install and configure SharePoint 2010 as a single-server farm. Remember that you have the option of installing SharePoint Foundation or SharePoint Server 2010 on a client operating system such as a 64-bit version of Windows 7. Building out your development environment using a 64-bit version of Windows 7 as the underlying operating system is the best approach if you must base your development environment on a client-side operating system.

If possible in your work environment, you should consider installing SharePoint Foundation or SharePoint Server 2010 on a 64-bit version of Windows Server 2008 or Windows Server 2008 R2. One option is to install a version of SharePoint 2010 on a native installation of Windows Server. Another popular option is to install a version of SharePoint 2010 on a virtual machine (VM). For example, you can install a 64-bit version of Windows Server 2008 R2 and configure Hyper-V. Hyper-V allows you to create a VM on which you can install a 64-bit version of Windows Server 2008 R2 and SharePoint Server 2010.

A key advantage of building a SharePoint development environment on a server-side operating system such as Windows Server 2008 R2 is that you can configure Active Directory Domain Services to provide a more realistic simulation of the networked environment that will be running in production. Figure 1-3 shows the layers of software we recommend that you install on a developer workstation you're configuring for SharePoint 2010 development.

As a SharePoint developer, you must remember that farms come in all different shapes and sizes. Although you will likely write and test your code on a single-server farm, that is probably not the type of farm in which your code will be deployed. It can be a big mistake to assume that your target SharePoint production environment is just like your development environment.

Many companies that are invested in SharePoint development categorize their farms into three different types. SharePoint developers write and debug SharePoint solutions in *development farms*. *Staging farms* simulate a more realistic environment and are used to conduct quality assurance testing on SharePoint solutions. For example, the servers in a staging farm should built without installing developer tools such as Microsoft Visual Studio 2010. Once a SharePoint solution has been thoroughly tested in a staging farm, it can be deployed in a *production farm*, where its functionality is made available to users.

SharePoint 2010 Central Administration

As a SharePoint developer, you must wear many hats. One hat you frequently wear is that of a SharePoint farm administrator. You should become familiar with the administrative site that SharePoint Foundation automatically creates for each farm. This administrative site is known as *SharePoint 2010 Central Administration*, and its home page is shown in Figure 1-4.

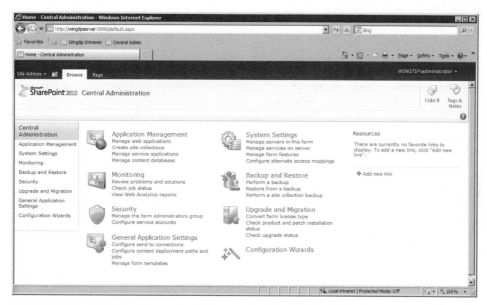

FIGURE 1-4 SharePoint developers should become familiar with SharePoint 2010 Central Administration.

Notice that Figure 1-4 shows the home page of SharePoint 2010 Central Administration in a farm with *only* SharePoint Foundation installed. If SharePoint Server 2010 is also installed, you'll see additional links to administrative pages that are not installed by SharePoint Foundation. Also note that SharePoint 2010 Central Administration is extensible. If you need to create a SharePoint solution for administrative purposes, you can integrate your work into SharePoint 2010 Central Administration by adding custom links and custom administration pages.

Scenario: Introducing Wingtip Toys

Many of the example configurations and code samples in this book are based on Wingtip Toys, a company that was fictitiously founded in 1882 by Henry Livingston Wingtip. Wingtip Toys has a long and proud history of producing the industry's most unique and inventive toys for people of all ages. Wingtip Toys has set up an intranet using SharePoint internally to provide a means of collaboration between its trinket design scientists, its manufacturing team, and its remote sales force. It has also erected an extranet using SharePoint to interact with partners and toy stores around the world. Finally, Wingtip Toys has decided to use SharePoint to create its Internet-facing site to advertise and promote its famous line of toys and novelties.

Web Applications

SharePoint Foundation is built on top of IIS 7.0 and relies on IIS websites to handle incoming HTTP requests. Therefore, you need to understand exactly what an IIS website really is.

An IIS website provides an entry point into the IIS Web server infrastructure. For example, the default website IIS creates automatically listens for incoming HTTP requests on port 80. You can create additional IIS websites to provide additional HTTP entry points using different port numbers, different IP addresses, or different host headers. In our scenario, we'll use host headers to create HTTP entry points for domain names such as *http://intranet.wingtip.com*.

SharePoint Foundation creates an abstraction on top of IIS that is known as a *Web application*. At a physical level, a Web application is a collection of one or more IIS websites configured to map incoming HTTP requests to a set of SharePoint sites. The Web application also maps each SharePoint site to one or more specific *content databases*. SharePoint Foundation uses content databases to store site content such as list items, documents, and customization information.

Warning: Don't Touch the SharePoint Databases

When developing for SharePoint Foundation, you're not permitted to directly access the configuration database or any of the content databases. For example, you must resist any temptation to write ADO.NET code that reads or writes data from the tables inside these databases. Instead, you should write code against the SharePoint Foundation programming APIs to reach the same goal, and leave it to SharePoint Foundation to access the configuration database and content database behind the scenes.

SharePoint Foundation uses ASP.NET 3.5 to extend the standard behavior of an IIS website. It does this by configuring IIS websites to run SharePoint-specific components in the ASP.NET pipeline, including a custom *HttpModule* and a custom *HttpHandler*. This integration with ASP.NET allows SharePoint Foundation to take control over every request that reaches an IIS website that has been configured as a SharePoint Web application.

Keep in mind that every SharePoint Web application runs as one large ASP.NET application. Consequently, SharePoint Foundation adds a standard ASP.NET web.config file to the root directory of each IIS website associated with a Web application. This high-level design can be counterintuitive for developers migrating to SharePoint Foundation from ASP.NET. A single SharePoint site is unlike an ASP.NET site because it can't have its own web.config file. That means a single web.config in SharePoint Foundation supplies configuration information for every site in a Web application. This is true even in scenarios where the number of sites in a Web application reaches into the hundreds or thousands.

A SharePoint farm typically runs two or more Web applications. The first Web application is created automatically and is used to run SharePoint 2010 Central Administration. You need at least one more Web application to create the sites that are used by typical users. The IT staff at Wingtip Toys decided to configure their production farm with three different Web applications used to reach employees, partners, and customers, as shown in Figure 1-5.

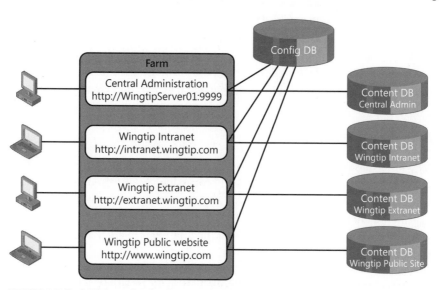

FIGURE 1-5 Each Web application has one or more content databases.

A key thing to remember about Web applications is that each one has its own independent security and authentication settings. This creates a valuable degree of flexibility because different sites in the same farm can be configured for access by different types of users.

The Wingtip IT staff configured the first Web application for intranet usage by requiring Integrated Windows authentication and by prohibiting anonymous access. They configured the second Web application for extranet usage by authenticating external users with a custom ASP.NET authentication provider. They configured the third Web application to allow anonymous access so that any user on the Internet could potentially access their public website anonymously.

The introduction of claims-based security support into SharePoint 2010 provides developers with new possibilities for configuring a Web application. One such possibility is the ability to outsource identity management to an identity service publicly available on the Internet, such as Windows Live ID. This approach gives developers the ability to track users for the purposes of security, auditing, and personalization but without the hassles of setting up a user database, storing credentials, and dealing with all the associated password management headaches.

The Wingtip IT staff configured the Web application for their public website to allow anonymous access but also to make logging into the site an available option. They configured a trust within the farm to the Windows Live ID service and then configured the Web application to use Windows Live ID as its identity provider. When customers attempt to log into the Wingtip public website, they are redirected to the Windows Live ID site and prompted to enter their Windows Live ID credentials. Once authenticated by Windows Live ID, the customer is then redirected back to the Wingtip public website with an established identity.

Service Applications

A SharePoint farm is often scaled by efficiently sharing resources across sites running in different Web applications and by offloading processing cycles from front-end Web servers to dedicated application servers. SharePoint 2007 provides a resource-sharing architecture based on Shared Service Providers (SSPs). However, SSPs are not ideal because they have no support in the core platform. They are part of the SharePoint Server 2007 product, and they don't support extensibility.

SharePoint Foundation introduces a new infrastructure for *service applications* that replaces the SSP architecture from SharePoint Server 2007. In SharePoint 2010, service applications are used to facilitate sharing resources across sites running in different Web applications and different farms. The new service application architecture also provides the means for scaling a SharePoint farm by offloading processing cycles from the front-end Web servers over to dedicated application servers.

A key benefit of this new architecture is that you can treat a service application as a pluggable component. Once you install and create a service application, you can configure it for several different deployment scenarios. In simple farms, an instance of the service application can run on each front-end Web server. In more complex farms, such as the one shown in Figure 1-6, a service application can be configured to run on a separate application server or in a farm of application servers.

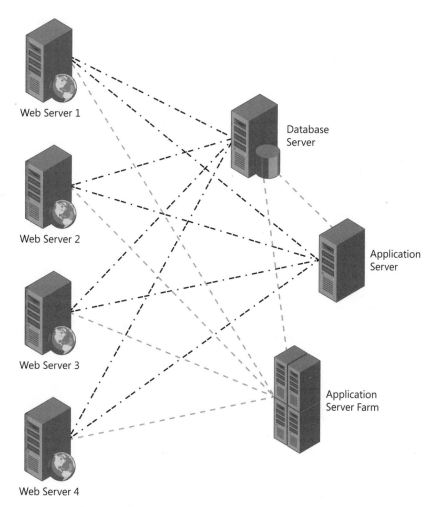

FIGURE 1-6 SharePoint farms run service applications in addition to Web applications.

A service application targeting SharePoint 2010 must be written to a specific set of requirements. For example, a service application must query the configuration database about its current deployment configuration and adjust its behavior accordingly.

When a service application runs across the network on a dedicated application server, it relies on a proxy component on the front-end Web server. The proxy component is deployed along with the service application and provides value by abstracting away the code required to discover where the service application lives on the network. The service application proxy component provides additional value by encapsulating the Windows Communication Foundation (WCF) code used to execute Web service calls on the target service application.

The proxy-based design of service applications provides flexibility in terms of deployment and configuration. For example, you can configure a proxy in one farm to communicate with a service application in another farm. The proxy simply consults the configuration database and discovers the correct address for the application server running the service application. The implication here is that the new service application architecture makes it much easier to share resources across farms while still controlling what services are made available and how they are consumed.

Four built-in service applications ship with SharePoint Foundation, as shown in Figure 1-7. When a new farm is created, SharePoint Foundation automatically creates and configures two important service applications: *Application Discovery and Load Balancer Service Application* and *Security Token Service Application*. The other two service applications built into SharePoint Foundation are *Business Data Connectivity Service* and *Usage and Health data collection*, which you can create manually or by running the Farm Configuration Wizard available in the SharePoint 2010 Central Administration site.

FIGURE 1-7 SharePoint Foundation includes four standard service applications.

Unlike the SSPs in SharePoint 2007, service applications were designed with developer extensibility in mind. Any SharePoint developer with the proper knowledge and incentive can create a service application that can plug into any SharePoint 2010 farm.

Even if you never find a good reason to create your own service application, you need to understand how service applications work and how they fit into the high-level architecture of SharePoint Foundation. For example, SharePoint Server 2010 delivers a good deal of its functionality through service applications. Furthermore, many other groups within the Office team at Microsoft have built their own service applications that can be installed and configured in a SharePoint 2010 farm.

SharePoint Server 2010

SharePoint Server 2010 is really just a piece of software that's been written to run on SharePoint Foundation. Every installation of SharePoint Server 2010 begins with an installation of SharePoint Foundation. After installing SharePoint Foundation, the installation for SharePoint Server 2010 then installs its own templates, components, and service applications.

Microsoft sells different editions of SharePoint Server 2010 using several different SKUs. SharePoint Server 2010 Standard Edition supplies core functionality such as enterprise search, content publishing, user profiles, and My Sites. SharePoint Server 2010 Enterprise Edition extends the standard edition by adding extra functionality for security, business intelligence, managed metadata, and rich integration with Microsoft Office client applications.

To help you understand some of the additional functionality SharePoint Server 2010 layers on top of SharePoint Foundation, Table 1-3 lists the service applications that SharePoint Server 2010 installs as well as the edition of SharePoint Server 2010 required to use each service application.

TABLE 1-3 SharePoint Server 2010 Service Applications

Service Application	Edition
Access Services	Enterprise
Application Registry Services	Standard
Excel Services	Enterprise
Managed Metadata Service	Standard
PerformancePoint Services	Enterprise
Search Service	Standard
Secure Store	Standard
State Service	Standard
User Profile Service	Standard
Visio Graphics Service	Enterprise
Web Analytics Service	Enterprise
Word Automation Services	Standard

Sites

Now that you understand the high-level architecture of a SharePoint farm, you need to know how SharePoint Foundation creates and manages sites within the scope of a Web application. Let's start by asking a basic question: What exactly is a SharePoint site?

This question has many possible answers. For example, a site is an endpoint that is accessible from across a network such the Internet, an intranet, or an extranet. A site is also a storage container that allows users to store and manage content such as list items and documents. In addition, a site is a customizable entity that allows privileged users to add pages, lists, and child sites. Finally, a site is a securable entity whose content is accessible to a configurable set of users.

As a developer, you can also think of a site as an instance of an application. For example, the scientists at Wingtip Toys use a SharePoint site to automate the business process of approving a new toy idea. When Wingtip scientists have new ideas for a toy, they describe their ideas in Microsoft Word documents, which they then upload to a document library in the site. The approval process is initiated whenever a scientist starts a custom approval workflow on one of those documents.

A site can also be used as an integration point to connect users to back-end data sources such as a database application or a line-of-business application such as SAP or PeopleSoft. The Business Connectivity Services that ship with SharePoint Foundation make it possible to establish a read-write connection with a back-end data source. One valuable aspect of the Business Connectivity Services architecture is that this external data often appears to be a native SharePoint list. There are many user scenarios and developer scenarios in which you can treat external data just as you would treat a native SharePoint list.

Site Collections

Every SharePoint site must be provisioned within the scope of an existing Web application. However, a site can't exist as an independent entity within a Web application. Instead, every site must also be created inside the scope of a site collection.

A *site collection* is a container of sites. Every site collection has a top-level site. In addition to the top-level site, a site collection can optionally contain a hierarchy of child sites. Figure 1-8 shows a Web application with three site collections. The first site collection contains just a top-level site. The second contains one level of child sites below the top-level site. The third contains a more complex hierarchy with three levels.

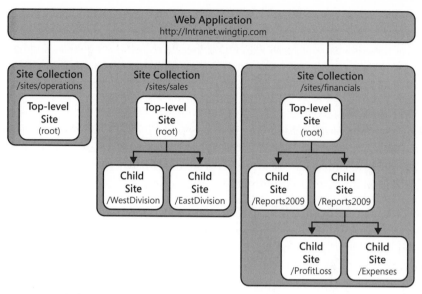

FIGURE 1-8 Each site collection has a top-level site and can optionally contain a hierarchy of child sites.

When a company begins using SharePoint Foundation or SharePoint Server 2010, one of the first questions that comes up is how to partition sites across site collections. For example, should you create one big site collection with lots of child sites, or should you create many individual site collections? This decision is usually best made after thinking through all the relevant issues discussed in the next few paragraphs. You must gain an understanding of how partitioning sites into site collections affects the scope of administrative privileges, security boundaries, backup and restore operations, and site design.

You could be asking yourself why the SharePoint Foundation architecture requires this special container to hold its sites. For starters, site collections represent a scope for administrative privileges. If you've been assigned as a site collection administrator, you have full administrative permissions within any existing site and any future site created inside that site collection.

Think about the requirements of site management in a large corporation that's provisioning thousands of sites per year. The administrative burden posed by all these sites is going to be more than most IT staffs can deal with in a timely manner. The concept of the site collection is important because it allows the IT staff to hand off the administrative burden to someone in a business division who takes on the role as the site collection owner.

Let's walk through an example. The Wingtip Toys IT staff is responsible for provisioning new site collections, and one of the Wingtip business divisions submits a request for a new site. Imagine the case where the Wingtip Sales Director has put in a request to create a new Team site for his sales staff. A Wingtip IT staff member would handle this request by creating a new site collection with a Team site as its top-level site.

When creating the new site collection, the Wingtip IT staff member would add the Wingtip Sales Director who requested the site as the site collection owner. The Wingtip Sales Director would have full administrative privileges inside the site collection and could add new users, lists, and pages without any further assistance from the Wingtip IT staff. The Wingtip Sales Director could also add child sites and configure access rights to them independently of the top-level site.

A second advantage of site collections is that they provide a scope for membership and the configuration of access rights. By design, every site collection is independent of any other site collection with respect to what security groups are defined, which users have been added as members, and which users are authorized to perform what actions.

For example, imagine that the Wingtip IT staff has provisioned one site collection for the Sales department and a second site collection for the Accounting department. Even though some users within the Accounting department have administrative permissions within their own site collection, there's nothing they can do that will affect the security configuration of the Sales site collection. SharePoint Foundation sees each site collection as an island with respect to security configuration.

A third reason for site collections is that they provide a convenient scope for backup and restore operations. You can back up a site collection and later restore it with full fidelity. The restoration of a site collection can take place in the same location where backup was made. Alternatively, a site collection can be restored in a different location—even inside a different farm. This technique for backing up a site collection and restoring it in another location provides one possible strategy for moving sites and all the content inside from one farm to another.

A final motivation for you to start thinking about in terms of site collections is that they provide a scope for many types of site elements and for running custom queries. For example, the server-side object model of SharePoint Foundation provides you with the capability to run queries that span all the lists within a site collection. However, there is no query mechanism in the SharePoint server-side object model that spans across site collections. Therefore, if your application design calls for running queries to aggregate list data from several different sites, it makes sense to add sites to the same site collection when they contain lists that must be queried together.

Imagine a case in which the West Division of the Wingtip Sales team has four field offices. The Wingtip Sales Director could create a child site for each field office below a site that was created for the West Division. Now assume that each child site has a Contacts list that is used to track sales leads. By using programming techniques shown later in this book, you can execute queries at the scope of the West Division site that would aggregate all the Contacts items found across all of its child sites. You could execute the same query at a higher scope and get different results. For example, if you executed the same query scoped to the top-level site, it would aggregate all the Contacts found throughout the site collection, including both the West Division and the East Division.

Customizing Sites

SharePoint Foundation provides many user options for configuring and customizing sites. If you're logged into a site as the site collection owner or as a site administrator, you can perform any site customization options supported by SharePoint Foundation. If you're logged into a site without administrative privileges in the role of a contributor, however, you won't have the proper permissions to customize the site. Furthermore, if you're logged in as a contributor, SharePoint Foundation uses *security trimming* to remove the links and menu commands that lead to pages with functionality for which you don't have permissions.

If you're logged into a standard Team site as a site administrator, you should be able to locate and drop down the Site Actions menu in the top-left corner of the page. This menu provides commands that allow you to edit the current page; to create new pages, lists, and child sites; to configure security; and to navigate to the Site Settings page shown in Figure 1-9.

FIGURE 1-9 The Site Settings page is accessible to site administrators in any site.

The Site Settings page provides links to pages that allow you to perform various administrative and customization tasks. Notice that the Site Settings page for a top-level site contains one section for Site Administration and a second section for Site Collection Administration. The Site Settings page for child sites doesn't include the section for Site Collection Administration.

You can see in Figure 1-9 that there are several sections of links, including Users and Permissions, Look and Feel, Galleries, and Site Actions, which provide links to various other administrative pages for the current site. If you're new to SharePoint Foundation, you should take some time to explore all the administrative pages accessible through the Site Settings page. Also keep in mind that Figure 1-9 shows only the links on the Site Settings page of a Team site running within a SharePoint Foundation farm. If the site were running in a SharePoint Server 2010 farm, there would be additional links to even more site administration pages that are not part of the standard SharePoint Foundation installation.

Creating and Customizing Pages

The support for wiki page libraries and Web Parts is an enabling aspect of SharePoint Foundation. Business users with no experience in Web design or HTML can quickly add and customize Web pages.

Although SharePoint 2007 supports wiki page libraries, this support has been significantly enhanced in SharePoint Foundation. An example of the increased support is evident when you create a standard Team site. As part of the provisioning process, SharePoint Foundation automatically creates a new wiki library at the path of SitePages off the root of the site, and it adds a wiki page named Home.aspx. It additionally configures Home.aspx to be the home page of the site, so it becomes the first page users see when navigating to the site.

Customizing the home page is simple for any user who has the proper permissions. The user can enter edit mode using either the Site Actions menu or the Ribbon. Once in edit mode, the user is free to simply type text or copy and paste from another application. The Insert tab in the Ribbon also makes it easy for the user to add tables, links, and images.

Web Part technology also plays a prominent role in page customization. Web Parts are based on the idea that developers supply a set of visual components that users can add and move around in their pages. Every site collection has a Web Part Gallery, which contains a set of Web Part template files. This set of Web Part template files determines which types of Web Parts can be added to pages within the site collection.

Although earlier versions of SharePoint technologies supported Web Parts, they were not as flexible as SharePoint Foundation because Web Parts could be added only to Web Part pages. SharePoint Foundation now makes it possible to add Web Parts anywhere inside a wiki page. When you're editing the content of a wiki page, you can place the cursor wherever you'd like and add a new Web Part using the Insert tab in the Ribbon. The new Web Part appears inline along with your other wiki content. This inline Web Part capability, combined with the wiki editing experience, can go a long way toward making SharePoint sites look less boxy—a common complaint about previous versions.

Creating and Customizing Lists

The Site Actions menu provides several different commands for creating new pages and new lists, such as New Page, New Document Library, and New Site. If you click the More Options command in the Site Actions menu, SharePoint Foundation displays the Create dialog shown in Figure 1-10. The SharePoint Foundation Create dialog provides a user interface built using Silverlight, which allows a user to filter through the available templates for creating pages, lists, and child sites. Figure 1-10 shows a filtered view of the templates available for creating tracking lists in the Create dialog.

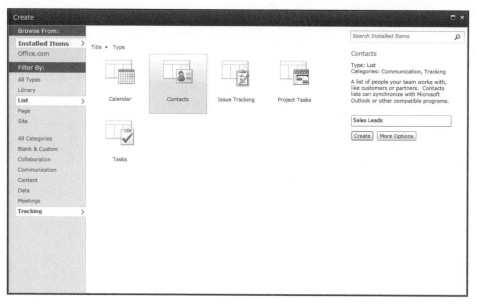

FIGURE 1-10 The SharePoint Foundation Create dialog is implemented using a Silverlight application.

In addition to list templates, the standard collaboration features of SharePoint Foundation also include templates for creating several different types of document libraries. Besides the standard document library type, there are also more specialized document library types for wiki page libraries, picture libraries, and InfoPath form libraries.

What's appealing to SharePoint users is that once they create a new list, it's immediately ready to use. SharePoint Foundation provides instant gratification by including page templates as part of the list template itself, making it possible to create each new list and document library with a set of pages that allow users to add, view, modify, and delete items and documents.

Once a list has been created, SharePoint Foundation gives a user the flexibility to further customize it. SharePoint Foundation provides a List Settings page for each list and document library. Figure 1-11 shows a typical List Settings page. It provides a set of links to secondary pages that allow the user to modify properties of a list such as its title and description and to configure other important aspects of the list, including versioning, workflow, and security permissions. The List Settings page also provides links to add and manage the set of columns behind the list.

List Information

Name:	CustomList1
Web Address:	http://intranet.wingtip.com/Lists/CustomList1/AllItems.aspx
Description:	

General Settings	Permissions and Management	Communications
Title, description and navigation	Delete this list	RSS settings
Versioning settings	Save list as template	
Advanced settings	Permissions for this list	
Validation settings	Workflow Settings	

Columns

A column stores information about each item in the list. The following columns are currently available in this list:

Column (click to edit)	Type	Required
Title	Single line of text	✔
Created By	Person or Group	
Modified By	Person or Group	

Create column
Add from existing site columns
Column ordering
Indexed columns

Views

A view of a list allows you to see a particular selection of items or to see the items sorted in a particular order. Views currently configured for this list:

View (click to edit)	Default View	Mobile View	Default Mobile View
All Items	✔	✔	✔

Create view

FIGURE 1-11 The List Settings page allows you to modify list properties and to add columns.

SharePoint Foundation provides many built-in list templates to track information about common business items such as tasks, contacts, and scheduled events. For business scenarios in which the list data that needs to be tracked doesn't conform to a built-in list template, SharePoint Foundation makes it easy for a user to create a custom list with a unique set of columns for these ad hoc situations.

SharePoint Foundation provides a list template named Custom List. When you create a new list from this template, it will initially contain a single column named Title. A user can add columns with just a few mouse clicks. Each added column is based on an underlying field type.

SharePoint Foundation supplies a rich set of built-in field types for columns whose values are based on text, numbers, currency, dates, and yes/no values. In Chapter 7, "Lists and Events," you'll see that you can also extend SharePoint Foundation by developing a custom field type for scenarios in which you need to store column values in the content database that need custom validation logic or specialized rendering instructions.

SharePoint Designer 2010

Microsoft SharePoint Designer 2010 is a specialized site customization tool. It is a rich desktop application that often makes customizing a site easier than when done through the browser. Not only is SharePoint Designer 2010 free, but the product is also significantly different from and better than SharePoint Designer 2007.

Figure 1-12 shows the redesigned user interface of SharePoint Designer 2010. Significant changes were made to simplify the user's view of a SharePoint site. Gone are the sites that show just a hierarchy of folders and files. The new user interface structures the elements of a site into logical collections of site objects such as Lists and Libraries, Workflows, Master Pages, and Subsites. A site object named All Files shows the old view of folders and files that will be familiar to users moving from SharePoint Designer 2007.

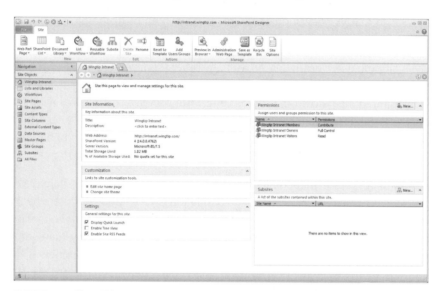

FIGURE 1-12 SharePoint Designer 2010 is a specialized tool for site customization.

SharePoint Designer 2010 is primarily designed to assist users in the role of site collection owner or site administrator. The tool makes it quick and easy to examine the properties and structure of a site and to perform common site tasks such as adding security groups and configuring permissions. Many users will also prefer the experience of SharePoint Designer 2010 over the browser when it comes to creating new lists and adding columns.

SharePoint Designer 2010 also allows a user to perform site customizations that aren't possible through the browser. The capability to create and customize workflows using a new set of workflow designers provides a great example. Using SharePoint Designer 2010, an experienced user can create and design complex workflows on targets such as sites, lists, and document libraries. SharePoint Designer 2007 had severe problems with creating reusable workflows. Fortunately, SharePoint Designer 2010 has overcome these problems.

Workflows created with SharePoint Designer 2010 can be reused across lists within the same site collection. These workflows can also be exported and reused across site collections, Web applications, and farms. As you'll see in Chapter 11, "Creating and Developing Workflows," you can export a workflow created with SharePoint Designer 2010 and then import it into Visual Studio 2010.

Site Customization vs. SharePoint Development

In one sense, SharePoint Foundation lessens the need for professional software developers because it empowers users to create and customize their own sites. In minutes, a user can create a SharePoint site, add several lists and document libraries, and customize the site's appearance to meet the needs of a particular business situation. An identical solution that has all the rich functionality that SharePoint Foundation provides out of the box would typically take an ASP.NET development team weeks or months to complete.

In another sense, SharePoint Foundation provides professional developers with new and exciting development opportunities. As with any other framework, the out-of-the-box experience with SharePoint Foundation takes you only so far. At some point, you'll find yourself needing to create custom list types and write code for custom SharePoint components such as Web Parts, event handlers, and workflows. What is attractive about SharePoint Foundation as a development platform is that it was designed from the ground up with developer extensibility in mind.

As you begin to design software for SharePoint 2010, it is critical that you differentiate between *customization* and *development*. SharePoint Foundation is very flexible for users because it was designed to support high levels of customization. As we've pointed out, you no longer need to be a developer to build a complex and highly functional website. Today, many sophisticated users are capable of customizing SharePoint sites for a large number of business scenarios. Site customization has its limitations, however. SharePoint Foundation records every site customization by modifying data within a content database, whether a new list is created or an existing list is customized with new columns and views. All types of site customization that can be performed using SharePoint Designer 2010 are recorded this way.

The fact that all site customization is recorded as a modification to the content database is both a strength and a weakness for SharePoint Foundation. It is a strength because it provides so much flexibility to users and site administrators doing ad hoc customizations. It is a weakness from the perspective of a professional software developer because customization changes are hard to version and can also be hard or impossible to make repeatable across site collections and farms.

Think about a standard ASP.NET development project in which all the source files you're working with live within a single directory on your development machine. Once you've finished the site's initial design and implementation, you can add all the site's source files to a source control management system such as Team Foundation Server.

By using a source control management system, you can formalize a disciplined approach to deploying and updating an ASP.NET site after it has gone into production. You can also elect to push changes out to a staging environment where your site's pages and code can be thoroughly tested before they are used in the production environment.

As a developer, you should ask yourself the following questions: How do I conduct source control management of customization changes? How do I make a customization change to a list definition or a page instance and then move this change from a development environment to a staging environment and finally to a production environment? How do I make a customization change within a site and then reuse it across a hundred different sites? Unfortunately, these questions have tough answers, and usually you'll find that a possible solution isn't worth the trouble.

Fortunately, as a developer you can work at a level underneath the SharePoint Foundation customization infrastructure. To be more specific, you can work with the low-level source files to create underlying templates for items such as pages and lists. These low-level source files don't live inside the content database; instead, they live within the file system of the front-end Web server.

Working at this level is complex and has a steep learning curve. Even so, this low-level approach lets you centralize source code management and have a more disciplined approach to code sign-off when moving functionality from development to staging to production. This approach also makes versioning and reuse of code far more manageable across multiple sites, Web applications, and farms.

For the remainder of this book, we differentiate between customization and development according to these criteria. SharePoint site customizations are updates to a site accomplished by making changes to the content database, generally through the Web browser or SharePoint Designer 2010. A site customization never requires touching the front-end Web server.

SharePoint development, on the other hand, involves working with farm solutions that include files that must be deployed to the file system of the front-end Web server. In Chapter 2, "SharePoint Foundation Development," we introduce SharePoint solutions and discuss best practices for how to package a development effort for deployment within a SharePoint 2010 farm.

Windows PowerShell Boot Camp for SharePoint Professionals

SharePoint 2010 is the first version of SharePoint technologies for which Microsoft supports administration through Windows PowerShell scripts. In SharePoint 2007, farm administrators use a command-line utility named stsadm.exe to run interactive commands from the console window and to write MS-DOS-style batch file scripts to automate common administrative tasks such as creating, backing up, or restoring a new site collection.

SharePoint Foundation still installs stsadm.exe, but it is primarily included to support backward compatibility with scripts migrating from earlier versions. Microsoft now recommends using the new Windows PowerShell support for writing, testing, and executing scripts that automate the same types of administrative tasks that you can accomplish using stsadm.exe, plus a whole lot more.

The Windows PowerShell support for SharePoint Foundation adds a new required skill for every farm administrator and every developer moving from SharePoint 2007 to SharePoint 2010. You're now required to be able to read, write, and execute Windows PowerShell scripts to automate tasks such as creating a new Web application or a new site collection.

Today, scores of SharePoint farm administrators and SharePoint developers have no prior experience in Windows PowerShell. After all, a SharePoint 2007 environment is a place where the squeaky wheel gets the grease. Who has time to learn about something they can't use in their day-to-day activities? It is likely that many of these SharePoint professionals won't learn about Windows PowerShell until they are forced to in their move to SharePoint 2010.

Given the expected percentage of readers without any prior experience with Windows PowerShell, we decided to conclude Chapter 1 with a fast and furious Windows PowerShell boot camp. Our goal here is to get you up to speed on Windows PowerShell so that you can start reading, writing, executing, and debugging Windows PowerShell scripts. So fasten your seat belt.

Learn Windows PowerShell in 21 Minutes

Working with Windows PowerShell is much easier than writing MS-DOS-style batch files. It's easier because the Windows PowerShell scripting language treats everything as an object. You can create and program against .NET objects as well as COM objects. Furthermore, Windows PowerShell has first-rate support for calling out to EXE-based utilities and passing parameters to execute specific commands.

There are two common ways in which you can use Windows PowerShell. First, you can execute commands interactively using the Windows PowerShell console window. Second, you can write scripts to automate administration tasks. Then you can execute these scripts either on demand or through some type of scheduling mechanism.

Let's start by getting familiar with the Windows PowerShell console window. You can launch the Windows PowerShell console window from the following path in the Windows Start menu.

Start\All Programs\Accessories\Windows PowerShell\Windows PowerShell

When the Windows PowerShell console appears, you should type and execute the following three commands interactively.

1. Type **cd** and then press Enter. This sets the current location to the root of the C:\ drive.

2. Type **cls** and then press Enter. This clears the console window.

3. Type **2 + 2** and then press Enter. This performs a mathematical calculation and displays the result.

If you followed these steps correctly and executed each of the three commands, your console window should look like the one in Figure 1-13.

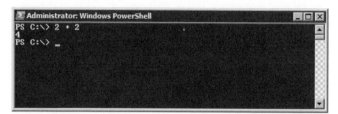

FIGURE 1-13: You can execute commands interactively from the Windows PowerShell console window.

Congratulations! You've just completed your first lesson. Now you know how to execute a command interactively from the Windows PowerShell console window. You simply type the command at the cursor in the Windows PowerShell console window and press the Enter key.

Windows PowerShell is based on reusable libraries containing functions known as *cmdlets* (pronounced "command lets"). Cmdlets have names that follow the convention of a common verb followed by a noun. For example, the built-in Windows PowerShell libraries provide a cmdlet named *Get-Process*, which returns a collection of objects representing the Windows processes running on the current machine.

```
PS C:\> Get-Process
```

Handles	NPM(K)	PM(K)	WS(K)	VM(M)	CPU(s)	Id	ProcessName
599	0	108	300	3		4	System
2683	6161	85248	84996	124	0.39	1648	dns
568	63	16240	30584	169	1.28	3888	explorer
588	48	29492	41536	191	1.17	848	iexplore
146	21	22168	28552	97	0.25	1680	inetinfo
1805	231	30220	32364	243	2.00	580	lsass
765	74	98828	79176	740	2.64	2892	OWSTIMER
270	22	64564	60460	569	0.83	3432	powershell
791	82	167088	98088	-1604	4.11	2368	ReportingServicesService
733	597	278316	153224	-1592	3.97	2024	sqlservr
977	135	173372	180504	1511	4.94	2176	w3wp
773	123	161220	164464	1485	3.36	5112	w3wp
270	31	25052	17860	496	0.14	2568	WSSADMIN

Pipelining is an important concept to understand when executing cmdlets. The basic idea is that every cmdlet returns an object or a collection of objects. Pipelining allows you to take the results of one cmdlet and pass it to a second cmdlet. The second cmdlet can run and then pass its results to a third cmdlet, and so on. You create a pipeline by typing a sequence of cmdlets separated by the | (pipe) character.

```
cmdlet1 | cmdlet2 | cmdlet3
```

Let's examine a common scenario in which you need to create a pipeline of two cmdlets to filter a collection of objects. First you call *Get-Process* to return a collection of objects, and then you use pipelining to pass this collection of objects to the *Where-Object* cmdlet.

```
PS C:\> Get-Process | Where-Object {$_.ProcessName -like "w*"}

Handles  NPM(K)   PM(K)     WS(K) VM(M)    CPU(s)    Id ProcessName
-------  ------   -----     ----- -----    ------    -- -----------
    977     135  173372    180504  1511      4.94  2176 w3wp
    773     123  161220    164464  1485      3.36  5112 w3wp
    270      31   25052     17860   496      0.14  2568 WSSADMIN
```

The *Where-Object* cmdlet takes a predicate expression enclosed in curly braces as a parameter. Inside these curly braces, you can use $_ to refer to an object as it's being filtered. The predicate expression in this example is *{$_.ProcessName -like "w*"}*. The filter returns all processes whose process name starts with "w".

Windows PowerShell cmdlets such as *Where-Object* use standard Windows PowerShell comparison operators. You should memorize these operators because you'll be using them regularly as you work with Windows PowerShell. Table 1-4 lists some commonly used Windows PowerShell comparison operators.

TABLE 1-4 Commonly Used Windows PowerShell Comparison Operators

Operator	Purpose
-lt	Less than
-le	Less than or equal to
-gt	Greater than
-ge	Greater than or equal to
-eq	Equal to
-ne	Not equal to
-like	Like using wildcard matches
-notlike	Not like using wildcard matches

You should understand that Windows PowerShell comparison operators that work with strings are case insensitive by default. However, these operators can be made case sensitive by adding a *c* immediately after the hyphen. For example, *-ceq* represents the case-sensitive *equal-to* operator.

Writing Windows PowerShell Scripts

Now that you've seen how to execute cmdlets from the Windows PowerShell console window, it's time to move on to Windows PowerShell scripting. Windows PowerShell scripts are text files that have an extension of .ps1. You can create and edit a Windows PowerShell script using any text editor, including notepad.exe.

Before you can begin writing and testing Windows PowerShell scripts, you must adjust the Windows PowerShell script execution policy on your developer workstation. The reason for this step is that Windows PowerShell is configured out of the box to prohibit or to prompt the user during script execution. On a developer workstation, it's common to disable the default execution constraints so that you can write and test scripts without security errors. You make this adjustment by calling the *Set-ExecutionPolicy* cmdlet from the Windows PowerShell console to set the current machine's execution policy to *"bypass"*.

```
Set-ExecutionPolicy "bypass"
```

Once you've correctly adjusted the Windows PowerShell execution policy, you can write your first script. Open notepad.exe and type in the following one-line script.

```
Write-Host "Hello World"
```

Now you need to save the file for the script with a .ps1 extension. First, create a new directory named Scripts on your local C:\ drive. Next, save your new Windows PowerShell script file as c:\Scripts\Script1.ps1. Now that you've saved the Windows PowerShell script file with a .ps1 extension, you can execute the script to test your work.

Let's first execute the script through the Windows PowerShell console window. In the console window, move to the new directory by executing *Set-Location c:\Scripts*. Now you can execute the script by typing **.\Script1.ps1** and pressing Enter. When you do this, you should be able to see the message *Hello World* in the Windows PowerShell console window.

Now let's create a Windows batch file so that you can execute the script without having to use the Windows PowerShell console window. Just create a new text file named RunIt.bat in the same directory as Script1.ps1, and call powershell.exe and pass the *-Command* parameter with the following syntax to execute the script.

```
powershell.exe -Command "& {.\Script1.ps1}"
pause
```

Notice that this example batch file also added a *pause* operation at the end. This can be handy because it keeps the MS-DOS console open so that you can see the output of your Windows PowerShell script.

Finally, you should learn how to directly execute a Windows PowerShell script without any assistance from an MS-DOS batch file. If you right-click on a Windows PowerShell script such as Script1.ps1 in Windows Explorer, you'll see a menu command with the caption *Run with PowerShell*. If you execute this command, the Windows operating system takes care of executing the Windows PowerShell script for you.

Executing Windows PowerShell scripts by using the *Run with PowerShell* command is quick and easy, but it doesn't leave the Windows PowerShell console window open when it's done. If you like using this technique but you still want to see the Windows PowerShell console window afterward, you can simply add the *Read-Host* cmdlet at the bottom of your script.

```
Write-Host "Hello World"
Read-Host
```

The Windows PowerShell Integrated Scripting Environment (ISE)

Although you can use any text editor you'd like to write Windows PowerShell scripts, you should prefer to use a powerful new utility, the *Windows PowerShell Integrated Scripting Environment (ISE)*, which is included with the Windows operating system. The Windows PowerShell ISE is shown in Figure 1-14.

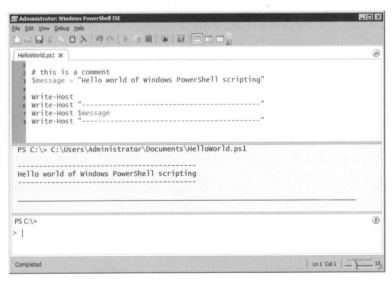

FIGURE 1-14 You should write Windows PowerShell scripts using the Windows PowerShell Integrated Scripting Environment (ISE).

SharePoint Foundation installs the Windows PowerShell runtime but doesn't automatically install the Windows PowerShell ISE. You need to explicitly install the Windows PowerShell ISE on your development workstation. In Windows Server 2008 and Windows Server 2008 R2, you enable the Windows PowerShell ISE feature through Server Manager. With Windows 7, you install the Windows PowerShell ISE through the Windows Control Panel.

The Windows PowerShell ISE will be immediately familiar to anyone with experience in Visual Studio. You can type a script in the top window and then press the F5 key to execute the script in debug mode. The Windows PowerShell ISE allows you to debug by setting breakpoints and to single-step through your code. Once you've launched the Windows PowerShell ISE, type the following script into the top window and then press F5.

```
$sum1 = 2 + 2
$sum2 = 3 + 4
$sum3 = $sum1 + $sum2
Write-Host $sum3
```

This example shows how to create a new variable in a Windows PowerShell script. You simply create a new variable name, which begins with the $ character. You don't need to define variables before you use them, as you do in C#. Instead, you just create a variable when you begin using it.

Now, let's write a Windows PowerShell control of flow construct. In this case, we create a new string array using the proper Windows PowerShell syntax and then write a *foreach* loop to enumerate each string.

```
$band = "Paul", "John", "George", "Ringo"
foreach($member in $band) {
  Write-Host $member
}
```

One aspect of Windows PowerShell that will instantly appeal to .NET developers is that you can create and program against any .NET object. For example, imagine you want to create an object from the *DateTime* class of the .NET Framework. You do this by executing the *New-Object* cmdlet and passing the class name and initialization values as parameters.

```
$date = New-Object -TypeName System.DateTime -ArgumentList @(1882,7,4,0,0,0)
$message = "Wingtip Toys, Inc. was founded on " + $date.ToLongDateString()
Write-Host $message
```

The preceding script produces the following output.

```
Wingtip Toys, Inc. was founded on Tuesday, July 04, 1882
```

In addition to creating new .NET objects, Windows PowerShell allows you to call the static methods and static properties of classes in the .NET Framework. You do this by typing the namespace-qualified class name in square brackets, like this: *[System.DateTime]*. After you type the class name, you add the `::` operator (two colons) and then the call to a static member.

```
$today = [System.DateTime]::Today
Write-Host $today.ToLongDateString()
Write-Host $today.ToString("MM/dd/yy")
Write-Host $today.AddDays(100).ToString("MMMM d")
```

If you're feeling nostalgic, you can even use Windows PowerShell to create and program against COM objects. For example, let's say you want to write a Windows PowerShell script that launches Internet Explorer and navigates to a specific URL. The Windows operating system provides a built-in COM interface that allows you to launch and control Internet Explorer.

```
$ie = New-Object -ComObject "InternetExplorer.Application"
$ie.Navigate("http://intranet.wingtip.com")
$ie.Visible = $true
```

The SharePoint PowerShell Snap-in

Windows PowerShell installs a set of core libraries containing cmdlets such as *Write-Host*, *Get-Process*, and *Where-Object*. Environments like SharePoint Foundation add their own custom cmdlet library by installing a Windows PowerShell snap-in. When you install SharePoint Foundation, a core Windows PowerShell snap-in named *Microsoft.SharePoint.PowerShell* is installed. However, you have to ensure that *Microsoft.SharePoint.PowerShell* is loaded before you begin to call its cmdlets.

SharePoint Foundation provides a specialized version of the Windows PowerShell console known as the *SharePoint 2010 Management Shell*. You can launch the SharePoint 2010 Management Shell from a shortcut that SharePoint Foundation adds to the Windows Start menu.

All Programs\Microsoft SharePoint 2010 Products\SharePoint 2010 Management Shell

The main difference between the standard Windows PowerShell console window and the SharePoint 2010 Management Shell console has to do with which Windows PowerShell providers get loaded automatically. More specifically, the SharePoint 2010 Management Shell automatically loads the SharePoint provider named *Microsoft.SharePoint.PowerShell* while the standard Windows PowerShell console does not. In general, you can't always rely on *Microsoft.SharePoint.PowerShell* being loaded automatically, so you need to learn how to load it explicitly within a Windows PowerShell script.

Let's say you've just launched the standard Windows PowerShell console window and you attempt to execute one of the cmdlets built into SharePoint Foundation, such as *Get-SPWebApplication*. The call to this cmdlet will fail unless you've already loaded the SharePoint PowerShell snap-in *Microsoft.SharePoint.PowerShell*. Before calling the *Get-SPWebApplication* cmdlet, you need to load the SharePoint Foundation PowerShell snap-in using the *Add-PSSnapin* cmdlet.

```
Add-PSSnapin Microsoft.SharePoint.PowerShell
Get-SPWebApplication
```

Executing these two cmdlets in sequence displays the current collection of Web applications for the current farm excluding the Web application for SharePoint 2010 Central Administration.

```
DisplayName                   Url
-----------                   ---
Wingtip Intranet              http://intranet.wingtip.com/
Wingtip Extranet              http://extranet.wingtip.com/
Wingtip Public Web site       http://www.wingtip.com/
```

One thing to keep in mind is that a call to *Add-PSSnapin* will fail if the SharePoint snap-in is already loaded. Therefore, you might want to play it safe and check to see whether the snap-in is already loaded before attempting to load it.

```
$snap = Get-PSSnapin | Where-Object {$_.Name -eq 'Microsoft.SharePoint.Powershell'}
if ($snap -eq $null) {
  Add-PSSnapin Microsoft.SharePoint.Powershell
}
```

Of course, if you just want to get rid of the error message, you can get the same effect with less typing by calling *Add-PSSnapin* using the *ErrorAction* parameter with a value of *SilentlyContinue*.

```
Add-PSSnapin Microsoft.SharePoint.PowerShell -ErrorAction "SilentlyContinue"
```

Now let's write a Windows PowerShell script to create a new Web application. You can do this by calling the *New-SPWebApplication* cmdlet. The call requires quite a few parameters.

```
Add-PSSnapin Microsoft.SharePoint.PowerShell -ErrorAction "SilentlyContinue"

$name = "Wingtip Testing Web App"
$port = 1001
$hostHeader = "intranet.wingtip.com"
$url = "http://intranet.wingtip.com"
$appPoolName = "SharePoint Default Appl Pool"
$appPoolAccount = Get-SPManagedAccount "WINGTIP\SP_WorkerProcess"

New-SPWebApplication -Name $name -Port $port -HostHeader $hostHeader -URL $url
                -ApplicationPool $appPoolName
                -ApplicationPoolAccount $appPoolAccount
```

Notice that the call to the *New-SPWebApplication* cmdlet in the preceding script breaks across multiple lines for clarity. When you write scripts, however, you must place a call to a cmdlet and all its parameters on a single line.

As you can imagine, writing and executing scripts like this can save quite a bit of time in a production farm because the need to perform the same tasks manually through SharePoint 2010 Central Administration is eliminated. Scripts like this also provide a great way to create consistency in how you create Web applications across farms.

We'll finish with one more example. Let's write a script to create a new site collection in the Web application we made earlier, which has a Team site as its top-level site. You can accomplish this by calling the *New-SPSite* cmdlet.

```
Add-PSSnapin Microsoft.SharePoint.PowerShell -ErrorAction "SilentlyContinue"

$title= "Wingtip Dev Site"
$url = "http://intranet.wingtip.com:1001"
$owner = "WINGTIP\Administrator"
$template = "STS#1"

New-SPSite -URL $url -Name $title -OwnerAlias $owner -Template $template
```

When you create a new site collection using the *New-SPSite* cmdlet, you must specify the URL and title and provide a user account to be configured as the site collection owner. You can also specify a template using the *Template* parameter, which is applied on the top-level site. In this example, a template of *STS#1* has been applied to create the top-level site as a standard Team site.

Now we've written a script to create a new site collection. The first time you run it, it works great. But what happens when you run it a second time? The second attempt to call the *New-SPSite* cmdlet fails because a site collection already exists at the target URL.

During development, there's a common scenario in which you must continually delete and re-create a site to effectively test and debug your code. Before deleting a site collection, your script should check to see whether a target site collection already exists at the target URL by using the *Get-SPSite* cmdlet. If the site collection already exists, you can delete it with the *Remove-SPSite* cmdlet.

```
Add-PSSnapin Microsoft.SharePoint.PowerShell -ErrorAction "SilentlyContinue"

$title= "Wingtip Dev Site"
$url = "http://intranet.wingtip.com:1001"
$owner = "WINGTIP\Administrator"
$template = "STS#1"

# delete target site collection if it exists
$targetSite = Get-SPSite | Where-Object {$_.Url -eq $url}
if ($targetSite -ne $null) {
  Remove-SPSite -Identity targetSite -Confirm:$false
}

# create new site collection
New-SPSite -URL $url -Name $title -OwnerAlias $owner -Template $template
```

Remember that cmdlets such as *New-SPSite* return objects that you can program against. For example, imagine you want to update the title of the top-level site after the site collection has been created. A site collection object exposes a *RootWeb* property that allows you to access the top-level site. The site object provides a *Title* property you can modify with a new title. You must call the site object's *Update* method to write your changes back to the content database.

```
Add-PSSnapin Microsoft.SharePoint.PowerShell -ErrorAction "SilentlyContinue"

$title= "Wingtip Dev Site"
$url = "http://intranet.wingtip.com:1001"
$owner = "WINGTIP\Administrator"
$template = "STS#1"

# delete target site collection if it exists
$targetSite = Get-SPSite | Where-Object {$_.Url -eq $url}
if ($targetSite -ne $null) {
  Remove-SPSite -Identity targetSite -Confirm:$false
}

$sc = New-SPSite -URL $url -Name $title -OwnerAlias $owner -Template $template
$site = $sc.RootWeb
$site.Title = "My New Site Title"
$site.Update
```

You've just seen an example of writing code against the server-side object model of SharePoint Foundation. Unfortunately, the Windows PowerShell ISE isn't able to provide IntelliSense in the same manner as Visual Studio does. However, the Windows PowerShell ISE still has valuable editing and debugging features that are easy to learn and use. You should become familiar with this tool because it provides a quick way to script out changes to the local farm in your development workstation or in a production environment.

Conclusion

SharePoint Foundation represents different things to different people. To users, SharePoint Foundation provides the infrastructure for Web-based business solutions that scale from simple team-collaboration sites to enterprise-level applications. To site collection administrators, SharePoint Foundation provides the capability to customize sites by adding lists and document libraries and by customizing many aspects of a site's appearance through the browser or by using a customization tool such as SharePoint Designer 2010.

To a company's IT staff, SharePoint Foundation provides a scalable and cost-effective solution for provisioning and managing a large number of sites in a Web farm environment. It also provides a reliable mechanism to roll out applications and to version these applications over time.

To a developer, SharePoint Foundation represents a rich development platform that adds value on top of the underlying ASP.NET platform. Developers build software solutions targeting SharePoint Foundation using features and components such as Web Parts, event handlers, and workflows. Now that you've studied the SharePoint developer roadmap and made it through our PowerShell boot camp, you're ready to dive into the fundamentals of SharePoint Foundation development.

Chapter 2
SharePoint Foundation Development

Did you notice that Chapter 1 doesn't include a single example using Microsoft Visual Studio? That omission was intentional. We want to make sure you first understand the fundamental concepts and terminology of Microsoft SharePoint Foundation and site customization before diving into a development environment. After all, it doesn't make sense to start writing code before you know what's possible without writing code.

Now we're ready to launch Visual Studio 2010 and start writing code. In this chapter, we're going to create several Visual Studio projects to demonstrate the fundamental development techniques for SharePoint Foundation. We'll do a few quick warm-up exercises by creating console applications that program against the server-side object model. After that, we'll concentrate on the central topic of this chapter: developing a SharePoint solution in Visual Studio.

Developer productivity takes a giant step forward in SharePoint 2010 because of a powerful new set of tools known as the SharePoint Developer Tools for Visual Studio 2010. These tools provide project templates and project item templates explicitly designed for SharePoint Foundation development. The SharePoint Developer Tools are valuable because they manage and hide so many of the tedious details of developing in SharePoint Foundation.

Although the SharePoint Developer Tools represent one of the most significant enhancements to the SharePoint development platform, we're going to hold off delving into them until Chapter 3, "SharePoint Developer Tools in Microsoft Visual Studio 2010." In this chapter, we create Visual Studio projects based on standard console applications and class libraries. This approach will show you the essential aspects of SharePoint Foundation development. It will also give you the background you need to fully appreciate what the Visual Studio 2010 SharePoint Tools are doing for you behind the scenes.

The Server-Side Object Model

The core server-side object model of SharePoint Foundation is served up through an assembly named *Microsoft.SharePoint.dll*. Once you reference this assembly within a Visual Studio 2010 project, you can start programming against the classes in the server-side object model, such as *SPSite*, *SPWeb*, and *SPList*.

In SharePoint 2007, developers generally referred to the public classes in the *Microsoft.SharePoint* assembly as the "object model." Nobody felt the need to qualify the term by saying "server-side" object model because there was only one object model. SharePoint Foundation introduces a new client-side object model. Therefore, we must now differentiate between the two models using the terms *server-side object model* and *client-side object model*. In this chapter, we focus on the server-side object model. In Chapter 10, "Client-Side Programming," we concentrate on the client-side object model.

There are two initial requirements for a Visual Studio project that programs against the server-side object model using the *Microsoft.SharePoint* assembly. First, the project must be configured to use .NET Framework 3.5 as its target framework. You have to be careful because Visual Studio 2010 uses a default value of .NET Framework 4.0 for many of the built-in project templates. The second requirement is that your project must have a platform target setting that is compatible with a 64-bit environment, which is essential for properly loading the *Microsoft. SharePoint* assembly.

Another critical requirement for any application or component that is programmed against the server-side object model is that the application or component must be deployed and run on a front-end Web server or application server in a SharePoint farm. This issue doesn't usually come up when you're creating standard SharePoint components such as Feature Receivers, event receivers, Web Parts, and workflow templates because these component types are deployed using SharePoint solutions, which make it possible to install and execute them on all front-end Web servers in a SharePoint farm.

You can also create client applications with Visual Studio 2010 that program against the server-side object model. For example, you can create a standard console application that uses the server-side object model to access a site and the elements inside the site, such as lists and items. However, you must keep in mind that any client application that depends on the *Microsoft.SharePoint* assembly can be run only when launched on a Web server in a SharePoint farm.

The key point here is that you won't likely encounter real-world scenarios that call for creating client applications that use the server-side object model. Even so, creating simple console applications that program against the *Microsoft.SharePoint* assembly can be useful because it gives you a quick and easy way to write and test code as you begin learning the server-side object model. Furthermore, these types of applications will run without issue on any SharePoint 2010 developer workstation that's been configured as a single-server farm.

Creating the Hello World Console Application

Let's start by creating the traditional Hello World application. Launch Visual Studio 2010 and create a new project named *HelloSharePoint* based on the Console Application project template. Make sure you create the new project based on .NET Framework 3.5 and not .NET Framework 4.0. After creating the project, you can verify this setting by navigating to the Application tab of the Project Properties dialog and inspecting the Target framework property, as shown in Figure 2-1.

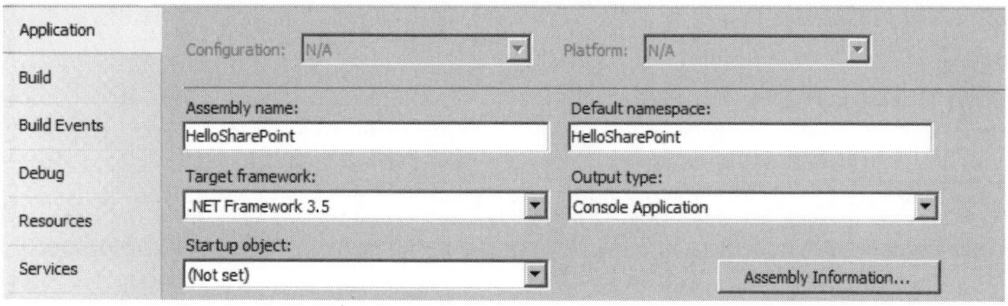

FIGURE 2-1 Visual Studio 2010 projects that use the server-side object model must target .NET Framework 3.5.

After you've verified that your project has the correct Target framework setting, you must navigate to the Build tab of the Project Properties dialog and change the Platform target setting to a value that is compatible with 64-bit applications. The default Platform target setting for a new console application is x86, which causes the application to load as a 32-bit application instead of a 64-bit application, causing strange and misleading error messages when the application attempts to load and use the *Microsoft.SharePoint* assembly. Make sure you set the Platform target property for your console application to a value of either x64 or Any CPU, as shown in Figure 2-2.

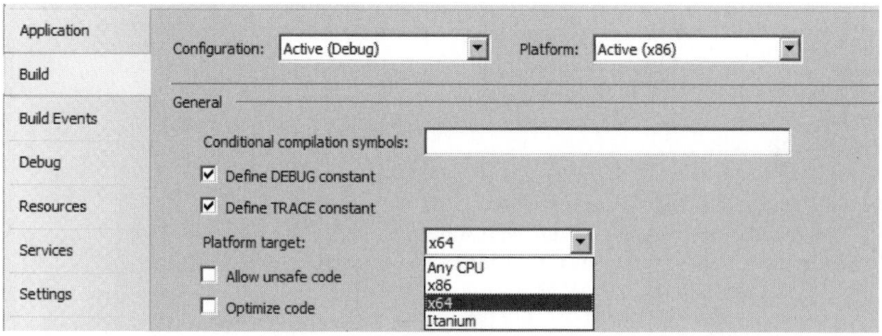

FIGURE 2-2 A console application that loads the *Microsoft.SharePoint* assembly should have a Platform target setting of either x64 or Any CPU.

Now that you've properly configured the console application's project settings, you can add a project reference to the *Microsoft.SharePoint* assembly, as shown in Figure 2-3. Once you've added this reference, you can begin programming against the SharePoint server-side object model.

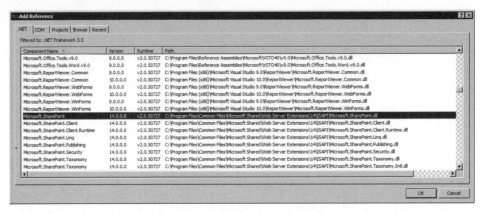

FIGURE 2-3 You must reference the *Microsoft.SharePoint* assembly to access the server-side object model.

Examine the code for the *HelloSharePoint* console application shown in Listing 2-1. This code demonstrates how to program against commonly used classes defined inside the *Microsoft.SharePoint* namespace, such as *SPSite*, *SPWeb*, and *SPList*.

LISTING 2-1 A Windows console application accesses a SharePoint site through the server-side object model.

```
using System;
using Microsoft.SharePoint;

namespace HelloSharePoint {
  class Program {
    static void Main() {
      const string siteUrl = "http://intranet.wingtip.com";
      using (SPSite siteCollection = new SPSite(siteUrl)) {
        SPWeb site = siteCollection.RootWeb;
        foreach (SPList list in site.Lists) {
          if (!list.Hidden) {
            Console.WriteLine(list.Title);
          }
        }
      }
    }
  }
}
```

The code in Listing 2-1 creates a new *SPSite* object with a URL pointing to a specific site collection on the local farm. A console application should use this technique to gain an entry point into the server-side object model. Next, the code accesses the *SPSite* object's *RootWeb* property to gain access to the top-level site within the current site collection. Finally, the code enumerates through all the lists in this site using a *foreach* loop and writes the *Title* property value of each nonhidden list to the console window.

When you create *SPSite* objects using the *new* operator, you must dispose of them when you're done using them. The reason for this is that *SPSite* objects allocate unmanaged resources behind the scenes and consume a significant amount of unmanaged memory. If you create *SPSite* objects with the *new* operator in your code and you don't properly dispose of them, your code will leak memory and can cause serious performance problems in a production farm. As a rule of thumb, when you create *SPSite* objects using the *new* operator, you must properly dispose of them either by creating them within a *using* construct or by making an explicit call to the *Dispose* method exposed by the *SPSite* class.

Now that you've written your first application that leverages the server-side object model, you can test it to make sure it works. If you press the F5 key to start the application in debug mode, the application will run and complete without pausing, making it difficult to see what is being displayed to the console window because the item disappears almost as soon as it is displayed.

If you start the application using the Ctrl+F5 keyboard combination, the application goes into standard execution mode instead of debug mode. In standard mode, the application pauses with the console window remaining open after the code has run, so you can see whatever the code has written to the console window. If you want to run the application in debug mode and still see output in the console window, you should either set breakpoints in your code or add a call to *Console.ReadLine* at the end of the *Main* method to pause the application and keep the console window open after the code completes its execution.

Enabling the SharePoint Developer Dashboard

A new infrastructure component that has been added to SharePoint 2010 is the *Developer Dashboard*. The Developer Dashboard is a user interface component built into SharePoint Foundation that displays diagnostic information that can be useful to developers and to farm administrators in diagnosing problems with the farm. Figure 2-4 shows the Developer Dashboard and some of the diagnostic information it displays about the current request.

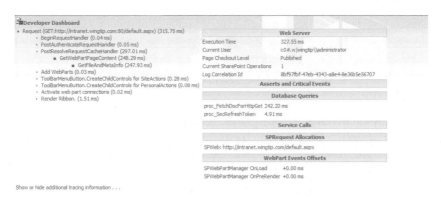

FIGURE 2-4 SharePoint Foundation provides the Developer Dashboard as a built-in diagnostics component.

By default, the Developer Dashboard is disabled. A quick and easy way to enable and disable the Developer Dashboard is by writing a console application that configures a few farm-wide properties through the server-side object model. Inside the *Microsoft.SharePoint.Administration* namespace is the class *SPWebService*, which exposes the *ContentService* property. The *ContentService* property exposes another property, *DeveloperDashboardSettings*, which holds a reference to an object of type *SPDeveloperDashboardSettings*. By accessing this object, you can enable the Developer Dashboard on a farm-wide basis by updating two properties: *DisplayLevel* and *TraceSettings*. Doing so causes the Developer Dashboard to display at the bottom of every page farm-wide.

```
using System;
using Microsoft.SharePoint;
using Microsoft.SharePoint.Administration;

namespace EnableDeveloperDashboard {
  class Program {
    static void Main() {
      SPDeveloperDashboardSettings settings =
        SPWebService.ContentService.DeveloperDashboardSettings;
      settings.DisplayLevel = SPDeveloperDashboardLevel.On;
      settings.TraceEnabled = true;
      settings.Update();
    }
  }
}
```

After you've successfully enabled the Developer Dashboard, you probably want to figure out how to disable it so that it doesn't appear at the bottom of every page. You just need to modify the preceding code. Simply update the *DisplayLevel* property with a value of *SPDeveloperDashboardLevel.Off* instead of *SPDeveloperDashboardLevel.On*. Once you've made this change, rerun your console application to disable the Developer Dashboard.

Developing SharePoint Solutions

You've already seen how to leverage the server-side object model in a Visual Studio project by adding a reference to the *Microsoft.SharePoint* assembly. Up to this point, we've used examples based on console applications so that we could focus on the server-side object model with a minimal amount of complexity. Now it's time to start developing SharePoint solutions.

When developing for SharePoint 2010, you're required to package and deploy your development efforts using a *SharePoint solution*. At the physical level, a SharePoint solution is a set of files from a development effort that are compressed into a single CAB file known as a *solution package*. The file name for a solution package must have an extension of .wsp.

The strategy of packaging and distributing each SharePoint solution as a single self-contained file is important because it leads to an easier and less error-prone approach to deploying and updating a custom development effort in one or more SharePoint farms.

Solution packages were introduced in SharePoint 2007. However, SharePoint 2007 allows you to deploy a solution package only at the farm level. SharePoint 2010 provides greater flexibility. You can deploy a solution package in SharePoint 2010 as a farm solution, which is consistent with how deployment works in SharePoint 2007, or as a sandboxed solution, which reduces the scope of deployment from the level of the farm to that of a single site collection.

When you plan to develop a new SharePoint solution, you should consider whether you'll ever want to deploy the resulting solution package as a sandboxed solution. If you do, you must learn how to create a SharePoint solution that can operate within the restrictions of the sandbox. In Chapter 4, "Sandboxed Solutions," we examine sandboxed solutions in greater depth and answer questions about why, when, and how to use them. Until then, we'll focus on developing SharePoint solutions that will be deployed only as farm solutions.

Developing a Solution for Wingtip Toys

Imagine that you're a developer working at Wingtip Toys. Chris Sells, the Wingtip Sales Director, has asked you to develop a SharePoint solution to assist his salespeople by automating the creation of a new list dedicated to tracking incoming sales leads. Your mission is to build a SharePoint solution that includes a feature to automate the creation of this new list for tracking sales leads.

Developing a SharePoint Solution Using a Class Library Project

You typically begin developing a SharePoint solution by creating a new Visual Studio project. The project will contain the source files for your SharePoint solution and should be configured to build a solution package as its output. The project should also contain integrated commands that allow Visual Studio to interact with the SharePoint Foundation to install and deploy the project's output solution package for testing.

For the remainder of this chapter, we'll develop a SharePoint solution using a standard class library project. The main goal of this exercise is to build your theoretical understanding of things like feature definitions and solution packages. This exercise will also give you an opportunity to improve your ability to write Windows PowerShell scripts and to integrate them with Visual Studio 2010.

Just keep in mind that the approach we're using in this chapter—creating a class library project to develop a SharePoint solution—is something you probably won't do in the real world.

Starting in Chapter 3, we'll begin using the approach you'll use in your actual projects targeting SharePoint 2010. This effort will involve creating new projects to develop solutions for SharePoint 2010 using the SharePoint Developer Tools for Visual Studio 2010.

The companion code that accompanies this chapter contains a class library project named WingtipDevProject1. You can see the high-level structure of this project by examining Figure 2-5, which shows a view of the project in Solution Explorer.

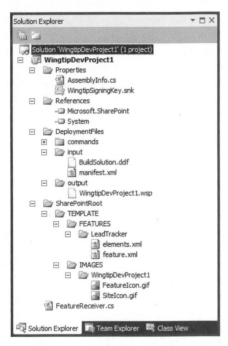

FIGURE 2-5 WingtipDevProject1 is a class library project created to develop a SharePoint solution.

The sample project WingtipDevProject1 contains the type of source files you typically add into a Visual Studio project when developing a SharePoint solution. WingtipDevProject1 has been developed for a SharePoint solution containing custom image files, XML definitions, and C# code compiled into a .NET assembly. To understand why the project is structured in this fashion, you must first understand the purpose and structure of the SharePoint root directory.

The SharePoint Root Directory

The fundamental architecture of SharePoint Foundation relies on a set of template files that are stored in a special directory on the local file system of each front-end Web server. In SharePoint 2007, this directory went by several different names, including the *SharePoint System directory* and the *12 Hive*. In SharePoint 2010, the SharePoint product team has formalized the name of this directory to be the *SharePoint root directory*.

A typical installation of SharePoint Foundation or SharePoint Server 2010 creates the SharePoint root directory at the following path.

C:\Program Files\Common Files\Microsoft Shared\Web Server Extensions\14

If you've installed only SharePoint Foundation and not SharePoint Server 2010, the SharePoint root directory contains a stock set of images, templates, features, and pages. If you install SharePoint Server 2010, the SharePoint root directory contains the same stock files of SharePoint Foundation and also a wealth of template files to provide additional functionality beyond that supplied by SharePoint Foundation.

When creating a SharePoint solution that is to be deployed as a farm solution, many of the types of template files that you add to your solution must be deployed in specific directories within the SharePoint root directory. Table 2-1 lists some of the more commonly used directories along with the types of template files they contain.

TABLE 2-1 SharePoint Solution File Locations Inside the SharePoint Root Directory

Path Relative to SharePoint Root Directory	Template File Types
/ISAPI	Web Services (.svc, .ashx, .asmx)
/Resources	Resource files (.resx)
/TEMPLATE/ADMIN	Application pages used exclusively in Central Administration
/TEMPLATE/CONTROLTEMPLATES	ASP.NET User Controls (.ascx)
/TEMPLATE/FEATURES	Feature definition files (.xml)
/TEMPLATE/IMAGES	Images (.gif, .jpg, and .png)
/TEMPLATE/LAYOUTS	Application pages (.aspx)
/TEMPLATE/LAYOUTS/1033/STYLES	CSS Files (.css)
/TEMPLATE/LAYOUTS/ClientBin	Silverlight components (.xap)
/TEMPLATE/SiteTemplates	Site Definition files (onet.xml)
/TEMPLATE/XML	Custom field type definition files (fdltype*.xml)

If you examine the project structure of WingtipDevProject1 shown in Figure 2-5, you notice that the project contains a top-level directory named SharePointRoot. Inside the SharePointRoot directory is a directory named TEMPLATE, and within TEMPLATE are two child directories, FEATURES and IMAGES. The key point is that this Visual Studio project contains a SharePointRoot directory with child directories that mirror the layout of the real SharePoint root directory.

> **Caution** The development technique of creating a SharePointRoot directory inside your project is optional, but it became a popular approach used in SharePoint 2007 development. When we get to Chapter 3, we'll abandon this approach in favor of an easier project structure created by the SharePoint Developer Tools. For now, we'll continue with this approach because it provides an effective way to teach you about deploying files from a farm solution into specific locations inside the SharePoint root directory.

Let's examine the two image files in WingtipDevProject1: FeatureIcon.gif and SiteIcon.gif. These files are being deployed inside the SharePoint IMAGES directory. However, note that FeatureIcon.gif and SiteIcon.gif aren't being deployed directly inside the IMAGES directory but instead inside an inner directory that has been given the same name as the project. Deploying images files in this fashion—inside a solution-specific directory within the IMAGES directory—is considered a best practice because it allows you to avoid file name conflicts with any of the stock image files that Microsoft deploys inside the IMAGES directory.

Creating a Feature Definition

Although you can create many different types of components within a SharePoint solution, you really should start by learning about feature definitions. A *feature definition* provides a mechanism for adding elements to a target site or site collection through a process known as *feature activation*. The types of elements that can be added to a site include menu commands, link commands, page templates, page instances, list definitions, list instances, event handlers, and workflows.

Many SharePoint developers use the terms *feature definition* and *feature instance* interchangeably. In this chapter, we stick with the term feature definition because it conveys the fact that you're dealing with a type of template that is used to create instances. Once you understand that a feature definition is really a template, you'll find it easier to differentiate between feature definitions and feature instances.

So what is the difference between a feature definition and a feature instance? The feature definition is the set of source files in your Visual Studio 2010 project that gets deployed using a solution package. Once deployed, a feature definition is a set of template files and components that reside on each front-end Web server. A *feature instance* is what gets created when a user activates the feature definition. SharePoint Foundation creates and maintains feature instances with entries in either a content database or the configuration database, depending on the activation scope of the underlying feature definition.

At a physical level, a feature definition is implemented with a set of files that are deployed within a dedicated directory created inside the FEATURES directory. More specifically, a feature's directory contains one or more XML-based files that contain *Collaborative Application Markup Language (CAML)*. The only file required for every feature definition is the feature manifest file, which must be named feature.xml and must be placed at the root of the feature's directory.

In addition to the feature.xml file, a feature definition often contains one or more XML files known as element manifests that define the elements that make up the feature definition. The directory for a feature definition can also contain several other types of files for elements such as list definitions and page templates as well as other kinds of resources, such as image files, Cascading Style Sheets (CSS) files, and JavaScript files.

One valuable technique for getting up to speed on features is to examine the standard set of feature definitions that ship as part of the basic SharePoint Foundation installation. An example of what the FEATURES directory looks like after you've installed SharePoint Foundation is shown in Figure 2-6. As you can see from this screenshot, the FEATURES directory contains 54 directories, each one representing one of the built-in feature definitions that gets installed along with SharePoint Foundation. If you've installed SharePoint Server 2010, the number of feature definitions included out of the box in the FEATURES directory increases from 54 to 266.

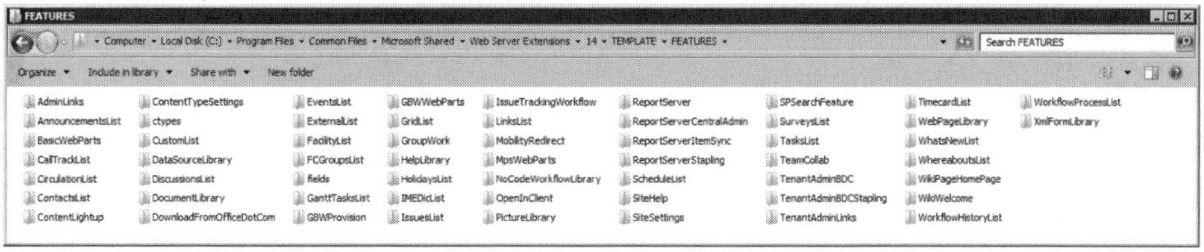

FIGURE 2-6 The installation of SharePoint Foundation includes a set of 54 built-in features.

Creating the Feature.xml File

When you want to create a new feature definition, you must create a directory inside the FEATURES directory, and directly inside this directory, you must create a file with the name feature.xml. Examine the XML definition in Listing 2-2, which shows the starting point for the feature.xml file used to create the Wingtip Lead Tracker feature definition.

LISTING 2-2 Every feature definition requires a feature.xml file, which serves as the feature manifest.

```xml
<Feature
  Id="86689158-7048-4421-AD21-E0DEF0D67C81"
  Title="Wingtip Lead Tracker"
  Description="A sample feature deployed using WingtipDevProject1.wsp"
  Version="1.0.0.0"
  Scope="Web"
  Hidden="FALSE"
  ImageUrl="WingtipDevProject1/FeatureIcon.gif"
  xmlns="http://schemas.microsoft.com/sharepoint/" >

  <ElementManifests>
    <ElementManifest Location="elements.xml" />
  </ElementManifests>

</Feature>
```

You see that a feature definition is defined in XML using a top-level *Feature* element containing attributes such as *Id, Title, Description, Version, Scope, Hidden,* and *ImageUrl*. You must create a new globally unique identifier (GUID) for the *Id* attribute so that your feature can be uniquely identified. You should create the feature definition's *Title* and *Description* attributes using user-friendly text. These attributes are shown directly to the users on the SharePoint Foundation feature management pages, where users are able to activate features.

The *Scope* of a feature definition defines the context in which the feature instances can be activated and deactivated. The Wingtip Lead Tracker feature definition has a *Scope* attribute setting of *Web*, which means it can be activated and deactivated within the context of a site. If you assign a *Scope* value of *Site*, your feature definition is then activated and deactivated within the scope of a site collection. The two other possible activation scopes for a feature definition are *WebApplication* and *Farm*.

As you can see, the *Hidden* attribute has a value of *FALSE*. This means that once installed within the farm, the feature definition can be seen by administrators who might want to activate it. You can also create a feature definition where the *Hidden* attribute has a value of *TRUE*, which has the effect of hiding the feature definition in the list of available features shown to administrators. Users can't directly activate hidden feature definitions. Instead, a farm administrator must activate them by using a Windows PowerShell script, through a development technique such as using a feature activation dependency, or by writing code against the server-side object model.

You can also see that the *ImageUrl* attribute of this feature definition points to the custom image file named *FeatureIcon.gif* that is part of the same project. The setting for the *ImageUrl* property in a feature.xml file should be set relative to the IMAGES directory.

The feature.xml file for the Wingtip Lead Tracker feature definition contains a reference to an element manifest named elements.xml. The reference to elements.xml is added using an *ElementManifests* element with an inner *ElementManifest* element whose *Location* attribute points to elements.xml. In the following section, we explain the purpose of element manifests and how to work with them.

Element Manifests

A feature definition can have one or more element manifests. An *element manifest* is an XML file that contains a set of declarative elements defined using CAML. SharePoint Foundation inspects the element manifest during feature activation and provisions an object in the target site for each defined element.

Every element manifest must have a top-level element named *Elements*. Inside *Elements*, you add declarative elements. The elements.xml file in WingtipDevProject1, which is shown in Listing 2-3, contains a single child element of type *ListInstance*, which provisions a new list in the target site when the feature definition is activated. This list is created using the Contacts list type built into SharePoint Foundation and has the title *Sales Leads*.

LISTING 2-3 An element manifest file contains an *Elements* node with one or more nested elements inside.

```
<Elements xmlns= http://schemas.microsoft.com/sharepoint/ >

  <ListInstance
    FeatureId="00BFEA71-7E6D-4186-9BA8-C047AC750105"
    TemplateType="105"
    Id="SalesLeads"
    Title="Sales Leads"
    Url="SalesLeads"
    OnQuickLaunch="TRUE"
  />

</Elements>
```

The *ListInstance* element contains several attributes that SharePoint Foundation uses as parameterized values when it creates the new list. The *FeatureId* attribute contains a GUID that identifies the feature definition in which the built-in Contacts list type is defined. The *TemplateType* attribute contains the integer identifier for the Contacts list type, which is 105. The remaining four attributes provide SharePoint Foundation with initialization settings for the list instance being created.

This example contains a single declarative element, but you have the flexibility to add multiple elements inside the *Elements* section of an element manifest. If you like, you can also extend the feature definition by adding element manifests. If you're developing a feature definition in which you need to add multiple declarative elements, you have a choice. You can add all the elements to a single element manifest, or you can spread them across two or more element manifests.

Throughout this book, we'll continue to explain the various types of declarative elements you can use in element manifests when developing a feature definition. Table 2-2 lists the most common element types used when developing feature definitions, along with a brief description of each element type.

TABLE 2-2 Common Element Types Used When Developing a Feature Definition

Element Type	Description
PropertyBag	Adds name-value properties to a feature
ListInstance	Creates a list instance
CustomActionGroup	Creates a new section for links
CustomAction	Creates a new link or menu command
HideCustomAction	Hides a built-in or custom link or menu command
Module	Provisions a file from a template file
Field	Creates a site column
ContentType	Creates a content type

Element Type	Description
ContentTypeBinding	Adds a content type to a list
ListTemplate	Creates a custom list type
Control	Creates a delegate control
Workflow	Creates a workflow template
WorkflowActions	Creates declarative workflows
WorkflowAssociation	Associates a workflow template with a list
FeatureSiteTemplateAssociation	Staples a second feature to a site template to support auto-activation

Adding a Feature Receiver

In addition to declarative elements, you can also extend a feature definition with a Feature Receiver. A Feature Receiver allows you to write event handlers in a managed programming language such as C# or Visual Basic. These event handlers are executed during feature-specific events such as feature activation and feature deactivation. The code you write in these event handlers can access the SharePoint Foundation server-side object model, making it possible to modify the target site. For example, you can write an event handler that fires during feature activation and performs routine initialization tasks such as creating new lists and adding list items. You can also extend the site by adding pages, navigation links, and Web Part instances.

To create a Feature Receiver, you start by adding a new class to your project that inherits from the *SPFeatureReceiver* class defined in the *Microsoft.SharePoint* namespace. Next, you override methods defined in *SPFeatureReceiver*, such as *FeatureActivated* and *FeatureDeactivating*. Listing 2-4 shows how the Feature Receiver class has been implemented for the Wingtip Sales Leads feature definition.

LISTING 2-4 You create a Feature Receiver by inheriting from the *SPFeatureReceiver* class and overriding event handler methods.

```
public class FeatureReceiver : SPFeatureReceiver {

  public override void FeatureActivated(SPFeatureReceiverProperties props) {
    SPWeb site = props.Feature.Parent as SPWeb;
    if (site != null) {
      site.Title = "Feature Activated";
      site.SiteLogoUrl = @"_layouts/images/WingtipDevProject1/SiteIcon.gif";
      site.Update();
    }
  }

  public override void FeatureDeactivating(SPFeatureReceiverProperties props) {
    SPWeb site = props.Feature.Parent as SPWeb;
    if (site != null) {
      site.Title = "Feature Deactivated";
```

```
        site.SiteLogoUrl = "";
        site.Update();
        SPList list = site.Lists.TryGetList("Sales Leads");
        if (list != null) {
          list.Delete();
        }
      }
    }
  }

}
```

The *FeatureActivated* method in this listing has been written to update the current site's *Title* and *SiteLogoUrl* properties. The site's *Title* property is updated to *Feature Activated* during feature activation in this example to give you a quick way to test the feature definition and get visual feedback that the code actually ran. The update to the *SiteLogoUrl* property will replace the stock site logo image in the upper left corner of the target site with the custom image file SiteIcon.gif.

Notice the technique used to obtain a reference to the current site. A parameter of type *SPFeatureReceiverProperties* is passed to the *FeatureActivated* method. You can use this parameter to acquire a reference to the *SPWeb* object associated with the target site. The *SPFeatureReceiverProperties* parameter exposes a *Feature* property that in turn exposes a *Parent* property that holds a reference to the current site. After updating the *Title* and *SiteLogoUrl* properties of the *SPWeb* object, the code must also call the *Update* method to save these changes back to the content database.

The *FeatureDeactivating* method in this example updates the value of the site's *Title* property to *Feature Deactivated* and updates the value of the *SiteLogoUrl* property back to an empty string. Assigning an empty string value has the effect of returning the site logo to the stock site logo image used by SharePoint Foundation. The code in the *FeatureDeactivating* method also deletes the Sales Leads list, which was declaratively provisioned during feature activation.

Those of you moving from SharePoint 2007 should take note of the *TryGetList* method that was added to the server-side object model in SharePoint 2010. In versions prior to SharePoint 2010, this method didn't exist, and developers usually resorted to enumerating through the *Lists* collection of a site to determine whether a list existed.

The code for a Feature Receiver must be compiled into a .NET assembly and deployed in the global assembly cache (GAC). The fact that the assembly requires deployment in the GAC means that you must add a signing key file to the project to sign the resulting output DLL with a strong name during compilation. If you look back at Figure 2-5, you can see that WingtipDevProject1 has a signing key file named WingtipSigningKey.snk.

The next step to integrating a Feature Receiver is to update the *Feature* element inside the feature.xml file with two new attributes. You must do this to inform SharePoint Foundation that the feature definition has an associated Feature Receiver. More specifically, you should add the *ReceiverAssembly* and *ReceiverClass* attributes as shown in the following example.

```
<Feature Id="86689158-7048-4421-AD21-E0DEF0D67C81"
  Title="Wingtip Lead Tracker"
  Description="A sample feature deployed using WingtipDevProject1.wsp"
  Version="1.0.0.0"
  Scope="Web"
  Hidden="FALSE"
  ReceiverAssembly="WingtipDevProject1, [four-part assembly name]"
  ReceiverClass="WingtipDevProject1.FeatureReceiver"
  ImageUrl="WingtipDevProject1/FeatureIcon.gif"
  xmlns="http://schemas.microsoft.com/sharepoint/" >
  <ElementManifests>
    <ElementManifest Location="elements.xml" />
  </ElementManifests>
</Feature>
```

The *ReceiverAssembly* attribute contains a four-part assembly name, which in most cases is the name of the assembly being built by the current project. Keep in mind that the assembly must be installed in the GAC prior to feature activation to work properly. The *ReceiverClass* attribute contains the namespace-qualified name of a public class within the receiver assembly.

Any class you reference with the *ReceiverClass* attribute must inherit from *SPFeatureReceiver*. When a feature definition with a Feature Receiver is activated, SharePoint Foundation loads the target assembly and dynamically creates an object from the class referenced by the *ReceiverClass* attribute. Once SharePoint Foundation has created the Feature Receiver object, it performs a type conversion to *SPFeatureReceiver*. If your Feature Receiver class doesn't inherit from *SPFeatureReceiver*, the SharePoint Foundation will experience a type conversion error at run time, causing your feature definition to fail during feature activation.

At this point, we've walked through the entire implementation of the Wingtip Lead Tracker feature definition. Your next challenge is to learn how to deploy and test this feature definition. In the next section, we discuss how to prepare this feature definition and the accompanying images files for deployment using a solution package.

Creating a Solution Package

Because SharePoint solutions are deployed in farms that range in size from a single stand-alone Web server to large enterprise server farms, you need an easy and reliable mechanism to deploy them as a single unit. By deploying a single unit, you can have a supported, testable, and repeatable deployment mechanism. The deployment mechanism that SharePoint uses is the solution package.

As mentioned earlier in the chapter, a solution package is a compressed CAB file with a .wsp extension that contains the set of template files and components to be deployed on one or more front-end Web servers. Every solution package contains metadata that enables SharePoint Foundation to unpack the .wsp file and install its template files and components. In server farm installations, SharePoint Foundation is able to automate pushing the solution package file out to each Web server in the farm.

Solution packages are deployed in two steps. The first step is installation, in which SharePoint Foundation adds a copy of the .wsp file to the configuration database. The second step is the deployment, in which SharePoint Foundation creates a timer job that is processed by all front-end Web servers in the server farm. The key takeaway here is that deploying SharePoint solutions using solution packages greatly simplifies installation across a farm of Web servers and ensures a consistent deployment in a variety of scenarios.

The Manifest.xml File

The metadata for a solution package is maintained in a solution manifest file that must be named manifest.xml. When you deploy a solution package, SharePoint Foundation inspects manifest.xml to determine which template files it needs to copy into the SharePoint root directory. The metadata inside manifest.xml can also instruct SharePoint Foundation to install an assembly in the GAC and to install feature definitions in the local farm. Installing a feature definition requires updates to the configuration database in addition to copying feature definition files into the proper location in the SharePoint root directory.

Let's take a look at a simple solution manifest. Examine the code in Listing 2-5, which shows the manifest.xml file from WingtipDevProject1.

LISTING 2-5 The manifest.xml file is the solution manifest, which provides installation instructions to the SharePoint Foundation installer.

```xml
<Solution
  SolutionId="0cee8f44-4892-4a01-b8f4-b07aa21e1ef2"
  Title="Wingtip Dev Project 1"
  DeploymentServerType="WebFrontEnd"
  ResetWebServer="True"
  xmlns="http://schemas.microsoft.com/sharepoint/">

  <FeatureManifests>
    <FeatureManifest Location="WingtipDevProject1\feature.xml" />
  </FeatureManifests>

  <TemplateFiles>
    <TemplateFile Location="IMAGES\WingtipDevProject1\FeatureIcon.gif" />
    <TemplateFile Location="IMAGES\WingtipDevProject1\SiteIcon.gif" />
  </TemplateFiles>

  <Assemblies>
    <Assembly Location="WingtipDevProject1.dll"
```

```
                    DeploymentTarget="GlobalAssemblyCache" />
    </Assemblies>

  </Solution>
```

As you can see, a manifest.xml file has a top-level *Solution* element with attributes such as an identifying GUID for the *SolutionId* and user-friendly text for the *Title*. The *DeploymentServerType* attribute tells SharePoint Foundation whether the contents of the solution package should be installed on front-end Web servers in the farm or on application servers. The *ResetWebServer* attribute tells SharePoint Foundation whether it needs to run an *IISRESET* operation on each server at the end of the deployment process.

In this example, three different child elements are nested inside the *Solution* element. The *FeatureManifests* element contains a *FeatureManifest* element with a *Location* attribute that references a *feature.xml* file using a path relative to the FEATURES directory. SharePoint Foundation now has the information it needs to properly install the feature.

The *TemplateFiles* element contains two *TemplateFile* elements with *Location* attributes that reference the two .gif files that are being used as custom image files using a path relative to the TEMPLATE directory. These elements give SharePoint Foundation the information it needs to copy these two files to a new subdirectory that it creates inside the IMAGES directory.

Finally, the *Assemblies* element contains an *Assembly* element with a *Location* attribute that references the assembly file that's distributed as part of the solution package using a path relative to the root of the solution package. As you can see, the *Assembly* element contains a *DeploymentTarget* attribute with a value of *GlobalAssemblyCache*, which tells SharePoint Foundation to install the assembly in the GAC on each front-end Web server or application server.

Activation Dependencies

If you're familiar with creating solution packages for SharePoint 2007, you'll be happy to discover that SharePoint 2010 introduces the capability to define a dependency between two solution packages. This type of dependency is helpful when one solution package installs components that are used by another solution package.

For example, imagine a scenario in which a solution package named WingtipUtilities.wsp installs an assembly in the GAC that contains a library of reusable utility functions. What if you then develop a second SharePoint solution named WingtipDevProject2 that references the assembly deployed by WingtipUtilities.wsp to call functions inside the utility library?

The key point is that the second SharePoint solution has been created with a dependency on WingtipUtilities.wsp. In other words, code deployed in WingtipDevProject2.wsp can't be expected to work correctly in a farm in which WingtipUtilities.wsp hasn't been deployed.

Therefore, you should define an activation dependency on WingtipUtilities.wsp by modifying the manifest.xml file inside WingtipDevProject2.wsp.

To create an activation dependency, you add an *ActivationDependencies* element inside the top-level *Solution* element with a nested *ActivationDependency* element. Therefore, the manifest.xml file in WingtipDevProject2.wsp should be updated to look like this:

```
<ActivationDependencies>
  <ActivationDependency
    SolutionId="0cee8f44-4892-4a01-b8f4-b07aa21e1ef1"
    SolutionName="WingtipUtilities.wsp"
  />
</ActivationDependencies>
```

The value of defining an activation dependency is that it allows you to discover problems early—at deployment time instead of run time. If you fail to define an activation dependency, you make it possible for a farm administrator to successfully deploy your solution package in a SharePoint farm that doesn't have the required dependencies. As a result, users could experience errors in the production environment that are difficult to track down and remedy.

If you define an activation dependency, the farm administrator will experience an error when attempting to deploy the solution package in a SharePoint farm that doesn't have the required dependencies. The error will generate the following error message:

"This solution cannot be activated because its functionality depends on another solution that does not exist: WingtipUtilities.wsp, Id: 0cee8f44-4892-4a01-b8f4-b07aa21e1ef1. First add the other solution to the Solution Gallery, activate that solution, and then repeat activation of this solution."

> **Note** We must point out that the term *activation dependency* is a little confusing when used in the context of a farm solution. From a conceptual standpoint, you're really creating a *deployment dependency* rather than an activation dependency when you use the *ActivationDependency* element in a solution package that will be deployed as a farm solution. You will see that the term *activation dependency* makes more sense when we get to Chapter 4 and discuss deploying a solution package as a sandboxed solution, which goes through the process of activation (not deployment) when it is used within the scope of a site collection.

Generating the Solution Package File

There are a few different ways to generate a solution package from the source files inside a Visual Studio project. Starting in Chapter 3, we'll use the SharePoint Developer Tools to create a solution package file. As you'll see, the SharePoint Developer Tools make your life much easier because the details of creating the solution package are handled behind the scenes and become transparent to developers. However, because we're building a SharePoint solution in this chapter without assistance from the SharePoint Developer Tools, we're going to build the solution package file using a command-line utility named makecab.exe.

When you plan to create a solution package file using the makecab.exe utility, you start by creating a *diamond definition file (DDF)*. The DDF file is passed to makecab.exe as an input parameter, and it lists the files that must be copied inside the solution package file. The following code shows the DDF file used in WingtipDevProject1.

```
.OPTION EXPLICIT
.Set CabinetNameTemplate=WingtipDevProject1.wsp
.Set DiskDirectory1=DeploymentFiles/output

;*** Add files to root folder of Solution Package
DeploymentFiles\input\manifest.xml
bin/debug/WingtipDevProject1.dll

;*** add feature files into a folder having the same name as feature
.Set DestinationDir=WingtipDevProject1
SharePointRoot\TEMPLATE\FEATURES\WingtipDevProject1\elements.xml
SharePointRoot\TEMPLATE\FEATURES\WingtipDevProject1\feature.xml

;*** add TEMPLATE files such as IMAGE files into a folder relative to /TEMPLATE
.Set DestinationDir=IMAGES\WingtipDevProject1
SharePointRoot\TEMPLATE\IMAGES\WingtipDevProject1\FeatureIcon.gif
SharePointRoot\TEMPLATE\IMAGES\WingtipDevProject1\SiteIcon.gif
```

As you can see, information at the top of this DDF file tells makecab.exe to generate an output file named WingtipDevProject1.wsp. There's also a line in the DDF file for each source file that must be copied into the output solution package file. Some of the files in a solution package, such as manifest.xml and WingtipDevProject1.dll, must be copied to the root of the solution package, while other files need to be copied to child folders nested inside the root.

You can call the makecab.exe utility from the command line using a Windows PowerShell script. Here is a simple example of a Windows PowerShell script that automates building a solution package using makecab.exe.

```
$ProjectName = "WingtipDevProject1"
$ProjectDirectory = "C:\InsideSP2010\WingtipDevProject1\WingtipDevProject1"
$DeploymentFilesDirectory = $ProjectDirectory + 'DeploymentFiles\'
$DiamondDefinitionFilePath = $DeploymentFilesDirectory +
                             'input\BuildSolution.ddf'
Set-Location $ProjectDirectory
$MAKECAB = "C:\Windows\SysWOW64\MAKECAB.EXE"
& $MAKECAB /V1 /F $DiamondDefinitionFilePath
```

Notice that the last line of this script begins with an & character, which serves as the Windows PowerShell call operator. The call operator is commonly used when your Windows PowerShell script needs to call out to an external utility such as makecab.exe.

Using Windows PowerShell Scripts to Automate Tasks in Visual Studio

When you're developing SharePoint solutions, it's helpful if you can integrate Windows PowerShell scripts to automate the tasks involved with testing and deploying your code. As you've seen in the previous section, you can call the makecab.exe utility from a Windows

PowerShell script to build your project files into a solution package. You can also call Windows PowerShell cmdlets from *Microsoft.SharePoint.PowerShell* to automate other important tasks during testing, such as installing and deploying a solution package in the local farm.

The Visual Studio 2010 project named WingtipDevProject1 has been configured with an integrated set of Windows PowerShell scripts, as shown in Figure 2-7. These scripts demonstrate how to automate many of the tasks you need to perform while testing and debugging a SharePoint solution.

FIGURE 2-7 WingtipDevProject1 contains Windows PowerShell scripts used to test and debug a SharePoint solution.

WingtipDevProject1 has been configured so that you can run any of these Windows PowerShell scripts by executing the project's *Build* command. Now we'll walk through the process of integrating Windows PowerShell scripts with a Visual Studio 2010 project so that you can accomplish the same goal in your projects.

The easiest way to execute a Windows PowerShell script from within a Visual Studio 2010 project is to navigate to the Build Events tab of the Project Properties dialog and call powershell.exe from the post-build event command line. You should call out to powershell.exe using the following path.

%WINDIR%\SysNative\WindowsPowerShell\v1.0\powershell.exe

It's important that you use the virtual path of %WINDIR%\SysNative and not the actual path of C:\Windows\System32. The reason for this is that Visual Studio 2010 is a 32-bit application that needs to call the 64-bit version of powershell.exe to successfully load the *Microsoft.SharePoint.Powershell* snap-in.

If you launch to powershell.exe using the path C:\Windows\System32, you'll encounter problems in SharePoint Foundation development. The problem arises because a 64-bit version of the Windows operating system will see that Visual Studio 2010 is a 32-bit application and will remap the path to load the 32-bit version of powershell.exe. By using the virtual path %WINDIR%\SysNative, you're able to avoid this problem and ensure that you successfully launch the 64-bit version.

To execute a Windows PowerShell script, you should call powershell.exe followed by the —*Command* parameter, which passes the path to the target Windows PowerShell script. For example, if you've written a Windows PowerShell script named MyScript.ps1 and added it to the project at the root directory, you can then execute the script by calling powershell.exe in the following manner.

```
powershell.exe -Command "$(ProjectDir)\MyScript.ps1"
```

Notice that this example uses the *$(ProjectDir)* token supported by Visual Studio 2010. Before executing this command, Visual Studio will replace this token with the actual path to the project so that powershell.exe can locate and execute the Windows PowerShell script MyScript (no 1).ps1. Now let's say you want to execute a Windows PowerShell script and pass it an input parameter, such as the name of the current project. You can use another Visual Studio token, named *$(ProjectName)*, and modify the call to powershell.exe to look like this:

```
powershell.exe -Command "$(ProjectDir)\MyScript.ps1 $(ProjectName)"
```

Now that you understand the basics of executing a Windows PowerShell script from within a Visual Studio 2010 project, we can explain how you can execute any of the Windows PowerShell scripts in WingtipDevProject1. The post-build event command line in WingtipDevProject1 has been written to call the script *BuildCommandDispatcher.ps1* and to pass four parameters using the Visual Studio tokens *$(ProjectName)*, *$(ProjectDir)*, *$(TargetPath)*, and *$(ConfigurationName)*.

The control of flow logic inside *BuildCommandDispatcher.ps1* uses a Windows PowerShell *switch* statement to examine the active configuration and executes the appropriate Windows PowerShell script passing the required parameters. This makes it possible for you to execute any of these Windows PowerShell scripts by changing the project's configuration, as shown in Figure 2-8, and then executing the project's *Build* command.

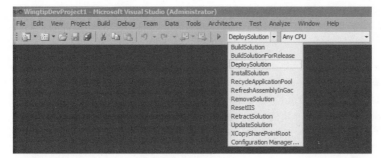

FIGURE 2-8 To execute a specific script, change the project configuration and run the *Build* command.

For example, if you set the project configuration to *BuildSolution* and then run the *Build* command, the logic in BuildCommandDispatcher.ps1 executes BuildSolution.ps1 and passes the project name and project directory as parameters. BuildSolution.ps1 has been written to build the solution package using the following code.

```
$ProjectName = $args[0]
$ProjectDirectory = $args[1]
$DeploymentFilesDirectory = $ProjectDirectory + 'DeploymentFiles\'
$DiamondDefinitionFilePath = $DeploymentFilesDirectory +
                             'input\BuildSolution.ddf'
Write-Host 'Building Solution Package using MAKECAB.EXE'
Set-Location $ProjectDirectory
$MAKECAB = "C:\Windows\SysWOW64\MAKECAB.EXE"
& $MAKECAB /V1 /F $DiamondDefinitionFilePath
```

Installing and Deploying a Solution Package

Once you've built the solution package, you must be able to install and deploy it so that you can test and debug your code. The act of installing a solution package simply copies the solution package file to the configuration database and registers it as a named solution that is ready for deployment. The act of deploying the solution package pushes the code out to each Web server for deployment and makes it possible to test and debug your work.

You can install a solution package by loading the *Microsoft.SharePoint.Powershell* snap-in and then calling the *Add-SPSolution* cmdlet, passing the *–LiteralPath* parameter using a value that contains the physical path to the solution package file.

```
Add-PSSnapin Microsoft.SharePoint.PowerShell -ErrorAction "SilentlyContinue"
Add-SPSolution -LiteralPath "C:\Solutions\WingtipDevProject1.wsp"
```

Once you've installed the solution package using the *Add-SPSolution* cmdlet, you can deploy it using the *Install-SPSolution* cmdlet. Keep in mind that the names of these cmdlets can cause confusion because you *install* a solution package using the *Add-SPSolution* cmdlet and you *deploy* it using the *Install-SPSolution* cmdlet. Also note that once the solution package has been installed, you refer to it using the *-Identity* parameter, whose value should be the name of the solution package file without any path.

```
Add-PSSnapin Microsoft.SharePoint.PowerShell -ErrorAction "SilentlyContinue"
Add-SPSolution -LiteralPath "C:\Solutions\WingtipDevProject1.wsp"
Install-SPSolution -Identity "WingtipDevProject1.wsp" -Local -GACDeployment
```

You should also observe that the call to *Install-SPSolution* includes two additional parameters, *-Local* and *-GACDeployment*. The *-Local* parameter tells SharePoint Foundation that it needs to worry about deploying the solution package only on the local server, which can speed things up when developing on a single-server farm. The other parameter, *-GACDeployment*, is required whenever you're deploying a solution package that installs an assembly in the GAC.

Retracting and Removing a Solution

If you want to remove a solution package from a farm after it has been deployed, you must retract it and then remove it. The act of retracting reverses the act of deployment. For example, retracting a solution forces SharePoint Foundation to delete all the files it copied during deployment as well as uninstall features and delete assemblies from the GAC. Once you've retracted a solution, you can then remove it, which deletes the solution package file from the configuration database.

You can retract a solution package using the *Uninstall-SPSolution* cmdlet. When calling *Uninstall-SPSolution*, you should pass the *-Identity* parameter and the *-Local* parameter in the same manner as when calling *Install-SPSolution*. You should also pass the *-Confirm* parameter with a value of *$false* because failing to do so can cause the cmdlet to prompt the user. This user prompt can cause problems because it freezes Visual Studio when a script that prompts the user for a response is executed.

```
Add-PSSnapin Microsoft.SharePoint.PowerShell -ErrorAction "SilentlyContinue"
$SolutionPackageName = "WingtipDevProject1.wsp"
Uninstall-SPSolution -Identity $SolutionPackageName -Local -Confirm:$false
```

Once you've retracted the solution using the *Uninstall-SPSolution* cmdlet, you can then remove it by calling *Remove-SPSolution*, which instructs SharePoint Foundation to delete the solution package file from the configuration database.

```
Add-PSSnapin Microsoft.SharePoint.PowerShell -ErrorAction "SilentlyContinue"
$SolutionPackageName = "WingtipDevProject1.wsp"
Uninstall-SPSolution -Identity $SolutionPackageName -Local -Confirm:$false
Remove-SPSolution -Identity $SolutionPackageName -Confirm:$false
```

These calls to *Uninstall-SPSolution* and *Remove-SPSolution* will fail if the solution package isn't currently installed and deployed. Therefore, it makes sense to add a call to *Get-SPSolution* and conditional logic to determine whether the solution package is currently installed and deployed before attempting to retract or remove it.

```
Add-PSSnapin Microsoft.SharePoint.PowerShell -ErrorAction "SilentlyContinue"
$SolutionPackageName  = "WingtipDevProject1.wsp"
$solution = Get-SPSolution | where-object {$_.Name -eq $SolutionPackageName}
# check to see if solution package has been installed
if ($solution -ne $null) {
  # check to see if solution package is currently deployed
  if($solution.Deployed -eq $true){
    Uninstall-SPSolution -Identity $SolutionPackageName -Local -Confirm:$false
  }
}
```

Now that you've seen how to retract and remove a solution package, it's time to walk through the *DeploySolution.ps1* script in WingtipDevProject1. When you're developing a SharePoint solution, you will frequently be deploying solution packages, and you must ensure that you properly retract and remove any older version before you deploy the latest one. Listing 2-6 shows how that step can be automated with a single Windows PowerShell script.

LISTING 2-6 This Windows PowerShell script is written to install and deploy a solution package with conditional logic to uninstall and delete a previous version when required.

```
$SolutionPackageName  = $args[0]
$SolutionPackagePath = $args[1]
Add-PSSnapin Microsoft.SharePoint.PowerShell -ErrorAction "SilentlyContinue"
$solution = Get-SPSolution | where-object {$_.Name -eq $SolutionPackageName}
if ($solution -ne $null) {
  if($solution.Deployed -eq $true){
    Uninstall-SPSolution -Identity $SolutionPackageName -Local -Confirm:$false
  }
  Remove-SPSolution -Identity $SolutionPackageName -Confirm:$false
}
Add-SPSolution -LiteralPath $SolutionPackagePath
Install-SPSolution -Identity $SolutionPackageName -Local -GACDeployment
```

Now that you've learned about deployment, it's time to test the solution. After WingtipDev Project1.wsp has been deployed, the Wingtip Lead Tracker feature definition should be installed and available for activation within a site on your local farm. You can manually activate the feature definition inside a test site using the site feature management page, as shown in Figure 2-9.

FIGURE 2-9 After deployment, the feature from WingtipDevProject1 can be activated through the site's feature management page.

When you activate Wingtip Lead Tracker, the underlying feature definition provisions a Contacts list entitled Sales Leads because of the declarative element we defined inside elements.xml. Feature activation should also force SharePoint Foundation to execute the *FeatureActivated* event handler, which should change the site icon and update the site title to Feature Activated.

Updating a Solution

After one of your solution packages has been deployed in a production farm, you might need to update some of the files that have already been deployed. SharePoint Foundation supports the concept of updating a solution package. This technique allows you to replace existing files that have already been deployed as well as to deploy new files that weren't part of the original solution package deployment.

For example, imagine a simple scenario in which WingtipDevProject1.wsp has already been deployed and its feature definition has been activated in several sites. What if, after the fact, the Wingtip Sales Director decides he doesn't like the SiteLogo.gif file you decided to use for the site logo? SharePoint Foundation makes it easy to accommodate this change. You can simply update your Visual Studio project by replacing the old SiteLogo.gif file with a new one of the same name. Then you can rebuild the solution package with the updated .gif file and run the *Update-SPSolution* cmdlet to automate replacing the old version of SiteLogo.gif file with the new one on each of the front-end Web servers.

```
$SolutionPackageName  = "WingtipDevProject1.wsp"
$SolutionPackagePath = "C:\Solutions\WingtipDevProject1.wsp"
Update-SPSolution -Identity $SolutionPackageName
                  -LiteralPath $SolutionPackagePath
                  -Local -GACDeployment
```

Now that you've seen how to update a solution package using the *Update-SPSolution* cmdlet, let's walk through the *UpdateSolution.ps1* script in WingtipDevProject1. You should observe that a call to *Get-SPSolution* will allow you to determine whether a previous version of the solution package has been installed and deployed. Knowing this is important because a call to *Update-SPSolution* will fail if the solution package isn't already deployed.

```
$SolutionPackageName  = $args[0]
$SolutionPackagePath = $args[1]
Add-PSSnapin Microsoft.SharePoint.Powershell
# ensure previous version of solution package is already deployed
$solution = Get-SPSolution | where-object {$_.Name -eq $SolutionPackageName}
if ($solution -ne $null) {
  if($solution.Deployed -eq $true){
    Update-SPSolution -Identity $SolutionPackageName
                      -LiteralPath $SolutionPackagePath
                      -Local -GACDeployment
  }
  else {
    Write-Host "Solution package cannot be updated because it is not deployed"
  }
}
```

As you'll see in the next section, using the technique of updating a solution provides the means to update a feature definition when you need to upgrade a feature. Updating a solution also provides a simple means to replace files and components with enhanced versions. For example, imagine you need to fix a bug in the C# code you've written inside the *ActivateFeature* event handler. You can simply update the code and rebuild a new version of the solution package. When you update the solution, the old copy of WingtipDevProject1.dll in the GAC is replaced with the new copy and the SharePoint worker process restarts to ensure that the new version gets loaded. You can use the same technique to update many other types of files, including Cascading Style Sheets (.css) files, JavaScript (.js) files, and Silverlight application (.xap) files.

Feature Upgrade Enhancements in SharePoint 2010

Although SharePoint 2007 tracks a version number for each feature definition, it doesn't go any further than that to provide support for feature versioning. Many companies and developers using SharePoint 2007 have been forced to create their own infrastructure to upgrade sites to a more recent version of a feature definition. Fortunately, the new feature upgrade enhancements in SharePoint Foundation mean that in SharePoint 2010 you won't have to do this anymore.

SharePoint Foundation supports feature activation at four different levels: site, site collection, Web application, and farm. Whenever a feature definition is activated, SharePoint Foundation creates a feature instance that tracks metadata about the underlying feature definition. The feature instance tracks feature properties such as *Id*, *Title*, and *Version*. Make sure you understand that the *Version* property of a feature instance represents the current version of the feature definition at the time of activation.

Once you've pushed a feature definition into a production farm and it's been activated, you might be required to update it to deal with changing business requirements. You can define upgrade actions inside a feature definition that will be processed when a feature instance is upgraded to the new version. Upgrade actions can be created inside the feature.xml file using declarative XML and can also execute custom event handlers written in C# or Visual Basic.

Once you've updated a feature definition in a Visual Studio project such as WingtipDevProject1, you can rebuild the solution package and push the new version out into a production farm or a staging farm using the *Update-SPSolution* cmdlet. However, pushing out a new version of a feature definition using *Update-SPSolution* is only half the story.

The farm now has an updated feature definition, but all the existing feature instances are still based on a previous version of the feature definition. You must run a query to find all the feature instances that require updating, and you then must call the *Upgrade* method on each feature instance to trigger the feature upgrade process. When the *Upgrade* method is called on a feature instance, SharePoint Foundation triggers the upgrade actions you've defined in your feature definition. To help you better understand this process, let's work through an example using the Wingtip Lead Tracker feature definition.

Upgrading Sites Using an Updated Feature Definition

You've been developing the WingtipDevProject1 solution in which you've created the Wingtip Lead Tracker feature definition. After you created and tested your implementation of the initial requirements, you built a solution package named WingtipDevProject1.wsp and gave it to the Wingtip IT staff. They deployed it in the production farm. That was six months ago. Now there are ten different sales sites in the production farm that have activated the Lead Tracker feature.

Earlier this morning, the Wingtip Sales Director sent you a request to update the Lead Tracker feature. The Sales Director has asked you to revise Wingtip Lead Tracker so that it creates a second list, named Customers, in addition to the Sales Leads list. Both these lists should be created using the Contacts list type built into SharePoint Foundation.

Updating a Feature Definition with Upgrade Actions

SharePoint Foundation tracks the version numbers for feature definitions using a four-part number similar to version numbers for assemblies in the .NET Framework. The initial version of the Wingtip Lead Tracker feature definition had a version number of 1.0.0.0. All the sites in which the Wingtip Lead Tracker feature has been activated also have version 1.0.0.0 feature instances.

Recall from earlier in this chapter that the initial version of the Wingtip Lead Tracker feature definition includes a single element manifest named elements.xml. This element manifest is referenced using an *ElementManifest* element in the feature.xml file.

```
<Feature
  Id="86689158-7048-4421-AD21-E0DEF0D67C81"
  Title="Wingtip Lead Tracker"
  Version="1.0.0.0"  . . .

>

  <ElementManifests>
    <ElementManifest Location="elements.xml" />
  </ElementManifests>

</Feature>
```

Now we'll begin updating the Wingtip Lead Tracker feature definition. We start by incrementing the *Version* number in feature.xml.

```
<Feature
  Id="86689158-7048-4421-AD21-E0DEF0D67C81"
  Title="Wingtip Lead Tracker"
  Version="2.0.0.0"
   .
   .
   .
```

The next step is to add a new *ListInstance* element to the feature definition to create the Customers list. Where should this new *ListInstance* element be added? We could add it into elements.xml along with the *ListInstance* element used to create the Sales Leads list. This would be a mistake, however, because the feature definition update would affect only sites that activated Wingtip Lead Tracker in the future; existing feature instances that were created by activating version 1.0.0.0 wouldn't be affected.

The recommended approach for dealing with this scenario is to create a second element manifest for elements that need to be provisioned during the upgrade process. In our example, we add a second element manifest to the Wingtip Lead Tracker feature definition. We name the second element manifest elements_v2.xml and add into it a second *ListInstance* element to create the Customers list.

```
<Elements xmlns="http://schemas.microsoft.com/sharepoint/">

  <ListInstance
    FeatureId="00BFEA71-7E6D-4186-9BA8-C047AC750105"
    TemplateType="105"
```

```
    Id="Customers"
    Title="Customers"
    Url="Customers"
    OnQuickLaunch="TRUE" />

</Elements>
```

When you add a new element manifest that is to be processed during feature upgrade, you must modify the feature.xml file by adding an *UpgradeActions* element inside the top-level *Feature* element. The *UpgradeActions* element must contain a *VersionRange* element that defines the *EndVersion* attribute and optionally the *BeginVersion* attribute. Inside the *VersionRange* element, you should add an *ApplyElementManifests* element with an inner *ElementManifest* element. Making the following modification to the feature.xml file, we can ensure that SharePoint Foundation will inspect elements_v2.xml during the feature upgrade process for a site and provision the Customers list as well as any new sites that activate the feature.

```
<Feature Id="86689158-7048-4421-AD21-E0DEF0D67C81" Version="2.0.0.0" >

  <ElementManifests>
    <ElementManifest Location="elements.xml" />
    <ElementManifest Location="elements_v2.xml" />
  </ElementManifests>

  <UpgradeActions>
    <VersionRange BeginVersion="1.0.0.0" EndVersion="2.0.0.0">
      <ApplyElementManifests>
        <ElementManifest Location="elements_v2.xml"/>
      </ApplyElementManifests>
    </VersionRange>
  </UpgradeActions>

</Feature>
```

The updated version of feature.xml has two different references to elements_v2.xml. Why? The bottom reference is used when a feature instance based on version 1.0.0.0 is upgraded to version 2.0.0.0. The top reference is needed as well. SharePoint Foundation uses the top reference to elements_v2.xml when a user activates the Wingtip Lead Tracker feature definition in a site for the first time using version 2.0.0.0. In this case, the feature instance is never upgraded, but the feature definition must still provision a new Customers list.

Adding Code Behind Custom Upgrade Actions

Earlier in this chapter, you saw how to extend a feature definition with a Feature Receiver by creating a public class that inherited from *SPFeatureReceiver*. In addition to the event handler methods we added, *FeatureActivated* and *FeatureDeactivating*, we now want to add another event handler method, *FeatureUpgrading*, which must be overwritten to execute code during a custom upgrade action.

```
public class FeatureReceiver : SPFeatureReceiver {

  public override void FeatureActivated(SPFeatureReceiverProperties props) {}

  public override void FeatureDeactivating(SPFeatureReceiverProperties props) {}

  public override void FeatureUpgrading(SPFeatureReceiverProperties props,
                                 string upgradeActionName,
                                 IDictionary<string, string> parameters) {
    // this event handler executes once for each custom upgrade action
  }
}
```

The *FeatureUpgrading* event handler is a bit more complicated than the event handlers for *FeatureActivated* and *FeatureDeactivating*. First, you need to add *ReceiverAssembly* and *ReceiverClass* attributes to the *UpgradeActions* element, as shown in Listing 2-7. Second, you must add one or more *CustomUpgradeAction* elements inside a *VersionRange* element inside the *UpgradeActions* element.

LISTING 2-7 You define upgrade actions by adding an *UpgradeActions* element to the feature.xml file.

```
<Feature Id="86689158-7048-4421-AD21-E0DEF0D67C81" Version="2.0.0.0" >

  <UpgradeActions
    ReceiverAssembly="WingtipDevProject1, [four-part assembly name]"
    ReceiverClass="WingtipDevProject1.FeatureReceiver" >

    <VersionRange BeginVersion="1.0.0.0" EndVersion="2.0.0.0">
      <CustomUpgradeAction Name="UpdateSiteTitle">
        <Parameters>
          <Parameter Name="NewSiteTitle">A much better site title</Parameter>
        </Parameters>
      </CustomUpgradeAction>
    </VersionRange>

  </UpgradeActions>

</Feature>
```

As you can see from Listing 2-7, a *CustomUpgradeAction* element is defined with the *Name* attribute and a parameter collection, which here contains only a single entry. It is essential to understand that the *FeatureUpgrading* event handler will execute once for each *CustomUpgradeAction* element. If you don't add at least one *CustomUpgradeAction* element, the *FeatureUpgrading* event handler will never fire.

Remember that you can add as many *CustomUpgradeAction* elements as you want. When you implement the *FeatureUpgrading* event handler, you can use the parameter named *upgradeActionName* to determine which custom upgrade action is being processed, and you can use the argument-named parameters to retrieve the parameters defined by the currently processing custom upgrade action.

In our case, the only custom upgrade action is named *UpdateSiteTitle*, and it contains a single parameter, *NewSiteTitle*. The implementation of the *FeatureUpgrading* event handler in Listing 2-8 uses a C# *switch* statement to execute the correct code for the custom upgrade action, named *UpdateSiteTitle*. Notice how the implementation must retrieve the value for the *NewSiteTitle* parameter to properly update the site title.

LISTING 2-8 The *FeatureUpgrading* method will execute once for each *CustomUpgradeAction* element.

```
public override void FeatureUpgrading(SPFeatureReceiverProperties props,
                                      string upgradeActionName,
                                      IDictionary<string, string> parameters) {
  // perform common initialization for all custom upgrade actions
  SPWeb site = props.Feature.Parent as SPWeb;
  if (site != null) {
    // determine which custom upgrade action is executing
    switch (upgradeActionName) {
      case "UpdateSiteTitle":
         //*** begin code for UpdateSiteTitle upgrade action
        string NewTitle = parameters["NewSiteTitle"];
        site.Title = NewTitle;
        site.Update();
        //*** end for UpdateSiteTitle upgrade action
        break;
      default:
        // unexpected feature upgrade action
        break;
    }
  }
}
```

We've now walked through adding an *UpgradeActions* element to the feature.xml file to upgrade a feature instance from version 1.0.0.0 to version 2.0.0.0. Keep in mind that this structure of the *UpgradeActions* element provides a good deal of flexibility to deal with future updates. Consider the scenario of pushing out a version 3.0.0.0 update. You might need to upgrade some feature instances that are currently version 1.0.0.0 in addition to feature instances that are version 2.0.0.0. You can add multiple *VersionRange* elements to differentiate between these two scenarios.

```
<UpgradeActions>

  <VersionRange BeginVersion="1.0.0.0" EndVersion="2.0.0.0">
    <!-- upgrade actions for upgrading from version 1 to 2 -->
  </VersionRange>

  <VersionRange BeginVersion="1.0.0.0" EndVersion="3.0.0.0">
    <!-- upgrade actions for upgrading from version 1 to 3 -->
  </VersionRange>

  <VersionRange BeginVersion="2.0.0.0" EndVersion="3.0.0.0">
    <!-- upgrade actions for upgrading from version 2 to 3 -->
```

```
    </VersionRange>

</UpgradeActions>
```

Upgrading Feature Instances

Once you've updated the feature definition, you must then push out the updated files using the *Update-SPSolution* cmdlet, as shown earlier in the chapter. You're still not done, however. SharePoint Foundation doesn't provide an administrative user interface to help you upgrade feature instances. Instead, you must write code to find all the feature instances requiring upgrade and explicitly call the *Upgrade* method supplied by the server-side object model.

Keep in mind that SharePoint Foundation doesn't allow two versions of a feature definition to be installed side by side within the same farm. Instead, an updated version of a feature definition overwrites the earlier version. For example, the updated feature.xml file replaces the original feature.xml file, and that's what SharePoint Foundation uses to determine a feature definition's current version number. This is another reason that the updated feature definition must contain all the original information as well as the new information for the updated version.

You can use the server-side object model to query for all the feature instances that require an upgrade. The *SPWebApplication* class exposes a *QueryFeatures* method that accepts the GUID identifier for a feature definition and returns all the associated feature instances. The *QueryFeatures* method has an overloaded implementation, which also allows you to filter the query based on whether the feature instance is up to date with the farm's current version of the feature definition. Here's a simple C# console application that executes a query to retrieve all feature instances requiring upgrade and explicitly calls the *Upgrade* method.

```
// get reference to target Web Application
Uri webAppUrl = new Uri("http://intranet.wingtip.com");
SPWebApplication webApp = SPWebApplication.Lookup(webAppUrl);

// query Web Application for feature instances needing an upgrade
Guid featureDefinitionId = new Guid("86689158-7048-4421-AD21-E0DEF0D67C81");
SPFeatureQueryResultCollection features =
  webApp.QueryFeatures(featureDefinitionId, true);

// enumerate through feature instances and call Upgrade
foreach (SPFeature  feature in features) {
  feature.Upgrade(true);
}
```

Although the C# code from the console application is easy to read and understand, it doesn't provide a practical way to upgrade feature instances in a production farm. It makes more sense to add the equivalent code to a Windows PowerShell script. The Windows PowerShell script in Listing 2-9 has been written to upgrade all the feature instances in the Web application at *http://intranet.wingtip.com*.

LISTING 2-9 You can write a Windows PowerShell script to explicitly upgrade feature instances.

```
Add-PSSnapin Microsoft.SharePoint.Powershell -ErrorAction "SilentlyContinue"
$WebAppUrl = "http://intranet.wingtip.com"
$featureId = New-Object System.Guid
                     -ArgumentList 86689158-7048-4421-AD21-E0DEF0D67C81"

$webApp = [Microsoft.SharePoint.Administration.SPWebApplication]::Lookup($WebAppUrl)
$features = $webApp.QueryFeatures($FeatureId, $true)

foreach($feature in $features){
  $feature.Upgrade($true)
}
```

Now that you've seen the entire process, let's summarize how feature upgrade works. Remember that feature upgrade only makes sense in a scenario in which a feature definition has been deployed and feature instances have already been created. The first step is updating the feature definition to include one or more upgrade actions. The second step is to rebuild the solution package and to push the updates out into the farm using the *Update-SPSolution* cmdlet. The final step is to run a Windows PowerShell script or use another approach to trigger the upgrade process on specific feature instances. When you trigger the upgrade process, SharePoint Foundation begins to process your upgrade actions.

Conclusion

In this chapter, we focused on teaching you the fundamental concepts and skills required to develop SharePoint solutions on the SharePoint Foundation platform. You've seen how to program against the server-side object model using C# code written in a Visual Studio 2010 project as well as using code written in a Windows PowerShell script. You also learned the basics of developing features and building a solution package for deployment.

You've also seen how to leverage the new feature upgrade support introduced in SharePoint Foundation. This new enhancement to the SharePoint platform is very welcome, as it finally gives developers a supported technique to evolve the functionality of a feature definition over time.

We apologize that we made you suffer through the theoretical exercise of building a Visual Studio 2010 project without the assistance of the new SharePoint Developer Tools. However, we feel the sacrifice you made was worth it because you now have a much better understanding of how SharePoint Foundation works internally. This new understanding will allow you to fully appreciate what the SharePoint Developer Tools do for you behind the scenes. It will also make it possible for you to extend a SharePoint project when you need to extend a feature definition or SharePoint solution with CAML elements that aren't supported by the SharePoint Developer Tools.

Chapter 3
SharePoint Developer Tools in Microsoft Visual Studio 2010

The release of SharePoint 2007 was a significant milestone for SharePoint as a development platform because in this version, Microsoft introduced support for features and solution packages. Soon after SharePoint 2007 was released, however, it became clear within Microsoft and throughout the industry that more and better developer productivity tools were needed.

The SharePoint 2010 developer platform increases developer productivity by introducing the SharePoint Developer Tools in Visual Studio 2010. These new tools make developing for SharePoint 2010 much faster and easier because they automate grungy tasks and hide many of the low-level details that developers have to worry about when developing for SharePoint 2007.

For example, a project created using the SharePoint Developer Tools in Visual Studio 2010 is a special type of project, known as a SharePoint project. Every SharePoint project is created with built-in support to generate its output as a solution package. The SharePoint Developer Tools also integrate commands into the Visual Studio 2010 environment that make it easy to deploy and retract the solution package for a SharePoint project during testing and debugging.

Life Before SharePoint Developer Tools

The development tools available for SharePoint 2007 are quite primitive. What has made things worse is that everybody does development differently. If you asked five different SharePoint 2007 developers which tools they use, you would likely hear five different responses.

Visual Studio 2008 shipped with a toolset named *Visual Studio Tools for Office (VSTO)*, which included two project templates for developing SharePoint 2007 workflow templates. However, these templates include no support for building a project into a .wsp file, which makes it challenging to distribute a development effort using best-practice techniques.

In a separate effort, the SharePoint team led a project to create a Visual Studio add-in named *Visual Studio Extensions for Windows SharePoint Services 3.0 (VSeWSS)*. One of the primary design goals of the VSeWSS project was to build support into a Visual Studio project to generate a .wsp file behind the scenes. The VSeWSS add-in also adds integrated commands into Visual Studio to deploy and test the project using the generated .wsp file.

VSeWSS has experienced several problems throughout the SharePoint 2007 life cycle. The 1.0 release of VSeWSS had some significant design flaws, so the adoption rate among intermediate to advanced SharePoint developers was low. Since the initial release of VSeWSS, the SharePoint team has shipped several updates to this toolset that have improved its usability and increased its adoption rate. Despite the updates, however, VSeWSS still has several noteworthy shortcomings.

First, the VSeWSS project format is hard-coded to a specific version of Visual Studio and a specific version of the VSeWSS add-in. That means you can't open a VSeWSS project unless you've installed the correct version of Visual Studio and the correct version of the VSeWSS add-in. Second, VSeWSS doesn't support team development environments that rely on the Microsoft Build Engine (MSBuild) or build servers that don't have Visual Studio installed. Finally, VSeWSS wasn't designed with extensibility in mind. That means using VSeWSS when developing SharePoint 2007 components that aren't directly supported by the toolset, such as workflow templates, is challenging and usually impractical.

Given the lack of effective developer tools for SharePoint 2007 available from Microsoft, many developers within the SharePoint developer community worked to fill in the gaps. They created their own tools and utilities to make SharePoint 2007 development easier. Many of the developers who created these utilities and tools posted their projects to CodePlex to share their efforts with other SharePoint developers around the world. Today, there are hundreds of SharePoint 2007 development projects on CodePlex.

The SharePoint 2007 project from CodePlex that has experienced the highest adoption rate among professional developers is *WSPBuilder*. The WSPBuilder utility allows developers to build SharePoint 2007 components using standard Visual Studio class library projects. WSPBuilder adds support to automate building the project into a .wsp file for best-practice deployment. Because WSPBuilder uses standard library projects, it is much more flexible than VSeWSS, allowing you to move between different versions of Visual Studio and to automate the solution package build process using MSBuild.

Many developers and companies decided to go it alone and to add custom support to their Visual Studio projects to build them into .wsp files and deploy them for testing. This approach typically involves creating standard class library projects and adding batch files or custom tasks to integrate commands to call command-line utilities such as makecab.exe and stsadm.exe. Unfortunately, this individualistic approach leads to a development style in which the developer is responsible for tracking tedious details, a chore that has a significantly negative impact on productivity.

In summary, the developer tools available in SharePoint 2007 are immature and are used inconsistently and with varying techniques across the developer community. One result is that beginning developers who are looking for guidance on the right way to get started have a difficult time finding it. Another consequence is that experienced .NET developers who have been using Visual Studio to build ASP.NET applications are frustrated because moving to the SharePoint 2007 development platform seems like a giant step backward in terms of productivity. Fortunately, the SharePoint Developer Tools put an end to these pains for both novice and experienced developers.

Getting Started with the SharePoint Developer Tools

The SharePoint Developer Tools are great for new developers just getting started with the SharePoint development platform because they abstract away many of the low-level details, such as creating the manifest.xml file and building a project into a .wsp file. Intermediate and advanced developers who already have experience with SharePoint 2007 development are going to appreciate the SharePoint Developer Tools because they support a high degree of extensibility.

You should understand that you can't use the SharePoint Developer Tools to develop solutions for SharePoint 2007. The SharePoint Developer Tools can be used only to develop for SharePoint 2010 and future versions. If you're still required to build business solutions for SharePoint 2007, you must use one of the older tools, such as VSeWSS or WSPBuilder, discussed in the previous section.

We begin our exploration of the SharePoint Developer Tools by examining a utility named *SharePoint Explorer*. This utility provides a convenient way to inspect a SharePoint site from within Visual Studio 2010 and to see the elements inside the site, such as lists and document libraries. After a quick discussion of SharePoint Explorer, we move ahead to the central topic of the chapter, building SharePoint projects using the SharePoint Developer Tools.

Before you begin using the SharePoint Developer Tools, you must ensure that your developer workstation is configured correctly. In particular, you must build out your development workstation as a single-server farm running either SharePoint Foundation or SharePoint Server 2010. A key point is that the SharePoint Developer Tools don't work correctly on a workstation that doesn't have a version of SharePoint 2010 installed. That's because the SharePoint Developer Tools were designed to run on a computer that is acting as a front-end Web server within a SharePoint 2010 farm.

Using SharePoint Explorer

As we just mentioned, the SharePoint Developer Tools include a utility named SharePoint Explorer. SharePoint Explorer is a visual component that runs inside the Server Explorer window of Visual Studio 2010, as shown in Figure 3-1. You work with SharePoint Explorer by adding SharePoint connections. To create a new SharePoint connection, you must provide a URL to a site running in the local SharePoint farm. Once created, a SharePoint connection displays a hierarchy of nodes that allow you to inspect the target site and the elements inside, such as its lists and document libraries. When you click the node for a site or a list, the standard Visual Studio property sheet shows the properties associated with the SharePoint object.

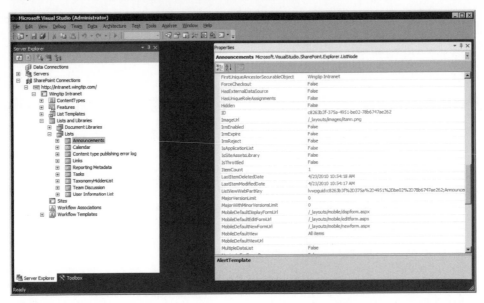

FIGURE 3-1 SharePoint Explorer allows you to inspect sites running within the local SharePoint site.

SharePoint Explorer doesn't provide any built-in functionality to modify a SharePoint site or to create new site elements such as a list instance. Therefore, you should think of a SharePoint connection as a read-only view into a SharePoint site. You primarily use SharePoint Explorer to inspect the properties and elements of a site using the standard Visual Studio property sheet.

SharePoint Explorer can also assist you with navigating to a site inside a browser window for testing purposes. For example, right-clicking on the node for a list lets you see a contextual menu command with the caption View in Browser. You can execute this command to launch a new session of Internet Explorer and navigate to the default view for that list.

SharePoint Explorer is fairly simple to understand and use. What makes it powerful is that it was designed to be extensible. Developers can create custom node types that load into a SharePoint connection along with the standard node types. This capability opens up the possibilities of custom node types that do more than just inspect sites. You could write a custom extension for SharePoint Explorer to modify the target site, or to add new site elements such as list instances or Web Parts.

Creating a SharePoint Project

Now it's time to create our first SharePoint project using the SharePoint Developer Tools. This walkthrough demonstrates what's required to create a new SharePoint project that contains a feature, a few elements, and a Feature Receiver. You'll also see how to test and debug your project inside a target test site running in the local farm.

The SharePoint Developer Tools provide several different templates for creating new SharePoint projects that are available in Visual Basic and C#. For example, you can see the project templates available for C# projects in the New Project dialog within Visual Studio 2010 by navigating to Visual C#\SharePoint\2010, as shown in Figure 3-2.

FIGURE 3-2 The SharePoint Developer Tools provide project templates for creating SharePoint projects.

When you select one of these project templates in the New Project dialog and then click the OK button to create a new SharePoint project, the SharePoint Developer Tools launch the SharePoint Customization Wizard shown in Figure 3-3. The SharePoint Customization Wizard prompts you for two pieces of information: the URL to a local site and a trust level.

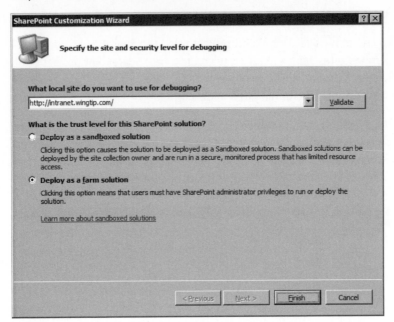

FIGURE 3-3 The SharePoint Customization Wizard prompts you for a URL to a test site and a trust level.

When you enter the URL in the SharePoint Customization Wizard, you must provide the URL to a site that is accessible within the local SharePoint farm. The SharePoint Developer Tools use this site URL when testing and debugging the project.

The SharePoint Configuration Wizard also makes you choose between two options: Deploy as a sandboxed solution or Deploy as a farm solution. Your choice mainly affects how the SharePoint Developer Tools deploy the project's solution package during testing and debugging. In this chapter, we'll work with projects that are deployed as farm solutions. In Chapter 4, "Sandboxed Solutions," we'll discuss how to develop projects that will be deployed as sandboxed solutions.

We first create a new SharePoint project named WingtipDevProject2 using the Empty SharePoint Project template and a site URL of *http://intranet.wingtip.com*. We also elect to create the new project using the option to deploy it as a farm solution. When you click the Finish button in the SharePoint Customization Wizard, Visual Studio takes a few seconds to create and configure the new project. Figure 3-4 shows what the new SharePoint project looks like in Solution Explorer.

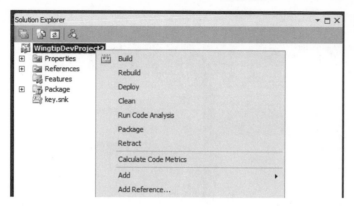

FIGURE 3-4 Every SharePoint project is created with a *Features* node and a *Package* node.

All Visual Studio projects contain standard nodes such as Properties and References. SharePoint projects have two additional nodes that exist only within SharePoint projects: the *Features* node and the *Package* node.

You use the *Features* node to add new features to a SharePoint project. Notice that the *Features* node is empty when you create a new SharePoint project using the Empty SharePoint Project template. You use the *Package* node to track project-wide settings related to building the project into a solution package .wsp file.

All SharePoint projects also have three special menu commands: Deploy, Package, and Retract. These menu commands, exclusive to SharePoint projects, are available when you right-click the top-level project node in Solution Explorer. These three menu commands are shown in Figure 3-4.

You can run the *Package* command to build a SharePoint project into a solution package. You can use the *Deploy* command to run a sequence of deployment steps that deploy the solution package in the local farm so that you can test and debug your work. The *Retract* command reverses the act of deployment by retracting the solution package from the local farm.

Creating a Feature

To add a new feature to a project, right-click the *Features* node and click the *Add* command. The SharePoint Developer Tools respond by creating a new feature with a generic name such as Feature1. You should get in the habit of renaming features with a meaningful name right after you create them. You can rename a new feature by right-clicking on the feature's top-level node and clicking the *Rename* command. In our example, we create a new feature and rename it ProductDevelopment, as shown in Figure 3-5.

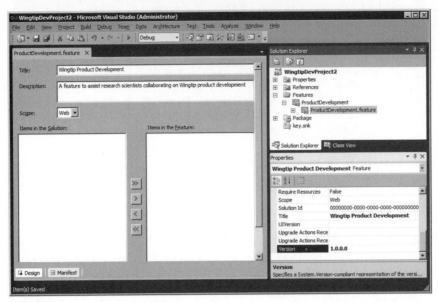

FIGURE 3-5 The SharePoint Developer Tools allow you to add new features to the *Features* node and to configure features using the Feature Designer and the standard Visual Studio property sheet.

Once you've created and renamed a new feature, you can double-click its node inside Solution Explorer to open it inside the Feature Designer, which is shown on the left-hand side of Figure 3-5. The Feature Designer allows you to modify the three feature properties: *Title*, *Description*, and *Scope*. Remember that a *Scope* setting of *Web* means that the feature activates at the site level and a *Scope* setting of *Site* means that the feature activates at the site collection level. The feature in our example has the *Title* of *Wingtip Product Development* and a *Scope* of *Web*.

Many other feature properties can be viewed and modified through the feature's property sheet, which is shown in the lower right-hand section of Figure 3-5. For example, you can use a feature's property sheet to assign a value to the *Version* property. When you're just getting started, getting to the property sheet for a feature can be a little tricky. The secret is to open the Feature Designer and then click it so that it becomes the active window. Once you make the Feature Designer the active window, Visual Studio shows the property sheet and allows you to view and update many additional feature properties.

Adding a Feature Receiver

Now it's time to create a Feature Receiver so that we can add some C# code that will execute whenever our new feature is activated or deactivated. The SharePoint Developer Tools make adding an event receiver to a feature easy. Just right-click the feature's top-level node and click the *Add Event Receiver* command, as shown in Figure 3-6.

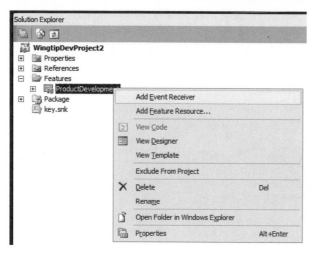

FIGURE 3-6 The SharePoint Developer Tools make it easy to extend a feature by adding a Feature Receiver.

When you add an event receiver using this technique, the SharePoint Developer Tools do quite a bit of work for you behind the scenes. First, they add a source file, which is based on either C# or Visual Basic, depending on the language of the underlying project. If you create a Feature Receiver for the feature named *ProductDevelopment*, the SharePoint Developer Tools create a C# source file named *ProductDevelopment.EventReceiver.cs*. The SharePoint Developer Tools also add configuration data behind the scenes. This configuration data results in the building of a feature.xml file that properly configures the *ReceiverClass* and *ReceiverAssembly* attributes so that SharePoint Foundation recognizes the Feature Receiver, and the event handlers added to the Feature Receiver are executed at the correct times.

When you first open a source file created for a Feature Receiver, such as *ProductDevelopment .EventReceiver.cs*, you see that the SharePoint Developer Tools have added a class definition for the Feature Receiver with method stubs that are commented out. You simply uncomment the stubs, which represent the events you want to handle, and add your custom code. In this walkthrough, we're going to add code for the *FeatureActivated* and *FeatureDeactivating* methods so that we can run custom C# code on the front-end Web server whenever the feature is activated or deactivated. In Listing 3-1, we include only the stubs of these two event handler methods and leave the implementation up to your imagination.

LISTING 3-1 The SharePoint Developer Tools automatically generate the starting code for an event receiver class.

```
using System;

using System.Runtime.InteropServices;
using System.Security.Permissions;
using Microsoft.SharePoint;
using Microsoft.SharePoint.Security;

namespace WingtipDevProject2.Features.ProductDevelopment {

  [Guid("b53e6391-97b6-4ae9-a1b9-579d14bd4404")]
  public class ProductDevelopmentEventReceiver : SPFeatureReceiver {

    public override void FeatureActivated(SPFeatureReceiverProperties properties) {
      // your activation code goes here
    }

    public override void FeatureDeactivating(SPFeatureReceiverProperties properties) {
      // your deactivation code goes here
    }

  }
}
```

The SharePoint Developer Tools also add a special GUID attribute when creating a new Feature Receiver class to give it a unique identifier. You shouldn't remove the GUID attribute from a feature class because the SharePoint Developer Tools use the GUID behind the scenes during the packaging process.

Adding a SharePoint Project Item

The primary way you extend the functionality in a SharePoint project is by adding new items created from special project item templates provided by the SharePoint Developer Tools. These items are known as SharePoint *project items*. You can see these templates inside the Add New Item dialog at C#\SharePoint\2010, as shown in Figure 3-7.

FIGURE 3-7 The Add New Item dialog supplies a folder of templates for creating SharePoint project items.

In our walkthrough, we'll create a new list instance named Scientists. When we choose the List Instance template and then click Add to create a new project item instance, SharePoint Developer Tools display the SharePoint Customization Wizard dialog to prompt us for the various properties of the new list. You can see in Figure 3-8 that we've given the list a display name of *Scientists* and indicated that we want the new list instance created from the *Contacts* list type.

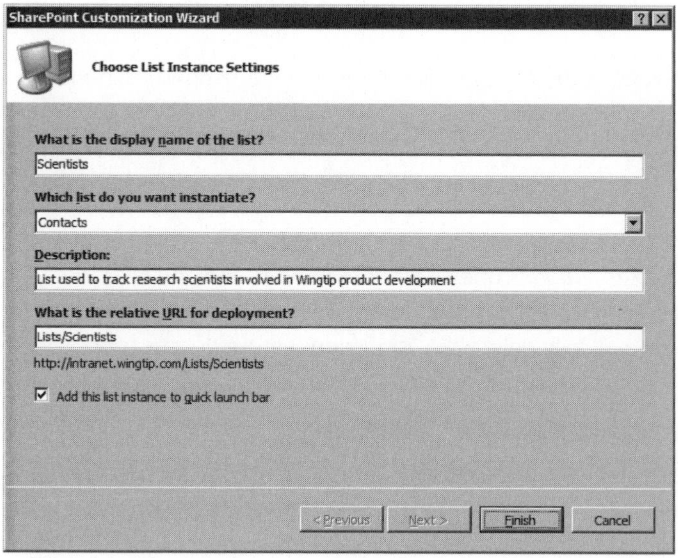

FIGURE 3-8 The SharePoint Customization Wizard prompts for values to initialize the new List Instance project item.

When you click the Finish button in the SharePoint Customization Wizard, the SharePoint Developer Tools create a top-level folder in the project with the same name as the project item instance. Inside this folder is an elements.xml file with a *ListInstance* element, as shown in Figure 3-9. In some cases, the XML that the SharePoint Developer Tools provide is sufficient for your needs. In other cases, you might be required to hand-edit the XML to change an attribute value or to add new attributes or elements.

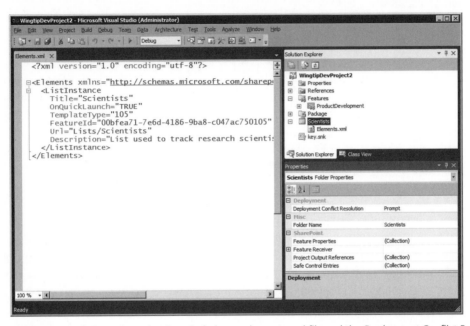

FIGURE 3-9 A *ListInstance* project item includes an elements.xml file and the *Deployment Conflict Resolution* property.

You can select the top-level folder for a project item to see its properties in the standard Visual Studio property sheet. Note that the project item itself can have its own properties. Also note that List Instance project items have a property named *Deployment Conflict Resolution* that allows you to configure the project item's behavior when the project is deployed during testing.

The *Deployment Conflict Resolution* property was designed to remedy an underlying problem. Although a *ListInstance* element can be used to create a new list during feature activation, it doesn't automatically delete the list during feature deactivation. Therefore, you can run into problems during testing when you're continually activating and deactivating a feature.

What happens if you activate a feature and then deactivate it? The feature creates a new list and leaves it in the site after it is deactivated. The next time you activate the feature, you'll run into a problem. The feature can't create the new list because another list of the same name already exists. In SharePoint 2010, this attempt to create the list instance results in a silent failure. The feature still activates successfully, but the new list isn't created.

The main idea behind the *Deployment Conflict Resolution* property is that you can configure a project item to delete any elements in the target site that might impact your testing. For example, when you deploy the project, the SharePoint Developer Tools can be configured to automatically look for and delete any list named *Scientists*. As long as the SharePoint Developer Tools delete the existing list instance prior to feature activation, you'll be able to properly test what happens when the list instances get created during activation.

A List Instance project item has a *Deployment Conflict Resolution* property value, which by default is set to a value of *Prompt*. Whenever you deploy the project and the SharePoint Developer Tools detect a conflict with an existing list in the test site, you'll be prompted to specify whether or not you want to delete the list. You can suppress the prompting behavior by changing the property value for *Deployment Conflict Resolution* to *Automatic*.

At this point, we've created a new feature that has both a Feature Receiver and an element manifest. However, we haven't yet dealt directly with the feature.xml file. This file is one of the key productivity points of the SharePoint Developer Tools. The SharePoint Developer Tools deal with the details of the feature.xml file behind the scenes. Beginners don't even have to know about the feature.xml file. However, you can get direct access to feature.xml, which might be required in some advanced scenarios.

Let's examine Figure 3-10 so that you can see what the Feature Designer looks like after you've added a project item. Notice that the Feature Designer shows the project item named *Scientists* inside its collection of items. Behind the scenes, the SharePoint Developer Tools have automatically updated the feature.xml file by adding a reference to the element manifest from the *Scientists* project item.

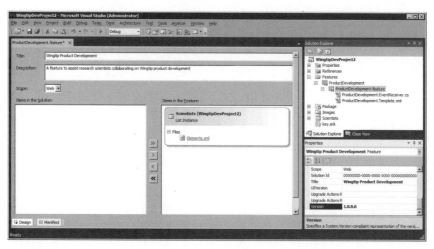

FIGURE 3-10 The Feature Designer allows you to add project items into a feature—or remove them.

The Feature Designer allows you to add and remove project items. For example, imagine the scenario in which you've added a second feature to this project. You could remove the project item from this feature and then add it to the first feature you created. The SharePoint Developer Tools even allow you to add the same project item to two features at the same time (in rare scenarios where that makes sense).

Deployment and Testing

Now that we have a SharePoint project with a feature, a Feature Receiver, and a project item, it's time to deploy and test our work. If you right-click the top-level project node inside Solution Explorer to drop down the context menu, you see a *Deploy* command and a *Retract* command. You'll use these commands constantly when you test and debug SharePoint projects.

You might be wondering what happens when you execute the *Deploy* command. The answer is, *it depends*. More specifically, it depends on which deployment configuration your project is using.

You can see and modify the available deployment configurations for a SharePoint project from the SharePoint tab of the Project Properties dialog, as shown in Figure 3-11. Every new SharePoint project is created with two deployment configurations, *Default* and *No Activation*. You can add more deployment configurations if you want something different. However, you can't modify *Default* and *No Activation*. You can only modify deployment configurations you've added.

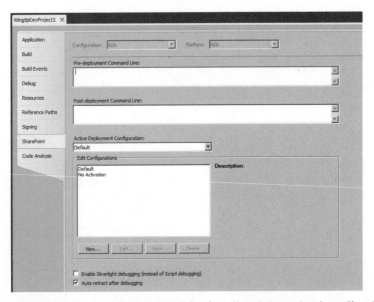

FIGURE 3-11 The Project Properties dialog for a SharePoint project has a SharePoint tab showing deployment configurations.

Notice the two text boxes on the SharePoint tab: Pre-deployment Command Line and Post-deployment Command Line. Using these text boxes, you can add command-line instructions that will execute either just before or directly after the active deployment configuration is processed. For example, you can add a command-line instruction to call a custom Windows PowerShell script using the techniques you learned in Chapter 2, "SharePoint Foundation Development," about integrating Windows PowerShell scripts into Visual Studio 2010.

The fact that you can change or modify the deployment configuration for a SharePoint project provides a convenient degree of flexibility. The SharePoint Developer Tools allow you to control the processing that occurs behind the *Deploy* and *Retract* commands by using units of execution known as *deployment steps*.

To see the deployment steps within a specific deployment configuration, select that deployment configuration in the SharePoint tab and then click the View button. Figure 3-12 shows the sequence of deployment steps for the default deployment configuration. First, the target Internet Information Services (IIS) application pool is recycled. Then, any previous deployment of the solution package is retracted and removed. Next, the latest build of the project's solution package is installed and deployed. Finally, any project features that have a *Scope* setting of either *Web* or *Site* are automatically activated.

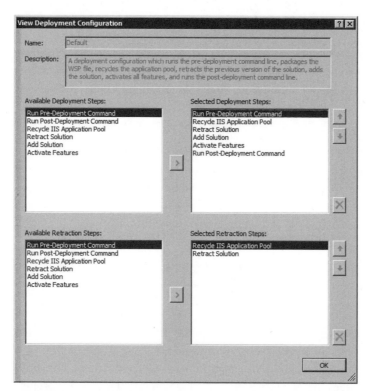

FIGURE 3-12 Each deployment configuration is made up of deployment steps.

On the left-hand side of the View Deployment Configuration dialog shown in Figure 3-12, you can see a list of available deployment steps that come out of the box with the SharePoint Developer Tools. The one obvious deployment step that is missing is the one for updating a solution package so that you can test and debug your upgrade actions from within Visual Studio. So how then can you run a command from Visual Studio 2010 to perform a solution upgrade in your local farm?

One approach is to create a new deployment configuration that doesn't contain the deployment steps for *Retract Solution* or *Add Solution*. Then you could add a Post-deployment Command Line instruction call to a custom Windows PowerShell script that runs the *Update-SPSolution* cmdlet, as we did in Chapter 2.

Another approach is to either create or find a custom deployment step that adds the functionality you need. This option is possible because the team that created the SharePoint Developer Tools designed deployment steps to be extensible. A developer can create a custom extension for Visual Studio 2010 and the SharePoint Developer Tools that adds custom deployment steps. Within the SharePoint developer community, Visual Studio extensions that extend the SharePoint Developer Tools with a custom deployment step for updating solutions—and much more—are already available.

Working with Mapped Folders

You now know how to create features and project items using the SharePoint Developer Tools. As you've seen, the SharePoint Developer Tools do a pretty good job of hiding the details of where the files for a feature need to be deployed inside the SharePoint root directory. However, in certain scenarios, a developer is required to deploy a file into a specific location inside the SharePoint root directory. For this reason, the SharePoint Developer Tools include *mapped folders*.

Let's say you want to deploy a custom image file named FeatureIcon.gif that will appear alongside the Wingtip Product Development feature on the feature management page. Going through the steps to accomplish this will give you a chance to learn how the SharePoint Developer Tools use mapped folders. They key point is that mapped folders can be used to deploy custom files inside the SharePointRootFiles folder into standard SharePoint folders such as TEMPLATE, CONTROL TEMPLATES, LAYOUTS, and IMAGES.

We're going to use an example of deploying an image file inside the IMAGE directory, but you can also use mapped folders for deploying many other types of files, including CSS files, JavaScript files, XSLT files, and Silverlight XAP files.

The first step is to add a new mapped folder to the project that will deploy its files into the SharePoint IMAGES folder. Just right-click the top-level project node in Solution Explorer, expand the Add menu, and click the *SharePoint "Images" Mapped Folder* command. Once you've created the Images folder inside your project, you should be able to observe that the SharePoint Developer Tools automatically created a child folder with the same name as the current project. In our example, the SharePoint Developer Tools created an Images folder inside the project that contains a child folder named WingtipDevProject2, as shown in Figure 3-13. We can then add custom image files to this folder, such as FeatureIcon.gif and SiteIcon.gif, the ones shown in Figure 3-13. The easy way to add custom image files is to right-click the child folder named WingtipDevProject2 and then click Add\Existing Items. When the resulting dialog opens, you can navigate to the folder on your development work-station that contains a copy the files you want and copy them into your mapped folder.

FIGURE 3-13 You can use mapped folders to deploy custom files inside the RootFiles folder to standard folders such as TEMPLATE, LAYOUTS, and IMAGES.

This example demonstrates how the SharePoint Developer Tools help ensure that best practices are followed in SharePoint development. More specifically, when deploying image files within a farm solution, you shouldn't add your custom files directly inside the Images folder because doing so creates potential problems with file name conflicts. The best practice is to add images to a child directory inside the Images folder that is named after the solution package. In this example, the SharePoint Developer Tools automatically created a child folder named WingtipDevProject2.

The SharePoint Developer Tools do a good deal of work behind the scenes to keep track of all your source files and to figure out which ones need to be compiled inside the output solu-tion package. To do this monitoring, the SharePoint Developer Tools add two extra proper-ties to each source file inside a SharePoint project: *Deployment Location* and *Deployment Type*. In Figure 3-14, you can see how the values for these two properties are set for the FeatureIcon.gif file that has been deployed in a mapped folder.

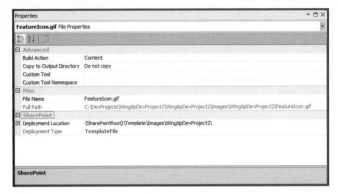

FIGURE 3-14 The SharePoint Developer Tools track source files in a SharePoint project using two extra properties, *Deployment Location* and *Deployment Type*.

Now that we've taken the steps to deploy FeatureIcon.gif into the farm when the solution package is deployed, we should configure the Wingtip Product Development feature by modifying its *ImageUrl* property. Just open the feature in the Feature Designer so that you can access the feature's property sheet. Inside the property sheet, you can update the *ImageUrl* property with a URL relative to the Images folder, which in this case is *WingtipDevProject2\FeatureIcon.gif*.

Let's finish our discussion of the SharePoint Developer Tools by looking at the Package Designer. If you expand the *Package* node in a SharePoint project, you'll see an inner node named *Package.package*. If you double-click this node, the SharePoint Developer Tools display the Package Designer. At the bottom left-hand corner of the Package Designer are three tabs: Design, Advanced, and Manifest. These tabs allow you to switch back and forth between different views of the project's solution package. Figure 3-15 shows the Manifest view, which reveals the XML that is written into the manifest.xml file when the SharePoint Developer Tools build the project into a solution package.

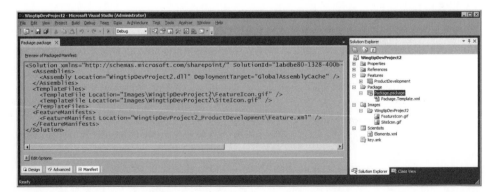

FIGURE 3-15 The Manifest View of the Package Designer shows the XML that goes into the manifest.xml file.

In many scenarios, a developer doesn't need to inspect or care about the XML that goes into the manifest.xml file. After all, the SharePoint Developer Tools are valuable partly because they hide so many of the details developers had to worry about in SharePoint 2007 development.

In other scenarios, however, a developer will need to directly edit the manifest.xml file. For example, when you need to add an XML element that the SharePoint Developer Tools don't directly support, such as the *ActivationDependencies* element discussed in Chapter 2, you have to add it manually to manifest.xml.

If you look at the *Package* node in Solution Explorer in Figure 3-15, you'll notice a source file named *Package.Template.xml*. If you open this file, you'll see that it has a top-level *Solution* element but no inner elements. All you need to do is add the *ActivationDependencies* element to this file inside the *Solution* element. When the SharePoint Developer Tools generate the manifest.xml file, they merge the XML elements they create behind the scenes with any XML elements you have added to *Package.Template.xml*. By using this technique, you can call on your knowledge of SharePoint development to supplement what the SharePoint Developer Tools support directly.

In addition to making direct edits to a project's manifest.xml file, you can also make direct edits to the feature.xml file for any feature in a SharePoint project. You'll need to edit directly in feature.xml when you want to version a feature definition by adding an *UpgradeActions* element, because the SharePoint Developer Tools don't directly support adding any elements dealing with feature upgrade functionality.

Inside the node for each feature, you should be able to locate and open the template.xml file. Once you open template.xml for a feature, you can add elements inside the top-level feature element. For example, you can add an *UpgradeActions* element like the one shown in Chapter 2. The SharePoint Developer Tools merge the *UpgradeActions* element and all the inner child elements into the feature.xml file that is built in the project's solution package.

Conclusion

In this chapter, we took a closer look at the SharePoint Developer Tools in Visual Studio 2010. We'll continue to go over other techniques you can use in the SharePoint Developer Tools throughout the remaining chapters of this book. This chapter was mostly about the fundamentals of using this new toolset. Here's a summary of those fundamentals.

The SharePoint Development Tools provide Visual Studio project templates for creating SharePoint projects. Every SharePoint project has the ability to build itself into a solution package and to deploy this solution package for testing and debugging on a local farm. You mainly grow out the functionality of a SharePoint project by creating SharePoint project items. Each SharePoint project item has its own folder, set of files, and properties. Certain types of project items, such as list instances, provide conflict resolution to clean up the target test site during activation. For advanced developers who want to move beyond the basics, the SharePoint Developer Tools allow you to add mapped folders and to make direct edits to low-level files such as manifest.xml and feature.xml.

Chapter 4
Sandboxed Solutions

Sandboxed solutions are Microsoft SharePoint Foundation features that are deployed into a partially trusted environment referred to as the *sandbox*. The sandbox is designed to bring greater stability to a SharePoint farm by restricting actions that could cause problems with performance, security, or other areas. This stability is achieved by limiting the functionality accessible to custom code solutions through the use of code access security (CAS) policies and by restricting access to portions of the object model.

The sandbox is a new capability for SharePoint Foundation and represents one of the most significant changes to the SharePoint developer platform. Because of the benefits the sandbox offers, developers should always look to deploy custom code to the sandbox before considering any other option. Therefore, a strong understanding of the sandbox is critical for writing robust SharePoint solutions.

Prior to SharePoint 2010, the vast majority of custom code had to be deployed to the global assembly cache (GAC). Because of this, developers often operated with full trust in the SharePoint server not only to call any part of the object model, but also to access databases, Web services, directories, and more. The one major exception to this rule in SharePoint 2007 development was deployment with Web Parts. The assembly containing Web Parts could be deployed to the GAC or to the bin folder under the Web application. However, a developer could easily grant full trust to Web Parts deployed in the bin folder anyway, simply by changing the trust level setting in the web.config file to Full.

The result of this situation was that nearly all code in the farm ran with full trust and few SharePoint developers had the need to learn much about CAS restrictions. The drawback of this approach is that the SharePoint farm was occasionally destabilized by custom code. To make matters worse, the offending assembly was often hard to identify.

As an example, consider the case in which an intermediate-level SharePoint developer is writing a Web Part designed to aggregate tasks from many lists to display on a site collection home page. Imagine this developer is unaware of the *Microsoft.SharePoint.SPSiteDataQuery* object and instead intends to loop through all the sites in the collection, loop through all the lists in the site, and finally loop through all the tasks in a list to create a single view of all tasks in the site collection. Furthermore, the developer intends to elevate privileges with the Web Part code to ensure programmatic access to the entire site collection. This simple Web Part could easily destabilize the entire farm.

Opting to loop through all the lists and items is a potential disaster because the process of looping causes entire lists to be loaded into memory. If these lists are large, significant resources could be consumed, resulting in performance problems for all users, as these resources would then be unavailable for servicing other requests. Elevating privileges is potentially problematic because the code gains access to all lists, and the intermediate developer may be unaware that creating *Microsoft.SharePoint.SPSite* and *Microsoft.SharePoint.SPWeb* objects without properly disposing of them leads to memory leaks. If this simple Web Part is deployed to the GAC, it will have no limitations on the resources it can consume. If the Web Part is then put on the home page of the portal, it could be hit by potentially thousands of users. It wouldn't be long before the farm was brought to a standstill because of low memory availability.

Interestingly, when poorly written code does destabilize a farm, the developer rarely suffers. Farms have limited mechanisms for identifying the code that is causing the problem. In some cases, information might be available in the Unified Logging Service (ULS), but often the destabilization is just considered a mysterious performance problem. As a result, fixing the problem generally falls to the IT professionals in charge of running the SharePoint farm. They are the ones who receive a call on Friday night saying that the farm is misbehaving. They are also the least qualified people to identify and fix the real problem—simply because they did not write the custom code that is causing the problem. In fact, IT professionals may actually cause further problems by desperately changing the farm configuration in an attempt to regain stability. Sometimes such situations become chronic, which results in negative experiences for IT professionals and users, who can begin to question the viability of SharePoint as a platform.

On the other end of the spectrum, experienced SharePoint developers often need access to trusted resources like external databases to solve business problems. These developers may be well aware of CAS limitations, understand the SharePoint object model, and generally create professional solutions. Unnecessarily restricting their ability to customize code significantly reduces the flexibility of SharePoint as a platform for them. Therefore, the challenge is one of balancing the agility required to solve business problems against the farm security and stability required of enterprise applications. This is where sandboxed solutions come into play.

Understanding the Sandbox

The sandbox is a separate process in which a SharePoint solution runs in isolation. This separate process exposes a subset of the *Microsoft.SharePoint* namespace that an assembly can call. Additionally, the process runs under a CAS policy that restricts programmatic access to any resource outside the sandbox (although as you'll learn shortly, you can create a full-trust proxy). Sandboxed solutions are managed through a new Solution Gallery at the site collection level and farm-level tools found in Central Administration. Additionally, Microsoft Visual Studio 2010 can deploy solutions directly to the sandbox during development.

Enabling sandboxed solutions in a SharePoint farm is simple because it requires enabling only a single Windows service, the *User Code Service*. The User Code Service is responsible for managing the execution of sandboxed solutions across the farm. Each server in the farm that will participate in hosting sandboxed solutions must have the User Code Service enabled. You can enable the User Code Service through Central Administration\System Settings\Manage Services on Server. Generally, this service simply runs under the Network Service account. Once this service is enabled, you can begin running sandboxed solutions.

Building a Basic Sandboxed Solution

When you create a new SharePoint solution in Visual Studio 2010, the SharePoint Customization Wizard offers you the option to deploy your solution as a farm solution or a sandboxed solution. Farm solutions are deployed in the same manner as they were in SharePoint 2007, and you can manage them by selecting System Settings\Manage Farm Solutions in Central Administration. Sandboxed solutions, on the other hand, are deployed directly to a site collection.

Now it's time to walk through an example of creating a sandboxed solution. We'll revisit the idea of developing a SharePoint solution for the Wingtip Lead Tracker feature that we introduced in Chapter 2, "SharePoint Foundation Development." This time, however, we'll use the SharePoint Developer Tools in Visual Studio 2010. We'll start by creating an Empty SharePoint project named LeadTracker. When you click OK to create the new project, the Visual Studio SharePoint Customization Wizard allows you to select the sandboxed solution deployment option, as shown in Figure 4-1.

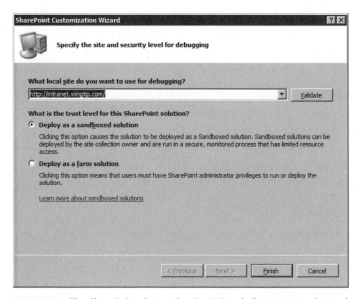

FIGURE 4-1 The SharePoint Customization Wizard allows you to choose between a sandboxed solution and a farm solution.

After you create the project in Visual Studio, you can alter the deployment target by editing the *Sandboxed Solution* property of the project in the project property sheet. Along with changing the deployment target, the *Sandboxed Solution* property also determines whether the *System.Security.AllowPartiallyTrustedCallers* attribute appears in the *AssemblyInfo* file. By default, assemblies targeting the sandbox have this attribute and assemblies targeting the farm do not. Figure 4-2 shows the relationship between the *Sandboxed Solution* property and the *AllowPartiallyTrustedCallers* attribute.

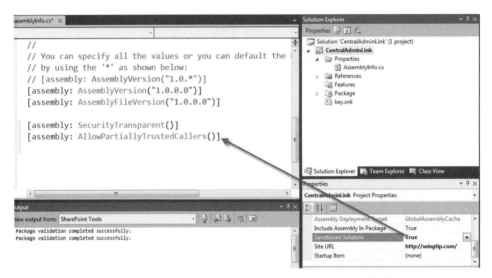

FIGURE 4-2 The *Sandboxed Solution* property affects the *AllowPartiallyTrustedCallers* attribute.

From the perspective of Visual Studio, there is no difference between a sandboxed solution and a farm solution. Both solutions are packaged and built in exactly the same manner. The differences are strictly related to the deployment target and the functionality available to the solution at run time.

The LeadTracker project has been created with two *ListInstance* items, which are used to create two Contacts lists: Sales Leads and Customers. There is also a site collection scoped feature with a Feature Receiver. The *FeatureActivated* event handler uses the server-side object model to change the default view of the Sales Leads list and to add custom nodes to the Quick Launch bar, as shown in Figure 4-3. The *FeatureDeactivating* event handler deletes the two lists and removes the *Lead Tracker* nodes from the Quick Launch bar.

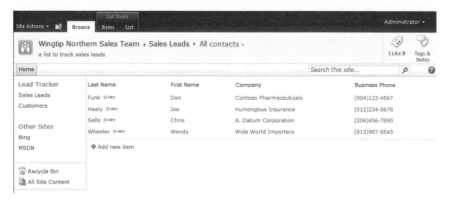

FIGURE 4-3 The Lead Tracker solution creates lists and modifies the Quick Launch bar.

Everything that has been added to the Lead Tracker project is compatible with the sandbox, as shown in Figure 4-4. Keep in mind, however, that any SharePoint solution that can be deployed as a sandboxed solution can also be deployed as a farm solution. Therefore, when working on a SharePoint project like Lead Tracker, you can switch back and forth between sandbox deployment and farm deployment.

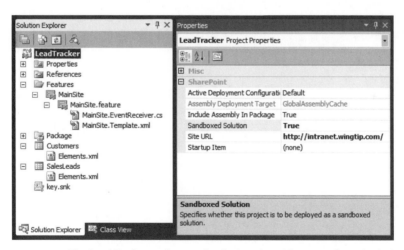

FIGURE 4-4 The Lead Tracker project can be deployed as either a sandboxed solution or a farm solution.

To illustrate this point, examine Listing 4-1, which shows an element manifest file for the Sales Leads SharePoint project item. The *ListInstance* element creates a new Contacts list named Sales Leads. The CAML element for this solution is identical whether it is deployed as a sandboxed solution or as a farm solution.

LISTING 4-1 The behavior of a *ListInstance* element is the same when deployed as either a sandboxed solution or a farm solution.

```
<Elements xmlns="http://schemas.microsoft.com/sharepoint/">

  <ListInstance
    TemplateType="105"
    FeatureId="00bfea71-7e6d-4186-9ba8-c047ac750105"
    Title="Sales Leads"
    Description="a list to track sales leads"
    Url="Lists/SalesLeads"
    OnQuickLaunch="TRUE" />

</Elements>
```

When the *Sandboxed Solution* property is set to *True*, selecting Build\Deploy Solution deploys the solution to the site collection Solution Gallery. This new gallery is the repository for all sandboxed solutions deployed within the site collection. You can access the gallery from the Site Settings page, under the Galleries section, using the link entitled Solutions. The Solutions Gallery is part of the Global Site Definition, so every site collection has one. Figure 4-5 shows the Solution Gallery with the feature deployed.

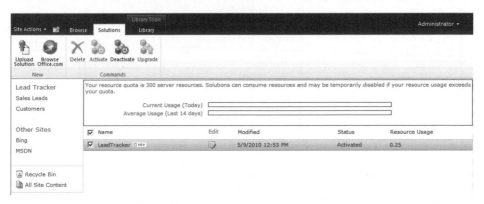

FIGURE 4-5 The Solution Gallery allows a site collection owner to upload and activate a sandboxed solution.

Keep in mind that there is a terminology difference between the two deployment methods. Farm solutions are installed and deployed. Sandboxed solutions are uploaded and activated. The install step in a farm deployment is similar to the upload step in a sandboxed deployment. Likewise, the deploy step in a farm deployment is similar to the activate step in a sandboxed deployment. The one notable difference is that the activation of a sandboxed solution automatically activates any feature scoped to the level of the site collection.

When the *Sandboxed Solution* property is set to *False*, selecting Build\Deploy will deploy the solution to the Farm Solution Gallery. From the Farm Solution Gallery, the solution can be deployed to various Web applications in the traditional manner. Figure 4-6 shows the Farm Solution Gallery with the feature deployed.

FIGURE 4-6 The Farm Solution Gallery allows a farm administrator to manage and deploy farm solutions.

For the simple *ListInstance* element defined in the CAML earlier, there is no difference in behavior when deployed as a sandboxed solution or a farm solution. Even at this point, however, you can see a significant difference in the deployment process. When a solution is deployed to the farm-level gallery, the farm administrator must become involved. This requirement gives the farm administrator significant control over the solution, but it is also a significant burden.

A SharePoint solution designed for the sandbox, like the Wingtip Lead Tracker, doesn't require farm-level deployment. Instead, the sandbox approach allows the site collection administrator to upload the solution and deploy it without involving the farm administrator. The farm administrator is thus relieved from the burden of dealing with solution deployment, and the site collection administrator is empowered to make decisions regarding the functionality available in the site collection. Furthermore, the sandbox is protecting the farm from instability by isolating the solution.

Sandboxed solutions also support feature upgrading. Upgrading is accomplished by creating a solution (.wsp) file with a different name but the same solution Id. When you subsequently deploy the new solution version, SharePoint will see that the Id matches an existing solution and prompt you to upgrade the solution. Once upgraded, the old solution is automatically deactivated.

Understanding the Architecture

Although the User Code Service is responsible for managing the execution of sandboxed solutions throughout the farm, several other components and processes are involved in the system. These components and processes include the *Execution Manager*, the *Worker Service*, and the *Worker Service Proxy*. Figure 4-7 shows an architectural diagram of the sandboxing system.

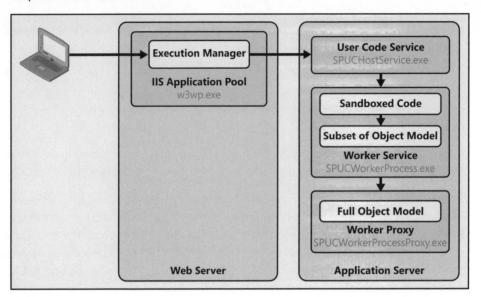

FIGURE 4-7 The sandboxing system executes code from a sandboxed solution in an isolated, partially trusted worker process.

The sandboxing system uses a component named the Execution Manager to handle the loading and execution of sandboxed solution code. The Execution Manager runs within the IIS application pool and is responsible for making a call out to the User Code Service (SPUCHostService.exe) requesting that a sandboxed solution be loaded.

As stated earlier, the User Code Service can be running on many different servers in the farm. You specify load balancing execution across the servers in the farm through administrative settings in Central Administration\System Settings\Manage User Solutions. Using these options, you can choose to execute the sandboxed solution on the same server where the user request was made or on a dedicated set of servers. In either case, the User Code Service makes a request of the Worker Service (SPUCWorkerProcess.exe) to load the sandboxed solution.

The Worker Service utilizes the same service framework as other services in the SharePoint farm. This framework includes a proxy that allows for remote communication with the service. For this reason, you'll also see a Worker Service Proxy (SPUCWorkerProcessProxy.exe) running on the server. Although the sandboxing architecture makes use of the SharePoint service framework, it isn't exposed through Central Administration in the same way as other services are. Therefore, you can't make a direct connection to the Worker Service Proxy. Instead, you simply configure the User Code Service for a server. The services framework is covered in more detail in Chapter 13, "Business Connectivity Services."

Once the assembly of a sandboxed solution is loaded into the Worker Service, its code can be executed. A pool of *AppDomains* is maintained within SPUCWorkerProcess.exe, and an available *AppDomain* is used to execute the request. Only one request at a time is executed in any *AppDomain*, so there won't be conflicts between the solutions.

As mentioned previously, execution of the code is limited to a subset of the *Microsoft.SharePoint* namespace and subject to CAS policy restrictions. Any calls to the SharePoint object model are first filtered against the subset object model to prevent any disallowed calls and then executed against the full object model, which runs in the Worker Service Proxy. When the code execution completes, the results are bubbled back up to the client request, which has been waiting synchronously for the request to complete. The final page is then drawn and delivered to the waiting user.

Knowing which processes are supporting the sandbox allows you to debug your solutions. In a full-trust solution, you can debug code by attaching to the w3wp.exe process. However, sandboxed solutions are running in a separate process, so you must attach the Visual Studio 2010 debugger to the SPUCWorkerProcess.exe process instead.

The components that make up the sandboxing system can be found in the SharePoint System Directory at C:\Program Files\Common Files\Microsoft Shared\Web Server Extensions\14\ UserCode. In this directory, you'll find SPUCHostService.exe, SPUCWorkerProcess.exe, and SPUCWorkerProcessProxy.exe. Along with the executables, you'll also find a web.config file that references the CAS policy restrictions in the file C:\Program Files\Common Files\ Microsoft Shared\Web Server Extensions\14\CONFIG\wss_usercode.config. Finally, this folder also contains a subfolder named \Assemblies. The Assemblies folder contains the assemblies *Microsoft.SharePoint.dll*, *Microsoft.SharePoint.SubsetProxy.dll*, and *Microsoft.SharePoint. UserCode.dll*, which support the object model subset and creation of full-trust proxies.

Understanding Solution Restrictions

Restricting the access of sandboxed solutions to a subset of the *Microsoft.SharePoint* namespace is intended to prevent solutions from accessing functionality that could destabilize the farm. When sandboxed solutions make calls to the SharePoint object model, the calls are routed through the subset proxy, which in turn makes calls to the full object model. The subset proxy exposes only the following subset of the object model:

- All of the *Microsoft.SharePoint* namespace, except
    - *SPSite* constructor
    - *SPSecurity* object
    - *SPWorkItem* and *SPWorkItemCollection* objects
    - *SPAlertCollection.Add* method
    - *SPAlertTemplateCollection.Add* method
    - *SPUserSolution* and *SPUserSolutionCollection* objects
    - *SPTransformUtilities* object
    - *Microsoft.SharePoint.Navigation* namespace

- All of the *Microsoft.SharePoint.Utilities* namespace, except

  - *SPUtility.SendEmail* method

  - *SPUtility.GetNTFullNameandEmailFromLogin* method

- *Microsoft.SharePoint.Workflow* namespace

- All of the *Microsoft.SharePoint.WebPartPages* namespace, except

  - *SPWebPartManager* object

  - *SPWebPartConnection* object

  - *WebPartZone* object

  - *WebPartPage* object

  - *ToolPane* object

  - *ToolPart* object

If you examine the subset object model carefully, you'll notice that the available portions are all part of the core foundational object model. There are no objects available from more advanced capabilities such as Business Connectivity Services (BCS), SharePoint Search, Excel Services, and so on. With this subset of functionality in mind, Table 4-1 lists common SharePoint project item types and whether or not they are available in the sandbox.

TABLE 4-1 SharePoint Project Item Availability for Sandboxed Solutions

Available in Sandbox	Not Available in Sandbox
List definitions	Visual Web Parts
List instances	Application pages
Site definitions	Custom action group
WebTemplate feature elements (instead of Webtemp.xml)	*HideCustomAction* element
Content types/Fields	Content type binding
Module/files	Web application-scoped features
Feature callouts	Farm-scoped features
Web Parts	Workflows with code
Support for all Web Parts that derive from *System.Web. UI.WebControls.WebParts.WebPart*	
SPItemEventReceiver	
SPListEventReceiver	
SPWebEventReceiver	
Custom actions	
Declarative workflows	

When designing sandboxed solutions, you have the option of using a declarative, programmatic, or hybrid approach. The purely declarative approach utilizes CAML elements alone to define the solution; a programmatic approach uses only code; and a hybrid approach uses both CAML and code. While many SharePoint solutions are hybrids, a declarative approach is particularly good for sandboxed solutions because no code needs to be deployed to the sandbox. This approach simplifies your solution development considerably. The following is a list of supported CAML elements you can use in your declarative solutions.

- ContentType

- CustomAction

- Field

- ListInstance

- ListTemplate

- Module

- PropertyBag

- Receivers

- WebTemplate

- WorkflowActions

- WorkflowAssociation

If a sandboxed solution should make a call to a portion of the SharePoint object model that isn't exposed through the subset proxy, the call will fail. In addition to the default elements not available through the subset proxy, Microsoft provides a mechanism for farm administrators to further restrict access to the API. The *API block list* is a collection associated with the *Microsoft.SharePoint.Administration.SPWebService* class that allows farm administrators to specify additional types that are blocked from use in the sandbox.

The *SPWebService* class has a *RestrictedObjectModel* collection property that contains zero or more *Microsoft.SharePoint.Administration.SPObjectModelMember* objects. Each *SPObjectModelMember* instance represents a blocked type. Farm administrators can use this collection to customize the available set of types or in response to a sandbox vulnerability that might be identified by Microsoft in the future. The following code shows how to list all the blocked APIs in the farm.

```
SPWebServiceCollection webServices = new SPWebServiceCollection(SPFarm.Local);

foreach (SPWebService service in webServices){
  foreach (SPObjectModelType type in service.RestrictedObjectModel.RestrictedTypes) {
    Console.WriteLine(type.FullName);
  }
}
```

Interestingly, there is little in Visual Studio 2010 to prevent you from writing code against forbidden portions of the object model. Therefore, you have to be careful with your code and test to ensure that it is properly supported by the targeted deployment model. When creating solutions, you can set references to any assembly you want and write code just as you can with any SharePoint solution. The only scenario that really doesn't work is to reference one sandboxed solution from another. However, the assemblies that you reference will be subject to CAS policy restrictions when executed. So even though you can write code against an assembly and compile successfully, it doesn't mean that the code will execute at run time. Sandboxed solutions are severely limited by CAS policies and can't generally access resources outside the sandbox. Table 4-2 details the specific CAS restrictions applied through the wss_usercode.config policy file.

TABLE 4-2 CAS Restrictions for Sandboxed Solutions

Policy	Description
SecurityPermission.Execution	Allows the sandboxed solution to load and execute.
AspNetHostingPermission.Level = Minimal	Allows the sandboxed solution to load and execute within an ASP.NET context, but prevents the solution from accessing any resources on the server.
SharePointPermission.ObjectModel	Allows the sandboxed solution to access the SharePoint object model; however, the subset proxy limits the calls that will actually succeed.

While CAS policies restrict the code that can run on the server, no restrictions are placed on code that runs on the client. This means that you can create Web Parts that inject JavaScript directly into the page, build Silverlight solutions, create AJAX Web Parts, use the client object model, and utilize script libraries such as jQuery. In many cases, a client-side solution is an attractive option because resources can be made available to the client through the SharePoint client object model or using Windows Communication Foundation (WCF) services that aren't available through the sandbox. In addition, although we haven't yet talked about resource throttling, it's important to know that resources utilized via the client object model don't count against a sandboxed solution's resource limits. More details on resources are coming later in this chapter, in the "Administrating Sandboxed Solutions" section.

Designing a Sandboxed Solution

As an example of the type of thinking required when designing sandboxed solutions, consider a simple sandboxed solution named ListPrintingUtility designed to add support for printing lists. The idea behind this solution is to add a command button to the Ribbon above a list that will allow the user to print the current view of the list. Figure 4-8 shows what the Print List button looks like on the Ribbon and also shows the utility printing window that opens when the button is clicked.

FIGURE 4-8 A sandboxed solution can add a custom Ribbon command for printing lists.

The Print List button shown on the Ribbon is added using a *CustomAction* element. When adding to the Ribbon, the CAML is more complex than what is required for simply adding to the Site Actions menu. Nonetheless, the CAML is supported by the sandbox, so it's a valid approach for creating the required interface. Listing 4-2 shows the CAML used to create the button. (More detail on Ribbon customization is available in Chapter 5, "Pages and Navigation".)

LISTING 4-2 This *CustomAction* element extends the Ribbon with a custom *Print List* command.

```
<CustomAction
  Id="Ribbon.List.Items.Print" Location="CommandUI.Ribbon"
  RegistrationType="ContentType" RegistrationId="0x01"
  Sequence="11"  Title="Print" >

<CommandUIExtension>
  <CommandUIDefinitions>
    <CommandUIDefinition Location="Ribbon.ListItem.Actions.Controls._children">
      <Button
        Id="Ribbon.List.Items.Action.PrintListButton"
        LabelText="Print List" Alt="Print List" Sequence="01"
        Image32by32="/_layouts/images/mewa_frozenb.gif"
        Command="PrintList"
        TemplateAlias="o1" />
    </CommandUIDefinition>
  </CommandUIDefinitions>
  <CommandUIHandlers>
    <CommandUIHandler
      Command="PrintList"
      CommandAction="javascript:
      var queryString = '?ListId={ListId}&amp;ViewId=' + ctx.view;
```

```
            var targetUrl = '{SiteUrl}/PrintingPages/List.aspx' + queryString;
            var windowOptions = 'scollbars=1,height=600,width=800';
            window.open(targetUrl, 'printwindow', windowOptions);"/>
    </CommandUIHandlers>
  </CommandUIExtension>
</CustomAction>
```

The *CommandAction* attribute specifies the code to run when the button is clicked. In this case, some JavaScript runs that opens a new window containing the page List.aspx. *QueryString* parameters are passed to the page detailing the list and view to display. The idea is simply to display the current view in a new page without any chrome. This design effectively creates a print view for the list.

The challenge with the List.aspx page is that it must be designed to run in the sandbox. In the past, most developers would simply deploy the page as an application page to the LAYOUTS directory directly in the SharePoint root directory. But the sandbox doesn't support these types of pages. Therefore, we need a different approach.

For this solution, the List.aspx page is deployed as a *site page*. Site pages are pages that are deployed to the content database instead of the system directory. These types of pages are supported in the sandbox and can be deployed to the content database by using a SharePoint project item created from the *Module* SharePoint project item type.

Figure 4-9 shows the ListPrintingUtility project opened in Visual Studio 2010. You can see that a SharePoint project item named *RibbonExtensions* was created from the Empty Element SharePoint project item type. This project item contains the element manifest with the *CustomAction* that adds the Print List button to the Ribbon. A second SharePoint project item, *PrintingPages*, was created from the *Module* SharePoint project item type. The *PrintingPages* item is used to deploy the site page List.aspx along with its associated files, including List.js, ListStyles.css, and ListStylesPrinting.css.

FIGURE 4-9 The ListPrintingUtility project uses client-side code instead of server-side code.

The site page List.aspx renders a print view of a list. When a user clicks the Print List button, the List.aspx page is requested with a *QueryString* containing the *ListId* and the *ViewId*. The List.aspx page must provide code to get the list items for rendering. However, there is a problem: site pages don't support server-side code. Therefore, you can't write any code in the page that uses the server-side SharePoint object model. This is where the client object model comes into play.

The client object model is a JavaScript library that allows you to write code on the client that is very similar to server-side code. The client object model is covered in detail in Chapter 10, "Client-Side Programming." For this solution, the necessary print view is created using client-side code, which is supported in site pages. Listing 4-3 shows the complete code in List.js for rendering the print view using the client object model.

LISTING 4-3 A sandboxed solution can make use of JavaScript code written against the new client-side object model.

```
var list;
var printView;

function initPage() {
  ExecuteOrDelayUntilScriptLoaded(getListData, "sp.js");
}

function getListData() {
  // get QueryString parameters
  var queryString = window.location.search.substring(1);
  var args = queryString.split('&');
  var listId = args[0].split('=')[1];
  var viewId = args[1].split('=')[1];
  // use client object model to get list items
  var context = new SP.ClientContext.get_current();
  var site = context.get_web();
  context.load(site);
  var lists = site.get_lists();
  context.load(lists);
  list = lists.getById(listId);
  context.load(list);
  var views = list.get_views();
  context.load(views);
  var view = views.getById(viewId);
  context.load(view);
  printView = view.renderAsHtml();
  context.executeQueryAsync(success, failure);
}

function success() {
  $get("listTitle").innerHTML = list.get_title();
  $get("listTable").innerHTML = printView.get_value();
}

function failure() {
  $get("listTitle").innerHTML = "error running Client OM query";
  $get("listTable").innerHTML = "";
}
```

The print list solution is a good example of the thinking involved in designing sandboxed solutions. Supported CAML elements were used to create the button. A site page was used to create the user interface experience, and supported client-side code was used to implement the functionality. A key point is that this project contains no server-side code. If you look back at the project property sheet in Figure 4-9, you can see that this project has the *Include Assembly in Package* property set to *false*. This is a new approach that is very different from what most developers have been doing in previous versions of SharePoint.

Understanding Full-Trust Proxies

After examining the restrictions imposed by the subset object model and CAS policies, you might conclude that many SharePoint solutions simply can't be deployed to the sandbox. Many SharePoint solutions require access to external resources such as databases or Web services or to advanced object model features. Fortunately, there is a mechanism designed to provide access to these resources and objects through a full-trust proxy.

A *full-trust proxy* allows a sandboxed solution to make a call to a trusted assembly outside the sandbox. That trusted assembly can in turn make calls to resources and objects that the sandboxed solution can't reach. The results of the operation can then be returned to the sandboxed solution.

Initially, you may find yourself wondering if the full-trust proxy object is simply a complex workaround for deploying full-trust solutions in the first place. After all, if you can deploy a full-trust proxy, can't you destabilize the farm? Wasn't the point of a sandbox to avoid code that can destabilize the farm? Well, the value of the full-trust proxy is that the farm administrator can choose what functionality will be deployed with full trust.

Consider the scenario in which a developer wants to create a Web Part that will read records from a database and display the information in a grid. If the Web Part is written assuming it has full trust, the developer can easily create database entities and read them. The entities can then be bound to controls and displayed. However, the developer would also have the ability to write back to the database. Furthermore, nothing stops the developer from performing other operations within the Web Part that require full trust. This is the situation that potentially leads to instability.

The full-trust proxy, on the other hand, can be written so that it only reads records from the database and returns those records to a sandboxed solution. The sandboxed solution can call the full-trust proxy to get the records it needs, bind them to the grid, and display them. However, the Web Part has no mechanism to write back to the database because the full-trust proxy doesn't expose that functionality. Additionally, the full-trust proxy can provide the same capability to other sandboxed solutions so that it needs to be written only once and can then be used by many solutions. Finally, the full-trust proxy allows only this read operation—no other higher-trust functionality is available to the developer.

The full-trust proxy is what makes the sandbox architecture more than simply an interesting new capability. The full-trust proxy completely changes the game for SharePoint developers. Under SharePoint 2010, developers should always look to deploy sandboxed solutions first. Only after proving that a sandboxed solution is inadequate should a developer move to another deployment model.

Even though sandboxed solutions are a boon for developers, they do have some limitations, even with full-trust proxies. For example, sandboxed solutions can't be used to deploy application pages with code to the LAYOUTS directory. Those assemblies must still be placed in the GAC.

To create a full-trust proxy that can be used by sandboxed solutions, you can create a new SharePoint project and add a custom class for each trusted operation. The class must then be registered within the SharePoint farm so that its operation can be made available to deployed sandboxed solutions. Finally, you must create a sandboxed solution that calls the trusted operation.

The first step in developing a full-trust proxy operation is to create a class that inherits from the *SPProxyOperation* class in the *Microsoft.SharePoint.UserCode* namespace. The *SPProxyOperation* class defines the operations that will be exposed to the sandboxed solution. This class must override the *Execute* method, which takes a *SPProxyOperationsArgs* object as an argument. The *Execute* method returns an object, which means that the sandboxed code must know what object type is returning and cast it appropriately.

Let's look at an example class that defines a full-trust proxy operation. Listing 4-4 shows the *GetWingtipWebApps* class that uses the server-side object model to enumerate through the Web applications in the current farm and to pass back a collection with the URL for each one. The point here is that this type of server-side object model code can't be called from within the sandbox. However, it can be called from a full-trust proxy operation on behalf of code running in the sandbox.

LISTING 4-4 A full-trust proxy operation can be created using a class that inherits from *SPProxyOperation*.

```
using System;
using System.Collections.Generic;
using Microsoft.SharePoint;
using Microsoft.SharePoint.Administration;
using Microsoft.SharePoint.UserCode;

namespace WingtipTrustedBase {
  public class GetWingtipWebApps : SPProxyOperation {

    public override object Execute(SPProxyOperationArgs args) {
      List<string> webApps = new List<string>();
      SPWebService webService = SPFarm.Local.Servers.GetValue<SPWebService>();
      foreach (SPWebApplication webApp in webService.WebApplications) {
```

```
          webApps.Add(webApp.DisplayName);
        }
        return webApps;
      }
    }
  }
```

Notice that the *SPProxyOperationsArgs* class is passed as an argument to the *Execute* method. If you need to create a full-trust proxy operation that requires parameters, you must create a second class that inherits from *SPProxyOperationsArgs* and is marked as *Serializable*. The caller is then responsible for creating an instance of this class and passing it when calling the full-trust proxy operation.

Once the *SPProxyOperation* classes and optionally the *SPProxyOperationsArgs* class are created, they must be added to the GAC. The operations must then be registered with the SharePoint farm. The registration process can easily be accomplished using a SharePoint project with a farm-level feature with a Feature Receiver. Listing 4-5 shows a Feature Receiver that handles registration.

LISTING 4-5 A full-trust proxy operation must be registered with the User Code Service.

```
using System;
using System.Runtime.InteropServices;
using Microsoft.SharePoint;
using Microsoft.SharePoint.UserCode;
using Microsoft.SharePoint.Administration;

namespace WingtipTrustedBase.Features.MainFarm {

  [Guid("ac52a0b6-7d95-400a-a911-25a103fa3ba7")]
  public class MainFarmEventReceiver : SPFeatureReceiver {

    public override void FeatureActivated(
                              SPFeatureReceiverProperties properties) {
      SPUserCodeService userCodeService = SPUserCodeService.Local;
      if (userCodeService != null) {
        string assemblyName = this.GetType().Assembly.FullName;
        SPProxyOperationType GetWingtipWebAppsOperation =
            new SPProxyOperationType(assemblyName,
                              typeof(GetWingtipWebApps).FullName);
        userCodeService.ProxyOperationTypes.Add(GetWingtipWebAppsOperation);
        userCodeService.Update();
      }
      else { throw new ApplicationException("User Code Service not running."); }
    }

    public override void FeatureDeactivating(
                              SPFeatureReceiverProperties properties) {
      SPUserCodeService userCodeService = SPUserCodeService.Local;
      if (userCodeService != null) {
```

```
        string assemblyName = this.GetType().Assembly.FullName;

        SPProxyOperationType GetWingtipWebAppsOperation =
            new SPProxyOperationType(assemblyName,
                                     typeof(GetWingtipWebApps).FullName);
        userCodeService.ProxyOperationTypes.Remove(GetWingtipWebAppsOperation);
        userCodeService.Update();
      }
      else { throw new ApplicationException("User Code Service isn't running."); }
    }
  }
}
```

Once the full-trust proxy is created and registered, you can call it from a sandboxed solution using the *SPUtility.ExecuteRegisteredProxyOperation* method. If the full-trust proxy operation you're calling takes parameters, you must create an instance of the *SPProxyOperationsArgs* class and pass it along with the assembly information for the *SPProxyOperation* class when calling the *ExecuteRegisteredProxyOperation* method. Listing 4-6 shows a Web Part making a call to the full-trust proxy operation named.

LISTING 4-6 You call a trusted proxy operation using the *ExecuteRegisteredProxyOperation* method.

```
using System;
using System.Collections.Generic;
using System.Web;
using System.Web.UI;
using System.Web.UI.WebControls;
using System.Web.UI.WebControls.WebParts;
using Microsoft.SharePoint;
using Microsoft.SharePoint.Utilities;
using Microsoft.SharePoint.UserCode;

namespace SandboxedParts.WebApps {

  public class WebApps : WebPart {
    protected override void RenderContents(HtmlTextWriter writer) {
      string operationAssemblyName = "WingtipTrustedBase, [four=part assembly name]";
      string operationTypeName = "WingtipTrustedBase.GetWingtipWebApps";
      List<string> WebApplications =
        SPUtility.ExecuteRegisteredProxyOperation(operationAssemblyName,
                                                  operationTypeName,
                                                  null) as List<string>;

      // use the data returned from full trsut proxy operation
      foreach (var WebApplication in WebApplications) {
        writer.Write(WebApplication + "<br />");
      }
    }
  }
}
```

While full-trust proxies represent a good option for overcoming the limitations of the sandbox, they are not the only option. Keep in mind that you can always use client-side code to perform operations outside the sandbox. This means that you can utilize the client object model and WCF services from JavaScript code to perform operations that might otherwise be restricted on the server.

Administrating Sandboxed Solutions

Like all administration in SharePoint Foundation, sandboxed solutions support a layered-administration model. Configuration can be done at the farm level as well as the site collection level. Farm-level administration controls quotas and resources in addition to providing monitoring capabilities. At the site collection level, administrators can upload, activate, and deactivate solutions within the site collection.

Using Central Administration Tools

To begin farm-level administration, the administrator opens the Central Administration site and clicks System Settings\Manage Services on Server. From this page, the administrator can turn the User Code Service on or off for any given server in the farm. Remember that the User Code Service must be running on a server in order for it to execute a sandboxed solution.

The administrator can control blocked solutions and load balancing by selecting System Settings\Manage User Solutions. On this page, the farm administrator can browse to solution packages that should be blocked and add them to the blocked list. Blocked solutions are not allowed to execute on the farm. The farm administrator can also select the type of load balancing to use with sandboxed solutions. The administrator can choose to have the solution execute on the same server where the request was received or to have it routed to a dedicated set of servers. Figure 4-10 shows the Manage User Solutions page.

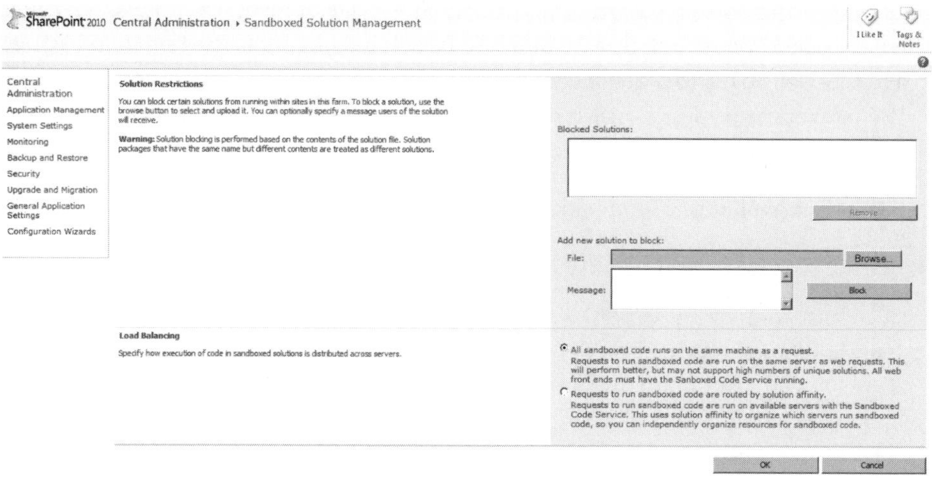

FIGURE 4-10 Farm administrators can manage user solutions within Central Administration.

Along with basic management, the farm administrator can also specify a quota for sandboxed solutions. Quotas are set up in Central Administration by selecting Application Management\ Configure Quotas and Locks. On this page, the farm administrator can set a limit on the resources that a sandboxed solution can use in a given Web application. This capability is critical to maintaining the stability of the farm. Figure 4-11 shows the Site Quota Information page where the limits are specified.

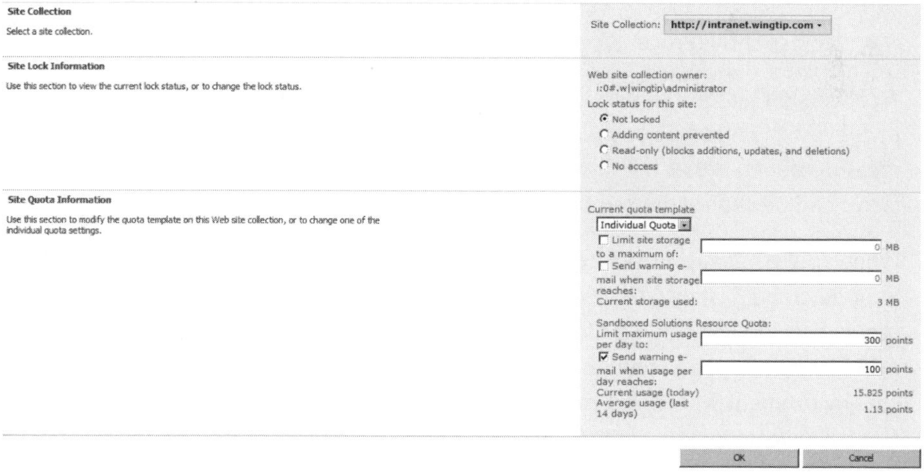

FIGURE 4-11 Farm administrators can adjust the settings site quotas for sandboxed solutions.

Quotas for sandboxed solutions are measured in units of resource "points." Resource points are calculated values that take 14 different factors into account. The farm administrator assigns a number of points to a site collection that represents the resource usage allowed per day. The farm administrator can also set a threshold at which the site collection administrator will receive a warning email. The following is a list of the 14 factors used to determine points:

- AbnormalProcessTerminationCount
- CPUExecutionTime
- CriticalExceptionCount
- InvocationCount
- PercentProcessorTime
- ProcessCPUCycles
- ProcessHandleCount
- ProcessIOBytes
- ProcessThreadCount
- ProcessVirtualBytes
- SharePointDatabaseQueryCount
- SharePointDatabaseQueryTime
- UnhandledExceptionCount
- UnresponsiveProcessCount

A conversion factor is applied to each of the 14 metrics used to monitor sandboxed solutions to convert the measure to points. These factors normalize the different units used in the measurements so that the farm administrator can set and monitor them. Each conversion factor can be changed using Windows PowerShell.

When you're initially introduced to the concept of resource points, you'll find yourself trying to understand exactly what they are, how they are calculated, and how you can plan their usage. Such an approach is inappropriate for sandboxed solutions. Instead, the goal for developers is to use as few resources as possible. You should test your resource usage in a QA environment where you can run the solution and see the resulting resource point usage. This will give you some idea of how your solution performs and whether it will fit into the current quota. Once a daily resource quota is exceeded, no more solutions will execute and an error message will appear. Figure 4-12 shows error messages for Web Parts running in a site collection that has exceeded its daily quota.

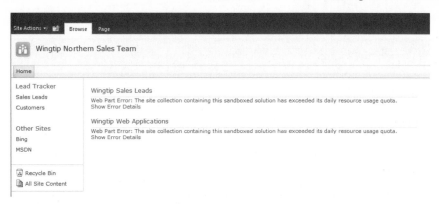

FIGURE 4-12 Code within a sandboxed solution will no longer execute once it has exceeded the daily quota.

Validating Sandboxed Solutions

For a farm administrator to block solutions from running in the sandbox, the administrator must have some way of identifying the solutions to block. The farm administrator could block a solution because it is behaving poorly, but this approach isn't proactive. A better approach is to identify rogue solutions before they ever run. To solve this problem, you can create a custom solution validator that runs whenever a solution is activated within a site collection. Your custom solution validator can decide which sandboxed solution to allow and which to prohibit. For example, you can decide to allow for only sandboxed solutions with assemblies that have been compiled using your company's private signing key.

To develop a validator, you create a class that inherits from *Microsoft.SharePoint.UserCode* *.SPSolutionValidator*. The *SPSolutionValidator* class in turn inherits from the *Microsoft.SharePoint* *.Administration.SPPersistedObject* class, which means that *SPSolutionValidator* can serialize its state into the SharePoint database. The impact of this capability is that you can use a generic List<string> collection to store any information you want to support validation. For example, you could use this approach to store information about known bad publishers.

When you inherit from the *SPSolutionValidator* class, you must provide a *System.Runtime* *.InteropServices.Guid* for your validator that is surfaced as the *ProviderID* property of the validator. Your validator must provide a default constructor that takes no arguments as well as a constructor that takes a *Microsoft.SharePoint.UserCode.SPUserCodeService* object. In the second constructor, you must set the *Signature* property to a unique value. Listing 4-7 shows a basic validator class with constructors.

LISTING 4-7 A solution validator class must inherit from *SPSolutionValidator*.

```
[Guid("D1735DCC-141F-4F1A-8DFE-8F3F48DACD1F")]
public class SimpleSolutionValidator : SPSolutionValidator {
    [Persisted]
    List<string> allowedPublishers;

    private const string validatorName = "Simple Solution Validator";

    public SimpleSolutionValidator() { }
    public SimpleSolutionValidator(SPUserCodeService userCodeService)
        : base(validatorName, userCodeService) {
        this.Signature = 5555;
    }
}
```

After coding the basic class and constructors, you must override the *ValidateSolution* and *ValidateAssembly* methods. *ValidateSolution* is called once for each solution, and *ValidateAssembly* is called once for each assembly within each solution. The *ValidateSolution* method receives a *SPSolutionValidationProperties* object, which contains information about the solution. The *ValidateAssembly* method receives a *SPSolutionValidationProperties* object as well, but it also receives a *SPSolutionFile* object with additional information about the assembly being validated. Listing 4-8 shows the *ValidateSolution* and *ValidateAssembly* methods, which for the sake of this demonstration are simply checking to see whether the name of any file in the solution or assembly begins with the string "Bad_". If any file begins with this string, the file fails validation.

LISTING 4-8 A solution validator prevents a sandboxed solution from activating when the *isValid* property is set to *true*.

```
public override void ValidateSolution(SPSolutionValidationProperties properties) {
    base.ValidateSolution(properties);
    bool isValid = true;

    //Check the name of the package
    if (properties.PackageFile.Location.StartsWith("Bad_",
                            StringComparison.CurrentCultureIgnoreCase)) {
        isValid = false;
    }

    //Look at the files in the package
    foreach (SPSolutionFile file in properties.Files)  {
        if (file.Location.StartsWith("Bad_",
                                StringComparison.CurrentCultureIgnoreCase))
            isValid = false;
    }

    //set error handler
```

```
        properties.ValidationErrorMessage = "Failed simple validation.";
        properties.ValidationErrorUrl =
           "/_layouts/Simple_Validator/ValidationError.aspx?SolutionName="
           + properties.Name;
        properties.Valid = isValid;
    }

    public override void ValidateAssembly(
        SPSolutionValidationProperties properties, SPSolutionFile assembly) {
        base.ValidateAssembly(properties, assembly);
        bool isValid = true;

        //Check the name of the assembly
        if (assembly.Location.StartsWith("Bad_",
                    StringComparison.CurrentCultureIgnoreCase))
            isValid = false;

        //set error handler
        properties.ValidationErrorMessage = "Failed simple validation.";
        properties.ValidationErrorUrl =
                "/_layouts/Simple_Validator/ValidationError.aspx?SolutionName="
                + properties.Name;
        properties.Valid = isValid;
    }
```

When a solution fails validation, you can elect to display an error page. The *ValidationError Message* and *ValidationErrorUrl* properties are used to set the values for handling validation errors. Typically, you simply create an application page in the LAYOUTS directory that is called when validation fails. Figure 4-13 shows a message being displayed from a custom application page when a solution fails validation.

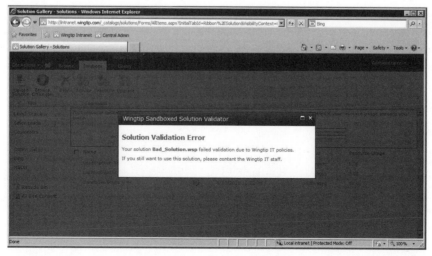

FIGURE 4-13 You can redirect the user to a custom error page when solution validation fails.

Before a custom solution validator can be used, it must be registered with the farm. To register the validator with the farm, you use a Feature Receiver in a farm-level feature. In fact, it's best to package the custom validator, application page, and Feature Receiver into a single feature. This way, the farm administrator can simply activate a single farm-level feature and the validator will be active. Listing 4-9 shows a Feature Receiver for registering and unregistering a custom validator.

LISTING 4-9 A Feature Receiver can be used to register a solution validator.

```
public class FeatureEventReceiver : SPFeatureReceiver {
  public override void FeatureActivated(SPFeatureReceiverProperties properties) {
    SPUserCodeService userCodeService = SPUserCodeService.Local;
    SPSolutionValidator validator = new SimpleSolutionValidator(userCodeService);
    userCodeService.SolutionValidators.Add(validator);
  }

  public override void FeatureDeactivating(SPFeatureReceiverProperties properties) {
    SPUserCodeService userCodeService = SPUserCodeService.Local;
    SPSolutionValidator validator = new SimpleSolutionValidator(userCodeService);
    userCodeService.SolutionValidators.Remove(validator.Id);
  }
}
```

Using Windows PowerShell for Administration

In addition to using Central Administration, farm administrators can also use Windows PowerShell to perform administrative tasks for sandboxed solutions. The tasks could include reporting as well as changing key settings. For example, the following Windows PowerShell code shows the command and displays the quota settings for Wingtip.com in the SharePoint 2010 Management Console. The properties *UserCodeMaximumLevel* and *UserCodeWarningLevel* map to the Maximum Usage per Day and Warning E-mail values in Central Administration, respectively.

```
(Get-SPSite -Identity "http://wingtip.com").Quota

QuotaID                        : 0
StorageMaximumLevel            : 0
InvitedUserMaximumLevel        : 0
StorageWarningLevel            : 0
UserCodeWarningLevel           : 100
UserCodeMaximumLevel           : 300
UpgradedPersistedProperties    :
```

Administrators can also change the quota settings for a site collection by setting the *UserCodeMaximumLevel* and *UserCodeWarningLevel* properties through Windows PowerShell. They would simply set the properties to the number of points desired. The following code shows how to set the Wingtip.com quota values back to the default.

```
(Get-SPSite -Identity "http://wingtip.com").Quota.UserCodeMaximumLevel = 300
(Get-SPSite -Identity "http://wingtip.com").Quota.UserCodeWarningLevel = 100
```

Along with viewing the quotas, you can also list the currently active solution validators. This is a great way for administrators to verify the validations that are in effect. The following command lists all the active solution validators.

```
[System.Reflection.Assembly]::Load(
"Microsoft.SharePoint, Version=14.0.0.0, Culture=neutral, PublicKeyToken=71e9bce111e9429c");
$s = [Microsoft.SharePoint.Administration.SPUserCodeService]::Local;
$s.solutionvalidators;
```

If you're interested in understanding more about the 14 measures that make up resource points, you can list them and set their values with Windows PowerShell. The following command lists all the measures.

```
[System.Reflection.Assembly]::Load(
"Microsoft.SharePoint, Version=14.0.0.0, Culture=neutral, PublicKeyToken=71e9bce111e9429c");
$s = [Microsoft.SharePoint.Administration.SPUserCodeService]::Local;
$s.ResourceMeasures;
```

If you want to see all the blocked APIs in the farm, you can list them as well as add new blocked types. The following command lists all the blocked APIs.

```
[System.Reflection.Assembly]::Load(
"Microsoft.SharePoint,Version=14.0.0.0,Culture=neutral,PublicKeyToken=71e9bce111e9429c")
$f = Get-SPFarm
$c = New-Object Microsoft.SharePoint.Administration.SPWebServiceCollection($f)
$c | foreach-object{$_.RestrictedObjectModel}
```

Using Site Collection Tools

Site Collection Administration is accomplished primarily through the Solution Gallery. From the Solution Gallery, a site collection administrator can upload, activate, and deactivate solution files. Site collection administrators can also monitor the current resource usage for the day as well as a rolling 14-day average. Figure 4-14 shows the site collection Solution Gallery with several installed solutions and their resource usage.

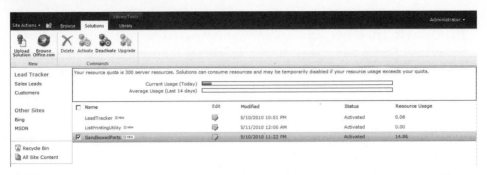

FIGURE 4-14 The site collection administrator can monitor resource usage for sandboxed solutions.

Conclusion

Sandboxed solutions represent a new form of solution deployment and management in SharePoint 2010. Because these solutions balance agility with farm stability, you should consider sandboxed solutions in your initial development efforts. Only if a sandboxed solution doesn't work should you move to another deployment model. You can't use the sandbox to deploy every conceivable SharePoint solution, but you can run many common solutions in the sandbox. Therefore, you should consider sandboxed solutions a best practice for SharePoint development.

The authors of this book have created CodePlex projects that have additional solutions and resources for sandboxed solutions. You can find these solutions at *http://sandbox.codeplex.com* and *http://ckssandboxsolutions.codeplex.com*.

Chapter 5
Pages and Navigation

Microsoft SharePoint Foundation is built on top of ASP.NET. It would be impossible for you to really understand how SharePoint Foundation processes the request for pages without a basic knowledge of the underlying architecture and page processing model of the ASP.NET Framework. For this reason, we will begin this chapter by explaining how key features of ASP.NET have been integrated into SharePoint Foundation.

After examining how SharePoint Foundation processes various types of pages, the chapter will focus on creating pages within a sandboxed solution. This will teach you how to create pages and a navigation scheme for scenarios where your SharePoint solutions are required to run under the constraints of the SharePoint Foundation Sandboxed Code Service.

The next part of this chapter examines the extra flexibility afforded to you when creating pages and navigation elements within a farm solution. As you will see, many more options become available when you make the assumption that your SharePoint solutions will be deployed at the farm level and you do not have to worry about the constraints of the sandbox.

The final section of this chapter will discuss creating a reusable SharePoint solution to brand SharePoint sites. You will see that it's fairly simple to create a SharePoint project designed to change the look and feel of a SharePoint site using a custom master page, a Cascading Style Sheets (CSS) file, and custom images. Along the way, we will discuss how branding issues change across different types of sites, as well as which branding techniques work on Microsoft SharePoint Server farms and SharePoint Foundation farms alike.

SharePoint Foundation Integration with ASP.NET

ASP.NET is a very deep topic in and of itself. There is no way this section, a chapter, or even an entire book could possibly cover all there is to say about ASP.NET. However, there are a handful of fundamental ASP.NET concepts that you must understand to learn how SharePoint Foundation really works inside.

ASP.NET Fundamentals

Before we start to explain how SharePoint Foundation integrates with ASP.NET, we want to conduct a quick review of the following ASP.NET topics:

- ASP.NET applications
- Web configuration files
- ASP.NET pages
- Master pages

An *ASP.NET application* represents a set of pages in a directory that share the same execution scope. An ASP.NET application can also include pages nested in child directories. If you are hosting ASP.NET applications with Microsoft Internet Information Services (IIS), then the ASP.NET runtime sees each IIS website and each IIS virtual directory as its own ASP.NET application.

The ASP.NET runtime runs each ASP.NET application in isolation from all other ASP.NET applications. Even in scenarios where multiple ASP.NET applications are running within the same IIS application pool, the ASP.NET runtime still ensures isolation by loading each ASP.NET application into its own private execution context using a mechanism supplied by the Microsoft .NET Framework known as an *AppDomain*.

Each ASP.NET application can be configured independently using a *Web configuration file*. The Web configuration file provides control over the behavior of various features of the ASP.NET Framework, such as compilation, page rendering, and state management. A Web configuration file for an ASP.NET application must be named *web.config*, and it should be added to the hosting application's root directory.

Each web.config file has a top-level element named *configuration*. The configuration element can contain many inner elements, such as the section with ASP.NET settings named *system.web*, shown here.

```
<configuration>
  <system.web>
    <customErrors mode="On" />
    <httpRuntime maxRequestLength="51200" />
  </system.web>
</configuration>
```

Much of the development done with the ASP.NET Framework is centered on ASP.NET Pages. An *ASP.NET page* is simply a text file with an .aspx extension that resides in an ASP.NET application. The contents of an ASP.NET page must include the *Page* directive as the first line.

A simple ASP.NET page can also define a Hypertext Markup Language (HTML) layout that can include server-side controls as well as *inline code* with server-side event handlers written in a language such as C# or Visual Basic.

```
<%@ Page Language="C#" %>
<html>
<head><title>Wingtip Toys</title></head>
<body>
  <form id="frmMain" runat="server">
    <asp:Label runat="server" ID="lblDisplay" />
  </form>
</body>
</html>

<script runat="server">
  protected override void OnLoad(EventArgs e)  {
    lblDisplay.Text = "Welcome to Wingtip Toys";
  }
</script>
```

What makes an ASP.NET page special is that the ASP.NET runtime compiles it into an assembly DLL on demand the first time it is processed. Behind the scenes, the ASP.NET Framework does quite a bit of work to compile an .aspx file into an assembly dynamic-link library (DLL). First, the ASP.NET runtime must parse the .aspx file to generate a C# or Visual Basic source file containing a public class that inherits from the *Page* class that is defined within the *System.Web.UI* namespace.

When the ASP.NET page parser generates this *Page*-derived class, it builds a control tree containing all the server-side controls defined within the .aspx file. The ASP.NET page parser also adds the required code to hook up any event handlers that are defined within the page.

Once the ASP.NET page parser builds the source file for an .aspx page, it can then compile it into an assembly DLL. This compilation occurs automatically the first time the .aspx file is requested by a user. Once the ASP.NET runtime has compiled an .aspx file into an assembly DLL, that copy of the assembly DLL can be used for all subsequent requests that target the same .aspx file until the Web server process is restarted. However, the ASP.NET runtime monitors the date/time stamp on the .aspx file and retriggers the compilation process to rebuild the assembly DLL if it determines that the associated .aspx file has been updated.

The ASP.NET Framework provides support for *master pages,* which provide an effective approach to page templating. More specifically, a *master page* is a text file with a *.master* extension that defines common HTML elements and server controls that can be reused across many different ASP.NET pages to give a website a consistent look and feel. Once you have created a master page with a common layout, you can then create ASP.NET pages that link to this master page. The key point is that all the ASP.NET pages that link to the same master page are able to share the same HTML layout.

When you create a master page, you must provide the pages that link to it with an ability to substitute in their own unique content. This is done by adding *ContentPlaceHolder* controls with unique IDs. Here is an example of a simple master page defined using the *Master* directive and a single *ContentPlaceHolder* control with an ID of *PlaceHolderMain*.

```
<%@ Master %>
<html>
<head><title>Wingtip Toys</title></head>
<body>
  <form id="frmMain" runat="server">
    <h2>Wingtip Toys</h2>
    <asp:ContentPlaceHolder ID="PlaceHolderMain" runat="server" />
  </form>
</body>
</html>
```

Note that when you create an ASP.NET page that links to a master page, you must specify the name of the master page file inside the *Page* directive using the *MasterPageFile* attribute. You must also take precautions to place any HTML and server control tags inside *Content* controls that reference specific *ContentPlaceHolder* controls from the master page by their IDs using the *ContentPlaceHolderID* attribute.

```
<%@ Page Language="C#" MasterPageFile="~/wingtip.master" %>

<asp:Content ID="Main" runat="server"
             ContentPlaceHolderID="PlaceHolderMain" >
 <asp:Label runat="server" ID="lblDisplay" />
</asp:Content>

<script runat="server">
  protected override void OnLoad(EventArgs e)  {
    lblDisplay.Text = "Welcome to Wingtip Toys";
  }
</script>
```

It is important to understand that an ASP.NET page that links to a master page will not compile if you try to add any HTML elements or server-side controls outside a *Content* element. Also, an ASP.NET page that links to a master page will not compile if it contains a *Content* control with a *ContentPlaceHolderID* attribute that does not reference the ID of a valid *ContentPlaceHolder* control on the master page.

Now that we have covered the rules of what you must do to avoid compilation errors, let's discuss some of the decisions that you face when you begin to work with ASP.NET pages that link to a master page. One important thing to keep in mind is that a *ContentPlaceHolder* control in a master page can contain default content, as in the following example.

```
<asp:ContentPlaceHolder ID="PlaceHolderMain" runat="server" >
  <p>under contruction</p>
</asp:ContentPlaceHolder>
```

Now assume that you are creating a master page that links to the master page with this *ContentPlaceHolder* control. You are then faced with a decision about what to do with this *ContentPlaceHolder* control, and you have three choices. Your first is to do what we have already discussed. You can add a *Content* control with a *ContentPlaceHolderID* attribute to swap out the default content and replace it with unique content for the page.

```
<asp:Content ID="Main" runat="server" ContentPlaceHolderID="PlaceHolderMain" >
  <p>My unique content<p>
</asp:Content>
```

Your second choice is to accept the default content. You can do this by ensuring that the page you are creating does not contain a *Content* control that references the *ContentPlaceHolder* control with the default content. This will ensure that the default content from the *ContentPlaceHolder* control on the master page will be added to the page that you are creating.

The third choice is the one that's not so obvious at first. Think about a scenario where you want to prevent the default content from a *ContentPlaceHolder* control from being added to the page, but you don't have any content that you want to substitute in its place. If you just want to eliminate the default content from a *ContentPlaceHolder* control, you can add an empty *Control* tag that references the appropriate *ContentPlaceHolderID*.

```
<asp:Content ID="Main" runat="server" ContentPlaceHolderID="PlaceHolderMain" />
```

The decision as to which approach to take will come up again and again as you begin working with ASP.NET pages that link to master pages created by the SharePoint Foundation team.

SharePoint Web Applications

Now that we have reviewed a few essential features of the ASP.NET Framework, we can move ahead to discuss how these features have been integrated into SharePoint Foundation.

SharePoint Foundation integrates with ASP.NET at the level of the IIS website. Whenever you create a new SharePoint Web application, SharePoint Foundation typically creates a new IIS website and adds quite a bit of configuration to it behind the scenes that involves adding child directories and files within the root directory of the hosting IIS website. This set of files includes a SharePoint-specific web.config file. Figure 5-1 shows a screenshot of an IIS website in the IIS Manager after it has been configured to run as a SharePoint Web application.

FIGURE 5-1 An IIS website configured as a Web application containing a standard set of virtual directories and files

When SharePoint Foundation configures an IIS website to run as a SharePoint Web application, it also creates several virtual directories including the _layouts directory and the _controltemplates directory. As you will see later in this chapter, these two virtual directories play a special role in how SharePoint Foundation processes pages.

At this point, we would like to make an important observation about Web applications. In particular, we want you to consider how the Web application as a whole fits into the bigger picture of SharePoint Foundation architecture from the perspective of manageability and scalability.

The creation of a Web application in SharePoint Foundation is a significant administration task that requires farm-level administrative privileges. Creating a Web application requires a significant number of changes to the file system on each front-end Web server. In a Web farm environment, these changes are mirrored automatically across each front-end Web server in the farm by SharePoint Foundation. But keep in mind that the process of creating a Web application is typically required only when initially installing and configuring SharePoint Foundation or SharePoint Server 2010. It is often unnecessary to continue creating Web applications on an ongoing basis.

Once a Web application has been created, it is no longer necessary to touch the file system of the front-end Web server when creating, updating, and deleting site collections. The SharePoint Foundation architecture makes it possible to provision new sites and site collections simply by adding entries to the configuration database and a content database. It is this aspect of the SharePoint Foundation architecture that gives it significant management and provisioning advantages over ASP.NET. This added level of manageability is even more pronounced in a Web farm environment.

One thing must be stressed here: a SharePoint Web application and all the site collections inside run as a single ASP.NET application. This has an important implication. All the sites and site collections running within the same Web application share the same web.config file. SharePoint Foundation provides no support for creating a web.config file that is private to a specific site or site collection.

Web Application Configuration Files

When SharePoint Foundation provisions a new Web application, it copies a SharePoint-specific web.config file to its root directory. This web.config file contains a system.web section, which is used to configure the ASP.NET runtime. However, SharePoint Foundation goes further by extending the standard ASP.NET web.config file format with a custom SharePoint section. Examine the Extensible Markup Language (XML) fragment in Listing 5-1, which shows the SharePoint section of the web.config file and the elements within the *configSections* element that are required by ASP.NET for extended configuration information.

LISTING 5-1 The *SharePoint* section of the web.config file

```xml
<configuration>

  <configSections>
    <sectionGroup name="SharePoint">
      <section name="SafeControls" />
      <section name="RuntimeFilter" />
      <section name="WebPartLimits" />
      <section name="WebPartCache" />
      <section name="WebPartWorkItem" />
      <section name="WebPartControls" />
      <section name="SafeMode" />
      <section name="MergedActions" />
      <section name="PeoplePickerWildcards" />
      <section name="WorkflowServices" />
      <section name="BlobCache" />
      <section name="OutputCacheProfiles" />
      <section name="ObjectCache" />
    </sectionGroup>
  </configSections>

  <SharePoint>
    <SafeMode />
    <WebPartLimits />
    <WebPartCache />
    <WebPartControls />
    <SafeControls />
    <PeoplePickerWildcards />
    <MergedActions />
    <BlobCache />
    <ObjectCache />
    <OutputCacheProfiles />
    <RuntimeFilter />
  </SharePoint>

</configuration>
```

The configuration elements that are nested within the *SharePoint* section are read by various components of SharePoint Foundation at run time. For each element nested within the *SharePoint* section, there is a section element inside the *configSections* element that defines what configuration class is used to read this information. This makes it possible for various components of the SharePoint Foundation to read this SharePoint Foundation–specific configuration information to control page processing. You will see several SharePoint development techniques throughout this book that require adding or changing elements within the *SharePoint* section of the web.config file. We will start by showing you how to modify the web.config file of a Web application to enable support for debugging.

Debugging SharePoint Projects

When you create a new Web application, SharePoint Foundation copies the standard web.config file, which has default configuration settings created specifically for a production environment. To enable debugging support, you must make three modifications to the web.config file.

The *SharePoint* section of the web.config file contains a *SafeControls* element with a *CallStack* attribute that is initially set to *false*. This attribute setting should be set to *true* to instruct the SharePoint Foundation to propagate error messages up the call stack. The *system.web* section contains a *customErrors* element with a *mode* attribute that is initially set to *On*. This attribute setting should be assigned a value of *Off* to actually see the error messages. Finally, the system.web section contains a *compilation* element with a *debug* attribute that is initially set to *false*. This attribute setting should be set to *true* so that the ASP.NET runtime compiles .aspx pages with symbolic debug information.

```
<configuration>
  <SharePoint>
    <SafeMode CallStack="true" />
  </SharePoint>
  <system.web>
    <customErrors mode="Off" />
    <compilation debug="true" />
  </system.web>
</configuration>
```

The SharePoint developer tools in Microsoft Visual Studio 2010 provide the convenience of automatically modifying the web.config file for you to enable debugging support on your developer workstation. As an example, let's walk through what happens when you press the F5 key to debug a SharePoint project.

When you press the F5 key to begin debugging a SharePoint project, the SharePoint Developer Tools inspect the current project's *Site Url* property and they use that information to locate the target Web application and its web.config file. If the SharePoint Developer Tools discover that this web.config file has not been modified to enable debugging support, they prompt you with the dialog shown in Figure 5-2. If you leave the radio button list with the default setting of Modify The Web.Config File To Enable Debugging and click OK, the SharePoint Developer Tools modify the three attributes that enable debugging support.

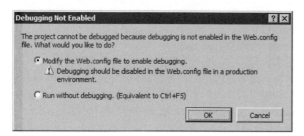

FIGURE 5-2 The SharePoint Developer Tools are capable of modifying settings in the web.config file to enable debugging support.

It's very handy that the SharePoint Developer Tools automatically update the web.config file to enable debugging support. However, you should keep in mind that the SharePoint Developer Tools do not provide any support to return the web.config file to its original state to simulate how your code will behave in a production environment. Several development scenarios, such as testing event handlers that cancel the user's action, require that debugging support be disabled. In times like this, you can modify the web.config file by hand to return it to this initial state.

```
<configuration>
  <SharePoint>
    <SafeMode CallStack="false" />
  </SharePoint>
  <system.web>
    <customErrors mode="On" />
    <compilation debug="false" />
  </system.web>
</configuration>
```

The Virtual File System of a Site

Whenever you create a new site collection, SharePoint Foundation creates a GUID to serve as its ID and assigns it to a specific content database. This content database is then used to store the content for all sites created within the scope of this site collection. SharePoint Foundation also creates a GUID-based ID for each site to track site-specific content within the content database.

As a SharePoint developer, you should see each SharePoint site as a *virtual file system* containing a hierarchy of folders and files. For example, consider what happens when you create a new site from the Blank site template. During the provisioning process, SharePoint Foundation adds many different files and folders to the virtual file system of the site, including the home page, named default.aspx, within the site's root directory.

A page that is tracked within the virtual file system of a site is known as a *site page*. Site pages play a key role in the SharePoint Foundation architecture because they make it possible for users to add, customize, and delete pages dynamically within any site without having to touch the file system on the front-end Web server. Everything about provisioning and tracking site pages is managed within the content database.

Let's look at an example of how the SharePoint Foundation provisions site pages. Consider the scenario when a user creates a new list or document library. For example, let's say you create a new document library named *Proposals*. You can do this by hand in a SharePoint site or programmatically using the server-side object model.

```
SPWeb site = SPContext.Current.Web;
string listName = "Proposals";
string listDesc = "Library for documents describing proposed new toys";
Guid libraryID = site.Lists.Add(listName, listDesc, SPListTemplateType.DocumentLibrary);
SPDocumentLibrary library = (SPDocumentLibrary)site.Lists[libraryID];
library.EnableVersioning = true;
library.OnQuickLaunch = true;
library.Update();
```

When SharePoint Foundation provisions the Proposals document library, it creates a folder named Proposals at the root of the site and then it creates a child folder named Forms. Inside the Forms folder, it creates a set of site pages with names such as DispForm.aspx, EditForm.aspx, AllItems.aspx, and Upload.aspx. The reason that SharePoint Foundation creates site pages inside the Forms folder for each new list and document library is that these site pages will provide users with the forms they will use to add and manage content.

Now let's turn our attention to writing code using the SharePoint Foundation server-side object model, which programs against site pages. You can access the files in the virtual file system of a site such as a site page using the *SPFile* class. The *SPWeb* object provides a *GetFile* method, which allows you to create an *SPFile* object using the site-relative path to a site page.

```
SPWeb site = SPContext.Current.Web;
SPFile sitePage1 = site.GetFile("default.aspx");
SPFile sitePage2 = site.GetFile("Proposals/Forms/AllItems.aspx");
```

The *SPFile* class provides methods for managing site pages within a site, such as *Delete*, *MoveTo*, and *CopyTo*. The *Delete* method, as its name implies, removes the target file from the site. *MoveTo* makes it possible to move a file, such as a site page, to another location so that it's accessible through a different URL. *CopyTo* allows you to clone a site page.

Note that the *GetFile* method returns an *SPFile* object even when you pass the path to a site page that does not exist. However, you will experience an exception if you attempt to access the majority of its methods and properties. If you are uncertain as to whether a site-relative path points to an existing site page, you should inspect the *Exists* property before attempting to access any of its other methods.

```
SPWeb site = SPContext.Current.Web;
SPFile sitePage = site.GetFile("SmellyOldSitePage.aspx");
if (sitePage.Exists) {
  sitePage.Delete();
}
```

SharePoint Foundation also makes it possible for a user to add site pages using several different techniques. For example, Team sites provide a *New Page* command on the Site Actions menu, giving users the ability to create new site pages in a wiki document library named Site Pages. The SharePoint Designer provides even more options for creating and customizing new site pages within SharePoint sites.

As a developer, you can create new site pages within an existing document library or at the root of the site. For example, you can write the text-based content of an ASP.NET page into a *MemoryStream* object and then pass that *Stream*-based object in a call to the *Add* method of the site's *Files* collection property.

```
MemoryStream stream = new MemoryStream();
StreamWriter writer = new StreamWriter(stream);
writer.WriteLine("<%@ Page %>");
writer.WriteLine("<html>");
writer.WriteLine("<body>");|
writer.WriteLine("<h2>Hello World</h2>");
writer.WriteLine("</body>");
writer.WriteLine("</html>");
writer.Flush();

SPWeb site = SPContext.Current.Web;
site.Files.Add("Hello.aspx",stream, true);
```

After you execute this code to create the new site page, you should be able to navigate to the site and type in the site-relative URL of Hello.aspx. At that point, you should see a simple page rendered inside the browser.

Page Templates and Ghosting

One of the strengths of SharePoint Foundation over ASP.NET is its ability to provision and customize the pages of a site without having to touch the front-end Web server. However, providing this capability and making it scale requires some additional complexities in the SharePoint Foundation page-processing model. Let's start with an example to illustrate a potential performance issue.

Imagine that your company has just created 100 new sites from the Blank Site template. If none of these sites requires a customized version of its default.aspx home page, would it still make sense to copy the exact same ASP.NET page definition file into the content database 100 times? The answer to this question is obviously no. Fortunately, site pages such as default.aspx can be processed using underlying *page templates* that live on the file system of the front-end Web server.

When SharePoint Foundation provisions a site page such as default.aspx, it adds information to the content database to indicate that the site page exists at a specific location within the virtual file system of the site. However, SharePoint Foundation does not copy the contents for the page into the content database. Instead, SharePoint Foundation adds extra metadata for the page to indicate which page template should be used when processing a request. This makes it possible for SharePoint Foundation to process the request for site pages using ASP.NET page files deployed on the file system of the front-end Web server.

A site page that is processed using an underlying page template is known as a *ghosted page*. From an architectural standpoint, ghosted pages are a key factor in allowing SharePoint Foundation farms to scale to tens of thousands of sites and pages because they eliminate the need to transfer the contents of an ASP.NET page from the Microsoft SQL Server computer running the content database to the front-end Web server where it is parsed. Instead, SharePoint Foundation can process requests for pages across thousands of sites using a handful of page templates that are compiled into assembly DLLs and loaded into the IIS worker process just once per Web application.

While a site page usually starts its life as a ghosted page that is rendered using an underlying page template, it can also be customized. For example, you can open a site page such as default.aspx in the page editor provided by SharePoint Designer 2010 and make changes to its content. When you save your work, SharePoint Designer writes the changes back to SharePoint Foundation. SharePoint Foundation responds by writing the content for the entire customized page into the content database.

A site page that has been customized cannot be processed using a page template. For this reason, customized pages are often referred to as *unghosted pages*. To process the request for an unghosted page, SharePoint Foundation must retrieve the content for an ASP.NET page from the content database server and move it over to the Web server. SharePoint Foundation then passes the customized page content over to the ASP.NET runtime, which parses the page definition and then loads it into memory, where it can be processed. The extra work of retrieving the page from SQL Server and moving it to the Web server where it is processed has negative performance implications in very large environments.

Another important aspect of site pages involves security. Consider a scenario in which a site collection owner tries, intentionally or unintentionally, to attack the Web server. For example, what would happen if this site collection owner added inline C# code to a customized site page? She may or may not have the training to realize that she is potentially damaging the SharePoint environment. As you might imagine, it would be quite a security hole if users without farm-level permissions were able to write code that would execute freely on the Web server. Fortunately, SharePoint Foundation was designed to prevent these types of attacks.

The key point is that customization support for site pages brings security concerns with it. Therefore, customized pages run under a special processing model known as *safe mode*. Safe mode prohibits the use of inline code that would execute on the Web server. Safe mode also prohibits the use of controls on customized page that have not been marked as safe using *SafeControl* elements in the SharePoint section of the hosting Web application's web.config file.

To implement safe mode processing, SharePoint Foundation must inspect the contents of each customized site page prior to processing. If SharePoint Foundation finds any inline code or unsafe controls, it does not process the page. If SharePoint Foundation doesn't find any inline script or unsafe controls, it then forwards the page to ASP.NET for parsing and processing.

Now that we have explained the difference between ghosted and unghosted pages, let's return to our discussion of programming against site pages using the server-side object model. The *SPFile* class makes it possible to read and write to the contents of a site page. For example, the *OpenBinary* method of an *SPFile* object returns a binary array containing the page contents. The *OpenBinaryStream* method returns a *System.IO.Stream* object. Each of these methods provides an approach for reading the contents of a site page.

An *SPFile* object also provides a *SaveBinary* method that allows you to update the contents of a site page. Note that updating the contents of a site page by using the *SaveBinary* method customizes the page and moves it into a customized or *unghosted* state.

Think about a scenario where the home page for a site has been unexpectedly customized by a user with SharePoint Designer 2010. What if these changes are unwanted? Can you remove the customization changes and return this site page to its original ghosted state? The answer is yes, and there are quite a few ways to accomplish this.

You can return a customized page to a ghosted state using SharePoint Designer 2010 by right-clicking a site page and running the Reset To Site Definition menu command. If you navigate to the Site Settings page in a site, you will find the Reset To Site Definition link, which will take you to a site administration page that provides the ability to convert customized pages back to their original ghosted state. As a developer, you can use the server-side object model. More specifically, you can access a customized site page using an *SPFile* object and call the *RevertContentStream* method.

```
SPWeb site = SPContext.Current.Web;
SPFile sitePage = site.GetFile("default.aspx");
sitePage.RevertContentStream();
```

Now let's discuss a scenario where your code must inspect the state of a site page dynamically to determine whether it has been customized. The *SPFile* class provides a property named *CustomizedPageStatus* for this exact reason. The *CustomizedPageStatus* property is based on an enumeration named *SPCustomizedPageStatus,* which defines three possible values: *Uncustomized, Customized,* and *None*.

A site page that runs in a ghosted state will have a *CustomizedPageStatus* property value of *Uncustomized*. When a site page that was initially in a ghosted state is customized, it will have the *CustomizedPageStatus* property value of *Customized*. Therefore, you can run a check before executing the *RevertContentStream* method.

```
SPWeb site = SPContext.Current.Web;
SPFile sitePage = site.GetFile("default.aspx");
if (sitePage.CustomizedPageStatus == SPCustomizedPageStatus.Customized) {
  sitePage.RevertContentStream();
}
```

Note that a site page can also have a *CustomizedPageStatus* property value of *None*. This indicates that the site page was created dynamically, without an underlying page template. An example of creating this type of site page using the *Add* method of the site's *Files* collection property was shown in the section entitled "The Virtual File System of a Site" earlier in this chapter. Because this type of site page never had an underlying page template, it can never be returned to a ghosted state.

Application Pages

In addition to site pages, SharePoint Foundation supports another common type of page known as an *application page*. An application page is an .aspx file that runs out of the _layouts virtual directory and is deployed physically inside the SharePoint Root directory under the following path.

```
C:\Program Files\Common Files\Microsoft Shared\Web Server Extensions\14\TEMPLATE\LAYOUTS
```

An application page is different from a site page because it is not tracked by the content database. Instead, application pages have a less complicated processing model that does not include support for customization. The processing model for application pages is far more like that of ASP.NET pages in a standard ASP.NET application because it doesn't require any extra support for ghosting and unghosting.

The Site Settings page (settings.aspx) is a good example of a typical application page. It is not owned by a particular site; rather, it can be used by any site within the farm. Furthermore, the Site Settings page does not require any site-specific entries in the content database, nor does it provide users with any opportunities for customization. However, the Site Settings page can still appear and behave differently from one site to the next. That's because an application page can determine the current site from its execution context and change its appearance and behavior according to what it discovers about the current site, the current site collection, and the current Web application.

As you already know, SharePoint Foundation creates the virtual _layouts directory for each Web application and maps it to the physical \LAYOUTS directory. By using this mapping scheme, along with some additional processing logic, the SharePoint Foundation runtime can make each application page accessible within the context of any site in the farm. For example, assume that there are three different sites in a SharePoint Foundation farm, accessible through these three URLs: *http://intranet.wingtip.com, http://intranet.wingtip.com/sites/sales,* and *http://www.wingtip.com.*

An application page, such as settings.aspx, can be accessed by adding its relative path within the _layouts directory to the end of a site's URL. For example, you can access the Site Settings page by using any of these three URLs: *http://intranet.wingtip.com/_layouts/settings.aspx, http://intranet.wingtip.com/sites/sales/_layouts/settings.aspx,* and *http://www.wingtip.com/_ layouts/settings.aspx.*

Because there is only one version of an application page scoped at the farm level, it can be compiled into a single assembly DLL and loaded into memory once for each Web application. You never have to worry about the existence of different versions of an application page for different sites. Furthermore, application pages are not subject to attack from users who have permission to customize site pages. Therefore, SharePoint Foundation never needs to run applications in safe mode or prohibit them from containing inline code.

Application pages are used extensively by both SharePoint Foundation and SharePoint Server 2010 to supply much of the standard functionality for provisioning and administering sites. The default installation of SharePoint Server 2010 adds more than 400 application pages into the LAYOUTS directory. In the section entitled "Creating Pages in Farm Solutions" later in this chapter, you will learn how to create custom application pages.

Differentiating Between Site Pages and Application Pages

As you begin to design and develop SharePoint solutions, you will find that it is often necessary to add new pages to a site. Each time you add a new page, you must decide whether to create the new page as a site page or an application page. Let us now summarize the difference between site pages and application pages so that you can consider the most relevant issues involved in making this decision.

Site pages support page customization through the browser and with SharePoint Designer 2010. Examples of site pages include the home page (default.aspx) for a site, as well as the pages associated with lists and document libraries, such as AllItems.aspx, NewForm.aspx, and EditForm.aspx. Site pages represent an essential part of the SharePoint Foundation architecture because they provide users with the flexibility to add, customize, and delete pages within a site.

The downside to site pages is that they require an elaborate processing infrastructure that has implications on security, performance, and scalability. Remember that customized site pages run in safe mode and, consequently, do not support inline code. To process the request for a customized site page, SharePoint Foundation must retrieve the content of pages from across the network in the content database. SharePoint Foundation must also parse each customized site page individually, as well as execute it in a special no-compile mode. While this special processing mode doesn't typically result in a measurable performance impact on small to medium farms, it can affect large farms with thousands of customized pages. This is mainly because each customized page instance must be loaded separately into memory.

Application pages do not support customization, which gives them a few distinct advantages over site pages. First, they are convenient to use in a design when you want to add pages to a site that users are not able to customize. Second, application pages are not tracked in the content database, which means that they are not subject to the same types of attacks as site pages. Therefore, they never run in safe mode and they can contain inline code. Third, each application page is always compiled into a single assembly DLL so that it performs and scales better than site pages that can be customized.

One noteworthy requirement of using application pages is that they must be deployed inside the SharePoint Root directory, which means that they cannot be used within sandboxed solutions. If you are required to build a SharePoint solution that targets the sandbox, the only type of page that you can add to a site is a site page.

Master Pages

SharePoint Foundation is designed around the concept of master pages. The obvious benefit of this is that all the pages in a SharePoint site can link to a single master page to achieve a consistent look and feel. Note that enhancements were made in SharePoint 2010 so that site pages and application pages could link to the same master page. This is a nice enhancement of SharePoint 2007, which had limitations that made it difficult to support linking site pages and application pages to the same master page.

Whenever SharePoint Foundation provisions a new site, it creates a special hidden document library known as the *Master Page Gallery*. In addition to creating the Master Page Gallery in each new site, SharePoint Foundation provisions the following three master page instances:

- v4.master
- minimal.master
- default.master

The master page named v4.master is the primary master page used in SharePoint 2010 sites. For example, v4.master is what gives Team sites in SharePoint 2010 a common page layout across site pages and application pages. This common layout is what some developers refer to as the "chrome" of the page because it includes familiar elements such as the Site Actions menu, the breadcrumb trail, the Ribbon, the Welcome menu, the Site Icon, the TopNav bar, and the Quick Launch, as shown in Figure 5-3.

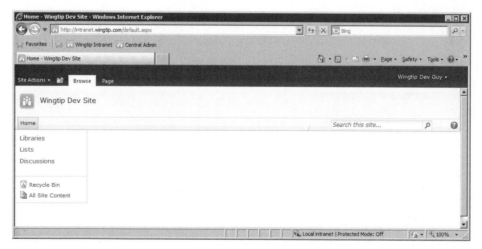

FIGURE 5-3 The standard master page named v4.master provides the default layout for SharePoint 2010 sites.

The master page named minimal.master provides a page layout without any of the chrome that is included in v4.master. The minimal.master page is used by several of the standard site page templates and application pages that are distributed along with SharePoint Foundation and SharePoint Server 2010.

The third master page that is provisioned in the Master Page Gallery for every new SharePoint 2010 site is default.master. This master page requires a bit of an explanation. Default.master is a master page designed to support a feature known as *visual upgrade*, which assists companies that are upgrading SharePoint 2007 sites to run within SharePoint 2010 farms. Here is a brief description of how visual upgrade works.

Default.master contains the standard HTML layout and chrome of a SharePoint 2007 site. When a site is upgraded from SharePoint 2007 to SharePoint 2010, SharePoint Foundation has its pages initially link to default.master instead of v4.master. The idea is that companies can upgrade from SharePoint 2007 to SharePoint 2010 without forcing their users to switch to the new SharePoint 2010 user interface immediately. Instead, users can continue to work with the older SharePoint 2007 user interface during a transition period. At some point in the future, a site collection owner can begin to use the new SharePoint 2010 user interface, and then SharePoint Foundation will redirect all the pages to use v4.master instead of default.master.

What is important to understand is that default.master is involved only when upgrading SharePoint 2007 sites to SharePoint 2010. If you are not involved in upgrade scenarios, your sites will never use default.master. However, things can be confusing because the "default" master page used by SharePoint 2010 is not default.master; it is v4.master.

An important point to understand about the master pages in the Master Page Gallery is that they are created initially in a ghosted state. In other words, every SharePoint 2010 site gets a copy of v4.master that is processed using a master page template that exists on the file system of the front-end Web server. However, you can customize a master page just as you can customize a site page.

For example, you can open a site using SharePoint Designer 2010 and then open its copy of v4.master in the page designer. This makes it possible to make customizations that affect every page in the current site. When you save your work to save the customization you have made to a master page with SharePoint Designer 2010, SharePoint Foundation will write the contents for the customized master page into the content database.

You should observe that the customized support for a master page is very similar to the customization support for a site page. A customized master page runs in safe mode, which means that it cannot contain inline code. Once a master page has been customized, you can get rid of this customization and return the master page to its initial ghosted state. You can accomplish this using the exact same techniques for returning a customized site page to its initial ghosted state discussed in the section entitled "Page Templates and Ghosting" earlier in this chapter.

Understanding v4.master

The master page named v4.master is widely used in SharePoint Foundation. For example, it defines the standard layout for every page on a team site. The v4.master page can also serve as the master page for the site page templates and application pages that you create within a SharePoint solution.

To understand the best practice for creating pages that link to v4.master, it's important that you have a basic understanding of what's defined inside. It's worth your time to open a copy of the v4.master file within Visual Studio 2010 and try to absorb all that's in there. While it might take some time to get to know everything inside v4.master, it's a worthwhile investment for any developer who is serious about designing pages and mastering branding techniques in SharePoint 2010.

The v4.master page contains the basic HTML layout for a page, including standard elements such as *html*, *head*, *body*, and *form,* and includes many server-side controls that are used to encapsulate logic and user interface components into the *Microsoft.SharePoint* assembly. Examples of these server-side controls include the *SPWebPartManager* control and controls to provide navigation components, such as breadcrumb trails and menus for navigating around the site.

Learning about the *ContentPlaceHolder* controls that exist in v4.master is important because they provide the extensibility mechanism used to add unique content to site page templates and application pages. Listing 5-2 shows a fragment of HTML distilled from v4.master that has been simplified to show you how these *ContentPlaceHolder* controls are structured within the HTML. Note that this listing shows just 4 of the 34 *ContentPlaceHolder* controls that are actually defined inside the full v4.master.

LISTING 5-2 v4.master containing ContentPlaceHolder controls

```
<%@ Master Language="C#" %>
<!DOCTYPE html PUBLIC "-//W3C//DTD XHTML 1.0 Strict//EN"
"http://www.w3.org/TR/xhtml1/DTD/xhtml1-strict.dtd">
<html runat="server">
<head runat="server">
  <title id="onetidTitle">
    <asp:ContentPlaceHolder ID="PlaceHolderPageTitle" runat="server" />
  </title>
    <asp:ContentPlaceHolder id="PlaceHolderAdditionalPageHead" runat="server"/>
</head>
<body>
<form runat="server">
<div id="s4-ribbonrow" ></div>
<div id="s4-workspace">
  <div id="s4-bodyContainer">
    <div id="s4-titlerow" >
     <asp:ContentPlaceHolder id="PlaceHolderPageTitleInTitleArea" runat="server" />
    </div>
    <div id="s4-mainarea" >
```

```
    <div id="s4-leftpanel"></div>
    <div id="MSO_ContentTable">
      <asp:ContentPlaceHolder ID="PlaceHolderMain" runat="server" />
    </div>
  </div>
 </div>
</div>
</form>
</body>
</html>
```

You can see that the head element of v4.master defines *ContentPlaceHolder* controls with an ID of *PlaceHolderPageTitle* and *PlaceHolderAdditionalPageHead*. The *ContentPlaceHolder* control with the ID of *PlaceHolderPageTitle* makes it possible to substitute the page title seen in the title bar of the browser. The *ContentPlaceHolder* control with the ID of *PlaceHolderAdditionalPageHead* makes it possible to add items such as extra meta tags, CCS rules, and JavaScript code into the head section of the page.

When you examine the site page templates supplied by SharePoint Foundation and SharePoint Server 2010, you will discover that they use the standard *MasterPageFile* attribute, which is understood and interpreted by the ASP.NET runtime. However, these site page templates use a dynamic token value of *~masterurl/default.master.*

```
<%@ Page MasterPageFile="~masterurl/default.master" %>
```

The obvious question now becomes what the meaning of *~masterurl/default.master* is. This dynamic token is a key part of the strategy that SharePoint Foundation employs to swap out the master page used by all the pages in a site. Let's examine exactly how this works.

The *SPWeb* object that represents a site has a property named *MasterUrl,* which is initialized to reference the instance of v4.master in the current site. When SharePoint Foundation processes a site page, it inspects the page's *MasterPageFile* attribute. If the *MasterPageFile* attribute has a token value of *~masterurl/default.master,* SharePoint Foundation replaces it with the *MasterUrl* property value of the current site. After SharePoint Foundation performs this substitution, it passes the site page over to ASP.NET for parsing and execution.

What is important to see is that all the pages in a site initially link to v4.master. However, you can modify the value of the *MasterUrl* property for an *SPWeb* object to reference a different master page. This has the effect of swapping out one master page for another. You will see this technique used in the section entitled "Adding a Feature Receiver to Apply Branding Attributes" later in this chapter.

Note that there is one common scenario in SharePoint Server 2010 where the pages in a site do not link to the master page referenced by the *MasterUrl* property. This scenario involves *publishing sites,* which contain a special document library named Pages. The Pages document library contains a special type of page known as a *publishing page.* All publishing pages dynamically link to a master page using another property of the *SPWeb* class named *CustomMasterUrl.* Therefore, when writing code to swap out the master page in a publishing site, you will be required to update the *CustomMasterUrl* property instead of, or in addition to, the *MasterUrl* property.

Creating a Site Page That Links to a Master Page

Now that you have seen how to link to a master page in the standard manner, let's create a new site page using what we have just learned. Let's start by looking at the content of a simple page.

```
<%@ Page MasterPageFile="~masterurl/default.master" %>

<asp:Content ContentPlaceHolderId="PlaceHolderMain" runat="server">
  <p>This is a very simple page.</p>
</asp:Content>
```

The *Page* directive at the top of this page template assigns the token value of *~masterurl/default .master* to the *MasterPageFile* attribute. As you already know, this token has the effect of linking the resulting site page to the current site's master page, which is v4.master by default. Other than that, all that's really required is to supply some unique content for the placeholder named *PlaceHolderMain.* You should be impressed by how little text is needed to define a simple site page or a site page template. This simple example demonstrates the power and elegance of master pages in SharePoint Foundation development.

At this point, let's revisit the coding example from earlier in this chapter, where we wrote the code to create a new site page using the server-side object model. Now we just need a minor modification to create a site page that links to v4.master.

```
// write out new site page instance into memory stream
MemoryStream stream = new MemoryStream();
StreamWriter writer = new StreamWriter(stream);
writer.WriteLine("<%@ Page MasterPageFile='"~masterurl/default.master'" %>");
writer.WriteLine("<asp:Content ContentPlaceHolderId='"PlaceHolderMain'" runat='"server'">");
writer.WriteLine("<h2>Hello World</h2>");
writer.WriteLine("</asp:Content>");
writer.Flush();

// add new page to site
SPWeb site = SPContext.Current.Web;
site.Files.Add("Page1.aspx", stream);
```

Creating an Application Page That Links to the Master Page

SharePoint Foundation processes application pages differently than site pages. The processing of an application page is more efficient because SharePoint Foundation does not need to parse through the page contents to look for inline code or to substitute dynamic tokens to link to a master page. However, application pages can still dynamically link to a master page using the *DynamicMasterPageFile* attribute in the *Page* directive.

```
<%@ Page DynamicMasterPageFile="~masterurl/default.master" %>
```

The technique that you have just seen to link to a master page can be confusing at first because the *DynamicMasterPageFile* attribute is not recognized by the ASP.NET runtime. Instead, *DynamicMasterPageFile* is a custom attribute that is read and interpreted by SharePoint Foundation. More specifically, the base class behind an application reads the value of the *DynamicMasterPageFile* attribute early in the page life cycle and uses the *OnPreInit* event of the *Page* class to link dynamically to the master page that is specified. This new behavior that has been added in SharePoint 2010 is a welcome improvement because it now allows all application pages and site pages to link to a single master page.

While the way that site pages and application pages link to a master page is different, they both typically rely on the *~masterurl/default.master* token to produce the same effect. This is what makes it possible to swap out the master page for every application page and site page in a site simply by updating the *SPWeb.MasterUrl* property. You will see how to practice this technique in the section entitled "Creating a Reusable Branding Solution" later in this chapter.

Creating Site Page Templates

So far, you have seen how to create the content for a simple site page. However, the example did not involve using an underlying page template. If you create site pages using an underlying page template, you will be able to achieve higher levels of control, reuse, and performance. The technique that is required to use page templates involves creating a feature that contains a special type of CAML element known as *Module*.

At a high level, you can think of a *Module element* as a file set. When you create a *Module*, you add one or more inner *File* elements. The key point is that each *File* element is used to provision an instance of a file from a file template. In our case, we will be creating a site page from a site page template. Keep in mind that the site page template exists on the file system of the Web server inside the directory of the hosting feature. The site page itself is created by adding entries to the content database.

Let's start by creating a site page template named MyTemplate.aspx with the same page content from the previous example and adding it to a feature directory.

```
<%@ Page MasterPageFile="~masterurl/default.master" %>

<asp:Content ContentPlaceHolderId="PlaceHolderMain" runat="server">
  <p>This is a very simple page</p>
</asp:Content>
```

Now we can add an element manifest to the feature with the following *Module* element.

```
<Elements xmlns="http://schemas.microsoft.com/sharepoint/">
  <Module Path="" Url="" >
    <File Url="MyTemplate.aspx" Name="MySitePage.aspx" Type="Ghostable" />
  </Module>
</Elements>
```

Note that the *File* element in this example is created with a *Url* attribute that references the site page template named MyTemplate1.aspx. The *Name* attribute contains the name of the site page being created, which in this case is MySitePage.aspx. When you activate the feature that contains this *Module* element, SharePoint Foundation provisions a site page instance within the target site at the following relative path.

```
MySitePage.aspx
```

Now let's add just a bit more complexity. Imagine that you do not want to create site pages at the root of the site but instead within a folder inside the root named WingtipSitePages. You can accomplish this by adding the folder path to the *URL* attribute of the *Module* element. You can also add multiple *File* elements inside a *Module* element, which makes it possible to create multiple site page instances from a single site page template.

```
<Elements xmlns="http://schemas.microsoft.com/sharepoint/">
  <Module Path="" Url="WingtipSitePages" >
    <File Url="MyTemplate.aspx" Name="Page1.aspx" Type="Ghostable" />
    <File Url="MyTemplate.aspx" Name="Page2.aspx" Type="Ghostable" />
    <File Url="MyTemplate.aspx" Name="Page3.aspx" Type="Ghostable" />
  </Module>
</Elements>
```

When you activate the feature that contains this updated Module element, SharePoint Foundation provisions three site page instances within the target site at the relative paths WingtipSitePages/Page1.aspx, WingtipSitePages/Page2.aspx, and WingtipSitePages/Page3 .aspx.

Note that the *File* element in the previous two examples contains a *Type* attribute with a value of *Ghostable*. When a site page is provisioned from a site page template, it initially exists in a ghosted state. This means that you can activate this feature in a thousand different sites within a farm, and there would be a thousand site pages that can all be processed using this page template, which is compiled into a single-assembly DLL and loaded into memory only once.

There are only two possible settings that you can use for the *Type* attribute: *Ghostable* and *GhostableInLibrary*. These two settings are used to differentiate between files that are provisioned inside a document library and those that are not. In this case, the site page instance has a *Type* of *Ghostable* because it is not being provisioned inside a document library. Later in this chapter, in the section entitled "Deploying a Custom Master Page," you will encounter an example of a *File* element whose *Type* attribute value will be defined as *GhostableInLibrary*.

In this chapter, you have seen two different ways to create a site page. The first technique involved adding a site page by executing the *Add* method on the site's *Files* collection property. The second technique involved using a feature containing a page template and a *Module* element. It is important to understand that the second technique has an advantage over the first because you can create ghosted pages.

Unfortunately, the server-side object model provides no direct support for creating a ghost-ed site page. The only way to create a new ghosted page is to use a feature with a *Module* element. However, this can cause problems in certain design scenarios because you must actually activate the feature to create the new ghosted site page.

Now consider a scenario in which your SharePoint solution must be designed to create new site pages continually in response to user actions. You can't simply activate a new feature each time the user does something to create a new page. Therefore, you need a design that can create new site pages in an ongoing fashion that doesn't require feature activation. However, you cannot use the *Add* method as discussed earlier because you want each of these new pages to be created in a ghosted state.

While you cannot create a new ghosted page directly using the server-side object model, there is a technique that will provide the same results. As noted earlier, the *SPFile* class contains a method named *CopyTo*. If you call *CopyTo* on a ghosted page, it creates a copy at a different URL, which is also a ghosted page. Therefore, you can supply a feature that needs to be activated only once. This feature can use a *Module* to provision a new ghosted site page that can then be used as a template.

```
<Elements xmlns="http://schemas.microsoft.com/sharepoint/">
  <Module Path="" Url="WingtipTemplates" >
    <File Url="MyTemplate.aspx" Name="MyTemplate.aspx" Type="Ghostable" />
  </Module>
</Elements>
```

Each time that you need to respond to a user action to create a site page, you can use the site page template to create a new *SPFile* object and then call the *CopyTo* method to clone it.

```
SPWeb site = SPContext.Current.Web;
SPFile sitePageTemplate = site.GetFile("WingtipTemplates/MyTemplate.aspx");
// copy iste page template to create new ghosted pages
sitePageTemplate.CopyTo("Page1.aspx");
sitePageTemplate.CopyTo("Page2.aspx");
sitePageTemplate.CopyTo("Page3.aspx");
```

Now that you have a more solid understanding of how SharePoint Foundation processes pages, let's create a few SharePoint solutions using the SharePoint Developer Tools in Visual Studio 2010. We will begin by creating a SharePoint project that can be deployed as a sandboxed solution. After that, we walk through a SharePoint solution that is designed as a farm solution and see that you have extra options in creating pages and controls when you don't have to worry about deployment within the sandbox.

Creating Pages in Sandboxed Solutions

Up to this point in this chapter, we have focused on essential background theory to help you understand the types of pages supported in SharePoint 2010, as well as how SharePoint Foundation processes each type of page. Now it's time to put this knowledge to work inside Visual Studio 2010 to create pages in a SharePoint project. We will begin by exploring how to create site pages and a simple navigation scheme in a sandboxed solution.

As we discussed in Chapter 4, "Sandboxed Solutions," designing a SharePoint solution for the sandbox does not prevent you from deploying it as a farm solution. Instead, when you create a SharePoint project as a sandboxed solution, you are really keeping your deployment options open and giving yourself the greatest amount of flexibility. Therefore, the techniques discussed in this section for creating pages can be used in any SharePoint 2010 deployment scenario. We will wait until later in this chapter, in the section entitled "Creating Pages in Farm Solutions," to discuss techniques for creating pages that must be deployed using a farm solution.

The primary technique for creating site pages in a sandboxed solution involves the use of page templates and a CAML-based *Module* element, as we discussed in the previous section of this chapter. Now we will focus on how the SharePoint Developer Tools provide assistance in creating and maintaining *Module* elements using a SharePoint Project Item Type, which is also known as *Module*.

The *Module* SharePoint Project Item Type

The SharePoint Developer Tools provide a SharePoint Project Item Type named *Module,* which provides a layer of productivity on top of the CAML-based *Module* element. You can add a new *Module* SharePoint Project Item Type to a SharePoint project using the Add New Item dialog of Visual Studio 2010, as shown in Figure 5-4.

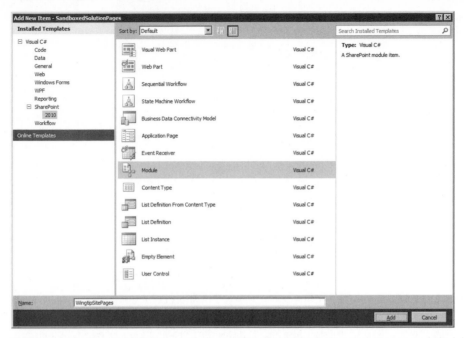

FIGURE 5-4 The SharePoint Developer Tools provide a SharePoint Project Item Type named *Module*, which makes it easier to work with the CAML-based *Module* element.

When you add a new *Module* SharePoint Project Item Type into a SharePoint project, the SharePoint Developer Tools create a new top-level folder in the project, which initially contains two files named elements.xml and sample.txt. The elements.xml file is important because it contains the *Module* element CAML markup that will be used to provision site pages from page templates. The sample.txt doesn't really have any purpose except to show you what happens when you add a file into the folder of the *Module* SharePoint Project Item Type. Therefore, you will typically either delete or rename the sample.txt file whenever you create a new *Module* SharePoint Project Item Type.

If you examine the contents of this elements.xml file right after you have created a *Module* SharePoint Project Item Type, you will see that it contains a *Module* element with an inner *File* element that references sample.txt. For example, if you add a new *Module* SharePoint Project Item Type named *WingtipSitePages*, the SharePoint Developer Tools will generate an elements .xml file with a *Module* element that looks like this.

```
<Module Name="WingtipSitePages">
  <File Path="WingtipSitePages\Sample.txt" Url="WingtipSitePages/Sample.txt" />
</Module>
```

A key advantage of using the *Module* SharePoint Project Item Type is that the SharePoint Developer Tools will create and maintain *File* elements inside the *Module* element automatically. For example, what happens if you right-click the sample.txt file and rename it as

Page1.aspx? The SharePoint Developer Tools respond by automatically updating the *Module* element inside elements.xml to reflect the change.

```
<Module Name="WingtipSitePages">
  <File Path="WingtipSitePages\Page1.aspx" Url="WingtipSitePages/Page1.aspx " />
</Module>
```

Let's say that you then add a second file to the root folder of the *Module* SharePoint Project Item Type named Page2.aspx. The SharePoint Developer Tools respond by automatically updating the *Module* element with a second *File* element.

```
<Module Name="WingtipSitePages">
  <File Path="WingtipSitePages\Page1.aspx" Url="WingtipSitePages/Page1.aspx" />
  <File Path="WingtipSitePages\Page2.aspx" Url="WingtipSitePages/Page2.aspx" />
</Module>
```

In addition to adding these two page template files to the *Module* SharePoint Project Item Type, you will want to update the content inside them with the contents of ASP.NET pages that have been designed to run in a SharePoint 2010 environment. For example, you can use this simple starting point for the contents of a site page template.

```
<%@ Page MasterPageFile="~masterurl/default.master" %>

<asp:Content ContentPlaceHolderId="PlaceHolderMain" runat="server">
  <p>This is page1.aspx</p>
</asp:Content>
```

Now you should be able to run the project's Deploy command, which will activate the feature in your test site. You should then be able to navigate to the site pages that have been created using the site-relative URLs *WingtipSitePages/Page1.aspx* and *WingtipSitePages/Page2.aspx*.

As you can see, the *Module* SharePoint Project Item Type makes your life easier because it takes care of adding and updating *File* elements inside a *Module* element. The *Module* SharePoint Project Item Type goes even further, providing *Deployment Conflict Resolution*. We first explained Deployment Conflict Resolution back in Chapter 3, "SharePoint Developer Tools in Microsoft Visual Studio 2010," with respect to List Instance project items. We will now revisit the topic to discuss how Deployment Conflict Resolution works with *Module* SharePoint Project Item Types.

Think about what happens when you activate a feature with the *Module* element containing two inner *File* elements that reference the page templates named Page1.aspx and Page2.aspx. When this feature is activated, SharePoint Foundation creates two new site pages in a ghosted state. Now think about what happens when you deactivate the feature. Does SharePoint Foundation automatically delete these two site pages? The answer is *no*. If you have a scenario that requires site pages to be deleted during feature deactivation, you must add explicit code to do so.

Now, think about a common scenario that can come up during testing, where you are activating and deactivating the same feature constantly. If your feature creates a site page during feature activation but does not delete it during feature deactivation, there is a potential problem. The second time you activate the feature, it attempts to create a new site page using the same site-relative URLs of the existing site page. SharePoint Foundation deals with this conflict by failing silently. There is no error, but the creation of the new site page fails.

When you run the Deploy command on a SharePoint project with a *Module* SharePoint Project Item Type, the SharePoint Developer Tools provide support to examine the target site and delete any existing files, such as site pages, that would cause conflicts. This ensures that each *File* element in a *Module* SharePoint Project Item Type is able to create a file in the virtual file system of your target site properly each time you run the Deploy command.

It's important to remember that the Deployment Conflict Resolution provides value only while you are testing your work inside Visual Studio 2010. Deployment Conflict Resolution does not provide any assistance with the way your SharePoint solutions behave when deployed in a production environment. Therefore, you must determine when you need to supply code to delete files such as site pages explicitly during feature activation for your production deployment.

Editing the elements.xml File Manually

While the *Module* SharePoint Project Item Type provides a significant boost in developer productivity by updating the elements.xml file on your behalf, there are common scenarios where you will need to edit the elements.xml file by hand.

As an example, let's say you want to use a *Module* SharePoint Project Item Type to create multiple site pages from a single page template. The SharePoint Developer Tools cannot update the elements.xml file to more than one site page automatically using the same underlying page template. The SharePoint Developer Tools only know how to add a single *File* element for each template file. However, you can update the elements.xml file by hand to achieve the desired effect without causing any undesirable side effects.

Let's walk through an example. Imagine you have created a *Module* SharePoint Project Item Type and added a single page template named Page1.aspx. The SharePoint Developer Tools will update the elements.xml file automatically to look like this.

```
<Module Name="WingtipSitePages">
  <File Path="WingtipSitePages\Page1.aspx" Url="WingtipSitePages/Page1.aspx " />
</Module>
```

Now you can edit the *Module* element inside elements.xml manually to add two new *File* elements that create two additional site pages at different URLs based on the same page template named Page1.aspx.

```
<Module Name="WingtipSitePages">
  <File Path="WingtipSitePages\Page1.aspx" Url="WingtipSitePages/Page1.aspx" />
  <File Path="WingtipSitePages\Page1.aspx" Url="WingtipSitePages/Page2.aspx" />
  <File Path="WingtipSitePages\Page1.aspx" Url="WingtipSitePages/Page3.aspx" />
</Module>
```

After you manually edit the *Module* element, you might worry that the SharePoint Developer Tools will overwrite your changes as they continue to update the elements.xml file automatically in response to your actions, such as adding, moving, deleting, and renaming files. Rest assured that the SharePoint Developer Tools are very good about preserving your manual edits as they continue to update the elements.xml file.

The SandboxedSolutionPages Sample Project

One of the sample SharePoint projects in the downloadable .zip archive of companion code for this book is named SandboxedSolutionPages. This project demonstrates how to create a *Module* SharePoint Project Item Type that contains page templates, image files, CSS files, JavaScript files, and a Silverlight application. The SandboxedSolutionPages project also demonstrates integrating jQuery functionality into site pages created from custom page templates. You can see the high-level structure of the SandboxedSolutionPages project in Figure 5-5.

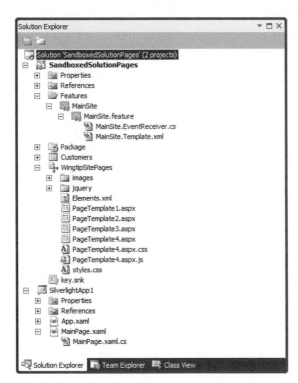

FIGURE 5-5 The SandboxedSolutionPages project demonstrates how to create site pages from page templates.

The SandboxedSolutionPages project contains a *Module* SharePoint Project Item Type named *WingtipSitePages*. Inside *WingtipSitePages,* there are four page templates that are used to create four site pages. For example, there is a page template named PageTemplate1.aspx, which is used to create a site page named SitePage1.aspx. Note that you will be required to edit the elements.xml file by hand if you want the name of the site page to differ from the file name of the template file used to create it. The *Module* element inside elements.xml contains *File* elements that have been modified manually to look like this.

```
<Module Name="WingtipSitePages">
  <File Path="WingtipSitePages\PageTemplate1.aspx"
       Url="WingtipSitePages/SitePage1.aspx" />
  <!-- other elements omitted for brevity -->
</Module>
```

In addition to provisioning four new site pages within the top-level site, activation of the *MainSite* feature creates a simple navigation scheme by adding four links to the top link bar. This is accomplished in the *FeatureActivated* method by using the server-side object model to add four new *SPNavigationNode* objects to the *TopNavigationBar* property of the current *SPWeb* object's *Navigation* property.

```
public override void FeatureActivated(SPFeatureReceiverProperties properties) {
    SPSite siteCollection = (SPSite)properties.Feature.Parent;
    SPWeb site = siteCollection.RootWeb;
    // create dropdown menu for custom site pages
    SPNavigationNodeCollection topNav = site.Navigation.TopNavigationBar;
    topNav.AddAsLast(new SPNavigationNode("Page 1", "WingtipSitePages/SitePage1.aspx"));
    topNav.AddAsLast(new SPNavigationNode("Page 2", "WingtipSitePages/SitePage2.aspx"));
    topNav.AddAsLast(new SPNavigationNode("Page 3", "WingtipSitePages/SitePage3.aspx"));
    topNav.AddAsLast(new SPNavigationNode("Page 4", "WingtipSitePages/SitePage4.aspx"));
}
```

By executing this code during feature activation, the SandboxedSolutionPages project is able to complement the four site pages with a simple but effective navigation scheme. There are now links on the top link bar that allow users to navigate to any of the four site pages, as shown in Figure 5-6.

FIGURE 5-6 You can create a simple navigation scheme by executing code to add links to the top link bar.

Creating Web Part Pages

Since we have been discussing designing and creating site pages, it now makes sense to cover Web Part pages. As their name implies, Web Part pages are a specific type of site page used to host Web Parts. Web Parts provide a valuable dimension to SharePoint Foundation. In particular, they make it possible for a site owner to customize a site page with changes that are seen by all users. Web Parts go even further, allowing individual users to add personalized changes that are seen only by them. SharePoint Foundation provides the underlying mechanisms to track all this customization and personalization inside the content database, along with all the other site-related data.

Before diving into the details of how Web Part pages work, two important aspects of their architecture must be noted. First, support for customizing and personalizing Web Parts is available with site pages but not with application pages, thus giving site pages a clear design advantage.

Second, adding and customizing Web Parts does not require customizing the Web Part pages that host them. A Web Part page defines Web Part zones but does not define what goes inside these zones. Instead, all the data for tracking Web Part instances and their customization and personalization data are kept in separate tables inside the content database. This means that a Web Part page can remain in a ghosted state, even though users are adding, customizing, and personalizing the Web Parts within its zones continually. For this reason, you should prefer to use Web Parts when designing business solutions that require user-level customization or personalization.

Web Part pages in SharePoint Foundation are built on top of the Web Part infrastructure supplied by ASP.NET. To create a Web Part page in an ASP.NET application, you must create an .aspx page that contains exactly one instance of a control named *WebPartManager* and one or more *WebPartZone* controls. The *WebPartManager* control is responsible for managing the lifetime of Web Part instances, as well as serializing Web Part–related data so that it can be stored and retrieved from the tables in the ASP.NET services database.

The Web Part infrastructure of SharePoint Foundation does not use the standard *WebPart Manager* control from ASP.NET. Instead, SharePoint Foundation relies on a specialized control named *SPWebPartManager,* which derives from the ASP.NET *WebPartManager* control. The *SPWebPartManager* control overrides the standard behavior of the *WebPartManager* control to persist Web Part data inside the SharePoint Foundation content database instead of inside the ASP.NET services database.

In most cases, you don't have to worry about dealing with the *SPWebPartManager* control directly because the one and only required instance of the *SPWebPartManager* is already defined in all the standard SharePoint Foundation master pages, including v4.master, minimal.master, and default.master. When you create a site page that links to any other master page, the *SPWebPartManager* control is added to the page automatically. Therefore, you simply need to add one or more *WebPartZone* controls.

Two things must be done when creating a page template for a Web Part page. The first is to inherit from the *WebPartPage* class that is defined inside the *Microsoft.SharePoint* assembly. The second is to add one or more *WebPartZone* controls. Note that you must use the *WebPartZone* control defined by SharePoint Foundation, not the one of the same name defined by ASP.NET.

To add *WebPartZone* controls to a page template, you must add a *Register* directive that imports the controls from the *Microsoft.SharePoint* assembly defined in the *Microsoft.SharePoint .WebPartPages* namespace. Listing 5-3 shows the contents of PageTemplate2.aspx, which demonstrates how to create a page template for a Web Part page.

LISTING 5-3 A starting point for a Web Part page template

```
<%@ Assembly Name="Microsoft.SharePoint, [4-part assembly name]" %>
<%@ Page language="C#" MasterPageFile="~masterurl/default.master"
        Inherits="Microsoft.SharePoint.WebPartPages.WebPartPage"  %>

<%@ Register Tagprefix="WebPartPages" Namespace="Microsoft.SharePoint.WebPartPages"
            Assembly="Microsoft.SharePoint, [4-part assembly name]" %>

<asp:Content ContentPlaceHolderId="PlaceHolderAdditionalPageHead" runat="server">
    <link href="styles.css" rel="stylesheet" type="text/css" />
</asp:Content>

<asp:Content ContentPlaceHolderId="PlaceHolderMain" runat="server">

  <div id="PageBanner" >
    <img src="images/WingtipLogo.gif" alt="Wingtip Logo" />
    <span id="PageBannerText" >Sales Page</span>
  </div>

    <div id="PageBody" >
    <div id="RightColumn" >
      <h2>Wingtip Sales Team</h2>
      <WebPartPages:WebPartZone ID="TopRight" runat="server"
                                Title="Top Right Web Part Zone"
                                FrameType="TitleBarOnly" />
    </div>
    <div id="LeftColumn" >
      <WebPartPages:WebPartZone ID="Main" runat="server"
                                Title="Main Web Part Zone"
                                FrameType="TitleBarOnly" />
    </div>
  </div>
</asp:Content>
```

When you provision a Web Part page from a page template, it initially contains no Web Parts in any of its Web Part zones. While you could rely on users manually adding Web Parts to your pages, it is more convenient and reliable for you to use a technique in which you prepopulate Web Part zones with whatever Web Parts your business solution requires. One common technique to accomplish this involves a declarative approach used inside the *File* element used to create the site page from the page template. More specifically, you can add an *AllUsersWebPart* element inside a *File* element. The following example demonstrates the *File* element that is used to create the site page from PageTemplate2.aspx.

```
<File Path="WingtipSitePages\PageTemplate2.aspx" Url="WingtipSitePages/SitePage2.aspx" >
  <!-- Add a Web Part to top right zone -->
  <AllUsersWebPart WebPartZoneID="TopRight" WebPartOrder="0">
    <![CDATA[
    <WebPart xmlns="http://schemas.microsoft.com/WebPart/v2"
             xmlns:iwp="http://schemas.microsoft.com/WebPart/v2/Image">
      <Assembly>Microsoft.SharePoint, [4-part assembly name]</Assembly>
      <TypeName>Microsoft.SharePoint.WebPartPages.ImageWebPart</TypeName>
      <FrameType>None</FrameType>
      <Title>Wingtip Sales Team - 1988</Title>
      <iwp:ImageLink>images/Salesteam.jpg</iwp:ImageLink>
    </WebPart>
    ]]>
  </AllUsersWebPart>
</File>
```

As you can see, a *File* element can contain an inner *AllUsersWebPart* element that references a target Web Part zone and contains an inner *WebPart* element with the serialized data for a Web Part instance. We will revisit the topic of creating Web Part elements in more detail in Chapter 6, "Controls and Web Parts," when we discuss Web Part template files.

Creating Output References to Integrate Silverlight Applications

As you have seen, the *Module* SharePoint Project Item Type provided by the SharePoint Developer Tools is both flexible and convenient. That's because the *Module* SharePoint Project Item Type makes it easy to deploy template files for site pages, CSS files, JavaScript files, and image files. In many cases, you can just add your template files to the folder for a *Module* SharePoint Project Item Type and then let the SharePoint Developer Tools do what's required to provision file instances in the target site during feature activation.

The SharePoint Developer Tools provide an especially valuable convenience when you need to integrate a Silverlight application into a SharePoint solution. However, the support for integrating a Silverlight application and deploying it with a SharePoint project is a bit more complicated than what you have seen so far. That's because Visual Studio 2010 must provide a way for you to work on a Silverlight application project and the hosting SharePoint project at the same time within the same Visual Studio solution. What's called for is something that will allow you to work on the user interface and write code inside the Silverlight application project, and then to test your work in a SharePoint test site by running the Deploy command.

Let's review for a moment and begin by discussing the basic concepts of developing a Silverlight application. When you create a new Silverlight project in Visual Studio 2010, the project is created with a MainPage.xaml file that contains the user interface definition and a code-behind file named MainPage.xaml.cs. When you build the Silverlight project, Visual Studio 2010 compiles MainPage.xaml and MainPage.xaml.cs into an assembly DLL and then packages the assembly DLL in a self-compressed .zip archive for distribution. The .zip archive used to deploy a Silverlight application has an extension of .xap and is usually referred to by developers as a XAP file (pronounced "zap").

The key point here is that every Silverlight project is configured to generate a XAP file as its output. For example, the output for a Silverlight project named SilverlightApp1 is SilverlightApp1.xap. However, it is important to recognize that the XAP file alone cannot be started as a stand-alone application. Instead, a Silverlight application must be hosted within the browser behind a Web page by adding an HTML-based object tag that references the XAP file.

```
<div>
  <object id="SilverlightApp1" width="800" height="300"
          data="data:application/x-silverlight-2,"
          type="application/x-silverlight-2" >
    <param name="source" value="SilverlightApp1.xap"/>
  </object>
</div>
```

There are two things that you must do to host a Silverlight application from a site page in a sandboxed solution. First, you must deploy the XAP file to the target site, making it accessible to the site page. Second, you must add an object tag to the site page to reference the XAP file. The SharePoint Developer Tools provide a special feature called Output Reference, which makes the second step incredibly easy to accomplish.

Each *Module* SharePoint Project Item Type has a collection property named *Output References*, which can be accessed through the standard Visual Studio property sheet. The SharePoint Developer Tools provide output references to give you a means to deploy the output of a Visual Studio 2010 project. While it's possible to create output references based on several different types of Visual Studio 2010 projects, the use of output references is particularly useful when integrating Silverlight applications into a SharePoint project. When you create an output reference based on a Silverlight project, the SharePoint Developer Tools automatically add the support to build the XAP file into the output solution package and to provision an instance of the XAP file in the target site.

To add an output reference, you should have a SharePoint project and a Silverlight project open at the same time within the same solution. If you look back at Figure 5-5, you can see that the solution contains the SharePoint project named SandboxedSolutionPages and the Silverlight project named SilverlightApp1. If you examine the property sheet for a *Module* SharePoint Project Item Type, you will notice that it contains a collection property named *Output References*. You can add a new output reference to the *Output References* collection property using the dialog shown in Figure 5-7.

FIGURE 5-7 You can use the *Output Reference* property to deploy a Silverlight application in a SharePoint solution.

When you add an output reference to a sandboxed solution, you should ensure that the *DeploymentType* property is configured as *ElementFile*. This instructs the SharePoint Developer Tools to deploy the XAP file into the *Module*'s target folder at the same location as the site pages. This makes it simple to reference the XAP file from an object tag inside one of the site pages because the site page and the XAP file have been deployed at the exact same location.

Once you properly integrate the Silverlight application project with a SharePoint project, it becomes very easy to test your work. You can run the Deploy command to push out the XAP file, along with the site page which references it using an object tag. As you continue to modify the user interface and write code behind your Silverlight application, you can continue to run the Deploy command. Each time you run the Deploy command, the SharePoint Developer Tools use Deployment Conflict Resolution to delete the previous version of the XAP and replace it with the latest version that has just been compiled.

Creating Pages in Farm Solutions

The SharePoint Developer Tools provide a project item template named Application Page, as shown in Figure 5-8, which makes it simple to add a new application page to a farm solution. When you add a new application page to a project, the SharePoint Developer Tools adds a skeleton .ASPX page file and an associated code-behind file with an extension of either .cs or .vb, depending on what language you are using.

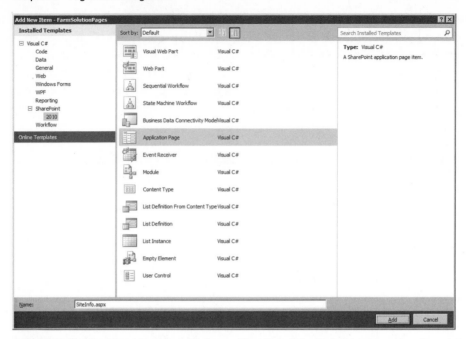

FIGURE 5-8 The SharePoint Developer Tools provide a SharePoint Project Item template for creating application pages.

Unfortunately, the SharePoint Developer Tools do not provide a visual designer for application pages. Therefore, you must work directly with HTML in code view when laying out controls and designing the user interface for an application page. However, you should remember that you can still use the Visual Studio 2010 toolbox to drag ASP.NET controls directly to the HTML in code view.

Now it's time to look at an example. The downloadable .zip archive of companion code for this book contains a sample SharePoint project named FarmSolutionPages. This project contains several different examples of using application pages in a SharePoint solution. The first example that we will look at is a custom application page named SiteInfo.aspx, which has been designed to display information about the lists on the current site. It is important to observe that SiteInfo.aspx has an associated code-behind file named SiteInfo.aspx.cs.

As a rule, application pages should derive from a base class named *LayoutsPageBase*, which is defined in the *Microsoft.SharePoint* assembly inside a namespace called *Microsoft.SharePoint. WebControls*. When the SharePoint Developer Tools generate the code-behind file for an application page, they add a public class with the same name as the application page that inherits from *LayoutsPageBase*. For example, here is the class that was created by the SharePoint Developer Tools inside *SiteInfo.aspx.cs*.

```
using Microsoft.SharePoint;
using Microsoft.SharePoint.WebControls;
```

```
namespace FarmSolutionPages {
  public partial class SiteInfo : LayoutsPageBase {
    // your code goes here
  }
}
```

Now let's take a look at Listing 5-4, which shows a partial listing for SiteInfo.aspx. If you look at the *Page* directive of SiteInfo.aspx, you can see that it has several attributes, including *Language*, *CodeBehind*, *Inherits*, and *DynamicMasterPage*. You can see that the *CodeBehind* attribute has a value that references the code-behind file SiteInfo.aspx.cs. Note that the *CodeBehind* attribute is used only by Visual Studio 2010 at design time and has no effect on the actual page at run time.

LISTING 5-4 A simple example of creating a custom application page

```
<%@ Assembly Name="$SharePoint.Project.AssemblyFullName$" %>
<%@ Page Language="C#"
        CodeBehind="SiteInfo.aspx.cs"
        DynamicMasterPageFile="~masterurl/default.master"
        Inherits="FarmSolutionPages.SiteInfo" %>

<asp:Content ID="PageTitle" runat="server"
            ContentPlaceHolderID="PlaceHolderPageTitle" >
  Wingtip Site Info
</asp:Content>


<asp:Content ID="PageTitleInTitleArea" runat="server"
            contentplaceholderid="PlaceHolderPageTitleInTitleArea" >
  Wingtip Site Info
</asp:Content>


<asp:Content ID="PageHead" runat="server"
            ContentPlaceHolderID="PlaceHolderAdditionalPageHead" >
  <style type="text/css">
    #MSO_ContentTable{ padding-left:10px; }
  </style>
</asp:Content>


<asp:Content ID="Main" runat="server"
            ContentPlaceHolderID="PlaceHolderMain" >

  <div style="margin-bottom:16px;">
    <h2>Site Lists</h2>
    <asp:GridView ID="grdLists" runat="server"
        AutoGenerateColumns="true" />
  </div>
  <div>
    <asp:Button ID="cmdReturn" runat="server"
                Text="Return to Site Settings" />
  </div>

</asp:Content>
```

You can also see that the *Page* directive inside SiteInfo.aspx contains the *DynamicMasterPageFile* attribute, which has a standard token value of *~masterurl/default.master.* As discussed earlier in this chapter in the section entitled "Understanding v4.master," this dynamic token has the effect of linking the application page to the master page that references the current site's *MasterUrl* property, which is v4.master by default.

The *Inherits* attribute of the *Page* directive references the class named *FarmSolutionPages .SiteInfo,* which has been created inside the code behind the SiteInfo.aspx.cs file. You should observe that this class in the code-behind file inherits from *LayoutsPageBase.*

At the top of Listing 5-4, you see an *Assembly* directive, which uses a token value of *$SharePoint.Project.AssemblyFullName$.* When the SharePoint Developer Tools generate the project's output solution package, they replace this token with the four-part assembly name of the current project's output assembly, which in this case is *FarmSolutionPages.dll.* Note that without the *Assembly* directive, SiteInfo.aspx would not be able to reference the class assigned to its *Inherits* attribute properly.

Note that the partial listing of SiteInfo.aspx in Listing 5-4 contains *Content* tags that override *ContentPlaceHolder* controls defined inside v4.master. The four *Content* tags used in this example reference *ContentPlaceHolder* controls with the IDs of *PlaceHolderPageTitle, PlaceHolderPageTitleInTitleArea, PlaceHolderAdditionalPageHead,* and *PlaceHolderMain.* Note that while these are 4 of the most commonly overridden placeholders in v4.master, there are 30 other *ContentPlaceHolder* controls that are useful to override in other scenarios. Figure 5-9 shows what this application page looks like when run in the context of a standard Team site.

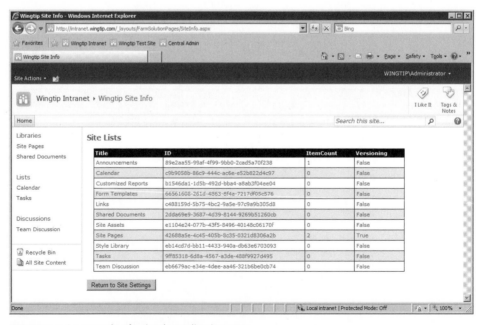

FIGURE 5-9 An example of a simple application page

The placeholder named *PlaceHolderPageTitle* is fairly simple. It is used to replace the page title that is shown on the top title bar of the browser window. The placeholder named *PlaceHolderPageTitleInTitleArea* is used to add a title to the page in the title row area just above the TopNav bar.

The placeholder named *PlaceHolderAdditionalPageHead* is very useful because it allows you to add several different types of content such as META tags, CSS rules, and JavaScript code at the bottom of the head section of the resulting page. In this example, *PlaceHolderAdditionalPageHead* is used to add a CSS rule to a *div* element in v4.master named *MSO_ContentTable*. This CCS rule adds 10 pixels of padding between the left navigation panel and the HTML content that has been added to *PlaceHolderMain*.

In most scenarios, the placeholder named *PlaceHolderMain* is where you will lay out HTML tags and ASP.NET controls to build the user interface. In SiteInfo.aspx, the *Content* control for *PlaceHolderMain* contains an *H2* tag, an ASP.NET *GridView* control, and a standard ASP.NET command button.

> **Tip** One other aspect of debugging that can catch you off guard is that the _layouts directory has its own web.config file, which has settings that override settings in the web.config file of the hosting Web application. To debug pages running from the _layouts directory, you must also open the web.config file at the following location and change the mode attribute setting in the *customErrors* element from *On* to *Off*.
>
> C:\Program Files\Common Files\Microsoft Shared\Web Server Extensions\14\TEMPLATE\ LAYOUTS\

When you first begin working with application pages, it can be tricky to add event handlers behind controls due to the lack of a visual designer. However, a simple and easy approach involves overriding the *OnInit* method. When you are writing code inside the body of a method such as *OnInit* in the code-behind class, you will see that the IntelliSense of Visual Studio 2010 will recognize controls such as the command button named cmdReturn. Here's an example wiring up a simple event handler for this command button that navigates from SiteInfo.aspx back to the Site Settings page named settings.aspx.

```
public partial class SiteInfo : LayoutsPageBase {
  protected override void OnInit(EventArgs e) {
    cmdReturn.Click += new EventHandler(cmdReturn_Click);
  }
  void cmdReturn_Click(object sender, EventArgs e) {
    SPUtility.Redirect("settings.aspx",
                        SPRedirectFlags.RelativeToLayoutsPage,
                        this.Context);
  }
}
```

Navigation Support for Application Pages

Now that you have seen how to create an application page, let's continue the process by adding a custom section and a navigation link to the Site Settings page. This can be accomplished by creating a feature containing a *CustomActionGroup* element and a *CustomAction* element. While these types of elements are not supported directly by the SharePoint Developer Tools with SharePoint Project Item templates, they can be created using the SharePoint Project Item template named Empty Element. For example, you can create an Empty Element project item and then add the following CAML elements to elements.xml.

```xml
<Elements xmlns="http://schemas.microsoft.com/sharepoint/">

  <CustomActionGroup
    Id="WingtipSiteAdministration"
    Location="Microsoft.SharePoint.SiteSettings"
    Title="Wingtip Site Administration"
    Sequence="61"
    Description=""
    ImageUrl="/_layouts/images/FarmSolutionPages/WingtipSectionIcon.gif" />

  <CustomAction
    Id="WingtipSiteInfo"
    GroupId="WingtipSiteAdministration"
    Location="Microsoft.SharePoint.SiteSettings"
    Rights="ManageWeb"
    Sequence="1"
    Title="Wingtip Site Info"
    Description="Use this page to get information about the current site" >
    <UrlAction Url="~site/_layouts/FarmSolutionPages/SiteInfo.aspx" />
  </CustomAction>

</Elements>
```

The *CustomActionGroup* element is used to add a new section to the site-setting menu for the current site. This has a *Title* of Wingtip Site Administration and has been assigned a *Sequence* attribute of 61, so that it appears after the other standard sections displayed on the Site Settings page. You can see that the *CustomAction* element in this example has a *GroupID* attribute that references the ID of the *CustomActionGroup* element. This ensures that the link created by the custom action is placed in the custom group.

This *CustomAction* element creates a link with a caption of "Wingtip Site Info," which points to the URL defined in the *Url* attribute within the *UrlAction* attribute. In this example, the URL has been assigned a value of *~site/_layouts/FarmSolutionPages/SiteInfo.aspx*. The first part of the URL contains the *~site* token, which SharePoint Foundation replaces with the base URL to the current site. This ensures that the application page always executes through the context of the current site. You can also use the *~sitecollection* token instead of the *~site* token if you want the application page to execute through the context of the top-level site of the current site collection, even in scenarios where the user has clicked the link within a child site.

There is one more aspect of this example that we want to discuss. You can observe that the *CustomAction* element also includes the *Rights* attribute, which has a value of *ManageWeb*. This attribute setting produces the effect of security trimming. In other words, the link will be shown only to users who have administrative permissions on the current site.

However, you should understand that the *Rights* attribute affects only security trimming and has no effect on security enforcement. While the *Rights* attribute can prevent users without the proper permissions from seeing the link, it does nothing to prevent an unprivileged user who knows the actual URL from getting to the application page. If you need actual security enforcement to prevent users without site administration permissions from being able to get to an application page such as SiteInfo.aspx, that security enforcement would have to be implemented separately.

One simple way to enforce security on an application page is to use the support built into the underlying base class named *LayoutsPageBase*. This class provides an overridable property named *RequireSiteAdministrator*. You can override this property in the code-behind class and return *true,* as shown in the following example.

```
public partial class SiteInfo: LayoutsPageBase {

  protected override bool RequireSiteAdministrator {
    get { return true; }
  }
}
```

Once you add this code to an application page, you truly make the page secure. When a user who is not a site administrator tries to navigate to this application page, the user is redirected to the standard SharePoint Foundation Access Denied page.

Custom Breadcrumb Navigation Using a Site Map

One of the less noticeable navigation components supplied by v4.master is the *Breadcrumb* control. This control appears as an icon of a folder with a green arrow just to the right of the Site Actions menu. The *Breadcrumb* control is a drop-down menu that displays a hierarchy of pages with the site's home page at the top. By default, the *Breadcrumb* control shows a hierarchy that contains the site's home page and the current page. However, you can build a custom site map that allows you to construct a more elaborate hierarchy of pages.

For example, if you are creating applications such as SiteInfo.aspx, which users navigate to from links on the Site Settings page, you can create a custom site map that adds the Site Settings page to the hierarchy of pages shown in the breadcrumb trail control, as shown in Figure 5-10.

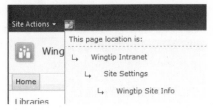

FIGURE 5-10 A custom site map can be used to customize the hierarchy of pages shown in the *Breadcrumb* control.

The first step to customizing the hierarchy of pages in the *Breadcrumb* control is to create a custom site map. To do this, you must create the site map file using a special naming convention. The name of the file must start with *layouts.sitemap,* and it must be given the extension of *.xml*. The site map in our example is named *layouts.sitemap.FarmSolutionPages.xml*. A second requirement is that this site map file must be deployed directly inside the LAYOUTS directory and not inside one of its child directories.

The second step is to create the XML content inside the site map file. You must add a top-level sitemap element, and then you add a *siteMapNode* element for each page that you want to place in the hierarchy.

```
<siteMap enableLocalization="true">
  <siteMapNode
    title="Wingtip Site Info"
    parentUrl="/_layouts/settings.aspx"
    url="/_layouts/FarmSolutionPages/SiteInfo.aspx" />
</siteMap>
```

One complication in getting the site map to work correctly is that SharePoint Foundation does not inspect your site map file at run time when it builds the hierarchy of pages in the *Breadcrumb* control. Instead, you must run a SharePoint Foundation system process that retrieves the *siteMapNode* elements from your site map and merges them into a master site map file named layouts.sitemap, which is located in the _app_bin folder inside the root directory of each Web application.

While you are testing your code in the development environment, you can force SharePoint Foundation to rebuild the layouts.sitemap file each time that you run the Deploy command by adding a *FeatureInstalled* event handler with the following code to a feature in your project.

```
public override void FeatureInstalled(SPFeatureReceiverProperties props) {
  SPWebService webService = SPFarm.Local.Services.GetValue<SPWebService>();
  webService.ApplyApplicationContentToLocalServer();
}
```

This code acquires a reference to the *SPWebService* object for the local farm. The code then calls the *ApplyApplicationContentToLocalServer* method, which forces SharePoint Foundation to rebuild the layouts.sitemap file on the local Web server.

However, keep in mind that this method name includes the word "local," which means that it will work reliably only in a farm that has a single Web server. To rebuild the layouts.sitemap file properly across a server farm with multiple Web servers, you should use the Windows PowerShell cmdlet named *Install-SPApplicationContent* from the SharePoint PowerShell snap-in.

The final step to getting the *Breadcrumb* control to work properly involves adding a *Content* control with an ID of *PlaceHolderTitleBreadcrumb* to swap out the *ListSiteMapPath* control defined in v4.master with a customized instance of the *ListSiteMapPath* control that uses a site map provider named *SPXmlContentMapProvider*.

```
<asp:Content ID="TitleBreadcrumb" runat="server"
             contentplaceholderid="PlaceHolderTitleBreadcrumb" >
  <SharePoint:ListSiteMapPath
    ID="ListSiteMapPath1" runat="server"
    SiteMapProviders="SPSiteMapProvider,SPXmlContentMapProvider"
    RenderCurrentNodeAsLink="false"
    PathSeparator=""
    CssClass="s4-breadcrumb"
    NodeStyle-CssClass="s4-breadcrumbNode"
    CurrentNodeStyle-CssClass="s4-breadcrumbCurrentNode"
    RootNodeStyle-CssClass="s4-breadcrumbRootNode"
    HideInteriorRootNodes="true"
    SkipLinkText="" />
</asp:Content>
```

Creating a Reusable Branding Solution

There is one common request for customizing SharePoint sites that has been heard again and again: "Can you make my SharePoint site look like it's not a SharePoint site?" Whether a company has public Internet sites or internal team sites, there is often a desire to replace the standard SharePoint look and feel with custom colors, fonts, and images.

While different designers and developers don't always agree on the best approach for branding SharePoint sites, we will focus on a technique that works in either a sandbox solution or a farm solution. That means our SharePoint solution must be designed in such a way that it does not deploy any files inside the SharePoint root directory. Instead, our SharePoint solution will be designed to deploy all the required branding files using template files and *Modules*. We will also refrain from picking up any dependencies on SharePoint Server 2010, which will ensure that our branding solution will work equally well on farms running either SharePoint Foundation or SharePoint Server 2010.

In this section, we are going to walk through a simple SharePoint project named Branding101. This project has been designed to create a reusable brand solution that can be used with any SharePoint 2010 site. You can see the high-level structure of the Branding101 project, which includes a custom master page, custom CSS files, and custom images, by examining Figure 5-11.

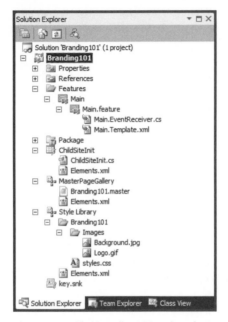

FIGURE 5-11 The Branding101 project demonstrates how to create a reusable branding solution.

Deploying a Custom Master Page

The first step in creating a branding solution is to figure out how to deploy a custom master page to the Master Page Gallery of the top-level site. You can start by creating a *Module* SharePoint Project Item Type, which is activated by a feature that is scoped at the site collection level. Note that the Branding101 solution has a single feature named *Main,* which activates at the site collection level.

The Branding101 solution contains a *Module* element named *MasterPageGallery,* which contains a template file for a custom master page named Branding101.master. When you create a custom master page such as Branding101.master, you will need a starting point. A popular technique is to copy and paste the text from the standard SharePoint 2010 master page named v4.master, which can be found at the following location.

```
C:\Program Files\Common Files\Microsoft Shared\Web Server Extensions\14\TEMPLATE\GLOBAL\
v4.master
```

Once you have added a master page template such as Branding101.master to a *Module* SharePoint Project Item Type, you must modify the elements.xml file to ensure that it is deployed correctly to the Master Page Gallery during feature activation. The elements.xml file of the *MasterPageGallery* item has been edited manually to produce the following XML.

```
<Elements xmlns="http://schemas.microsoft.com/sharepoint/">
  <Module Name="MasterPageGallery"
          Path="MasterPageGallery"
          Url="_catalogs/masterpage" >

    <File Url="Branding101.master" Type="GhostableInLibrary" >
      <Property Name="UIVersion" Value="4" />
      <Property Name="ContentTypeId" Value="0x010105" />
    </File>

  </Module>
</Elements>
```

When you create a *Module* element such as *MasterPageGallery* to provision files within a document library such as the Master Page Gallery, it is important that you configure the *Url* attribute of the *Module* element using the site relative path to the root of the document library. When provisioning a master page to the Master Page Gallery, the *Url* attribute of the *Module* element should always be configured with the standard path of _catalogs/masterpage.

When you provision a file into the scope of a document library, each *File* element should also be edited to include a *Type* attribute with a value of *GhostableInLibrary*. When provisioning master pages in SharePoint 2010, you should also add two *Property* elements inside the *File* element to configure two important properties named *UIVersion* and *ContentTypeId*.

The *UIVersion* property of a master page is used by SharePoint Foundation to differentiate between master pages designed for the new SharePoint 2010 user interface and those designed for the older user interface of SharePoint 2007. If you have designed your master page based on the new SharePoint 2010 user interface, you should configure the *UIVersion* property with a value of 4. Earlier in this chapter, in the section entitled "Master Pages," we briefly described the new visual upgrade feature in SharePoint 2010. You can configure the *UIVersion* property with a value of 3 for migration scenarios where you are taking advantage of the visual upgrade feature, and you have designed the master page to target the older SharePoint 2007 user interface.

The *ContentTypeId* property is used to differentiate between master pages and page layouts that are used by SharePoint Server 2010 publishing sites. When deploying a master page, you should configure it with the correct *ContentTypeId* value for master pages, which is always *0x010105*.

Deploying CSS Files and Images to the Style Library

In SharePoint Server 2007, the publishing features have been designed to create a special document library named the Style Library, which Microsoft uses to deploy standard CSS files and image files used in publishing sites. The Style Library is also commonly used as a deployment target by Web designers and developers who are using CSS files and image files to apply branding elements to SharePoint 2007 publishing sites.

When you are developing a generic and reusable branding solution for SharePoint 2007 farms, the Style Library cannot be used because it exists only on publishing sites. Windows SharePoint Services 3.0 does not create the Style Library when you create other types of sites, such as a Team site, Blank site, or Document Workspace. Fortunately, this is no longer a problem in SharePoint 2010.

In SharePoint 2010, every site collection gets its own Style Library. That's because Microsoft has moved the standard provisioning instructions for creating the Style Library out of the publishing features and into the Global site definition. Each time that SharePoint Foundation creates a new site collection, it adds the Style Library to the top-level site. This makes the Style Library an ideal candidate for deploying CSS files and image files in a generic branding solution.

The Branding101 project contains a second *Module* SharePoint Project Item Type named Style Library, which is used to provision a custom CSS file and multiple custom images inside the Style Library. Deploying custom CSS files and image files in the Style Library is recommended because it works with both sandboxed solutions and farm solutions. This technique also works within farms running SharePoint Server 2010, as well as within farms running only SharePoint Foundation. It must be noted that several other popular approaches to branding SharePoint 2010 sites do not provide this level of flexibility.

Unlike *MasterPageGallery*, which is used to deploy a custom master page template, it is not necessary to modify the elements.xml file of the Style Library by hand. The SharePoint Developer Tools can add all the appropriate *File* elements behind the scenes. Furthermore, you can continue to add other image files to the Images folder inside the Style Library Module, and they will be deployed automatically inside the proper location within the Style Library for you.

Adding a Feature Receiver to Apply Branding Attributes

Now that you understand how the two *Module* SharePoint Project Item Types have been configured to deploy the custom master page and a custom CSS file, it's time to walk through the code that configures the current site collection to begin using them. The feature, named *Main,* contains a feature receiver with a *FeatureActivated* event handler and a

FeatureDeactivating event handler. These event handlers make it possible to write code that applies the branding solution during feature activation, as well as to remove the branding solution during feature deactivation.

Now let's go through the code in the *FeatureActivated* event handler, which applies the branding solution. First, the code determines the path to Branding101.master in the Master Page Gallery. Note that the path to the master page must be calculated relative to the root of the hosting Web application. Next, the code enumerates through all the sites within the current site collection and updates several properties within the *SPWeb* object of each site.

```
public override void FeatureActivated(
                    SPFeatureReceiverProperties properties) {
  SPSite siteCollection = properties.Feature.Parent as SPSite;
  if (siteCollection != null) {
    SPWeb topLevelSite = siteCollection.RootWeb;
    // calculate relative path to site from Web Application root
    string WebAppRelativePath = topLevelSite.ServerRelativeUrl;
    if (!WebAppRelativePath.EndsWith("/")) {
      WebAppRelativePath += "/";
    }
    // enumerate through each site and apply branding
    foreach (SPWeb site in siteCollection.AllWebs) {
      site.MasterUrl = WebAppRelativePath +
                       "_catalogs/masterpage/Branding101.master";
      site.CustomMasterUrl = WebAppRelativePath +
                             "_catalogs/masterpage/Branding101.master";
      site.AlternateCssUrl = WebAppRelativePath +
                             "Style%20Library/Branding101/Styles.css";
      site.SiteLogoUrl = WebAppRelativePath +
                         "Style%20Library/Branding101/Images/Logo.gif";
      site.UIVersion = 4;
      site.Update();
    }
  }
}
```

The *MasterUrl* property of the *SPWeb* object is the property that you use to redirect site pages and application pages to link to a custom master page such as Branding101.master. Note that the code that you have just seen calculates the path to Branding101.master by combing the Web application-relative path to the site and the site relative path to the Master Page Gallery in the top-level site, which always has a value of *_catalogs/masterpage*.

Note that this example updates the *SPWeb* property named *CustomMasterUrl* in addition to the *MasterUrl* property. Updating the *CustomMasterUrl* property is important only in publishing sites that contain publishing pages inside the Pages document library. The *CustomMasterUrl* property is used to reassign the master page for publishing pages. Assigning a new value to the *CustomMasterUrl* property in a SharePoint Foundation site will have no effect, nor will it cause any problems.

The *AlternateCssUrl* property is used to link all the pages within a site to the custom CSS file named styles.css. Note that the linking behavior associated with the *AlternateCssUrl* property is implemented by the SharePoint *CssLink* control, which is defined in the head section of all the standard SharePoint 2010 master pages. The SharePoint *CssLink* control also adds a link to an essential CSS file named *coreV4.css* and should therefore be included in any custom master page targeting SharePoint 2010.

While the SharePoint project named Branding101 relies on the approach of linking to a custom CSS file using the *AlternateCssUrl* property, it should be noted that some branding solutions take an alternative approach of linking to a custom CSS file using the *CSSRegistration* control. For example, you can add the following *CssRegistration* tag to the head section of a custom master page to link to a CSS file inside the Style Library.

```
<SharePoint:CssRegistration
  name="<% $SPUrl:~sitecollection/Style Library/styles.css %>"
  After="corev4.css"
  runat="server"
/>
```

One benefit to using the *CssRegistration* control over the *AlternateCssUrl* property is that it allows you to link to more than one CSS file. A second advantage is that you can use the *CssRegistration* control in individual pages for scenarios where you have a CSS file that is used by some but not all the pages within a site.

However, use of the *CssRegistration* control also has a disadvantage because it usually relies on the *$SPUrl* expression to determine the path to the current site. However, use of the *$SPUrl* expression requires the hosting farm to be running SharePoint Server 2010. If there is a chance that your branding solution will need to be used in farms running only SharePoint Foundation, you should choose the technique of linking to a custom CSS file using the *AlternateCssUrl* property over the *CssRegistration* control. While it is possible to use the *CssRegistration* without the *$SPUrl* expression, it can be tricky, and it often results in branding solutions that do not work in scenarios where the hosting site collection is not located at the root of the hosting Web application.

The *SiteLogoUrl* property is used in this example because it provides a quick and effective way of replacing the site image in the upper-left side of the page. Note that the behavior associated with the *SiteLogoUrl* property is implemented by the SharePoint *SiteLogoImage* control, which is defined in the Title Row section of standard SharePoint 2010 master pages such as v4.master.

The *UIVersion* property is used to configure whether the current site should run in the standard UI mode for SharePoint 2010 sites or whether it should run in the older UI mode that is used when migrating SharePoint 2007 sites to SharePoint 2010. The main effect that the

UIVersion property setting will have will be to determine which file the *CssLink* control links to: the new standard CSS file created for SharePoint 2010 named corev4.css, or the older standard CSS file named core.css, which is designed to style pages in SharePoint 2007. The Branding101 solution assigns a value of 4 to the *UIVersion* property to ensure that pages are linked to corev4.css instead of core.css.

You have now seen how and why the Branding101 solution configures important *SPWeb* properties on every site within the current site collection during feature activation. Now let's discuss what code should be executed during feature deactivation. It makes sense to remove all the custom branding elements to return the current site collection to its original state. Here is an implementation of the *FeatureDeactivating* method, which returns all pages to using the standard master page v4.master as well as removing the link to the custom CSS file and the custom site logo.

```
public override void FeatureDeactivating(
                      SPFeatureReceiverProperties properties) {
  SPSite siteCollection = properties.Feature.Parent as SPSite;
  if (siteCollection != null) {
    SPWeb topLevelSite = siteCollection.RootWeb;
    // calculate relative path of site from Web Application root
    string WebAppRelativePath = topLevelSite.ServerRelativeUrl;
    if (!WebAppRelativePath.EndsWith("/")) {
      WebAppRelativePath += "/";
    }
    // enumerate through each site and remove custom branding
    foreach (SPWeb site in siteCollection.AllWebs) {
      site.MasterUrl = WebAppRelativePath +
                        "_catalogs/masterpage/v4.master";
      site.CustomMasterUrl = WebAppRelativePath +
                             "_catalogs/masterpage/v4.master";
      site.AlternateCssUrl = "";
      site.SiteLogoUrl = "";
      site.Update();
    }
  }
}
```

Adding an Event Receiver to Brand Child Sites

There is one more project item that needs to be discussed to complete the walkthrough of the Branding101 project. What's still needed is a way to apply the custom branding elements to child sites automatically as they are created inside a site collection that has activated the Branding101 feature. To accomplish this task in SharePoint 2007, you would be required to resort to feature stapling. However, SharePoint 2010 adds support for a new event named *WebProvisioned,* which makes this job much easier.

The Branding101 project contains an Event Receiver SharePoint Project Item Type named *ChildSiteInit,* which is used to automate copying the branding property values from the top-level site to child sites as they are created. The key benefit of adding this event handler is that it will fire each time a new child site is created. This makes it fairly simple to write this code, which copies the relevant *SPWeb* properties from the top-level site to the new child site.

```
using System;
using Microsoft.SharePoint;

namespace Branding101.ChildSiteInit {

  public class ChildSiteInit : SPWebEventReceiver {
    public override void WebProvisioned(
                          SPWebEventProperties properties) {
      SPWeb childSite = properties.Web;
      SPWeb topSite = childSite.Site.RootWeb;
      childSite.MasterUrl = topSite.MasterUrl;
      childSite.CustomMasterUrl = topSite.CustomMasterUrl;
      childSite.AlternateCssUrl = topSite.AlternateCssUrl;
      childSite.SiteLogoUrl = topSite.SiteLogoUrl;
      childSite.Update();
    }
  }
}
```

Conclusion

This chapter has covered the fundamentals of how pages are processed in SharePoint 2010. You learned that pages in a SharePoint site can be categorized as either site pages or application pages. Site pages provide SharePoint users with the ability to add, customize, and delete pages while working with a site. While many site pages are initially created in a ghosted state and processed in terms of an underlying page template, SharePoint Foundation must provide a more elaborate processing model to support site page customization. Application pages, on the other hand, are based on a less complicated deployment and processing model, which can lead to simpler designs and more efficient processing.

This chapter also examined and compared the factors involved in designing and implementing pages for sandboxed solution and farm solutions. Because a sandboxed solution cannot deploy application pages, the design for a sandboxed solution must rely on provisioning site pages using page templates and *Modules*. However, you have also seen that it is possible to create site pages in a sandboxed solution that contains advanced elements such as Web Parts, Silverlight applications, and client-side code that uses jQuery. In addition, you have learned that many design options are available in only farm solutions, such as using application pages and creating a custom site map.

The last part of the chapter examined designing and implementing a reusable SharePoint solution to brand SharePoint sites. You learned how to create a SharePoint project that applies a branding solution to a target site collection using a custom master page and a custom CSS file. Furthermore, you now know the proper techniques to create a branding solution that can be deployed as either a sandboxed solution or a farm solution on farms running either SharePoint Foundation or SharePoint Server 2010.

Chapter 6
Controls and Web Parts

Web Parts are the most common type of control created by Microsoft SharePoint developers. However, they are not the only type. In fact, there are several other control types that can be beneficial to create and reuse to extend SharePoint sites. We will begin this chapter with a quick primer on developing custom controls and demonstrate several examples of when and where they can be used in a SharePoint project. Along the way, we will discuss where user controls and delegate controls fit into the overall SharePoint developer story.

The second half of the chapter focuses on Web Part development, where you will learn the role of the Web Part Manager and the Web Part Gallery. We will demonstrate several different styles for Web Parts rendering, including using an Extensible Stylesheet Language for Transformations (XSLT) transform to generate Hypertext Markup Language (HTML) output. We will show you how to extend Web Parts using persistent properties and custom Editor Parts. We will also discuss taking advantage of the Web Part framework support for Web Part verbs and Web Part connections, as well as using asynchronous processing when retrieving data from across the network.

Developing with Controls

An *ASP.NET control* is a reusable user interface component that is used on pages in ASP.NET development and in SharePoint development. In the ASP.NET programming model, a control is defined as a class that inherits from the *Control* class in the *System.Web.UI* namespace. For example, you could use the following class definition as the starting point for creating a custom control class.

```
namespace WingtipControls {
  public class WingtipCustomControl : System.Web.UI.Control {
    // control class implementation
  }
}
```

The ASP.NET Framework provides many specialized control classes that can be used in SharePoint development. For example, there are built-in controls such as *Button*, *Label*, *TextBox*, and *CheckBox*. All these control classes inherit—either directly or indirectly—from the *Control* class, forming a large inheritance hierarchy. Figure 6-1 shows how the ASP.NET control classes discussed in this chapter fit into this hierarchy.

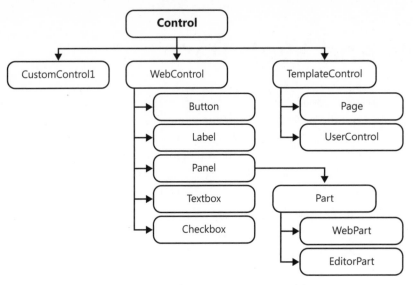

FIGURE 6-1 All control classes inherit from the ASP.NET *Control* class.

The WingtipControls Sample Project

The downloadable .zip archive of companion code for this book contains a sample SharePoint project named WingtipControls, which contains working samples of the custom controls and user controls shown over the next few sections. You can see the high-level structure of this project by examining Figure 6-2.

FIGURE 6-2 The WingtipControls project demonstrates using custom controls and user controls in SharePoint development.

Note that the WingtipControls project has been configured as a farm solution. This is a requirement because this project relies on several techniques that cannot be used in sandboxed solutions. In general, developing any type of custom control other than a Web Part in SharePoint development will force you to deploy your project as a farm solution.

You create a custom control using a new class that inherits from the *Control* class. In most cases, you then override selected methods of the *Control* class to handle events in the ASP.NET page life cycle. You can also add public properties to a custom control class, which can be used as initialization parameters. The following listing shows a simple custom control class named *WingtipCustomControl*.

```
using System;
using System.Web;
using System.Web.UI;

namespace WingtipControls {
  public class WingtipCustomControl : Control {

    public string UserGreeting { get; set; }

    protected override void Render(HtmlTextWriter writer) {
      writer.AddStyleAttribute(HtmlTextWriterStyle.Color, "Blue");
      writer.AddStyleAttribute(HtmlTextWriterStyle.FontSize, "18pt");
      writer.RenderBeginTag(HtmlTextWriterTag.Div);
      writer.Write(UserGreeting);
      writer.RenderEndTag(); // </div>
    }
  }
}
```

The *WingtipCustomControl* class includes a public property named *UserGreeting* and overrides the *Render* method. The *Render* method of the *Control* class is called by the ASP.NET run time once the hosting page has entered the rendering phase, providing the control with an opportunity to write HTML content into the page. The *Render* method in this case has been implemented to generate an HTML *div* element with inner text containing the value of the *UserGreeting* property.

The *Render* method accepts a parameter named *writer,* which is based on the *HtmlTextWriter* class. The *HtmlTextWriter* class provides a *RenderBeginTag* method and *RenderEndTag* method, which can be used to generate HTML tags such as a *div* element. The *HtmlTextWriter* class also provides an *AddStyleAttribute* method, which can be called just before the *RenderBeginTag* method to add attributes in an HTML element. For example, the two calls to *AddStyleAttribute* in this example produce an opening *div* tag that looks like this.

```
<div style="color: blue; font-size: 18pt;">
```

Once you have created a control class such as *WingtipCustomControl*, you can begin to use it within application pages, site pages, or master pages. This is accomplished by adding *control tags* to create page-level instances of the control class. However, before you can add a control tag, you must first add a *Register directive*. The *Register* directive should be added at the top of the page under the *Page* directive, and it should contain three attributes: the *Tagprefix* attribute, the *Namespace* attribute, and the *Assembly* attribute.

```
<%@ Register Tagprefix="WingtipControls"
             Namespace="WingtipControls"
             Assembly=" WingtipControls, [4-part assembly name]" %>
```

Once you have added the *Register* directive to a page, you can add a control tag to create an instance of the control. The control tag is created by combining *Tagprefix* and the control class name separated by a colon. Here is an example of adding a control tag to create an instance of the *WingtipCustomControl* class.

```
<WingtipControls:WingtipCustomControl
    runat="server"
    Id="WingtipControl1"
    UserGreeting="Hello World" />
```

When creating a control tag, you must always include the *runat="server"* attribute to let the ASP.NET run time know that this should be processed as a server-side control. You should also include the *Id* attribute and assign it a unique value. When you create a control tag, you can also include attributes to initialize public properties. In this example, the control tag adds an attribute to initialize the *UserGreeting* property.

Safe Mode Processing and Safe Controls

In SharePoint development, you can use custom controls on several different types of pages, including application pages, site pages, and master pages. However, it is important to understand that there is a potential problem when adding custom controls to site pages and master pages. The problem is that site pages and master pages can be customized, which leads Microsoft SharePoint Foundation to process them in safe mode.

The reasons that SharePoint Foundation incorporates safe mode processing was initially discussed in Chapter 5, "Pages and Navigation." As you remember, the primary motivation for safe mode is based on the fact that ordinary users can customize the contents of a site page or a master page. The concern here is that users without farm-level permissions should not be able to add server-side code to pages. Safe mode protects the farm by prohibiting any inline code on customized pages that would run on the Web server.

Safe mode processing goes further by adding restrictions on what types of controls can be used on a customized page. At first, you might wonder why safe mode poses this restriction. The reason has to do with a scenario in which a malicious user tries to mount an attack by customizing a site page using a server-side control that has been installed on the Web server. For example, imagine that Web servers in a SharePoint farm have also been configured to run an older application built using the ASP.NET Framework. A malicious user might attempt to exploit a custom control from the older application by adding it to a customized page and parameterizing the control tag.

Safe mode prevents this type of attack by requiring any control class used on a customized page to be registered as a safe control. A control class is registered as a safe control by adding a *SafeControl* entry into a Web application's web.config file. Note that the standard web.config file that SharePoint Foundation creates for new Web applications already includes *SafeControl* entries for the standard controls and Web Parts included with ASP.NET and SharePoint 2010.

The key point here is that any custom controls that you create cannot be used on customized pages unless they are deployed from within a SharePoint project that is configured to add the required safe control entries into the web.config file. Fortunately, the SharePoint developer tools in Microsoft Visual Studio 2010 makes adding these safe control entries very easy.

If you examine the web.config file for a Web application, you will find a *SafeControls* section inside the *SharePoint* section. Registering a custom control as a safe control requires adding a new *SafeControl* element with three attributes: the *Assembly* attribute, the *Namespace* attribute, and the *TypeName* attribute. It is a common practice to register all the custom controls in an assembly using a single *SafeControl* entry that includes the root namespace and an * character for the type name.

```
<SafeControls>
  <SafeControl
    Assembly=" WingtipControls, [4-part assembly name]"
    Namespace="WingtipControls"
    TypeName="*" />
</SafeControls>
```

Now we will examine how the SharePoint Developer Tools assist you with adding *SafeControl* entries. As you know, SharePoint projects are built by adding SharePoint project items. You should notice that each SharePoint project item exposes a standard set of properties that can be seen and modified through the standard property sheet in Visual Studio. One of these properties is the *Safe Control Entries* collection. If you choose to modify this collection, the SharePoint Developer Tools provide the Safe Control Entries dialog, shown in Figure 6-3, which allows you to add *Safe Control Entry* members in a declarative fashion.

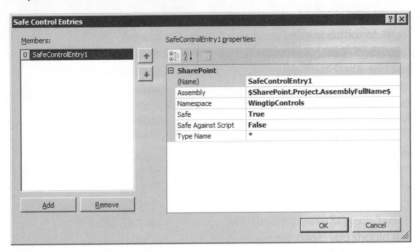

FIGURE 6-3 The SharePoint Developer Tools make it easy to add a Safe Control Entry, which allows a custom control to run on customized pages.

In the WingtipControls project, there is a SharePoint project item named *WingtipControls*. The *Safe Control Entries* collection for this SharePoint project item contains a *Safe Control Entry* member with the root namespace for the project and a type name based on the * character. This *Safe Control Entry* member effectively registers every public control class in the current project.

Note that when you are developing Web Parts, you are not usually required to add *Safe Control Entry* members explicitly to the *Safe Control Entries* collection. That's because the SharePoint Developer Tools automatically add the required *Safe Control Entry* member whenever you create a Web Part project item. However, there is no dedicated SharePoint project item for creating a custom control. Therefore, you are typically required to add at least one *Safe Control Entry* member by hand when developing custom controls.

Now it's time to discuss how the SharePoint Developer Tools deal with *Safe Control Entry* members. When you build a SharePoint project into a solution package, the SharePoint Developer Tools add a *SafeControl* entry into the manifest.xml file for each *Safe Control Entry* member. For example, when you build the WingtipControls project into a solution package, the SharePoint Developer Tools generate the manifest.xml file with the following *SafeControl* entry.

```
<Solution>
  <Assembly Location="WingtipControls.dll" DeploymentTarget="GlobalAssemblyCache">
    <SafeControls>
      <SafeControl Assembly="WingtipControls, [4-part assembly name]"
                   Namespace="WingtipControls"
                   TypeName="*" />
    </SafeControls>
  </Assembly>
  <!--other elements removed for brevity -->
</Solution>
```

Once the SharePoint Developer Tools have added the *SafeControl* entry into the manifest.xml file, the rest of the safe control registration process is automated by SharePoint Foundation. More specifically, when SharePoint Foundation deploys a farm solution, it propagates each *SafeControl* entry from the manifest.xml file into the web.config file.

Now we have walked through the entire process of registering a custom control as a safe control. It is very convenient that the SharePoint Developer Tools do a great job at making the entire process transparent to the developer. However, one last key point must be emphasized: It still requires a farm administrator to deploy a solution package in a production farm. Therefore, the farm administrator is still ultimately in charge of what custom controls and Web Parts are registered as safe controls.

Using a Custom Control to Create a Menu

Now we will examine a useful scenario where you can take advantage of custom controls in SharePoint development. Imagine that you would like to create a custom menu with custom menu commands and have it appear as a fly out menu on the site actions menu. This can be accomplished by creating a custom menu control that will appear like the one shown in Figure 6-4.

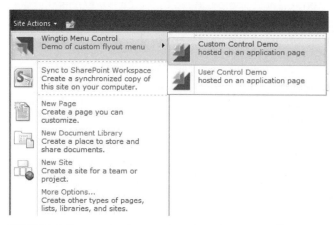

FIGURE 6-4 You can develop a custom control to create a fly out menu.

To create a custom menu control within a SharePoint project, you begin by referencing the primary ASP.NET assembly named *System.Web*. Next, you create a public class that inherits from the *Control* class and you override the *CreateChildControls* method. Inside your implementation of *CreateChildControls,* you will be required to create instances of control classes defined in the *Microsoft.SharePoint* assembly inside the *Microsoft.SharePoint.WebControls* namespace. These control classes are *SubMenuTemplate* and *ItemTemplate*.

```
public class WingtipMenuControl : Control {

  protected override void CreateChildControls() {

    // create fly out  menu
    SubMenuTemplate smt = new SubMenuTemplate();

    // create fly out menu commands
    MenuItemTemplate mit1 = new MenuItemTemplate();
    MenuItemTemplate mit2 = new MenuItemTemplate();

    // add menu commands to Controls collection of fly out menu
    smt.Controls.Add(mit1);
    smt.Controls.Add(mit2);

    // add fly out menu to Controls collection of of menu control
    this.Controls.Add(smt);
  }
}
```

You must create an instance of the *SubMenuTemplate* control to serve as the top-level menu command, which triggers the fly out menu. After creating an instance of the *SubMenuTemplate* control, you then must create an instance of the *MenuItemTemplate* control for each menu command you want to add to the fly out menu. Each instance of the *MenuItemTemplate* control must also be added to the *Controls* collection of the *SubMenuTemplate* control. Finally, the instance of the *SubMenuTemplate* control must be added to the *Controls* collection of the custom menu control. A complete implementation of a simple menu control is shown in Listing 6-1.

LISTING 6-1 The code required to create a custom menu control with a fly out menu

```
public class WingtipMenuControl : Control {

  string SubMenuIconUrl = @"/_layouts/images/WingtipControls/SubMenuIcon.gif";
  string MenuIconUrl = @"/_layouts/images/WingtipControls/MenuIcon.gif";
  string AppPage1Url = @"/_layouts/WingtipControls/CustomControlDemo.aspx";
  string AppPage2Url = @"/_layouts/WingtipControls/UserControlDemo.aspx";

  protected override void CreateChildControls() {
    SPWeb site = SPContext.Current.Web;

    // create fly out  menu
    SubMenuTemplate smt = new SubMenuTemplate();
    smt.ID = "CustomSubMenu";
    smt.Text = "Wingtip Menu Control";
    smt.Description = "Demo of custom fly out menu";
    smt.MenuGroupId = 1;
    smt.Sequence = 1;
    smt.ImageUrl = site.Url + SubMenuIconUrl;
```

```
    // create fly out menu command 1
    MenuItemTemplate mit1 = new MenuItemTemplate();
    mit1.ID = "FlyoutMenu1";
    mit1.Text = "Custom Control Demo";
    mit1.Description = "hosted on an application page";
    mit1.Sequence = 1;
    mit1.ClientOnClickNavigateUrl = site.Url + AppPage1Url;
    mit1.ImageUrl = site.Url + MenuIconUrl;

    // create fly out menu command 2
    MenuItemTemplate mit2 = new MenuItemTemplate();
    mit2.ID = "FlyoutMenu2";
    mit2.Text = "User Control Demo";
    mit2.Description = "hosted on an application page";
    mit2.Sequence = 2;
    mit2.ClientOnClickNavigateUrl = site.Url + AppPage2Url;
    mit2.ImageUrl = site.Url + MenuIconUrl;

    // add menu commands to Controls collection of fly out menu
    smt.Controls.Add(mit1);
    smt.Controls.Add(mit2);

    // add fly out menu to Controls collection of of menu control
    this.Controls.Add(smt);
  }
}
```

Once you have created the class for the custom menu control, you must create a *CustomAction* element in a feature that is used to add the fly out menu somewhere inside the SharePoint user interface. The easiest way to create a *CustomAction* element with the SharePoint Developer Tools is to create a new SharePoint project item based on the *Empty Element* type and then by adding the following *CustomAction* element into the elements.xml file.

```
<CustomAction Id="WingtipMenuControl"
  GroupId="SiteActions"
  Location="Microsoft.SharePoint.StandardMenu"
  Sequence="1"
  ControlAssembly="$SharePoint.Project.AssemblyFullName$"
  ControlClass="WingtipControls.WingtipMenuControl"
  Title="Wingtip Control Demos"
  Description="Wingtip Controls Menu Control Demo"
/>
```

Note that SharePoint Foundation requires a safe control entry for each custom menu control. Therefore, you must ensure that you have added the proper safe control entry using the *Safe Control Entries* collection, as discussed in the previous section.

While this particular example added a fly out menu to the Site Actions menu, you can use the exact same technique to create a fly out menu for other locations in the SharePoint user interface. For example, you could use this custom menu control to supply a fly out menu to the Actions menu for a list of document library or the Edit Control Block (ECB) menu for a list item or document.

Also, remember that you have quite a bit of flexibility in terms of a feature's activation scope. You can add the *CustomAction* element to a feature that activates at the site scope or site collection scope, which would make it possible for site collection owners and site administrators to activate the feature and begin using the fly out menu. Alternatively, you could add the *CustomAction* element to a feature that is activated at the Web Application scope or farm scope, which would allow you to enable or disable the fly out menu on a larger scale.

User Controls

The ASP.NET Framework provides user controls as an alternative to creating custom controls. Developing with user controls can yield higher levels of productivity in SharePoint Development because it provides the only supported technique where you can use a visual designer to create a user interface component. For example, you can drag ASP.NET controls, such as *Label*, *TextBox,* and *Button,* onto a user control from the Visual Studio 2010 toolbox, making it much faster to develop user input forms.

Once you get comfortable working with user controls, you will find that they provide the fastest way to create user interface components for a SharePoint solution. This is especially true when you want to use specialized ASP.NET controls such as the validation controls or data bound controls, which are much easier to configure using Visual Studio 2010 wizards and the standard property sheet. Also, keep in mind that you can add a user control to an application page, a site page, or a master page. Later in this chapter, in the section entitled "Creating Visual Web Parts," you will see that a user control can also be used to provide the user interface for a custom Web Part.

At the physical level, a user control is a text file with an .ascx extension that is deployed directly to the file system of the Web server. The ASP.NET Framework provides the functionality to parse .ascx files at run time and to compile them into assembly dynamic-link libraries (DLLs), just as it does for .aspx files such as application pages.

In Chapter 5, we introduced the LAYOUTS directory and explained why SharePoint Foundation uses this directory to deploy application pages. SharePoint Foundation provides a similar directory inside the 14/TEMPLATES directory named CONTROLTEMPLATES, which is used to deploy the user controls. For example, the CONTROLTEMPLATES directory contains the standard user controls that are deployed during the installation of SharePoint Foundation and SharePoint Server 2010, such as Welcome.ascx.

SharePoint Foundation provides access to user controls in each Web Application using a virtual directory named _controltemplates, which is mapped to the CONTROLTEMPLATES directory. This mapping makes it possible to reference a user control file from any site within the farm using a standard path. For example, you can reference the standard user control named *Welcome.ascx* from any site using the following site-relative path.

```
~/_controltemplates/Welcome.ascx
```

The fact that each user control is accessible using a standard path makes it possible to reference them from application pages, site pages, and master pages. For example, the user control named *Welcome.ascx* is used on the v4.master page by adding a *Register* directive with three attributes: the *Tagprefix* attribute, the *TagName* attribute, and the *src* attribute.

```
<%@ Register
    TagPrefix="wssuc"
    TagName="Welcome"
    src="~/_controltemplates/Welcome.ascx"
%>
```

Once the *Register* directive for a user control has been added to a page, it is possible to create an instance of the user control using a control tag that combines *TagPrefix* and *TagName* separated by a colon.

```
<wssuc:Welcome id="IdWelcome" runat="server" />
```

User controls are like application pages in the sense that they must be deployed inside the SharePoint root directory. This means that user controls that are deployed in the standard fashion cannot be used in sandboxed solutions. Also, user controls are similar to application pages because they do not support any form of user customization. Therefore, user controls are assumed to be trusted by the Web server and, consequently, their contents are never inspected by the safe mode parser.

A user control is similar to a custom control because it requires a safe control entry to run properly on a customized page. However, this does not require your attention so long as you deploy your user controls at any location inside the CONTROLTEMPLATES directory. The reason for this is that SharePoint Foundation adds the following *SafeControl* entry to the web.config file for every Web application, which simply trusts the CONTROLTEMPLATES folder.

```
<SafeControl Src="~/_controltemplates/*" IncludeSubFolders="True" Safe="True" />
```

Creating New User Controls in a SharePoint Solution

Now that you understand the details of how user controls are deployed in SharePoint Foundation, it's time to discuss using them to develop a SharePoint solution. The SharePoint Developer Tools provide a SharePoint project item template named User Control, which you can use to add new user controls to your project.

While the CONTROLTEMPLATES directory is the proper place to deploy custom user control files, it is typically recommended that you do not deploy them directly inside this directory. Instead, it is recommended that you deploy custom user controls in a child directory nested inside the CONTROLTEMPLATES directory to avoid potential file name conflicts with Microsoft user control files. The SharePoint Developer Tools adhere to this practice by adding user controls to a solution-specific child directory nested inside the CONTROLTEMPLATES directory. For example, if you add a new User Control project item to a project named WingtipControls, the SharePoint Developer Tools add the .ascx file at the location CONTROLTEMPLATES\WingtipControls.

Once you have added a user control to a SharePoint project, you can edit the contents of the .ascx file in *Design view,* which makes it quick and easy to create user input forms and other types of user interface components because you can drag server-side controls from the standard Visual Studio toolbox. You also have the option of working in *Source view* or in a hybrid mode known as *Split view,* which is shown in Figure 6-5. While you are working in any view, you also get the convenience of being able to edit the properties of each control using a standard Visual Studio property sheet.

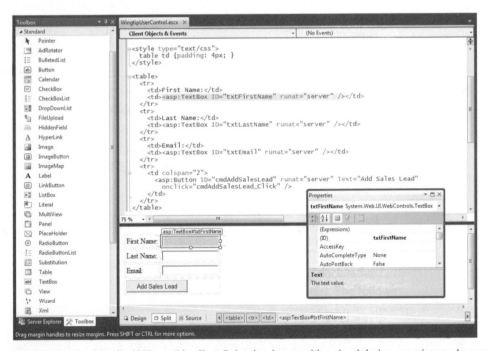

FIGURE 6-5 Visual Studio 2010 provides SharePoint developers with a visual design experience when working with user controls.

While SharePoint Foundation permits you to add inline code directly inside the .ascx file using C# or Visual Basic, this is not the recommended approach. It provides a much better development experience when you write your code for a user control in a code-behind file with an extension of either *.cs* or *.vb*. Fortunately, the SharePoint Developer Tools take care of all the necessary details behind the scenes to create and configure a code-behind file whenever you add a new user control to a SharePoint project.

In the WingtipControls project, there is a user control file named WingtipUserControl.ascx. When this user control was added to the project, the SharePoint Developer Tools automatically created an associated code-behind file named WingtipUserControl.ascx.cs, which had an initial class definition that looked like this.

```
using System;
using System.Web.UI;
using System.Web.UI.WebControls;
using System.Web.UI.WebControls.WebParts;

namespace WingtipControls.ControlTemplates.WingtipControls {
  public partial class WingtipUserControl : UserControl {
    protected void Page_Load(object sender, EventArgs e) {
    }
  }
}
```

You will find that it's easy to work with a user control and its code-behind file. For example, you can drag a command button onto the visual designer and then name it using its property sheet. If you double-click a command button in design view, Visual Studio 2010 will automatically create and wire up an event handler method in the code-behind file and place your cursor in the new event handler method so that you can begin typing the code that will execute when a user clicks that button.

Adding User Controls to Pages

While the SharePoint Developer Tools do everything that's required to create a new user control, they do not provide the same convenience when you need to add a user control to an application page, a site page template, or a master page template. Therefore, you must learn how to create the required *Register* directive and the control tag by hand. However, this is actually easy to do.

The WingtipControls project adds the user control named *WingtipUserControl.ascx* to an application page named UserControlDemo.aspx. This application page contains the following *Register* directive.

```
<%@ Register
  TagPrefix="wtuc"
  TagName="WingtipUserControl"
  src="~/_controltemplates/WingtipControls/WingtipUserControl.ascx"
%>
```

Note that the *src* attribute has a value of the standard path to the .ascx file where it has been deployed inside the _controltemplates virtual directory. This allows the hosting page to find and load the user control when executing from any site within the farm. Once you have added the *Register* directive, the final part of creating an instance of the user control is adding a control tag to the page. The application page named UserControlDemo.aspx contains the proper control tag to create an instance of the user control.

```
<wtuc:WingtipUserControl runat="server" />
```

Note that you would create the exact same *Register* directive and control tag to add this user control to a site page or a master page. You could also take this example further by adding public properties to the user control, which can provide extra flexibility. Just as with custom controls, the public properties of a user control can be initialized in a control tag. This makes it possible to develop a single user control that can be parameterized differently across control tags to produce different appearances and behaviors.

Delegate Controls

SharePoint Foundation provides a powerful extensibility mechanism known as delegate controls. A *delegate control* is a control placeholder that allows you to substitute in one or more control instances during the processing of a page. It's actually easy to get started because SharePoint Foundation provides a useful set of delegate controls in its standard master pages such as v4.master. As you will see, the built-in delegate controls provide a simple and effective technique for adding elements such as HTML meta tags, Cascading Style Sheets (CSS) rules, and client-side JavaScript code across many pages at once.

Let's begin by examining one of the delegate controls that has been added to v4.master. If you open the v4.master template file and look inside the head section, you will see a delegate control with a *ControlId* attribute of *AdditionalPageHead*, which is located right after the placeholder control with an *id* attribute of *PlaceHolderAdditionalPageHead*.

```
<head runat="server">

  <asp:ContentPlaceHolder id="PlaceHolderAdditionalPageHead" runat="server"/>

  <SharePoint:DelegateControl
              runat="server"
              ControlId="AdditionalPageHead"
              AllowMultipleControls="true"/>

</head>
```

Now, let's consider how delegates really work from a design perspective. In some ways, a delegate control is similar to a placeholder control because it defines a named region inside a master page that a developer can use to substitute in unique content. Like a placeholder control, a delegate control can supply default content that is used until a substitution is performed.

While delegate controls have similarities to placeholder controls, they also have their differences. One major difference is that the substitution mechanism used for replacing the contents of a delegate control is driven by feature activation. Therefore, you can replace what's defined inside a delegate control in v4.master without requiring any changes to v4.master or any of the site pages or application pages that link to it. All you need to do is define a feature with a *Control* element and then activate that feature.

A significant aspect of using delegate controls involves the scope of the feature that is being used to drive substitution. When you design a feature to substitute the contents of a delegate control, the feature can be scoped at any of the four supported levels, which are site scope, site collection scope, Web application scope, and farm scope. This dimension of delegate controls provides a powerful mechanism for enabling and disabling branding elements or functionality behind pages on a wide-scale basis.

To work with delegate controls, you must be working in a SharePoint solution that is deployed using a farm solution. In other words, the techniques involved with delegate controls cannot be used inside the sandbox. The examples presented in this chapter are part of the WingtipControls project, which has been designed for deployment as a farm solution.

Creating a Delegate Control with a User Control

The easiest way to substitute content into a delegate control is with a custom user control. For example, the WingtipControls project contains a user control named *WingtipDelegateUserControl.ascx*, which contains a two HTML meta tags and a few CSS rules that add a header image to the page body.

```
<%@ Control %>

<meta name='author' content='Wingtip Toys' />
<meta name='copyright' content='&copy; 2010 Wingtip Toys, Inc.' />

<style type="text/css" media="screen">
  body {
    background-image: url('/_layouts/images/WingtipControls/WingtipHeader.gif');
    background-repeat: repeat-x;
    margin-top: 20px;
  }
</style>
```

Once you have created the user control and added the content inside it, your next step is to create a new SharePoint project item using the *Empty Element* type. Then you can open the elements.xml file for this new SharePoint project item and add the following *Control* element.

```
<Control
 Id="AdditionalPageHead"
 ControlSrc="~/_controltemplates/WingtipControls/WingtipDelegateUserControl.ascx"
 Sequence="101"
/>
```

Now let's look at how delegate controls really work. When the feature with the *Control* element has been activated, SharePoint Foundation knows that whenever it processes a page that links to v4.master, it must create an instance of the user control named *WingtipDelegateUserControl.ascx*. SharePoint Foundation also knows to add the user control instance to the page in the location where the delegate control is defined. In this case, the user control instance is added to the head section of the page because that's where the delegate control with a *ControlId* of *AdditionalPageHead* is located.

Note that v4.master defines the delegate control with the *ControlId* of *AdditionalPageHead* with an attribute named *AllowMultipleControls*, which has a value of *true*. This means that SharePoint Foundation makes it possible for multiple features to add control instances into this delegate control at the same time.

In a scenario where a delegate control has an *AllowMultipleControls* attribute with a value of *true*, the *Control* element can be defined with a *Sequence* attribute that dictates which delegate control instances are processed first. For example, imagine two features both added controls to the *AdditionalPageHead* delegate control. The delegate control instance created by the *Control* element with the lower *Sequence* number would be processed first, and the delegate control instance with the larger *Sequence* number would be processed last, which can provide benefits when working with CSS.

If you examine some of the other delegate controls inside v4.master, you will notice that they are defined without the *AllowMultipleControls* attribute. This means that these types of delegate control can accept only a single control instance. In this case, the feature that has the *Control* element with the lowest *Sequence* number wins, and it becomes the only feature to add a control instance to the delegate control as pages are processed.

You should observe that the *MainSite* feature of the WingtipControls project is designed to activate at the site collection scope. That means activating this feature will add the HTML meta tags and CSS rules to every page within the current site collection. Also, remember that delegate controls can be substituted at any scope supported by features. You can create a feature with a *Control* element scoped at the Web application or farm level to add HTML meta tags, CSS rules, or JavaScript code to every page on a larger scale.

Creating a Delegate Control with a Custom Control

While it is easy to create user controls to work with delegate controls, SharePoint Foundation also supports delegate control substitution with custom controls. This provides an alternative that can be more lightweight and powerful from a programming perspective. The WingtipControls project contains a custom control class named *WingtipDelegateCustomControl,* which overrides the *OnLoad* event handler method and uses the *ClientScriptManager* class of the ASP.NET Framework to register a client-side startup script.

```
public class WingtipDelegateCustomControl : Control {

  protected override void OnLoad(EventArgs e) {
    // register startup script using JavaScript code in string literal
    ClientScriptManager CSM = this.Page.ClientScript;
    string key = "WingtipScript";
    string script = @"
            ExecuteOrDelayUntilScriptLoaded(SayHello, 'sp.js');
            function SayHello() {
              var message = 'Hello from a delegate custom control';
              SP.UI.Notify.addNotification(message);
            }";
    CSM.RegisterStartupScript(this.GetType(), key, script, true);
  }
}
```

As you can see, a delegate control makes it easy to add client-side JavaScript code across many pages at once. The example that you have just seen relies on a string variable named *script,* which holds the JavaScript code that is registered as a startup script within the browser. However, another approach is to add a JavaScript source file to the current project. This approach can offer a better development experience because Visual Studio 2010 provides color coding and extra convenience when you write your JavaScript code inside a source file with a *.js* extension. Using JavaScript source files makes it easier to write and maintain large JavaScript libraries that you plan to include across all pages on a sitewide or even a farmwide basis.

The WingtipControls project contains a JavaScript source file named WingtipDelegateCustom Control.js. This file has been configured as an embedded resource as well as added to the project's resources as a file resource named WingtipDelegateCustomControl_js. This makes it possible to retrieve the contents of that JavaScript source file and register it as a startup script using the following code.

```
// register startup script using JavaScript code inside WingtipDelegateCustomControl.js
CSM.RegisterStartupScript(this.GetType(), key, script, true);
string key2 = "WingtipScript2";
string script2 = Properties.Resources.WingtipDelegateCustomControl_js;
CSM.RegisterStartupScript(this.GetType(), key2, script2, true);
```

While these examples demonstrate calling the *RegisterStartupScript* method, the *ClientScript Manager* class provides other useful methods for managing client-side scripts, including *RegisterClientScriptBlock*, *RegisterClientScriptInclude*, *RegisterArrayDeclaration*, and *RegisterExpandoAttribute*. If you are building a SharePoint solution that includes a custom library of JavaScript functions, you must decide how you are going to push this JavaScript code out to the browser. An approach that involves delegate control substitution with a custom control that programs against the *ClientScriptManager* class provides a simple and effective strategy for managing custom JavaScript libraries across many pages on a sitewide or even farmwide basis.

Once you have created a custom control to substitute into a specific delegate control, you must create a *Control* element to perform the substitution. Like a *Control* element created for a user control, the *Control* element for a custom control must provide an *Id* attribute that matches the *ControlId* attribute of the target delegate control. However, you do not use the *src* attribute, as you do when working with user controls. Instead, you must use the *ControlAssembly* and *ControlClass* attributes to reference a specific control type within a target assembly. When using the SharePoint Developer Tools, you can also use a dynamic token for the *ControlAssembly* property so that you do not have to hard-code the four-part assembly name into your source file.

```
<Control
  Id="AdditionalPageHead"
  ControlAssembly="$SharePoint.Project.AssemblyFullName$"
  ControlClass="WingtipControls.WingtipDelegateCustomControl"
  Sequence="102"
/>
```

Developing Web Parts

Web Parts are the most popular type of component created by SharePoint developers. One reason for this is that SharePoint technologies have supported the development of custom Web Parts since the release of SharePoint 2003. A second reason is that Web Parts give SharePoint Foundation one of its greatest strengths. More specifically, Web Parts provide business users with the ability to customize pages and shape their work environment in a way that suits their work style.

While a Web Part is a control, it is a specialized type of control designed to support user customization. The support for customization is the main characteristic that separates Web Parts from other types of controls. For example, a user can add Web Parts to a page as well as delete them. A user can modify an existing Web Part to change its appearance or behavior. Furthermore, all this work can be done using the browser without customizing the content of the underlying page. An important observation for developers is that a Web Part page remains in a ghosted state even when users are adding, customizing, and deleting Web Parts.

When you begin working with Web Parts, you must differentiate between customization and personalization. *Customization* refers to a change by a privileged user, such as a site collection owner, that is seen by all users. *Personalization* refers to a change by an individual user that is seen only by that user. One of the most valuable aspects of the Web Part infrastructure is that it provides the developer with automatic support to save and retrieve customization data as well as personalization data.

Web Part Fundamentals

A Web Part is a class that inherits from the *WebPart* class defined by the ASP.NET Framework in the *System.Web.UI.WebControls.WebParts* namespace. A Web Part is a special type of control that can be created inside the context of a Web Part Zone that has been defined inside a Web Part page. Web Parts are different from other types of controls because of the manner in which they are created and managed. Standard controls are created by adding control tags to a hosting page. Creating a new Web Part instance, on the other hand, doesn't require a modification to the hosting page. Instead, Web Part instances are created and tracked inside a database behind the scenes using dedicated tables. This is valuable from a design perspective because it allows Web Part classes to be loosely coupled with the Web Part pages that host them. It also allows users to add Web Part instances to Web Part pages that remain running in a ghosted state, which is a key factor in scalability.

The WingtipWebParts Sample Project

The downloadable .zip archive of companion code for this book contains a sample SharePoint project named WingtipWebParts. This project contains working samples of the custom Web Parts that are shown throughout the remainder of this chapter. You can see the high-level structure of this project by examining Figure 6-6.

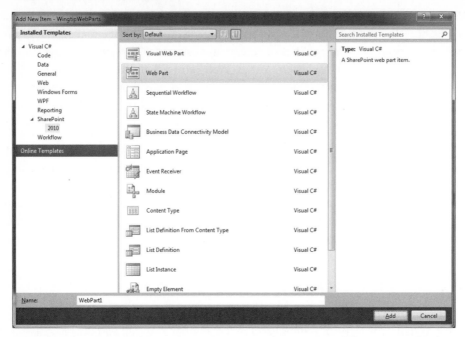

FIGURE 6-6 The WingtipWebParts project demonstrates how to create different types of Web Parts.

To test the WingtipWebParts project, you should create a new site collection with either a team site or a blank site as the top-level site. When you deploy the WingtipWebParts project and activate the MainSite feature in this site collection, the project will create a set of Web Part pages and prepopulate them with sample Web Parts automatically. The MainSite feature has also been implemented to add a drop-down menu to the TopNav bar, making it easy to navigate from page to page.

The Role of the Web Part Manager

The Web Part infrastructure of the ASP.NET Framework relies on a special control known as the *Web Part Manager,* which is responsible for creating and managing Web Parts instances each time a Web Part page is processed. Any page that contains Web Parts must have exactly one instance of the *Web Part Manager* control. In SharePoint Foundation, the implementation of the Web Part Manager is provided by the *SPWebPartManager* class, which is defined inside the *Microsoft.SharePoint* assembly.

You rarely have to worry about creating the required instance of the *SPWebPartManager* control in SharePoint 2010 development. That's because all the standard master pages in SharePoint Foundation such as v4.master already contain the control tag for the *SPWebPartManager* control. However, when creating your own custom master pages, you should ensure that they contain an instance of the *SPWebPartManager* control as well.

To really understand how Web Parts work, you must understand the role of the *SPWebPartManager* control. Early in the life cycle of a Web Part page, the *SPWebPartManager* control queries the content database to determine what Web Part instances need to be created. The *Web Part Manager* control acts as a director for the page, adding each Web Part instance to the appropriate Web Part zone and ensuring that each Web Part instance is initialized with the proper customization data and personalization data. Whenever a user creates a new Web Part instance using the browser, the *SPWebPartManager* control coordinates writing the new serialized Web Part instance into the content database.

SharePoint 2003 Web Parts

To help you avoid confusion when you get started with Web Parts, we need to give you a quick history lesson. The SharePoint team created the first Web Part infrastructure, which debuted in the 2003 release. This was back before ASP.NET supported Web Parts. All the custom Web Parts that were created for SharePoint 2003 were developed using this older format, which was part of the *Microsoft.SharePoint* namespace.

After the release of SharePoint 2003, Microsoft made a strategic decision to move the Web Part infrastructure from the SharePoint development platform down a layer into the ASP.NET Framework. When ASP.NET 2.0 was released in 2005, it contained a similar yet separate Web Part infrastructure.

What's important (and somewhat confusing, unfortunately) is that SharePoint 2007 and SharePoint 2010 are both built on the newer ASP.NET Web Part infrastructure, not the older SharePoint 2003 Web Part infrastructure. When you create Web Parts for SharePoint 2010, you inherit from the *WebPart* base class in the ASP.NET Framework, not the older class of the same name defined inside the *Microsoft.SharePoint* assembly.

Both SharePoint 2007 and SharePoint 2010 provide backward compatibility for older Web Parts developed under the SharePoint 2003 format. However, it is likely that the backward compatibility support will be dropped in a future version of SharePoint technologies. When this happens, any Web Parts developed under the SharePoint 2003 format will have to be written using the ASP.NET Web Part format.

The Web Part Gallery

The Web Part infrastructure was designed to enable users to create new Web Parts on demand using the browser. However, this poses a problem. How does a user discover which types of Web Parts are available for creating new Web Part instances? This problem is solved in SharePoint Foundation by the Web Part Gallery.

The *Web Part Gallery* is a special type of document library that is created automatically by SharePoint Foundation in the top-level site of every new site collection. It is important to understand that there is exactly one Web Part Gallery per site collection. There is not one per site.

The Web Part Gallery contains Extensible Markup Language (XML) files known as *Web Part template files.* Each Web Part template file in the Web Part Gallery represents a creatable Web Part type within the current site collection. If you look inside a Web Part template file, you will find XML data that can be used to create a new Web Part instance. The XML format includes an assembly name and a class name for the Web Part class, as well as initialization data for various Web Part properties.

```
<webParts>
  <webPart xmlns="http://schemas.microsoft.com/WebPart/v3">
    <metaData>
      <type name="WingtipWebParts.WebPart1.WebPart1, [4-part assembly name]" />
      <importErrorMessage>
      There has been an error importing this Web Part
      </importErrorMessage>
    </metaData>
    <data>
      <properties>
        <property name="Title" type="string">Web Part 1</property>
        <property name="Description" type="string">A simple description</property>
        <property name="AllowEdit" type="bool">True</property>
        <property name="AllowZoneChange" type="bool">True</property>
        <property name="AllowClose" type="bool">False</property>
      </properties>
    </data>
  </webPart>
</webParts>
```

Web Part template files that are created using the ASP.NET Web Part format have a *.web-part* extension. However, you will also see Web Part template files created using the older SharePoint 2003 format, and those files have a *.dwp* extension. When you develop Web Parts for SharePoint 2010, you will be creating Web Part template files with an extension of *.webpart*.

When you develop Web Parts in a SharePoint project, it is recommended that you create a feature designed to provision a *.webpart* file for each Web Part into the Web Part Gallery. Because there is only one Web Part Gallery per site collection, the feature to provision *.webpart* files should be scoped at the site collection level instead of at the site level. Fortunately, the SharePoint Developer Tools do a great job of automating all this work behind the scenes each time you create a new Web Part using one of their SharePoint project item templates.

When you want to create a new Web Part in a SharePoint project, the SharePoint Developer Tools assist you by providing two different SharePoint project item templates, as shown in Figure 6-7. The *Web Part project item* is used to create standard Web Parts. The *Visual Web Part project item* is used to create a Web Part whose user interface is supplied by a user control. In this chapter, we will examine how to create both standard Web Parts and Visual Web Parts.

FIGURE 6-7 The SharePoint Developer Tools provide two SharePoint project item templates for adding Web Parts to a SharePoint project.

Whenever you add a new Web Part to a SharePoint project, the SharePoint Developer Tools create a new Web Part project item already configured with the required *Safe Control Entries* collection member. The SharePoint Developer Tools also add a Web Part template file and an elements.xml file, as shown in Figure 6-8. The elements.xml file contains a *Module* element configured to provision an instance of the Web Part template file into the Web Part Gallery. It is this Web Part template file that makes the new Web Part creatable.

FIGURE 6-8 Each Web Part project item is created with a Web Part template file and an elements.xml file.

When you add new Web Parts to a project, the SharePoint Developer Tools automatically manage your features for you. If you add a new Web Part to a project that already contains a site collection scoped feature, the SharePoint Developer Tools automatically associate the Web Part's elements.xml file with this feature. If the current SharePoint project does not contain a feature scoped to the level of the site collection, the SharePoint Developer Tools will create a new feature and associate the Web Part's elements.xml file with it automatically.

For example, think through what would happen if you create a new SharePoint project using the Empty SharePoint Project template and then you add three new Web Part project items. The SharePoint Developer Tools will create a site collection scoped feature when you add the first Web Part project item. However, there is no need to create another feature after that. The SharePoint Developer Tools associate the second and third Web Part project items with the same feature that was created for the first Web Part project item.

Let's say that you have just added a new Web Part project item to a SharePoint project. The first thing that you should do is to modify the Web Part template file and the elements.xml file. Start by opening the Web Part template file and locating the two properties named *Title* and *Description*. You should modify these properties because they will be seen by users who are looking through the list of creatable Web Parts in the Web Part Gallery. There are also quite a few other standard Web Part properties that you might consider explicitly initializing, as shown in the following example.

```
<property name="Title" type="string">Web Part 1</property>
<property name="Description" type="string">A simple description</property>

<property name="ChromeState" type="chromestate">Normal</property>
<property name="ExportMode" type="exportmode">All</property>

<property name="AllowMinimize" type="bool">True</property>
<property name="AllowHide" type="bool">True</property>
<property name="AllowEdit" type="bool">True</property>
<property name="AllowClose" type="bool">True</property>
<property name="AllowZoneChange" type="bool">True</property>
<property name="AllowConnect" type="bool">True</property>
```

Next, open the elements.xml file. You will find that it contains a *Module* element with a *List* attribute and a *URL* attribute, which are preconfigured to target the Web Part Gallery. Inside the *Module* element is a *File* element that contains a *Path* attribute, a *Url* attribute, and a *Type* attribute. Inside the *File* element, you will also find a *Property* element that defines a property named *Group* with a preconfigured value of *Custom*.

```
<Elements xmlns="http://schemas.microsoft.com/sharepoint/" >
  <Module Name="WebPart1" List="113" Url="_catalogs/wp">
    <File Path="WebPart1\WebPart1.webpart"
          Url=" WebPart1.webpart"
          Type="GhostableInLibrary">
      <Property Name="Group" Value="Custom" />
    </File>
  </Module>
</Elements>
```

There is no need to modify any attributes of the *Module* element. Likewise, there is no need to modify the *Path* attribute or the *Type* attribute of the *File* element. However, it is recommended that you modify the *Url* attribute of the *File* element because it determines the name given to the Web Part template file as it is created in the Web Part Gallery. Why is the modification necessary?

The problem with the default value for the *Url* attribute of the *File* element is file name conflicts in the Web Part Gallery. A critical point is that the Web Part Gallery can contain only one Web Part template file, named *WebPart1.webpart*. There will be a problem with file name conflicts if two different features both attempt to provision a Web Part template file named *WebPart1.webpart* into the Web Part Gallery. In such a scenario, the first feature to be activated will succeed, but the second feature will fail silently during activation because it is not able to provision its copy of *WebPart1.webpart*. The key to avoiding this problem is to ensure that your Web Part template files have unique names.

We recommend that you add the project name as a prefix to the file name of each Web Part template file. For example, our sample project is named WingtipWebParts. The *Url* attribute for each Web Part template file has been modified to include the project name prefix, resulting in Web Part template files with names such as WingtipWebParts_WebPart1.webpart. These modifications serve to reduce the risk of problems caused by file name conflicts in the Web Part Gallery.

The second modification you should make to the elements.xml file involves the *Property* element that defines the *Group* property with a default value of *Custom*. The *Group* property determines which category the Web Part is added to when the user is examining the list of creatable Web Parts. You should replace the default value of *Custom* with the name of the category in which you want your Web Parts to appear. In most cases, the *Group* property value should be the same for all the Web Parts within the same project. Here is an example of an elements.xml file from the WingtipWebPart project, with the updated values shown in bold.

```
<Elements xmlns="http://schemas.microsoft.com/sharepoint/" >
  <Module Name="WebPart1" List="113" Url="_catalogs/wp">
    <File Path="WebPart1\WebPart1.webpart"
          Url="WingtipWebParts_WebPart1.webpart"
          Type="GhostableInLibrary">
      <Property Name="Group" Value="Wingtip Web Parts" />
    </File>
  </Module>
</Elements>
```

Deleting Web Part Template Files at Feature Deactivation

When a privileged user, such as a site collection owner, activates the feature associated with
your Web Parts, the feature automatically creates instances of your Web Part template files
inside the Web Part Gallery. However, nothing is built into either the SharePoint development
platform or the SharePoint Developer Tools that assist you with deleting these Web Part template files during feature deactivation.

When developing Web Parts, it's recommended that you write code in the *FeatureDeactivating*
event handler to delete all the Web Part template files that were created during feature activation. You will find that the recommendation that we made earlier for creating Web Part template file names that begin with the project name also simplifies writing the cleanup code.
You can simply inspect the first part of the file name as you enumerate through the Web Part
Gallery looking for the correct files to delete. Here is code from the WingtipWebParts project
that demonstrates the proper technique.

```
public override void FeatureDeactivating(properties) {
  SPSite siteCollection = (SPSite)properties.Feature.Parent;
  SPWeb site = siteCollection.RootWeb;

  // figure out which Web Part template files need to be deleted
  List<SPFile> FilesToDelete = new List<SPFile>();
  SPList WebPartGallery = site.Lists["Web Part Gallery"];
  foreach (SPListItem WebPartTemplateFile in WebPartGallery.Items) {
    if (WebPartTemplateFile.File.Name.Contains("WingtipWebParts")) {
      FilesToDelete.Add(WebPartTemplateFile.File);
    }
  }

  // delete Web Part template files
  foreach (SPFile file in FilesToDelete) {
    file.Delete();
  }
}
```

Programming with the *SPLimitedWebPartManager* Class

There are several different ways in which a Web Part can be created and placed on a page. The most common technique is by adding a Web Part template file into the Web Part Gallery and allowing the user to create the Web Part using the browser. In Chapter 5, you also saw that it was possible to prepopulate a Web Part page with Web Parts in a declarative fashion by adding an *AllUsersWebPart* element containing a serialized Web Part instance to the *File* element used to provision a Web Part page. Now, we will examine a third technique of doing this.

The server-side object model provides a class named *SPLimitedWebPartManager*, which provides the developer with direct access to the collection of Web Parts on a Web Part page. Programming against the *SPLimitedWebPartManager* class makes it possible to add, customize, personalize, and delete Web Part instances. Note that the *SPLimitedWebPartManager* is available in SharePoint solutions deployed at the farm level, but it cannot be used in sandboxed solutions.

To program using the *SPLimitedWebPartManager* class, you must first access a Web Part page as an *SPFile* object. You can accomplish this by calling the *GetFile* method of the *SPWeb* class and passing a site-relative path. The *SPFile* class provides a method named *GetLimitedWebPartManager*, which returns an instance of the *SPLimitedWebPartManager* class.

Think about a scenario where you need a feature that's been implemented to delete all the existing Web Parts from a site's home page automatically and replace them with a single instance of the *Image* Web Part. Here is an example of how you could implement the *FeatureActivated* method in a site-scoped feature to accomplish this.

```
public override void FeatureActivated(SPFeatureReceiverProperties properties) {

  // Get Web Part Manager for home page
  SPWeb site = (SPWeb)properties.Feature.Parent;
  SPFile homePage = site.GetFile("default.aspx");
  SPLimitedWebPartManager wpm;
  wpm = homePage.GetLimitedWebPartManager(PersonalizationScope.Shared);

  // delete all Web Parts on page
  while (wpm.WebParts.Count > 0) {
    wpm.DeleteWebPart(wpm.WebParts[0]);
  }

  // add Image Web Part to Right zone
  ImageWebPart wp = new ImageWebPart();
  wp.ChromeType = PartChromeType.None;
  wp.ImageLink = "_layouts/images/IPVW.GIF";
  wpm.AddWebPart(wp, "Right", 0);
}
```

Note that the call to *GetLimitedWebPartManager* in this example passes a parameter of *PersonalizationScope.Shared* when retrieving the *SPLimitedWebPartManager* object. This allows you to make customization changes to Web Part instances that are seen by all users. Alternatively, you could pass a parameter of *PersonalizationScope.User,* which then leads the *SPLimitedWebPartManager* object to make personalization changes that would be seen only by the current user.

Web Part Output Rendering

There are several different styles commonly used to render the output for a Web Part. The WingtipWebParts project contains examples of each style. For example, *WebPart1* demonstrates the simplest rendering technique, which involves overriding the *RenderContents* method and calling methods on *writer,* an *HtmlTextWriter*-based parameter.

```
using System.Web;
using System.Web.UI;
using System.Web.UI.WebControls;
using System.Web.UI.WebControls.WebParts;

namespace WingtipWebParts.WebPart1 {
  public class WebPart1 : WebPart {
    protected override void RenderContents(HtmlTextWriter writer) {
      writer.AddStyleAttribute(HtmlTextWriterStyle.Color, "Blue");
      writer.AddStyleAttribute(HtmlTextWriterStyle.FontSize, "18px");
      writer.RenderBeginTag(HtmlTextWriterTag.Div);
      writer.Write("Hello World");
      writer.RenderEndTag(); // </div>
    }
  }
}
```

You might notice that this example is very similar to the implementation of the custom control named *WingtipCustomControl* discussed at the beginning of the chapter. The one key difference is that a custom Web Part class overrides the *RenderContents* method, while the custom control class overrides the *Render* method. What's important to understand is that you can override the *RenderContents* method in a Web Part but should never override the *Render* method, as you might do in a custom control. Why is this so?

Web Parts render inside chrome. *Web Part chrome* refers to the common user interface elements, such as a formatted title bar and borders around the Web Part's body. The rendering of the chrome is handled by the underlying ASP.NET Framework inside implementation of the *Render* method within the *WebPart* base class. You should never override the *Render* method of a Web Part because you want to leave the responsibility of rendering the Web Part chrome with the ASP.NET Framework. When you override the *RenderContents* method, you are able to generate HTML output that is safely written inside the chrome.

There is an alternative style for rendering Web Parts that involves creating child controls. The motivation for creating child controls within a Web Part is that it relieves the developer from parsing together HTML tags. Instead, you just create child controls and you let them generate the HTML tags for you. An example of this approach can be seen in *WebPart2*, as shown in the following code.

```
public class WebPart2 : WebPart {

  protected Label lbl;

  protected override void CreateChildControls() {
    lbl = new Label();
    lbl.Text = "Hello Child Controls";
    lbl.Font.Size = new FontUnit(18);
    lbl.ForeColor = Color.Blue;
    this.Controls.Add(lbl);
  }
}
```

To create child controls from a Web Part properly, you should override the *CreateChildControls* method. As you can see from this example, this technique requires the developer to create child control instances explicitly in code using the *new* operator. When creating a child control, you should also be sure to add it to the *Controls* collection of the Web Part.

> **Tip** The WingtipWebParts project manages the font size and font color in child controls by programming against types inside the *System.Drawing* namespace, such as the *FontUnit* class and the *Color* class. However, these types are defined inside an assembly named System.Drawing, which is not automatically referenced in a new SharePoint project. If you want to use these classes in a new SharePoint project, be sure to add a project reference to the System.Drawing assembly, as well as a using statement to import the *System.Drawing* namespace.

In a scenario in which a Web Part creates only one child control, there's no need to override the *RenderContents* method. That's because the base class implementation of the *RenderContents* method enumerates through the *Controls* collection and renders the HTML for each child control using code that looks something like this.

```
protected override void RenderContents(HtmlTextWriter writer) {
  foreach (Control control in this.Controls) {
    control.RenderControl(writer);
  }
}
```

Now, let's examine a more complicated scenario in which a Web Part creates several child controls and adds them to its *Controls* collection. If this Web Part does not override the *RenderContents* method, the Web Part will render all the child controls in the order in which they were added to the *Controls* collection. But the child controls appear one after another, without any line breaks between them. Therefore, you might elect to override *RenderContents* so that you can render the child controls explicitly inside an HTML *table* element or inside a set of custom *div* elements. The development style of creating child controls and explicitly rendering them into a HTML *table* element is demonstrated by the *WebPart3* class, which is shown in Listing 6-2.

LISTING 6-2 Overriding *CreateChildControls* and *RenderContents* in a Web Part with multiple child controls

```
public class WebPart3 : WebPart {

  protected TextBox txtFirstName;
  protected TextBox txtLasttName;
  protected Button cmdAddSalesLead;

  protected override void CreateChildControls() {
    txtFirstName = new TextBox();
    Controls.Add(txtFirstName);

    txtLasttName = new TextBox();
    Controls.Add(txtLasttName);

    cmdAddSalesLead = new Button();
    cmdAddSalesLead.Text = "Add Sales Lead";
    cmdAddSalesLead.Click += new EventHandler(cmdAddSalesLead_Click);
    Controls.Add(cmdAddSalesLead);
  }

  void cmdAddSalesLead_Click(object sender, EventArgs e) {
    // left as an exercise for the reader
  }

  protected override void RenderContents(HtmlTextWriter writer) {
    writer.RenderBeginTag(HtmlTextWriterTag.Table);
    writer.RenderBeginTag(HtmlTextWriterTag.Tr);
    writer.RenderBeginTag(HtmlTextWriterTag.Td);
    writer.Write("First Name:");
    writer.RenderEndTag(); // </td>
    writer.RenderBeginTag(HtmlTextWriterTag.Td);
    txtFirstName.RenderControl(writer);
    writer.RenderEndTag(); // </td>
    writer.RenderEndTag(); // </tr>

    writer.RenderBeginTag(HtmlTextWriterTag.Tr);
    writer.RenderBeginTag(HtmlTextWriterTag.Td);
```

```
    writer.Write("Last Name:");
    writer.RenderEndTag(); // </td>
    writer.RenderBeginTag(HtmlTextWriterTag.Td);
    txtLasttName.RenderControl(writer);
    writer.RenderEndTag(); // </td>
    writer.RenderEndTag(); // </tr>

    writer.RenderBeginTag(HtmlTextWriterTag.Tr);
    writer.AddAttribute(HtmlTextWriterAttribute.Colspan, "2");
    writer.RenderBeginTag(HtmlTextWriterTag.Td);
    cmdAddSalesLead.RenderControl(writer);
    writer.RenderEndTag(); // </td>

    writer.RenderEndTag(); // </table>
  }
}
```

You should observe that the code in *WebPart3* creates a new command button instance and wires it up to a server-side event handler. This is accomplished by adding a method with the correct signature for a command button click event such as *cmdAddSalesLead_Click,* and then by wiring it up by assigning a new delegate to the button's *Click* event. Note that Visual Studio 2010 provides a handy shortcut in the C# editor for this scenario to create the event handler method. For example, once you type in the event name and then the plus sign (+) and equals sign (=), as shown here, you can simply type the Tab key twice and Visual Studio 2010 will create the event handler method body and wire it up automatically.

```
// press the TAB key twice after typing the text below
cmdAddSalesLead.Click +=
```

Creating Visual Web Parts

It can get pretty tedious creating standard Web Parts when you are required to create user input forms that contain many child controls. For example, imagine you need to create a Web Part that has 10 text boxes and 5 drop-down controls on it. When working with a standard Web Part, you would have to create and initialize 15 different control instances using code. Fortunately, the Visual Web Part project item type can provide a much more productive alternative.

A *Visual Web Part* is simply a Web Part whose user interface is created with an ASP.NET user control. When you create a new Visual Web Part project item, the SharePoint Developer Tools add a user control and an associated code-behind file in addition to the other files created in a standard Web Part project item. The SharePoint Developer Tools also create a Web Part class with a boilerplate implementation that creates an instance of the user control using the *LoadControl* method supplied by the *Page* class of the ASP.NET Framework.

```
public class WebPart4 : WebPart {
  private const string _ascxPath =
    @"~/_CONTROLTEMPLATES/WingtipWebParts/WebPart4/WebPart4UserControl.ascx";

    protected override void CreateChildControls() {
      Control control = Page.LoadControl(_ascxPath);
      Controls.Add(control);
    }
  }
}
```

When you create a new Visual Web Part project item, you should first modify the *.webpart* file and the elements.xml file just as you would in a standard Web Part project item. However, you do not need to make any modifications to the Web Part class. Instead, you do all your work in the source files for the user control. You can begin by opening the User Control in Design view where you can drag controls from the toolbox and modify their properties using the standard property sheet of Visual Studio 2010.

Look inside the WingtipWebPart project and compare the Web Parts named *WebPart3* and *WebPart4*. While these two Web Parts produce the exact same output, *WebPart4* is created using a Visual Web Part, which makes it less complicated and easier to maintain. The child controls are laid out using an HTML *table* element in the .ascx file.

```
<table>
  <tr>
    <td>First Name:</td>
    <td><asp:TextBox ID="txtFirstName" runat="server" /></td>
  </tr>
  <tr>
    <td>Last Name:</td>
    <td><asp:TextBox ID="txtLastName" runat="server" /></td>
  </tr>
  <tr>
    <td>Email:</td>
    <td><asp:TextBox ID="txtEmail" runat="server" /></td>
  </tr>
  <tr>
    <td colspan="2">
      <asp:Button ID="cmdAddSalesLead" runat="server" Text="Add Sales Lead"
        onclick="cmdAddSalesLead_Click" />
    </td>
  </tr>
</table>
```

There are many scenarios where using Visual Web Parts will make your life easier. The obvious case is when you are required to build a Web Part that involves many child controls in a complicated layout.

In some scenarios, you might be able to write all the code you need in the code-behind files of the user control, which means that you do not have to modify the Web Part class at all. When you write code for a user control, you will need to access the server-side object model of SharePoint Foundation frequently. You can use the *SPContext* class to obtain a reference to the current site collection or the current site.

```
SPSite siteCollection = SPContext.Current.Site;
SPWeb site = SPContext.Current.Web;
```

While the Visual Web Part makes some things easier, it is important to understand that it can also make other designs more complicated. For example, you will still be required to modify the Web Part class if you want your Visual Web Part to support persistent properties, Web Part verbs, or Web Part connections. In such designs, you often have to create additional methods so that the Web Part class and the code-behind class for the user control can communicate with one another.

Rendering Output Using an XSLT Transform

You have seen four different styles of rendering the output for a Web Part. Now it is time to examine one more using an XSLT transform. This can be a very handy approach if your Web Parts have XML that needs to be converted into HTML for display on a Web page. The WingtipWebPart project contains a sample Web Part named *WebPart5,* which performs an XSLT transform on a Really Simple Syndication (RSS) feed. The following XSLT transform has been created to convert the XML from a generic RSS feed into HTML that can be rendered as the output for a Web Part.

```
<?xml version="1.0" encoding="us-ascii" ?>
<xsl:stylesheet version="1.0" xmlns:xsl="http://www.w3.org/1999/XSL/Transform" >
  <xsl:output method="html"/>
  <xsl:template match="/">
    <xsl:apply-templates select="/rss/channel"/>
  </xsl:template>
  <xsl:template match="/rss/channel">
    <h3><xsl:value-of select="title"/></h3>
    <ul><xsl:apply-templates select="item"/></ul>
  </xsl:template>
  <xsl:template match="/rss/channel/item">
    <li>
      <a href="{link}"><xsl:value-of select="title"/></a>
      <p><xsl:value-of select="description" disable-output-escaping="yes" /></p>
    </li>
  </xsl:template>
</xsl:stylesheet>
```

This XSLT transform has been added to the WingtipWebParts project in a source file named RssFeedToHtml.xslt. Note that the *Build Action* property of this source file has been configured to a setting of Embedded Resource so that its contents will be compiled into the project's output assembly. Finally, the source file has also been added as a project resource, making it possible to retrieve string-based content for the XSLT transform using the following code.

```
string xsltContent = Properties.Resources.RssFeedToHtml;
```

Now that you have seen how to retrieve the contents of an XSLT transform from an embedded resource, it's time to walk through the code in *WebPart5*. The *RenderContents* method has been written to reach across the network and retrieve an RSS feed using classes from the *System.Net* namespace such as *WebRequest* and *WebResponse*. Once the Web Part has retrieved the XML for an RSS feed from across the network, it then performs the transform using the *XslCompiledTransform* class in the Microsoft .NET Framework and renders the HTML as its output.

```
protected override void RenderContents(HtmlTextWriter writer) {

    // add URL to RSS feed of your favorite blogging hero
    string urlRSS = "http://feeds.feedburner.com/AndrewConnell";

    // call across network to get XML from an RSS feed
    WebRequest request = WebRequest.CreateDefault(new Uri(urlRSS));
    WebResponse response = request.GetResponse();
    Stream responseStream = response.GetResponseStream();

    // retreive text for XSLT transform from embedded resource
    string xsltContent = Properties.Resources.RssFeedToHtml;

    // create XslCompiledTransform object and perform transform
    XslCompiledTransform transform = new XslCompiledTransform();
    XmlReader xslt = XmlReader.Create(new StringReader(xsltContent));
    transform.Load(xslt);
    XmlReader reader = new XmlTextReader(responseStream);
    XmlTextWriter results = new XmlTextWriter(writer.InnerWriter);
    transform.Transform(reader, results);

    // close reader to release resources
    reader.Close();
}
```

Now you have seen that it is relatively simple to use the XSTL transform engine built into the .NET Framework to render the output for a Web Part. However, there is a caveat. While this example might seem elegant and powerful, it has a serious flaw. The problem with this code is that it is making the call across the network using a synchronous programming technique. Calling across the network in a synchronous fashion can lead to problems with scalability and response times.

When you call across the network to retrieve data from a Web service or a database, it's recommended that you do so using an asynchronous technique. We will revisit this example later in the chapter, in the section entitled "The *AsynchRssReader* Web Part," and revise the code shown in *WebPart5* to use an asynchronous programming technique. This will be particularly important when developing Web Parts that are required to scale in high-traffic environments.

Persistent Properties

Much of the excitement about Web Parts revolves around their ability to support customization and personalization. As you recall, customization refers to a change that is shared by all users, whereas personalization refers to a change specific to an individual user.

When you are developing Web Parts, it often makes sense to take advantage of the built-in support for customization and personalization. This can be done by adding public properties to a Web Part class and making them persistent. You can make a public property in a Web Part class persistent by applying the *Personalizable* attribute.

```
public class CustomProperties1 : WebPart {
  [ Personalizable ]
  public string UserGreeting { get; set; }
}
```

When you apply the *Personalizable* attribute to a Web Part property, you are really giving the Web Part Manager an instruction to begin tracking the associated property value in the content database along with the other serialized properties for a Web Part instance. It's remarkable how much extra work the Web Part framework does for you when you add that one little attribute.

When you add a persistent property to a Web Part class, it is recommended that you take the required steps to initialize the property value properly when a Web Part instance is created. This is achieved by adding a new *property* element to the Web Part template file. For example, the persistent Web Part property named *UserGreeting* can be initialized by adding the following *property* element to the Web Part template file.

```
<property name="UserGreeting" type="string">It was the best of times</property>
```

When you apply the *Personalizable* attribute, you can set the *personalization scope* explicitly to a value of either *Shared* or *User*.

```
[ Personalizable(PersonalizationScope.Shared) ]
public string Prop1 { get; set; }

[ Personalizable(PersonalizationScope.User) ]
public string Prop2 { get; set; }
```

A persistent property with a personalization scope of *Shared* supports customization but not personalization. A persistent property with a personalization scope of *User* supports both customization and personalization. When a property with a personalization scope of *User* is customized, it creates a default value shared by all users. However, this default value can be overridden by any user who makes a personalization change.

Now that you have seen how to make Web Part properties persistent, the next step is deciding how you want to configure a persistent property so that its value can be seen and updated by users. You have to decide whether you want SharePoint Foundation to build the user interface experience or if you want to take the extra steps to build the user interface experience yourself using a custom Editor Part. We will begin by walking through the easier procedure, in which you let SharePoint Foundation build the user interface experience for you. This is accomplished by adding a few more attributes to the persistent property. Here is an example of a persistent property named *UserGreeting* defined in the sample Web Part named *CustomProperties1*.

```
[ Personalizable(PersonalizationScope.User),
  WebBrowsable(true),
  WebDisplayName("User Greeting"),
  WebDescription("Supplies text content for Web Part"),
  Category("Wingtip Web Parts")]
public string UserGreeting { get; set; }
```

When you assign the *WebBrowsable* attribute a value of *true,* SharePoint Foundation automatically displays the property name and property value in a generic Editor Part whenever the user is customizing or personalizing an instance of the Web Part. The *WebDisplayName* attribute and the *WebDescription* attribute allow you to configure the captions and tooltips seen by the user. The *Category* attribute controls the section in which the property will appear.

The sample Web Part named *CustomProperties1* is defined with three persistent properties named *UserGreeting*, *TextFontSize*, and *TextFontColor*. Each of these three properties has been defined using the *WebBrowsable* attribute, the *WebDisplayName* attribute, the *WebDescription* attribute, and the *Category* attribute just like the example that you have just seen. When a user runs an action to edit a Web Part of this type, SharePoint Foundation creates the user interface experience that is shown in Figure 6-9.

FIGURE 6-9 WebBrowsable property values can been seen and updated through a generic Editor Part.

While this technique provides a quick and easy solution, it doesn't always provide the level of control that you need. For example, you cannot add any custom validation to constrain the types of values entered by users. You cannot provide a drop-down box that's been populated from items in a SharePoint list or from a Web service across the network. For any persistent property based on a string or a numeric type, SharePoint Foundation provides nothing more than a simple text box to accept the user's input.

There are a few helpful tricks that you should know about when you create *WebBrowsable* properties. First, if you create a *WebBrowsable* property based on the *bool* type, SharePoint Foundation creates its input control using a check box instead of a text box. Also, if you create a *WebBrowsable* property based on a public enumeration type, SharePoint Foundation will create a drop-down list that is populated using enumeration type values. For example, the WingtipWebParts project defines two enumerations named *TextFontSizeEnum* and *TextFontColorEnum*.

```
public enum TextFontSizeEnum {
  Fourteen = 14,
  Eighteen = 18,
  TwentyFour = 24,
  ThirtyTwo = 32
}

public enum TextFontColorEnum {
  Purple,
  Green,
  Blue,
  Black
}
```

The sample Web Part named *CustomProperties2* defines its properties named *TextFontSize* and *TextFontColor* in terms of these two enumeration types. This approach provides a better user experience, as well as built-in validation, because the user is forced to select a value from a drop-down box, as shown in Figure 6-10.

FIGURE 6-10 A *WebBrowsable* property based on a public enumeration is rendered as a drop-down list.

Custom Editor Parts

For some Web Parts, you will find that it is sufficient to define persistent properties with the *WebBrowsable* attribute so that SharePoint Foundation automatically displays them for editing in the generic Editor Part. However, this will not be sufficient for all scenarios. There will be times when you will want to create your own custom Editor Parts for the tool pane. This section will step through what's required to accomplish this.

To create a custom Editor Part, you must create a new class that inherits from the *EditorPart* class defined inside the *System.Web.UI.WebControls.WebParts* namespace. The sample Web Part named *CustomProperties3* has an associated Editor Part named *CustomProperties3Editor*.

In addition to creating and implementing a new class to create the Editor Part, you must also make a few changes to the Web Part class itself. First, you should modify the attributes of your persistent properties so that they do not appear in the generic Editor Part. This can be done by applying the *WebBrowsable* attribute with a value of *false*.

```
[ Personalizable(PersonalizationScope.User),
  WebBrowsable(false) ]
public string UserGreeting { get; set; }

[ Personalizable(PersonalizationScope.User),
  WebBrowsable(false) ]
public int TextFontSize { get; set; }

[ Personalizable(PersonalizationScope.User),
  WebBrowsable(false) ]
public string TextFontColor { get; set; }
```

Next, you must override the *CreateEditorParts* method within the Web Part class to instruct SharePoint Foundation to load your custom Editor Part when it loads the standard Editor Parts that are displayed for all Web Parts.

When you override *CreateEditorParts*, you must first create an object from your Editor Part class. When you create and initialize this Editor Part object, it is critical that you assign a unique value to its ID property. If you forget to do this, you will get an ambiguous exception with very little debugging detail. A common technique for creating a unique Editor Part ID is to append a string to the end of the Web Part's ID that is guaranteed to be unique. You then must create the return value for *CreateEditorParts* by creating a new instance of the *EditorPartCollection* class, which can be initialized using an array of *EditorPart* references.

```
public override EditorPartCollection CreateEditorParts() {
  EditorPart editor = new CustomProperties3Editor();
  editor.ID = this.ID + "_editor";
  EditorPart[] parts = { editor };
  return new EditorPartCollection(parts);
}
```

Now we have finished updating the Web Part class to support a custom Editor Part. Therefore, it's time to move on to implementing the Editor Part class. This usually involves overriding three methods in the Editor Part class named *CreateChildControls*, *SyncChanges*, and *ApplyChanges*.

As in the case of creating a Web Part class, you override the *CreateChildControls* method to create the child controls that will allow the user to see and update property values. The sample Editor Part class named *CustomProperties3Editor* has code in the *CreateChildControls* method, which creates a multi-line *Textbox* control and two *RadioButtonList* controls to provide an enhanced user interface experience, as shown in Figure 6-11.

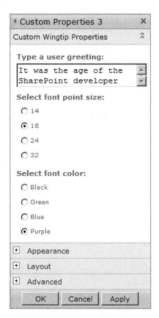

FIGURE 6-11 A custom Editor Part can be used to create a better user editing experience.

The two other methods that you must override in addition to *CreateChildControls* are *SyncChanges* and *ApplyChanges,* which are defined as abstract methods inside the *EditorPart* class. *SyncChanges* is called when the user clicks the *Edit Web Part* menu command, which provides an opportunity to retrieve the current property values from the Web Part and use them to initialize user input controls in the Editor Part. Note that the *EditorPart* class provides a protected property named *WebPartToEdit,* which makes it possible to obtain a reference to the correct Web Part. Here is the implementation of the *SyncChanges* method in the sample Editor Part named *CustomProperties3Editor.*

```
public override void SyncChanges() {
  EnsureChildControls();
  CustomProperties3 webpart = this.WebPartToEdit as CustomProperties3;
  // initialize text box with UserGreeting property
  txtUserGreeting.Text = webpart.UserGreeting;
```

```
  // initialize RadioButtonList to select current font size
  ListItem FontItem = lstFontSizes.Items.FindByText(webpart.TextFontSize.ToString());
  FontItem.Selected = true;
  // initialize RadioButtonList to select current font color
  lstFontColors.Items.FindByText(webpart.TextFontColor).Selected = true;
}
```

The first thing you should notice in this implementation of *SyncChanges* is that it begins with a call to *EnsureChildControls*. This is required because there are times when *SyncChanges* is executed before *CreateChildControls*. This can cause problems because the *CreateChildControls* method is where you create the child controls. The call to *EnsureChildControls* forces the execution of the *CreateChildControls* method before any work is done in the *SyncChanges* method. As a rule, you should always start with a call to *EnsureChildControls* whenever you override *SyncChanges* or *ApplyChanges*.

While the *SyncChanges* method is used to take property values from the Web Part and initialize user input controls, *ApplyChanges* does the opposite. The *ApplyChanges* method fires whenever the user clicks the OK button or Apply button in the task pane, giving you a chance to retrieve user input from the Editor Part and write it back to the Web Part. After you have written the updated property values to the Web Part, you must return a value of *true*, which instructs the Web Part Manager to save your changes back to the content database. A typical implementation of the *ApplyChanges* method can be seen in the sample Editor Part named *CustomProperties3Editor*.

```
public override bool ApplyChanges() {
  EnsureChildControls();
  CustomProperties3 webpart = this.WebPartToEdit as CustomProperties3;
  webpart.UserGreeting = txtUserGreeting.Text;
  webpart.TextFontSize = Convert.ToInt32(lstFontSizes.Text);
  webpart.TextFontColor = lstFontColors.Text;
  // return true to force Web Part Manager to persist changes
  return true;
}
```

Web Part Verbs

A *Web Part Verb* is a user command that is rendered in the Web Part menu as part of the chrome that is rendered on the right side of the title bar. There are several built-in Web Part verbs, such as *Minimize, Close,* and *Edit Web Part*. These built-in Web Part verbs can be disabled in display mode by initializing a Web Part instance with the following property settings.

```
<property name="AllowMinimize" type="bool">False</property>
<property name="AllowClose" type="bool">False</property>
<property name="AllowEdit" type="bool">False</property>
```

Note that initializing a Web Part with these property settings affects display mode but not edit mode. For example, when a site collection owner enters edit mode on a Web Part page, SharePoint Foundation will always provide the Edit Web Part menu for each Web Part. The key point here is that there are some menu commands in the Web Part menu that cannot be removed or disabled.

The Web Part framework provides a way for a developer to add Web Part verbs. This allows you to extend the Web Part menu with custom commands to a particular business scenario. The menu command behind a Web Part verb can be configured as either a client-side event handler or a server-side event handler. SharePoint 2010 also allows you to combine a client-side event handler and a server-side handler using a single Web Part verb.

To add one or more Web Part verbs to a Web Part class, you must override the read-only *Verbs* property. Inside the *get* block of the *Verbs* property, you must create an instance of the *WebPartVerb* class for each Web Part verb that you want to create. The *WebPartVerb* class provides several different constructors, giving you the ability to create a client-side verb, a server-side verb, or a combo verb that combines a client-side handler and a server-side handler.

To create a client-side verb, you should use the constructor that accepts two string parameters. The first string parameter is used to pass the verb's ID and the second string parameter is used to pass in the JavaScript code that should be executed when the user invokes the verb.

```
string ClientSideScript = "alert('hello from a client-side handler')";
WebPartVerb verb1 = new WebPartVerb(this.ID + "_verb1", ClientSideScript);
```

To create a server-side verb, you should use the constructor that accepts a string parameter followed by a delegate-based parameter. The second parameter is used to pass a delegate reference to the server-side method with the following signature.

```
void OnVerbExecuted(object sender, WebPartEventArgs e) {
  // this method is executed when the user invokes the server-side verb
}
```

Here is a complete implementation of the *Verbs* property that creates both a client-side verb and a server-side verb and adds them to a new *WebPartVerbCollection* object, which is passed as the property's return value.

```
public override WebPartVerbCollection Verbs {
  get {
    // create client-side verb
    string ClientSideScript = "alert('hello from a client-side handler')";
    WebPartVerb verb1 = new WebPartVerb(this.ID + "_verb1", ClientSideScript);
    verb1.Text = "Client-side Verb";
```

```
    // create server-side verb
    WebPartVerb verb2 = new WebPartVerb(this.ID + "_verb2", OnVerbExecuted);
    verb2.Text = "Server-side verb";

    // return collection with new verbs
    WebPartVerb[] verbs = new WebPartVerb[] { verb1, verb2 };
    return new WebPartVerbCollection(verbs);
  }
}

void OnVerbExecuted(object sender, WebPartEventArgs e) {
  // this method is executed when the user invokes the server-side verb
}
```

If you want to create a combo verb, there is a third constructor that takes three parameters, allowing you to pass both a delegate to a server-side method and a string with client-side JavaScript.

The WingtipWebParts project contains a sample Web Part named *WebPartVerbsFontDemo*, which demonstrates several useful techniques that you can employ when creating Web Part verbs. Each Web Part verb instance exposes properties that allow you to enable or disable it, as well as give it a check mark or a custom image. This makes it possible to create Web Part menus that change dynamically according to the current context. Figure 6-12 shows how the Web Part menu for the *WebPartVerbsFontDemo* Web Part appears to the user.

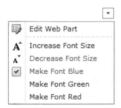

FIGURE 6-12 The menu command for a Web Part verb that can be disabled, checked, or given a custom image.

Another useful technique demonstrated in the *WebPartVerbsFontDemo* Web Part is creating a server-side verb that updates a persistent Web Part property. For example, when a user clicks the Web Part menu with the Make Font Green caption, the Web Part verb issues a Hypertext Transfer Protocol (HTTP) postback, which fires a server-side method in the Web Part class named *OnMakeFontGreen*. But how would you actually write the code in this server-side event handler to change the value of the persistent property named *TextFontColor*? Perhaps you would start by writing the event handler code like this.

```
void OnMakeFontGreen(object sender, WebPartEventArgs e) {
  this.TextFontColor = "Green";
}
```

As it turns out, this code will not produce the desired effect. It updates the Web Part inside the scope of a single request, but it does not write the change back to the content database. What you need to do is create an instance of *SPLimitedWebPartManager* for the current page, which makes it possible to update the Web Part and save the changes back to the content database. The following implementation uses the *SPLimitedWebPartManager* class to produce the desired effect.

```
void OnMakeFontGreen(object sender, WebPartEventArgs e) {
  this.TextFontColor = "Green";
  SPWeb site = SPContext.Current.Web;
  SPFile page = site.GetFile(Context.Request.Url.AbsolutePath);
  SP.SPLimitedWebPartManager wpm = page.GetLimitedWebPartManager(PersonalizationScope.User);
  WebPartVerbsFontDemo webpart = wpm.WebParts[this.ID] as WebPartVerbsFontDemo;
  webpart.TextFontColor = "Green";
  wpm.SaveChanges(webpart);
}
```

Web Parts Connections

The Web Part Framework allows Web Parts to be connected together using Web Part connections. A *Web Part connection* represents a communications channel between two Web Parts where one Web Part plays the role of the *connection provider* and the other plays the role of the *connection consumer*.

One key point is that developers create Web Parts that are connectable. However, users are typically the ones who actually create Web Part connections. The Web Part Manager plays an essential role because it allows users to discover which pairs of Web Parts on a page are connectable and to establish connections between them. Once a pair of Web Parts has been connected, the Web Part Manager also takes on the responsibility of creating the communications channel between them early in the life cycle of a Web Part page.

> **Note** Earlier versions of SharePoint technologies supported Web Part connections that worked across pages. However, the support for creating cross-page connections was dropped because it caused problems with reliability and maintainability. The support for Web Part connections in SharePoint 2010 is based on connecting Web Part instances that are running on the same Web Part page. Anything you see or read about cross-page connections is either deprecated or unsupported and can be safely ignored.

Each Web Part connection is based on an interface definition known as the *connection interface*. Once two Web Parts are connected, the consumer is able to access the provider using the method and properties defined in the connection interface. The WingtipWebParts project provides an example of two Web Parts named *FontConnectionProvider* and *FontConnectionConsumer,* which demonstrate how to pass font formatting data in a Web

Part connection. For example, when you change the font size and color in the provider Web Part, the consumer Web Part changes its font size and color along with it. The connection between these two Web Parts is based on a public interface named *IFontProvider.*

```
public interface IFontProvider {
  FontUnit FontSize { get; }
  Color FontColor { get; }
}
```

Let's start by discussing how to implement the *FontConnectionProvider* class. We will start by implementing the connection interface in the Web Part class itself. For example, the *FontConnectionProvider* class implements the *IFontProvider* interface and uses its persistent properties, named *TextFontColor* and *TextFontSize,* to provide a consumer with its current setting for font formatting.

```
public class FontConnectionProvider : WebPart, IFontProvider {

  public FontUnit FontSize {
    get { return new FontUnit(this.TextFontSize); }
  }

  public Color FontColor {
    get { return Color.FromName(this.TextFontColor); }
  }

  // other class members omited for brevity
}
```

The second thing that you need to do in the provider Web Part is to create a special method known as a connection point. A *connection point* is a method that serves as an entry point into a connectable Web Part instance. The Web Part Manager uses connection points to connect the provider to the consumer after a connection has been established. The Web Part Manager also uses connection points to discover the potential connections that could be established between any pair of Web Parts on the current page. When the Web Part Manager determines that there is a potential connection between two Web Parts on the current page, it lights up the Connections menu in both Web Parts, giving the user the ability to create a connection in the browser.

When you create a method to serve as a *provider connection point,* it does not matter what you name it. What does matter is that the method is defined without parameters and with a return type based on the connection interface. You must also apply the *ConnectionProvider* attribute to the method, which makes it a discoverable connection point to the Web Part Manager. This is how the connection point method is defined in the *FontConnectionProvider* class.

```
[ConnectionProvider("Font Formatting", AllowsMultipleConnections = true)]
public IFontProvider FontProviderConnectionPoint() {
  return this;
}
```

As you can see, the implementation of this method is pretty simple, apart from having the *ConnectionProvider* attribute and the correct signature. Because the Web Part class implements the connection interface, the method simply needs to return a reference to the current Web Part instance using the C# *this* reference.

The *ConnectionProvider* attribute is applied using two parameters. The first parameter is a *Display Name* for a connection that will be shown to the user through the Connections fly out menu. The *AllowsMultipleConnections* parameter is a named parameter that allows you to control whether users can create additional connections after the first connection has been established. In this case, it does make sense to allow for multiple connections because there could be a scenario in which the users would want two or more consumer Web Parts to synchronize on the same font formatting used by a single provider.

Now, let's discuss implementing a consumer Web Part to support an *IFontProvider* connection. The consumer Web Part must supply a method for a *consumer connection point* with a signature that is different than the method for a provider connection point. The method for the consumer connection point takes a single parameter based on the interface type and has a *void* return type. The method also requires the *ConnectionConsumer* attribute, which takes the same parameters as the *ConnectionProvider* attribute. Examine the following definition for the *FontConnectionConsumer* class.

```
public class FontConnectionConsumer : WebPart {

    protected IFontProvider FontProvider;

    [ConnectionConsumer("Font Formatting", AllowsMultipleConnections=false)]
    public void FontProviderConnectionPoint(IFontProvider provider) {
      FontProvider = provider;
    }

    // other class members omited for brevity
}
```

The *ConnectionConsumer* attribute is applied passing the *Display Name* parameter and the *AllowsMultipleConnections* parameter. As you can see, the *AllowsMultipleConnections* parameter is assigned a value of *false*. That's because it doesn't make sense given the scenario of connecting a font consumer to more than one font provider. By assigning the *AllowsMultipleConnections* parameter a value of *false,* you are telling the Web Part Manager to disallow additional connections through the current connection point once a single connection has been established.

The other thing that you should notice about the previous listing of the *FontConnectionConsumer* class is that it contains a protected field named *FontProvider*, which is based on the connection interface type. This is used so that the consumer Web Part can track a connection to the provider Web Part. Let's discuss what happens when a page is processed to give you an understanding of how the connection is established.

When a Web Part page with a connected pair of Web Parts is being processed, the Web Part Manager calls the provider's connection point method to obtain an *IFontProvider* reference. Then the Web Part Manager passes that reference to the consumer by calling its connection point method. The consumer's connection point method copies this reference to the protected field named *FontProvider* to provide a way to access the provider Web Part in other methods.

One thing that you must keep in mind is that a consumer Web Part often will execute in a disconnected state, so you cannot always assume that the *FontProvider* field has a valid reference. Instead, you should implement a consumer Web Part to handle gracefully scenarios in which it is not connected. Here is an example of a method in the *FontConnectionConsumer* class that is written to test whether the current Web Part instance is connected before attempting to access its properties.

```
protected override void OnPreRender(EventArgs e) {
  if (FontProvider != null) {
    lbl.ForeColor = FontProvider.FontColor;
    lbl.Font.Size = FontProvider.FontSize;
  }
}
```

Now that we have reviewed how to implement the provider Web Part and the consumer Web Part, it's time to discuss how the user connects these Web Parts once they have been created on a Web Part page. Imagine a scenario where a Web Part page has one instance of the *FontConnectionProvider* Web Part and two instances of the *FontConnectionConsumer* Web Part. The Web Part Manager discovers that two possible connections can be created. If you enter edit mode for the Web Part page and access the Web Part drop-down menu of the provider Web Part, you will see that the Web Part Manager has provided an option for the user to create connections by adding fly out menus to the Connections menu, as shown in Figure 6-13.

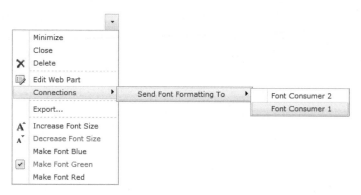

FIGURE 6-13 The Web Part Manager enables the Connections menu when it discovers connectable Web Parts.

If you take a closer look at the Connections fly out menu shown in Figure 6-13, you will notice that the Web Part Manager uses the *Display Name* that was added to the *ConnectionProvider* attribute. The *Display Name* of *Font Formatting* is parsed together in a string between the words *Send* and *To*. This is something that you should keep in mind when creating the *Display Name* values for connection points.

On the right side of Figure 6-13, you can see selectable menu commands containing the title of consumer Web Parts that can be connected to this provider Web Part. If you click one of those consumer Web Part titles, you will create a Web Part connection between the two. After you have made a connection, the same menu will still appear, but with a check mark on it to show that there is an established connection. You can also click the checked menu item to delete the Web Part connection as well.

While Figure 6-13 shows a provider Web Part that is connected to a consumer, it is also possible to create the same type of connection in the other direction. In other words, the two consumer Web Parts will provide fly out menus in their Connections menu, which allows a user to establish a connection to a consumer. Also, keep in mind that there is no difference between connecting a provider to a consumer and connecting a consumer to a provider. The connection, once established, behaves the same way in either case.

Connected Web Parts Using the *SPLimitedWebPartManager* Class

In many scenarios, users will connect Web Parts using the Connections menu, as was shown in the previous section. However, there are occasionally scenarios in which it makes sense to prepopulate a Web Part page with two connectable Web Parts and to also preestablish a connection between them.

The WingtipWebParts project contains a feature receiver that uses the *SPLimitedWebPartManager* class to create an instance of both the provider Web Part and the consumer Web Part on a Web Part page named WebPartsPreconnected.aspx. The code then calls a method of the *SPLimitedWebPartManager* class named *SPConnectWebParts*, which is used to create a connection between the two Web Part instances, as shown in Listing 6-3.

LISTING 6-3 Web Parts connected with code using *SPLimitedWebPartManager*

```
public override void FeatureActivated(SPFeatureReceiverProperties properties) {

  SPSite siteCollection = (SPSite)properties.Feature.Parent;
  SPWeb site = siteCollection.RootWeb;

  SPFile page = site.GetFile("WebPartPages/WebPartsPreconnected.aspx");
  SPLimitedWebPartManager mgr =
    page.GetLimitedWebPartManager(PersonalizationScope.Shared);

  // create provider Web Part in Left zone
  FontConnectionProvider.FontConnectionProvider ProviderWebPart =
    new FontConnectionProvider.FontConnectionProvider();
  ProviderWebPart.Title = "Font Provider 1";
  ProviderWebPart.UserGreeting = "I look pretty";
  ProviderWebPart.TextFontSize = 18;
  ProviderWebPart.TextFontColor = "Blue";
  mgr.AddWebPart(ProviderWebPart, "Left", 0);

  // create consumer Web Part in Right zone
  FontConnectionConsumer.FontConnectionConsumer ConsumerWebPart =
    new FontConnectionConsumer.FontConnectionConsumer();
  ConsumerWebPart.Title = " Font Consumer 1";
  ConsumerWebPart.UserGreeting = "And so do I";
  mgr.AddWebPart(ConsumerWebPart, "Right", 0);

  // create connection between Web Parts
  mgr.SPConnectWebParts(
    ProviderWebPart,
    mgr.GetProviderConnectionPoints(ProviderWebPart).Default,
    ConsumerWebPart,
    mgr.GetConsumerConnectionPoints(ConsumerWebPart).Default
  );
}
```

Asynchronous Processing

We have now reached the final topic of this chapter, which is creating Web Parts that use asynchronous processing. If you develop Web Parts that retrieve data from across the network without using asynchronous processing, your Web Parts will have serious limitations when it comes to scaling and optimizing page response times. Learning to write Web Parts that use the asynchronous processing support provided by the ASP.NET Framework is a key factor in achieving scalability in SharePoint farms that experience high levels of traffic.

Let's begin by discussing the core problem. By default, the ASP.NET Framework processes each page request using a single thread. This is true even for Web Part pages that contain several Web Parts. Now consider a scenario where two Web Parts on the same page both call across the network to remote Web services to retrieve data. When the first Web Part calls across the network, it has the effect of blocking the primary request thread that is processing the page. That means that all page processing halts until the call from the first Web Part returns from across the network.

A key point is that the second Web Part is not able to begin its call across the network until the call sent by the first Web Part returns. In other words, the two Web Parts have to conduct their calls across the network in a serialized fashion, as opposed to being able to send them in parallel. You can see that a Web Part page in this scenario has a response time that gets longer each time you add another Web Part that calls across the network. Now consider a scenario where a Web Part page has 10 Web Parts calling across the network instead of 2 Web Parts. The response time for processing the page would become unacceptably long.

The use of asynchronous processing provides a much better solution when developing Web Parts that call across the network. A key factor is that each Web Part is able to call across the network on a secondary thread that doesn't block other Web Parts. Therefore, all the Web Parts on a page can make calls across the network in parallel, which can reduce response times significantly. The total page response time is reduced from the sum of network call times to the time of the network call that takes the longest.

A second motivation for using asynchronous processing involves automatic time-out support. Think about a scenario where your Web Part calls across the network to a Web service that is experiencing problems with availability or responsiveness. How long should your Web Part wait for a response from the troubled Web service before giving up and returning with an error? Furthermore, how would you write the code in your Web Part to cancel a pending call across the network. Without assistance from the ASP.NET Framework, you would be forced to program at a very low level to terminate a thread blocking on a remote method call. Fortunately, this is not a concern because the asynchronous processing support in the ASP.NET Framework provides automatic time-out detection, which shields the developer from the low-level programming details of cancelling a network call in progress.

The third motivation for using asynchronous processing has to do with the way in which the ASP.NET Framework manages threads. The ASP.NET Framework manages a thread pool of primary request threads, which it uses to process incoming page requests. What is important to understand is that this thread pool never changes in size. In other words, the primary request threads used to process ASP.NET pages are a finite resource.

If you rely on primary request threads to call across the network, you cause blocking, which effectively reduces the number of primary request threads available to service incoming requests. This type of blocking can compromise Web application responsiveness in high-traffic farms. When you use asynchronous processing, the ASP.NET Framework uses secondary threads drawn from a separate thread pool that grows and shrinks dynamically in response to traffic increasing and decreasing. This has a positive effect on both responsiveness and scalability.

Understanding Asynchronous Tasks

Before we examine the programming details, let's take a moment to discuss the high-level architecture that allows the ASP.NET Framework to provide support for asynchronous processing. By default, each page request is processed by a *primary request thread* from the main thread pool. The primary request thread creates and initializes the page object and then begins executing page life cycle methods such as *OnInit, OnLoad,* and *CreateChildControls.* After the primary request thread has completed executing the other page-level methods and event handlers, it enters the final rendering phase of the page request, where it executes the methods associated with output rendering, such as *Render* and *RenderContents.*

The technique for using asynchronous processing support in Web Parts involves creating and registering *asynchronous tasks.* Whenever you create and register an asynchronous task, you are in effect making a request to the ASP.NET Framework to execute code on a secondary thread. It is recommended that you create and register asynchronous tasks as late as possible in the page life cycle, but you must do it before the page enters the rendering phase. Therefore, you should add the code to perform this work in the *OnPreRender* method. While it is most common for Web Parts to create and register a single asynchronous task per request, you can also write a single Web Part that creates and registers two or three asynchronous tasks per request if the scenario calls for it.

When the ASP.NET Framework detects one or more asynchronous tasks have been registered, it changes the thread processing model for the current page request. Let's now look at what happens in a page request in which asynchronous tasks have been registered. The page process begins in the usual fashion, where the primary request thread creates and initializes the page object and then executes methods and event handlers in the page life cycle. However, the primary request thread executes methods only up to and including the *OnPreRender* method. After the *OnPreRender* method completes, the primary request thread returns to its thread pool, where it becomes available to serve other incoming page requests.

After the *OnPreRender* method completes and the primary request thread has been returned to its thread pool, the ASP.NET Framework begins to execute each asynchronous task on its own secondary thread. For example, within a page request that involves three asynchronous tasks, the ASP.NET Framework will employ three secondary threads, allowing each asynchronous task to progress at its own pace without being blocked by any of the other asynchronous tasks. As noted earlier, the ASP.NET Framework draws these secondary threads from a separate thread pool, which grows and shrinks dynamically according to traffic levels.

Once the asynchronous tasks for a page request begin to execute, the ASP.NET Framework monitors their progress. A key point is that every asynchronous task in a page request must finish before the page request can enter the rendering phase. The ASP.NET Framework adds value in page processing by providing the automatic blocking behavior, which patiently waits until each asynchronous task has either completed its execution or has timed out.

Once all the asynchronous tasks have either completed their work or have timed out, the ASP.NET Framework transitions the page request into the rendering phase by executing methods such as *Render* and *RenderContents*. Note that the ASP.NET Framework processes the rendering methods using primary request threads from the main thread pool as opposed to using the secondary threads that are used to execute asynchronous tasks.

Creating and Registering Asynchronous Tasks

Asynchronous processing support is enabled by creating and registering an instance of the *PageAsyncTask* class. The code that creates and registers the *PageAsyncTask* instance should be added to the *OnPreRender* method. Here is a starting point for a Web Part class that is written to support asynchronous processing.

```
public class AsyncProcessing101 : WebPart {
  protected override void OnPreRender(EventArgs e) {
    PageAsyncTask task1 = new PageAsyncTask(Task1Begin, Task1End, Task1Timeout, null);
    this.Page.RegisterAsyncTask(task1);
  }

  IAsyncResult Task1Begin(object sender, EventArgs args,
                          AsyncCallback callback, object state){
    // access data across network on secondary thread
    // return IAsyncResult object for ASP.NET to monitor progress
  }

  void Task1End(IAsyncResult result) {
    // perform required work after async task has completed
  }

  void Task1Timeout(IAsyncResult result) {
    // handle case where async task to cancelled due to time-out
  }
}
```

To create a new *PageAsyncTask* instance, you must call a constructor that accepts four parameters. The first three parameters are based on delegate types that are used to reference three different methods. In the Web Part class named *AsyncProcessing101,* these methods have the names *Task1Begin, Task1End,* and *Task1Timeout.* The fourth parameter in the constructor is based on the *System.Object* type and can be used to pass any arbitrary data to the secondary thread that is processing the asynchronous task.

Once you have created the *PageAsyncTask* instance, you must then register it with the ASP.NET Framework. You register a *PageAsyncTask* instance by calling the *RegisterAsyncTask* method supplied by the *Page* class.

Let's discuss the method named *Task1Begin*. This is the method that executes on a secondary thread where you should make your call across the network. Note that this method is defined with an *IAsyncResult* return type, which represents a common asynchronous programming pattern in the .NET Framework. The ASP.NET Framework uses the *IAsyncResult* object to monitor the progress of the asynchronous task and to determine when the work has been completed. The .NET Framework provides quite a few classes that implement the *IAsyncResult* design pattern. Some examples of these classes include Web Requests, Web Service Proxies, and ADO.NET database classes.

If you need to call across the network using an application programming interface (API) or library that does not support the *IAsyncResult* design pattern, you can also factor the code for your asynchronous task into a separate method and then execute that method using a .NET delegate. The value of employing a .NET delegate is that it automatically provides a *BeginInvoke* method that is defined with an *IAsyncResult* return type. Here is an example of using the built-in .NET Framework delegate named *Action,* which allows you to execute a method and return an *IAsyncResult* object.

```
IAsyncResult Task1Begin(object sender, EventArgs args,
                        AsyncCallback callback, object state) {
  Action func1 = new Action(GetDataFromNetwork);
  return func1.BeginInvoke(callback, state);
}

void GetDataFromNetwork(){
  // call across network
}
```

Now let's discuss the method named *Task1End*. The ASP.NET Framework executes this method after the asynchronous processing is finished. For example, the ASP.NET Framework will not execute *Task1End* until *Task1Begin* has completed its work. Moreover, the ASP.NET Framework will not execute *Task1End* until every other asynchronous task has completed its work. If three different *PageAsyncTask* instances have been created and registered during the processing of a page, the ASP.NET Framework waits until each of the three asynchronous tasks have finished executing their *Begin* methods before it executes any of their *End* methods.

The ASP.NET Framework executes the last method, named *Task1Timeout,* in the event that a time-out occurs. When a time-out occurs, you can assume that the associated asynchronous task did not complete successfully. Therefore, you should add time-out logic to the Web Part to provide some type of error message to the user indicating that there has been a problem.

Note that SharePoint Foundation provides a default time-out value of 7 seconds. SharePoint Foundation provides a default time-out value that is configured in the web.config file inside the *pages* element within the system.web section.

```
<configuration>
  <system.web>
    <pages asyncTimeout="7" >
  </system.web>
</configuration>
```

Note that there is only one time-out value per page request. An asynchronous task does not have its own independent time-out value. If you believe that you need a time-out value that is longer or shorter than seven seconds, you can modify the *AsyncTimeout* property of the *Page* class in the *OnPreRender* method.

```
this.Page.AsyncTimeout = new TimeSpan(0, 0, 10);
```

The *AsynchRssReader* Web Part

The *AsynchRssReader* Web Part provides a real-world example of a Web Part that uses an asynchronous task to make a Web service call across the network. The complete definition for this Web Part class is shown in Listing 6.4. By examining this listing, you can get a better picture of how all the pieces fit together.

LISTING 6-4 The *AsyncRssReader* Web Part

```
public class AsyncRssReader : WebPart {

  [ Personalizable(PersonalizationScope.User),
    WebBrowsable(true),
    WebDisplayName("RSS Source URL:"),
    WebDescription("provides address for RSS feed"),
    Category("Wingtip Web Parts")]
  public string RssSourceUrl { get; set; }

  private WebRequest request;
  private Stream response;
  private bool requestTimedOut;

  protected override void OnPreRender(EventArgs e) {
    // do not register async task if in design mode
    if (this.WebPartManager.DisplayMode.AllowPageDesign) { return; }

    // ensure valid URL for RSS Feed
    if (string.IsNullOrEmpty(RssSourceUrl))
      RssSourceUrl = "http://feeds.feedburner.com/AndrewConnell";

    // create WebRequest and register async task
    request = WebRequest.CreateDefault(new Uri(RssSourceUrl));
    PageAsyncTask task1 =
      new PageAsyncTask(Task1Begin, Task1End, Task1Timeout, null);
```

```
        this.Page.AsyncTimeout = new TimeSpan(0, 0, 10);
        this.Page.RegisterAsyncTask(task1);
    }

    IAsyncResult Task1Begin(object sender, EventArgs args,
                            AsyncCallback callback, object state) {
        return request.BeginGetResponse(callback, state);
    }

    void Task1End(IAsyncResult result) {
        response = request.EndGetResponse(result).GetResponseStream();
    }

    void Task1Timeout(IAsyncResult result) {
        requestTimedOut = true;
    }

    protected override void RenderContents(HtmlTextWriter writer) {
        if (this.WebPartManager.DisplayMode.AllowPageDesign) {
            writer.Write("No RSS Reading while in design mode");
        }
        else if (requestTimedOut || response == null) {
            writer.Write("Request for RSS feed timed out");
        }
        else{
            XslCompiledTransform transform = new XslCompiledTransform();
            string xsltRssFeedToHtml = Properties.Resources.RssFeedToHtml'
            XmlReader xslt = XmlReader.Create(new StringReader(xsltRssFeedToHtml));
            transform.Load(xslt);
            XmlReader reader = new XmlTextReader(response);
            XmlTextWriter results = new XmlTextWriter(writer.InnerWriter);
            transform.Transform(reader, results);
            reader.Close();
        }
    }
}
```

When designing Web Parts, you should consider only registering asynchronous tasks when a Web Part is in display mode. In other words, you should avoid expensive trips across the network when the user has the hosting Web Part page in design mode. Before registering an asynchronous task to call across the network, the *AsynchRssReader* Web Part runs a simple test to verify that the current page is not in design mode. This test can be accomplished by inspecting the Web Part Manager's *DisplayMode* property.

```
protected override void OnPreRender(EventArgs e) {
  if (this.WebPartManager.DisplayMode.AllowPageDesign) {
    // return without registering asynchronous task
    return;
  }
  // continue with registering asynchronous task...
}
```

The *AsynchRssReader* Web Part calls to a Web service using the *WebRequest* class and the *WebResponse* class, which are defined by the .NET Framework inside the *System.Net* namespace. Note that the *WebRequest* class provides a method named *BeginGetResponse,* which returns an *IAsyncResult* object. The *Task1Begin* method calls the *BeginGetResponse* method to begin the call across the network. You can also observe that the *Task1Begin* method uses the *IAsyncResult* object returned from *BeginGetResponse* as its own return value.

While the *Task1Begin* method calls *BeginGetResponse*, there is also a need to call a corresponding method of the *WebRequest* class named *EndGetResponse*. The call to *EndGetResponse* is in the *Task1End* method, which takes the *Stream*-based return value and assigns it to the protected field named *response*.

```
void Task1End(IAsyncResult result) {
  response = request.EndGetResponse(result).GetResponseStream();
}
```

RenderContents begins its execution after the asynchronous task has completed. Note that the implementation of *RenderContents* begins by checking to ensure that the page is not in design mode and that a time-out has not occurred. *RenderContents* then completes its work by extracting the contents of the RSS feed from the *Stream* object referenced by the *response* field, as shown in Listing 6-4.

Conclusion

This chapter began by covering the fundamentals of creating and using custom controls. There were several examples of creating and using custom controls, such as the case of adding a custom fly out menu to a SharePoint site. The text also covered when it makes sense to employ user controls in SharePoint development to increase your productivity, and how to use the power of delegate controls in scenarios where you need to add CSS rules and JavaScript code across many pages on a sitewide or farmwide basis.

The second part of this chapter took a detailed look at Web Part development. You learned about the role of the Web Part Manager and the function of the Web Part Gallery. We demonstrated several different styles for rendering the output of a Web Part and discussed scenarios where each style is most appropriate. In addition, the text examines essential Web Part development skills, such as adding persistent properties and custom Editor Parts. The chapter demonstrated taking advantage of Web Part verbs, Web Part connections, and asynchronous processing support, which is critical when retrieving data from across the network.

Chapter 7
Lists and Events

This chapter covers the fundamentals of designing and creating lists and document libraries. You will learn how to create list columns using fields, field types, and site columns. You will also learn how to create custom content types, as well as how to configure lists and document libraries to use a custom content type.

The second part of the chapter covers working with document libraries. You will learn how to develop a feature that creates a document library with a custom document template. You will also learn how to program against the documents in a document library and how to create new documents using code.

After discussing lists and document libraries, this chapter introduces events and event receivers and explains how to register event handlers on objects that support events such as lists, document libraries, and content types. You will also learn the difference between before events and after events and see several examples of writing event handlers for common production scenarios.

Creating Lists

One of the greatest strengths of Microsoft SharePoint Foundation is that it enables users to create lists and to customize them for specific business scenarios. For example, a user can create a new custom list and add whatever columns are required for the business needs at hand. All the details of how SharePoint Foundation tracks the schema definition for columns in a list and how it stores list items in the content database are handled behind the scenes. The idea that a company has to keep a database administrator available to create new database tables for tracking new types of business-related content is a thing of the past.

When a user creates a new list, SharePoint Foundation allows the user to select a *list template* from a collection of list templates available in the current site. Table 7-1 shows a listing of commonly used list templates supplied by SharePoint Foundation. As you can see, Table 7-1 shows the user-friendly name of the list template as well as the underlying *template type* and *template type ID*.

TABLE 7-1 SharePoint Foundation List Templates

Template Name	Template Type	Template Type ID
Custom List	GenericList	100
Document Library	DocumentLibrary	101
Survey	Survey	102
Links List	Links	103
Announcements List	Announcements	104
Contacts List	Contacts	105
Calendar	Events	106
Tasks List	Tasks	107
Discussion Lists	DiscussionBoard	108
Picture Library	PictureLibrary	109
Form Library	XMLForm	115
Wiki Page Library	WebPageLibrary	119

As you can imagine, there are many ad hoc scenarios where creating a list does not require the assistance of a developer. Users who are skilled in SharePoint site customization are more than capable of creating lists and configuring them to achieve a desired goal. At the same time, however, there are definitely scenarios where it makes sense to automate the creation of lists using a SharePoint solution. This is especially true when the process for creating a specific set of lists must be repeatable across different sites or different farms.

In Chapter 2, "SharePoint Foundation Development," we demonstrated how to create a new list in a declarative fashion using a feature that contains a *ListInstance* element. For example, you can create a feature with a *ListInstance* element having the attributes *TemplateType* and *FeatureId* set to values identifying the *Contacts* list template and the *Contacts* feature, respectively. For example, the following *ListInstance* element will create a new *Contacts* list when its hosting feature is activated.

```
<ListInstance
  TemplateType="105"
  FeatureId="00bfea71-7e6d-4186-9ba8-c047ac750105"
  Title="Customers"
  Description="Wingtip customers list "
  Url="Lists/Customers"
  OnQuickLaunch="TRUE" >
</ListInstance>
```

In Chapter 3, "SharePoint Developer Tools in Microsoft Visual Studio 2010," when we introduced the SharePoint developer tools in Microsoft Visual Studio 2010, you saw that Visual Studio 2010 provides SharePoint projects with a dedicated SharePoint project item template for creating a *ListInstance* element that provides the convenience of automatic conflict resolution. We also discussed that automatic conflict resolution is something that occurs only when working inside Visual Studio 2010. There is nothing about automatic conflict resolution that changes the behavior of your code in a production environment.

When you create a SharePoint project item based on the List Instance project item template, you can observe that the SharePoint Customization Wizard creates the list using a Uniform Resource Locator (URL) based on a site-relative location inside the Lists folder, which is a standard practice. If you modify the *Url* attribute in a *ListInstance* element that is creating a standard list, it is recommended that you use a location inside the Lists folder.

While it is possible to create a new list declaratively using a *ListInstance* element, you also have the option of creating lists programmatically. For example, you can write code that uses the server-side object model to create a list that is identical to the list created by the *ListInstance* element.

```
SPWeb site = SPContext.Current.Web;
string ListTitle = "Customers";
string ListDescription = "Wingtip customers list";
Guid ListId = site.Lists.Add(ListTitle, ListDescription, SPListTemplateType.Contacts);
SPList list = site.Lists[ListId];
list.OnQuickLaunch = true;
list.Update();
```

As you can see, the *Lists* collection of an *SPWeb* object provides an *Add* method that accepts parameters for a new list's title, description, and list template type. The server-side object model provides the *SPListTemplateType* enumeration type, which supplies an enumeration value for each of the built-in SharePoint Foundation list template types. When you create a standard list using this approach, SharePoint Foundation creates the new list using a URL inside the Lists folder. For example, the previous code sample creates a list with a base *Url* value of *Lists/Customers*.

When you call the *Add* method on the *Lists* collection for a site, it creates the list and returns a GUID–based list *ID* that can be used to retrieve the associated *SPList* object. Once you obtain an *SPList* reference to the newly created list, you can then modify list properties such as *OnQuickLaunch*. Remember that you must save your changes to the content database by calling the *Update* method.

Note that when you create a new list by calling the *Add* method, SharePoint Foundation uses the first parameter to create both the list *Title* and the list's base URL. If you include a space in the title when creating a new list, SharePoint Foundation replaces the space with *%20* to create an encoded URL. For example, if you pass a title of *Marketing Tasks* when calling the *Add* method, you would create a list with a base URL of *Marketing%20Tasks*, which is harder for users to type. You might prefer the following technique, in which each list is created using a title that contains no spaces. After the *Add* method completes and the base URL has been established, you can modify the list's *Title* property to a string with spaces that is more readable to the user.

```
SPWeb site = SPContext.Current.Web;
Guid ListId = site.Lists.Add("MarketingTasks", "", SPListTemplateType.Tasks);
SPList list = site.Lists[ListId];
list.Title = "Marketing Tasks";
list.OnQuickLaunch = true;
list.Update();
```

As you have just seen, you have two choices for creating a new list in a SharePoint solution: use a declarative approach or a programmatic approach. So how should you choose between these two approaches? To some degree, this is a matter of developer preference. However, the declarative approach does have a noteworthy disadvantage: There is no graceful way to handle conflicts. For example, suppose that a user attempts to activate a feature with the *ListInstance* element in a site that already contains a list with the same title. The feature activates successfully, but the feature's attempt to create the list silently fails due to the conflict, leaving the functionality of the feature in a unpredictable state.

You have more control when you create a list programmatically. That's because you can check to see if there is an existing list that would prevent the new list from being created. For example, you can query the *Lists* collection of the current site to see if there is an existing list with the same title before attempting to create a new list. If there is a list with a conflicting title, you can delete that list or change its title to ensure that your code can create the new list with the desired title successfully.

```
SPWeb site = SPContext.Current.Web;
string ListTitle = "Customers";
string ListDescription = "Wingtip customers list";

// delete Customers list if it exists
SPList list = site.Lists.TryGetList("Customers");
if (list != null)
  list.Delete();

// create new Customers list
Guid ListId = site.Lists.Add(ListTitle, ListDescription, SPListTemplateType.Contacts);
list = site.Lists[ListId];
list.OnQuickLaunch = true;
list.Update();
```

Another advantage of using code to create lists over the declarative *ListInstance* element is that you have more control over configuring list properties. The following code listing demonstrates how to configure a new list to disable attachments, folder creation, and grid editing; enable versioning; and configure item-based security.

```
Guid ListId = site.Lists.Add(ListTitle, ListDescription, SPListTemplateType.Contacts);
list = site.Lists[ListId];
list.OnQuickLaunch = true;
list.EnableAttachments = false;
list.EnableFolderCreation = false;
list.DisableGridEditing = true;
list.EnableVersioning = true;
list.MajorVersionLimit = 3;
list.ReadSecurity = 2;
list.WriteSecurity = 2;
list.Update();
```

Note that the last two list properties modified in this example are named *ReadSecurity* and *WriteSecurity*. By modifying these properties on a list, you can restrict contributor access to specific items. The *ReadSecurity* and *WriteSecurity* properties each have a default value of 1 in a new list. When these properties have the default value of 1, it means that anyone with contributor access rights can view, update, and delete any of the items in the list.

However, imagine there is a business scenario in which you want to restrict contributors from viewing or updating items created by other contributors. If you set a list's *WriteSecurity* property to a value of 2, contributors will be able to update and delete only the items that they created. They will not be able to update or delete items created by others. If you set a list's *ReadSecurity* property to a value of 2, contributors will not be able to view items created by others.

The *ReadSecurity* property can be assigned only values of 1 or 2. However, the *WriteSecurity* property can be assigned a value of 1, 2, or 4. If you set a list's *WriteSecurity* property to a value of 4, contributors are prohibited from updating or deleting any items in the list, including those that they created. This type of security configuration often makes sense for items that contain content such as surveys or votes.

Keep in mind that the *ReadSecurity* property and *WriteSecurity* property settings affect only users with contributor access. A list owner or a site administrator will continue to have read/write access on all list items regardless of the current settings for the *ReadSecurity* and *WriteSecurity* properties.

Fields and Field Types

Each SharePoint list contains a collection of *fields* that define what users perceive as columns. A field can be created inside the context of a single list. These are the types of fields that we will discuss first. However, a field can also be defined within the context of a site, which makes it possible to reuse it across multiple lists. These types of fields are known as site columns and they will be introduced later in the chapter.

Every field is defined in terms of an underlying *field type*. Table 7-2 shows a list of field types that SharePoint Foundation displays to users when they are adding a new field to a list using the Create Column page. Note that in addition to the field types included with SharePoint Foundation, there are extra field types installed by SharePoint Server 2010. As you will see in Chapter 8, "Templates and Type Definitions," it's also possible to develop custom field types in a SharePoint solution to extend the set of field types available for use within a farm.

TABLE 7-2 SharePoint Foundation Field Types

Field Type	Display Name
Text	Single Line Of Text
Note	Multiple Lines Of Text
Choice	Choice
Integer	Integer
Number	Number
Decimal	Decimal
Currency	Currency
DateTime	Date And Time
Lookup	Lookup
Boolean	Yes/No
User	Person Or Group
URL	Hyperlink Or Picture
Calculated	Calculated

At a lower level, SharePoint Foundation classifies lists using *base types*. Standard lists have a base type of *0*, whereas document libraries have a base type of *1*. There also are less frequently used base types for discussion forums (*3*), vote or survey lists (*4*), and issue lists (*5*). The base type defines a common set of fields, and all list types configured to use that base type automatically inherit those fields.

For example, all five base types define a field named *ID*. This field enables SharePoint Foundation to track each item in a list behind the scenes with a unique integer identifier. All five base types also define fields named *Created, Modified, Author,* and *Editor.* These fields allow SharePoint Foundation to track when and by whom each item was created and last modified.

Every list contains a special field named *Title*. This field is special for standard lists because it contains the value that is rendered inside the *Edit Control Block (ECB) menu* shown in Figure 7-1. While the *Title* field contains the value rendered inside the ECB menu, it is not actually the field that SharePoint Foundation uses to create the ECB menu within a view. Instead, SharePoint Foundation uses a related field named *LinkTitle*, which reads the value of the *Title* field and uses it to render the ECB menu.

FIGURE 7-1 The *LinkTitle* field creates the Edit Control Block (ECB) menu, which displays the value of the *Title* field.

There is a third related field named *LinkTitleNoMenu,* which can be used to display the value of the *Title* field in a hyperlink that can be used to navigate to the View Item page. Note that the *LinkTitle* field and the *LinkTitleNoMenu* field are computed fields, which means that their values cannot be edited.

Each field has an *internal name* as well as a *display name.* Once a field has been created, its internal name can never be modified. However, the display name can be modified. For example, every list has a field with the internal name of *Title.* However, many list types modify the display name of the *Title* field to something more appropriate for the ECB menu. For example, the English-language version of SharePoint Foundation configures the *Title* field of the *Contacts* list type with a display name of *Last Name.* This is why the *Last Name* column provides the ECB menu in a *Contacts* list.

Imagine that you are in a scenario where you need to create a new list and modify the display name of the *Title* field. For example, let's say that you need a new list to track prod-uct categories, so you create a new list using the list template for a *Custom List.* The *SPList* class provides a *Fields* collection, from which you can retrieve the *Title* field. Once you have obtained an *SPField* reference to the *Title* field, you can modify its display name using the *Title* property of the *SPField* class and then save your changes by calling the *Update* method.

```
Guid ListId = site.Lists.Add("ProductCategories", "", SPListTemplateType.GenericList);
SPList list = site.Lists[ListId];
list.Title = "Product Categories";
list.OnQuickLaunch = true;
list.Update();

// modify display name of Title field
SPField fldTitle = list.Fields.GetFieldByInternalName("Title");
fldTitle.Title = "Category";
fldTitle.Update();
```

One interesting side effect of this code is that it updates the display name of the *LinkTitle* field and the *LinkTitleNoMenu* field, in addition to the display name of the *Title* field. This behavior is provided automatically by SharePoint Foundation, which always updates the display name for these three fields at once.

In the code you just saw, the reference to the *Title* field was retrieved using the *GetFieldBy InternalName* method. You should note that you can also access a field from a list's *Fields* collection using the C# indexer syntax.

```
SPField fld = list.Fields["Title"];
```

There are many scenarios in which either technique will work just fine. However, you must understand that the indexer syntax is based on passing the field's display name, not the internal name. However, you must be careful when accessing a field by its display name because it can be modified by users and is localized into different spoken languages for different versions of SharePoint 2010. In scenarios when a field's display name could change, it is a safer bet to access the field within a Fields collection using the *GetFieldByInternalName* method.

Now that we have covered the basics of field and field types, let's write the code required to add a few custom fields to a new list. The *Fields* collection of the *SPList* class provides an *Add* method, which makes it relatively simple to add fields based on common field types.

```
// create new Customers list
Guid ListId = site.Lists.Add("Products", "", SPListTemplateType.GenericList);
SPList list = site.Lists[ListId];
list.OnQuickLaunch = true;
list.Update();

// modify display name of Title field
SPField fldTitle = list.Fields.GetFieldByInternalName("Title");
fldTitle.Title = "Product";
fldTitle.Update();

// add custom fields
list.Fields.Add("ProductDescription", SPFieldType.Note, false);
list.Fields.Add("InventoryLevel", SPFieldType.Integer, true);
list.Fields.Add("ListPrice", SPFieldType.Currency, true);
```

Note that this code avoids using spaces when creating the field name. If you create a field with a space in its name, SharePoint Foundation creates the internal name by replacing each space with *_x0020_*. That means calling the *Add* method and passing a name of *List Price* would create a field with an internal name of *List_x0020_Price*. Most developers prefer creating fields using a name without spaces. After a field has been created, you can update its display name using the *Title* property of the *SPField* class.

```
string fldName = list.Fields.Add("ListPrice", SPFieldType.Currency, true);
SPField fld = list.Fields.GetFieldByInternalName(fldName);
fld.Title = "List Price";
fld.DefaultValue = "0";
fld.Update();
```

The properties of the *SPField* class, such as *DefaultValue,* represent common properties that are shared across all field types. However, specific field types have associated classes that inherit from *SPField*. Examples of these field type classes include *SPFieldBoolean, SPFieldChoice, SPFieldCurrency, SPFieldDateTime, SPFieldDecimal, SPFieldNumber, SPFieldText, SPFieldUrl,* and *SPFieldUser.* You must convert a field object returned by the *GetFieldByInternalName* method to one of these specific field type classes to program against the unique properties of the underlying field type.

```
string fldName = list.Fields.Add("ListPrice", SPFieldType.Currency, true);
SPFieldCurrency fld =
  (SPFieldCurrency)list.Fields.GetFieldByInternalName(fldName);
fld.Title = "List Price";
fld.DefaultValue = "0";
fld.MinimumValue = 0;
fld.MaximumValue = 10000;
fld.CurrencyLocaleId = 1033; // local ID for United States Dollars
fld.DisplayFormat = SPNumberFormatTypes.TwoDecimals;
fld.Update();
```

Using this technique, you can take advantage of what each field type has to offer. For example, you can create a new *Choice* field, add several choice values, and change its formatting.

```
string fldName = list.Fields.Add("Territory", SPFieldType.Choice, true);
SPFieldChoice fld =
  (SPFieldChoice)list.Fields.GetFieldByInternalName(fldName);
// add choice values
fld.Choices.Add("North");
fld.Choices.Add("South");
fld.Choices.Add("East");
fld.Choices.Add("West");
// modify field rendering format
fld.EditFormat = SPChoiceFormatType.RadioButtons;
fld.Update(true);
```

Lookup Fields and List Relationships

SharePoint Foundation supports *lookup fields,* which make it possible for users to update a field value using a drop-down menu populated by the field values in another list. For example, imagine that you want to add a field to the Products list that lets the user pick a product category. You can accomplish this by calling the *AddLookup* method on the *Fields* collection of the list where you want a lookup to occur. When calling the *AddLookup* method, you must pass the display name of the source field and the GUID-based *ID* of the source list.

```
// create Products list
Guid ListId = site.Lists.Add("Products", "", SPListTemplateType.GenericList);
SPList list = site.Lists[ListId];
```

```
// add lookup field based on category field in product categories list
string LookupFieldDisplayName = "Category";
SPList LookupList = site.Lists["Product Categories"];
Guid LookupListID = LookupList.ID;
list.Fields.AddLookup(LookupFieldDisplayName, LookupListID, true);
```

While lookup fields have been supported in previous versions, SharePoint 2010 extends their behavior with the capability to define a relationship between the two lists. For example, the lookup field created in the previous example can be used to define a relationship between the *Product Categories* list and the *Products* list with restricted delete behavior.

```
list.Fields.AddLookup("Category", LookupListID, true);
SPFieldLookup fldCategory = (SPFieldLookup)list.Fields["Category"];
fldCategory.Indexed = true;
fldCategory.RelationshipDeleteBehavior = SPRelationshipDeleteBehavior.Restrict;
fldCategory.Update();
```

The list relationship created by this lookup field will prevent users from deleting any item in the *Product Categories* list that is currently being used by any item in the *Products* list. A user who attempts to delete a product category in use will experience the following error:

```
This item cannot be deleted because an item in the "Products" list is related to an item in
the "Product Categories" list.
```

In some scenarios, it makes more sense to create a relationship with cascading delete behavior instead of restricted delete behavior. This can be done by configuring the relationship delete behaviors using a value of *SPRelationshipDeleteBehavior.Cascade*. When a user deletes a product category, all the product items that have been assigned that category will be deleted as well.

While there is definite value in the new support for defining list relationships, it is important that you don't overestimate what it really does. It cannot be used to create the same level of referential integrity that can be achieved between two tables in a Microsoft SQL Server database. That means that it does not really prevent the possibility of orphaned items, such as when you have products that are not assigned to an existing product category. The value of creating the relationship with delete behavior simply relieves you of additional development work, such as writing an event handler to achieve something such as cascade delete behavior.

One other benefit of creating a relationship between lists is related to programming with LINQ. While we will not cover LINQ programming until Chapter 9, "Accessing Data in Lists," we will briefly discuss how it is affected by list relationships.

Imagine that you have a *Product Categories* list and a *Products* list with a relationship such as the one we have just created. If you execute a LINQ query against the *Product Categories* list, the query will return a column containing a collection of strongly typed *Product* objects.

If you execute a LINQ query against the *Products* list, the query will return a column containing a strongly typed *Product Category* object. This illustrates how LINQ can simulate a logical *JOIN* operation between related lists when running a simple query against one of the lists. By creating the relationship, you can effectively extend the functionality of your LINQ queries.

Views

Each list has a collection of *views* that provide the rendering mechanism for displaying list items. A view contains a collection of *view fields,* which determines which fields from the underlying list will be displayed. Views also provide lists with the ability to display items using filtering, sorting, and grouping.

Each view is hosted by a site page that is created dynamically along with the view. For example, many lists contain an *All Items* view that is hosted by a site page named AllItems.aspx. Many of the SharePoint Foundation list types add secondary views as well. For example, a *Task* list contains secondary views such as *My Task, Due Today,* and *Active Tasks,* that are hosted by their own site pages.

Each list has a view that is configured as the *default view*. This is the view that is shown when a user navigates to the base URL for the list. When you add fields to a list programmatically, these fields are not automatically added to the default view. However, you can add a new field to a view by calling the *Add* method on the *ViewFields* collection of the *SPView* class and passing the internal name of the field as a parameter.

```
// create Sales Leads list
Guid ListId = site.Lists.Add("SalesLeads", "", SPListTemplateType.GenericList);
SPList list = site.Lists[ListId];

// add custom fields
list.Fields.Add("EMailAddress", SPFieldType.Text, false);
list.Fields.Add("Phone", SPFieldType.Text, false);

// add fields to default view
SPView view = list.DefaultView;
view.ViewFields.Add("EMailAddress");
view.ViewFields.Add("Phone");
view.Update();
```

If you want to create or update a view that applies a specific sort order or a filter, you can update the *Query* property of the *SPView* class. However, this can be a bit tricky at first because you must parse together an Extensible Markup Language (XML) fragment using Collaborative Application Markup Language (CAML). More specifically, you must create a CAML fragment that contains an *OrderBy* element, a *Where* element, or both. Here is an example of the CAML code required to update a view to sort by the *Title* field and to filter out any items that have no email address.

```
view.Query = @"<OrderBy>
                  <FieldRef Name='Title' />
               </OrderBy>
               <Where>
                 <IsNotNull>
                   <FieldRef Name='EMailAddress' />
                 </IsNotNull>
               </Where>";
view.Update();
```

Hopefully, this example will get you started creating views using code. We will take a more detailed look at using CAML in Chapter 9, when we discuss writing code to execute queries against lists.

Site Columns

As you have seen, SharePoint Foundation supports the creation of fields within the scope of a list. SharePoint Foundation also support the creation of *site columns,* which are fields created within the scope of a site. The advantage of a site column is that it represents a field that can be reused across multiple lists.

Every site within a site collection contains its own *site columns gallery.* However, when you add a site column to a site columns gallery, that site column is available for use within the current site, as well as in all the child sites in the site hierarchy below. When you add a site column to the site column gallery of a top-level site, it is available for use throughout the entire site collection. For this reason, site columns generally should be added to the site columns gallery of top-level sites instead of child sites.

SharePoint Foundation automatically adds a standard set of site columns to the site columns gallery of every top-level site using a hidden feature named *fields*. Table 7-3 shows a small sampling of this standard set of site columns that are always available for use in every SharePoint site.

TABLE 7-3 Some Site Columns Added to Every Top-Level Site

Internal Name	Display Name	Field Type
ID	ID	Counter
Title	Title	Text
LinkTitle	Title	Computed
LinkTitleNoMenu	Title	Computed
Author	Created By	User
Created	Created	DateTime
Editor	Modified By	User
Modified	Modified	DateTime
FirstName	First Name	Text

Internal Name	Display Name	Field Type
HomePhone	Home Phone	Text
CellPhone	Mobile Number	Text
WorkPhone	Business Phone	Text
EMail	E-Mail	Text
HomeAddressStreet	Home Address Street	Text
HomeAddressCity	Home Address City	Text
HomeAddressStateOrProvince	Home Address State Or Province	Text
HomeAddressPostalCode	Home Address Postal Code	Text
WorkAddress	Address	Note
WorkCity	City	Text
WorkFax	Fax Number	Text
WorkState	State/Province	Text
WorkZip	ZIP/Postal Code	Text
StartDate	Start Date	DateTime
Birthday	Birthday	DateTime
SpouseName	Spouse	Text

As you can see, the standard set of site columns includes the common fields that the SharePoint Foundation base types add to every list, such as *ID*, *Title*, *Author*, *Created*, *Editor*, and *Modified*. It also includes site columns that are used by standard list types, such as *Announcements*, *Contacts*, *Calendar*, and *Tasks*. For example, the *Contacts* list type uses site columns such as *FirstName*, *HomePhone*, *CellPhone*, *WorkPhone*, and *EMail*.

You might notice that a field named *LastName* is suspiciously absent from the standard set of site columns. That's because standard SharePoint Foundation lists that track people-related information store last names in the *Title* field with a modified display name to provide ECB menu support.

SharePoint Foundation adds more than 400 site columns into the site column gallery of every top-level site. However, many of these site columns are hidden, including quite a few that are included only for backward compatibility with earlier versions. However, site administrators can view the site columns that are not hidden using a standard application page named mngfields.aspx, which is accessible using the *Site columns* link in the *Galleries* section of the *Site Settings* page of a top-level site.

When you are required to add a new field to a list, you should determine whether there is already an existing site column that meets your needs. In general, it is preferable to reuse an existing site column instead of creating a new field inside the scope of a list. This is especially true in scenarios where multiple lists require a field with common properties. By updating a

site column, you can automatically push your changes to any list within the current site collection that contains a field based on that site column. The use of site columns also makes
writing queries easier because you can standardize field names across multiple lists.

The SPWeb provides a *Fields* collection that makes it possible to enumerate through the site
columns in the site column gallery for the current site.

```
SPWeb site = SPContext.Current.Web;
foreach (SPField fld in site.Fields) {
  // enumerate site columns in current site
}
```

It is important to understand that the site columns available for use in a site include the
site columns in the local site column gallery as well as the site columns in the galleries of all
parent sites. The *SPWeb* class provides a second collection property named *AvailableFields*,
which allows you to enumerate through all site columns that can be used in the current site.

```
SPWeb site = SPContext.Current.Web;
foreach (SPField fld in site.AvailableFields) {
  // enumerate site columns in current site and in parent sites
}
```

Now consider the following two lines of code.

```
SPField fld1 = site.Fields.GetFieldByInternalName("Title");
SPField fld2 = site.AvailableFields.GetFieldByInternalName("Title");
```

When should you access site columns through the *Fields* collection rather than the
AvailableFields collection? The first observation is that the line of code that accesses the
Title field through the *Fields* collection works only when executed in the context of a top-
level site. This code will fail when executed within the scope of a child site. Therefore, access-
ing site columns through the *AvailableFields* collection can offer more flexibility. However,
you should note that you cannot modify a site column that has been accessed through the
AvailableFields collection. If you plan to modify a site column, you must access it using the
Fields collection in the context of the site where it exists.

In addition to using the standard site columns provided by SharePoint Foundation, you can
also create your own manually using the browser or with code using the server-side object
model. You will find that writing the code for creating a new site column is just like writing
the code for creating a new field in a list that we demonstrated earlier. The main difference is
that you call the *Add* method on the *Fields* collection of a site instead of the *Fields* collection
of a list.

Remember that you should generally create site columns in a top-level site so they are available for use throughout the current site collection. The following code demonstrates how to
create a new site column named EmployeeStatus to provide a *Choice* field that can be reused
across multiple lists in the current site collection.

```
SPWeb site = SPContext.Current.Site.RootWeb;
site.Fields.Add("EmployeeStatus", SPFieldType.Choice, true);
SPFieldChoice fld =
  (SPFieldChoice)site.Fields.GetFieldByInternalName("EmployeeStatus");

// update site column display name
fld.Title = "Employee Status";
fld.Group = " Wingtip Site Columns";

// add choices
fld.Choices.Add("Full Time");
fld.Choices.Add("Part Time");

// configure rendering format
fld.EditFormat = SPChoiceFormatType.RadioButtons;

// save changes
fld.Update();
```

Now let's put this new site column to use. The code shown in Listing 7-1 demonstrates creating a new list to track employees. The code begins by creating a custom list and modifying the display name of the *Title* field to *Last Name*. The code then adds fields to track information about each employee. The majority of the fields added to the list are based on standard site columns provided by SharePoint Foundation. However, there is also a field that is added based on the custom site column named EmployeeStatus. You should observe that the site columns are retrieved using the *AvailableFields* collection instead of the *Fields* collection so that this code can be executed successfully in a child site.

LISTING 7-1 Adding fields to a list using site columns

```
Guid ListId = site.Lists.Add("Employees", "", SPListTemplateType.GenericList);
SPList list = site.Lists[ListId];
list.OnQuickLaunch = true;
list.Update();

// modify display name of title field
SPField fld = list.Fields["Title"];
fld.Title = "Last Name";
fld.Update();

// add fields using site columns available in current site
SPFieldCollection fields = site.AvailableFields;
list.Fields.Add(fields.GetFieldByInternalName("FirstName"));
list.Fields.Add(fields.GetFieldByInternalName("EmployeeStatus"));
list.Fields.Add(fields.GetFieldByInternalName("WorkPhone"));
list.Fields.Add(fields.GetFieldByInternalName("HomePhone"));
list.Fields.Add(fields.GetFieldByInternalName("CellPhone"));
```

```
list.Fields.Add(fields.GetFieldByInternalName("EMail"));
list.Fields.Add(fields.GetFieldByInternalName("HomeAddressStreet"));
list.Fields.Add(fields.GetFieldByInternalName("HomeAddressCity"));
list.Fields.Add(fields.GetFieldByInternalName("HomeAddressStateOrProvince"));
list.Fields.Add(fields.GetFieldByInternalName("HomeAddressPostalCode"));
list.Fields.Add(fields.GetFieldByInternalName("StartDate"));
list.Fields.Add(fields.GetFieldByInternalName("SpouseName"));
list.Fields.Add(fields.GetFieldByInternalName("Birthday"));

// add selected fields to default view
SPView view = list.DefaultView;
view.InlineEdit = "TRUE";
view.ViewFields.Add("FirstName");
view.ViewFields.Add("WorkPhone");
view.ViewFields.Add("HomePhone");
view.ViewFields.Add("CellPhone");
view.ViewFields.Add("EMail");
view.Update();
```

A significant benefit to using site columns is that they can be used to update multiple lists at once. Imagine a scenario where you have created 10 different lists within a site collection that contains fields based on the site column named EmployeeStatus. What would you need to do if you wanted to add a new choice value to the EmployeeStatus site column and make it available for use in any of those lists?

For example, let's say that you want to create a new choice value of *Intern* in addition to the two existing choices of *Full Time* and *Part Time*. This is easy because you can simply add the new choice value to the site column and then call the *Update* method with a value of *true* to push your changes to all the lists within the current site collection that contain fields based on the site column.

```
SPWeb site = SPContext.Current.Site.RootWeb;
SPFieldChoice fld =
        (SPFieldChoice)site.Fields.GetFieldByInternalName("EmployeeStatus");

// add new choice value to site column
fld.Choices.Add("Intern");

// update site column and push changes to lists that use it
fld.Update(true);
```

We need to emphasize that it's essential to pass a parameter value of *true* when calling the *Update* method. This is required to push the changes to the site column out to lists that use it. If you call *Update* without passing any parameters, you will update the site column, but no lists will be affected.

Content Types

SharePoint Foundation supports a flexible and powerful mechanism for designing lists known as a *content type*. A content type is an entity that uses site columns to define a schema of fields for an item in a list or a document in a document library. It's important to understand that content types, like site columns, are defined independently outside the scope of any list or document library. A content type defines a field collection that is reusable across multiple lists or multiple document libraries. Furthermore, content types can be updated to make sweeping changes to many lists at once, such as a scenario where you need to add a new field to accommodate changing business requirements.

Every site within a site collection contains its own *content types gallery*. The content types gallery for a site can be viewed and administered through an application page named mngctype.aspx, which is accessible through the *Site content types* link in the Galleries section of the Site Settings page.

Content type visibility behaves just as it does for site columns. When you add a content type to the content types gallery of a specific site, that content type is available for use within the current site, as well as in all the child sites in the site hierarchy below. When you add a content type to the content types gallery of a top-level site, it is available for use throughout the entire site collection. Therefore, you generally should create custom content types in the content types gallery of top-level sites so that they are made available on a site collection–wide basis.

SharePoint Foundation automatically adds a standard set of content types to the content types gallery of every top-level site using a hidden feature named *ctypes*. Table 7-4 shows a partial listing of the standard content types that SharePoint Foundation makes available within every site. This table lists each content type with its ID and name along with the name of its parent content type.

TABLE 7-4 A Partial Listing of the Standard SharePoint Foundation Content Types

ID	Name	Parent
0x01	Item	System
0x0101	Document	Item
0x0102	Event	Item
0x0104	Announcement	Item
0x0105	Link	Item
0x0106	Contact	Item
0x0108	Task	Item

ID	Name	Parent
0x0120	Folder	Item
0x010101	Form	Document
0x010102	Picture	Document
0x010105	Master Page	Document
0x010108	Wiki Page	Document
0x010109	Basic Page	Document
0x012002	Discussion	Folder
0x012004	Summary Task	Folder

Content types are defined based upon the principles of inheritance. Every content type that you can create or use inherits from another content type. SharePoint Foundation provides a special built-in content type named *Item,* which sits at the top of the inheritance hierarchy. Every other content type inherits, either directly or indirectly, from the *Item* content type. Figure 7-2 shows how the standard content types provided by SharePoint Foundation fit into this hierarchy.

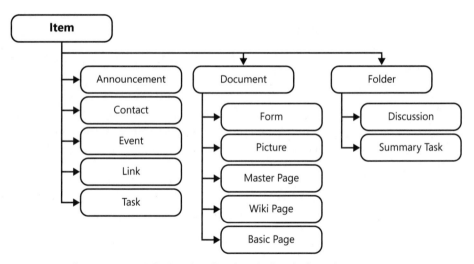

FIGURE 7-2 All content types inherit, either directly or indirectly, from the *Item* content type.

Note There is actually another content type named *System*, which exists at the very top of the inheritance hierarchy above Item. However, as a developer, you will never deal directly with the *System* content type or program against it. Figure 7-2 has omitted the *System* content type to focus on content types that you can work with directly.

Now let's take a moment to discuss the format of a content type ID. Each content type has a string-based ID that begins with the ID of its parent content type. The *Item* content type has an ID based on the hexadecimal number *0x01*. Because every content type inherits from *Item*, that means that all content type IDs begin with *0x01*. For example, the *Document* content type, which inherits from *Item*, has an ID of *0x0101*. Content types that inherit from *Document* have IDs that begin with *0x0101*, such as *Form*, which has an ID of *0x010101*, and *Picture*, which has an ID of *0x010102*.

If you create a new content type through the browser or are using code with the server-side object model, SharePoint Foundation will create a new content type ID for you. SharePoint Foundation creates a content type ID by parsing together the base content type ID, followed by *00* and a new GUID. For example, if you create a new content type that inherits from *Document*, SharePoint Foundation will create a content type ID that looks like this.

```
0x010100F51AEB6BBC8EA2469E1617071D9FF658
```

The inheritance-based architecture of content types yields quite a bit of power. For example, consider what happens if you add a new site column to the *Document* content type in the content types gallery of a top-level site. You would effectively be adding the site column to all the content types that inherit from *Document*, which provides a simple and effective way to add a new field to every document library in a site collection.

Content types go beyond defining a set of fields. A content type can also define behaviors with event handlers and workflow associations. For example, consider what would happen if you register an event handler on the *Document* content type in the content types gallery of a top-level site. You would effectively be registering the event handler on every document in the site collection, including those documents based on derived content types such as *Form*, *Picture*, *Master Page*, *Wiki Page*, and *Basic Page*.

Programming with Content Types

The *SPWeb* class provides a *ContentTypes* collection that makes it possible to enumerate through the content types in the content types gallery of the current site.

```
SPWeb site = SPContext.Current.Web;
foreach (SPContentType ctype in site.ContentTypes) {
  // enumerate content types for current site
}
```

You can also use a second *SPWeb* collection property named *AvailableContentTypes*, which allows you to enumerate the aggregation of content types in the content types gallery of the current site and all parent sites.

```
SPWeb site = SPContext.Current.Web;
foreach (SPContentType ctype in site.AvailableContentTypes) {
  // enumerate content types for current site and parent sites
}
```

These two collections for content types behave just like the two collections for site columns discussed earlier. For example, consider the following two lines of code.

```
SPContentType ctype1 = site.ContentTypes["Item"];
SPContentType ctype2 = site.AvailableContentTypes["Item"];
```

When would you want to access a content type through the *ContentTypes* collection rather than the *AvailableContentTypes* collection? The first observation is that the line of code that accesses the *Item* content type through the *ContentTypes* collection will fail if it is ever executed within the context of a child site. Therefore, accessing content types with the *AvailableContentTypes* collection is more flexible if you need to write code that might execute in the context of a child site.

However, another important point is that a content type that has been retrieved through the *AvailableContentTypes* collection is read-only and cannot be modified. Therefore, you must retrieve a content type using the *ContentTypes* collection inside the context of the site where it exists if you need to modify it. Remember that all the standard SharePoint Foundation content types are added to the content types gallery of each top-level site.

```
SPWeb site = SPContext.Current.Site.RootWeb;
SPContentType ctype = site.ContentTypes["Item"];
```

While each content type defines a collection of site columns, it doesn't just track a collection of site columns using *SPField* objects. Instead, it tracks each site column using an SP*FieldLink* object.

```
SPContentType ctypeContact = site.ContentTypes["Contact"];
foreach (SPFieldLink fieldLink in ctypeContact.FieldLinks) {
  // enumerate through each site column
}
```

You can think of an *SPFieldLink* object as a layer on top of an *SPField* object that the content type can use to customize default property values of the underlying site column. Let's look at a scenario in which you might want to modify the standard content type named *Contacts*. The *Contacts* content type contains the standard site column named *FirstName*. However, the *FirstName* site column is not defined as a required field. The following code uses an *SPFieldLink* object to modify the *FirstName* site column to be a required field and then pushes this modification to all the lists in the current site collection that contain the *FirstName* field by calling the *Update* method and passing a parameter value of *true*.

```
SPWeb site = SPContext.Current.Site.RootWeb;
SPContentType ctypeContact = site.ContentTypes["Contact"];
SPFieldLink fldLinkFirstNamex = ctypeContact.FieldLinks["FirstName"];
fldLinkFirstNamex.Required = true;
ctypeContact.Update(true);
```

You have seen how to update an existing site column within a content type and push the change out to existing lists. Now let's move on to a different scenario, in which a content type is used to add a new field to existing lists. Imagine a scenario at Wingtip Toys where a site collection contains confidential information about product design. Let's say that you have been asked by management to add a new field to every list and document library to track whether each item and document is confidential or not. The following code creates a new site column in the top-level site, adds the new site column to the *Item* content type, and then pushes the change to every list and document library.

```
SPWeb site = SPContext.Current.Site.RootWeb;
site.Fields.Add("WingtipConfidential", SPFieldType.Boolean, true);
SPFieldBoolean fld =
  (SPFieldBoolean)site.Fields.GetFieldByInternalName("WingtipConfidential");
fld.Title = "Wingtip Confidential";
fld.Update();

SPContentType ctypeItem = site.ContentTypes["Item"];
ctypeItem.FieldLinks.Add(new SPFieldLink(fld));
ctypeItem.Update(true, false);
```

Note that the call to *Update* on the *Item* content type passes a second parameter with a value of *false*. This second parameter requires some explanation. There are some content types in the standard set of content types added by SharePoint Foundation that are defined as read-only content types. If you do not pass a value of *false* for the second parameter, the call to *Update* fails when it attempts to modify one of these read-only content types. When you pass a value of *false*, the call to *Update* succeeds because it ignores any failures due to the inability to update read-only content types.

Creating Custom Content Types

You will never create a content type from scratch. Instead, you always select an existing content type to serve as the base content type for the new content types you are creating. For example, you can create the most straightforward content type by inheriting from the content type named *Item*. This automatically provides your new content type with the standard fields and behavior that are common across all content types. Alternatively, you can elect to inherit from another content type that inherits from the *Item* content type, such as *Announcement*, *Contact*, *Task*, or *Document*.

You can create a new content type manually using the browser or with code using the server-side object model. To create a new content type with code, you must call the *SPContentType* class constructor passing three parameters. The first parameter is the *SPContentType* object associated with the parent content type you want to inherit from. The second parameter is the target content types collection, which should typically be the *ContentTypes* collection of a top-level site. The third parameter is the string name of the content type to be created.

```
SPWeb site = SPContext.Current.Site.RootWeb;
string ctypeName = "Wingtip Person";
SPContentType ctypeParent = site.ContentTypes["Item"];
SPContentType ctype = new SPContentType(ctypeParent, site.ContentTypes, ctypeName);
```

Once you have created an *SPContentType* object and initialized its properties, such as *Description* and *Group*, you must call the *Add* method on the *ContentTypes* property of the target site to actually save your work in the content database. Here's all the code required to create a new content type named *Wingtip Person* that inherits from the *Item* content type.

```
SPWeb site = SPContext.Current.Site.RootWeb;
string ctypeName = "Wingtip Person";
SPContentType ctypeParent = site.ContentTypes["Item"];
SPContentType ctype = new SPContentType(ctypeParent, site.ContentTypes, ctypeName);
ctype.Description = "Basic tracking information for a person";
ctype.Group = "Wingtip Content Types";
site.ContentTypes.Add(ctype);
```

Once you have created the content type such as *Wingtip Person*, you can then modify field links inherited from the parent content type. For example, you can modify the display name for the field link associated with the *Title* field.

```
// change display name of Title field
SPFieldLink fldLinkTitle = ctype.FieldLinks["Title"];
fldLinkTitle.DisplayName = "Last Name";
```

You can then add whatever field links you like using existing site columns. Each field link should be created by calling the *Add* method of the *FieldLinks* collection and passing a new *SPFieldLink* object that has been initialized using an existing site column.

```
ctype.FieldLinks.Add(
  new SPFieldLink(site.Fields.GetFieldByInternalName("FirstName")));
ctype.FieldLinks.Add(
    new SPFieldLink(site.Fields.GetFieldByInternalName("EMail")));
ctype.FieldLinks.Add(
  new SPFieldLink(site.Fields.GetFieldByInternalName("HomePhone")));
ctype.FieldLinks.Add(
  new SPFieldLink(site.Fields.GetFieldByInternalName("CellPhone")));
ctype.FieldLinks.Add(
  new SPFieldLink(site.Fields.GetFieldByInternalName("WorkPhone")));
// save changes
ctype.Update();
```

Note that you have the option of removing field links from a new content type as well as adding them. For example, you can create a content type that inherits from *Contact* and then remove the site columns that you don't want. Once you modified the field links collection of a content type, you must save your changes to the content database by calling the *Update* method.

You have just seen the code required to create a new content type named *Wingtip Person*. Now we are going to put this content type to use by creating a new list and configuring the list to use our new content type. This technique requires you to modify an *SPList* property named *ContentTypesEnabled* and set its value to *true*. After you have modified the *ContentTypesEnabled* property, you can then add one or more content types to the list using the *Add* method of the content types collection.

```
SPWeb site = SPContext.Current.Web;
Guid ListId = site.Lists.Add("Employees", "", SPListTemplateType.GenericList);
list = site.Lists[ListId];
list.OnQuickLaunch = true;
list.ContentTypesEnabled = true;
SPField fldTitle = list.Fields["Title"];
fldTitle.Title = "Last Name";
fldTitle.Update();

// reference Wingtip Person content type
SPContentType WingtipPerson = site.AvailableContentTypes["Wingtip Person"];
list.ContentTypes.Add(WingtipPerson);

// delete Item content type
list.ContentTypes["Item"].Delete();
```

You should understand that lists created using one of the standard list template types will already have a content type in their *ContentTypes* collection. For example, the *ContentTypes* collection of a *Contacts* list will initially contain the *Contacts* content type. The *ContentTypes* collection of a *Tasks* list will initially contain the *Task* content type. The *ContentTypes* collection of a *Custom* list will initially contain the *Item* content type. The final line of code in the previous example deletes the *Item* content type so that the *ContentTypes* collection of the newly created list contains a single content type named *Wingtip Person*.

While this example involved a list with a single content type, you should understand that SharePoint Foundation makes it possible to configure a list with multiple content types. The design implication here is that content types make it possible to maintain heterogeneous content inside a single list or document library.

Imagine a business scenario in which you need to track customers, and those customers may be either companies or individuals. The problem you face is that customers that are companies and customers who are individuals require different fields to track their information. The solution is to create two different content types for each type of customer and then to create a *Customers* list and configure it to support both content types.

Working with Document Libraries

In terms of general SharePoint Foundation architecture, a document library is really just a specialized type of list. The main difference between a document library and other types of lists is that a document library is designed to store documents instead of merely list items. Every item in a document library is based on a file stored inside the content database. You can add extra fields to a document library just as you can to a standard list. This is a common practice because the fields in a document library allow you to track document metadata that is stored outside the document file.

Document libraries have an underlying base type of *1*, which defines several document-related fields. For example, SharePoint Foundation tracks the name of each file in a document library using a field named *FileLeafRef* that has a display name of *Name*. There is a second field named *FileRef*, with a display name of *URL Path*, which contains the file name combined with its site-relative path. There is another field named *FileDirRef* with a display name of *Path*, which contains the site-relative path without the file name.

The ECB menu works differently in document libraries than in standard lists. More specifically, SharePoint Foundation populates the ECB menu for a document using the file name instead of the *Title* field. SharePoint Foundation uses a related field named *LinkFilename*, which reads the file name from the *FileLeafRef* field and uses it to render the ECB menu. There is a third related field named *LinkFilenameNoMenu*, which can be used to display the file name in a hyperlink that can be used to navigate to the *View Properties* page associated with a document.

You can program against a document library using the *SPList* class just as you would with any other type of list. For example, each document library is represented within the *Lists* collection of the containing site with an *SPList* object.

The server-side object model provides the *SPDocumentLibrary* class that inherits from *SPList*. *SPDocumentLibrary* extends *SPList* with additional functionality that is specific to document libraries. Once you obtain an *SPList* reference to a document library from the *Lists* collection of a site, you can convert the *SPList* reference to an *SPDocumentLibrary* reference to access the extra methods and properties that are only available with document libraries.

```
SPDocumentLibrary DocLib = (SPDocumentLibrary)site.Lists["Product Proposals"];
```

Throughout this section, we are going to step through the process of creating a document library and configuring it with a custom document template. This chapter is accompanied by a sample SharePoint project named *WingtipDocuments*, which contains working samples of the techniques that we are going to show. Note that running and testing this sample project requires that you first install the Open XML SDK 2.0 for Microsoft Office, which is available as a free download from *http://www.microsoft.com/downloads/en/details .aspx?FamilyID=c6e744e5-36e9-45f5-8d8c-331df206e0d0&DisplayLang=en*.

Creating a Document Library

You can create a document library from within a SharePoint project by creating a *ListInstance* element with a *TemplateType* value of *101* and the GUID that identifies the *DocumentLibrary* feature provided by SharePoint Foundation.

```
<ListInstance
  TemplateType="101"
  FeatureId="00bfea71-e717-4e80-aa17-d0c71b360101"
  Url="ProductProposals"
  Title="Product Proposals"
  Description=""
  OnQuickLaunch="TRUE" />
```

Earlier in this chapter, in the section entitled "Creating Lists," we explained that it is a standard convention to create a list with a base URL that is relative to the Lists folder, such as Lists/Customers. However, the base URL for a document library should be created relative to the root of the site instead of inside the Lists folder. Therefore, the *ListInstance* element to create a document library should have a URL that looks like *ProductProposal* instead of *Lists/ProductProposal*.

If you prefer to create document libraries using the server-side object model, you can call the *Add* method on the *Lists* collection of a site just as you do when creating a standard list. The only difference is that you pass a list template parameter with an *SPListTemplateType* enumeration value of *DocumentLibrary*.

```
site.Lists.Add("ProductSpecifications", "", SPListTemplateType.DocumentLibrary);
```

When you create a document library using the *Add* method, SharePoint Foundation creates the document library at a URL relative to the root of the site. It does not create document libraries inside the Lists folder, as it does with standard lists. Once the *Add* method completes its work and returns, you can retrieve the document library's *SPList* reference from the *Lists* collection and cast it to an *SPDocumentLibrary* reference. Here's the code required to create a new document library and configure it to force document checkout and to enable both major and minor versioning.

```
Guid DocLibID =
  site.Lists.Add("ProductSpecifications", "", SPListTemplateType.DocumentLibrary);

// configure properties of document library
SPDocumentLibrary DocLib = (SPDocumentLibrary)site.Lists[DocLibID];
DocLib.Title = "Product Specifications";
DocLib.ForceCheckout = true;
DocLib.EnableVersioning = true;
DocLib.MajorVersionLimit = 3;
DocLib.EnableMinorVersions = true;
DocLib.MajorWithMinorVersionsLimit = 5;
DocLib.OnQuickLaunch = true;
DocLib.Update();
```

Adding a Custom Document Template

One unique characteristic of document libraries is that they provide support for *document templates*. A user can create a new document from a document template by using the New Document menu on the Documents tab of a document library, as shown in Figure 7-3. For example, you can create a document template using Microsoft Word that allows users to create documents that already contain the company letterhead; or you can create a document template using Microsoft Excel that allows users to create documents for expense reports that have a structure predefined by the accounting department.

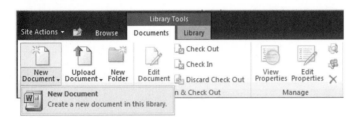

FIGURE 7-3 Users create documents from document templates using the New Document menu.

The *WingtipDocument* project demonstrates creating document libraries that are configured with custom document templates that have been created for specific business scenarios. For example, the Product Proposals document library is configured with a document template named Proposal.dotx, which has been designed to create new document proposals. The document library named Product Specifications is configured with a document template named Specification.dotx, which has been designed to create production specification documents.

A document library is initially configured with a generic document template. However, what should you do if you want the document library to use a custom document template? The approach we have used with the Product Proposals document library is to upload the custom document template file using a *Module* element. Note that SharePoint Foundation creates a special folder named Forms inside the root folder of each document library. The Forms folder is the proper location to upload the document template for a document library.

Note that the SharePoint Developer Tools are not capable of generating the correct XML inside the elements.xml file of a Module project item to upload a document template. After creating the Module project item, you should add the document template file and then edit the elements.xml file manually so that it looks like this.

```
<Module Name="ProductProposalTemplates" Url="ProductProposals" List="101" >

  <File Path="ProductProposalTemplates\Proposal.dotx"
        Url="Forms/Proposal.dotx"
        Type="GhostableInLibrary" />

</Module>
```

Note that the *Url* attribute for the *Module* element has been modified with the site-relative URL of the document library, which in this case is *ProductProposals*. This is required, so the files inside this *Module* element are provisioned relative to the root of the document library instead of the root of the site. You should also notice that *Module* element include a *List* attribute with a value of *101,* which is required to indicate that the target location exists inside the scope of a document library.

In addition to modifying the *Module* element, you must also edit the *Url* attribute and the *Type* attribute of the inner *File* element manually. You must configure the *File* element's *Url* attribute with a path to provision the document template file in the Forms folder. You must also modify the *File* element to include a *Type* attribute configured with a value of *GhostableInLibrary.*

Now that you have seen how to upload the document template file using a *Module* element, there is still one remaining step. You must supply code to configure the *DocumentTemplateUrl* property of the document library. You can accomplish this by adding the following code into a feature receiver.

```
// assume feature is scoped at the site level (Scope=Web)
public override void FeatureActivated(SPFeatureReceiverProperties properties) {
  SPWeb site = (SPWeb)properties.Feature.Parent;
  SPDocumentLibrary libProposals;
  libProposals = (SPDocumentLibrary)site.Lists["Product Proposals"];
  string templateUrl = @"ProductProposals/Forms/Proposal.dotx";
  libProposals.DocumentTemplateUrl = templateUrl;
  libProposals.Update();
}
```

We have walked through the technique for configuring the document template for a list that you have created declaratively using a *ListInstance* element. Now we will demonstrate a second approach to upload the document template for a document library using code. Once you have created a document library by calling the *Add* method on a *Lists* collection of a site, you can access the Forms folder of the document library using an *SPFolder* object.

```
// create document library
Guid DocLibID =
  site.Lists.Add("ProductSpecifications", "", SPListTemplateType.DocumentLibrary);

// access the Forms folder of new document library
SPDocumentLibrary DocLib = (SPDocumentLibrary)site.Lists[DocLibID];
SPFolder formsFolder = DocLib.RootFolder.SubFolders["Forms"];
```

The *SPFolder* object provides a *Files* collection property with an *Add* method, which makes it possible to upload a copy of the document template file. When you call the *Add* method on a *Files* collection object to create a new file such as a document template, you can pass the contents of the file using either a byte array or an object based on the *Stream* class of the *System.IO* namespace.

There is a convenient trick that we discussed in Chapter 6, "Controls and Web Parts," that we will now revisit. The problem that we need to solve is to load the contents for a document template into a byte array. You can do this by adding the document template file into a SharePoint project as a source file and configuring it as an *Embedded Resource*. Next, you can configure the document template file as a project resource by adding it to the *Files* collection on the Resources tab of the Project Properties dialog. This technique makes it possible to load the contents of a document template file into a byte array using a single line of code.

```
byte[] docTemplateContent = Properties.Resources.Specification_dotx;
```

Once you have figured out how to load the contents for a document template file into a byte array, it is then fairly easy to create a new document library and configure it with a custom document template in just a few lines of code.

```
// create document library
Guid DocLibID =
   site.Lists.Add("ProductSpecifications", "", SPListTemplateType.DocumentLibrary);

// upload and configure document template
SPDocumentLibrary DocLib = (SPDocumentLibrary)site.Lists[DocLibID];
SPFolder formsFolder = DocLib.RootFolder.SubFolders["Forms"];
formsFolder.Files.Add("Specification.dotx", Properties.Resources.Specification_dotx;);
DocLib.DocumentTemplateUrl = @"ProductSpecifications/Forms/Specification.dotx";
DocLib.Update();
```

Creating Document-Based Content Types

You can create custom content types for tracking documents. This design approach provides the same type of advantages as creating content types for standard lists. For example, you can create a content type that defines a custom set of site columns for tracking document metadata and then reuse that content type across many document libraries. If you design document libraries using custom content types, you also have the ability to add new columns to a content type and push the changes to many document libraries at once.

One unique aspect of content types that inherit from the *Document* content type is that they add support for document templates. For example, you can create a new content type that inherits from the *Document* content type and configure it with a custom document template. Imagine that you have a scenario in which you want to create a custom content type named *Wingtip Document* so you can configure it with a custom document template named WingtipStandard.dotx that contains the Wingtip company letterhead. You can begin by creating a new content type that inherits from the *Document* content type.

```
string ctypeName = "Wingtip Document";
SPContentType ctypeParent = site.ContentTypes["Document"];
SPContentType ctype = new SPContentType(ctypeParent, site.ContentTypes, ctypeName);
ctype.Description = "Content type using standard Wingtip document template";
ctype.Group = "Wingtip Content Types";
ctype = site.ContentTypes.Add(ctype);
```

After you have created the *Wingtip Document* content type, your next step is to upload a copy of the document template file. However, the tricky part is knowing where to upload this file. SharePoint Foundation creates a dedicated folder for each content type in the virtual file system of the hosting site within a special folder named _cts. When you create a new content type named *Wingtip Document,* SharePoint Foundation automatically creates a new folder for it at _cts/Wingtip Document. This is the location where you should upload the document template. After you have uploaded a copy of the document template file, you can then configure the content type to use it by modifying its *DocumentTemplate* property.

```
SPFolder ctypeFolder = site.GetFolder("_cts/Wingtip Document");
byte[] docTemplateContent = Properties.Resources.WingtipStandard_dotx;
ctypeFolder.Files.Add("WingtipStandard.dotx", docTemplateContent);
ctype.DocumentTemplate = "WingtipStandard.dotx";
ctype.Update();
```

Once you have created the *Wingtip Document* content type and configured it to use WingtipStandard.dotx as its document template, you can begin to create document libraries that use it. Here is a simple example of creating a new document library and configuring it to use the *Wingtip Document* content type.

```
Guid DocLibId = site.Lists.Add("WingtipDocuments", "", SPListTemplateType.DocumentLibrary);
SPDocumentLibrary DocLib = (SPDocumentLibrary)site.Lists[DocLibId];
DocLib.Title = "Wingtip Documents";
DocLib.ContentTypesEnabled = true;
DocLib.OnQuickLaunch = true;
DocLib.Update();

// add Wingtip Document content type
DocLib.ContentTypes.Add(site.AvailableContentTypes["Wingtip Document"]);

// delete generic Document content type
DocLib.ContentTypes["Document"].Delete();
```

This example demonstrates configuring a document library with a single content type. For certain scenarios, it often makes sense to configure a document library to support multiple content types. When a document library has more than one content type with a custom document template, the document template for each of these content types is made available through the New Document menu on the Documents tab.

Programming with Documents

There is a dual aspect to programming documents in a document library. While you can program against a document library using an *SPList* object, you can also program against a document using an *SPListItem* object. However, each document is also represented in the server-side object with an *SPFile* object. That means you can program against a document in a document library as either an *SPListItem* or *SPFile* object. The following code demonstrates how to enumerate through a document library using an *SPListItem* object to obtain the *SPFile* object for each document.

```
void ProcessDocuments(SPDocumentLibrary docLib) {
  foreach (SPListItem item in docLib.Items) {
    SPFile file = item.File;
    // program against document as either SPListItem object or SPFile object
  }
}
```

The *SPListItem* object can be used to read or update fields just as you would read or update fields for an item in a standard list. The *SPFile* object, on the other hand, can be used to control other aspects of the document, such as controlling versioning, check-in, and checkout, as well as reading from and writing to the document's content.

```
SPFile file = item.File;

// check on number of versions
int versionCount = file.Versions.Count;

// determine when document was checked out
DateTime checkedOutDate = file.CheckedOutDate;

// open document for stream-based access
using(Stream fileContents = file.OpenBinaryStream()) {
  // program against stream to access document content
}
```

One thing to watch out for is the scenario in which a document library contains folders in addition to documents. Note that folders, like files, are stored as items within a document library and show up as *SPListItem* objects in the *Items* collection. You can inspect an *SPListItem* property named *FileSystemObjectType* before attempting to process an item as an *SPFile* object.

```
foreach (SPListItem item in docLib.Items) {
  if (item.FileSystemObjectType == SPFileSystemObjectType.File) {
    // process item as document
    SPFile file = item.File;
  }
}
```

One last point to keep in mind is that discovering documents by enumerating through the *Items* collection of a document library finds all documents without regard to whether they exist in the root folder or in folders nested below the root folder. If you would rather enumerate through only the documents in the root folder of a document library, you can use a different approach by using the *SPFolder* and *SPFile* classes.

```
void ProcessDocumentsAtRoot(SPDocumentLibrary docLib) {
  foreach (SPFile file in docLib.RootFolder.Files) {
    // program against file using SPFile class
  }
}
```

Creating Documents with Code

We will now conclude this section by discussing how to use code to generate new documents in a document library using code. This approach can provide the basis for many different types of business solutions because you can provide significant value to users by automating the tedious details for constructing business documents from scratch.

The WingtipDocuments project has an application page named CreateNewDocument.aspx, which has been designed to assist users to create new documents. The basic user interface of this page is shown in Figure 7-4. Note that the WingtipDocuments project adds a custom menu item to the Site Actions menu that allows the user to navigate to CreateNewDocument .aspx.

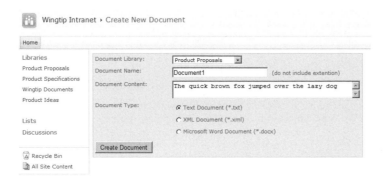

FIGURE 7-4 The sample project WingtipDocuments demonstrates techniques for creating documents using code.

The application page named CreateNewDocument.aspx relies on code inside a utility class named *DocumentFactory.cs*. You can examine this class to see what code is required to generate a new document and add it to a document library. Let's look at three examples, in which we demonstrate how to create a text file, an XML document, and a Word document.

Let's begin by examining the code to create a simple text file. Once you have obtained an *SPDocumentLibrary* reference to a document library, you can access the *Files* collection of its *RootFolder* property. The *Files* collection provides an *Add* method that makes it possible to create a new document from the content in a byte array or any that inherits from the *Stream* class from the *System.IO* namespace.

One popular technique for generating the content for a new document is to use a *MemoryStream* object. A *MemoryStream* object serves as an in-memory buffer that you can use to build out the content for a document dynamically until you are ready to save it as a file. Note that this technique or any other one that uses any type of *Stream*-based object restricts you to farm solution deployment because the sandboxed solution architecture prevents you from using any of the classes in the *System.IO* namespace.

When you are generating simple text-based content, you can create a *StreamWriter* object that allows you to write into the buffer of the *MemoryStream* object using the *Write* method. After you have written your content, you should call the *Flush* method to prepare the *MemoryStream* for writing its contents into a new document. You actually create the document by calling the *Add* method on the *Files* collection and passing the name of the new document and the *MemoryStream* object with the document's contents. You can also pass a third Boolean parameter that indicates whether the call should overwrite an existing file with the same name.

```
SPWeb site = SPContext.Current.Web;
SPDocumentLibrary library = (SPDocumentLibrary)site.Lists["Product Proposals"];

// write text-based content into memory stream
MemoryStream DocumentStream = new MemoryStream();
StreamWriter writer = new StreamWriter(DocumentStream);
writer.Write("Hello");
writer.Write(" World");
writer.Close();

// create new document using text content in memory stream
library.RootFolder.Files.Add("Document1.txt", DocumentStream, true);

// dispose memory stream object to release memory
DocumentStream.Dispose();
```

Now that you have seen how to create a text document, it's not much harder to create an XML document because you can use the same technique of adding the XML content to a *MemoryStream* object. In our example, we will create the contents for an XML document using the *XmlTextWriter* class and the *XDocument* class provided by the Microsoft .NET Framework version 3.5.

```
SPWeb site = SPContext.Current.Web;
SPDocumentLibrary library = (SPDocumentLibrary)site.Lists["Product Proposals"];
MemoryStream DocumentStream = new MemoryStream();
XmlTextWriter writer = new XmlTextWriter(DocumentStream, Encoding.UTF8);
writer.Formatting = Formatting.Indented;
writer.Indentation = 2;

// create XML document
var xml =
  new XDocument(
    new XDeclaration("1.0", "utf-8", "yes"),
    new XElement("WingtipDocument",
      new XElement("DocumentContents", "Hello World")));

// write XML content into memory stream
xml.WriteTo(writer);
writer.Close();

// create new document using XML content in memory stream
library.RootFolder.Files.Add("Document2.xml", DocumentStream, true);

// dispose memory stream object to release memory
DocumentStream.Dispose();
```

As you can see, creating an XML document using the *XDocument* class provides an elegant and readable approach for structuring the XML elements inside. You create each XML element using an *XElement* object. Both the *XDocument* class and the *XElement* class provide constructors that allow you to nest child *XElement* objects. The code that you have just seen will generate a new XML document that looks like this.

```
<?xml version="1.0" encoding="utf-8" standalone="yes"?>
<WingtipDocument>
  <DocumentContents>Hello World</DocumentContents>
</WingtipDocument>
```

Now that you have seen instances of creating text documents and XML documents, we will conclude by showing one more example that dynamically creates a new Word document. Note that this code relies on an assembly named *DocumentFormat.OpenXml* that is not installed by default on a Web server running SharePoint 2010, nor is it installed by Visual Studio 2010. You can install this assembly into the global assembly cache (GAC) of your developer workstation by installing the Open XML SDK 2.0 for Office.

Note that the Open XML SDK 2.0 is installed using an MSI file named OpenXMLSDKv2.msi, which is less than 4 megabytes (MB) in size. Earlier in this chapter, in the section entitled "Working with Document Libraries," we showed you the URL for the Open XML SDK 2.0 download page. You must install this SDK on your development workstation to open and test the sample SharePoint project for this chapter named WingtipDocuments.

If you decide to use the Open XML SDK 2.0 for Office in a production scenario, you will also need to ensure that the *DocumentFormat.OpenXml* assembly is installed on the production Web servers. However, this requirement should not pose much of a problem because the SharePoint Developer Tools make it possible to configure a SharePoint solution to deploy the *DocumentFormat.OpenXml* assembly into the GAC of each Web server. In other words, you can deploy this assembly along with any SharePoint solution that depends on it.

Our intention here is not to teach you the fundamentals of creating documents with the Open XML SDK 2.0. There is no way we could do that adequately in a single chapter. Our goal here is to show you how little code is involved to get started creating Office documents from code inside a SharePoint solution. For example, you can create a new Word document in a *MemoryStream* object and save it to a document library with very few lines of code.

```
SPWeb site = SPContext.Current.Web;
SPDocumentLibrary library = (SPDocumentLibrary)site.Lists["Product Proposals"];
MemoryStream DocumentStream = new MemoryStream();

// create new Word document and add content
WordprocessingDocument wordDocument =
  WordprocessingDocument.Create(DocumentStream, WordprocessingDocumentType.Document);
MainDocumentPart mainPart = wordDocument.AddMainDocumentPart();
mainPart.Document = new Document();
Body body = mainPart.Document.AppendChild(new Body());
Paragraph para = body.AppendChild(new Paragraph());
Run run = para.AppendChild(new Run());
run.AppendChild(new Text(contents));
wordDocument.Close();

// add new file to document library
library.RootFolder.Files.Add("Document3.docx", DocumentStream, true);
```

We hope this little teaser motivates you to learn more about using the Open XML SDK to create new documents for Microsoft Word, Microsoft Excel, and Microsoft PowerPoint. We highly recommend the Open XML developer site at *http://openxmldeveloper.org*, a Microsoft-sponsored community site that has great samples and helpful tutorials to get you started. With a little effort on your part, you will soon be creating Word documents, Excel spreadsheets, and PowerPoint slideshows that will really impress your users. We will revisit this topic and discuss the Open XML SDK in a little more depth in Chapter 9.

Creating and Registering Event Handlers

SharePoint Foundation supports *server-side events* on host objects such as sites, lists, and content types. This support is valuable to developers because it makes it possible to write *event handlers,* which are methods that are executed automatically in response to *event actions* such as creating a new list, updating an item in a list, and deleting a document.

Events can be separated into two main categories: *before events* and *after events*. *Before events* fire before the corresponding event action occurs and before SharePoint Foundation has written any data to the content database. A key point is that a before event is fired early enough that it supports the cancellation of the event action that triggers it. Therefore, before events provide a great opportunity to perform custom validations.

After events fire after the event action has completed and after SharePoint Foundation has written to the content database to commit the event action. After events do not support cancelling the event action. Instead, after events are used to execute code in response to an event action. A common example is sending out email notifications to let all the members of a site know when a new document has been uploaded.

SharePoint Foundation uses a special naming convention for event handlers. Before events are based on overridable methods whose names end with *-ing*. For example, before events have names such as *WebAdding, WebDeleting, ItemAdding,* and *ItemUpdating*. The methods for after events have names that end with *–ed,* such as *WebProvisioned, WebDeleted, ItemAdded,* and *ItemUpdated*.

Each event handler is executed under a specific *synchronization mode*. The two supported synchronization modes are *synchronous* and *asynchronous*. Before events are always executed under a synchronization mode of synchronous. A key point is that synchronous event handlers have a blocking nature because they run on the same thread that is processing the event action.

By default, SharePoint Foundation executes after events under a synchronization mode of asynchronous. The main difference is that asynchronous event handlers execute on a separate thread so they do not block the response that is sent back to the user. Imagine a scenario where a user uploads a new document and an after event responds by sending out a series of email notifications to more than 100 users. The asynchronous nature of an after event doesn't require the user who has uploaded the document to wait while the code in the event handler is sending out email messages. The response page is returned to the user while the after event continues to execute.

While SharePoint Foundation executes after events asynchronously by default, you have the option of configuring an after event to run as a synchronous event. This new support was introduced in SharePoint 2010, and it makes it possible to execute an after event on the same thread that is processing the response page sent back to the user. Configuring an after event to run asynchronously can be a useful technique in a scenario where code executed by the after event makes an update to an item that must be seen immediately. We will see an example of such a scenario later in this chapter, in the section entitled "Programming After Events."

Event Receiver Classes

Event handling in SharePoint Foundation is based on *event receiver classes*. You create a new event receiver class by inheriting from one of the following event receiver base classes that are defined inside the *Microsoft.SharePoint* assembly:

- *SPItemEventReceiver*
- *SPListEventReceiver*
- *SPEmailEventReceiver*
- *SPWebEventReceiver*
- *SPWorkflowEventReceiver*

The *SPItemEventReceiver* class provides event handling support for when users add, modify, or delete items in a list or documents in a document library. The *SPListEventReceiver* class provides event handling support for when users create and delete lists, as well as when users modify a list's fields collection. The *SPEmailEventReceiver* class provides event handling support for when users send email messages to an email–enabled list.

The *SPWebEventReceiver* class provides event handling support for when users create new child sites within a site collection. The *SPWebEventReceiver* class also provides event handling support for when users move or delete sites including both child sites and top-level sites. The *SPWorkflowEventReceiver* class is new in SharePoint 2010 and it provides event handling support for when users start a workflow instance as well as event handling support to signal when a workflow instance has completed or has been postponed.

Once you have created a class that inherits from one of the event receiver base classes, you implement the event receiver class by overriding methods that represent event handlers. For example, imagine you want to create an event handler for an after event that executes each time a user creates a new list. You can starting by creating a new event receiver that inherits from the *SPListEventReceiver* and override the event handler method named *ListAdded*. Here is an example of creating a custom receiver class named *ListEvents*.

```
namespace WingtipEvents.ListEvents {
  public class ListEvents : SPListEventReceiver {
    public override void ListAdded(SPListEventProperties properties) {
      // your event handler code goes here
    }
  }
}
```

There are now two remaining steps. First you must bind the event handler to a host object using event registration. Second, you must write the code to implement the event handler. We will now cover these two topics in order.

Registering Event Handlers

Once you create an event receiver class, you must bind one or more of its event handler methods to a host object using *event registration*. The types of objects that support event registration include site collections, sites, lists, content types, and documents. Note that only certain types of event handlers are supported by each type of host object. For example, you can register a *ListAdded* event handler with a site collection or a site, but that event type is not supported by host objects such as lists, content types, or documents. Likewise, you can register an *ItemUpdating* event handler with a list, content type, or document, but that event type is not supported by site collections or sites.

The simplest and most common technique for registering an event handler is to use a feature with a declarative *Receivers* element. Here is a simple example of an element manifest that contains a *Receivers* element created to register the event handler named *ListAdded* shown in the previous code listing.

```
<Elements xmlns="http://schemas.microsoft.com/sharepoint/">
  <Receivers>
    <Receiver>
      <Name>Receiver1</Name>
      <Type>ListAdded</Type>
      <Assembly>$SharePoint.Project.AssemblyFullName$</Assembly>
      <Class>WingtipDocuments.ListEvents.ListEvents</Class>
    </Receiver>
  </Receivers>
</Elements>
```

The SharePoint Developer Tools assist you in creating event receiver classes and registering their event handlers using declarative XML. When you are working on a SharePoint project and you add a new SharePoint project item based on the Event Receiver template, the SharePoint Developer Tools automatically create a new source file containing an event receiver class in either C# or Visual Basic. Creating an *Event Receiver* project item also generates an elements.xml file that contains a *Receivers* element designed to register one or more of your event handlers for you.

In some scenarios, the SharePoint Developer Tools are capable of making all the required changes to the *Receivers* element for you behind the scenes. In other scenarios, you will be required to make manual edits to the elements.xml file to configure the *Receivers* element with a specialized type of event registration. There are also scenarios in which you cannot achieve the event registration you need in a declarative fashion using a *Receivers* element. In these cases, you must resort to registering an event handler using the server-side object model.

Creating an Event Receiver Project Item

Let's begin using the easiest approach, in which you let the SharePoint Developer Tools do all the work to create the event receiver class and to register its event handlers. Imagine that you want to create event handlers for before events to validate items in lists created from the *Contacts* list template. You can begin by creating a new SharePoint project item using the Event Receiver project item template. When you create a new *Event Receiver* project item, the SharePoint Developer Tools prompts you with the SharePoint Customization Wizard dialog shown in Figure 7-5.

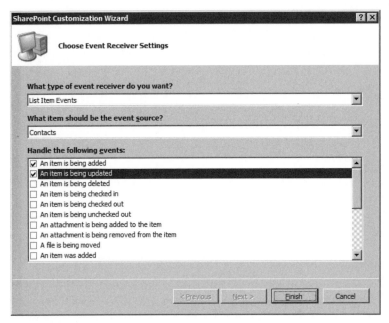

FIGURE 7-5 When creating an *Event Receiver* project item, the SharePoint Customization Wizard prompts you for the type of event receiver and type of events.

When you create a new *Event Receiver* project item, you will be prompted with a dialog that allows you to select the type of event receiver class, as well as which events you would like to handle. In our situation, we will select an event receiver type of *List Item Events,* which will result in creating an event receiver class that inherits from *SPItemEventReceiver*. We will also select an event source of *Contacts* to indicate that we would like to register our event handlers with all lists created using the *Contacts* list template. In the list box in this scenario, we can select the events that we would like to handle. We will select the event *An item is being added,* which will create and register the *ItemAdding* event handler. We will also select the event *An item is being updated,* which will create and register the *ItemUpdating* event handler.

When you click the *Finish* button in the SharePoint Customization Wizard, the SharePoint Developer Tools creates a new SharePoint project item that contains a C# or Visual Basic source file containing an event receiver class with the event handler methods *ItemAdding* and *ItemUpdating*. The SharePoint Developer Tools also create an elements.xml file that contains the following *Receivers* element.

```
<Receivers ListTemplateId="105">

  <Receiver>
    <Name>CustomersEventsItemAdding</Name>
    <Type>ItemAdding</Type>
    <Assembly>$SharePoint.Project.AssemblyFullName$</Assembly>
    <Class>WingtipEvents.CustomersEvents.CustomersEvents</Class>
    <SequenceNumber>10000</SequenceNumber>
  </Receiver>

  <Receiver>
    <Name>CustomersEventsItemUpdating</Name>
    <Type>ItemUpdating</Type>
    <Assembly>$SharePoint.Project.AssemblyFullName$</Assembly>
    <Class>WingtipEvents.CustomersEvents.CustomersEvents</Class>
    <SequenceNumber>10000</SequenceNumber>
  </Receiver>

</Receivers>
```

Let's take a moment and review the contents of this *Receivers* element. It contains a single attribute named *ListTemplateId,* which is used to indicate the target list type. The value of *105* indicates that we want to register each event handler defined inside the *Receivers* element for all *Contacts* lists.

You should observe that there is a separate *Receiver* element to register each event handler. There is no supported technique to register multiple event handlers at once with a single *Receiver* element. You can also see that each of the *Receiver* elements generated by the SharePoint Developer Tools has several inner elements.

A *Receiver* element has four required inner elements: *Name, Type, Assembly,* and *Class.* The *Name* element is used to assign a unique name to the event handler. The *Type* element is used to specify the type of event handler that is being registered. The *Assembly* element must contain the complete four-part assembly name (but fortunately the SharePoint Developer Tools ease this requirement, allowing you to use the dynamic token for this value, which is *$SharePoint.Project.AssemblyFullName$*). The *Class* element must contain the namespace-qualified class name of the event receiver class.

The SharePoint Developer Tools add an optional element named *SequenceNumber.* This element is useful when there are multiple event handlers that have been registered for the same event type on the same host object. The event handler that has been registered with the lowest sequence number is guaranteed to execute before event handlers with higher sequence numbers. Therefore, the *SequenceNumber* element makes it possible to control the order in which event handlers execute.

Now consider a scenario in which you have already created an *Event Receivers* project item and then you decide you want to add another event handler. This situation is made very simple to handle by the SharePoint Developer Tools. Each *Event Receiver* project item has an associated property sheet, as shown in Figure 7-6. All you need to do is find the correspond-ing property for the desired event handler and set its property value to *true*. For example, if you set the property named *Handle ItemDeleting* to *true,* the SharePoint Developer Tools automatically update the elements.xml file with the required *Receiver* element and add the appropriate event handler method to the event receiver class as well.

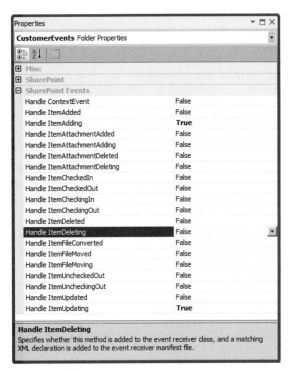

FIGURE 7-6 Each *Event Receiver* project item has a property sheet that makes it easy to add new event handlers.

The *Event Receiver* project item does a great job of creating and updating the *Receivers* ele-ment inside the elements.xml file. However, there are several scenarios in which it is useful to make edits to the *Receivers* element manually. Let's start by revisiting the top-level *Receivers* element that was created by the SharePoint Developer Tools.

```
<Receivers ListTemplateId="105">
```

A *ListTemplateId* attribute setting of *105* registers the event handlers for every *Contacts* list in the activation scope of the hosting feature. In other words, if the *Event Receiver* project item has been added to a feature with an activation scope of *Site*, the event handlers are registered for every *Contacts* list in the current site collection. However, if the *Event Receiver* project item has been added to a feature with an activation scope of *Web*, the event handlers are registered only for *Contacts* lists in the current site.

Now consider a scenario where you need to register the event handlers of an *Event Receiver* project item on a single list instead of every list created from a specific template type. To achieve this type of event registration, you must modify the *Receivers* element manually by removing the *ListTemplateId* attribute and adding the *ListUrl* attribute. Fortunately, Visual Studio 2010 provides you with IntelliSense when you edit the elements.xml file. Here is an example of a *Receivers* element that uses the *ListUrl* attribute to register its event handlers on a single list.

```
<Receivers ListUrl="Lists/Customers" >
```

In addition to situations where you will be editing the attributes of a *Receivers* element manually, there are also scenarios where you need to edit the contents of the inner *Receiver* elements. For example, a *Receiver* element supports adding an inner *Data* element, which enables you to pass parameterized string data to an event handler. This makes it possible to register the same event handler on different host objects while providing each registration with unique parameters. For example, imagine that you have added a *Data* element to a *Receiver* element that registers an event handler for the *ItemAdding* event.

```
<Receivers ListUrl="Lists/Customers" >
  <Receiver>
    <Type>ItemAdding</Type>
    <Data>MySpecialData</Data>
    <!-- other elements omitted for clarity -->
  </Receiver>
</Receivers>
```

When implementing the event handler, you can access the value of the *Data* element using the *ReceiverData* property of the *SPItemEventProperties* parameter named *properties*.

```
public override void ItemAdding(SPItemEventProperties properties) {
  // retreive data from ReceiverData property
  string data = properties.ReceiverData;
}
```

Programmatic Event Registration

While registering event handlers declaratively using a *Receivers* element works in the majority of scenarios, there are a few cases where it doesn't suffice. For example, you cannot register an event handler on a host object such as a content type or an individual document using a declarative *Receivers* element. These types of event registration must be accomplished using code and the server-side object model.

Before we discuss registering event handlers programmatically, we must point out the caveats. First, code that registers event handlers cannot be used in sandbox solutions. This technique works only in farm solutions. Furthermore, a programmatic approach to registering event handlers usually requires additional logic to unregister event handlers and to ensure that the same event handler is never registered twice. The point to take away is that writing the code to manage event registration can be tricky, and it is easy to introduce subtle bugs. Therefore, we recommend that you use a declarative approach whenever you can and resort to registering event handlers with code only for scenarios where a declarative approach is not supported.

Now that we have discussed the caveats, let's move on to the code. Imagine a scenario where you want to create an event handler that will fire whenever any new content is added to a site collection. You can achieve the desired effect by creating an *ItemAdded* event handler and registering it on the *Item* content type inside the content types gallery of a top-level site. Once again, we are using a programmatic approach in this scenario only because there is no declarative approach that allows us to achieve the same outcome.

Host object types that support events such as *SPContentType* expose a collection property named *EventReceivers*. The *EventReceivers* collection property exposes an *Add* method that has three different overloaded implementations. The simplest implementation of the *Add* method accepts three parameters: the event type, the four-part assembly name, and the namespace-qualified name of the event receiver class. Here's an example of implementing the *FeatureActivated* method for a site collection scoped feature that registers an event handler on the *Item* content type using an event receiver class named *ItemContentTypeEvents*.

```
public override void FeatureActivated(SPFeatureReceiverProperties properties) {
  SPSite siteCollection = (SPSite)properties.Feature.Parent;
  SPWeb site = siteCollection.RootWeb;

  // retreive content type
  SPContentType ctypeItem = site.ContentTypes["Item"];

  // register event handler for content type
  string ReceiverAssemblyName = this.GetType().Assembly.FullName;
  string ReceiverClassName = typeof(ItemContentTypeEvents).FullName;
  ctypeItem.EventReceivers.Add(SPEventReceiverType.ItemDeleting,
                    ReceiverAssemblyName,
                    ReceiverClassName);

  // push updates to all lists and document libraries
  ctypeItem.Update(true, false);
}
```

While calling the *Add* method with these three parameters provides the easiest approach for registering an event handler, it provides the least flexibility. For example, you cannot assign registration properties for receiver data or synchronization. To obtain more control, you can register the event handler by calling another implementation of the *Add* method, which takes no parameters and returns an *SPEventReceiverDefinition* object.

```
SPContentType ctypeItem = site.ContentTypes["Item"];
string ReceiverAssemblyName = this.GetType().Assembly.FullName;
string ReceiverClassName = typeof(ItemContentTypeEvents).FullName;

// register event handler by creating SPEventReceiverDefinition object
SPEventReceiverDefinition def = ctypeItem.EventReceivers.Add();
def.Type = SPEventReceiverType.ItemDeleting;
def.Assembly = ReceiverAssemblyName;
def.Class = ReceiverClassName;
def.SequenceNumber = 100;
def.Data = "MyData";
def.Update();

// push updates to all lists and document libraries
ctypeItem.Update(true, false);
```

You have now seen the code to register an event handler upon feature activation. However, another important consideration is that you should also supply the code to unregister the event handler during feature deactivation. An effective technique to accomplish this type of registration management involves calling the third implementation of the *Add* method, which accepts a GUID parameter to register an event handler with a unique identifier.

```
Guid defID = new Guid("DEADBEEF-BADD-BADD-BADD-BADBADBAD2B8");
SPEventReceiverDefinition def = ctypeItem.EventReceivers.Add(defID);
```

When you have assigned a GUID to an event handler during registration, it makes it easy to unregister using the same GUID.

```
Guid defID = new Guid("DEADBEEF-BADD-BADD-BADD-BADBADBAD2B8");
ctypeItem.EventReceivers[defID].Delete();
```

Another thing you have to watch out for is registering the same event handler twice by mistake. If you register the same event handler twice, SharePoint Foundation will execute it twice whenever the event occurs. When you register an event handler using an identifying GUID, you can use the *EventReceiverDefinitionExist* method of the *EventReceivers* property collection to ensure the event handler in question has not yet been registered.

```
Guid defID = new Guid("DEADBEEF-BADD-BADD-BADD-BADBADBAD2B8");
// check to see if event handler is already registered
if (!ctypeItem.EventReceivers.EventReceiverDefinitionExist(defID)) {
  // register event handler since it has not already been registered
}
```

Now that we have examined the essential details of registering events programmatically, let's now examine the feature receiver shown in Listing 7-2. You can see that there is complementary code in the *FeatureActivated* method and the *FeatureDeactivating* method to register an event handler upon feature activation and to deactivate it on feature deactivation.

LISTING 7-2 Event handlers, registered and unregistered using an identifying GUID

```
public class MainSiteEventReceiver : SPFeatureReceiver {

  // define GUID to identify eventh handler
  Guid defID = new Guid("DEADBEEF-BADD-BADD-BADD-BADBADBAD2B8");

  public override void FeatureActivated(SPFeatureReceiverProperties properties) {
    SPSite siteCollection = (SPSite)properties.Feature.Parent;
    SPWeb site = siteCollection.RootWeb;
    SPContentType ctypeItem = site.ContentTypes["Item"];
    string ReceiverAssemblyName = this.GetType().Assembly.FullName;
    string ReceiverClassName = typeof(ItemContentTypeEvents).FullName;
    if (!ctypeItem.EventReceivers.EventReceiverDefinitionExist(defID)) {
      SPEventReceiverDefinition def = ctypeItem.EventReceivers.Add(defID);
      def.Type = SPEventReceiverType.ItemDeleting;
      def.Assembly = ReceiverAssemblyName;
      def.Class = ReceiverClassName;
      def.Update();
      ctypeItem.Update(true, false);
    }
  }

  public override void FeatureDeactivating(SPFeatureReceiverProperties properties) {
    SPSite siteCollection = (SPSite)properties.Feature.Parent;
    SPWeb site = siteCollection.RootWeb;
    SPContentType ctypeItem = site.ContentTypes["Item"];
    // unregister event handler using unique GUID identifier
    if (ctypeItem.EventReceivers.EventReceiverDefinitionExist(defID)) {
      ctypeItem.EventReceivers[defID].Delete();
      ctypeItem.Update(true, false);
    }
  }
}
```

Programming Before Events

When you write the event handler implementation for a before event, you have the ability to cancel the user action that triggered the event. You can accomplish this by assigning a value of *true* to the *Cancel* property of the event handler parameter named *properties*.

```
public override void ListDeleting(SPListEventProperties properties) {
  properties.Cancel = true;
}
```

When canceling the event action, you can also use the *ErrorMessage* property to assign a custom error message that will be displayed to the user. For example, here is a simple event handler that prevents any user who is not a site collection owner from deleting a list.

```
public override void ListDeleting(SPListEventProperties properties) {
  if(!properties.Web.UserIsSiteAdmin){
    properties.Cancel = true;
    properties.ErrorMessage = "Only site collection owners can delete lists";
  }
}
```

When you assign a value of *true* to the *Cancel* property in a before event, SharePoint Foundation responds by short-circuiting the user's request and canceling the event action. The key point here is that before events provide you with a layer of defense against unwanted modifications. Instead of deleting the list as the user requested, SharePoint Foundation displays the custom error message in an error dialog to the user, as shown in Figure 7-7.

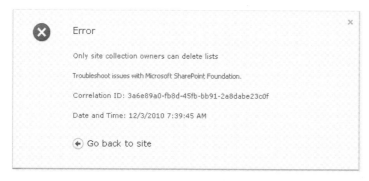

FIGURE 7-7 SharePoint Foundation displays a standard error dialog to the user when you cancel an event action.

There is a common problem that occurs on a development workstation when testing before events. If the web.config file for the hosting Web application is configured for developer debug mode, you will not see the user-friendly dialog shown in Figure 7-7. Instead, you will see a page that reports a low-level run-time exception. To simulate what the user will really experience when your event handler cancels an event action in a production environment, you must ensure that the web.config file is not configured for debug mode. In particular, you should make sure the *CallStack* attribute of the *SafeMode* element inside the *SharePoint* section has a value of *false* and that the *mode* attribute of the *customErrors* section in the *system.web* section has a value of *On*.

```
<configuration>
  <SharePoint>
    <SafeMode CallStack="false" >
  </SharePoint>
  <system.web>
    <customErrors mode="On" />
  </system.web>
<configuration>
```

In some scenarios, you might decide that the standard error dialog displayed by SharePoint Foundation upon the cancellation of an event action is not sufficient. If you want to create a user experience that is different from what is shown in Figure 7-7, you can modify two properties of the *SPListEventProperties* parameter, *SPEventReceiverStatus* and *RedirectUrl,* to redirect the user to a custom error page.

```
public override void ListDeleting(SPListEventProperties properties) {
  if (!properties.Web.UserIsSiteAdmin) {
    properties.Cancel = true;
    properties.Status = SPEventReceiverStatus.CancelWithRedirectUrl;
    properties.RedirectUrl = properties.Web.Site.Url +
                        "/WingtipErrorPages/ListDeleting.aspx";
  }
}
```

While it is easy to redirect the user to a custom error page, you should realize that this approach requires you to build a custom user experience from the ground up. This is something that can be done using either an application page or a site page. However, such a design typically involves adding query string parameters to the *RedirectUrl* property to pass contextual information the custom error page. This is the most straightforward way to provide information about the list and item where the cancellation took place so that a custom error page can provide the user with error messages and links back to various locations within the site. The point to take away is that custom error pages require extra work and should be used only when they are really needed.

Validating Field Values

Now that you have seen the basics of cancelling an event action, let's discuss creating event handlers for before events that perform custom validations. For example, you can validate that the ship date for an invoice is not a Saturday or Sunday, or that a phone number or email address meets a pattern defined by a regular expression.

One of the most powerful aspects of writing validation logic in the event handler for a before event is that you can perform a validation that spans columns. Let's use the *Customers* list that we created in the section entitled "Creating Lists," earlier in this chapter, using the standard *Contacts* list template. A *Contacts* list contains a field for a work phone number and another field for a home phone number. We can write event handlers for the *Customers* list to perform validation on each *Customer* item to require that either the work phone or the home phone field has a non-blank value. The basic idea here is that customer items are not valid unless they provide at least one working phone number.

Consider that there are two ways for users to modify a list item: They can add a new item, or they can update an existing item. When writing validation logic, you must typically add redundant code behind the *ItemAdding* method and the *ItemUpdating* method.

```
public class CustomerEvents : SPItemEventReceiver {
  public override void ItemAdding(SPItemEventProperties properties) {
    // add validation logic for users adding new customers
  }
  public override void ItemUpdating(SPItemEventProperties properties) {
    // add validation logic for users updating existing customers
  }
}
```

Because *ItemAdding* and *ItemUpdating* require the same logic, it's best to maintain the validation logic in a separate method that can be called from each of these two event handlers. The *CustomerIsValid* method accepts two string parameters named *WorkPhone* and *HomePhone* and returns *true* if either of these parameters is not blank. It also uses a protected field to track an error message that is accessible to either event handler.

```
public class CustomerEvents : SPItemEventReceiver {

  protected string ValidationErrorMessage;

  protected bool CustomerIsValid(string WorkPhone, string HomePhone) {
    if((string.IsNullOrEmpty(WorkPhone)) &&
       (string.IsNullOrEmpty(HomePhone))) {
      ValidationErrorMessage = "Valid customer must have either work phone or home phone.";
      return false;
    }
    else {
      return true;
    }
  }

  public override void ItemAdding(SPItemEventProperties properties) {
    // call to CustomerIsValid to validate customer fields
  }
  public override void ItemUpdating(SPItemEventProperties properties) {
    // call to CustomerIsValid to validate customer fields
  }
}
```

The *CustomerIsValid* method provides us with a single place to maintain validation logic. While this example is relatively simple, this type of design will make it much easier to maintain your validation logic as the code for determining what constitutes a valid customer grows over time.

Now let's turn our attention to writing the code in the event handlers to call *CustomerIsValid*. When you write the code in an event handler such as *ItemAdding* or *ItemUpdating*, you cannot access a field value through an *SPListItem* event. This is because a before event executes before anything has been written into the content database. To inspect a field value in a before event, you must access it using the *AfterProperties* collection property exposed by the *SPItemEventProperties* parameter.

```
public override void ItemAdding(SPItemEventProperties properties) {
  string WorkPhone = properties.AfterProperties["WorkPhone"].ToString();
}
```

The *AfterProperties* collection property contains the pending field values that will be written to the content database if the event action is not cancelled. Here is a complete example of inspecting the values of the *WorkPhone* field and the *HomePhone* field and using these values to call the *CustomerIsValid* method to determine whether to cancel the event action.

```
public override void ItemAdding(SPItemEventProperties properties) {
  string WorkPhone = properties.AfterProperties["WorkPhone"].ToString();
  string HomePhone = properties.AfterProperties["HomePhone"].ToString();
  if (!CustomerIsValid(WorkPhone, HomePhone)) {
    properties.Cancel = true;
    properties.ErrorMessage = this.ValidationErrorMessage;
  }
}

public override void ItemUpdating(SPItemEventProperties properties) {
  string WorkPhone = properties.AfterProperties["WorkPhone"].ToString();
  string HomePhone = properties.AfterProperties["HomePhone"].ToString();
  if (!CustomerIsValid(WorkPhone, HomePhone)) {
    properties.Cancel = true;
    properties.ErrorMessage = this.ValidationErrorMessage;
  }
}
```

Note that the *SPItemEventProperties* parameter exposes another collection property named *BeforeProperties*. While *AfterProperties* contains field values that reflect the user's pending changes, *BeforeProperties* contains the original field values that reflect an existing item before it was modified. This makes it possible to validate a field value using the before and after values, such as when you want to prohibit a field with a numeric value from increasing by more than 50 percent. Note that the field values in *BeforeProperties* are based on an existing item in the content database. Therefore, field values in *BeforeProperties* are valid in *ItemUpdating*, but not in *ItemAdding*.

Programming After Events

You must remember that after events are inherently different than before events. That's because after events execute after the event action has completed. After events do not provide the developer with an opportunity to cancel an event action. Instead, after events provide the opportunity to execute code in response to an event action, such as a user successfully creating a new list.

Let's start with an example of writing an event handler implementation for an after event named *ListAdded*. Imagine a scenario in which users are allowed to create document libraries using the browser. However, you want to create an event handler so you can respond to the event action of creating a new document library so you can ensure that each document library is created with a specific set of property settings. The following implementation of *ListAdded* has been written to inspect the list type so that it can automate configuring each new document library with custom settings.

```
public override void ListAdded(SPListEventProperties properties) {
  // get reference to list
  SPList list = properties.List;
  // determine if list was created from document library template
  if (list.BaseTemplate == SPListTemplateType.DocumentLibrary) {
    // convert SPList reference to SPDocumentLibrary
    SPDocumentLibrary doclib = (SPDocumentLibrary)list;
    // configure document library with standard Wingtip settings
    doclib.ForceCheckout = true;
    doclib.EnableVersioning = true;
    doclib.MajorVersionLimit = 3;
    doclib.EnableMinorVersions = true;
    doclib.MajorWithMinorVersionsLimit = 5;
    doclib.Update();
  }
}
```

Now let's discuss writing the event handler for an after event so that it maintains data integrity. For example, imagine a scenario in which the *Title* field for a list is required to be maintained in all uppercase characters. We can use after events to ensure this requirement.

Because an after event such as *ItemAdded* executes after the item has been written to the content database, you can read and write field values using an *SPListItem* object. The *SPList* object for the underlying item is accessible through the *ListItem* property of the *properties* parameter.

```
public override void ItemAdded(SPItemEventProperties properties) {
  string Title = properties.ListItem["Title"].ToString();
}
```

In addition to reading a field value, you can modify it. Here is an example of an after event that reads the *Title* field value, converts it to uppercase, and then writes it back to the underlying item.

```
public override void ItemAdded(SPItemEventProperties properties) {

  // read field value
  string Title = properties.ListItem["Title"].ToString();

  // write field value
  properties.ListItem["Title"] = Title.ToUpper();
  properties.ListItem.UpdateOverwriteVersion();
}
```

Note that this implementation uses the *UpdateOverwriteVersion* method instead of the *Update* method. You should avoiding calling *Update* in an after event on a list where versioning is enabled because it will generate two versions each time a user adds or updates an item. The *UpdateOverwriteVersion* method is provided for this exact scenario because it updates the most current version instead of generating a new version.

A second issue that causes concern is that modifying an item in an after event can trigger another event. Consider the scenario where an after event updates an item, which triggers the after event, which updates the item that triggers the after event, and so on. If you are not careful, you can create a recursive loop that will run until an error occurs. Here is an example of a flawed implementation of *ItemUpdated* that will experience this problem.

```
public override void ItemUpdated(SPItemEventProperties properties) {
  properties.ListItem["Title"] = properties.ListItem["Title"].ToString();
  properties.ListItem.UpdateOverwriteVersion();
}
```

Whenever you are required to implement an after event in which you update the item that triggered the event, you must disable event firing by modifying the *EventFiringEnabled* property of the event receiver class.

```
public override void ItemUpdated(SPItemEventProperties properties) {
  this.EventFiringEnabled = false;
  properties.ListItem["Title"] = properties.ListItem["Title"].ToString();
  properties.ListItem.UpdateOverwriteVersion();
  this.EventFiringEnabled = true;
}
```

If you do not disable event firing in the *ItemAdded* event handler, it is not as critical because it will not cause a recursive loop. However, it is still recommended because you then avoid triggering an *Update* event and executing *ItemUpdated* unnecessarily when a user adds a new item.

```
public override void ItemAdded(SPItemEventProperties properties) {
  this.EventFiringEnabled = false;
  properties.ListItem["Title"] = properties.ListItem["Title"].ToString();
  properties.ListItem.UpdateOverwriteVersion();
  this.EventFiringEnabled = true;
}
```

At this point, we are almost done with our discussion. There is just one more issue to address, which centers around the fact that SharePoint Foundation executes the event handlers for after events such as *ItemAdded* and *ItemUpdated* using a default synchronization mode that is asynchronous. The situation we are dealing with here, in which an after event updates an item, is the classic scenario in which you want to configure these event handlers to execute synchronously.

The problem with after events that execute asynchronously revolves around the user seeing inconsistent field values. When a user updates a field value in the browser and saves the changes with a postback, any updates made by an event handler running asynchronously are not guaranteed to be reflected in the page that is sent back to the user. When you configure the event handler for an after event to run synchronously, you guarantee that the event handler's updates are reflected in the page returned to the user. To configure the event handler for an after event to run synchronously, you can add a *Synchronization* element with an inner value of *Synchronous* manually into the *Receiver* element.

```
<Receiver>
  <Name> ItemAddedUpperCaseHandler</Name>
  <Type>ItemAdded</Type>
  <Assembly>$SharePoint.Project.AssemblyFullName$</Assembly>
  <Class>WingtipEventReceivers.UpperCaseReceiver.UpperCaseReceiver</Class>
  <Synchronization>Synchronous</Synchronization>
</Receiver>
```

Conclusion

In this chapter, we covered the fundamental architecture of lists and document libraries. You learned about fields, field types, site columns, and content types, as well as how to create them in the scope of a site collection using the server-side object model. This will provide a good background for Chapter 8, in which we will create field types, site columns, and content types using XML definitions.

This chapter also explored working with documents and document libraries. It isn't overly complicated to develop features that create document libraries with custom document templates. It also examined techniques for generating documents with code and introduced the Open XML SDK, which provides a powerful dimension of productivity for scenarios where you need to read, update, and create documents for Office products such as Word, Excel, and PowerPoint.

The final part of the chapter examined taking advantage of the event infrastructure provided by SharePoint Foundation. You learned about the fundamentals of creating event receiver classes and registering event handlers. You also saw that the SharePoint Developer Tools do a great job of hiding the grungy details of creating and registering event handlers. However, there are still a few scenarios where the SharePoint Developer Tools cannot hide all the details of event registration. For these scenarios, you have learned how to modify declarative *Receiver* elements and to write code using the server-side object model manually to achieve the exact type of event registration that you need.

Chapter 8
Templates and Type Definitions

This chapter explores advanced techniques for developing and deploying custom templates and type definitions. We will begin by discussing how to develop custom field types. This development strategy offers the greatest level of control when initializing field values and performing data validation. You will also learn how to create a customized editing experience for a custom field type by extending it with a custom field control.

The second section of the chapter focuses on developing reusable type definitions for site columns, content types, and list templates using features and Collaborative Application Markup Language (CAML). While developing CAML-based definitions has a steep learning curve and poses more challenges with testing and debugging, it provides an alternative approach with certain advantages over creating site columns, content types, and lists using the server-side object model. Therefore, we also need to provide some motivation by discussing when the extra work required to develop CAML-based definitions is worth the effort.

The final part of the chapter focuses on site definitions and the process of creating new sites. You will learn about the underlying site provisioning architecture of Microsoft SharePoint Foundation in which every new site is created using a specific site definition. We will examine the standard site definitions included with SharePoint 2010 and explain the role of the Global site definition. We will also discuss the pros and cons of developing custom site definitions and provide alternative techniques for creating new sites, including feature stapling and developing a custom site provisioning provider.

Field Type Definitions

Chapter 7, "Lists and Events," introduced the fundamental concepts involved with fields, site columns, and field types. You learned that every field and every site column is created in terms of an underlying field type. You also learned about the built-in field types in SharePoint Foundation, which include *Text*, *Note*, *Boolean*, *Integer*, *Number*, *Decimal*, *Currency*, *DateTime*, *Choice*, and *Lookup*. Now it's time to discuss extending the set of built-in field types by developing *custom field types*. What's important to understand is that when you develop a custom field type, you are really developing a *field type definition*.

A primary motivation for creating custom field types is that it provides the greatest level when it comes to initializing and formatting field values. Custom field types are also commonly written to perform data validation on user input to prevent inconsistent field values from being written into the content database.

A second motivation for developing a custom field type is that it can be extended with an associated user interface component known as a *field control*. A custom field control complements a custom field type because it allows you to create a rich user interface with a Hypertext Transfer Markup Language (HTML) layout, ASP.NET server controls, and code-behind that can be as simple or as complicated as the scenario calls for.

Before we begin, we must point out a few caveats about developing custom field types. First, custom field types cannot be deployed in sandbox solutions. Instead, custom field types must be deployed using a farm solution. Second, custom field types work great through the browser, but they often cause integration problems with Microsoft Office products such as Microsoft Word or Microsoft Excel. Furthermore, you will find several other areas in which custom field types cause frustration, such as a scenario where a user is viewing list items through the *DataGrid* view or a developer is trying to program against a list using the LINQ to SharePoint provider.

There is one particular area in SharePoint 2010 development where custom field types are most popular. This involves a scenario when you are creating a custom SharePoint solution for *publishing sites* whose functionality is included as part of SharePoint Server 2010 Standard Edition. The high-level design of a publishing site is based on a scheme in which content authors submit page content through browser-based input forms. The power of developing a custom field type along with a custom field control makes it possible to provide content authors with a very rich editing experience in the browser.

Creating Custom Field Types

The developer tools in Microsoft Visual Studio 2010 do not provide a dedicated project item template for creating a custom field type. However, this doesn't pose much of a problem. When you need to develop a custom field type, you should start by creating a new SharePoint project based on the Empty SharePoint Project template. Inside this project, you will add a new public class for each custom field type. You will also add a special Extensible Markup Language (XML) definition file that is required to deploy the project's custom field types.

The downloadable .zip archive of companion code for this book contains a sample SharePoint project named WingtipFieldTypes. This project contains working samples of the custom field types and field controls that we are going to examine over the next few pages. You can see that the project structure of WingtipFieldTypes in Figure 8-1 contains the source files for four custom field types named *FieldEmployeStartDate*, *FieldSocialSecurityNumber*, *FieldUnitedStatesAddress*, and *FieldEmployeeStatus*.

FIGURE 8-1 The WingtipFieldTypes project demonstrates creating custom field types and custom field controls.

Creating the Class for a Custom Field Type

For each custom field type, you must create a *field type class* that inherits from one of the built-in field type classes, such as *SPFieldText*, *SPFieldNumber*, *SPFieldDateTime*, and *SPFieldMultiColumn*. The following code snippet shows how each of the custom field type classes in the WingtipFieldTypes project inherits from one of these required base classes.

```
public class EmployeeStartDate : SPFieldDateTime {
  // custom field type implementation
}
public class SocialSecurityNumber : SPFieldText {
  // custom field type implementation
}
public class UnitedStatesAddress : SPFieldMultiColumn {
  // custom field type implementation
}
public class EmployeeStatus : SPFieldText {
  // custom field type implementation
}
```

The first step in implementing a custom field type class is to add two public constructors that are required by SharePoint Foundation. SharePoint Foundation requires these two specially parameterized constructors because it uses them in various scenarios to create instances of your custom field type. When you add these constructors to your field type class, you don't need to supply any actual code inside the curly braces. You just need to define the required parameter list and pass these parameters on to the base class constructor with a matching parameter list.

```
public class EmployeeStartDate : SPFieldDateTime {

  public EmployeeStartDate(SPFieldCollection fields, string fieldName)
         : base(fields, fieldName) { }

  public EmployeeStartDate(SPFieldCollection fields, string typeName, string displayName)
         : base(fields, typeName, displayName) { }

}
```

Once you have added these two public constructors, the next step is to override whatever base class methods and properties make sense for your particular scenario. We will begin by examining the sample field type class named *EmployeeStartDate,* which has overridden the base members named *OnAdded, DefaultValue,* and *GetValidatedString.*

```
public class FieldEmployeeStartDate : SPFieldDateTime {
  // constructors omitted for brevity

  // configure new fields to display date but not time
  public override void OnAdded(SPAddFieldOptions op) {}

  // add logic to create default date as first Monday
  public override string DefaultValue {  get {}  }

  // add validation to ensure start date is a Monday
  public override string GetValidatedString(object value) {}
}
```

Let's first look at the implementation of *OnAdded.* This method acts like an event handler for an after event, such as we discussed in Chapter 7. Whenever a new field is created using this custom field type, the *OnAdded* method will execute, giving us a chance to modify the field's property settings. The implementation of *OnAdded* in the *EmployeeStartDate* class updates the *DisplayFormat* property of each new field to display its date value without the time.

```
public override void OnAdded(SPAddFieldOptions op) {
  this.DisplayFormat = SPDateTimeFieldFormatType.DateOnly;
  this.Update();
}
```

At Wingtip Toys, the Human Resources department has established a policy that the start date for a new employee must always fall on a Monday due to payroll processing requirements. Therefore, the *EmployeeStartDate* class overrides the *get* method of the *DefaultValue* property to return the current date, if that is a Monday, or the first Monday after that.

```
public override string DefaultValue {
  get {
    DateTime startDate = DateTime.Today;
    // move forward to first Monday
    while (startDate.DayOfWeek != DayOfWeek.Monday) {
      startDate = startDate.AddDays(1);
    }
```

```
      return SPUtility.CreateISO8601DateTimeFromSystemDateTime(startDate);
  }
}
```

Note that the *DefaultValue* property is based on the *string* type, not the *DateTime* type. Therefore, its implementation must calculate the correct date for the next Monday and return this date as a string. Another observation is that SharePoint Foundation formats dates as strings using a special format known as ISO8601. There are helper methods provided by the *SPUtility* class to assist with converting dates between *System.DateTime* values and *System.String* values, and vice versa. This example demonstrates calling the *CreateISO8601DateTimeFromSystemDateTime* method supplied by *SPUtility*.

Validating User Input Values

The implementation of the *EmployeeStartDate* class also demonstrates performing a custom validation on a field value. Field value validation is implemented by overriding a method named *GetValidatedString,* which is always executed prior to SharePoint Foundation saving an item that contains a field based on the field type. The *GetValidatedString* method passes a parameter named *value* that you can use to inspect the field value that the user is attempting to save to the content database. If the custom validation logic inside *GetValidatedString* determines that user input for the field value is not valid, it should be written to throw an exception of type *SPFieldValidationException*. Here is the implementation of the *GetValidatedString* method in the *EmployeeStartDate* field type class, which validates that each field value is a Monday.

```
// add validation to ensure start date is a Monday
public override string GetValidatedString(object value) {
  DateTime input = System.Convert.ToDateTime(value);
  if (input.DayOfWeek != DayOfWeek.Monday) {
    throw new SPFieldValidationException("Employee start date must be a Monday");
  }
  return base.GetValidatedString(value);
}
```

Now let's discuss what happens when this validation code is executed. Imagine a scenario with a list named Wingtip Employees, which contains a field created from the *EmployeeStartDate* field type. What happens when a user attempts to save an employee item with a start date that is not a Monday? The *GetValidatedString* method executes and determines that the user input is invalid. At this point, the method throws an exception that cancels the user's request to save the current item and displays an error message to the user, as shown in Figure 8-2.

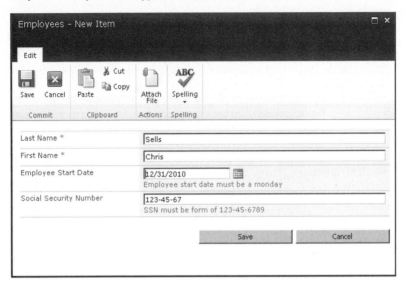

FIGURE 8-2 Throwing an SPFieldValidationException item cancels the action to update an item and displays an error.

As you can see, a custom field type provides an effective way to validate user input values. Now let's look at a second example of a custom field type that contains custom validation logic. The *GetValidatedString* method in the *SocialSecurityNumber* field type class uses the *Regex* class supplied by the Microsoft .NET Framework and a regular expression to determine whether the user input matches the correct pattern for a U.S. social security number.

```
public override string GetValidatedString(object value) {
  string UserInput = value.ToString();
  string SSN_RegularExpression = @"^\d{3}-\d{2}-\d{4}$";
  if ( (!string.IsNullOrEmpty(UserInput)) &
       (!Regex.IsMatch(UserInput, SSN_RegularExpression) ) {
    throw new SPFieldValidationException("SSN must be form of 123-45-6789");
  }
  return base.GetValidatedString(value);
}
```

Deploying a Custom Field Type

Now that we have created a custom field type class, the next step is to create an XML file containing a CAML-based definition for each custom field type that is required for deployment. When you create the XML file to deploy your custom field types, you must create it using a naming pattern where the file name starts with *fldtypes* and ends with an extension of *.xml*. For example, the WingtipFieldTypes project contains the file fldtypes_WingtipFieldTypes.xml. In addition to giving this XML file a special name, you must deploy it to a specific directory inside the SharePoint Root directory at the path of TEMPLATE/XML.

Let's quickly review how SharePoint Foundation initializes the available set of field types. When SharePoint Foundation initializes the worker process for an application pool, it queries the TEMPLATE/XML directory for files that match the pattern of fldtypes*.xml and scans through them to discover the field type definitions deployed within the local farm. From this, you can make two interesting observations about custom field type deployment. First, custom field types are not deployed using features. Second, custom field types are deployed as an all-or-nothing proposition at farm-level scope.

If you look at the TEMPLATE/XML directory on a Web server in a SharePoint 2010 farm, you will find a system file named fldtypes.xml that defines all the core field types supplied by SharePoint Foundation. The installation of SharePoint Server 2010 deploys several more of these XML files, including fldtypes_hold.xml, fldtypes_publishing.xml, fldtypes_SPRatings.xml, fldtypes_TargetTo.xml, and fldtypes_taxonomy.xml, to supply additional field type definitions of its own. When you are learning how to develop custom field types, it can be very helpful to inspect these XML files to see how the SharePoint Foundation team and the SharePoint Server 2010 team have structured the CAML definitions for the built-in field types.

Each field type definition is created using a *FieldType* element, which must reside inside a top-level *FieldTypes* element. The WingtipFieldType project deploys the definitions for all four custom field types in an XML file named fldtypes_WingtipFieldTypes.xml.

```
<FieldTypes>
  <FieldType> <!- EmployeeStartDate field type definition --> </FieldType>
  <FieldType> <!- SocialSecurityNumber field type definition --> </FieldType>
  <FieldType> <!- UnitedStatesAddress field type definition --> </FieldType>
  <FieldType> <!- EmployeeStatus field type definition --> </FieldType>
<FieldTypes>
```

When you create the *FieldType* element for a field type definition, you must add several *Field* elements with a *Name* attribute that defines the type of value inside. These *Field* elements are required to provide information about the custom field type, such as its name, its parent type, its display name, the field type class name, and the name of its assembly. The *FieldType* element for the custom field type named *EmployeeStartDate* is defined in the following code.

```
<FieldType>
  <Field Name="TypeName">EmployeeStartDate</Field>
  <Field Name="ParentType">DateTime</Field>
  <Field Name="TypeDisplayName">Employee Start Date</Field>
  <Field Name="TypeShortDescription">Employee Start Date</Field>
  <Field Name="UserCreatable">TRUE</Field>
  <Field Name="FieldTypeClass">
    WingtipFieldTypes.EmployeeStartDate,$SharePoint.Project.AssemblyFullName$
  </Field>
</FieldType>
```

Note that there are several more optional attributes that you can use when creating custom field type definitions. For example, you can add optional named attributes, such as *ShowInListCreate, ShowInDocumentLibraryCreate, ShowInSurveyCreate,* and *ShowInColumnTemplateCreate,* which allow you to configure a custom field type to be displayed or hidden on the Create Column page for scenarios where users are adding new fields to a list or content type.

```
<FieldType>
  <Field Name="TypeName">SocialSecurityNumber</Field>
  <Field Name="ParentType">Text</Field>
  <Field Name="TypeDisplayName">Social Security Number</Field>
  <Field Name="TypeShortDescription">Social Security Number (demo)</Field>
  <Field Name="UserCreatable">TRUE</Field>
  <Field Name="ShowInListCreate">TRUE</Field>
  <Field Name="ShowInDocumentLibraryCreate">TRUE</Field>
  <Field Name="ShowInSurveyCreate">TRUE</Field>
  <Field Name="ShowInColumnTemplateCreate">TRUE</Field>
  <Field Name="FieldTypeClass">
    WingtipFieldTypes.SocialSecurityNumber,$SharePoint.Project.AssemblyFullName$
  </Field>
</FieldType>
```

Creating a Custom Field Control

You have now seen the required steps to create and deploy a custom field type. Now we will examine how to extend a custom field type with a custom field control to provide the user with a customized editing experience.

Remember that the step for creating a custom field control is optional when creating a custom field type. The custom field type named *EmployeeStartDate* provides an example of a custom field type that does not have an associated field control. Instead, it relies on the editing experience provided by its parent, which is the field type named *Text*.

The primary motivation for extending a custom field type with a custom field control is to provide a custom editing experience. You create this editing experience using a *rendering template*. To create a rendering template, you must create a new user control and add a control tag based on a special control type named *RenderingTemplate*.

```
<SharePoint:RenderingTemplate>
  <Template>
    <!-- your HTML layout and server controls go here -->
  </Template>
</SharePoint:RenderingTemplate>
```

The WingtipFieldTypes project contains a custom field control that extends the custom field type named *SocialSecurityNumber*. The rendering template for this custom field control is defined inside the user control file named WingtipFieldTypes.SocialSecurityNumber.ascx. The rendering template definition has been created using a *RenderingTemplate* control with an ID of *SocialSecurityNumberRenderingTemplate*.

```
<SharePoint:RenderingTemplate ID="SocialSecurityNumberRenderingTemplate" runat="server">
  <Template>
    <asp:TextBox ID="txtUserInput" runat="server" MaxLength="11" CssClass="ms-long" />
  </Template>
</SharePoint:RenderingTemplate>
```

The *RenderingTemplate* control ID of *SocialSecurityNumberRenderingTemplate* is used to load and initialize the rendering template. You will see how that is accomplished in just a moment. Inside the *RenderingTemplate* control, there is an inner *Template* element. This is where you add the HTML layout and ASP.NET controls to produce a custom editing experience. You have the flexibility to create the *RenderingTemplate* control using a composite of ASP.NET controls and a rich HTML layout involving *div* elements or an HTML table. In this first example, we have kept things simple by defining the rendering template using a simple ASP.NET *TextBox* control:

```
<asp:TextBox ID="txtUserInput" runat="server" MaxLength="11" CssClass="ms-long" />
```

If you look back at the Visual Studio project structure in Figure 8-1, you can see that all three user control files have been deployed inside the SharePointRoot directory within the directory structure of TEMPLATE/CONTROLTEMPLATES. This is the directory in which you are required to deploy the .ascx file for a user control that contains a *RenderTemplate* control tag. Note that the rendering template will not load correctly if you deploy the user control file in a child directory such as TEMPLATE/CONTROLTEMPLATES/WingtipFieldTypes. This reason for this is that SharePoint Foundation inspects the CONTROLTEMPLATES directory for user control files that contain rendering templates, but it does not inspect any of its child directories.

As a general best practice when developing farm solutions, avoid deploying custom files from a SharePoint project directly inside one of the standard directories inside the SharePoint Root directory, such as IMAGES, LAYOUTS, or CONTROLTEMPLATES. The purpose of this practice is to avoid file name conflicts between the files that you deploy and the files that are already deployed by Microsoft and by other custom solutions. However, when developing custom field types, you cannot follow this practice because you must deploy the user control file directly inside the CONTROLTEMPLATES directory.

To increase your level of protection against file name conflicts, it is recommended that you add the solution name to the beginning of the file name to make it more unique. For example, the user control files with rendering templates in the WingtipFieldTypes project have names such as WingtipFieldTypes.SocialSecurityNumber.ascx instead of SocialSecurityNumber.ascx.

Once you have created the rendering template, the next step is to create a *field control class*. You create the field control class by inheriting from a base class named *BaseFieldControl* and overriding properties and methods such as *DefaultTemplateName*, *CreateChildControls,* and *Value*.

```
public class SocialSecurityNumberFieldControl : BaseFieldControl {

  // used to pass the RenderTemplate ID to SharePoint Foundation
  protected override string DefaultTemplateName {}

  // used to obtain references to controls created by the rendering template
  protected override void CreateChildControls() {}

  // used to read and write values to and from the content database
  public override object Value {}
}
```

When you override the read-only property named *DefaultTemplateName*, your implementation simply needs to return the string-based ID of the rendering template.

```
protected override string DefaultTemplateName {
  get { return "SocialSecurityNumberRenderingTemplate";  }
}
```

Once you have implemented the *DefaultTemplateName* property, the next thing to do is to set up a way to access programmatically controls defined in the rendering template. You can accomplish this by adding a protected field for each control and overriding *CreateChildControls* to initialize these fields properly. Here is an example of how this is done in the field control class named *SocialSecurityNumberFieldControl,* which has an associated rendering template that contains a single *TextBox* control named *txtUserInput*.

```
public class SocialSecurityNumberFieldControl : BaseFieldControl {

  protected TextBox txtUserInput;

  protected override void CreateChildControls() {
    base.CreateChildControls();
    txtUserInput = (TextBox)this.TemplateContainer.FindControl("txtUserInput");
  }
}
```

Note that you will not be instantiating control instances in the *CreateChildControls* method but rather going through a protected property of the base class named *TemplateContainer*, which exposes a *FindControl* method. This technique allows you to obtain references to existing control instances that are created by the control tags inside the rendering template.

Now it's time to add the logic to the field control class that is responsible for reading and writing the field's underlying value to and from the content database. You do this by overriding a property of the *BaseFieldControl* class named *Value*. The *Value* property is based on the type *System.Object*, which allows quite a bit of flexibility. You can work with any type of object you'd like as long as it supports .NET serialization. Fortunately, most of the standard types, arrays, and collections in the base class libraries of the .NET Framework provide automatic support for .NET serialization. The *SocialSecurityNumberFieldControl* class illustrates a fairly simple example of implementing the *Value* property.

```
public class SocialSecurityNumberFieldControl : BaseFieldControl {
  protected TextBox txtUserInput;

  public override object Value {
    get {
      this.EnsureChildControls();
      // return control Text property value which is written to content DB
      return txtUserInput.Text;
    }
    set {
      this.EnsureChildControls();
      // initilize control with current field value retrieved from content DB
      txtUserInput.Text = (string)this.ItemFieldValue;
    }
  }
}
```

As you can see, the *get* and *set* methods of the *Value* property both begin their implementation with a call to *EnsureChildControls*. The call to *EnsureChildControls* guarantees that the *CreateChildControls* method has already executed. This is done to ensure that the *txtUserInput* field contains a valid reference so that you can program against the control without a null reference exception.

You can see that the *get* method of the *Value* property simply returns the string value from the *TextBox* control. The SharePoint Foundation run time will call the *get* method when a user updates an item that contains a column based on this custom field type. SharePoint Foundation takes this return value and writes it directly to the content database.

SharePoint Foundation calls the *set* method when a user opens the item in edit view just before the controls created by your *RenderingTemplate* control are shown to the user. The key point to understand about implementing the *set* method is that the *ItemFieldValue* property provides you with access to the current field value in the content database. This is what makes it possible for you to initialize the control (or controls) in your *RenderingTemplate*.

At this point, we have walked through the complete implementation of the rendering template and the custom field control class. The only step that remains is to update the custom field type class named *SocialSecurityNumber* to use the custom field control. You do this by overriding a read-only property named *FieldRenderingControl*.

```
public class SocialSecurityNumber : SPFieldText {

  public override BaseFieldControl FieldRenderingControl {
    get {
      BaseFieldControl fldControl = new SocialSecurityNumberFieldControl();
      fldControl.FieldName = this.InternalName;
      return fldControl;
    }
  }
}
```

As shown in this example, when you override the *get* method of *FieldRenderingControl* in a custom field type class, you must create an instance of the field control class and initialize the *FieldName* property using the *InternalName* property of the custom field type class. Once you have created and initialized an instance of the field control class, you pass it back as the *get* method's return value. This is how a custom field type class informs SharePoint Foundation that it wants to load its own custom field control.

Custom Field Types with Multicolumn Values

The custom field type named *UnitedStatesAddress* demonstrates the technique of creating a field type with multicolumn values. This is useful in the case of capturing an address from the user where there are several pieces of related data that must be captured and validated as a whole.

Multicolumn field types such as *UnitedStatesAddress* must inherit from *SPFieldMultiColumn*. In most cases, there will also be a requirement to supply a custom field control with a custom *RenderingTemplate* designed to display multiple input controls to the user. Here is an example of the rendering template defined inside WingtipFieldTypes.UnitedStatesAddress.ascx.

```
<SharePoint:RenderingTemplate ID="UnitedStatesAddressRenderingTemplate" runat="server">
  <Template>
    <table class="ms-authoringcontrols" >
      <tr>
        <td>Street:</td>
        <td><asp:TextBox ID="txtStreet" runat="server" Width="328px" /></td>
      </tr>
      <tr>
        <td>City:</td>
        <td><asp:TextBox ID="txtCity" runat="server" Width="328px" /></td>
      </tr>
      <tr>
        <td>State:</td>
        <td><asp:TextBox ID="txtState" runat="server" MaxLength="2" Width="120px" /></td>
      </tr>
      <tr>
        <td>Zipcode:</td>
        <td><asp:TextBox ID="txtZipcode" runat="server" MaxLength="10" Width="120px" /></td>
      </tr>
    </table>
  </Template>
</SharePoint:RenderingTemplate>
```

When you create a multicolumn field type, you typically create the *RenderingTemplate* as a composite of several input controls like the example that you have just seen. Next, you need to learn the trick of moving the values from these controls back and forth to and from the content database as a single multicolumn value. The server-side object model supplies a creatable class type named *SPFieldMultiColumnValue,* which makes this possible using programming syntax similar to dealing with a string array. The *UnitedStatesAddressFieldControl* class demonstrates overriding the *Value* property with an implementation that reads and writes multicolumn values to and from the content database.

```
public override object Value {
  get {
    this.EnsureChildControls();
    SPFieldMultiColumnValue mcv = new SPFieldMultiColumnValue(4);
    mcv[0] = txtStreet.Text;
    mcv[1] = txtCity.Text;
    mcv[2] = txtState.Text;
    mcv[3] = txtZipcode.Text;
    return mcv;
  }
  set {
    this.EnsureChildControls();
    SPFieldMultiColumnValue mcv =
              (SPFieldMultiColumnValue)this.ItemFieldValue;
    txtStreet.Text = mcv[0];
    txtCity.Text = mcv[1];
    txtState.Text = mcv[2]; ;
    txtZipcode.Text = mcv[3];
  }
}
```

It would be possible for you to extend this simple example further to exploit the potential of multicolumn field types. For example, what if you were able to call to a Web service and pass a postal code that would return the associated city and state? That would allow you to add extra functionality to autopopulate the text boxes for City and State and to perform validation to ensure that the address is correct.

Custom Field Types with Custom Properties

The custom field type named *FieldEmployeeStatus* demonstrates how you can extend a custom field type with one or more *custom properties*. The main idea is that each field instance created from the custom field type gets its own independent property settings. You can create custom properties for a custom field type by adding a *PropertySchema* element to the bottom of the *FieldType* element for a custom field type. You create each custom property by adding *Field* elements inside the *PropertySchema* element. For example, the custom field type named *EmployeeStatus* has been defined with two custom properties named *AllowContractors* and *AllowInterns*.

```
<FieldType>
  <Field Name="TypeName">EmployeeStatus</Field>
  <Field Name="ParentType">Text</Field>
  <!-other Field elements omitted for clarity -->
  <PropertySchema>
    <Fields>
      <Field Name="AllowContractors"
             DisplayName="Allow for Contractors"
             Type="Boolean">
        <Default>0</Default>
      </Field>
      <Field Name="AllowInterns"
                DisplayName="Allow for Interns"
                Type="Boolean">
        <Default>0</Default>
      </Field>
    </Fields>
  </PropertySchema>
</FieldType>
```

Once you have added one or more custom properties to a custom field type, SharePoint Foundation will add input controls automatically to the page that allows a user to add or update columns based on your custom field type. Figure 8-3 shows what the user sees when adding or updating a field based on the custom field type named *EmployeeStatus*. The user has the option of choosing to include or exclude choice values for adding list items that include contractors or interns.

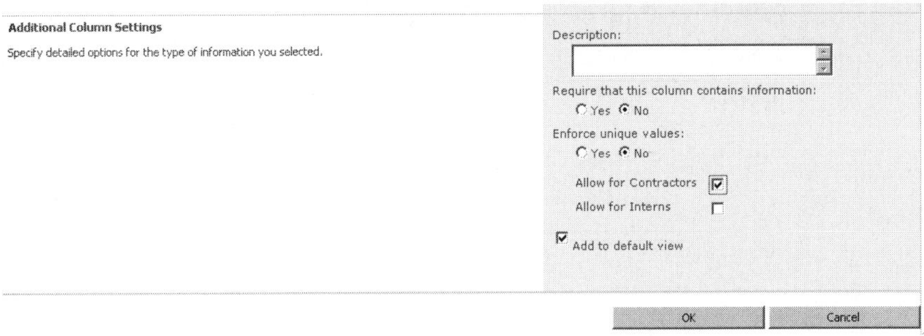

Additional Column Settings

Specify detailed options for the type of information you selected.

Description:

Require that this column contains information:
  ◯ Yes ◉ No

Enforce unique values:
  ◯ Yes ◉ No

Allow for Contractors ☑

Allow for Interns ☐

☑ Add to default view

[OK]   [Cancel]

FIGURE 8-3 Custom property fields make it possible to parameterize field instances.

Once you have extended a custom field type with one or more custom properties, you then must write code to inspect what values the user has assigned to them. In the case of the custom field type named *EmployeeStatus*, there is code in the *CreateChildControls* method of the field control class that initializes a *RadioButtonList* control by adding items for contractors and interns only when the code has determined that the user has set the values for the associated custom properties to *true*.

```
protected override void CreateChildControls() {
  base.CreateChildControls();
  lstEmployeeStatus =
    (RadioButtonList)TemplateContainer.FindControl("lstEmployeeStatus");
  if (lstEmployeeStatus != null) {
    lstEmployeeStatus.Items.Clear();
    lstEmployeeStatus.Items.Add("Full-time Employee");
    lstEmployeeStatus.Items.Add("Part-time Employee");
    // check to see if contractors are allowed
    bool AllowContactors =
        (bool)this.Field.GetCustomProperty("AllowContractors");
    if (AllowContactors) {
      lstEmployeeStatus.Items.Add("Contractor");
    }
    // check to see if interns are allowed
    bool AllowInterns =
        (bool)this.Field.GetCustomProperty("AllowInterns");
    if (AllowInterns) {
      lstEmployeeStatus.Items.Add("Intern");
    }
  }
}
```

Now that you have seen how to implement custom properties in a custom field type, let's walk through a sample usage scenario so that you can see how these properties can change the user experience. Imagine that a user has added a new field to an Employees list based on the *EmployeeStatus* field type. If this user configures the *EmployeeStatus* field so that the *AllowContractors* property is *true* and the *AllowInterns* property is *false,* the field control has been implemented to display one additional choice in the *RadioButtonList* control for *Contractor,* as shown in Figure 8-4.

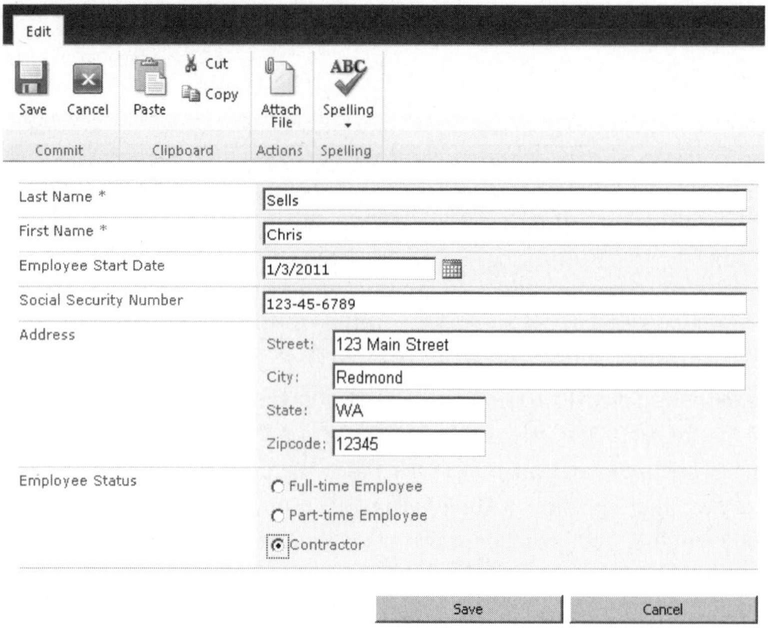

FIGURE 8-4 The choices available when editing an *EmployeeStatus* field can be customized through custom properties.

List Definitions

In this section, we will examine how to develop reusable definitions for site columns, content types, and list templates using *Collaborative Application Markup Language (CAML)*. The techniques you will learn here will provide an alternative approach to the techniques discussed in Chapter 7, which involved creating new site columns and content types in the scope of a site collection using the server-side object model.

When compared to other SharePoint development techniques, CAML-based definitions are definitely harder to develop and test. For example, there is little debugging support and many of the error messages that you get are cryptic and hard to interpret. However, developing CAML-based definitions has its advantages. They provide the greatest level of control and higher levels of reuse across site collections and across farms. Another important advantage is that CAML-based definitions can also be localized to support multiple languages. The ability to localize site columns, content types, and list types for different spoken languages can be essential when developing commercial SharePoint solutions for international sale and redistribution.

As you begin working with CAML, it can be very educational to dissect the CAML-based defi-nitions for site columns, content types, and list types that ship with SharePoint Foundation and SharePoint Server 2010. For example, you can examine the standard site columns defined in the *fields* feature and the standard content types defined in the *ctypes* feature. You can also inspect the CAML definitions for standard SharePoint Foundation list types by examining features such as *CustomList*, *ContactsList,* and *TaskList*.

When you examine the features and CAML definitions that ship with the product, be sure to look—but don't touch. Modifying any of the built-in features or CAML definitions can seri-ously injure the SharePoint farm running on your development workstation. Start by copying and pasting the contents of the built-in CAML definitions into source files that you have cre-ated inside a SharePoint project. Then you can do all your editing and testing without modi-fying any of the files deployed by the installation of SharePoint Foundation and SharePoint Server 2010.

The downloadable .zip archive of companion code for this book contains a sample SharePoint project named WingtipTypes. We are going to walk through the WingtipTypes project to demonstrate how to create CAML definitions. From Figure 8-5, you can see that the project contains a SharePoint project item named WingtipSiteColumns, which contains several site column definitions. There is also SharePoint project item for a content type named *WingtipProduct* and another SharePoint project item for a list definition named *WingtipProductList*.

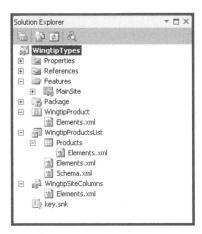

FIGURE 8-5 The WingtipTypes project demonstrates using a feature to activate CAML definitions with the scope of a site collection.

All the type definitions inside the WingtipTypes project are activated at the site collection scope using a feature named *MainSite*. The best way to think about this is that activating the feature instantiates these type definitions and makes them available for use. Note that WingtipTypes is a project that can be deployed as a farm solution or as a sandboxed solution.

Creating Site Column Definitions

A site column definition is created using a *Field* element. For example, the fields feature of SharePoint Foundation contains hundreds of site column definitions, including the following definition for the standard site column named *FirstName*.

```
<Field
  ID="{4a722dd4-d406-4356-93f9-2550b8f50dd0}"
  Name="FirstName"
  SourceID="http://schemas.microsoft.com/sharepoint/v3"
  StaticName="FirstName"
  Group="$Resources:Person_Event_Columns"
  DisplayName="$Resources:core,First_Name;"
  Type="Text">
</Field>
```

You can observe that certain text elements inside the *FirstName* site column are defined using a special syntax with the *$* character, such as $Resources:core,First_Name;, which represents special ASP.NET syntax that is used to retrieve localized strings out of a resource file. The ability to localize such aspects of a site column definition makes it possible for SharePoint Foundation to support localization of CAML-based definitions for different spoken languages.

Now that we have seen one of the built-in site column definitions of SharePoint Foundation, let's create one of our own. Note that the SharePoint Developer Tools do not provide a dedicated SharePoint project item template for creating site column definitions. Therefore, you should create a new project item using SharePoint project item template named Empty Element and add *Field* elements to the project item's elements.xml file. That's how we create a project item named WingtipSiteColumns in the WingtipTypes project.

The elements.xml file of the WingtipSiteColumns project item contains several site column definitions. The first two define text-based fields for tracking a product code and a product description.

```
<Field
  ID="{D0D32083-F81B-420E-832E-5CC94E12F417}"
  Name="ProductCode"
  DisplayName="Product Code"
  Group="Wingtip Site Columns"
  Type="Text"
  DisplaceOnUpgrade="TRUE" />

<Field
  ID="{36819A9B-E748-47D5-9949-A65DD195BF80}"
  Name="ProductDescription"
  DisplayName="Description"
  Group="Wingtip Site Columns"
  Type="Text"
  DisplaceOnUpgrade="TRUE" />
```

These two *Field* elements demonstrate creating a custom site column definition using attributes such as *ID, Name, DisplayName, Group,* and *Type.* You will need a new globally unique identifier (GUID) each time you create a new site column definition. Note that Visual Studio 2010 provides a handy utility named GuidGen.exe that can be used to create new GUIDs and copy them to the Clipboard.

One other important detail is that you must include the curly braces for GUIDs that are used as the *ID* in a *Field* element. Unfortunately, SharePoint Foundation is inconsistent about when it requires curly braces on the GUIDs you have created. Here is a case where each GUID must be added with curly braces for the site column definition to work properly.

The last attribute in both site column definitions is named *DisplaceOnUpgrade* and has been assigned a value of *true.* This attribute setting can provide more flexibility during a feature upgrade when you need to push changes within a site column definition out to fields that were created previously using an earlier version of the same site column definition.

The elements.xml file of the WingtipSiteColumns project item contains a third site column definition named ProductListPrice. This definition differs from the first two because it is based on the *Currency* field type and contains extra attributes for decimal formatting and the minimum allowable value.

```
<Field
  ID="{F0182CD5-C126-4E96-9BB5-B16A34DC8F3B}"
  Name="ProductListPrice"
  DisplayName="List Price"
  Group="Wingtip Site Columns"
  Type="Currency"
  Decimals="2"
  Min="0"
  Required="FALSE"
  DisplaceOnUpgrade="True" />
```

There is a fourth site column definition named ProductCategory, which demonstrates creating a *Choice* field. The definition for ProductCategory contains the *Format* attribute with a setting of *RadioButtons,* as well as a collection of choice values to provide the user with several different categories from which to pick when assigning the field value.

```
<Field
  ID="{0C5BDEB7-0E0E-4c38-A2E5-F39941E61CE9}"
  Name="ProductCategory"
  DisplayName="Category"
  Group="Wingtip Site Columns"
  Type="Choice"
  Format="RadioButtons"
  DisplaceOnUpgrade="TRUE" >
<CHOICES>
  <CHOICE>Electronics</CHOICE>
  <CHOICE>Games</CHOICE>
```

```
      <CHOICE>Trains</CHOICE>
      <CHOICE>Arts and Crafts</CHOICE>
    </CHOICES>
    <Default>Electronics</Default>
</Field>
```

As you become more involved in creating site column definitions, you will discover that the *Field* element has many more possible attributes. For more information, you can look at the MSDN documentation at *http://msdn.microsoft.com/en-us/library/ms437580.aspx.*

Creating Content Type Definitions

A content type definition is created using a *ContentType* element. The *ContentType* element must contain a set of required attributes and a collection of field links created using *FieldRef* elements. Each content type definition also requires an ID that begins with the content type ID of its parent. For example, the content type ID for the *Announcement* content type is *0x0104*, which inherits from the *Item* content type with an ID of *0x01*. Here is the content type definition for the *Announcement* content type, which is activated in every new site collection using the built-in *ctypes* feature.

```
<ContentType
  ID="0x0104"
  Name="$Resources:Announcement"
  Group="$Resources:List_Content_Types"
  Description="$Resources:AnnouncementCTDesc"
  V2ListTemplateName="announce"
  Version="0">
  <FieldRefs>
    <FieldRef ID="{7662cd2c-f069-4dba-9e35-082cf976e170}" Name="Body" />
    <FieldRef ID="{6a09e75b-8d17-4698-94a8-371eda1af1ac}" Name="Expires" />
  </FieldRefs>
</ContentType>
```

As seen in this example, a content type definition includes references to site column definitions using *FieldRef* elements. In Chapter 7, we discussed how each content type tracks its fields using field links. In terms of the server-side object model, a field link is represented with an *SPFieldLink* object, as opposed to a field instance that is represented with an *SPField* object. Each *FieldRef* element references a specific site column definition using both the identifying GUID and its string-based name.

Before you can create a content type definition, you must decide which base content type to inherit from. For example, you can inherit from a standard list content type such as *Item*, *Contact*, or *Task*. You can also elect to create a content type that inherits from *Document*, making it possible to add support for a document template and use it in a document library. In our example, we are going to keep it simple and create a content type named *WingtipProduct* that inherits from *Item*.

The SharePoint Developer Tools provide a dedicated SharePoint project item template named *Content Type*. When you create a new Content Type project item, the SharePoint Customization Wizard prompts you to select a base content type from a drop-down list. If you select a base content type of *Item*, the SharePoint Customization Wizard will generate a new content type definition with an empty *FieldRefs* element.

```
<!-- Parent ContentType: Item (0x01) -->
<ContentType ID="0x01003e0f572308e74cffb2f0b13db11f5be2"
             Name="Wingtip Product"
             Group="Wingtip Content Types"
             Description="A Wingtip product"
             Inherits="TRUE"
             Version="0">
  <FieldRefs>
  </FieldRefs>
</ContentType>
```

As you examine the *Wingtip Product* content type definition, you will notice that the *ID* attribute generated by the SharePoint Customization Wizard has a somewhat complicated format. In Chapter 7, we explained that the first part of a content type ID is based on a hexa-decimal number that identifies its base content type. The hexadecimal number for the base content type is followed by *00*. The last part of a content type ID is a GUID that uniquely identifies the content type. The SharePoint Customization Wizard follows these rules when creating the content type ID for a new Content Type project item.

For each field link that you want to add, you must create a *FieldRef* element that references a site column definition. Also, note that you can include a field link that references a site col-umn that is already included in the base content type to change some of its properties. For example, the *Wingtip Product* content type includes a field link to the *Title* field so that it can modify its *DisplayName* property to *Product Name*.

```
<FieldRefs>
  <FieldRef ID="{fa564e0f-0c70-4ab9-b863-0177e6ddd247}"
            Name="Title" DisplayName="Product Name" />
  <FieldRef ID="{D0D32083-F81B-420E-832E-5CC94E12F417}"
            Name="ProductCode" />
  <FieldRef ID="{36819A9B-E748-47D5-9949-A65DD195BF80}"
            Name="ProductDescription" />
  <FieldRef ID="{0C5BDEB7-0E0E-4c38-A2E5-F39941E61CE9}"
            Name="ProductCategory" />
  <FieldRef ID="{F0182CD5-C126-4E96-9BB5-B16A34DC8F3B}"
            Name="ProductListPrice" />
</FieldRefs>
```

Additional Content Type Metadata

A content type definition can contain embedded XML documents that carry additional metadata about the content type. This metadata can consist of either custom XML data unique to your SharePoint solution or XML data defined by a SharePoint Foundation schema. For example, you can include any custom XML content you like in the *XmlDocument* node so long as it is valid XML. However, the most common use of the *XmlDocument* nodes within SharePoint Foundation itself is to specify custom data forms and event handlers. The following example shows a custom data form specification, in which the display and edit forms are custom-defined.

```
<ContentType>
  <!-content type attributes and field links omitted for clarity -->
  <XmlDocuments>
    <XmlDocument
      NamespaceURI="http://schemas.microsoft.com/sharepoint/v3/contenttype/forms/url">
      <FormUrls xmlns="http://schemas.microsoft.com/sharepoint/v3/contenttype/forms/url">
        <Display>_layouts/MyCustomDisplayForm.aspx</Display>
        <Edit>_layouts/MyCustomEditForm.aspx</Edit>
      </FormUrls>
    </XmlDocument>
  </XmlDocuments>
</ContentType>
```

Creating List Definitions

The SharePoint Developer Tools provide two different SharePoint project item templates for creating a new list definition. One is named *List Definition,* and the other is named *List Definition From Content Type.* If you create a new project item using the List Definition project item template, the SharePoint Customization Wizard prompts you to choose the type of list that you want to create by selecting one of the built-in list definitions such as *Announcements*, *Contacts,* or *Tasks.* For example, if you choose *Contacts*, the SharePoint Customization Wizard generates a new custom list definition with CAML that is similar to the Contacts list definition.

When you create a new project item using the List Definition From Content Type project item template, the SharePoint Customization Wizard prompts you to select a content type defined inside the current project. In our example, we have used this project item template to create a new list definition named WingtipProductsList that is based on the *Wingtip Product* content type.

When you create a new project item for a list definition, it contains two CAML-based files named elements.xml and schema.xml. Both of these files are required to create a list definition. We will begin by examining the elements.xml file that contains a *ListTemplate* element.

```xml
<ListTemplate
    Name="WingtipProductsList"
    Type="25001"
    BaseType="0"
    OnQuickLaunch="TRUE"
    SecurityBits="11"
    Sequence="10"
    DisplayName="Products List"
    Description="Wingtip products list"
    Image="/_layouts/images/itgen.png"/>
```

As you can see, this *ListTemplate* element has a *Name* of *WingtipProductsList*. The value of the *Name* attribute is important within a *ListTemplate* element because SharePoint Foundation requires a child directory inside the root feature directory with the same name that contains a file with the well-known name schema.xml. Note that the SharePoint Developer Tools have done the required work of creating a child directory named WingtipProductsList inside the root feature directory and placing the schema.xml file inside. Just be careful not to change the value of the *Name* attribute without also changing the name of the directory that holds the schema.xml file.

The *ListTemplate* element defines a *Type* attribute with an integer value used to identify the creatable list type associated with the list definition. Microsoft uses lower-numbered identifiers for the built-in list types such as *104* for *Announcements* and *105* for *Contacts*. Microsoft recommends creating list type identifiers with values of 10,000 or greater. The SharePoint Developer Tools follow this recommendation by creating IDs starting at 10000. However, because the vast majority of custom list definitions defined around the world have a *Type* value of *10000*, we will make ours a little more unique by giving it a value of 25001.

Now that you have seen what's required in the elements.xml file, let's move on to discuss what's inside the schema.xml file. The schema.xml file contains a top-level *List* element that contains several attributes and inner elements for content type, fields, views, and forms.

```xml
<List
  xmlns:ows="Microsoft SharePoint"
  Title="Products List"
  FolderCreation="FALSE"
  DisableAttachments="TRUE"
  Url="Lists/Products"
  BaseType="0"
  Direction="0"
  xmlns="http://schemas.microsoft.com/sharepoint/">
```

```
   <MetaData>
     <ContentTypes> <!-- add content types --> </ContentTypes>
     <Fields> <!-- add fields --> </Fields>
     <Views> <!-- define views here -->  </Views>
     <Forms> <!-- add support for forms here --> </Forms>
   </MetaData>

</List>
```

Now we will take a little time to walk through the individual sections of the schema.xml file in more detail. We will begin with the *ContentTypes* element. The *ContentTypes* element can contain content type instances or content type references. The *ContentTypes* element in our example contains a *ContentType* element with an instance of the *Wingtip Product* content type.

```
<ContentTypes>
   <ContentType ID="0x01003e0f572308e74cffb2f0b13db11f5be2"
                Name="Wingtip Product" Description="Wingtip product"
                Inherits="TRUE" Version="0">
     <FieldRefs>
       <FieldRef ID="{fa564e0f-0c70-4ab9-b863-0177e6ddd247}" Name="Title"
                  DisplayName="Product Name" />
       <FieldRef ID="{D0D32083-F81B-420E-832E-5CC94E12F417}" Name="ProductCode" />
       <FieldRef ID="{36819A9B-E748-47D5-9949-A65DD195BF80}" Name="ProductDescription" />
       <FieldRef ID="{0C5BDEB7-0E0E-4c38-A2E5-F39941E61CE9}" Name="ProductCategory" />
       <FieldRef ID="{F0182CD5-C126-4E96-9BB5-B16A34DC8F3B}" Name="ProductListPrice" />
     </FieldRefs>
</ContentTypes>
```

Now that you have seen the *ContentTypes* section, we will now examine the *Fields* section. Dealing with the fields of a content type in the schema.xml file is more complicated than the example shown in the previous chapter, when we added a content type to a list through the server-side object model. When you add a content type to a list using the server-side object model, SharePoint Foundation automatically adds the fields of the content type to the *Fields* collection of the list. However, this doesn't happen automatically when you add a content type to the *ContentTypes* section of the schema.xml file. You are still required to add each field to the list field's collection explicitly. This is accomplished by adding *Field* elements to the *Fields* element. Each *Field* element must contain required attributes such as its *ID, Name,* and *Type,* which are required to create a field instance whenever a new list is created.

```
<Fields>
    <Field ID="{fa564e0f-0c70-4ab9-b863-0177e6ddd247}" Name="Title"
         DisplayName="Product Name" Type="Text" DisplaceOnUpgrade="TRUE"  />
    <Field ID="{82642ec8-ef9b-478f-acf9-31f7d45fbc31}" Name="LinkTitle"
         DisplayName="Product Name" Type="Computed" Sealed="TRUE" />
    <Field ID="{bc91a437-52e7-49e1-8c4e-4698904b2b6d}" Name="LinkTitleNoMenu"
         DisplayName="Product Name" Type="Computed" Sealed="TRUE" />
    <Field ID="{D0D32083-F81B-420E-832E-5CC94E12F417}" Name="ProductCode"
         DisplayName="Product Code" Type="Text" />
```

```
    <Field ID="{36819a9b-e748-47d5-9949-a65dd195bf80}" Name="ProductDescription"
        DisplayName="Description" Type="Text" />
    <Field ID="{0C5BDEB7-0E0E-4c38-A2E5-F39941E61CE9}" Name="ProductCategory"
        DisplayName="Category" Type="Choice" Format="RadioButtons" >
      <CHOICES>
        <CHOICE>Electronics</CHOICE>
        <CHOICE>Games</CHOICE>
        <CHOICE>Trains</CHOICE>
        <CHOICE>Arts and Crafts</CHOICE>
        <CHOICE>Action Figures</CHOICE>
      </CHOICES>
      <Default>Electronics</Default>
    </Field>
    <Field ID="{f0182cd5-c126-4e96-9bb5-b16a34dc8f3b}" Name="ProductListPrice"
        DisplayName="List Price" Type="Currency" Decimals="2" Min="0" Required="FALSE"
        DisplaceOnUpgrade="True" RowOrdinal="0"
        SourceID="{eaa3c1e3-ceb2-4e64-b876-42726a96867e}" />
  </Fields>
```

When you first begin to work with schema.xml files, the requirement to add redundant field definitions into the schema.xml file doesn't seem too intuitive. After all, we've already defined the fields once in the *Wingtip Product* content type, so why should we be forced to define them a second time in the schema.xml file? SharePoint Foundation, however, doesn't supply any mechanism to copy the fields from content types that are added or referenced from inside the schema.xml file.

For large sets of data, the list schema can define indexes on fields that can improve data access and querying list content significantly. This makes lists a viable storage mechanism for external business applications with the added value of the collaborative interface of SharePoint Foundation. Indexed fields can be defined in the list schema or they can be specified after creation through the browser or the server-side object model. List indexes are similar to the concept of a SQL index, although the index is defined in a SQL-indexed name-value table that contains a reference to the list as well as the indexed column values.

After adding fields, you also will want to specify which fields are to be added to the various views supported by the list, such as the standard All Items view. This means you must modify the *Views* element of the schema.xml file. The following *View* element demonstrates adding *FieldRef* elements to the *ViewFields* node of the default view so that it displays the fields that have been added in the *Fields* section previously.

```
<View BaseViewID="1" Type="HTML" WebPartZoneID="Main"
      Url="AllItems.aspx" DisplayName="All Items" DefaultView="TRUE"
      MobileView="TRUE" MobileDefaultView="TRUE"
      SetupPath="pages\viewpage.aspx"
      ImageUrl="/_layouts/images/generic.png" >
  <Toolbar Type="Standard" />
  <XslLink Default="TRUE">main.xsl</XslLink>
  <RowLimit Paged="TRUE">30</RowLimit>
  <ViewFields>
    <FieldRef Name="LinkTitle" />
```

```
    <FieldRef Name="ProductCode" />
    <FieldRef Name="ProductDescription" />
    <FieldRef Name="ProductCategory" />
    <FieldRef Name="ProductListPrice" />
  </ViewFields>
  <Query>
    <OrderBy><FieldRef Name="ProductCode" /></OrderBy>
  </Query>
<View>
```

The *Forms* element at the bottom of the schema.xml file is used to define the default forms for displaying, editing, and adding items. A schema.xml file can be written to use custom forms for viewing and editing content. However, you can also rely on a generic form named form.aspx, which is installed along with SharePoint Foundation and deployed inside the SharePoint Root directory at a path of TEMPLATE\Pages. When you create a new list definition using the SharePoint Developer Tools, the schema.xml is created to use the generic file form.aspx for each of its default forms.

```
<Forms>
  <Form Type="DisplayForm" Url="DispForm.aspx"
               SetupPath="pages\form.aspx" WebPartZoneID="Main" />
  <Form Type="EditForm" Url="EditForm.aspx" SetupPath="pages\form.aspx" WebPartZoneID="Main"
/>
  <Form Type="NewForm" Url="NewForm.aspx" SetupPath="pages\form.aspx" WebPartZoneID="Main"
/>
</Forms>
```

Feature Activation Dependencies

Now that we have discussed creating CAML-based definitions for site columns, content types, and list types, it's time to discuss an import feature design issue. Consider a scenario where you are developing a SharePoint project such as WingtipTypes, which defines a feature with a custom list definition. Now imagine that you create a second project named CreateProductsList, which contains a feature with a *ListInstance* element that creates a list instance from the custom list definition in WingtipTypes.

```
<ListInstance
  Title="Products"
  OnQuickLaunch="TRUE"
  TemplateType="25001"
  FeatureId="edcdcd75-dff2-479d-ac32-b37f8fa9d459"
  Url="Lists/Products"
  Description="" />
```

The key point is that the feature that contains this *ListInstance* element will not work correctly unless the first feature that contains the custom list definition has been activated. SharePoint Foundation provides support *activation dependencies* between features to deal with this scenario. A feature can defined with an activation dependency by adding an *ActivationDependency* element to its feature.xml file.

```
<Feature
  xmlns="http://schemas.microsoft.com/sharepoint/"
  Id="1a134b00-f92c-412f-a812-e9e1bf72619e"
  Scope="Web"
  Title="Create Products List">

  <ActivationDependencies>
    <ActivationDependency
      FeatureId="edcdcd75-dff2-479d-ac32-b37f8fa9d459"
      FeatureTitle="Wingtip Types" />
  </ActivationDependencies>

</Feature>
```

If you use the feature designer supplied by the SharePoint Developer Tools, you will find that it provides assistance adding activation dependencies to other features defined inside the same solution. This makes it so you can add activation dependencies without having to edit the feature.xml file manually.

Now let's discuss what happens when a user activates a feature that depends on another feature that has not been activated. The behavior of SharePoint Foundation is different depending on whether the feature on which the dependency has been created has been configured as a hidden feature. When you activate a feature that defines an activation dependency on a hidden feature, SharePoint Foundation automatically activates the hidden feature in any case where it has not already been activated. However, when you activate a feature that defines an activation dependency on a visible feature that has not already been activated, things work out differently. In this case, SharePoint Foundation fails to activate the dependent feature and displays an error message informing the user of the feature that must be activated first.

The TeamCollab feature, which ships as a built-in feature with SharePoint Foundation, provides another good example of using activation dependencies. The TeamCollab feature in and of itself provides no implementation. However, it defines activation dependencies on 19 other built-in features that define the list definitions for the standard collaboration list types.

Activating the TeamCollab feature forces the activation of these 19 other features that make all the collaboration list types available, such as *Announcements*, *Contacts*, *Tasks*, *Events*, and *Document Library*. As you can see, feature activation dependencies can be used to aggregate many features into a common feature set that can then be activated and deactivated through a single high-level feature.

Site Definitions

A *site definition* is top-level component that SharePoint Foundation uses to create and initialize new sites. A site definition contains a set of provisioning instructions that have been designed to initialize new sites by performing common tasks such as activating specific features and creating site elements such as pages, lists, navigation nodes, and Web Parts.

In SharePoint Foundation, every site is provisioned from a specific site definition. This is true for top-level sites as well as for child sites nested within a site collection. Once a site is provisioned from a particular site definition, it picks up a dependency on that site definition that remains in effect for the lifetime of the site. A site's dependency on its underlying site definition can never be removed or changed, and the site definition must be installed and remain functional in the farm for the site to continue working properly.

The installation of SharePoint Foundation deploys several site definitions that can be used to create various types of collaboration sites. For example, SharePoint Foundation provides a popular site definition named STS, which can be used to create Team sites and Blank sites. The installation of SharePoint Server 2010 deploys additional site definitions that can be used to create specialized sites that use features in areas such as publishing, searching, business intelligence, and records management. SharePoint Foundation also supports creating and deploying custom site definitions created by third-party developers.

Consider a scenario in which you create a custom site definition and deploy it within a particular SharePoint Foundation farm. Now imagine that you use this site definition to provision the top-level site for a new site collection. What would happen if you attempted to back up the site collection in a Windows PowerShell script using the *Backup-SPSite* cmdlet and then attempted to restore this site in another SharePoint Foundation farm using *Restore-SPSite*? This would not work properly unless your custom site definition has been deployed to both farms.

Now is the time for us to make a big disclaimer. Developing custom site definitions has several well-known pitfalls and disadvantages. Throughout the history of SharePoint development, custom site definitions have proved to be hard to deploy and to version over time. The biggest problem that many companies face with custom site definitions involves migrating sites from one version of SharePoint to another. For example, many of the custom site definitions that were developed for SharePoint 2007 have caused serious problems when companies have attempted to migrate the content in their sites to SharePoint 2010. For these reasons, it is generally recommended that you avoid custom site definitions when designing and developing SharePoint solutions.

In rare circumstances, in very controlled environments, it still might make sense for an experienced SharePoint developer to develop a custom site definition. However, you are better off learning alternative techniques that allow you to achieve the same goal without all the pitfalls and disadvantages associated with custom site definitions. In particular, you can find other ways to create sites and initialize them with a customized set of provisioning instructions.

In this chapter, we will not spend time showing you how to develop a custom site definition. Instead, we are going to explain how site definitions work in order to demonstrate how to fully use the site definitions that come with SharePoint 2010. This approach will give you techniques for creating sites that will not cause migration pains as you move your sites and content to future versions of the product.

Configurations and Web Templates

A site definition itself does not represent a creatable site template. Instead, a site definition contains one or more *configurations,* which appear to users as creatable site templates. For example, the STS site definition contains three separate configurations: Team Site, Blank Site, and Document Workspace.

Let's examine the details of how a site definition is deployed. Each site definition has its own directory in the SiteTemplates directory, which exists inside the TEMPLATE directory. The directory for a site definition must be given the same name as the site definition itself. For example, if you look inside the SiteTemplates directory, you will find a child directory named STS, which contains files used by the STS site definition.

The directory for a site definition such as STS must always include a child directory named XML containing a special file named ONET.XML, which serves as the site definition manifest. While the ONET.XML file is the only file required, the directory for a site definition can contain other files, such as page templates. The STS site definition directory contains page templates named default.aspx and defaultdws.aspx. The page template named default.aspx is used to create the home page for Team sites and Blank sites, while defaultdws.aspx is used to create the home page for a new Document Workspace site.

In addition to a named directory inside the SiteTemplates directory, a site definition must be deployed using a *Web template file.* A Web template file is a localized file that is deployed within a locale-specific directory using a path such as TEMPLATE\<*culture*>\XML, where the <*culture*> folder is the locale identifier. In a farm running the U.S. English version of SharePoint 2010, for example, Web template files are deployed in the TEMPLATE\1033\XML directory.

Now let's discuss how SharePoint Foundation initializes the available set of site templates with a farm. When SharePoint Foundation initializes the worker process for an application pool, it queries the TEMPLATE/*<culture>*/XML directory for files that match the pattern of *webtemp*.xml* and scans through them to discover the configurations of each site definition that have been deployed within the local farm. As you can see, a site definition is like a field definition because it is deployed as an all-or-nothing proposition at farm-level scope.

A Web template file contains a *Template* element for each site definition. Inside the *Template* element, there is one *Configuration* element for each configuration supported by the site definition. Note that a single Web template file can contain multiple site definitions. SharePoint Foundation deploys a core Web template file named webtemp.xml that contains *Template* elements for all the standard site definitions included with SharePoint Foundation.

```
<Templates xmlns:ows="Microsoft SharePoint">

  <Template Name="GLOBAL" ID="0">
    <Configuration ID="0" Title="Global template" Hidden="TRUE" />
  </Template>

  <Template Name="STS" ID="1">
    <Configuration ID="0" Title="Team Site" Hidden="FALSE"  />
    <Configuration ID="1" Title="Blank Site" Hidden="FALSE" />
    <Configuration ID="2" Title="Document Workspace" Hidden="FALSE" />
  </Template>

  <!-- other Template elements omitted for clairty -->

</Templates>
```

The webtemp.xml file deployed by SharePoint Foundation includes several other *Template* elements for other site definitions, including MPS, CENTRALADMIN, WIKI, BLOG, SGS, and TENANTADMIN. SharePoint Server 2010 deploys several other Web template files of its own, such as webtempsps.xml, webtempsrch.xml, and webtempppsma.xml. If you open up these Web template files and examine them, you will find familiar site definitions and configurations that can be used to create new sites offering extended functionality in areas such as publishing, content searching and management, business intelligence, and social networking.

ONET.XML: The Site Definition Manifest

The ONET.XML file serves as the top-level manifest for a site definition and its configurations. This manifest file is used to define provisioning instructions that activate features and create site elements. Let's start by examining a high-level view of the ONET.XML file that serves as the manifest for the STS site definition.

```
<Project
  Title="$Resources:onet_TeamWebSite;"
  Revision="2"
  ListDir="$Resources:core,lists_Folder;"
  xmlns:ows="Microsoft SharePoint"
  UIVersion="4">

  <NavBars />
  <ListTemplates />
  <DocumentTemplates />
  <Configurations/>
  <Modules />
  <ServerEmailFooter/>

</Project>
```

The basic structure of the ONET.XML file includes a top-level *Project* element, which contains several child elements such as *NavBars, ListTemplates, DocumentTemplates, Configurations, Modules,* and *ServerEmailFooter.*

The *NavBars* node defines the set of what navigation bars that are created when a new site is provisioned. The *NavBars* element inside the STS site definition has been written to create several navigation bars that are used by the top link bar and the Quick Launch.

```
<NavBars>
  <NavBar Name="$Resources:core,category_Top;" ID="1002" />
  <NavBar Name="$Resources:core,category_Documents;" ID="1004" />
  <NavBar Name="$Resources:core,category_Lists;" ID="1003" />
  <NavBar Name="$Resources:core,category_Discussions;" ID="1006" />
</NavBars>
```

Note that these *NavBar* elements are based on well-known ID values. The *NavBar* element with an *ID* of *1002* is used to create the navigation bar used by the top link bar. The *NavBar* elements with IDs of 1004, 1003, and 1006 are used to create dynamic collections of navigation nodes that are displayed in the Quick Launch. For example, the *NavBar* element with an ID of *1004* creates a dynamic collection of navigation nodes that link to document libraries that have been created with the option to display them on the Quick Launch.

The Configurations section of the ONET.XML file contains a child *Configuration* element for each supported configuration. This is what makes it possible for a site definition to provide multiple configurations that provision new sites differently from one another. The ONET.NET file in the STS site definition defines three separate *Configuration* elements for creating Team sites, Blank sites, and Document Workspace sites.

```
<Project>
  <Configurations>
    <Configuration ID="0" Name="Default" />   <!--used to create Team sites -->
    <Configuration ID="1" Name="Blank" />     <!--used to create Blank sites -->
    <Configuration ID="2" Name="DWS" />       <!--used to create Document Workspace sites -->
  </Configurations>
</Project>
```

A *Configuration* element contains attributes such as *ID*, *Name*, and *MasterUrl*. A *Configuration* element also contains child elements such as *Lists*, *Modules*, *SiteFeatures*, and *WebFeatures*, which are used to create site elements and activate features.

```
<Configuration ID="0" Name="Default" MasterUrl="_catalogs/masterpage/v4.master">
  <Lists />
  <Modules />
  <SiteFeatures />
  <WebFeatures />
</Configuration>
```

If you examine the *Configuration* element for a Blank site, you will find that it contains an empty *Lists* element. However, the *Configuration* element for a Team site contains a *Lists* element that creates several list instances whenever a new Team site is created.

```
<Lists>
  <List Type="101" Title="$Resources:core,shareddocuments_Title;" />
  <List Type="108" Title="$Resources:core,discussions_Title;" />
  <List Type="104" Title="$Resources:core,announceList;" />
  <List Type="103" Title="$Resources:core,linksList;" />
  <List Type="106" Title="$Resources:core,calendarList;" />
  <List Type="107" Title="$Resources:core,taskList;" />
</Lists>
```

The *Configurations* section contains a *Modules* element that is used to reference *Module* elements defined below in the ONET.XML file. For example, the *Configuration* element for a Team site includes a *Modules* element that references a *Module* named *Default*.

```
<Modules>
  <Module Name="Default" />
</Modules>
```

While *Module* elements are referenced inside the *Configurations* element, they are actually defined below the *Configurations* element in a *Modules* element that is nested directly inside the top-level *Project* element.

```
<Project>
  <Configuration ID="0" Name="Default">
    <Modules>
      <Module Name="Default" />
    </Modules>
  </Configuration>
```

```
    <Modules>
      <Module Name="Default" />
      <Module Name="DefaultBlank" />
      <Module Name="DWS" />
    </Modules>
<Project>
```

In Chapter 5, "Pages and Navigation," we discussed using *Module* elements with features. As you may remember, a *Module* element contains *File* elements that are used to provision files such as site pages and master pages from template files. There is one major difference between the behavior of *Module* elements in features and their behavior in site definitions. A *Module* element in a feature is always processed when the feature is activated. However, a *Module* element defined inside a site definition is processed only when it is referenced by a *Configuration* element.

As you learned in Chapter 5, a *Module* element can contain a *File* element written to create a Web Part page and populates it with Web Part instances. The STS site definition contains a *Module* element named *DefaultBlank,* which is referenced by the *Configuration* element for a Blank site. This *Module* has been written to provision a home page for a new Blank site named default.aspx and add a link to the top link bar.

```
<Module Name="DefaultBlank" Url="" Path="">
  <File Url="default.aspx" NavBarHome="True" Type="Ghostable">
    <NavBarPage Name="$Resources:core,nav_Home;" Url="~site" ID="1002" Position="Start" />
    <NavBarPage Name="$Resources:core,nav_Home;" Url="" ID="0" Position="Start" />
  </File>
</Module>
```

The last two items that we want to discuss about an ONET.XML file are the two elements inside the *Configuration* element named *SiteFeatures* and *WebFeatures*. These two elements contain *Feature* elements whose purpose is to activate specific features during the site provisioning process. For example, the *SiteFeatures* element for the Team site configuration activates two site collection-scoped features that add support for the standard SharePoint Foundation Web Parts and the Three-State Workflow template.

```
<SiteFeatures>

  <!-- BasicWebParts Feature -->
  <Feature ID="00BFEA71-1C5E-4A24-B310-BA51C3EB7A57" />

  <!-- Three-state Workflow Feature -->
  <Feature ID="FDE5D850-671E-4143-950A-87B473922DC7" />

</SiteFeatures>
```

The *WebFeatures* element for the Team site configuration activates three site-scoped features named *TeamCollab*, *MobilityRedirect*, and *WikiPageHomePage*. These features add support for the basic collaboration list types, a standard wiki library named *SitePages,* and mobile device compatibility.

```
<WebFeatures>

  <!-- TeamCollab Feature -->
  <Feature ID="00BFEA71-4EA5-48D4-A4AD-7EA5C011ABE5" />

  <!-- MobilityRedirect -->
  <Feature ID="F41CC668-37E5-4743-B4A8-74D1DB3FD8A4" />

  <!-- WikiPageHomePage Feature -->
  <Feature ID="00BFEA71-D8FE-4FEC-8DAD-01C19A6E4053" />

</WebFeatures>
```

The Global Site Definition

SharePoint Foundation maintains a set of common provisioning instructions in the *Global site definition*. Whenever a new site is created, SharePoint Foundation begins the site provisioning process by executing the provisioning instructions defined by the Global site definition. After that, SharePoint Foundation completes the site provisioning process by executing the unique provisioning instructions defined by the site definition configuration that has been selected as the site template.

The Global site definition has an ONET.XML file that contains site provisioning instructions that are executed each time a new site is created. If you examine the ONET.XML file of the Global site definition, you will find a *Project* element that contains child elements named *ListTemplates*, *BaseTypes*, *Configurations*, and *Modules*.

```
<Project>
  <ListTemplates/>    <!-- defines list definitions for system lists and galleries -->
  <BaseTypes/>        <!-- defines base types used by list and document libraries -->
  <Configurations/>   <!-- defines configuration with shared provisioning instructions -->
  <Modules/>          <!-- provisions files for standard master pages and themes -->
</Project>
```

The *ListTemplates* element contains *ListTemplate* elements that define list definitions for creating special system lists and galleries such as the Master Page Gallery and the Web Part Gallery. The *BaseTypes* section provides a definition for each of the supported base types, including *Generic List*, *Document Library*, *Discussion Form*, and *Issues List*.

```
<BaseTypes>
  <BaseType Title="Generic List" Type="0" />
  <BaseType Title="Document Library" Type="1" />
  <BaseType Title="Discussion Forum" Type="3" />
  <BaseType Title="Issues List" Type="5" />
</BaseTypes>
```

If you want to learn about how each base type is defined, you can examine the contents of each *BaseType* element to see what fields are added to every list and document library.

The *Configuration* element of the Global site definition is important because it is used to activate the built-in features named *fields* and *ctypes* automatically whenever a new site collection is created. The *Configuration* element also contains a *Lists* element to create special system lists and galleries.

```
<Configuration ID="0" Name="Default" MasterUrl="_catalogs/masterpage/v4.master">
  <SiteFeatures>
    <Feature ID="CA7BD552-10B1-4563-85B9-5ED1D39C962A" /> <!-- activates fields feature -->
    <Feature ID="695B6570-A48B-4A8E-8EA5-26EA7FC1D162" /> <!-- activates ctypes feature -->
  </SiteFeatures>
  <Lists>
    <!-- provisions system lists such as the master page gallery -->
  </Lists>
</Configuration>
```

Inside the *Lists* section, there is a *List* element that is used to create a Master Page Gallery in each new site.

```
<List Title="$Resources:core,MasterPageGallery;" Type="116" Url="_catalogs/masterpage" />
```

There are six other *List* elements that contain a *RootWebOnly* attribute with a value of *TRUE*. This attribute setting configures these *List* elements so that they create system lists and galleries in top-level sites only when a new site collection is being created.

```
<!-system lists and galleries created in every top-level site -->
<List Title="$Resources:core,global_onet_solutiongallery_list;" Type="121"
      Url="_catalogs/solutions" RootWebOnly="TRUE" />
<List Title="$Resources:core,userinfo_schema_listtitle;" Type="112"
      Url="_catalogs/users" RootWebOnly="TRUE" />
<List Type="113" Title="$Resources:core,webpartgalleryList;"
      Url="_catalogs/wp" RootWebOnly="TRUE" />
<List Type="114" Title="$Resources:core,listtemplategalleryList;"
      Url="_catalogs/lt" RootWebOnly="TRUE" />
<List Title="$Resources:core,themegalleryList;" Type="123"
      Url="_catalogs/theme" RootWebOnly="TRUE" />
<List Title="$Resources:core,stylelibraryList;" Type="101" Catalog="TRUE"
      Url="Style Library" Description="$Resources:core,stylelibraryList_Desc"
      RootWebOnly="TRUE" AllowEveryoneViewItems="TRUE" AllowDeletion="FALSE" />
```

The ONET.XML file in the Global site definition includes two *Module* elements, which are named *DefaultMasterPage* and *OOBThemes*.

```
<Modules>
  <Module Name="DefaultMasterPage" />
  <Module Name="OOBThemes" />
</Modules>
```

The *Module* element named *DefaultMasterPage* is used to add the three standard master pages to every new site.

```
<Module Name="DefaultMasterPage" List="116" Url="_catalogs/masterpage" >
    <File Url="default.master" Type="GhostableInLibrary" IgnoreIfAlreadyExists="TRUE" />
    <File Url="v4.master" Type="GhostableInLibrary" IgnoreIfAlreadyExists="TRUE" />
    <File Url="minimal.master" Type="GhostableInLibrary" IgnoreIfAlreadyExists="TRUE" />
  </Module>
</Modules>
```

The *Module* element named *OOBThemes* has been written to add the .thmx files for the standard SharePoint Foundation themes into the Themes Gallery of each top-level site.

```
<Module Name="OOBThemes" List="123" Url="_catalogs/theme" RootWebOnly="TRUE">
  <File Url="Azure.thmx" Type="GhostableInLibrary"
        Path="lists/themes/Azure.thmx" IgnoreIfAlreadyExists="TRUE" />
  <!-- File elements for other .thmx files have been omitted for clarity -->
</Module>
```

Creating and Initializing Sites

Now that you have learned about site definition and configurations, let's discuss automating the process of creating new sites. You can create a new site in a Windows PowerShell script by calling the SharePoint PowerShell cmdlet named *New-SPSite*. When you do this, you can specify a site template by passing a parameter that identities a specific configuration from one of the standard site definitions. The parameter value is created by specifying the name of the site definition followed by the pound sign (#) and the integer identifier of the configuration. For example, you can use *STS#0* to reference the site template called *Team Site,* and *STS#1* to reference the site template called *Blank Site.* If you want to create a new site collection based on the Publishing site template, you can reference its configuration for creating a new top-level site, which is BLANKINTERNETCONTAINER#0.

The following example of a Windows PowerShell script uses a site template parameter of *STS#1* to create a new site collection that has a Blank site as its top-level site.

```
Add-PSSnapin Microsoft.SharePoint.PowerShell -ErrorAction "SilentlyContinue"

# add variables to track parametrized values used to provision new site
$title= "Wingtip Sales Site"
$url = "http://intranet.wingtip.com/sites/sales"
$owner = "WINGTIP\WendyW"
$template = "STS#1"
$WikiHomePageFeatureId = "00BFEA71-D8FE-4FEC-8DAD-01C19A6E4053"

# create new site collection with Blank site as top-level site
$sc = New-SPSite -URL $url -Name $title -OwnerAlias $owner -Template $template

# obtain reference to top-level site
$site = $sc.RootWeb
```

```
# activate any required features
Enable-SPFeature -Identity $WikiHomePageFeatureId -Url $site.Url

# use the server-side object model to initialize site properties.
$site = $sc.RootWeb
$site.Title = "My Custom Title"
$site.Update
```

As you can see, this approach makes it possible to create a new site using any configuration you want. Once you have created a new top-level site from a specific configuration, you can use the *Enable-SPFeature* cmdlet to enable any required features. You can also use the server-side object model to initialize site properties and to add site elements such as lists and navigation nodes. What we have shown here in a Windows PowerShell script can also be written in C# or Visual Basic code that programs against the server-side object model. The key point is that you can initialize new sites however you want, without having to resort to custom site definitions.

Feature Stapling

A feature can also be used to attach one or more other features to a configuration of a site definition through a technique known as *feature stapling*. For example, instead of creating a custom site definition, you can elect to create a custom feature to extend configurations from a standard site definition. For example, you can create a feature to staple the *MainSite* feature in the WingtipTypes project to the configurations for Team Site and Blank Site.

To staple a feature to a configuration such as Team Site and Blank Site, you must create a second feature to associate the feature to be stapled with one or more configurations. Feature stapling is achieved by adding a *FeatureSiteTemplateAssociation* element that contains an *Id* attribute specifying the feature that is being stapled and a *TemplateName* attribute specifying the target configuration. The following example demonstrates stapling the *MainSite* feature of the WingtipTypes project to the configurations for Team Site and Blank Site.

```
<Elements xmlns="http://schemas.microsoft.com/sharepoint/">
  <FeatureSiteTemplateAssociation
    Id="edcdcd75-dff2-479d-ac32-b37f8fa9d459"
    TemplateName="STS#0" />
  <FeatureSiteTemplateAssociation
    Id="edcdcd75-dff2-479d-ac32-b37f8fa9d459"
    TemplateName="STS#1" />
</Elements>
```

The purpose of feature stapling is to activate features automatically when a new site is created. Once a feature that staples other features has been activated, SharePoint Foundation automatically activates the stapled features as new sites are created. However, it is important that you know how the scope of a feature that staples other features affects the provisioning behavior of SharePoint Foundation.

The activation scope of the feature performing the stapling must be higher than the features being stapled. For example, a feature that activates at the site collection scope can staple only features that activate a site-level scope. A feature that activates at the Web application scope can staple features that activate a site-level scope or at the site collection scope. A feature that activates at the farm scope can staple features that activate at any of the other three scopes.

If you define a feature with an activate scope of Web application scope, it provides a quick and easy way to automate the activation of its stapled features within every new Team site and Blank site that are created in the target Web application. Going one step further, you can associate stapling a feature to the main configuration of the Global site definition. This technique makes it possible to staple a feature to all new sites, as opposed to only sites created from a specific configuration.

```
<Elements xmlns="http://schemas.microsoft.com/sharepoint/">
  <FeatureSiteTemplateAssociation
    Id="edcdcd75-dff2-479d-ac32-b37f8fa9d459"
    TemplateName=" GLOBAL" />
</Elements>
```

This technique is powerful because it provides an approach to activate specific features on any type of site created within a farm. The one caveat here is that the configuration for Blank sites is configured to ignore any features stapled to the Global site definition. You can staple a feature to all site configurations, including Blank Site, using the following code.

```
<Elements xmlns="http://schemas.microsoft.com/sharepoint/">
  <FeatureSiteTemplateAssociation
    Id="edcdcd75-dff2-479d-ac32-b37f8fa9d459"
    TemplateName=" GLOBAL" />
  <FeatureSiteTemplateAssociation
    Id="edcdcd75-dff2-479d-ac32-b37f8fa9d459"
    TemplateName=" STS#1" />
</Elements>
```

Creating a Site Provisioning Provider

Up to now, we have discussed the caveats of creating custom site definitions, and we have stated that we will not show you how to create a custom site definition in this chapter because it is not a recommended approach. This is primarily due to the migration problems that occur when sites are created that depend on custom site definitions. Microsoft recommends that you avoid these problems by creating sites using the standard site definitions that are included as part of SharePoint Foundation and SharePoint Server 2010.

We would like to finish the chapter by demonstrating an advanced technique that makes it possible to add customized site templates to a farm. These site templates will be added in a fashion that allows users to create new top-level sites and child sites in the browser using the standard site template selector of SharePoint Foundation.

The technique involves creating a special type of component known as a *site provisioning provider*. The purpose of a site provisioning provider is to create and initialize new sites. However, a critical aspect of this technique is that it does not rely on a custom site definition. Instead, the technique involves creating new sites using the standard site definition configurations, such as Team Site and Blank Site.

The downloadable .zip archive of companion code for this book contains a sample SharePoint project named WingtipSiteTemplates. This project demonstrates creating a site provisioning provider named *WingtipProvisioningProvider*. Note that because this project contains a site provisioning provider and a Web Template file, it must be deployed as a farm solution. You create a site provisioning provider with a class that inherits from the *SPWebProvisioningProvider* base class and that overrides a single method named *Provision*.

```
using System;
using Microsoft.SharePoint;

namespace WingtipSiteTemplates {
  public class WingtipProvisioningProvider : SPWebProvisioningProvider {
    public override void Provision(SPWebProvisioningProperties properties) {
      // add code to provision new site
    }
  }
}
```

When you implement the *Provision* method, you get to specify the configuration that is used to provision the new site by calling the *ApplyWebTemplate* method. This makes it possible to create customized provisioning instructions while using standard configurations such as Blank Site.

```
public override void Provision(SPWebProvisioningProperties properties) {

  // provision new site using Blank site configuration
  properties.Web.ApplyWebTemplate("STS#1");

  // TODO: add extra code here to initialize new site.
}
```

When the *ApplyWebTemplate* method completes, SharePoint Foundation has finished provisioning the new site using the Blank Site configuration. Now you can add whatever logic you would like to activate features, initialize site properties, and create any required site elements, such as lists and child sites. Note that due to security issues, you must call a method named *RunWithElevatedPrivileges* on the *SPSecurity* class to run your code with the privileges required to initialize a new site.

```
public override void Provision(SPWebProvisioningProperties properties) {
  // apply template using a configuration
  properties.Web.ApplyWebTemplate("STS#1");

  // elevate privileges before programming against site
  SPSecurity.RunWithElevatedPrivileges(delegate() {
    using (SPSite siteCollection = new SPSite(properties.Web.Site.ID)) {
      using (SPWeb site = siteCollection.OpenWeb(properties.Web.ID)) {
        // activate features and initilize site properties
        site.Features.Add(new Guid("00BFEA71-D8FE-4FEC-8DAD-01C19A6E4053"));
        site.Title = "My Custom Site Title";
        site.Update();
      }
    }
  });
}
```

The final step to deploying a site provisioning provider involves creating a Web template file that references the site provisioning provider class. The WingtipSiteTemplates project contains the following Web template file, named webtemp_WingtipSiteTemplates.xml, which is deployed in the Web templates directory for U.S. English at a path of TEMPLATE/1033/XML.

```
<Template Name="WingtipSiteTemplates" ID="11001">

    <Configuration ID="0"
        Title="Wingtip Standard Team Site"
        Hidden="FALSE"
        ImageUrl="/_layouts/images/litware/LITWARE_PREV.PNG"
        Description="Use this site template to create a Wingtip team site."
        DisplayCategory="Wingtip"
        ProvisionAssembly="$SharePoint.Project.AssemblyFullName$"
        ProvisionClass="WingtipSiteTemplates.WingtipProvisioningProvider"
        ProvisionData="StandardTeamSite" />

    <Configuration ID="1"
        Title="Wingtip Sales Site"
        Hidden="FALSE"
        ImageUrl="/_layouts/images/litware/LITWARE_PREV.PNG"
        Description="Use this site template to create a Wingtip team site."
        DisplayCategory="Wingtip"
        ProvisionAssembly="$SharePoint.Project.AssemblyFullName$"
        ProvisionClass="WingtipSiteTemplates.WingtipProvisioningProvider"
        ProvisionData="SalesSite" />

  </Template>

</Templates>
```

As you can see, this Web template file defines two configurations called Wingtip Standard Team Site and Wingtip Sales Site. Both of these configurations are set to display in the standard SharePoint Foundation site template picker under the Wingtip custom tab, as shown in Figure 8-6. You can see that both *Configuration* elements are configured to use the same provisioning provider class, but they have different values for the *ProvisionData* attribute. This makes it possible for the *WingtipProvisioningProvider* class to provide the *Provision* method that inspects the *ProvisionData* attribute to determine what type of new site to create and initialize.

```
public override void Provision(SPWebProvisioningProperties properties) {
  if (properties.Data.Equals("StandardTeamSite")) {
    // add code to provision standard team site
  }
  if (properties.Data.Equals("SalesSite")) {
    // add code to provision standard team site
  }
}
```

FIGURE 8-6 A site provision provider can be used to create site templates that rely on standard configurations such as Blank Site and Team Site.

Conclusion

This chapter has examined advanced techniques for developing custom definitions. We began by discussing how to develop custom field types and custom field controls. While developing custom field types has its share of compatibility issues, it offers the greatest amount of flexibility when initializing field values and performing data validation.

The chapter also taught you how to develop reusable type definitions for site columns, content types, and list templates. You saw that this style of development requires a solid understanding of CAML. Developing CAML-based definitions can be challenging when it comes to testing and debugging, yet it provides advantages over creating site columns, content types, and lists by hand in the browser or through the server-side object model. You can see that developing CAML-based definitions can be helpful in some projects but is overkill in others.

The chapter ended with an examination of how SharePoint Foundation provisions new sites using site definitions and configurations. You also learned about the role of the Global site definition. We ended the chapter by recommending that you avoid developing custom site definitions and that you use alternative techniques for creating and initializing new sites, including feature stapling and developing a custom site provisioning provider.

Chapter 9
Accessing Data in Lists

Microsoft SharePoint lists are intended to be viewed and edited by users. In many SharePoint solutions, however, they also act as a data source supporting create, read, update, delete, and query (CRUDQ) operations. Support for direct editing by users and programmatic access for CRUDQ operations makes SharePoint lists a unique type of data source; they act like a bound data grid and a database table all at the same time.

The dual nature of lists means that careful consideration must be given to how they are used in a SharePoint solution. While lists support CRUDQ operations, they really aren't database tables and should not be used when the power of a database is required. Furthermore, the out-of-the-box interface does not support the same level of customization as an ASP.NET grid control and shouldn't be used in situations where the flexibility of a custom control is required. Ultimately, list-based solutions are best when they are designed so that user editing is supported by custom code for viewing, reporting, rules, and automation.

This chapter is focused on the technologies available in SharePoint to support CRUDQ operations against lists in server-side code. These technologies include object model support for lists and items, query support through the Collaborative Application Markup Language (CAML) and Language Integrated Query (LINQ), and Open XML support for the creation of documents in libraries. Client-side support for CRUDQ operations is covered in Chapter 10, "Client-Side Programming."

Using the Basic List Object Model

SharePoint provides a complete server-side object model for accessing lists and items. Using the objects provided, you can perform create, read, update, and delete (CRUD) operations on any list (querying is done using other techniques covered later in this chapter). The process begins by getting a reference to the list of interest in the form of a *Microsoft.SharePoint* *.SPList* object. List references can be retrieved from the *Microsoft.SharePoint.SPListCollection*, which is available from the *Lists* property of the *SPWeb* object, as shown in the following console application code.

```
using (SPSite siteCollection = new SPSite("http://intranet.wingtip.com"))
{
  using (SPWeb site = siteCollection.OpenWeb)
  {
    foreach(SPList list in site.Lists)
    {
      Console.WriteLine(list.Title);
    }
  }
}
```

Typically, you'll be more interested in referencing a specific list than the *SPListCollection* object. In these cases, you may retrieve a list directly by its name or by using the Uniform Resource Locator (URL) that refers to the location of the list in the current site. When retrieving a list by name, you can use the *TryGetList* method of the *SPListCollection*, which returns *null* if the list does not exist. When retrieving the list by the URL, you can use the *GetList* method of the *SPWeb* object, which throws a *System.IO.FileNotFoundException* if the list does not exist. The following code shows both approaches using a console application.

```
using (SPSite siteCollection = new SPSite("http://intranet.wingtip.com))
{
  using (SPWeb site = siteCollection.OpenWeb)
  {
    SPList toyList = site.Lists.TryGetList("Toys");
    if(toyList != null)
      Console.WriteLine("Success!");
    else
      Console.WriteLine("List does not exist");

    try
    {
      SPList taskList = site.GetList("/Lists/Tasks");
      Console.WriteLine("Success!");
    }
    catch(FileNotFoundException)
    {
      Console.WriteLine("List does not exist");
    }
  }
}
```

Once you have a reference to a list, you may use it to access items. Lists maintain items in a *Microsoft.SharePoint.SPListItemCollection* object, which is accessible via the *Items* property of *SPList*. Items in the collection are returned as *Microsoft.SharePoint.SPListItem* objects. The collection can be bound directly to a grid for display, iterated over using a *foreach* statement, or directly accessed using either the item's ID or index. Each individual *SPListItem* maintains a *Hashtable* of values representing the properties of the item. Listing 9-1 shows snippets of code for a simple Web Part that performs CRUD operations on a specified SharePoint list.

LISTING 9-1 Basic CRUD operations

```
//Set up an SPGirdView
itemGrid = new SPGridView;
itemGrid.AutoGenerateColumns = false;
this.Controls.Add(itemGrid);
BoundField titleField = new BoundField;
titleField.DataField="Title";
titleField.HeaderText="Title";
itemGrid.Columns.Add(titleField);
```

```
//Get the list
SPList list = SPContext.Current.Web.Lists.TryGetList("Toys");
if (list == null)
    messages.Text = "List does not exist.";

//Create a new item
//NOTE: Update must be called
SPListItem newItem = list.Items.Add;
newItem["Title"] = "Created Item " + DateTime.Now.ToLongDateString;
newItem.Update;

//Read items by binding to grid
//NOTE: This loads all items, folders, and fields!
SPListItemCollection items = list.Items;
itemGrid.DataSource = items;
itemGrid.DataBind;

//Delete the first item
list.Items[0].Delete;

//Update the first item
//Note the use of a temporary SPListItem
SPListItem updateItem = list.Items[0];
updateItem["Title"] = "Updated Item " + DateTime.Now.ToLongDateString;
updateItem.Update;
```

Several aspects of the code in Listing 9-1 are worth noting. First, when creating new items in a list, the *Update* method must be called to save the new item. If the *Update* method is not called, then the list item will be lost. Second, when updating a list item, be sure to use a temporary *SPListItem* object, as shown in the code, or your changes will not be saved. In addition, if the item was edited by another user before the update is saved, the operation will fail. Finally, when reading items from a list, you should be careful about accessing the *Items* property of the list. When the *Items* property is accessed, it attempts to load all items, folders, and fields, which can cause performance issues. SharePoint does provide some list throttling, as discussed in the section entitled "Throttling Queries" later in the chapter, to minimize performance issues, but the best way to ensure good performance is to write a query against the list and return only what you need.

Querying Lists with CAML

Querying a list for specific items that meet a certain criteria can be done using the *Microsoft .SharePoint.SPQuery* object. The *SPQuery* object exposes a *Query* property that accepts a CAML fragment, which defines the query to be performed. A *ViewFields* property defines the fields to return. The following code shows a simple query run against a list.

```
SPQuery query = new SPQuery;
query.Viewfields = @"<FieldRef Name='Title'/><FieldRef Name='Expires'/>";
query.Query =
@"<Where>
  <Lt>
    <FieldRef Name='Expires'/>
    <Value Type='DateTime'><Today/></Value>
  </Lt>
</Where>";
SPList list = SPContext.Current.Web.Lists.TryGetList("Announcements");
SPListItemCollections items = list.GetItems(query);
```

The *ViewFields* property accepts a CAML fragment containing a series of *FieldRef* elements. Each *FieldRef* element has a *Name* attribute that specifies the name of the list field to return from the query. Note that the *Name* attribute must contain the name of the field as it is defined in the schema.xml file for the list definition and not simply the display name of the field.

To create a query, you must construct a CAML fragment properly, defining the items to return from the list. At the highest level, the CAML fragment may contain *Where*, *OrderBy*, and *GroupBy* elements. Inside each of these elements, you can use additional CAML elements to specify conditions. Table 9-1 contains a complete list of CAML elements that may be used to create a query, and Listing 9-2 shows the basic form of the CAML query.

LISTING 9-2 CAML query form

```
<Where>
  <Lt>,<Gt>,<Eq>,<Leq>,<Geq>,<Neq>,<BeginsWith>,<Contains>,<IsNotNull>,<IsNull>
    <FieldRef/>
    <Value>[Test Value], Today</Value>

  </Lt>,</Gt>,</Eq>,</Leq>,</Geq>,</Neq>,</BeginsWith>,</Contains>,</IsNotNull>,
    </IsNull>
  <And>,<Or>
  <Lt>,<Gt>,<Eq>,<Leq>,<Geq>,<Neq>,<BeginsWith>,<Contains>,<IsNotNull>,<IsNull>
    <FieldRef/>
    <Value>[Test Value], Today</Value>

  </Lt>,</Gt>,</Eq>,</Leq>,</Geq>,</Neq>,</BeginsWith>,</Contains>,</IsNotNull>,
    </IsNull>
  </And>,</Or>
</Where>
<OrderBy>
  <FieldRef/>
</OrderBy>
<GroupBy>
  <FieldRef/>
<GroupBy>
```

TABLE 9-1 CAML Elements for Querying

Element	Description
And	Groups multiple conditions
BeginsWith	Searches for a string at the beginning of the text field
Contains	Searches for a string within the text field
Eq	Equal to
FieldRef	A reference to a field (useful for *GroupBy* elements)
Geq	Greater than or equal to
GroupBy	Groups results by these fields
Gt	Greater than
IsNotNull	Is not *null* (not empty)
IsNull	Is *null* (empty)
Join	Used to query across two lists that are joined through a *Lookup* field
Leq	Less than or equal to
Lt	Less than
Neq	Not equal to
Now	The current date and time
Or	Boolean or operator
OrderBy	Orders the results of the query
Today	Today's date
TodayIso	Today's date in International Organization for Standardization (ISO) format
Where	Used to specify the *Where* clause of the query

Querying Joined Lists

In addition to querying single lists, the *SPQuery* object can be used to query across two lists that are joined by a *Lookup* field and surfacing projected fields. The basics of list joins, look-ups, and projected fields are covered in Chapter 8, "Templates and Type Definitions." This chapter simply presents the necessary information to query these lists.

For example, consider two lists named Instructors and Modules. The Instructors list is a simple list that contains contact information for classroom instructors. The Modules list is a custom list that contains information about training modules that will be taught in the classroom. The Modules list is joined to the Instructors list via a *Lookup* field that shows the *FullName* of the instructor. In addition, the instructor's *E-mail Address* is available as a projected field. In this way, an instructor may be assigned a module to teach. Using an *SPQuery* object and CAML, you may create a query that returns fields from both of these lists, as shown in Listing 9-3.

LISTING 9-3 Querying joined lists

```
SPWeb site = SPContext.Current.Web;
SPList listInstructors = site.Lists["Instructors"];
SPList listModules = site.Lists["Modules"];

SPQuery query = new SPQuery;
query.Query = "<Where><Eq><FieldRef Name=\"Audience\"/>" +
              "<Value Type=\"Text\">Developer</Value></Eq></Where>";
query.Joins = "<Join Type=\"Inner\" ListAlias=\"classInstructors\">" +
              "<Eq><FieldRef Name=\"Instructor\" RefType=\"Id\" />" +
              "<FieldRef List=\"classInstructors\" Name=\"Id\" /></Eq></Join>";
query.ProjectedFields =
"<Field Name='Email' Type='Lookup' List='classInstructors' ShowField='Email'/>";
query.ViewFields = "<FieldRef Name=\"Title\" /><FieldRef Name=\"Instructor\" />" +
                   "<FieldRef Name=\"Email\" />";

SPListItemCollection items = listModules.GetItems(query);
```

In Listing 9-3, the *Where* clause is created to return training modules that are intended for a developer audience; this is similar to the simple example shown earlier. The *Join* property is new and defines the join between the two lists through the *Lookup* field. Remember that the query is being run on the Modules list, so it must be joined to the Instructors list. The *ListAlias* attribute defines an alias for the Instructors list that may be used in the join clause. The first *FieldRef* element refers to the name of the *Lookup* field in the Modules list and will always have a *RefType* equal to *Id*. The second *FieldRef* in the join clause uses the alias name for the Instructors list and will always have a *Name* equal to *Id*. The *ProjectedFields* property also uses the alias name for the Instructors list and refers to additional fields in the Instructors list that should be returned with the query.

Querying Multiple Lists

While the SPQuery object is good for querying a single list or joined lists, if you want to query multiple lists within a site collection simultaneously, then you can make use of the *Microsoft.SharePoint.SPSiteDataQuery* object. Like the *SPQuery* object, the *SPSiteDataQuery* object has *Query* and *ViewFields* properties. In addition to these fields, the *SPSiteDataQuery* object also has *Lists* and *Webs* properties. The *Lists* property is used to specify the lists within the site collection that should be included in the query. The *Webs* property is used to determine the scope of the query. Listing 9-4 shows a query that returns events from all calendars in the current site collection where the end date is later than today.

LISTING 9-4 Querying multiple lists

```
//Creates the query
SPSiteDataQuery query = new SPSiteDataQuery;

//Builds the query
query.Query = "<Where><Gt><FieldRef Name='EndDate'/>" +
              "<Value Type='DateTime'><Today OffsetDays=\"-1\"/></Value></Gt>
                  </Where>";

//Sets the list types to search
query.Lists = "<Lists ServerTemplate='106' />";

//Sets the Fields to include in results
query.ViewFields = "<FieldRef Name='fAllDayEvent' />" +
                   "<FieldRef Name='Title' />" +
                   "<FieldRef Name='Location' />" +
                   "<FieldRef Name='EventDate' />" +
                   "<FieldRef Name='EndDate' />";

//Sets the scope of the query
query.Webs = @"<Webs Scope='SiteCollection' />";

//Execute the query
DataTable table = SPContext.Current.Site.RootWeb.GetSiteData(query);
```

The *Lists* property in Listing 9-4 is a CAML fragment that can take several forms to specify the lists to include in the query. Setting the property to *<Lists ServerTemplate=*[value]*/>* limits the query to lists of a certain server template. For example, type *106* is a calendar. Table 9-2 shows all the possible values for the *ServerTemplate* attribute. Setting the property to *<Lists BaseType=*[value]*/>* limits the query to lists of a certain *BaseType*. Table 9-3 lists the possible values for the *BaseType* attribute. Setting the property to *<Lists Hidden='true'/>* includes hidden lists in the query. Setting the property to *<Lists MaxListLimit=*[value]*/>* limits the query to considering no more than the specified number of lists.

The *Webs* property is a CAML fragment that must either be *<Webs Scope='SiteCollection'/>* or *<Webs Scope='Recursive'/>*. *SiteCollection* includes all lists in the site collection while *Recursive* includes only those lists in the current site or subsites beneath the current site.

TABLE 9-2 Server Templates

Server Template	ID	Description
GenericList	100	Custom list
DocumentLibrary	101	Document library
Survey	102	Survey
Links	103	Links list
Announcements	104	Announcements list

Server Template	ID	Description
Contacts	105	Contacts list
Events	106	Calendar
Tasks	107	Tasks list
DiscussionBoard	108	Discussion lists
PictureLibrary	109	Picture library.
DataSources	110	Data sources library
WebTemplateCatalog	111	Site template gallery
UserInformation	112	User list
WebPartCatalog	113	Web Part gallery
ListTemplateCatalog	114	List template gallery
XMLForm	115	InfoPath form library
MasterPageCatalog	116	Master Page gallery
WebPageLibrary	119	Wiki Page library
DataConnectionLibrary	130	Data connection library
WorkflowHistory	140	Workflow History list
GanttTasks	150	Project Tasks list
Meetings	200	Meetings
Agenda	201	Meeting agenda
MeetingUser	202	Meeting attendees
Decision	204	Meeting decisions
MeetingObjective	207	Meeting objectives
Posts	301	Blog posts
Comments	302	Blog comments
Categories	303	Blog categories
IssueTracking	1100	Issue tracking list
AdminTasks	1200	Central Administration tasks

TABLE 9-3 BaseType Values

Value	Description
0	Generic list
1	Document library
3	Discussion forum
4	Vote or Survey
5	Issues list

Throttling Queries

Chapter 8 began to discuss the support that SharePoint offers for large lists. In particular, you learned that SharePoint allows administrators to throttle the number of items returned in a list view to prevent performance degradation caused by returning an excessive number of items. While these throttle settings apply to views created by users, they also apply to queries executed in custom code.

When executing queries, the number of results returned will be determined by the throttle settings for the given list and the rights of the current user. Throttle settings are set for the Web application in Central Administration. Rights for the current user that affect throttling include administration rights on the Web front-end server, administration rights in the Web application, and auditor rights in the Web application.

In the context of list throttling, users who have server administration rights on the Web front end where the query is run are known as *server administrators*. Users granted Full Read (auditors) or Full Control (administrators) permissions through the Web application policy in Central Administration are considered *super users*. Everyone else is termed a *normal user*.

The List View Threshold is set at the Web application level and specifies the maximum number of items that a database operation can involve at a single time. The default value for this setting is 5,000, which means that results returned from an *SPQuery* or *SPSiteDataQuery* object will be generally limited to 5,000 items for both super users and normal users. In addition, the List View Lookup Threshold specifies the maximum number of lookup, person/group, or workflow status fields that can be involved in the query. This value defaults to 6. Server administrators are normally not affected by the List View Threshold or List View Lookup Threshold settings.

Both the *SPQuery* and *SPSiteDataQuery* objects have a *QueryThrottleMode* property that can be set to one of the values in the *Microsoft.SharePoint.SPQueryThrottleOption* enumeration. The possible values for the property are *Default*, *Override*, and *Strict*. Setting the *QueryThrottleMode* property to *Default* causes query throttling to be implemented for both super users and normal users based on the List View Threshold and List View Lookup Threshold settings. Server administrators are not affected.

Setting the *QueryThrottleMode* property to *Override* allows super users to return the number of items up to the limit specified in the List View Threshold for the Auditors and Administrators setting so long as the Object Model Override setting is set to "Yes" for the current Web application. Normal users are still limited to returning the number of items specified in the List View Threshold and List View Lookup Threshold settings. Server administrators remain unaffected.

Setting the *QueryThrottleMode* property to *Strict* causes the limits specified by the List View Threshold and List View Lookup Threshold settings to apply to all users. In this case, it makes no difference what rights you have in the Web application or server. Listing 9-5 shows the *RenderContents* method from a Web Part with configurable throttling returning query results from a list and demonstrating the concepts that have just been discussed.

LISTING 9-5 Throttling query results

```
protected override void RenderContents(HtmlTextWriter writer)
{
    SPWeb site = SPContext.Current.Web;
    SPList list = site.Lists[listName];
    SPUser user = SPContext.Current.Web.CurrentUser;
    SPQuery query = new SPQuery;

    //Throttle settings
    if (overrideThrottling)
        query.QueryThrottleMode = SPQueryThrottleOption.Override;
    else
        query.QueryThrottleMode = SPQueryThrottleOption.Strict;

    //Execute query
    query.Query = "</OrderBy>";
    query.ViewFields = "<FieldRef Name=\"Title\" />";
    SPListItemCollection items = list.GetItems(query);

    //Show user role
    if(user.IsSiteAdmin || user.IsSiteAuditor)
        writer.Write("<p>You are a 'Super User'</p>");
    else
        writer.Write("<p>You are a regular user</p>");

    //Is throttling enabled?
    if(list.EnableThrottling)
        writer.Write("<p>Throttling is enabled</p>");
    else
        writer.Write("<p>Throttling is not enabled</p>");

    //Show count of items returned
    writer.Write("<p>" + items.Count + " items returned.</p>");

}
```

Regardless of the value set for the *QueryThrottleMode* property, no results will be throttled if the query is run within the time specified in the Daily Time Window For Large Queries. During this time period, all queries are allowed to run to completion. In addition, the *EnableThrottling* property of the list may be set to *False* to remove the list from any and all throttling restrictions. The *EnableThrottling* property can be set only by someone with Farm Administrator rights using a Microsoft Windows PowerShell script similar to the following.

```
$site = Get-SPWeb -Identity "http://intranet.wingtip.com/products"
$list = $site.Lists["Toys"]
$list.EnableThrottling = $false
```

Introducing LINQ

LINQ is a new technology in SharePoint 2010 that acts as an additional layer on top of the existing CAML technology for performing CRUDQ operations. Between the basic object model operations of the *SPList* and the query operations supported by *SPQuery* and *SPSiteDataQuery*, SharePoint seems to have the full range of CRUDQ operations already covered. Why, then, would SharePoint provide a completely different technology for performing CRUDQ operations on lists? The answer is that coding LINQ operations is much easier than coding CAML operations.

To understand why LINQ is easier to use than CAML, consider the CAML query in Listing 9-3, in the previous section. While this query accomplishes the task of joining two lists across a *Lookup* field, it has several weaknesses because the query is text-based. First, you do not know until run time if the query is written correctly. If the query is not correct, then it will simply fail at run time with an obscure error that provides little diagnostic help. Second, the text-based query provides no IntelliSense support at design time. When writing the query, you have no idea what CAML elements are legal in the syntax without having a reference open. Third, the query is difficult to read. You cannot determine easily what the query is doing and what lists are being joined. Finally, the data returned from the query is placed in a *SPListItem* collection, which does not provide strongly typed business entities. Access to items in the collection and subsequently fields in the items is all performed through text. Once again, you don't know if it's correct until run time.

LINQ addresses the problems posed by CAML because it is an object-oriented query language. Because it provides strongly typed objects at design time, you can create queries in code and know that they are correct because the code compiles. In addition, the strongly typed objects provide IntelliSense at design time, which makes it much easier to construct a correct query. Finally, the results are returned from queries as strongly typed objects, so the items and fields also provide IntelliSense and compile-time checking.

The following code shows a simple LINQ query. Even without knowing anything about LINQ, you can see that the query is easier to read. Along with the design experience provided by the strongly typed objects, this makes LINQ a powerful technology for interacting with lists.

```
var q = from m in dc.Modules
        orderby m.ModuleID
        select new m;
```

LINQ Overview

The development of LINQ technology began in 2003. The goal of LINQ was to make it easier for developers to interact with Structured Query Language (SQL) and Extensible Markup Language (XML) because the programming models were so different. The result today is a query language that can work across a wide variety of sources, including SQL, XML files, arrays, and SharePoint lists, to name just a few.

While the vision for LINQ is to create a single query language that works regardless of the data source, there are several versions of LINQ today. The *System.Linq* namespace provides the core LINQ functionality, but it may be supplemented by other namespaces, such as *System.Data.Linq* for SQL access, *System.Data.Entity* for the Entity Framework, *System.Xml.Linq* for XML manipulation, or *Microsoft.SharePoint.Linq* for SharePoint list operations. In all cases, however, the objective is to write similar syntax regardless of the data source.

Each data source must have a LINQ provider. The LINQ provider for a data source implements the *System.Linq.IQueryable* interface. This interface is the foundation for the LINQ syntax. If a LINQ provider is not available for a data source, then it cannot be queried with LINQ.

As an example of how different data sources can be accessed with similar syntax, look at the code in Listing 9-6. This listing shows access to processes, arrays, XML elements, a database, and a collection of objects. In each case, the LINQ query is very similar and straightforward using a syntax that is similar to a SQL statement.

LISTING 9-6 LINQ queries against different data sources

```
//Processes
var q = from p in Process.GetProcesses
        orderby p.WorkingSet64 descending
        select new { p.ProcessName };

//Arrays
string[] names = { "Ted", "Scot", "Andrew"};

var q = from n in names
        orderby n
        select n;

//XML
string xml = "<Contacts>" +
             "<Contact FirstName=\"Scot\" LastName=\"Hillier\" />" +
             "<Contact FirstName=\"Ted\" LastName=\"Pattison\" />" +
             "<Contact FirstName=\"Andrew\" LastName=\"Connell\" />" +
             "</Contacts>";

XDocument d = XDocument.Parse(xml);
```

```
var q = from c in d.Descendants("Contact")
        select new { c.Attribute("FirstName").Value };

//SQL
using (MiniCRM dc =
       new MiniCRM("Data Source=(local);Initial Catalog=MiniCRM;Integrated
Security=True;"))
{

    MiniCRM_Names[] q = (from n in dc.MiniCRM_Names
                         select n).ToArray;

}

//Objects
List<Instructor> contacts = new List<Instructor>;
contacts.Add(new Instructor("Scot", "Hillier"));
contacts.Add(new Instructor("Andrew", "Connell"));
contacts.Add(new Instructor("Ted", "Pattison"));

var q = from c in contacts
        select new { c.FirstName };
```

Understanding LINQ Language Elements

To be able to write the LINQ queries shown in Listing 9-6, several enhancements were made to the C# language. These enhancements were all targeted at simplifying and unifying how queries are written. Understanding these enhancements will help you create LINQ queries. The following sections cover the key enhancements made to C# and how they are used in LINQ.

Understanding Generic Collections

Generic collections are critical for managing data in LINQ and provide support for strongly typed object collections. Generic collections were introduced in the Microsoft .NET Framework 2.0 and are contained in the *System.Collection.Generics* namespace. Using generic collections, you can create lists, dictionaries, stacks, queues, linked lists, and others based on a particular type. For example, the following code creates a list of *Customer* objects.

```
List<Customer> customers = new List<Customer>;
```

Generic collections are vastly superior to traditional collections such as arrays because they are *type safe*. This means that they can accept only certain object types. Type safety means that the code related to the collection can be checked at compile time instead of run time.

In addition to type safety, generic collections also support enumeration, which is done via the *System.Collections.IEnumerable* interface. This means that generic collections have support for the *foreach* syntax, which is critical for enumerating the results returned from a LINQ query. All .NET Framework arrays also implement *IEnumerable,* which is why LINQ syntax works with standard arrays as well.

Understanding Extension Methods

Extension methods are a language enhancement to C# that allows you to create new methods for a class without subclassing. For example, suppose that you wanted to create a new method for the *string* class called *IsValidEmailAddress* that can be used to see if the *string* contains an email address. To create the extension method, you must create a new *static* class that contains the extension method as a static method. The following code shows how this is done.

```
static void Main(string[] args)
{
    //Extension method
    string email = "administrator@wingtip.com";
    Console.WriteLine(email.IsValidEmailAddress);
}

public static class ExtensionMethod
{
    public static bool IsValidEmailAddress(this string s)
    {
        Regex r = new Regex(@"^[\w-\.]+@([\w-]+\.)+[\w-]{2,4}$");
        return r.IsMatch(s);
    }
}
```

Once the extension method is created, it becomes available as a method for the class. This method shows up in IntelliSense as if it were a standard method for the class. Figure 9-1 shows the extension method in Microsoft Visual Studio.

FIGURE 9-1 An extension method

Extension methods are critical to LINQ queries because they enable functionality in the query. The *System.Linq* namespace defines several extension methods for the *IEnumerable* interface that you can use right away. Perhaps the most important extension method is the *Where* method, which enables you to specify the items to return from a query. This method takes as an argument a *delegate* function to execute. Listing 9-7 shows how the *delegate* function is defined and used in the *Where* method to find files that were created on the first day of the month.

LISTING 9-7 The *Where* extension method

```
Func<FileInfo, bool> whereMethod = CreatedOnFirstDay;

static void Main(string[] args)
{
    DirectoryInfo di = new DirectoryInfo("C:\\");
    var q1 = di.GetFiles.Where(CreatedOnFirstDay);
}

static bool CreatedOnFirstDay(FileInfo info)
{
    return info.CreationTime.Day == 1;
}
```

Perhaps the most interesting part of the code in Listing 9-7 is the syntax used by the *Where* method. Note that this syntax looks decidedly different from the LINQ queries shown earlier in the chapter. This is because the syntax in Listing 9-7 uses *method syntax,* while the earlier code uses *query syntax.* Method syntax looks more like traditional code, while query syntax looks more like a SQL statement. Both method syntax and query syntax are equivalent, but query syntax is preferred because it is more readable. The following code shows the equivalent query syntax for finding files created on the first day of the month.

```
var q4 = from f in di.GetFiles
            where f.CreationTime.Day == 1
            select f;
```

Understanding Lambda Expressions

When using method syntax in LINQ, you must often create a *delegate* function. The *delegate* functions are a bit messy because they must be declared, defined, and then passed as an argument. In C#, you can create a shorthand version of a *delegate* function in line with the extension method. This shorthand method is known as an *anonymous* function because the in-line declaration does not have a specific name. The following code shows the equivalent anonymous function code for the method syntax shown in Listing 9-7.

```
var q2 = di.GetFiles.Where(delegate(FileInfo info){
            return info.CreationTime.Day == 1;
            });
```

While the anonymous function simplifies the method syntax code, C# will let you go even further by using a *lambda* expression. A lambda expression is a shorthand representation of an anonymous function. The lambda expression uses the lambda operator =>, which is read as "goes to," to relate the input parameters to the statement block. The following code shows the equivalent lambda expression code for the method syntax shown in Listing 9-7. The expression is read as "info goes to info.CreationTime.Day equals 1."

```
var q3 = di.GetFiles.Where(info => info.CreationTime.Day == 1);
```

Understanding Projections

C# introduced several language enhancements that support shorthand ways of creating properties, objects, and collections. Specifically, C# supports automatic properties, shorthand initializers, and anonymous types. Each of these enhancements has a role to play in LINQ.

Automatic properties are a way to define properties in a class without coding member variables. The compiler emits the getter and setter for you. Automatic properties are useful when you do not need to code any logic into the getter and setter methods. The following code shows a simple example of automatic properties in a class.

```
public class Person {
  public string FirstName { get; set; }
  public string LastName  { get; set; }
  public int    Age       { get; set; }
}
```

Along with automatic properties, C# also provides shortcuts for object and collection initialization. These shortcuts complement automatic properties and allow you to create whole collections with compact code. The following code shows object and collection initialization using the shorthand code.

```
//Object Initializer
Contact c= new Contact{ FirstName="Gustavo", LastName="Achong" };
//Collection Initializer
List<Contact> contacts = new List<Contact>{
Contact c= new Contact{ FirstName="Gustavo", LastName="Achong" },
Contact c= new Contact{ FirstName="Cathy", LastName="Abel" },
Contact c= new Contact{ FirstName="Kim", LastName="Aber" },
};
```

Closely related to automatic properties and initialization is the idea of anonymous types. Anonymous types give a simple way of creating an object with read-only properties without actually having to define the type. The compiler creates the type name, which is not available to the source code. Instead, the new type is referenced using the *var* keyword. The object is still strongly typed, but the type name is not exposed to the code. The following code shows a simple example of an anonymous type that uses shorthand initialization and the *var* keyword.

```
var v= new { FirstName="Gustavo", LastName="Achong" };
```

The object coding enhancements in C# allow LINQ to perform projections of results into anonymous types. When using projections, LINQ creates a new anonymous type and initializes it with read-only data from the query results. The key to creating the projection is to use the *new* keyword in the *select* statement to create an anonymous type with automatic properties. The following code shows a projection creating a new collection of process names.

```
var q = from p in Process.GetProcesses
        orderby p.WorkingSet64 descending
        select new { Name = p.ProcessName };
```

Working with LINQ to SharePoint

The LINQ to SharePoint provider is part of the *Microsoft.SharePoint.Linq* namespace and is used as an additional layer on top of CAML. LINQ queries created with the LINQ to SharePoint provider are translated into CAML queries for execution. While LINQ to SharePoint is not a complete replacement for CAML, it does provide CRUDQ operations for lists. Because of its full support for CRUDQ operations and the inherent advantages of LINQ development over CAML, you will generally use LINQ as your primary interface for working with lists. You will fall back to CAML only when required, such as when overriding throttles or aggregating multiple lists with the *SPSiteDataQuery* object.

Generating Entities with *SPMetal*

SharePoint list data is maintained in the content database. This means that the structure of the list and item data is based on relational tables. As a SharePoint developer, however, you do not need to understand the structure of these tables because the object model abstracts the structure into *SPList* and *SPListItem* objects. When you write a LINQ to SharePoint query, you should expect the same experience as when using the object model. List and item data should be abstracted so that you do not have to understand the content database schema.

LINQ to SharePoint provides an object layer abstraction on top of the content database through the use of *entity classes*. Entity classes are lightweight, object-relational interfaces to the list and item data in the content database. In addition, entity classes are used to track changes and provide optimistic concurrency during updates.

Entity classes are created using a command-line utility called *SPMetal*. *SPMetal* is located in the SharePoint system directory at C:\Program Files\Common Files\Microsoft Shared\Web server extensions\14\Bin. As a best practice, you should update the *PATH* variable in your environment to include the path to *SPMetal*. This way, you can simply run the utility immediately after opening a command window.

Generating entity classes with *SPMetal* can be very simple. At a minimum, you must specify the site for which you want to generate entities and the name of the code file to create. Once the code file is created, you may immediately add it to a project in Visual Studio and start writing LINQ queries. The following code shows an example that will generate entity classes for all the lists and content types in a site.

```
SPMetal /web:http://intranet.wingtip.com /code:Entities.cs
```

While generating entity classes can be quite easy, you will likely want more control over which entities are created and how they are structured. *SPMetal* provides a number of additional arguments that you can use to alter code generation. Table 9-4 lists and describes all of the possible arguments for *SPMetal*.

TABLE 9-4 *SPMetal* **Arguments**

Argument	Description
/code:<filename>	Specifies the name of the generated file.
/language:<language>	Specifies the language for the generated code. Can be either csharp or vb.
/namespace:<namespace>	Specifies the namespace for the generated code.
/parameters:<file>	Specifies an XML file with detailed code-generation parameters.
/password:<password>	Specifies credentials to use for data access during the code-generation process.
/serialization:<type>	Specifies the serialization type. Can be either none or unidirectional.
/user:<username>	Specifies credentials to use for data access during the code-generation process.
/useremoteapi	Specifies that the generation of entity classes is to be done for a remote SharePoint site, such as SharePoint Online.
/web:<url>	The URL of the SharePoint site for which entities will be generated.

If you examine the code file generated by *SPMetal*, you will see that there are two kinds of classes are created. First, a single class is created that inherits from *Microsoft.SharePoint.Linq .DataContext*. The *DataContext* class provides a connection to lists and change tracking for operations. You can think of the *DataContext* class as serving a purpose similar to the *SqlConnection* class in data access code. Second, multiple classes are generated that represent the various content types used by the lists on the site. Using the *DataContext* class together with the entity classes allows you to write LINQ queries. Listing 9-8 shows a simple LINQ query written to return all training modules contained in the Modules list using a *DataContext* class named *Entities*.

LISTING 9-8 A simple LINQ to SharePoint query

```
using (Entities dc = new Entities(SPContext.Current.Web.Url))
{
    var q = from m in dc.Modules
            orderby m.Title
            select m;

    foreach (var module in q)
    {
        moduleList.Items.Add(module.Title);
    }
}
```

Understanding the *DataContext* Class

Before performing any LINQ operations, you must connect to a site using the *DataContext* object. The *DataContext* accepts a URL in the constructor so that you can specify the site where it should connect, which is useful as you move your code from development to production. Of course, the site you specify must actually have the lists and content types for which entities have been generated. Otherwise, your operations will fail. The *DataContext* class also implements *IDisposable* so that it can be coded with a *using* block.

The *DataContext* class provides a *GetList<T>* method that provides access to each list for which an entity has been generated. You can use this method in LINQ query syntax to specify easily the list against which the query should be run. Along with the method, the *DataContext* also has a property of *EntityList<T>* for each list. Listing 9-8 showed an example using *dc.Modules* in the LINQ query.

The *Log* property can be used for viewing the underlying CAML created from the LINQ query. This is useful for not only monitoring and debugging, but it also can be used to help create CAML queries for the *SPQuery* and *SPSiteDataQuery* objects. The *Log* property accepts a *System.IO.TextWriter* object so you can write the log to a file or output it in a Web Part easily.

The *DataContext* class will track changes made to the entity objects so that they can be written back to the content database. The *ObjectTrackingEnabled* property determines whether the *DataContext* will track changes. The property defaults to *True*, but setting it to *False* will improve performance for read-only operations. If the *DataContext* is tracking changes, then the content database may be updated by calling the *SubmitChanges* method. A detailed discussion appears in the section entitled "Adding, Deleting, and Updating with LINQ to SharePoint" later in this chapter.

Using Parameters.xml to Control Code Generation

The arguments accepted by *SPMetal* provide a fair amount of control over the entity-generation process, but in practice, you will likely want even more control. The highest level of control over entity generation is given by passing a parameters.xml file to *SPMetal* with detailed information about the entities to generate.

The parameters.xml file contains elements that give *SPMetal* specific details about code generation. In particular, it specifies what lists, content types, and fields should be generated in code. The parameters.xml file is passed to *SPMetal* through the */parameters* argument. The following code shows a sample parameters.xml file.

```xml
<?xml version="1.0" encoding="utf-8"?>
<Web Class="Entities" AccessModifier="Public"
  xmlns="http://schemas.microsoft.com/SharePoint/2009/spmetal" >
  <List Name="Instructors" Member="Instructors">
    <ContentType Name="Contact" Class="Instructor">
      <Column Name="FullName" Member="FullName"/>
      <ExcludeOtherColumns/>
    </ContentType>
  </List>
  <List Name="Modules" Member="Modules" />
  <ExcludeOtherLists/>
</Web>
```

The *Web* element is the root of the schema. The *Class* attribute specifies the name of the *DataContext* class to generate, and the *AccessModifier* attribute specifies the access level to the class. The *List* element is a child of the *Web* element and specifies the name of a list for which entities should be generated. The *Member* attribute specifies the name of the property in *DataContext* that will represent this list. The *ContentType* element is a child of the *List* element and specifies a content type for which an entity should be generated. The *Class* attribute specifies the name of the generated class. The *Column* element is a child of the *ContentType* element and specifies a column that should be included in the generated entity. The *ExcludeOtherColumns*, *ExcludeOtherContentTypes*, and *ExcludeOtherLists* elements are used to stop looking for items to include in entity generation. In this way, you can specify the exact set of lists, content types, and columns to include in the generated entities. This is very useful for excluding list, content types, and columns that are present in the development environment, but will not be present in the production environment. Table 9-5 shows the complete schema for the parameters.xml file.

TABLE 9-5 **Parameters.xml Schema**

Element	Child Elements	Attribute	Description
Web	List ExcudeList ExcludeOtherLists IncludeHiddenLists ContentType ExcludeContentType ExcludeOtherContentTypes IncludeHiddenContentType	*Class* (optional)	Name of *DataContext* class
		AccessModifier (optional)	Specifies accessibility of *DataContext* and entity classes. May be *Internal* or *Public*.
List	ContentType ExcludeContentType	Name	Name of the list in SharePoint
		Member (optional)	Name of the *DataContext* property representing the list
		Type (optional)	Type of the *DataContext* property representing the list
ContentType	Column ExcludeColumn ExcludeOtherColumns IncludeHiddenColumns	Name	Name of the content type
		Class (optional)	Name of the generated class
		AccessModifier (optional)	Accessibility of the generated class
Column	N/A	Name	Name of the column
		Member (optional)	Name of the generated property for the column
		Type (optional)	Type of the generated property for the column
ExcludeColumn	N/A	Name	Name of the column to exclude from entity generation
ExcludeOtherColumns	N/A	N/A	Excludes all columns not explicitly included
IncludeHiddenColumns	N/A	N/A	Includes hidden columns in entity generation

Element	Child Elements	Attribute	Description
ExcludeList	N/A	Name	Name of the list to exclude from entity generation
ExcludeOtherLists	N/A	N/A	Excludes all lists not explicitly included
IncludeHiddenLists	N/A	N/A	Includes hidden lists in entity generation
ExcludeContentType	N/A	Name	Name of content type to exclude from entity generation
ExcludeOtherContentTypes	N/A	N/A	Excludes all content types not explicitly included
IncludeHiddenContentTypes	N/A	N/A	Includes hidden content types in entity generation

Querying with LINQ to SharePoint

Once you have entities generated, then you can begin to write LINQ to SharePoint queries. Writing LINQ to SharePoint queries is very similar to writing LINQ queries for other data sources. You formulate a query using query syntax, receive the results into an anonymous type and then use the *IEnumerable* interface to iterate over the results. Listing 9-4 earlier in the chapter shows a simple example.

LINQ to SharePoint also supports querying across lists that are joined by a *Lookup* field. Listing 9-3, earlier in this chapter, showed how this is possible with CAML, but LINQ to SharePoint makes the syntax much simpler. The following code shows the equivalent LINQ query for the CAML shown in Listing 9-3. Note how the join is done simply by using the dot operator to move easily from the Modules list to the joined Instructors list.

```
var q = from m in dc.Modules
        orderby m.ModuleID
        select new { m.Title, Presenter = m.Instructor.FullName, Email = m.Instructor.Email};
```

Not only does this code join two lists together, but it is also using a projection. The *new* keyword is creating a new set of anonymous objects whose field names have been set to *Title*, *Presenter*, and *Email*.

LINQ to SharePoint also allows you to perform query composition. Query composition is the ability to run a LINQ query on the results of a LINQ query. For example, the following code shows how to run a new query specifically looking for a training module named "Visual Studio 2010."

```
var q1 = from m1 in dc.Modules
         orderby m1.ModuleID
         select new {
           m1.Title, Presenter = m1.Instructor.FullName,
           Email = m1.Instructor.Email
         };
var q2 = from m2 in q1
         where m2.Title.Equals("Visual Studio 2010")
         select m2;
```

Finally, LINQ to SharePoint supports a number of extension methods that you can use for aggregation, grouping, and returning specific entities. The methods are often used on the results of the query. The following code, for example, shows how to return the total number of training modules in the query results. The most commonly used extension methods are listed in Table 9-6.

```
var t = (from m in dc.Modules
         select m).Count;
```

TABLE 9-6 Commonly Used Extension Methods

Method	Description
Any	Returns *true* if there are any items in the query results.
Average	Returns the aggregated average value.
Count	Returns the count of items in the query result.
First	Returns the first item in the results. This is useful if you are expecting a single result.
FirstOrDefault	Returns the first item in the results. If there is no first item, it returns the default for the object type.
Max, Min	Return the item with the maximum or minimum value.
Skip	Skips a certain number of items in the results. This is useful when used with *Take* for paging.
Sum	Returns the aggregated sum.
Take	Allows you to return only a specified number of results. Useful when used with *Skip* for paging.
ToList	Returns the query results into a generic List<T>.

Adding, Deleting, and Updating with LINQ to SharePoint

Along with queries, you can also add, delete and update lists with LINQ to SharePoint. Adding and deleting items are accomplished using methods associated with the *EntityList<T>* property of the *DataContext*. The *InsertOnSubmit* method adds a single new item to a list; the *InsertAllOnSubmit* method adds a collection of new items to a list; the *DeleteOnSubmit* method deletes a single item from a list; and the *DeleteAllOnSubmit* method deletes a collection of items from a list. The *RecycleOnSubmit* method puts a single item into the Recycle Bin, and the *RecycleAllOnSubmit* method puts a collection of items in the Recycle Bin. The following code shows an example of adding a new item to the Modules list.

```
using (Entities dc = new Entities(SPContext.Current.Web.Url))
{
    ModulesItem mi = new ModulesItem;
    mi.Title = "LINQ to SharePoint";
    mi.Id = 301;
    dc.Modules.InsertonSubmit(mi);
    dc.SubmitChanges();
}
```

Updating items in lists is done by simply changing the property values in the item and then calling the *SubmitChanges* method of the *DataContext*. The following code shows a simple example of an update operation.

```
using (Entities dc = new Entities(SPContext.Current.Web.Url))
{
    var q = (from m in dc.Modules
            where m.Id==1
            select m).First;

    q.Title = "Revised Title for Module 1";
    dc.SubmitChanges();
}
```

When updating items, LINQ to SharePoint uses optimistic concurrency. The provider will check to see whether the items in the list have been changed since your LINQ query was run before it will attempt to update them. If a discrepancy is found for any of the submitted entities, then no changes are committed. All discrepancies must be resolved before any change in the current batch can be committed.

When discrepancies are found during the update process, LINQ to SharePoint throws a *Microsoft.SharePoint.Linq.ChangeConflictException*. In addition, the *ChangeConflicts* collection of the *DataContext* is populated with *ObjectChangeConflict* objects that contain data about fields in the item that are causing conflicts. The *SubmitChanges* method supports overloads that allow you to specify whether update attempts should continue after the first conflict or whether update attempts should stop. The *ChangeConflicts* collection will be populated only with information about failed attempts, so electing to stop after the first failure will not provide complete data on all conflicts. Regardless of whether or not you continue update attempts, remember that no changes will be saved if any conflict occurs. The purpose of continuing update attempts is to populate the *ChangeConflicts* collection completely.

The *ChangeConflicts* collection contains a *MemberConflicts* collection, which has detailed information about the actual values causing the conflict. In particular, the *MemberConflicts* collection is populated with *MemberChangeConflict* objects, each of which has *OriginalValue*, *CurrentValue*, and *DatabaseValue* properties. *OriginalValue* is the value of the column when the LINQ query was run. *CurrentValue* is the value that *SubmitChanges* is attempting to write to the content database. *DatabaseValue* is the current value of the column in the database. Trapping *ChangeConflictException* and using the *MemberChangeConflict* objects allows you to display the conflicts to the user. The code in Listing 9-9 shows how to iterate the collection, build a list, and bind the list to a grid for display.

LISTING 9-9 A simple LINQ to SharePoint query

```
Try
{
    //Update code
}
catch (Microsoft.SharePoint.Linq.ChangeConflictException x)
{
    conflicts = new List<Conflict>;
    foreach (ObjectChangeConflict cc in dc.ChangeConflicts)
    {
        foreach (MemberChangeConflict mc in cc.MemberConflicts)
        {
            Conflict conflict = new Conflict;
            conflict.OriginalValue = mc.OriginalValue.ToString;
            conflict.CurrentValue = mc.CurrentValue.ToString;
            conflict.DatabaseValue = mc.DatabaseValue.ToString;
            conflicts.Add(conflict);
        }

    }
    conflictGrid.DataSource = conflicts;
    conflictGrid.DataBind;
}
```

Along with displaying the results, you can also resolve conflicts in code. After displaying the results to users in a grid, you can allow them to select whether the pending changes should be forced or lost. The *Resolve* method of the *MemberChangeConflict* class accepts a *Microsoft.SharePoint.Linq.RefreshMode* enumeration, which can have a value of *KeepChanges*, *KeepCurrentValues*, or *OverwriteCurrentValues*. *KeepChanges* accepts every pending change but gives the highest priority to the current user. *KeepCurrentValues* keeps only the changes made by the current user and loses all other changes. *OverwriteCurrentValues* loses the current changes and sets the values to what is in the database. After calling the *Resolve* method, you must call the *SubmitChanges* method again to complete the operation. The following code shows an example of keeping the current changes and losing all other changes.

```
foreach (ObjectChangeConflict cc in dc.ChangeConflicts)
{
    foreach (MemberChangeConflict mc in cc.MemberConflicts)
    {
        mc.Resolve(RefreshMode.KeepCurrentValues);
    }
}
dc.SubmitChanges;
```

Working with Document Libraries

So far in this chapter, the focus has been on list items that do not have associated files. However, document libraries represent a significant part of the SharePoint infrastructure, and you will often want to perform operations on libraries, files, and folders as part of your custom solutions. The good news is that a document library is really just a specialized type of list so everything you know about CAML and LINQ applies to document libraries. You only need to supplement your knowledge to deal specifically with the files that these libraries contain.

Using the Basic Library Object Model

Because a document library is a specialized list, you will find that the *SPList* object can be used to access document libraries as well as lists. This means that document libraries appear in the *Lists* collection of *SPWeb* objects just like any other list. The server-side object model supplements the functionality offered by the *SPList* through the *Microsoft.SharePoint. SPDocumentLibrary* object, which inherits from *SPList* and provides the additional functionality necessary to work with document libraries. If you have a reference to an *SPList* object, you can use the following code to see if the list is actually a document library.

```
public bool IsListAlsoDocumentLibrary(SPList list) {
  if (list is SPDocumentLibrary)
    return true;
  else
    return false;
}
```

Once you have a reference to a document library, you may access it through either the *SPList* object or the *SPDocumentLibrary* object. In many cases, you will start by working with the *SPList* object to access the individual *SPListItem* objects in the library and their associated metadata. You can subsequently use the *SPListItem* object to access the document associated with the item through the *File* property. The *File* property returns a *Microsoft.SharePoint. SPFile* object. The *SPFile* object may be used to manage the document and read and write content. The following code shows how to access the *SPFile* object from the *SPListItem* object and manipulate the file using the object model.

```
foreach (SPListItem item in docLib.Items)
{
  if (item.FileSystemObjectType == SPFileSystemObjectType.File) {
    SPFile file = item.File;
    //Check on number of versions
    int versionCount = file.Versions.Count;
    //Determine when document was checked out
    DateTime checkedOutDate = file.CheckedOutDate;
    //Open document for stream-based access
    using(Stream fileContents = file.OpenBinaryStream) {
      // program against stream to access document content
    }
  }
}
```

Along with documents, many libraries will also contain folders. Folders in a document library are stored as *SPListItem* objects, but they do not return files from the *File* property. This structure can be confusing because iterating over the items in a collection will simply return all items and folders in a flat table. If you instead want to access the documents in a particular folder, then you must use the *Microsoft.SharePoint.SPFolder* object.

The *SPDocumentLibrary* object has a *RootFolder* property, which in turn has a *Files* collection. The *RootFolder* property returns a *SPFolder* object, and the *Files* collection returns all the files that are in the root of the library. A *SubFolders* property on the *SPFolder* object allows you to work through the complete hierarchy of folders in the library. The code in Listing 9-10 shows how to build a tree view of a document library recursively based on the underlying folder structure.

LISTING 9-10 Building a hierarchy of documents from a library

```
protected override void OnLoad(EventArgs e) {
  SPWeb site = SPContext.Current.Web;
  foreach (SPList list in site.Lists) {
    if (list is SPDocumentLibrary && !list.Hidden) {
      SPDocumentLibrary docLib = (SPDocumentLibrary)list;
      SPFolder folder = docLib.RootFolder;
      TreeNode docLibNode = new TreeNode(docLib.Title,
                                         docLib.DefaultViewUrl,
                                         @"\_layouts\images\ITDLSM.GIF");

      LoadFolderNodes(folder, docLibNode);
      treeSitesFiles.Nodes.Add(docLibNode);
    }
  }
  treeSitesFiles.ExpandDepth = 1;
}

protected void LoadFolderNodes(SPFolder folder, TreeNode folderNode) {
  foreach (SPFolder childFolder in folder.SubFolders) {
    if (childFolder.Name != "Forms") {
      TreeNode childFolderNode = new TreeNode(childFolder.Name,
                                              childFolder.Name,
                                              @"\_layouts\images\FOLDER.GIF");
```

```
      LoadFolderNodes(childFolder, childFolderNode);
      folderNode.ChildNodes.Add(childFolderNode);
    }
  }
  foreach (SPFile file in folder.Files) {
    TreeNode fileNode;
    fileNode = new TreeNode(file.Name, file.Name, @"\_layouts\images\ICGEN.GIF");
    folderNode.ChildNodes.Add(fileNode);
  }
}
```

Along with managing metadata and viewing files, you will also want to add new files to document libraries. When adding new files to document libraries, it is important to recognize that the library is really just an abstraction on top of the SharePoint website. What this means is that when you add files to a document library, you are really just adding documents to a specific location on the SharePoint site. Therefore, the code for adding documents is found in the *SPWeb* object, not the *SPDocumentLibrary* object.

The *SPWeb* object has a *Files* property, which returns the *SPFileCollection* of files in the root of the site. The *SPFileCollection* object provides *Add* and *Delete* methods, which can be used to manage files on the site. The *Add* method has several overloads, but generally you will need the URL for the library and a *Stream* object for the file. Listing 9-11 shows how to upload a simple text file to the root folder of the Shared Documents document library.

LISTING 9-11 Uploading a file

```
//Create stream and add document content
Stream documentStream = new MemoryStream;
StreamWriter writer = new StreamWriter(documentStream);
writer.Write("Some content for my simple text document");
writer.Flush;

//Add document into document library
string fileName = "MyFile.txt";
string url = "http://intranet.wingtip.com/Shared%20Documents/";
site.Files.Add(url + filename, documentStream, true);
```

A separate overload of the *Add* method can be used to add new metadata for a document when it is uploaded. When you use this method, you must create a *Hashtable* containing the metadata values assigned to properties of the library. Listing 9-12 shows a complete file upload operation that sets metadata values.

LISTING 9-12 Uploading a file with metadata

```
//Create stream and add document content
Stream documentStream = new MemoryStream;
StreamWriter writer = new StreamWriter(documentStream);
writer.Write("Some content for my simple text document");
writer.Flush;

string fileName = "MyFile.txt";
string url = "http://intranet.wingtip.com/";

//Set metadata
Hashtable docProperties = new Hashtable;
docProperties["vti_title"] = "My Text File";

//Add document into document library
site.Files.Add(url + filename, documentStream, docProperties, true);
```

Note that in Listing 9-12, the names of the document properties do not correspond to the display names of the metadata for the library. The names of the file properties must be the actual names maintained by the document itself. You can list all the metadata properties for a document using the following code.

```
SPList list = site.Lists["Shared Documents"];
foreach (SPListItem item in list.Items) {
  SPFile file = item.File;
  foreach (DictionaryEntry entry in file.Properties) {
    Console.WriteLine(entry.Key + ": " + entry.Value);
  }
  break;
}
```

Working with Open XML

When you are working with documents in SharePoint 2010, you will quite often be dealing with Microsoft Office documents. Therefore, it is important to understand how to create, modify, and manage these document types in your custom solutions. With Office 2007 and later, the file formats for all Office documents are based on an XML standard designed to be more extensible and interoperable than previous formats.

The idea behind the XML document specification is to create an open standard for document definitions so that they may be shared between tools and transformed between systems easily. For SharePoint developers, the Open XML formats are a real advantage because they allow the creation and manipulation of documents through standard XML programming techniques. Prior to Office 2007, the document formats were based on a proprietary binary format that was not documented. From a development perspective, the only way to manipulate a document was to use the object model through automation. This meant starting Microsoft Word, Microsoft Excel, or Microsoft PowerPoint programmatically and then executing operations against it to create documents or slideshows, import data, or print reports.

The problem with automating Word, Excel, and PowerPoint is that they were never intended to function as server products, but they often were deployed on servers to centralize the automation. Because the products were not server-ready, instances of Word, Excel, and PowerPoint often did not shut down properly. In many cases, these solutions required periodic rebooting of the server just to clear the stalled instances of the software. Fortunately, this kind of deployment is no longer necessary.

Understanding Document Packages

Before writing custom solutions against the open XML formats in Office 2010, you should understand the basic structure of an Office document. For example, consider the structure of a simple Word 2010 document. Office Open XML file formats are based on standard .zip file technology. Each top-level file is saved as a .zip archive, which means you can rename the file with a .zip extension and examine the contents.

The Word, Excel, or PowerPoint file is known as a *package* in Open XML parlance. Because a package is implemented as a standard .zip archive, it automatically provides compression and makes its contents instantly accessible to many existing utilities and application programming interfaces (APIs) on Windows platforms and non-Windows platforms alike.

Inside a package are two kinds of internal components: *parts* and *items*. In general, parts contain content and items contain metadata describing the parts. Items can be subdivided further into *relationship items* and *content-type items*.

A part is an internal component containing content that is persisted inside the package. The majority of parts are simple text files serialized as XML with an associated XML schema. However, parts can also be serialized as binary data when necessary, such as when a Word document contains a graphic image or media file.

A part is named by using a Uniform Resource Identifier (URI) that contains its relative path within the package file combined with the part file name. For example, the main part within the package for a Word document is named /word/document.xml.

The Open XML file formats use relationships to define associations between a source and a target part. A package relationship defines an association between the top-level package and a part. A part relationship defines an association between a parent part and a child part. Relationships are important because they make these associations discoverable without examining the content within the parts in question. Relationships are independent of content-specific schemas and are, therefore, faster to resolve. An additional benefit is that you can establish a relationship between two parts without modifying either of them.

Relationships are defined in internal components known as relationship items. A relationship item is stored inside the package just like a part, although a relationship item is not actually considered a part. For consistency, relationship items are always created inside folders named _rels.

For example, a package contains exactly one package relationship item named /_rels/.rels. The package relationship item contains XML elements to define package relationships, such as the one between the top-level package for a .docx file and the internal part /word/ document.xml, as shown in the following code.

```xml
<?xml version="1.0" encoding="UTF-8" standalone="yes"?>
<Relationships xmlns="../package/2006/relationships ">
  <Relationship Id="rId1"
                Type="../officeDocument/2006/relationships/officeDocument"
                Target="word/document.xml"/>
</Relationships>
```

A *Relationship* element defines a name, type, and target part. Furthermore, the type name for a relationship is defined by using the same conventions used to create XML namespaces. In addition to a single package relationship item, a package can also contain one or more part relationship items. For example, you can define relationships between /word/document.xml and child parts inside a package relationship item located at the URI /word/_rels/document .xml.rels. Note that the *Target* attribute for a relationship in a part relationship item is a URI relative to the parent part, not the top-level package.

Every part inside a package is defined in terms of a specific content type. Don't confuse these content types with a Content Type in SharePoint because they are completely different. A content type within a package is metadata that defines a part's media type, a subtype, and a set of optional parameters. Any content type used within a package must be explicitly defined inside a component known as a content type item. Each package has exactly one content type item, which is named /[Content_Types].xml. The following is an example of content type definitions inside the /[Content_Types].xml item of a typical Word document.

```xml
<?xml version="1.0" encoding="UTF-8" standalone="yes"?>
<Types xmlns="http://schemas.openxmlformats.org/package/2006/content-types">
  <Default
     Extension="rels"
     ContentType="application/vnd.openxmlformats-
                  package.relationships+xml"/>
  <Default
     Extension="xml"
     ContentType="application/xml"/>
  <Override
   PartName="/word/document.xml"
   ContentType="application/vnd.openxmlformats-
                officedocument.wordprocessingml.document.main+xml "/>
</Types>
```

Content types are used by the consumer of a package to interpret how to read and render the content within its parts. A default content type is typically associated with a file extension, such as .rels or .xml. *Override content types* are used to define a specific part in terms of a content type that differs from the default content type associated with its file extension. For example, /word/document.xml is associated with an *Override* content type that differs from the default content type used for files with an *.xml* extension.

Using the Open XML SDK 2.0

While understanding the package structure is important, creating solutions that read and write XML directly to the Open XML file formats is tedious and prone to error. When Open XML first emerged, this was exactly how solutions were created. Fortunately, a new set of libraries that provides strongly typed objects for manipulating documents is now available for use with Open XML. To use these documents, you must download and install the Open XML software development kit (SDK), version 2.0.

Once you have installed the Open XML 2.0 SDK, you will be able to set a reference to the assembly DocumentFormat.OpenXML.dll file. This assembly contains more than 50 different namespaces that represent a tremendous amount of functionality crossing all types of Office documents. A complete presentation of Open XML is well beyond the scope of this chapter; the goal here is just to present the basics so that you can see how it fits into your SharePoint solutions.

As a simple example, Listing 9-13 shows how to create a simple Word document using the *DocumentFormat.OpenXML* namespace. Within this listing, there are several things to note. First, along with setting a reference to DocumentFormat.OpenXML.dll, you must also set a reference to WindowsBase.dll, which is part of Windows Presentation Foundation (WPF) and contains supporting functionalities. Second, notice how the strongly typed objects provided by the Open XML SDK allow you to easily create a document and know at compile time that it is valid. Third, note how the document content is created and then packaged into a compound document at the end, which results in the actual file.

LISTING 9-13 Creating a document with the Open XML SDK

```
using DocumentFormat.OpenXml;
using DocumentFormat.OpenXml.Packaging;
using DocumentFormat.OpenXml.Wordprocessing;

namespace SimpleDocumentCreation
{
    class Program
    {
        static void Main(string[] args)
        {
            using (WordprocessingDocument package =
                WordprocessingDocument.Create(
```

```
                    "C:\\HelloOpenXML.docx",
                    WordprocessingDocumentType.Document))
            {
                //Create content
                Body body = new Body(
                    new Paragraph(
                        new Run(
                            new Text("Hello, Open XML SDK!"))));

                //Create package
                package.AddMainDocumentPart;
                package.MainDocumentPart.Document = new Document(body);
                package.MainDocumentPart.Document.Save;
                package.Close;
            }
        }
    }
}
```

While strongly typed objects make document creation easy, they also make reading documents easy because they support LINQ. LINQ support means that you can write queries against the contents of a document and operate on the results for reading and updating. As an example, the code in Listing 9-14 shows how to open a Word document, find all the text items, and print them through a console application.

LISTING 9-14 Reading a document with LINQ

```
using System;
using System.Linq;
using DocumentFormat.OpenXml;
using DocumentFormat.OpenXml.Packaging;
using DocumentFormat.OpenXml.Wordprocessing;

namespace SimpleDocumentRead
{
    class Program
    {
        static void Main(string[] args)
        {
            using (WordprocessingDocument package =
                WordprocessingDocument.Open(args[0], false))
            {
                var q = from t in package.MainDocumentPart.Document.Descendants<Text>
                        select t;
                foreach (var i in q)
                {
                    Console.WriteLine(i.Text);
                }
            }
        }
    }
}
```

Conclusion

SharePoint supports several technologies for performing CRUDQ operations against lists in server-side code. For simple, low-volume operations, the object model support for lists and items is appropriate. For more complete operations, LINQ is an excellent choice and will likely be the preferred method to use. In some advanced scenarios, however, CAML is still required to achieve the desired results.

Chapter 10
Client-Side Programming

The server-side object model for Microsoft SharePoint has long been sophisticated and fully functional. In fact, there is nothing that can be done in the browser that cannot be done through the server-side object model. When it comes to accessing SharePoint using rich clients, however, there has historically been a large deficit in functionality. In previous versions of SharePoint, client-side programmability was largely accomplished through a set of Web services provided by SharePoint. These Web services exposed basic functions for interacting with lists, performing searches, reading profile data, and the like. However, the scope of these Web services was easily less than a third of the functionality available in the server-side object model. In response, many developers resorted to creating custom Web services that wrapped the server-side object model, but this approach never yielded a complete programming model. As a result, customers have consistently requested improved client-side programmability for future versions of SharePoint.

SharePoint 2010 takes a dramatically new approach to client-side programmability by introducing three new client-side object models: Managed, Silverlight, and JavaScript. Each of the three object models provides an object interface to SharePoint functionality that is based on the objects available in the *Microsoft.SharePoint* namespace. This approach provides a development experience that is vastly superior to the Web service model used in previous versions of SharePoint. While none of the models is fully equivalent to the server-side model, they are equivalent to each other, so you can use your knowledge of one model with another.

Along with new client object models, SharePoint 2010 also introduces a new Web service interface that uses WCF Data Services. This new interface is primarily used for querying lists from the client. The main advantage of WCF Data Services over the client object models is that it provides an object-relational mapping (ORM) layer over the lists and items so that they are strongly typed in code. You should think of the WCF Data Services interface as a complement to the client object models, and you will often use them together in solutions.

Understanding Client Object Model Fundamentals

The three client object models are maintained in separate libraries, which are located under the system directory. The Managed object model is contained in the assemblies *Microsoft .SharePoint.Client.dll* and *Microsoft.SharePoint.ClientRuntime.dll,* which can be found in the ISAPI folder. The Silverlight client object model is contained in the assemblies *Microsoft .SharePoint.Client.Silverlight.dll* and *Microsoft.SharePoint.Client.Silverlight.Runtime.dll,* which are located in the LAYOUTS\ClientBin folder. The JavaScript client object model is contained in the library SP.js, which is located in the LAYOUTS folder. While each of the models provides a different programming interface, each interacts with SharePoint through a Windows Communication Foundation (WCF) service named Client.svc, which is located in the ISAPI directory. Figure 10-1 shows a basic architectural diagram for the client object models.

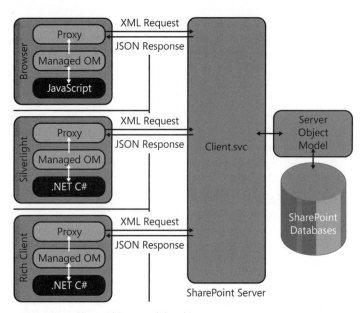

FIGURE 10-1 Client Object Model architecture

Each of the three object models presents an object interface in front of a service proxy. Developers write client-side code using the object model, but the operations are batched and sent as a single Extensible Markup Language (XML) request to the Client.svc service. When the XML request is received, the Client.svc service makes calls to the server-side object model on behalf of the client. The results of the server-side calls are then sent back to the calling client in the form of a JavaScript Object Notation (JSON) object.

The client object models focus on functionality for objects at and below the site collection level. This focus is sensible because the majority of client-side programming is targeted at improving the user experience. This focus also makes the associated libraries smaller, which is particularly important when scripts must be downloaded for the JavaScript model. In addition, great care has been taken to ensure that the three models return objects that behave similarly. This means that if you know how to write code against one of the models, you can easily port that code to either of the other two models. Table 10-1 shows some of the main objects supported by each model alongside the related object from the server-side model.

TABLE 10-1 **Equivalent Objects in the Server and Client Models**

Server Model	Managed Model	Silverlight Model	JavaScript Model
SPContext	ClientContext	ClientContext	ClientContext
SPSite	Site	Site	Site
SPWeb	Web	Web	Web
SPList	List	List	List
SPListItem	ListItem	ListItem	ListItem
SPField	Field	Field	Field

Understanding Contexts

Much like the standard code you write against the server-side object model, client object models require a starting point in the form of a context object. The context object provides an entry point into the associated application programming interface (API) that can be used to gain access to other objects. Once you have access to the objects, you may interact with the scalar properties of the object freely (e.g., *Name*, *Title*, *Url,* and so on). Listing 10-1 shows how to create a context in each of the models and return an object representing a site collection. Once the site collection object is returned, the *Url* property is examined. Code for the server model is included for comparison.

LISTING 10-1 Creating contexts

```
//Server Object Model
SPSite siteCollection  = SPContext.Current.Site;
string url = siteCollection.Url;

//Managed Client Object Model
using (ClientContext ctx = new ClientContext("http://intranet.wingtip.com"))
{
    Site siteCollection = ctx.Site;
    ctx.Load(siteCollection);
    ctx.ExecuteQuery();
    string url = siteCollection.Url;
}

//Silverlight Client Object Model
using (ClientContext ctx = new ClientContext("http://intranet.wingtip.com"))
{
    Site siteCollection = ctx.Site;
    ctx.Load(siteCollection);
    ctx.ExecuteQuery();
    string url = siteCollection.Url;
}

//JavaScript Client Object Model
```

```
var siteCollection;
function getSiteCollection
{
    var ctx = new SP.ClientContext("/");
    siteCollection = ctx.get_site;
    ctx.load(site);
    ctx.executeQueryAsync(success, failure);
}
function success {
    string url = siteCollection.get_url;
}
function failure {
    alert("Failure!");
}
```

The *ClientContext* class in both the managed and Silverlight object models inherits from the *ClientContextRuntime* class. Using the *ClientContext* class, you can get a valid run-time context by passing in the Uniform Resource Locator (URL) of a site. In addition, this class provides several members that are needed to access data and invoke methods on the server.

The *SP.ClientContext* class in the JavaScript client object model inherits from the *SP.Client ContextRuntime* class and provides equivalent functionality to the *ClientContext* class found in the managed and Silverlight client object models. Like the managed and Silverlight models, you can get a run-time context in the JavaScript model using the *SP.ClientContext* class and passing a URL. Unlike the managed and Silverlight models, however, you may also get a run-time context to the current site by using a constructor with no arguments, so our example above could be rewritten as simply var ctx = new SP.ClientContext.

Loading and Executing Operations

The *ClientContextRuntime* class used by Managed and Silverlight clients defines two methods for loading objects: *Load* and *LoadQuery*. The load methods are used to designate objects that should be retrieved from the server. The *Load* method specifies an object or collection to retrieve, while the *LoadQuery* method allows you to return collections of objects using a LINQ query.

See Also The material in this chapter assumes that you are familiar with LINQ queries and concepts such as method syntax, query syntax, and lambda expressions. LINQ is covered in detail in Chapter 9, "Accessing Data in Lists."

Executing the *Load* or *LoadQuery* method does not cause the client to communicate with the server. Instead, it adds the load operation to a batch that will be executed on the server. In fact, you may execute multiple load methods (as well as other operations) before calling the server. Each operation is batched, waiting for your code to initiate communication with the server. To execute the batched operations, your code must call the *ExecuteQuery* or *ExecuteQueryAsync* method. The *ExecuteQuery* method creates an XML request and passes it to the *Client.svc* service. The client then waits synchronously while the batch is executed and the JSON results are returned. The *ExecuteQueryAsync* method, which is used in the Silverlight client object model, sends the XML request to the server, but it returns immediately. Designated success and failure callback methods receive notification when the batch operation is complete.

The JavaScript model works like the managed and Silverlight models by loading operations and executing batches. In the case of the JavaScript model, however, all batch executions are accomplished asynchronously. This means that you must call the *executeQueryAsync* method and pass in the name of functions that will receive success and failure callbacks, as shown in Listing 10-1.

The sample code in Listing 10-1 uses the *Load* method to request an object representing the current site collection. Once an object is returned, you may generally access any of the scalar properties associated with the object. In cases where you do not want to return all the scalar properties for a given object, you may designate the properties to return. In the managed and Silverlight object models, properties are designated by providing a series of lambda expressions. In the JavaScript object model, properties are designated by name. This technique helps to minimize the amount of data sent between the client and server. The following code shows how to request only the *Title* and *ServerRelativeUrl* properties for a site collection object.

```
//Managed and Silverlight client object models reference properties via lambda expressions
ctx.Load(site, s=>s.Title, s=>s.ServerRelativeUrl);
//JavaScript client object model references properties by name
ctx.Load(site, "Title", "ServerRelativeUrl");
```

When working with the client object models, you will quite often be interested in returning collections of items, such as all the lists in a site or all the items in a list. Collections of items may be returned using either the *Load* or *LoadQuery* method. When specifying the items of a collection to return, you can use the *Load* method with a LINQ query formatted using method syntax. In addition, you can use the *LoadQuery* method with a LINQ query formatted using query syntax. Listing 10-2 shows how to return all the list titles in a site where the *Title* is not *NULL*.

LISTING 10-2 Returning collections with LINQ

```
using (ClientContext ctx= new ClientContext("http://intranet.wingtip.com"))
{
    //Method Syntax
    ctx.Load(ctx.Web,
            w => w.Lists.Include(l => l.Title).Where(l => l.Title != null));
    ctx.ExecuteQuery();
```

```
foreach (List list in ctx.Web.Lists)
{
    Console.WriteLine(list.Title);
}

//Query Syntax
var q = from l in ctx.Web.Lists
        where l.Title != null
        select l;

var r = ctx.LoadQuery(q);
ctx.ExecuteQuery();
}
    foreach (var i in r)
    {
        Console.WriteLine(i.Title);
    }
```

While the JavaScript client object model supports both a *Load* and *LoadQuery* method, the JavaScript model does not support LINQ queries. However, you may use query strings to request that collections be included in the returned results. Listing 10-3 shows how to use the JavaScript client object model to return all the list titles in a site, along with the field names and descriptions for each list.

LISTING 10-3 Returning collections with JavaScript

```
var site;
var listCollection;
function getListCollection
{
    var ctx = new SP.ClientContext;
    site = ctx.get_web;
    ctx.Load(site);
    listCollection = site.get_lists;
    ctx.load(listCollection, 'Include(Title,Id,Fields.Include(Title,Description))');
    ctx.executeQueryAsync(success, failure);
}
function success {
    alert(site.get_title);
    alert(listCollection.get_count);

    var listEnumerator = listCollection.getEnumerator;
    while (listEnumerator.moveNext){
        alert(listEnumerator.get_current.get_fields.get_count);
    }
}
function failure {
    alert("Failure!");
}
```

Working with the Managed Client Object Model

Because the Managed client object model is supported by IntelliSense, is checked at compile time, and can run synchronously, it is by far the easiest of the three models with which
to work. Using the Managed client object model is a simple matter of setting a reference to
the assemblies *Microsoft.SharePoint.Client.dll* and *Microsoft.SharePoint.ClientRuntime.dll*, adding a *using* statement for the *Microsoft.SharePoint.Client* namespace, and writing code. The
development environment in Microsoft Visual Studio 2010 provides complete support for the
Managed client object model, including IntelliSense and debugging. Because it is the easiest
model to use, you may often find prototyping solutions are best done in the Managed client
object model and then moved to one of the other models as necessary.

Handling Errors

Because of the disconnected nature of the client object model, error handling is especially
important. Errors may be thrown when you attempt to access an object or value that has
not yet been retrieved from the server. You may also see errors if you create a query that is
not meaningful in the current context, such as trying to retrieve list items before loading the
associated list. Finally, you must deal with errors that happen in the middle of batch operations on the server. In all these situations, you must pay special attention to error handling in
your client object model solutions.

If you attempt to access a scalar property that has not been retrieved, then you will receive
a *PropertyOrFieldNotInitializedException* error. If you make a request to the server that is
deemed invalid, then you will receive a *ClientRequestException* error. If your LINQ query is
invalid, you will receive an *InvalidQueryExpressionException* error. General errors thrown on
the server during execution of a request will result in a *ServerException* error. Listing 10-4
shows code that will generate the various run-time errors that you may see when working
with the Managed client object model.

LISTING 10-4 Handling request errors

```
using (ClientContext ctx = new ClientContext("http://intranet.wingtip.com"))
{
    try
    {
        //Fails because the object was not initialized
        //Requires Load and ExecuteQuery
        Console.WriteLine(ctx.Web.Title);
    }
    catch (PropertyOrFieldNotInitializedException x)
    {
        Console.WriteLine("Property not initialized. " + x.Message);
    }
```

```
    try
    {
        //Fails because Skip and Take are meaningless
        //in the context of a list collection
        ctx.Load(ctx.Web, w => w.Lists.Skip(5).Take(10));
        ctx.ExecuteQuery();
    }
    catch (InvalidQueryExpressionException x)
    {
        Console.WriteLine("Invalid LINQ query. " + x.Message);
    }

    try
    {
        //Fails because InvalidObject is a meaningless object
        InvalidObject o = new InvalidObject(ctx, null);
        ctx.Load(o);
        ctx.ExecuteQuery();
    }
    catch (ClientRequestException x)
    {
        Console.WriteLine("Bad request. " + x.Message);
    }

    try
    {
        //Fails because the list does not exist
        //The failure occurs on the server during processing
        ctx.Load(ctx.Web,w=>w.Lists);
        List myList = ctx.Web.Lists.GetByTitle("Non-Existent List");
        myList.Description = "A new description";
        myList.Update();
        ctx.ExecuteQuery();

    }
    catch (ServerException x)
    {
        Console.WriteLine("Exception on server. " + x.Message);
    }
}
```

Of the errors that may occur during operations, *ServerException* stands out as notable. This is because *ServerException* is thrown when an operation fails on the server. Furthermore, the failing operation could be in the middle of a large batch of operations, which can lead to unpredictable behavior. The fundamental challenge with the batch model embodied in the client object model is that you need a way to respond to errors that happen on the server so that the remainder of the batch operations can finish processing. The *ServerException* error is thrown on the client after the batch has failed, which gives you no opportunity to correct the error.

Fortunately, all three client object models provide a mechanism for sending error-handling instructions to the server along with the batch operations. The *ExceptionHandlingScope* object allows you to define a *try-catch-finally* block that embodies server-side operations. If errors occur during processing on the server, they are handled on the server by the code embodied in *ExceptionHandlingScope*. Listing 10-5 shows how exception-handling scopes are implemented in the Managed client object model.

LISTING 10-5 Handling errors in a scope

```
using (ClientContext ctx = new ClientContext("http://intranet.wingtip.com"))
{
    //Set up error handling
    ExceptionHandlingScope xScope = new ExceptionHandlingScope(ctx);

    using (xScope.StartScope)
    {
        using (xScope.StartTry)
        {
            //Try to update the description of a list named "My List"
            List myList = ctx.Web.Lists.GetByTitle("My List");
            myList.Description = "A new description";
            myList.Update;
        }
        using (xScope.StartCatch)
        {
            //Fails if the list "My List" does not exist
            //So, we'll create a new list
            ListCreationInformation listCI = new ListCreationInformation;
            listCI.Title = "My List";
            listCI.TemplateType = (int)ListTemplateType.GenericList;
            listCI.QuickLaunchOption = Microsoft.SharePoint.Client.QuickLaunchOptions.On;
            List list = ctx.Web.Lists.Add(listCI);
        }
        using (xScope.StartFinally)
        {
            //Try to update the list now if it failed originally
            List myList = ctx.Web.Lists.GetByTitle("My List");
            if(myList.Description.Length==0)
            {
                myList.Description = "A new description";
                myList.Update;
            }
        }
    }

    //Execute the entire try-catch as a batch!
    ctx.ExecuteQuery;
}
```

The most important aspect of the code shown in Listing 10-5 is that the *ExecuteQuery* method is called only once, and it appears after the code in the exception handling scope. This means that all the operations defined in the exception handling scope are sent to the server in a single batch. Initially, the server will try to update the description of the target list. If this operation fails, the exception handling scope assumes that it is because the list does not exist. Therefore, the exception-handling scope creates a new list with the correct name. Finally, the description is updated for the newly created list.

While the exception-handling scope provides a powerful way for you to deal with errors that occur during batch processing, it requires some additional planning. For example, the code in Listing 10-5 assumes that any failure is the result of a nonexistent list. However, there are other reasons that the operation could fail, such as the user not having the rights to update the list. Fortunately, the *ExceptionHandlingScope* provides properties that help you understand exactly what went wrong on the server. The *ServerErrorCode*, *ServerErrorValue*, and *ServerStackTrace* properties can all be used to analyze the server error and decide about how to proceed.

Understanding Authentication and Authorization

By default, all Managed client object model code runs under the Windows identity of the person executing the code. This means that the user must have appropriate permissions inside SharePoint to create, read, update, or delete items. If the user does not have appropriate permissions, then your code will throw a *ServerUnauthorizedAccessException* error.

If your Web application supports Forms-Based Authentication (FBA), then you can change the *AuthenticationMode* property of the *ClientContext* to *FormsAuthentication*. Under Forms Authentication, the code must then supply the logon credentials through the *FormsAuthenticationLoginInfo* object. The credentials will subsequently be sent as clear text to SharePoint when the batch operations are executed. Because the credentials are sent as clear text, you should use Secure Sockets Layer (SSL) on Web applications using Forms Authentication. The following code shows how to change the authentication mode to Forms Authentication and send the credentials.

```
using (ClientContext ctx = new ClientContext("http://intranet.wingtip.com"))
{
    ctx.AuthenticationMode = ClientAuthenticationMode.FormsAuthentication;
    FormsAuthenticationLoginInfo loginInfo =
      new FormsAuthenticationLoginInfo("brianc", "pass@word1");
    ctx.FormsAuthenticationLoginInfo = loginInfo;
}
```

Authorization of actions within the client object model always depends on the rights the user has in SharePoint. When performing operations with the client object model, you will often need to verify the permissions of the user before acting. The client object model has support for users, groups, and roles so that you can add, update, and delete as necessary. Most often, however, you will use the *BasePermissions* class to check the permissions for a user. You can then use the *DoesUserHavePermissions* method of the Web object to check them.

Because checking permissions is often a prerequisite to performing a task, the managed and Silverlight client object models support the concept of a *conditional scope*. A conditional scope uses a *ConditionalScope* object to establish a set of conditions under which operations should execute on the server. If the conditions are not met, the code does not run. Conditional scopes can be combined with error-handling scopes to create code that can handle many situations on the server without returning to the client.

Within the scope itself, many operations that you will want to perform are not allowed, such as updating properties and calling methods. Fortunately, the conditional scope sets a flag letting you know if the condition was met so you can use that information to run additional operations. Listing 10-6 shows a sample that uses a conditional scope to determine if a user has the rights necessary to create a new list. If so, then a new list is created. If not, the operation is skipped.

LISTING 10-6 Checking permissions in a conditional scope

```
using (ClientContext ctx = new ClientContext("http://intranet.wingtip.com "))
{
    ctx.Load(ctx.Web);
    ctx.ExecuteQuery;

    List list = null;

    //Set up permissions mask
    BasePermissions permissions = new BasePermissions;
    permissions.Set(PermissionKind.ManageLists);

    //Conditional scope
    ConditionalScope scope = new ConditionalScope(
        ctx,
         => ctx.Web.DoesUserHavePermissions(permissions).Value == true);

    using (scope.StartScope)
    {
        //Operations are limited in scopes
        //so just read
        Console.WriteLine(ctx.Web.Title);
    }

    //Execute
    ctx.ExecuteQuery();
```

```
    //Did scope execute?
    Console.WriteLine(scope.TestResult.Value);

    if (scope.TestResult.Value)
    {
        //Create a new list, we have permissions
        ListCreationInformation listCI = new ListCreationInformation;
        listCI.Title = "My List";
        listCI.TemplateType = (int)ListTemplateType.GenericList;
        listCI.QuickLaunchOption = Microsoft.SharePoint.Client.QuickLaunchOptions.On;

        list = ctx.Web.Lists.Add(listCI);
        ctx.ExecuteQuery();

        Console.WriteLine(list.Title);
    }
}
```

Creating, Updating, and Deleting

In the conditional scope shown in Listing 10-6, a new list was created if the user had the appropriate permissions. Creating new lists and items using the Managed client object model is done with *creation information* objects. *ListCreationInformation* and *ListItemCreation Information* allow you to define all the necessary values for a list or item and then send that data with the batch back to the server. Listing 10-7 shows how to use these objects to create a new list and list item.

LISTING 10-7 Creating a list and list item

```
using (ClientContext ctx = new ClientContext("http://intranet.wingtip.com "))
{
    //Create a new list
    ListCreationInformation listCI = new ListCreationInformation;
    listCI.Title = "My List";
    listCI.Description += "A list for use with the Client OM";
    listCI.TemplateType = (int)ListTemplateType.GenericList;
    listCI.QuickLaunchOption = Microsoft.SharePoint.Client.QuickLaunchOptions.On;
    List list = ctx.Web.Lists.Add(listCI);
    ctx.ExecuteQuery();

    //Create a new list item
    ListItemCreationInformation listItemCI = new ListItemCreationInformation;
    ListItem item = list.AddItem(listItemCI);
    item["Title"] = "New Item";
    item.Update();
    ctx.ExecuteQuery();
}
```

Throughout this chapter so far, you have seen several examples of returning objects. In the examples, you have seen how to return a single object and how to use LINQ to specify a collection of objects. The only piece missing is how to return list items. Initially, you might suspect that returning items from lists is similar and should use LINQ queries, but that is not the case. The Managed client object model uses LINQ to Objects, not LINQ to SharePoint, so the LINQ approach outlined in Chapter 8, "Templates and Type Definitions," is not valid for the client object model. Instead, you must use Collaborative Application Markup Language (CAML) queries to return items from a list.

CAML queries are created for the Managed client object model through the *CamlQuery* object. This object has a *ViewXml* property that accepts a CAML query designating the items to return. This CAML query follows the same rules that were outlined in Chapter 8. Listing 10-8 shows a sample of running a CAML query against a list.

LISTING 10-8 Using CAML to return list items

```
using (ClientContext ctx = new ClientContext("http://intranet.wingtip.com "))
{
    //Read the Site, List, and Items
    ctx.Load(ctx.Web);

    List myList = ctx.Web.Lists.GetByTitle("My List");
    ctx.Load(myList);

    StringBuilder caml = new StringBuilder;
    caml.Append("<View><Query>");
    caml.Append("<Where><Eq><FieldRef Name='Title'/>");
    caml.Append("<Value Type='Text'>New Item</Value></Eq></Where>");
    caml.Append("</Query><RowLimit>100</RowLimit></View>");

    CamlQuery query = new CamlQuery;
    query.ViewXml = caml.ToString;
    ListItemCollection myItems = myList.GetItems(query);
    ctx.Load(myItems);

    ctx.ExecuteQuery();
    Console.WriteLine("Site: " + ctx.Web.Title);
    Console.WriteLine("List: " + myList.Title);
    Console.WriteLine("Item Count: " + myItems.Count.ToString);
}
```

Updating through the Managed client object model is straightforward. In most cases, you will simply set the value of a property and then call the appropriate *Update* method. Listing 10-9 shows samples of updating a site, list, and list item.

LISTING 10-9 Update operations

```
//Update the Site, List, and List Items
ctx.Web.Description = "Client OM samples";
ctx.Web.Update();

myList.Description = "Client OM data";
myList.Update();

foreach (ListItem myItem in myItems)
{
    myItem["Title"] = "Updated";
    myItem.Update();
}

ctx.ExecuteQuery();
Console.WriteLine("Site: " + ctx.Web.Description);
Console.WriteLine("List: " + myList.Description);
Console.WriteLine("Item Count: " + myItems.Count.ToString);
```

Deleting objects with the Managed client object model involves calling the *DeleteObject* method. This method is the same across most objects that can be deleted. The following code shows how to delete the list created earlier.

```
myList.DeleteObject;
ctx.ExecuteQuery;
```

Along with lists, you'll want to work with libraries. In the Managed client object model, document libraries are handled similarly to lists. Of course, the major difference is in handling documents. Fortunately, uploading documents to libraries using the Managed client object model is very similar to using the server object model; you must upload the document using the URL of the folder where you want to store the document. Listing 10-10 shows a full set of create, read, update, and delete (CRUD) operations around a file and a document library.

LISTING 10-10 Working with document libraries

```
using (ClientContext ctx = new ClientContext("http://intranet.wingtip.com "))
{
    //Get site
    Web site = ctx.Web;
    ctx.Load(site);
    ctx.ExecuteQuery();

    //Create a new library
    ListCreationInformation listCI = new ListCreationInformation;
    listCI.Title = "My Docs";
    listCI.Description = "A library for use with Client OM";
    listCI.TemplateType = (int)ListTemplateType.DocumentLibrary;
```

```
listCI.QuickLaunchOption = Microsoft.SharePoint.Client.QuickLaunchOptions.On;
List list =site.Lists.Add(listCI);
ctx.ExecuteQuery();

//Create a document
MemoryStream m = new MemoryStream;
StreamWriter w = new StreamWriter(m);
w.Write("Some content for the document.");
w.Flush;

//Add it to the library
FileCreationInformation fileCI = new FileCreationInformation;
fileCI.Content = m.ToArray;
fileCI.Overwrite = true;
fileCI.Url = "http://intranet.wingtip.com/My%20Docs/MyFile.txt";
Folder rootFolder = site.GetFolderByServerRelativeUrl("My%20Docs");
ctx.Load(rootFolder);
Microsoft.SharePoint.Client.File newFile = rootFolder.Files.Add(fileCI);
ctx.ExecuteQuery();

//Edit Properties
ListItem newItem = newFile.ListItemAllFields;
ctx.Load(newItem);
newItem["Title"] = "My new file";
newItem.Update();
ctx.ExecuteQuery();

//Delete file
newItem.DeleteObject();
ctx.ExecuteQuery();
}
```

Working Asynchronously

Although the *ClientContext* object does not support the *ExecuteQueryAsync* method in the managed client object model, you can still perform asynchronous operations using more standard techniques. While asynchronous calls in the Managed client object model are not as critical as in the Silverlight and JavaScript client object models, they are convenient. Using a straightforward approach, you may define callback methods for success and failure. Listing 10-11 shows how to return a site collection object asynchronously and display the associated *Url* property in a console application.

LISTING 10-11 Asynchronous calls in the Managed client object model

```
delegate void Async;
ClientContext ctx;
Site siteCollection;

static void Main(string[] args)
```

```
{
    Program p = new Program();
    p.Run();
    Console.WriteLine("Waiting...");
    Console.Read();
}

public void Run
{
    ctx= new ClientContext("http://intranet.wingtip.com");
    siteCollection = ctx.Site;
    ctx.Load(siteCollection);
    Async async = new Async(ctx.ExecuteQuery);
    async.BeginInvoke(callback, null);
}

void callback(IAsyncResult arg)
{
    Console.WriteLine("Callback received...");
    Console.WriteLine(site.Url);
    Console.WriteLine("Callback done!");
}
```

Working with the Silverlight Client Object Model

Silverlight is a Web browser plug-in that allows for the creation of rich media-centric solutions. Because Silverlight is a plug-in, it runs inside of Internet Explorer directly on the client. Combining SharePoint, Silverlight, and the client object model can result in applications that are both highly responsive and visually appealing. By default, SharePoint provides support for Silverlight through built-in applications like the Media Player as well as support for custom applications through the Silverlight Web Part. In this section, you'll review an introduction to Silverlight development, learn the tools that are available, and see how to use these tools in client-side programming.

Introducing Silverlight Development

If you have never created a custom Silverlight application, you will find it pleasantly easy to get started. Visual Studio 2010 provides strong support for Silverlight development, including debugging, packaging, and deployment. When you are specifically targeting SharePoint as the platform for your applications, you have a couple of extra steps, but nothing too difficult.

SharePoint ships with the Silverlight Web Part, which is a Web Part that can host any Silverlight solution. In addition, SharePoint ships with several Silverlight applications that you can use right away. The Silverlight Web Part can be found in the Media And Content category of the Web Part catalog. When you drop this Web Part on a page, you are prompt-ed to enter the path to a Silverlight XAP (pronounced "zap") file. All the Silverlight applications that ship with SharePoint reside in the _LAYOUTS/ClientBin folder. If you wanted to host the HierarchyChart application, for example, you would enter the path /_LAYOUTS/ClientBin/ HierarchyChart.xap. In addition, you can use the Silverlight Web Part to host your own applications. Note that you must have the Silverlight run time installed on your client to run Silverlight applications. In addition, Silverlight is supported in only 32-bit browsers.

Creating a Silverlight application begins in Visual Studio 2010. In the New Project dialog, you may select Silverlight from the list of Installed Templates and then select Silverlight Application as the project type. When you create a new Silverlight project, you have the option to include an additional project in the solution for testing. The testing project can either be a Web application project or an actual website. Including a test project in the solu-tion allows you to test and debug easily just by hitting F5. Visual Studio automatically starts the test Web project and loads the Silverlight solution for you. Figure 10-2 shows the New Silverlight Application dialog.

FIGURE 10-2 Selecting a testing project

Inside Visual Studio, the development activities necessary to create your Silverlight applica-tion are similar to creating any application. First, you must create a user interface; second, you must code the functionality. The biggest difference between Silverlight development and any other type of development is that the user interface is defined through a declara-tive syntax known as Extensible Application Markup Language (XAML, pronounced "za-mil"). Visual Studio provides both a visual and markup view of the user interface to make develop-ment easier. For this walkthrough, Listing 10-12 shows the XAML and Figure 10-3 shows the user interface.

LISTING 10-12 A Silverlight user interface defined with XAML

```xml
<UserControl x:Class="HelloSilverlight.MainPage"
    xmlns="http://schemas.microsoft.com/winfx/2006/xaml/presentation"
    xmlns:x="http://schemas.microsoft.com/winfx/2006/xaml"
    xmlns:d="http://schemas.microsoft.com/expression/blend/2008"
    xmlns:mc="http://schemas.openxmlformats.org/markup-compatibility/2006"
    mc:Ignorable="d"
    d:DesignHeight="50" d:DesignWidth="150"
    Height="50" Width="150" >

    <Grid x:Name="LayoutRoot" Background="White">
        <StackPanel Orientation="Vertical">
            <Button x:Name="clicker" Click="clicker_Click" Content="Push Me!"/>
            <TextBox x:Name="output"/>
        </StackPanel>
    </Grid>
</UserControl>
```

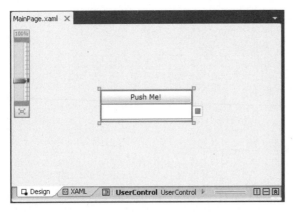

FIGURE 10-3 A Silverlight user interface in Visual Studio

Looking at Listing 10-12 and Figure 10-3, you can see that the sample application is a simple solution designed to display a message when a button is clicked. In Listing 10-12, note how *Button* and *TextBox* are defined in XAML. Take special note of how the click event is defined through the *Click* attribute. This event handler will appear in code behind the user interface. To code event handlers, you can simply right-click them in the XAML and select View Code from the context menu. This will take you to the event handler, where you can fill in the necessary code. In the sample, a message is entered into the *TextBox* using the following code.

```csharp
private void clicker_Click(object sender, RoutedEventArgs e)
{
    output.Text = "Hello, Silverlight!";
}
```

Once the code is complete, you may build the application in Visual Studio. Building the application will cause Visual Studio to emit a XAP file containing all the necessary assemblies for your application to run. At this point, you can simply copy the XAP file into the /_LAYOUTS/ClientBin directory in SharePoint, drag a Silverlight Web Part to a SharePoint page, point to the XAP file, and use your solution. Figure 10-4 shows the completed solution running in the Silverlight Web Part.

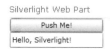

FIGURE 10-4 Hosting a custom solution in the Silverlight Web Part

While you are developing your solution, you will undoubtedly want to debug it. Debugging in Silverlight is reasonably straightforward. If you are using a testing Web project, then you can set breakpoints and hit F5 as usual. If the solution is hosted in SharePoint, then you can attach to the IEXPLORER.EXE process and set breakpoints.

One thing to be careful of when debugging is that Internet Explorer will cache any XAP file that you view. The caching is done to improve performance so that additional downloads are not necessary. When debugging, however, this can be frustrating because you are making changes to the assembly constantly. Therefore, you must clear the XAP file from the cache before each debugging run or you will not see the latest changes.

The best way to clear the cache is to select Tools, Internet Options from the Internet Explorer menu. On the General tab, click the Settings button under the Browsing History section. In the Temporary Internet Files and History Settings dialog, click the View Files button. When viewing the files, search for all *.xap files. Locate the one that you are debugging and delete it. Then copy your latest XAP file into the ClientBin directory and begin your debugging session.

Obviously, there is a lot more to Silverlight development than can be covered in this short section. The goal of this walkthrough is simply to give you a head start in developing Silverlight solutions for SharePoint 2010 so that you can focus on how to use the client object model with Silverlight.

Asynchronous Programming with Silverlight

The classes and method found in the Silverlight client object model are nearly identical to the ones in the Managed client object model. The single biggest difference is that the Silverlight client object model supports the *ExecuteQueryAsync* method and the Managed client object model does not. Asynchronous query operations are particularly important in Silverlight applications because the thread that executes a query cannot be used to update the Silverlight user interface. Attempting to update the Silverlight user interface after a synchronous query will result in an error informing you that the user interface thread is potentially blocked, so your operation is not allowed. Therefore, you must make asynchronous calls to the client object model from Silverlight and update the user interface on a separate thread. Listing 10-13 shows a simple example of returning the URL for a site collection and displaying it in a Silverlight application. You must follow this pattern whenever you use the Silverlight client object model.

LISTING 10-13 Asynchronous calls from Silverlight

```
public partial class MainPage : UserControl
{
    private System.Threading.SynchronizationContext thread;

    public static event ClientRequestSucceededEventHandler succeedListener;
    public static event ClientRequestFailedEventHandler failListener;

    public delegate void succeedDelegate(object sender, ClientRequestSucceededEventArgs e);
    public delegate void failDelegate(object sender, ClientRequestFailedEventArgs e);

    public MainPage
    {
        InitializeComponent;

        //The object to hold the returned site collection
        Site siteCollection;

        //Delegates for the callback methods
        succeedDelegate sd = new succeedDelegate(HandleClientRequestSucceeded);
        failDelegate fd = new failDelegate(HandleClientRequestFailed);

        //Event handlers for the callback methods
        succeedListener += new ClientRequestSucceededEventHandler(sd);
        failListener += new ClientRequestFailedEventHandler(fd);

        thread = System.Threading.SynchronizationContext.Current;
        if (thread == null)
            thread = new System.Threading.SynchronizationContext;
    }

    private void Button_Click(object sender, RoutedEventArgs e)
    {
            ClientContext ctx= new ClientContext(SiteUrl.Text);
            Site siteCollection = ctx.Site;
            ctx.Load(siteCollection);
            ctx.ExecuteQueryAsync(succeedListener, failListener);
    }

    //Delegate implementations
    public void HandleClientRequestSucceeded(object sender,
                                      ClientRequestSucceededEventArgs args)
```

```
{
    thread.Post(new System.Threading.SendOrPostCallback(delegate(object state)
    {
        EventHandler h = OperationSucceeded;
        if (h != null)
            h(this, EventArgs.Empty);
    }), null);
}

public void HandleClientRequestFailed(object sender, ClientRequestFailedEventArgs args)
{
    thread.Post(new System.Threading.SendOrPostCallback(delegate(object state)
    {
        EventHandler h = OperationFailed;
        if (h != null)
            h(this, EventArgs.Empty);
    }), null);
}

//Event handler implementations
public void OperationSucceeded(object sender, EventArgs e)
{
    Messages.Text = "Success" + site.Url;
}

public void OperationFailed(object sender, EventArgs e)
{
    Messages.Text += "Failure!";
}
}
```

Listing 10-13 begins by declaring a *System.Threading.SynchronizationContext* object. The *SynchronizationContext* object is used to facilitate communication between threads in the Silverlight application. Specifically, it will facilitate communication between the thread that returns data from the server and the thread that displays the data in the user interface.

Next, the code defines a *ClientRequestSucceededEventHandler* and *ClientRequestFailedEvent Handler* as event delegates. These delegates are the prototypes for the listeners that will be passed as arguments to the *ExcecuteQueryAsync* method. In addition, a pair of delegates are defined that prototype the methods that will receive the success or failure callback.

In the *HandleClientRequestSucceeded* and *HandleClientRequestFailed* callback methods, the *SynchronizationContext* is used to post a message to the thread that will update the user interface. This results in calling either the *OperationSucceeded* or *OperationFailed* method, where the code is free to update the user interface.

Error Handling in Silverlight

Just as you did in the Managed client object model, you will want to handle server errors using *ErrorHandlingScope* so that batch operations on the server can proceed gracefully when an error occurs. Fortunately, the code for handling errors in the Silverlight client object model is identical to the code in the Managed client object model. The only consideration is to remember that all Silverlight calls to the client object model are asynchronous. Therefore, you will need to combine the asynchronous programming paradigm discussed earlier with the exception-handling scope code shown in the Managed client object model.

Passing Parameters to Silverlight

As you develop more sophisticated Silverlight applications, you will find it necessary to send configuration parameters to Silverlight. For instance, the Silverlight client object model requires a URL to establish *ClientContext*. If you want your Silverlight application to be portable across sites, then it must be able to retrieve a configuration parameter that tells it what URL to use. In these cases, you will need to use Silverlight *initialization parameters*.

Initialization parameters are key-value pairs that can be passed from the hosting website to the Silverlight application. The hosting website creates an instance of a Silverlight application through an *object* tag in Hypertext Markup Language (HTML), the *createObject* method in *Silverlight.js*, or the *createObjectEx* method also found in *Silverlight.js*. When the application instance is created, the initialization parameters are sent as a single string. The following code shows a simple example of an *object* tag in creating an instance of a Silverlight application and passing initialization parameters.

```
<object id="SLHost" width="300" height="50"
 data="data:application/x-silverlight-2,"
 type="application/x-silverlight-2" >
 <param name="source" value="ClientBin/SilverlightApplication.xap"/>
 <param name="initParams" value="key1=value1,key2=value2"/>
</object>
```

When either the *CreateObject* or *CreateObjectEx* method is used, the initialization parameters are passed as an argument. While the Silverlight Web Part takes the *object* tag approach, many custom Silverlight hosting Web Parts use JavaScript methods. The following code shows an example of the *CreateObject* method so you can get an idea of how this works.

```
<div id="silverlightControlHost">
    <script type="text/javascript">
        Silverlight.createObject(
            "ClientBin/SilverlightApplication1.xap",
            silverlightControlHost,
            "SLApp",
```

```
        {
            width: "100%", height: "100%"
        },
        { onError: onSLError, onLoad: onSLLoad },
        "param1=value1,param2=value2",
        "context"
    );
    </script>
</div>
```

Regardless of how the parameters are passed, you must add some special code to your Silverlight application to accept and use them. For example, consider a Silverlight application that shows a SharePoint list in a grid. In this scenario, the URL of the website and the name of the target list are passed as initialization parameters to the Silverlight application. Inside the application, the Silverlight client object model is used to get a *ClientContext*, query the list, and display the list items in a grid. Figure 10-5 shows the complete application, displaying items from a list of toys.

Silverlight Toys

Id	Title	
1	Rubber Ball	
2	Ice Skates	
3	Wooden Blocks	
4	Board Games	
5	Playing Cards	
5 items returned.		

FIGURE 10-5 Displaying list items in Silverlight

To accept and use initialization parameters, you must first edit the MainPage.xaml.cs file. This file contains a single constructor for the Silverlight application that takes no arguments. In this file, you must define a new constructor that accepts the number and type of arguments that you expect. In this case, you expect a *string* with the URL of the website and a *string* with the name of the list. In the constructor, you simply save the initialization parameters to member variables so that they are available throughout the scope of the application. The following code shows how the new constructor is defined.

```
public MainPage(string WebUrl, string ListName)
{
    InitializeComponent();

    //Save initialization parameters
    webUrl = WebUrl;
    listName = ListName;
}
```

Once the new constructor is created, you must modify the *Application_Startup* method in the App.xaml.cs file. The *Application_Startup* method is called when the new instance of the Silverlight application is created. In this code, you must retrieve the initialization parameters and pass them to the new constructor that you created earlier. The following code shows how this is done.

```
private void Application_Startup(object sender, StartupEventArgs e)
{
    //Code to receive initialization params
    try
    {
        string webUrl = e.InitParams["WebUrl"];
        string listName = e.InitParams["ListName"];
        this.RootVisual = new MainPage(webUrl, listName);
    }
    catch
    {
        this.RootVisual = new MainPage;
    }
}
```

Once the initialization parameters are passed to Silverlight successfully, you may use them in code. Most often, these values will be used along with the Silverlight client object model to create a context and perform operations. Don't forget that you must also perform all operations asynchronously.

Creating a Custom Silverlight Host

While the Silverlight Web Part that ships with SharePoint 2010 is useful in many cases, there will undoubtedly be times when you need to create your own Silverlight host Web Part. Creating your own host Web Part gives you much more control over the initialization parameters, configuration, and behavior of Silverlight. Creating your own host is fairly straightforward as well. You can begin by creating a new Web Part project in Visual Studio 2010. Because this is a host, there is no reason to create a Visual Web Part project—a simple Web Part project will suffice.

Once you have created a new Web Part project, you can start by deciding what properties you want to expose. Typically, you'll want to make the height, width, source, and initialization parameters available for configuration. The following code shows the definition for the *Source* property, which contains the server-relative URL of the XAP file.

```
[Personalizable(PersonalizationScope.Shared),
WebBrowsable(true), WebDisplayName("XAP Package"),
WebDescription("The relative URL of the XAP package"),
Category("Silverlight")]
public string Source
{
```

```
    get { return source; }
    set { source = value; }
}
```

Because the *object* tag, the *createObject* method, and the *createObjectEx* method depend on the Silverlight.js library, you need to make sure that your host has loaded it. To load the Silverlight.js library, use *ClientScriptManager* to load the library, which is located in the LAYOUTS directory. The following code shows how to load the library before rendering the Web Part.

```
protected override void OnPreRender(EventArgs e)
{
    ClientScriptManager cs = Page.ClientScript;
    if (!cs.IsClientScriptIncludeRegistered("sl_javascript"))
        cs.RegisterClientScriptInclude(this.GetType,
            "sl_javascript", "/_LAYOUTS/Silverlight.js");
}
```

Once the library is loaded, you can inject markup into the hosting SharePoint page if you want. You can decide to inject the *object* tag, the *createObject* method, or the *createObjectEx* method, in either an external script file or through code. Listing 10-14 shows how to create a script within the Web Part code that you can inject into the page. Note how the Web Part properties are used as parameters for the object tag.

LISTING 10-14 Injecting script to create a Silverlight instance

```
private string GetCreateScript
{
    StringBuilder script = new StringBuilder;

    script.Append("<div id=\"customSLHost\">\r\n");
    script.Append("  <object data=\"data:application/x-silverlight-2,\"
                              type=\"application/x-silverlight-2\" width=\"");
    script.Append(HostWidth);
    script.Append("\" height=\"");
    script.Append(HostHeight);
    script.Append("\">\r\n");
    script.Append("    <param name=\"source\" value=\"");
    script.Append(Source);
    script.Append("\"/>\r\n");
    script.Append("    <param name=\"width\" value=\"");
    script.Append(HostWidth);
    script.Append("\"/>\r\n");
    script.Append("    <param name=\"height\" value=\"");
    script.Append(HostHeight);
    script.Append("\"/>\r\n");
    script.Append("  </object>\r\n");
    script.Append("</div>\r\n");

    return script.ToString();
}
```

Working with the JavaScript Client Object Model

The JavaScript client object model provides a script-based programming experience that is equivalent to the managed and Silverlight client object models. Using the JavaScript client object model allows you to create SharePoint solutions that are more responsive and browser-agnostic. Also, you can add capabilities such as Asynchronous JavaScript and XML (AJAX) and jQuery to improve the user experience greatly.

When working with the JavaScript client object model, you will find that several areas differ from the managed and Silverlight implementations. For the most part, these differences have to do with either technology limitations or programming conventions used in JavaScript. For example, the method signatures throughout the JavaScript client object model follow a convention that is typical for JavaScript. This means that properties are retrieved through a *get* method as opposed to a *dot* operator.

Because the JavaScript client object model does not support all the data types found in the .NET Framework , some of them will be different. You have already seen this in previous examples in this chapter where using lambda expressions is not supported, so the JavaScript client object model uses query strings. Furthermore, JavaScript supports some data types that do not exist in the .NET Framework. These include values such as *NaN*, which represents a numeric value that is undefined in JavaScript.

Setting Up a Basic Page

Creating a basic page that uses the JavaScript client object model is not difficult, but several requirements must be met for the code to execute successfully. You can begin by creating a new SharePoint feature in Visual Studio 2010 and adding an Application Page. Generally, the Application Pages added by Visual Studio have everything that you need to begin writing JavaScript client object model code immediately. Listing 10-15 shows a simple example that displays the title of the current site when a button is clicked.

LISTING 10-15 An Application Page using the JavaScript client object model

```
<%@ Assembly Name="$SharePoint.Project.AssemblyFullName$" %>
<%@ Import Namespace="Microsoft.SharePoint.ApplicationPages" %>
<%@ Register Tagprefix="SharePoint" Namespace="Microsoft.SharePoint.WebControls"
Assembly="Microsoft.SharePoint, Version=14.0.0.0, Culture=neutral, PublicKeyToken=71e9
bce111e9429c" %>
<%@ Register Tagprefix="Utilities" Namespace="Microsoft.SharePoint.Utilities"
Assembly="Microsoft.SharePoint, Version=14.0.0.0, Culture=neutral, PublicKeyToken=71e9
bce111e9429c" %>
<%@ Register Tagprefix="asp" Namespace="System.Web.UI" Assembly="System.Web.
Extensions, Version=3.5.0.0, Culture=neutral, PublicKeyToken=31bf3856ad364e35" %>
<%@ Import Namespace="Microsoft.SharePoint" %>
```

```
<%@ Assembly Name="Microsoft.Web.CommandUI, Version=14.0.0.0, Culture=neutral, PublicK
eyToken=71e9bce111e9429c" %>
<%@ Page Language="C#" AutoEventWireup="true" CodeBehind="HelloWorld.aspx.cs" Inherits
="JavaScriptClientOMSamples.Layouts.JavaScriptClientOMSamples.HelloWorld" DynamicMaste
rPageFile="~masterurl/default.master" %>

<asp:Content ID="PageHead" ContentPlaceHolderID="PlaceHolderAdditionalPageHead"
runat="server">
    <script type="text/javascript">
        var site;
        function goClientOM {
            //Get Context
            var ctx = new SP.ClientContext;
            //Get site
            site = ctx.get_web;
            ctx.load(site);
            //Execute
            ctx.executeQueryAsync(success, failure);
        }

        function success {
            alert(site.get_title);
        }

        function failure {
            alert("Failure!");
        }

    </script>
</asp:Content>

<asp:Content ID="Main" ContentPlaceHolderID="PlaceHolderMain" runat="server">
    <div id="displayDiv">
        <input type="button" value="Push Me!" onclick="javascript:goClientOM;" />
    </div>
</asp:Content>
```

For the JavaScript client object model to function correctly, the ASPX page hosting the code must meet several requirements. First, you must register the *Microsoft.SharePoint.WebControls* namespace on the page. This reference is not required by the JavaScript client object model directly, but it contains controls that will be used in support of the code, as you will see in the following explanation. The pages that you create in Visual Studio 2010 already have the namespace registered using this code.

```
<%@ Register Tagprefix="SharePoint" Namespace="Microsoft.SharePoint.WebControls"
 Assembly="Microsoft.SharePoint, Version=14.0.0.0, Culture=neutral,
 PublicKeyToken=71e9bce111e9429c" %>
```

Second, a reference to the script library SP.js must be available. For the pages that you create in Visual Studio 2010, the proper references already exist on the default master page. However, if you need to add the script reference explicitly, you can do it by using a *ScriptLink* control, which is part of the *Microsoft.SharePoint.WebControls* namespace. The following code shows how you can load the SP.js library explicitly using *ScriptLink*.

```
<SharePoint:ScriptLink ID="SPScriptLink" runat="server" LoadAfterUI="true"
 Localizable="false" Name="sp.js" />
```

Finally, if the JavaScript code performs any updates to sites or lists, a *FormDigest* control must be on the page. The *FormDigest* control is part of the *Microsoft.SharePoint.WebControls* namespace and generates a security validation, which is necessary when a change is posted that modifies the content database. The *FormDigest* control is already part of the default master page, but you can add another one explicitly using the following code.

```
<SharePoint:FormDigest runat="server" />
```

Once the prerequisites are met, you may write code against the JavaScript client object model. In the sample shown previously in Listing 10-15, a button is used to call a function. The function first creates a new *SP.ClientContext* object without using a URL. Unlike the managed and Silverlight client object models, which require a full URL, the JavaScript client object model takes a server-relative URL when creating a context. This means that using no argument in the constructor results in a context for the site associated with the current page.

Once the context is created, the current site can be retrieved using the *get_web* method. Notice that the *get_web* method is equivalent to the *Web* property found in the managed and Silverlight client object models. This syntax difference is consistent throughout the JavaScript client object model.

Just as in the other models, the object must be loaded and then the query must be executed. In the case of the JavaScript client object model, each query to the server must be performed asynchronously. Therefore, success and failure functions must be defined each time the *executeQueryAsync* method is called. On success or failure, the sample simply shows an alert with the results.

Handling Errors in the JavaScript Client Object Model

The JavaScript client object model supports exception-handling scopes just like the managed and Silverlight client object models. Of course, the syntax is a bit different. Listing 10-16 shows the implementation of the sample contained in Listing 10-4 in the JavaScript client object model.

LISTING 10-16 Implementing exception-handling scopes in JavaScript

```
<script type="text/javascript">
    function goClientOM {

        //Get Context
        var ctx = new SP.ClientContext;

        //Start exception-handling scope
        var e = new SP.ExceptionHandlingScope(ctx);
        var s = e.startScope;

          //try
          var t = e.startTry;

              var list1 = ctx.get_web.get_lists.getByTitle("My List");
              ctx.load(list1);
              list1.set_description("A new description");
              list1.update;

          t.dispose;

          //catch
          var c = e.startCatch;

              var listCI = new SP.ListCreationInformation;

              listCI.set_title("My List");
              listCI.set_templateType(SP.ListTemplateType.announcements);
              listCI.set_quickLaunchOption(SP.QuickLaunchOptions.on);

              var list = ctx.get_web.get_lists.add(listCI);

          c.dispose;

          //finally
          var f = e.startFinally;
              var list2 = ctx.get_web.get_lists.getByTitle("My List");
              ctx.load(list2);
              list2.set_description("A new description");
              list2.update;

          f.dispose;

        //End exception-handling scope
        s.dispose;

        //Execute
        ctx.executeQueryAsync(success, failure);

    }

    function success {
        alert("Success");
    }
```

```
    function failure {
        alert("Failure!");
    }

</script>
```

Running Code on Page Load

In our samples, the JavaScript function is initiated by clicking a button. However, there are many times when you want code to run immediately when the page is loaded. Initially, you may think that you can simply fire the code using an *onLoad* event, but this will not work. The script-loading model used by SharePoint will load the required libraries on demand to minimize the size of the page download. Because of this, you must use the *ExecuteOrDelayUntilScriptLoaded* method that will delay your call until the SP.js library is downloaded. To run Listing 10-15 immediately when the page loads, the markup in the main placeholder should be replaced with the following code.

```
<asp:Content ID="Main" ContentPlaceHolderID="PlaceHolderMain" runat="server">
    <script type="text/javascript">
        //Waits until the SP.js script is loaded and then calls our function
        var e = ExecuteOrDelayUntilScriptLoaded(goClientOM, "sp.js");
    </script>
    <div id="displayDiv">
    </div>
</asp:Content>
```

Debugging JavaScript

All the JavaScript libraries that ship with SharePoint 2010 have debug versions available that can be used during the development process. In addition, you may debug your own scripts directly in the browser while they run. To debug scripts, open the browser to the page in SharePoint where your solution is located. Next, select Tools, Developer Tools from the browser menu or simply press F12. In the Developer Tools dialog, click the Script tab and you will see your JavaScript. When the script is visible, click Start Debugging. Finally, set a breakpoint in your script, return to SharePoint, and run your solution. Your breakpoints will be hit and you can perform the debug in the SharePoint script libraries.

Working with AJAX

When you are working with the JavaScript client object model, you will undoubtedly want to incorporate AJAX into your solution. One of the core principles of AJAX is to facilitate as much processing on the client as possible, including data retrieval and user interface rendering. Therefore, AJAX is an excellent choice to complement the JavaScript client object model.

SharePoint 2010 is AJAX-enabled by default. This means that you can take advantage of the client-side AJAX run time in your solutions immediately. The client-side AJAX run time is contained in the script library MicrosoftAjax.js, which is located in the LAYOUTS directory. Scripts are compiled into the *System.Web.Extensions* namespace and are loaded into each page using the *ScriptManager* control, which is located on the default master page.

When the AJAX script library is loaded, you will have access to the *Sys.Application* object, which is the main client-side object and is equivalent to the *Page* object in ASP.NET. You can use the *Sys.Application* object to create a true page life cycle for your client-side code including init, load, and disposing events. Life cycle events are added to the page using the *add_init*, *add_load*, and *add_disposing* methods of the *Sys.Application* object. The designated functions are then called at the appropriate time in the page life cycle. Listing 10-17 shows a sample page that implements a page life cycle.

LISTING 10-17 Implementing a page life cycle with *Sys.Application*

```
<asp:Content ID="PageHead" ContentPlaceHolderID="PlaceHolderAdditionalPageHead"
runat="server">

    <script type="text/javascript">
        function ajaxInit {
            $get("displayDiv").innerHTML = "<p>Initialized</p>";
        }
        function ajaxLoad {
            $get("displayDiv").innerHTML += "<p>Loaded</p>";
        }
        function ajaxDisposing {
            $get("displayDiv").innerHTML += "<p>Disposing</p>";
        }
    </script>

</asp:Content>

<asp:Content ID="Main" ContentPlaceHolderID="PlaceHolderMain" runat="server">
    <script type="text/javascript">
        Sys.Application.add_init(ajaxInit);
        Sys.Application.add_load(ajaxLoad);
        Sys.Application.add_disposing(ajaxDisposing);
    </script>
    <div id="displayDiv">
    </div>
</asp:Content>
```

Another advantage of using the AJAX library is that it has support for shorthand notation. In Listing 10-17, note the use of the *$get* shortcut. The *$get* shortcut is the equivalent of *document .getElementById* in the document object model (DOM). Using it in your pages makes them more readable and compact. In the example, it is used to add content to the page each time an event in the life cycle is fired.

You can combine the structure offered by a true page life cycle with the script management offered by SharePoint and make calls to the JavaScript client object model from within the life cycle events. You will still have to wait for the SP.js script to load, but your final code will be more structured and readable. For example, the following code calls a function that accesses the JavaScript client object model from the load event for the page.

```
<script type="text/javascript">
    function ajaxInit {
    }
    function ajaxLoad {
        var e = ExecuteOrDelayUntilScriptLoaded(goClientOM, "sp.js");
    }
    function ajaxDisposing {
    }
</script>
```

Using Object-Oriented JavaScript

Along with the page life cycle, you can take advantage of AJAX to define client-side controls that you can use to render information returned from the client object model. Client-side AJAX controls are defined using object-oriented JavaScript to wrap user interface elements. These controls may then be incorporated into the overall page model to render information. For example, consider a solution designed to display the titles of all lists from the current SharePoint site. To support the sample, Listing 10-18 shows the code for a simple AJAX list control.

LISTING 10-18 An AJAX list control

```
//Register namespace
if (typeof (Wingtip) == 'undefined')
    Type.registerNamespace('Wingtip');

//Constructor
Wingtip.SimpleList = function (element) {
    this.element = element;
    this.element.innerHTML = '<ol></ol>';
    this.items = '';
}

//Prototype
Wingtip.SimpleList.prototype = {
    element: null,
    items: null,
    add: function (text) {
        this.items += '<li>' + text + '</li>';
        this.element.innerHTML = '<ol>' + this.items + '</ol>';
    }
}

//Register the class
Wingtip.SimpleList.registerClass('Wingtip.SimpleList');
```

The first part of the code in Listing 10-18 registers the namespace *Wingtip*. The *Wingtip* namespace in JavaScript fills the same purpose as it does in Microsoft C#; it ensures the uniqueness of class names that you define. The next part of the code defines the constructor for the *SimpleList* class. The *SimpleList* class takes an element in the constructor. This element will be a *div* element, and the list will be rendered inside this element. The constructor initializes the list as an ordered list with no items. Below the constructor is the definition of the class. JavaScript uses the *prototype* property to mark the definition of properties and methods within the class. Finally, the class is registered with the AJAX framework.

Class definitions are typically done in separate JavaScript files and then loaded at run time. You can load the separate files using the *ScriptLink* control in the same manner as discussed earlier. For simplicity, you can also include small controls directly on the page. Once you have created the class, it may be instantiated just like any other class. In this sample, we want to use the *add* method of the class to add the titles of all the SharePoint lists. Therefore, the control must be combined with the AJAX page model, delayed script execution, and the JavaScript client object model to achieve the final result. Listing 10-19 shows the complete code for the sample.

LISTING 10-19 Combining AJAX, SharePoint, and the client object model

```
<asp:Content ID="PageHead" ContentPlaceHolderID="PlaceHolderAdditionalPageHead"
runat="server">

    <script type="text/javascript">
        var site;
        var listCollection;

        function ajaxInit {
            //Nothing to do here
        }

        function ajaxLoad {

            //Register namespace
            if (typeof (Wingtip) == 'undefined')
                Type.registerNamespace('Wingtip');

            //Constructor
            Wingtip.SimpleList = function (element) {
                this.element = element;
                this.element.innerHTML = '<ol></ol>';
                this.items = '';
            }

            //Prototype
            Wingtip.SimpleList.prototype = {
                element: null,
                items: null,
                add: function (text) {
                    this.items += '<li>' + text + '</li>';
```

```
                            this.element.innerHTML = '<ol>' + this.items + '</ol>';
                }
            }

            //Register the class
            Wingtip.SimpleList.registerClass('Wingtip.SimpleList');

            //Call JavaScript Client OM
            ExecuteOrDelayUntilScriptLoaded(doClientModelOps, "sp.js");
        }

        function ajaxDisposing {
            //Nothing to do here
        }

        function doClientModelOps {

            //Get Context
            var ctx = new SP.ClientContext;

            //Get site
            site = ctx.get_web;
            ctx.load(site);

            //Get lists
            listCollection = site.get_lists;
            ctx.load(listCollection,
                    'Include(Title,Id,Fields.Include(Title,Description))');

            //Execute
            ctx.executeQueryAsync(success, failure);

        }

        function success {

            //Create instance of control
            var displayList = new Wingtip.SimpleList($get("displayDiv"));

            //Show names of lists
            var listEnumerator = listCollection.getEnumerator;
            while (listEnumerator.moveNext) {
                displayList.add(listEnumerator.get_current.get_title);
            }
        }

        function failure {
            $get("displayDiv").innerHTML = "<p>Failure!</p>";
        }
    </script>

</asp:Content>

<asp:Content ID="Main" ContentPlaceHolderID="PlaceHolderMain" runat="server">
    <script type="text/javascript">
```

```
        Sys.Application.add_init(ajaxInit);
        Sys.Application.add_load(ajaxLoad);
        Sys.Application.add_disposing(ajaxDisposing);
    </script>
    <div id="displayDiv">
    </div>
</asp:Content>
```

Working with jQuery

jQuery is a popular JavaScript framework that simplifies JavaScript development by providing cross-browser support and simplified ways for developers to perform common tasks. Using jQuery, developers can find, select, and manipulate elements of the DOM more easily. In addition, jQuery supports several plug-ins that easily create responsive user interfaces like tabs, accordions, and dialogs. Complete coverage of jQuery is beyond the scope of this book, but you can learn more at the official jQuery site, which is *www.jquery.com*. In this section, you will learn how to integrate jQuery with SharePoint and use it with the JavaScript client object model.

jQuery is an open-source framework that is available from *www.jquery.com* in the form of JavaScript libraries. To use jQuery with SharePoint, you can download the libraries and deploy them to the LAYOUTS\1033 directory (or whatever folder represents the culture for your installation), where they can be added to a page easily using *ScriptLink* controls, as shown in the following code.

```
<SharePoint:ScriptLink ID="JQueryLink1" runat="server" language="javascript"
  Name="jquery-1.3.2.min.js"/>
```

Much as you can use the *$get* shortcut to select elements easily in the DOM, jQuery supports a $ object. In jQuery, the $ object is a shortcut for the *jQuery* object. So, everywhere you see a $ in code, you could substitute *jQuery*. For example, you can test for jQuery support before performing an operation using the following code.

```
if ($) { //perform actions }
```

When working with SharePoint, AJAX, and the client object model, you can use jQuery to make your development easier and more structured. You can, for example, select elements from the DOM using the $ operator. For example, the following code selects a *div* element with an *id* of *displayDiv*.

```
var d = $("div#displayDiv");
```

Along with simpler development, jQuery provides several plug-ins that make it very easy to produce Web 2.0 interfaces in your solutions. One popular example of a jQuery plug-in is the accordion. The accordion plug-in allows you to create a user interface element that has sections that slide open when they are clicked. Figure 10-6 shows a simple accordion created from an unordered list containing the titles and descriptions of SharePoint lists on the current site. Clicking a list title causes the accordion to slide open and reveal the list description.

```
• Documents
  This system library was created by the Publishing feature
• Images
• JavaScript OM Samples
• Master Page Gallery
• Pages
• Workflow Tasks
```

FIGURE 10-6 A simple jQuery accordion

To create the solution shown in Figure 10-6, the code from Listing 10-18 was modified slightly to create an unordered list instead of an ordered list. In addition, the list was given an *id* attribute with a value of *simpleAccordion* so that it could be selected in jQuery. Once those changes are made, it is a simple matter to apply the accordion by selecting the unordered list using the following line of code.

```
$('ul#simpleAccordion').accordion;
```

Although the jQuery framework is extensive, you can see that integrating it with SharePoint, AJAX, and the client object model requires just a few steps. This same approach can be used with your own custom frameworks and libraries. This combination will allow you to create SharePoint solutions that provide an appealing and responsive user interface that runs entirely on the client.

Working with WCF Data Services

WCF Data Services (formerly known as ADO.NET Data Services) is a framework that allows you to create and access data remotely. WCF Data Services exposes data as Web-based resources that are addressable through Uniform Resource Identifiers (URIs). WCF Data Services implements REST semantics, which means you can perform complete CRUD operations on data sources using only the *GET, PUT, POST,* and *DELETE* operations in the Hypertext Transfer Protocol (HTTP). SharePoint 2010 implements WCF Data Services for all lists and libraries. This means you can perform operations on list items using simple URIs.

WCF Data Services has several advantages over the client object models. First, WCF Data Services provides a strongly typed ORM layer that you can use in code to access SharePoint lists and items. In the client object model, on the other hand, all lists and items are returned as more generic types like *List* and *ListItem*. Second, WCF Data Services supports LINQ queries against SharePoint lists, whereas the client object model relies on CAML queries. Third, WCF Data Services uses GET, PUT, POST, and DELETE operations in HTTP so any client that supports HTTP can access SharePoint lists.

Getting Started with WCF Data Services

To use WCF Data Services in your solutions, you must ensure that the latest version is installed in your farm. The installation itself is straightforward, with no additional configuration required after install. Once you have WCF Data Services installed, you may use it immediately by simply opening a browser and issuing URI commands. SharePoint 2010 supports the URI commands through a WCF service named ListData.svc. ListData.svc is located in the ISAPI directory, which is accessible through URIs containing _vti_bin_. For example, the following URI returns information about all the lists available in the Wingtip.com site.

```
http://wingtip.com/_vti_bin/ListData.svc
```

Information returned from Listdata.svc is in the form of an ATOM feed. In the browser, this will simply appear as an XML document. The following code shows the XML returned from the previous URI.

```
<?xml version="1.0" encoding="utf-8" standalone="yes" ?>
<service xml:base="http://contososerver/clientom/_vti_bin/ListData.svc/" xmlns:atom="http://
www.w3.org/2005/Atom" xmlns:app="http://www.w3.org/2007/app" xmlns="http://www.w3.org/2007/
app">
  <workspace>
    <atom:title>Default</atom:title>
    <collection href="Demos">
      <atom:title>Demos</atom:title>
    </collection>
    <collection href="MasterPageGallery">
      <atom:title>MasterPageGallery</atom:title>
     </collection>
    <collection href="MasterPageGalleryCompatibleUIVersionS">
      <atom:title>MasterPageGalleryCompatibleUIVersionS</atom:title>
     </collection>
    <collection href="TrainingModules">
      <atom:title>TrainingModules</atom:title>
    </collection>
  </workspace>
</service>
```

Once you have this information about available lists, you can use it to create a new URI that requests information about the items in a list. This is accomplished by simply appending the name of the list to the end of the URI. The following URI returns all the list items for the TrainingModules list.

```
http://intranet.wingtip.com/_vti_bin/ListData.svc/TrainingModules
```

Instead of returning all the items in the list, you can ask for a particular item. This is done by appending the *Id* of the item to the end of the URI. The following URI requests only the item with *Id* equal to "2".

```
http://intranet.wingtip.com/_vti_bin/ListData.svc/TrainingModules(2)
```

When making a request, you can also order the results by including the *$orderby* query string in the URI. The following URI returns all items ordered by title.

```
http://intranet.wingtip.com/_vti_bin/ListData.svc/TrainingModules?$orderby=Title
```

Additional query commands are also available. The *$top* command returns just the first number of rows specified. The *$skip* command skips rows and is used with the *$top* command to implement paging. The *$filter* command allows you to specify a *WHERE* clause. The following URIs show samples of these commands.

```
http://intranet.wingtip.com/_vti_bin/ListData.svc/TrainingModules?$top=2
http://intranet.wingtip.com/_vti_bin/ListData.svc/TrainingModules?$skip=2&top=2
http://intranet.wingtip.com/_vti_bin/ListData.svc/TrainingModules?$filter=Title eq 'WCF'
```

Using WCF Data Services in Visual Studio

Creating URIs in the browser is interesting and instructive, but it is not typically the way that you would create a WCF Data Services solution. Instead, you would create a new project in Visual Studio 2010 and set a reference to the ListData.svc service. When you create a reference to ListData.svc in your project, Visual Studio creates a proxy object and an ORM layer. This allows you to use strongly typed objects when you write code. Behind the scenes, Visual Studio takes care of issuing the appropriate URI to fulfill your request.

Much like the client object model, you must create a context using the URL of the site where the lists reside. After that, however, you may create and execute LINQ queries immediately to perform CRUD operations. Listing 10-20 shows a simple example of a solution that runs a LINQ query to return all the overdue items in the TrainingModules list.

LISTING 10-20 Using WCF Data Services in Visual Studio 2010

```
ListDataRef.ClientObjectModelDataContext ctx =
    new ListDataRef.ClientObjectModelDataContext(
    new Uri("http://intranet.wingtip.com/_vti_bin/ListData.svc"));
ctx.Credentials = CredentialCache.DefaultCredentials;

var q = from m in ctx.TrainingModules
        where m.DueDate.Value.CompareTo(DateTime.Today)<0
        orderby m.Title
        select m;

Console.WriteLine("Overdue Modules");
Console.WriteLine("***************");
foreach (var i in q)
{
    Console.WriteLine(i.Title);
}
```

WCF Data Services supports full CRUD operations on the SharePoint lists. Once items are returned from the LINQ query, they may be updated and saved. Changes are sent back to the list when you call the *SaveChanges* method of the context object. Creating new items and deleting items are performed using the *AddTo* and *DeleteObject* methods. Of course, all operations are performed under the credentials supplied in the application, so users must have rights to the list for an operation to succeed.

Creating rich-client solutions that use the full range of CRUD operations on a list can be extremely simple with WCF Data Services. This is because Visual Studio 2010 provides support for directly binding SharePoint list data to controls in an application. To get started, all you need to do is select Data, Add New Data Source from the Visual Studio menu. This will start the Data Source Configuration Wizard.

In the Data Source Configuration Wizard, you can select to create a new SharePoint Data Source. Here, you simply provide the complete path to ListData.svc through the site that contains your lists. Once the connection is made, you may view all the lists by selecting Data, Show Data Sources. From this view, you can simply drag the list you want to work with onto a Windows form, and a data-bound grid will appear automatically. A complete sample for creating a data-bound solution is contained in the companion code.

Conclusion

In this chapter, you learned how to create SharePoint solutions that use client-side technologies. Using client-side technologies in your solutions is powerful because they provide a more responsive user interface, unload processing from the server, and are a great complement to sandboxed solutions. Client-side technologies are more powerful in SharePoint 2010 than in any previous version of the software. You should give strong consideration to including them in your SharePoint solutions.

Chapter 11
Creating and Developing Workflows

This chapter explains how Microsoft SharePoint 2010 supports automating business processes using workflows. SharePoint Server 2010 provides several standard workflows that can be used in a variety of business scenarios. SharePoint 2010 also provides you with the ability to create custom workflows with SharePoint Designer 2010. This is what we will discuss in the first half of the chapter.

While the strategy of creating custom workflows with SharePoint Designer is recommended for most environments, you might find yourself in a scenario that calls for more control and power. In the second half of this chapter, we will examine developing custom workflow components with Microsoft Visual Studio 2010. As you will see, you can develop custom workflow actions in Visual Studio 2010 that can be used in custom workflows created with SharePoint Designer 2010. Alternatively, you can develop custom workflow templates with Visual Studio 2010 that can be deployed and put to use without any involvement from SharePoint Designer 2010.

What Is Workflow?

In a generic sense, workflow is a business process; it doesn't even have to be an automated process. It's just the definition of how business works for one particular area or concern. Printing out a timesheet, handing it to your manager to sign, and then delivering it to Human Resources for payment processing is a workflow, even though it is an entirely manual process.

For all intents and purposes, however, when you talk about workflow, you are talking about a business process that has been automated to some degree, and the term *workflow* typically refers to that automation. All of the following are examples of workflows:

- A manufacturing assembly line
- Credit card approval authorization
- Setup and orientation of a new employee
- Document review

For our purposes in SharePoint, we really don't care about the first two—they are not what SharePoint does. The second two, however, are very much within the purview of SharePoint. Why is that? What is it about the first two that make them not applicable to SharePoint, and what is it about the second two that makes them pertinent?

The answer is us: people. The first two activities do not involve human interaction, while the second two do. Yes, credit card authorization could involve people in special cases, but that is not typical processing. That is known as *edge-case exception processing;* it kicks in when the primary process can't handle the situation, and at that point, it may involve people and may even involve SharePoint in some way. The second two examples involve people almost exclusively. They may involve some automated processing for things like spell-checking, but that is just a part of the overall process. For the most part, examples such as processing the paperwork for a new hire or reviewing a document is people interacting with their content, and that is what makes them relevant to SharePoint. SharePoint is a people-oriented tool; it's all about people interacting with their content, so it makes perfect sense that this carries through into workflow. Therefore, a definition of SharePoint workflow could be

> *The automated process supporting the interactions between people and their content, typically for the purposes of review, modification, and/or publication, relying primarily upon SharePoint Foundation for supporting functionality, such as storage, security, management, and notification.*

But what does that somewhat sterile definition of SharePoint workflow tell us? How does it help us understand how to support workflow in our environment? It doesn't, in a sense, but it does point to some important aspects of SharePoint workflow:

- **SharePoint workflows live inside SharePoint.**   This may sound obvious, but read the definition again and you'll see that it really says "relying primarily upon…" In other words, it is perfectly all right for non-SharePoint elements to be involved in the process, but SharePoint is the primary actor. This might mean, for example, that notifications are sent out via email or text message, but the content is stored in SharePoint. Or it might mean that a third party translation engine is used to translate content that is stored in SharePoint.

- **SharePoint workflows are human-centric.**   There will almost always be some machine-to-machine communication or interaction, but people play a key role in SharePoint workflows.

- **SharePoint workflows are tasked with supporting certain types of processes, those related to "review, modification, and/or publication" of content.**   Can SharePoint support other types of processes? Absolutely. But most of the time, the processes that are good candidates for SharePoint workflows will fall into one of these three buckets.

- **SharePoint Foundation provides the plumbing.**   The definition given previously uses the examples of storage, security, management, and notification, but it is SharePoint Foundation that provides the majority of these types of services.

SharePoint Workflow Fundamentals

Now that we have a general sense of what makes a good SharePoint workflow, let's take a high-level look at how SharePoint is going to allow us to support that process. The following elements come into play when working with workflow in SharePoint 2010.

Tasks

The primary interaction point between people and their content inside a workflow is the standard SharePoint *Task*. At points in the process where human interaction is required, someone needs to be told that he or she has work to do, and that notification is typically done via tasks, as shown in Figure 11-1.

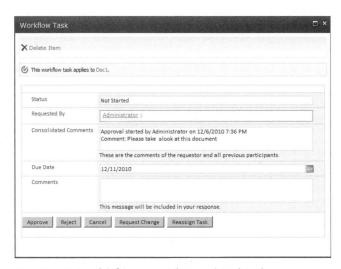

FIGURE 11-1 A task informs users about assigned work.

Tasks allow users to see what work they need to do, track the status of the work, assign the work to someone else, and other related actions. They also serve as a gatekeeper for SharePoint in the sense that the workflow can be stopped until the task is completed—either by the assigned person or through some type of defined escalation or reassignment process, which causes the task to be marked as completed (even if what really happens is that the task is simply closed) and the workflow is ended.

Lists/Libraries and Content Types

Workflows must be attached to a container. In SharePoint 2007, the only containers available were Lists/Libraries or Content Types. The container *owns* the workflow, and instances of the workflow run against objects in that container. While this has changed in SharePoint 2010, workflows are still attached to a List, Library, or Content Type the vast majority of times.

Document Sets

While technically, Document Sets in SharePoint 2010 are Content Types, they are important enough to be handled individually. A Document Set is a collection of related documents. It is possible to attach a workflow to a Document Set and have the workflow operate on all the individual documents in the set.

Sites

In SharePoint 2010, a workflow can be owned by a site and run against either the site itself or anything within that site. While this is a significant new capability that is the *only* valid solution in some situations, it is also an edge case. Attaching workflows to sites is not typically how workflows are handled in SharePoint.

SharePoint Designer

SharePoint Designer (SPD) is one of two tools used to build SharePoint workflows. The tool is targeted at administrators and power users, not developers. That is not to say that developers won't use the tool. In many ways, SPD is *the* tool used to build workflows in SharePoint 2010. This is a significant change from 2007 and will be discussed later in this chapter, in the section entitled "Creating Custom Workflows."

Visual Studio 2010

In the cases where SPD cannot be used to build a workflow, Visual Studio is the other tool that can be used in the situation. Visual Studio can also be used to extend the capabilities of SPD by introducing custom functionality.

Visio 2010

While technically, Microsoft Visio does not create a SharePoint workflow, it is a third tool that becomes involved. Visio Premium now includes the ability to design a workflow in such a way that it can be imported into SPD and *finished off*. In this sense, Visio is a tool that makes up a part of the SharePoint workflow building continuum. Designing a workflow in Visio is covered later in this chapter, in the section entitled "Creating a Workflow with Visio and SharePoint Designer."

Windows Workflow Foundation

Windows Workflow Foundation (WF) is not a part of SharePoint; it is a core element of the Microsoft .NET Framework. However, it is still an important part of SharePoint workflows because it is the foundation upon which SharePoint workflow is based. WF provides a set of core objects and services to support the automation of business processes. It does not, however, provide any type of user interface, management, or monitoring. It is a toolkit with which to build business process automation functionality into an application, which is exactly what the SharePoint team did—it used the WF components to build workflow support into SharePoint.

The User Experience in a SharePoint Workflow

Users have multiple points of interaction with SharePoint workflows. Understanding their experience requires reviewing the various situations in which a user can be involved in a SharePoint workflow.

The first time many SharePoint users will experience a SharePoint workflow is when a task is assigned to them as part of a workflow process. In this situation, they will see a screen similar to that shown in Figure 11-1, earlier in this chapter.

The example shown in Figure 11-1 shows a task assigned by an instance of the out-of-the-box Approval—SharePoint 2010 workflow template. It offers the opportunity for users to enter a comment and then take one of five actions:

- **Approve**   Confirms that the document or item the workflow is running on meets the criteria for acceptance.

- **Reject**   Confirms that the document or item the workflow is running on does not meet the criteria for acceptance.

- **Cancel**   Closes the task form without recording any action.

- **Request Change**   Asks that the owner of the document or item makes a modification before they can approve it.

- **Reassign Task**   Makes someone else responsible for completing the task.

The details of any task form will vary depending upon which workflow template the workflow is based upon and how the workflow template was built, but most tasks will be similar to Figure 11-1.

If users have the SharePoint Task list configured to synchronize with Microsoft Outlook, their first workflow experience may still be with a task, but that experience would be with an Outlook task form rather than a SharePoint task form.

Other ways with which users can interact with workflows include the following:

- Starting a new workflow (as shown in Figure 11-2).

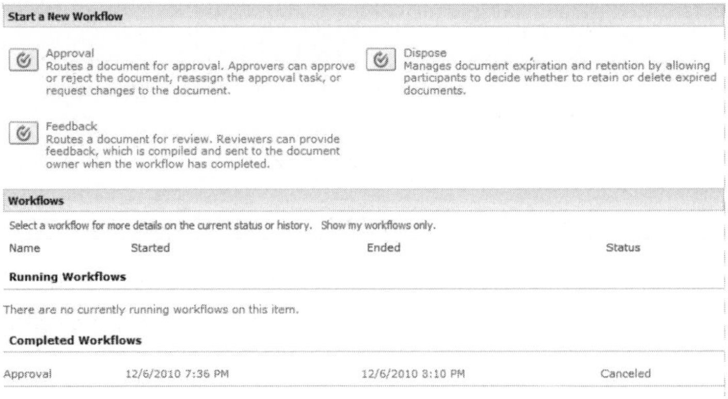

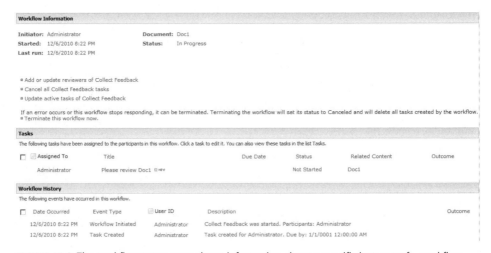

FIGURE 11-2 Users can select from multiple available workflow templates when creating a new workflow instance.

- Checking the status of a running workflow (as shown in Figure 11-3).

FIGURE 11-3 The workflow status page shows information about a specific instance of a workflow.

- Creating a new workflow association (as shown in Figure 11-4).

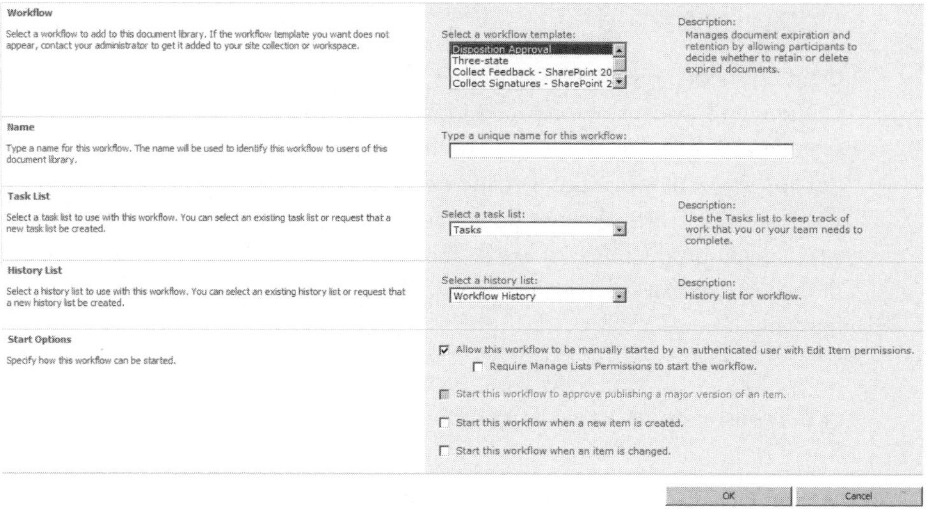

FIGURE 11-4 Creating a new workflow association makes it possible to create an instance of the work-flow on an item.

Creating Custom Workflows

While it may be a minor point that is easy to miss, it is important to note that this section is entitled "Creating Custom Workflows," not "Developing Custom Workflows." In this section, we are not going to discuss anything that involves development, code, or anything to do with Visual Studio 2010. None of the techniques discussed here require any development experience; they can be performed by an administrator or a trained user. Coded workflows are covered later in this chapter, in the section entitled "Developing Custom Workflow Components."

SharePoint Designer 2010

The tool of choice for creating new workflows in SharePoint 2010 is SPD. SPD is not a developer tool; it is a user and administrator tool. You don't use it to write code—you use it to configure SharePoint.

SPD has existed since the release of SharePoint 2007—and even before that if you count its prior life as Microsoft FrontPage. While SPD had been tarred with a bad reputation in the past, it has overcome that in the current release. SharePoint Designer 2010 has come into its own and become the premier tool for non-developers to use to customize their SharePoint environment. Used properly, and for tasks for which it was designed, SPD is a great tool.

Getting Started

Creating a workflow in SPD is a matter of designing the workflow in a graphical interface and configuring the steps of the process by filling in details inside forms. While SPD still works directly against a site, and there is nothing out of the box to stop that from being your production site, a best practice is still to *never* work directly against your production farm. You should always create a workflow against a development or test farm and then deploy your workflow to production, just like its fully coded cousins. You'll see as we go through the rest of this section that there are new capabilities in SharePoint Designer 2010 that make this a real option now.

Before we get started building our first workflow in SPD, it is important to understand some of the constructs and capabilities of the tool.

Workflow Types

The primary capability of SharePoint Designer 2010 that enables us to create a workflow on a non-production site and then deploy to production is one of the new types of workflows that are now supported—the *Reusable Workflow*. While this is the most important of the supported workflow types, there are two others as well.

Reusable Workflows

Reusable workflows offer just what the name implies—the ability to reuse the workflow multiple times. This includes the ability to deploy the workflow across environments. If you are building workflows to operate on things stored inside a list or library (that is, not a site workflow), you should create them as reusable workflows. There is little, if any, reason to build any other type of workflow targeted toward a list or library.

Behind the scenes, reusable workflows are owned by a particular Content Type (although they can be associated at a high enough level to be available on all Content Types). Later in this chapter, in the section entitled "Association Columns," we'll cover a new capability that can be used to ensure that the instance of a Content Type that the workflow is attached to has the columns the workflow requires to run.

Site Workflows

Site workflows are another appropriately named new capability of SharePoint 2010—they are workflows that are associated with a site as their owning container. This gives the ability to run a workflow without having to create a list or library solely for the purpose of being the owning container for the workflow. This site workflow can run on any construct (or possibly multiple constructs) within the owning site, meaning that it can run on the site itself, on one or more lists within the site, on multiple items from a single list, or on multiple items from multiple lists. While this is an important new capability of SPD workflows, it is also a very specific solution to a niche set of requirements. Fortunately, for those requirements, it is the perfect solution.

Interestingly, one of the primary requirements that site workflows could meet is often going to be solved via another new capability in SharePoint 2010: Document Sets. A common requirement in SharePoint 2007 was the need to run a single workflow on a collection of documents, treating the documents as a single entity as far as the workflow was concerned. In SharePoint 2010, the introduction of Document Sets, and the ability to run workflows on them, obviates this use for site workflows. The need doesn't completely go away, for the following reasons:

- Site workflows can be used for other purposes, such as operating on the site itself.

- Not all groups of documents can or should be added to a Document Set. Often, the documents may be related, but not enough to be grouped in a Document Set; or the document may already be in a Document Set, and therefore cannot be added to a second.

- Document Sets work only for documents. There is no corresponding Item Set for grouping related items in a list. If you need a workflow to operate on a collection of items, you have no choice but to implement it as a site workflow.

One issue that is going to arise if you attempt to use a site workflow in this manner is the fact that SPD workflows do not support looping, which would be necessary to grab a collection of documents and repeat the same steps on each of them. Overcoming this problem would be possible with some custom code, or by using secondary workflows, but please review the section entitled "Avoiding Rube Goldberg Emulation" later in this chapter, before you start building secondary workflows.

List Workflows

List workflows are the norm for SPD workflows; they are what we had in SharePoint 2007, including the restrictions on deployment. For this reason, and the aforementioned best practice of not working directly against production, creating List workflows in SharePoint 2010 is not recommended.

Steps

A *step* is a basic unit of organization in SPD workflows. It is used to organize the actions and conditions that make up the workflow into groups that make sense to the workflow creator. Participants in a workflow never interact with the steps or even know anything about them.

Participants deal only with the items inside the steps. Figure 11-5 shows a portion of a SPD workflow containing steps.

As units of organization within a SPD workflow, steps have a few additional capabilities that can come in handy:

- They can be moved around within the workflow designer to reorganize the workflow. The Move Up button and the Move Down button on the SPD ribbon can be used to move the currently selected step up or down in relation to the other steps.

- They can be nested. Figure 11-5 shows two steps (Begin Owner Review and Finish Owner Review) nested inside another step (Owner Review).

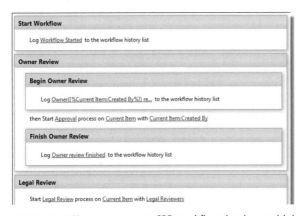

FIGURE 11-5 You can create an SPD workflow that has multiple, distinct steps.

Impersonation Step

In only one situation does a step have any impact upon the actual processing of the workflow—and that is when it is a special type of step called an *Impersonation Step*. An Impersonation Step is a new addition to SPD workflows. It is used to change the user context for the actions and conditions contained within the step to that of the most recent workflow editor. In other words, when executing the actions and conditions contained within an Impersonation Step, SharePoint will impersonate the person who last saved the workflow.

Outside an Impersonation Step, SPD workflows run as the user who started the workflow or, in the case of auto-started workflows, caused the workflow to start. Normally, this is desired. In some situations, however, the workflow may need to perform an action that the current user does not have sufficient privileges to complete. In this case, impersonation is required, and the Impersonation Step is the only available means of impersonation in SPD workflows.

Note If you expect to make significant use of Impersonation Steps in your environment, you may want to consider creating a workflow author user account in your environment. You can use the fact that actions and conditions inside an Impersonation Step will execute as the last user who saved the workflow to your advantage by making it part of your deployment process to open and save workflows while logged in as this workflow author. This gives you a simple way to make sure that security for workflows is predictable and manageable—the only account that you need to set security on would be this special pseudo-service account.

It is also worth considering implementing a policy for including a Log to History List action inside any Impersonation Step that writes the name of the actual user the workflow was running as prior to the Impersonation Step to the workflow's history list. This can help track down problems should they arise.

Actions

An *action* in a SPD workflow is the most basic unit of work that can be added to the workflow. SPD ships with 43 actions out of the box, which are listed in Table 11-1.

TABLE 11-1 Actions Shipping with SPD

Action Category	Action Name
Core Actions	Add a Comment
	Add Time to Date
	Build Dynamic String
	Do Calculation
	Error Message
	Log to History List
	Pause for Duration
	Pause until Date
	Send an Email
	Send Document to Repository
	Set Time Portion of Date/Time Field
	Set Workflow Status
	Set Workflow Variable
	Stop Workflow
Document Set Actions	Capture a version of the Document Set (*)
	Send Document Set to Repository (*)
	Set Content Approval Status for the Document Set (*)
	Start Document Set Approval Process (*)

Action Category	Action Name
List Actions	Add List Item Permissions (Imp)
	Check In Item
	Check Out Item
	Copy List Item"
	Create List Item
	Declare Record (*)
	Delete Drafts (*)
	Delete Item
	Delete Previous Versions (*)
	Discard Check Out Item
	Inherit List Item Parent Permissions (Imp)
	Remove List Item Permissions (Imp)
	Replace List Item Permissions (Imp)
	Set Content Approval Status
	Set Field in Current Item
	Undeclare Record (*)
	Update List Item
	Wait for Change in Document Check-Out Status
	Wait for Field Change in Current Item
Relational Actions	Lookup Manager of a User (*)
Task Actions	Assign a Form to a Group
	Assign a To-do Item
	Collect Data from a User
	Start Approval Process (*)
	Start Custom Task Process (*)
	Start Feedback Process (*)
Task Behavior Actions	Append Task (*)
	Delegate Task (*)
	End Task Process (*)
	Escalate Task (*)
	Forward Task (*)
	Insert Task (*)
	Reassign Task (*)
	Request a change (*)
	Rescind Task (*)
	Send a Task Notification Email (*)
	Set Content Approval Status (as author) (*)
	Set Task Field (*)
	Wait for Change in Task Process Item (*)
	Wait for Deletion of Task Process Item (*)

Action Category	Action Name
Utility Actions	Extract Substring from End of String
	Extract Substring from Start of String
	Extract Substring from Index of String
	Extract Substring of String from Index with Length
	Persist On Close Activity (Imp)

* (*) Indicates the action is available only in farms running SharePoint Server 2010
 (Imp) Indicates the action is available only in an Impersonation Step

While this covers many, if not most, of the common actions that workflows will need to perform, it is important to note that it is possible to add custom actions to SPD and use them inside workflows.

Conditions

Conditions are similar to actions, and they are used in the SPD workflow designer in a similar manner. However, instead of performing any actual work themselves, conditions control whether or how actions will do their work. Conditions give the workflow author the opportunity to add branching and conditional logic to the workflow, hence controlling what happens based upon circumstances at run time. SPD ships with conditions out of the box, which are listed in Table 11-2.

TABLE 11-2 Conditions Shipping with SPD

Condition Category	Category Name
Common Conditions	If any value equals value
	If current item field equals value
Other Conditions	Check list item permission levels (Imp)
	Check list item permissions (Imp)
	Created by a specific person
	Created in a specific date span
	If task outcome equals value (*)
	Modified by a specific person
	Person is a valid SharePoint user
	The file size in a specific range of kilobytes
	The file type is a specific type
	Title field contains keywords

* (*) Indicates the action is available only in farms running SharePoint Server 2010
 (Imp) Indicates the action is available only in an Impersonation Step

It is possible to create complex branching structures by adding a condition to your workflow and then adding multiple Else-If branches to it by right-clicking and selecting Else-If Branch, as shown in Figure 11-6. The figure also shows how you can organize those branches by adding nested steps to each branch.

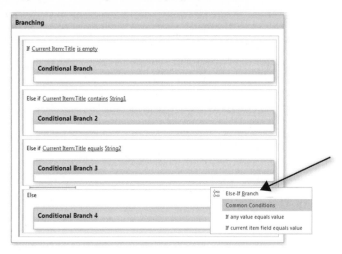

FIGURE 11-6 A complex branching structure with multiple Else-If branches and nested steps

Save a Workflow

Creating a workflow can take an extended period of time, so being able to save the workflow *without* publishing it and making it available to users is a nice new feature. Clicking the Save button on the SPD ribbon stores the workflow in the global workflow catalog for the current site but does not make it available for use on the site.

Publish a Workflow

When your workflow is complete and ready to be made available for testing in your development environment (because you're not working directly in your production environment, right?), click the Publish button on the SPD ribbon. This saves the workflow and makes it available for use.

Association Columns

Each reusable workflow must be created in terms of a specific Content Type. Because these workflows can run on the specified Content Type *or any Content Type that inherits from that Content Type*, it is possible that a particular Content Type instance that the workflow is running on will have a different set of columns than the workflow expects to find.

To overcome this potential problem, SPD includes a new capability called *association columns*. Clicking the Association Columns button on the SPD ribbon will open a dialog that allows you to manage the association columns included with this workflow. When the workflow is added to a new list (or, more specifically, a Content Type instance within a list), SharePoint will add a new column to the Content Type instance for each association column included with the workflow.

When adding association columns to a workflow, you can choose to either select an existing site column or add a new column. If you choose the former and then deploy the workflow to a site that does not already have that site column, it will be added to the site column gallery for that site and added to the Content Type. If you choose the latter, it will be created as a site column and added to the Content Type to which the workflow is attached.

One important final note: If you add an association column to a reusable workflow and then add that workflow to a list or Content Type that already has a column with that name, the association column will still be added. Its name will be made unique, typically by adding a number to the end, and the workflow will be adjusted to use this renamed column. This is often not what you would expect to happen, so it is important to be aware of this.

Visio

An important new capability of SPD workflows is something entirely external to SPD: using Visio Professional to design a workflow. This is an interesting new capability that allows business users—the people who presumably know the business process the best—to play an active role in the construction of their process.

Figure 11-7 shows a workflow laid out in Visio, including the following elements:

1. The Import and Export buttons on the new Process tab in Visio, which facilitate round-trip collaboration on the process design between Visio and SPD.

2. The Visio design surface showing a basic workflow.

3. A selection of the Visio shapes used to design the workflow process.

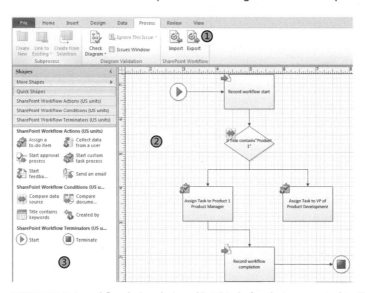

FIGURE 11-7 A workflow being designed in Visio before being exported to SPD

As implied by the buttons on the Ribbon, it is possible to move workflows back and forth between Visio and SPD during the design process with full fidelity.

We'll use Visio in the workflow that we will build later in this chapter, in the section entitled "Creating a Workflow with Visio and SharePoint Designer."

Avoiding Rube Goldberg Emulation

SPD is a great tool for building SharePoint workflows, and never more so than in the 2010 release. It is not the only tool, however, and sometimes it is not the right tool to use. Just because you can make something work in a SPD workflow doesn't mean that you should. Think about what you are doing and think whether the correct answer is really "No, you can't do that in an SPD workflow. You need Visual Studio." To understand the limitations of SPD, see the section entitled "Developing Custom Workflow Components," later in this chapter.

It is not worth jeopardizing your SharePoint environment just because SPD is the only tool in your toolbox. Building fragile constructs of additional lists and nested workflows is a problem waiting to happen. You need to ask yourself what the impact is of this Rube Goldberg machine failing, because the likelihood of it doing so is often alarmingly high.

Use SPD when it meets your needs, and even push the envelope a little bit, but realize that using it when it you shouldn't is as wrong as a developer writing custom code to duplicate a piece of functionality SharePoint provides out of the box.

 Note If you're not familiar with Rube Goldberg, see *http://en.wikipedia.org/wiki/Rube_Goldberg* and *http://en.wikipedia.org/wiki/Rube_Goldberg_machine*.

A Poor Man's Event Receiver

Perhaps the title of this section is a bit pejorative, but a fairly common use of SPD workflows is to build a process into SharePoint that technically shouldn't be a workflow at all; it should be an event receiver. Event receivers are discussed in Chapter 7, "Lists and Events," but at a high level, event receivers are another mechanism in SharePoint to run a process in response to changes in the SharePoint environment—uploading a document, creating a list item, and so on.

So how do we know when we "should" use a workflow and when we "should" use an event receiver? The short answer is that you really don't; it's all a matter of degree. In a perfect world, there would be a clear delineation between what should be implemented as a workflow and what should be an event receiver, but in the real world, there are often multiple conflicting requirements that push us in one direction or another. Here are some guidelines that can help to make a decision:

- Workflows tend to:
    - Be long-running
    - Interact with people
    - Require durability—in other words, it's a big deal if they don't process or stop in the middle
    - Be complex
- Event receivers tend to:
    - Be transient, often running for less than a second
    - Not create tasks or otherwise interact with users
    - Be simple, often performing only one or two pieces of work
    - Be less mission-critical
    - Require a higher level of technical ability and require Visual Studio to implement

With that list in mind (but realizing that they are only guidelines and that there are many exceptions to them), make sure that you think about the path you choose and do not blindly head down one road or the other. If you take a little time to think about the best approach, you probably won't go wrong.

Creating a Workflow with Visio and SharePoint Designer

With a good understanding of our tool, it's finally time to review the process of creating a workflow with Visio and SPD. We're going to begin in Visio and simulate the work that would be done by a business user who has a process that needs to be automated.

Start Visio Premium and chose the Microsoft SharePoint Workflow template form the Flowchart category. Visio will open a new design session with a normal-looking Visio design surface and a collection of shapes in the Shapes pane on the left side of the screen.

The first thing that must be done when creating any workflow design is to add your Start and Terminate shapes to the design surface, so go ahead and drag them to the design surface. Your window should now look something like Figure 11-8.

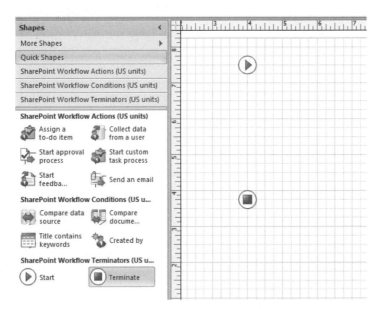

FIGURE 11-8 The beginning of a workflow process in Visio

The workflow that we are going to build is relatively simple, but it will still illustrate the important concepts and parts of the process. You can see from Figure 11-8 that there are sections in the Visio toolbar with captions such as "SharePoint Workflow Actions," which contain Visio shapes. You can drag these SharePoint-specific shapes to the Visio design surface to create a flowchart for a SharePoint workflow, such as the one shown in Figure 11-9.

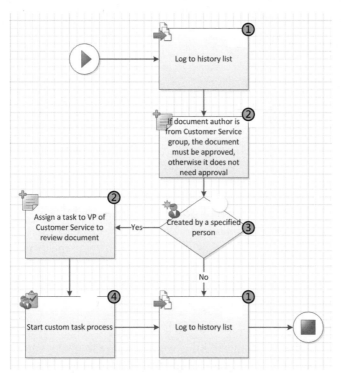

FIGURE 11-9 The fully defined process

For the record, Figure 11-9 contains the following:

1. Two Log To History List shapes used to record the beginning and end of our process

2. Two Add a Comment shapes to provide clarifying information to the person who will build the process in SPD. Notice that these need to be connected directly in line with the rest of the shapes.

3. One Created By A Specific Person shape to check who created the document.

4. One Start A Custom Task Process shape to assign an approval task.

With that done, our process is designed and ready to export to SPD to be finished and tested.

There is no need to save your Visio diagram (although you can if you want), because the export process automatically saves a copy that can be opened by Visio if necessary. Inside Visio, click the Process tab and then click Export, as shown in Figure 11-10. When you attempt to export the workflow, it will be checked automatically for validity. If it fails the validity check, you will be notified in a small task window with an indication of where the problem is.

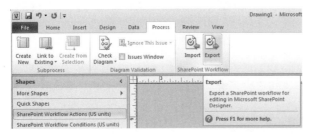

FIGURE 11-10 Exporting the process design from Visio for use in SPD

If your workflow passes the validity test, you will be prompted with a regular Save dialog. Go ahead and save the file in a place where it will be accessible to you later. Notice that the file extension is *.vwi*. This is a new file format called Visio Workflow Interchange, which contains the information necessary for both SPD and Visio to open and work with the process design. Technically, it is just a *.zip* file with a different extension. If you change the extension to *.zip*, you will be able to open the file in any program that is compatible with such files (such as Windows Explorer) and explore the contents.

We're done with Visio, so you can go ahead and close it. We're going to finish the workflow in SPD, so go ahead and start that program. SPD is going to require that you work in an active SharePoint site, so go ahead and connect to a site in your development environment.

In the left navigation pane, under the Site Object category, click Workflow. On the Ribbon, click the Import From Visio button, as shown in Figure 11-11.

FIGURE 11-11: Importing a process drawing into SPD

The Import Workflow From Visio Drawing dialog will prompt you to locate the file that you wish to import and then click Next. The final screen prompts you to name your new workflow (which by default will end up as the name that administrators see in SharePoint, so choose your name appropriately) and select a type of workflow to create. Choose the options shown in Figure 11-12 and click Finish.

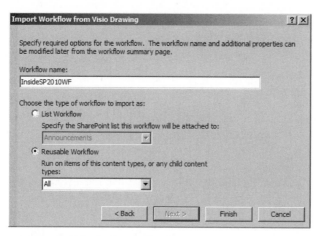

FIGURE 11-12 The final step of importing the workflow into SPD

After SPD finishes the import process, it will open the workflow designer, as shown in Figure 11-13.

FIGURE 11-13 The workflow as initially imported from Visio

Now it is time to refine the workflow and configure the various actions that have been created. The first thing to notice about the imported process is that it all exists within one step. Visio has no means to break a process down into steps, so it always creates a single step called ID3. This does not meet our needs, so we are going to change things a little.

First, let's separate the process into three steps:

1. Beginning

2. Assigning a task, if necessary

3. Finishing

The actual steps that you would use in your workflow will depend entirely on your business process. There is no right or wrong answer for how to break apart your workflow into steps; the only important thing is that the step breakdown makes sense to you.

To begin, place your mouse immediately after the bounding box for step ID3 and click. You should see a small orange line, like the one shown in Figure 11-13 just above the first Log This Message To The Workflow History List action. On the Ribbon, click the Step button in the Insert group, and then hit the down arrow on your keyboard and the Step button again to add new steps to the process.

The first step will hold the first Log action, but we want to give it a better name than ID3. Click the ID3 text and rename the step to Start Workflow. Click the title of Step 2 and rename it to Assign Task, and then do the same for Step 3, renaming it to Finish Workflow.

Now we need to move the actions to their appropriate steps. Click the last Log action and click the Move Down button on the Ribbon until it shows in the Finish Workflow step. Moving the condition and task creation actions is a little bit trickier because of their nested nature, but all you need to do is run your mouse over the action you want to move, and you'll notice a series of rectangles surrounding the actions. Make sure that the outermost bounding rectangle is highlighted, and then click it so it is selected. Now click the Move Down button to move the entire selection down to the Assign Task step.

Your workflow should now look similar to Figure 11-14. The last thing we need to do is configure the individual actions.

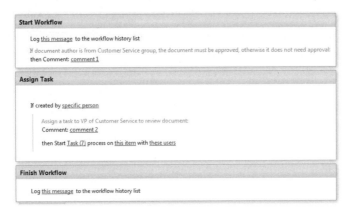

FIGURE 11-14 The imported workflow with the structure reorganized, but before configuring any of the actions or conditions

The first action is one of the Log To History List actions. All this is going to do is write the message that we specify into the workflow history list configured for an instance of this workflow. Configuring this action is a simple matter of clicking the This Message link and specifying a new message in the text box that appears. If you want your message to include information about the workflow or the item that it is running on, you can use the workflow lookup button, which has an icon for a function with the letters *fx*, to specify the value that you wish to display. For our purposes, having the message "workflow started" will be sufficient, so type that text.

The next item to be configured is the condition at the top of the Assign Tasks step. For this, we simply need to select the person or group that we want to be part of our condition check. The text of the comment from the Visio diagram indicates that the task is assigned only if the item the workflow is running on was created by a member of the Customer Service group, so that's what we'll put into our action. If you don't have a group named Customer Service in your environment, you can simply choose another user or group for the sake of this walk-through. To specify the user or group, click on the Specific Person link to open the Select Users dialog. Select People/Groups From SharePoint Site and click Add. Search for the group or user you are going to check and click OK.

The next action to configure is the actual task assignment. For this, we need to perform the following steps:

1. Configure the task to be assigned.

2. Configure the item the task will be associated with.

3. Configure who the task will be assigned to.

We're going to take these out of order, starting with the easiest step (step 2) and working toward the hardest (step 1). This task is to be associated with our current item, so simply click the This Item link and accept the default option of Current Item in the dialog that appears. The next part of configuring the task assignment is to indicate to whom the task will be assigned. Click the These Users link and configure the Select Task Process Participants dialog box, as shown in Figure 11-15, with the only change being that you should specify whatever account you are currently logged in as in place of <You> in the Participants text box.

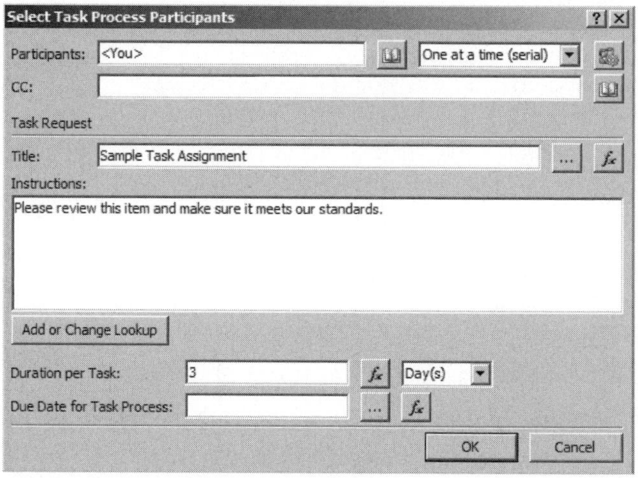

FIGURE 11-15 Configuring the participants in the workflow process

The last step is to configure the task itself. One of the key points of this new task control in SPD workflows is the ability to encapsulate a high degree of functionality, including the ability to assign multiple tasks to different people as part of this process. To do this, click the Start Task link to display the page used to configure the task. To keep this walkthrough simple, we are just going to accept all the defaults. There are a lot of options on this page, though, and it is worth exploring thoroughly to see some of the new power of this addition to the SPD workflow arsenal. In particular, the new task that we are creating in this step will be configured to support the following actions:

- Create new outcomes for the task. By default, the task supports two different outcomes: approval or rejection. You can now add more buttons for whatever outcome you require and check that outcome at task completion.

- Add new fields to the task form to collect additional information from the person completing the task.

- Add specific functionality to respond at several points during the task's lifetime:
  - When the task process starts
  - Before the first task assignment is made
  - If the task process is cancelled
  - When the task process completes

  All of this is configured by clicking the Change The Behavior Of The Overall Task Process link.

- Control who can see and edit task items, limiting access to task owners and the overall process owner.

- Control individual task assignments, responding to events such as:
  - Assigned
  - Pending
  - Expired
  - Deleted
  - Completed

- Change the conditions that signal that the overall task is completed.

This completes the configuration of the actions in our workflow. Notice that we haven't done anything with either of the Comment activities that were added from Visio. We could delete them or leave them in place depending on what we want. They will have no effect on the running workflow, but if we want business users to open the process back in Visio, they might expect to see them there, so let's leave them.

Click the Publish button on the Ribbon to validate the workflow and push it up to SharePoint, where it will now be available for use. You can test the workflow by navigating to your site, selecting a list or document library (and remember we built this as a reusable workflow available for any Content Type so it will work on *any* list or library), and starting it on an item.

Deploying an SPD Workflow

The last important new functionality in SPD workflows is the ability to save the workflow as a template and deploy it to a different environment. Completing this is quite simple.

Back in SPD, click the Workflows item under Site Objects in the left navigation pane to show all the available workflows on our site. Click to the right side of the name of the workflow that we just created to select it, and then click the Save As Template button on the Ribbon. After a few seconds of processing, a message will tell us that the template has been saved to the Site Assets library. The item in Site Assets is a regular SharePoint Solution file (WSP) that we can download and deploy to a different site/site collection in this environment or to a totally unique farm.

SPD Workflow Summary and Recommendation

This completes our walkthrough of SPD workflows. While we touched upon many new functionalities, we only mentioned some other key new aspects. It is worth the time to explore SPD workflows fully. The overall effect of the changes to SPD workflows is that this is now the recommended tool for building SPD workflows. True, there are a couple of items that cannot be handled by SPD workflows (we'll discuss these in the next section) but these are almost all edge cases that are quite uncommon. The vast majority of workflow scenarios can now be implemented in SPD.

Developing Custom Workflow Components

Now we have come to the second half of this chapter, where we will discuss developing custom workflow components with Visual Studio 2010. You will learn that developing custom workflow components requires a deeper understanding of WF and SPD workflow internals. Consequently, there is a significantly steeper learning curve when compared to learning to create custom workflows with SharePoint Designer 2010. Once you begin learning what is involved in custom workflow component development, you will likely gain a new appreciation for the strategy of creating custom workflows with SPD 2010 because it hides so many details.

As stated earlier in this chapter, we recommend you use SharePoint Designer 2010 to create custom workflows whenever you can. However, there are scenarios where SharePoint Designer 2010 doesn't provide all the flexibility and power you need. Without custom development, you are limited to the functionality that is provided by the standard workflow actions that SharePoint 2010 makes available to SharePoint Designer 2010. Here's a list of common requirements that are hard or impossible to meet using SharePoint Designer 2010 alone:

- **Looping**   SharePoint Designer 2010 workflows cannot provide direct looping support through collections such as the lists in a site or the items in a list.

- **Accessing content outside the current site**   The standard workflow actions do not make it possible to access SharePoint content in other sites or site collections or to access anything at the level of the farm or Web application.

- **Calling across the network**   Standard workflow actions do not make it possible to call a remote Web service from a SharePoint Designer 2010 workflow.

- **Running with elevated permissions**   SPD workflows actions run under the identity and with the permissions of the current user. Impersonation Steps, discussed earlier in this chapter, can help to some degree, but that still restricts workflow actions from running under the identity and with the permissions of a more privileged user.

- **Obtaining low-level control at the WF level**   By its nature, SharePoint Designer 2010 insulates the workflow builder from the details of the underlying SPD workflow architecture. In many business scenarios, this is acceptable, and even preferable. However, occasionally, you will need a level of control over your process that SharePoint Designer 2010 does not allow.

If you find that the business requirements for the workflows that you must build are beyond what SharePoint Designer 2010 can provide on its own, you have two different strategies for integrating Visual Studio 2010. The first strategy involves using Visual Studio 2010 to develop custom actions that can be consumed by users creating custom workflows in SharePoint Designer 2010. The second strategy involves using Visual Studio 2010 to develop custom workflow templates. What is important to understand is that these two strategies differ greatly when it comes to involving SharePoint Designer 2010.

The first strategy in which you develop custom actions with Visual Studio 2010 is complimentary to your efforts with SharePoint Designer 2010 to create custom workflows. The idea is that you accomplish as much as you can when creating custom workflows with SharePoint Designer 2010 using the standard actions included with SharePoint Foundation and SharePoint Server 2010. Then you resort to developing custom actions that can be consumed by SharePoint Designer 2010 and used to create custom workflows when you need more power.

The second strategy of using Visual Studio 2010 to develop custom workflow templates completely removes SharePoint Designer 2010 from the workflow creation process. While this approach provides the greatest amount of power and control, you should not underestimate the loss in productivity. This approach definitely does not lend itself to environments where your efforts to build custom workflows must be able to adapt quickly to changing business needs. It is best used on projects where the business processes are well defined and not likely to change.

Developing Custom Actions

If you decide to develop custom actions with Visual Studio 2010, there are still more decisions you must make. You must decide whether to take the easy approach or the harder, more powerful approach. The easy approach involves building custom actions that are loaded with partial trust and executed inside the sandbox. These types of workflow components are known as *sandboxed actions,* and we will cover them first.

The second approach involves developing *full trust actions,* which is accomplished by creating custom activity classes. This approach yields more power because your workflow actions are deployed at farm level and run under a full trust execution model just as the standard workflow actions that are available in SharePoint Designer 2010. However, developing and deploying full trust actions is more involved and requires a greater understanding of WF and the SPD workflow architecture. We will discuss what you need to know to create and deploy full trust actions after first discussing how to create sandboxed actions.

Developing Sandboxed Actions

To create a sandboxed action, you must create a public class that contains a method known as an *action function.* The method that implements the action function can be given any name, but it must be defined with a single *SPUserCodeWorkflowContext* parameter and have a return value based on the *Hashtable* collection type defined inside the *System.Collections* namespace.

```
public class SandboxedAction1 {
  public Hashtable ActionMethod1(SPUserCodeWorkflowContext context) {
    // the implementation for your custom action code goes here
  }
}
```

The *SPUserCodeWorkflowContext* parameter provides you with access to contextual information such as URLs and IDs of the current site, the current list, and the current list item. This makes it possible to program against the current site, list, and item using classes in the server-side object model such as *SPWeb, SPList,* and *SPListItem.*

Remember that your code is running inside the sandbox, so you are limited by the constraints of the User Code service that were discussed in Chapter 4, "Sandboxed Solutions." When the code in the action function has completed its work, it should be written to return a *Hashtable* object that contains a named value of *Outcome*. This is used to return a status message such as *Success* if your code completes without any errors.

```
public Hashtable ActionMethod1(SPUserCodeWorkflowContext context) {
  // perform work for action
  using (SPSite siteCollection = new SPSite(context.CurrentWebUrl)) {
    SPWeb web = siteCollection.OpenWeb();
    SPList list  = web.Lists.GetList(context.ListId,true);
    SPListItem item = list.GetItemById(context.ItemId);
    // perform work required by action
  }

  // return outcome status using Hashtable
  Hashtable actionResults = new Hashtable();
  actionResults["Outcome"] = "Success";
  return actionResults;
}
```

In addition to the public class with an action function, each sandboxed action requires a declarative *Action* element defined inside a *WorkflowActions* element. You should create these required XML elements inside a SharePoint project item created using the Empty Element project item template. The *Action* element should be given a *Name* attribute and a *Category* attribute that is used to display action information to the user in SharePoint Designer 2010. Here is the minimal starting point for an *Action* element for a sandboxed action which includes attributes for the assembly name, the class name, the action function named, and an attribute named *SandboxedFunction*, which must be configured with a value of *true*.

```
<WorkflowActions>
  <Action
      Name="Custom Sandboxed Action 1"
      Category="Custom Wingtip Actions"
      Assembly="$SharePoint.Project.AssemblyFullName$"
      ClassName="WingtipSandboxedActions.SandboxedAction1"
      FunctionName="ActionMethod1"
      SandboxedFunction="true"
      AppliesTo="all" >
    <RuleDesigner Sentence="The 'Hello World' Custom Action">
      <FieldBind Field="Outcome" Text="outcome" Id="1" DesignerType="ParameterNames" />
    </RuleDesigner>
    <Parameters>
      <Parameter Name="Outcome" Type="System.String, mscorlib" Direction="Out"
                 DesignerType="ParameterNames" Description="Outcome of operation"/>
    </Parameters>
  </Action>
</WorkflowActions>
```

Note that the *Action* attribute also contains the required *AppliesTo* attribute, which can be assigned a value of *list, doclib,* or *all,* depending on whether the action can be used on lists, document libraries, or both. You can also see that the inner *RuleDesigner* element contains a *Sentence* attribute that is shown to the user in the workflow designer of SharePoint Designer 2010 once the user has added the action to a workflow. The *Parameters* element is used to define input parameters and output parameters. When creating sandboxed actions, you should always define the *Outcome* parameter as shown in the previous example.

The downloadable .zip archive of companion code for this book includes a project named WingtipSandboxedActions, which contains a working sample of the *SandboxedAction1* class. This project also contains a sandboxed action named *CreateDocWorkspaceAction,* which shows a more realistic example of a custom action that you would create to solve an actual business problem.

If you open the WingtipSandboxedActions project and deploy it as a sandboxed solution, Visual Studio 2010 will upload and activate these two custom actions within the context of the target test site. After that, you should be able to open the site with SharePoint Designer 2010 and see those custom actions among the list of available actions when creating custom workflows in SharePoint Designer 2010.

Developing Full-Trust Workflow Actions

You can develop a second type of custom action that does not run in the sandbox but instead at a level of full trust. However, this approach becomes more involved because you must implement a low-level workflow component known as an activity. In WF programming, an *activity* is a class that inherits from the *Activity* class defined within the *System.Workflow .ComponentModel* assembly inside a namespace of the same name. The *Activity* class is defined with an overridable method named *Execute*. You implement the *Execute* method to give the activity class the behavior it requires.

```
public class HelloWorldActivity : Activity {
  protected override ActivityExecutionStatus Execute(ActivityExecutionContext context) {
    // your action implementation goes here
  }
}
```

When you create an activity class, you must define a static *DependencyProperty* field and an accompanying public property for each input parameter and output parameter. In our example, we will define two input parameters named *__Context* and *UserID*. The first parameter named *__Context* will be used to pass an input parameter of type *WorkflowContext*. The second parameter named *UserID* will be used to pass an input parameter of type *int* with the ID of the current user.

```
public class HelloWorldActivity : Activity {

  public static DependencyProperty __ContextProperty =
    DependencyProperty.Register("__Context",
                                typeof(WorkflowContext),
                                typeof(HelloWorldActivity));

  public static DependencyProperty UserIdProperty =
    DependencyProperty.Register("UserId",
                                typeof(int),
                                typeof(HelloWorldActivity));

  public WorkflowContext __Context {
    get { return (WorkflowContext)base.GetValue(__ContextProperty); }
    set { base.SetValue(__ContextProperty, value); }
  }

  public int UserId {
    get { return (int)base.GetValue(UserIdProperty); }
    set { base.SetValue(UserIdProperty, value); }
  }
```

Note that the *Execute* method of an activity is always called by the WF runtime; it should
never be called directly by developers. When the WF runtime calls the *Execute* method, it
passes an *ActivityExecutionContext* parameter, which makes it possible to access workflow
services. SharePoint Foundation extends WF with several SharePoint-specific workflow services,
including the SharePoint Service, the Task Service, and the List Item Service, all of which can
be accessed using the following code.

```
protected override ActivityExecutionStatus Execute(ActivityExecutionContext context) {

  ISharePointService SPService =
          (ISharePointService)context.GetService(typeof(ISharePointService));
  ITaskService TaskService =
          (ITaskService)context.GetService(typeof(ITaskService));
  IListItemService ListItemService =
          (IListItemService)context.GetService(typeof(IListItemService));

  // Now perform work using workflow services
}
```

Note that while your code is executing in the context of a workflow instance, you must create
tasks and update site content using workflow services. For example, you should not create
tasks and update list items using standard server-side object model techniques. Instead, you
must create tasks using the Task Service and update items using the List Item Service. Here
is a sample implementation of the *Execute* method that uses the SharePoint Service to log a
comment to the workflow history list.

```
protected override ActivityExecutionStatus Execute(ActivityExecutionContext context) {
  // get reference to SharePoint Service
  ISharePointService SPService =
          (ISharePointService)context.GetService(typeof(ISharePointService));

  // use SharePoint Service to perform work
  SPService.LogToHistoryList(
    this.WorkflowInstanceId,
    SPWorkflowHistoryEventType.WorkflowComment,
    this.UserId,
    TimeSpan.MinValue,
    "The 'Hello World' activity",
    "My description",
    "My custom data");

    // return Closed to indicate the activity has completed
    return ActivityExecutionStatus.Closed;
  }
}
```

The final thing to observe is that *Execute* method must complete by returning a value from the *ActivityExecutionStatus* enumeration. By passing a value of *Closed*, you are indicating to the WF runtime that the activity has completed its work and that the execution flow of the workflow can continue to the next activity. *ActivityExecutionStatus* defines several other enumeration values, such as *Canceling, Compensating, Executing, Faulting,* and *Initialized,* which you can return from the *Execute* method to deal with other scenarios as well.

The manner in which full-trust actions are deployed is different from the way that sandboxed actions are deployed. The deployment of full-trust actions requires a farm solution because you must deploy an XML file with *Action* elements to a location inside the SharePoint Root directory. You must also deploy the assembly with the custom action in the global assembly cache (GAC) and modify the web.config file for the hosting Web application with an authorized type entry.

Let's start by discussing how to create and deploy the XML file required for full trust actions. First, the XML file must be created with an extension of *.actions*. Second, the XML file must be deployed inside the SharePoint Root directory at a location of TEMPLATE/<*culture*>/ Workflow, where <*culture*> is the identifier for the current language. For a SharePoint 2010 farm based on U.S. English, for example, the correct directory would be TEMPLATE/1033/ Workflow. Third, the XML file must contain a top-level *WorkflowInfo* element that contains an *Action* element for each full trust action. Note that in addition to custom actions, you can create custom conditions.

```
<WorkflowInfo Language="en-us">
  <Conditions And="and" Or="or" Not="not" When="If" Else="Else if" >
    <!-- add Condition elements here -->
  </Conditions>
  <Actions>
    <!-- add Condition elements here -->
  </Actions>
</WorkflowInfo>
```

The downloadable .zip archive of companion code for this book includes a project named CustomWingtipActions, which demonstrates how to develop and deploy full-trust actions. This project includes an XML file named Wingtip.actions. By examining this file, you can see how to create the XML elements required to deploy both custom actions and custom conditions.

The second important aspect of deploying full-trust actions involves modifying the web.config file for the hosting Web application. More specifically, full-trust actions and conditions will not appear in SharePoint Designer 2010 unless you have added a custom *authorizedType* element into the *authorizedTypes* section of the web.config file.

```
<configuration>
  <System.Workflow.ComponentModel.WorkflowCompiler>
    <authorizedTypes>
      <!-- authorized type entries for standard actions and conditions -->
      <authorizedType
        Assembly="WingtipCustomActions, [full four-part assembly name]"
        Namespace="WingtipCustomActions"
        TypeName="*"
        Authorized="True" />
    </authorizedTypes>
  </System.Workflow.ComponentModel.WorkflowCompiler>
</configuration>
```

Unfortunately, there is no declarative technique that you can use in a SharePoint project to add an *authorizedType* element to the web.config file associated with a Web application. However, it is still recommended that you automate updating the web.config file so you don't require a SharePoint farm administrator to make the required changes by hand. The best way to automate adding the required *authorizedType* element is by using the support in the server-side object model made available through the *SPWebConfigModification* class.

In a SharePoint environment, web.config files are scoped at the level of the Web application. Therefore, it makes sense to automate adding and removing *authorizedType* elements by adding a feature receiver to a Web application–scoped feature. The CustomWingtipActions project contains such a feature, *RegisterAuthorizedTypes*, which implements the following feature receiver class.

```
public class RegisterAuthorizedTypesEventReceiver : SPFeatureReceiver {

  public override void FeatureActivated(SPFeatureReceiverProperties properties) {
    SPWebApplication webApp = (SPWebApplication)properties.Feature.Parent;
    SPWebConfigModification mod = CreateModificationForAuthType();
    webApp.WebConfigModifications.Add(mod);
    webApp.Update();
    webApp.WebService.ApplyWebConfigModifications();
  }

  public override void FeatureDeactivating(SPFeatureReceiverProperties properties) {
    SPWebApplication webApp = (SPWebApplication)properties.Feature.Parent;
    SPWebConfigModification mod = CreateModificationForAuthType();
    webApp.WebConfigModifications.Remove(mod);
    webApp.Update();
    webApp.WebService.ApplyWebConfigModifications();
  }

  private SPWebConfigModification CreateModificationForAuthType() {
    // implementation of this method shown below
  }

}
```

As you can see, both the *FeatureActivated* method and the *FeatureDeactivating* acquire an *SPWebApplication* reference to the current Web application and call a helper method named *CreateModificationForAuthType* to create a new *SPWebConfigModification* object. The *SPWebApplication* class provides a *WebConfigModifications* collection property with an *Add* method, used to add entries to the web.config file, and a *Remove* method, used to remove entries from the web.config file. After adding or removing an entry, you must then call *Update* on the *SPWebApplication* object, followed by a call to the *ApplyWebConfigModifications* method of the Web application's *WebService* property to push the changes to all the Web servers in the current farm.

The helper method named *CreateModificationForAuthType* has been implemented to create an *SPWebConfigModification* object, which can be used to add or remove an *authorizedType* element to the web.config file. Note that you must assign values correctly to several properties of a *SPWebConfigModification* object, including *Owner, Sequence, Type, Path, Name,* and *Value.*

```
private SPWebConfigModification CreateModificationForAuthType() {
  SPWebConfigModification mod = new SPWebConfigModification();
  mod.Owner = "WingtipCustomActions";
  mod.Sequence = 0;
  mod.Type = SPWebConfigModification.SPWebConfigModificationType.EnsureChildNode;

  // construct path for element
  mod.Path = "configuration/System.Workflow.ComponentModel.WorkflowCompiler/
authorizedTypes";
```

```
// create element name and value
string assemblyName = this.GetType().Assembly.FullName;
string assemblyNamespace = "WingtipCustomActions";

mod.Name = "authorizedType[@Assembly='" + assemblyName + "']" +
                      "[@Namespace='" + assemblyNamespace + "']" +
                      "[@TypeName='*']" +
                      "[@Authorized='True']";

mod.Value = "<authorizedType Assembly='" + assemblyName + "' " +
                      "Namespace='" + assemblyNamespace + "' " +
                      "TypeName='*' " +
                      "Authorized='True' />";

// return SPWebConfigModification object
return mod;
}
```

If you open the CustomWingtipActions project in Visual Studio 2010 and run the
Deploy command, the project's output solution package will deploy the Wingtip.actions
file to the correct location in the SharePoint Root directory. When you activate the
RegisterAuthorizedTypes feature within the scope of a Web application, its feature receiver
will add the *authorizedType* entry to the web.config file. After that, you should be able to
open any site in that Web application using SharePoint Designer 2010 and see the custom
actions and the custom conditions provided by the CustomWingtipActions project.

> **Note** In production farms with multiple Web servers, there will be more than one physi-
> cal web.config file associated with a Web application. For example, there will be at least one
> web.config file per Web server, and there could also be more than one if a Web application
> has been extended with multiple zones. However, when using *SPWebConfigModification*, you
> do not have to worry about how many physical web.config files exist for a Web application.
> SharePoint Foundation handles all the updates behind the scenes. Just make sure that you call
> the *ApplyWebConfigModifications* method, and your updates will be made correctly.

Developing Custom Workflow Templates

The final option for developing custom workflow components is the most powerful: using
custom workflow templates. When you develop a custom workflow template, you use Visual
Studio 2010 exclusively to build a custom workflow. If you elect to use this approach, it
means that SharePoint Designer 2010 is completely removed from the process of creating
custom workflows and maintaining business logic to automate business processes.

There are, of course, some caveats to developing custom workflow templates that we would like you to consider before deciding to use this strategy. First, workflow templates cannot be deployed using sandboxed solutions. Workflow templates can only be deployed using farm solutions. Second, there is no integration with Visio. All the Visio workflow integration features that we discussed earlier in this chapter in the section entitled "Creating a Workflow with Visio and SharePoint Designer" work only with custom workflows created with SharePoint Designer 2010, not with custom workflow templates created with Visual Studio 2010.

Another important thing to remember is that SharePoint 2010 is based on .NET Framework 3.5, rather than the most recent version of the .NET Framework, which is version 4.0. A key point is that .NET Framework 4.0 has introduced significant changes to the WF runtime and the way that workflows are built and executed. It is currently impossible to determine the level of compatibility between the workflow templates that you develop for SharePoint 2010 and .NET Framework 3.5 and future versions of SharePoint Foundation and SharePoint Server once these products have been updated to work with the new version of WF in .NET Framework 4.0. If you employ a workflow strategy based on creating custom workflows with SharePoint Designer 2010, it involves working at a higher level and has a greater chance of being shielded from all these pending changes.

One last issue to consider is that developing custom workflow templates is very different and can be more challenging than other areas of SharePoint development. If you really need the power and control that comes with developing custom workflow templates, you should lower your expectations for productivity and your ability to respond quickly to requests from business users.

A Quick Primer on WF Development

Before we go into the details of using Visual Studio 2010 to create a custom workflow template, let's cover some of the fundamental WF concepts and basic terminology. Earlier in this chapter, in the section entitled "Developing Full-Trust Workflow Actions," we showed you how to develop a custom activity that is recognized by SharePoint Designer 2010 as an action. When developing workflow templates, you don't write custom activities. Instead, you become a consumer of activities. Your goal is to create a composition of activities that defines a starting point, a control-of-flow structure with multiple execution paths, and an ending point.

Activities are the building blocks with which you construct workflow templates. You must learn how to use the standard activity libraries included with Visual Studio 2010 to become proficient in developing workflow templates. The two main activity libraries that you must learn about include the *Base Activity Library (BAL)* of WF and the *SharePoint Foundation Activity Library.*

It's helpful if you regard activities in the same fashion as you think about server-side controls in ASP.NET. Like controls, activities are black boxes of reusable code that expose properties and events. As with controls, the consumer of an activity can simply drag it to a design surface within Visual Studio 2010. The activity consumer then initializes the properties for the activity by using a standard property sheet. The activity consumer also generates event handlers for activities and writes code behind these event handlers. This development paradigm makes it relatively simple to add and maintain custom logic.

Another very important aspect of the WF programming model is that certain types of activities can have child activities, which are known as *composite activities*. The WF programming model includes a class named *CompositeActivity*, which inherits from *Activity*. The *CompositeActivity* class extends the *Activity* base class by including an *Activities* property that exposes a collection used to add and track child activities. Many of the activities that you reuse from the BAL inherit from *CompositeActivity* and can contain child activities.

Each composite activity manages the execution of its child activities, which allows composite activities to provide control-of-flow constructs within a WF program. For example, the BAL provides a composite activity named *While* that repeatedly executes a child activity so long as some condition within the WF program remains true. There is another composite activity named *IfThen,* which conditionally executes child activities contained in two possible paths depending on whether a certain condition in the WF program is met.

Your ability to express control-of-flow constructs within a WF program using composite activities results in creating application logic that is natural and easy to understand. It also makes it possible to encapsulate and reuse complex control-of-flow constructs in a fashion that isn't possible in programming languages, such as C# and Visual Basic. For example, the BAL provides a composite activity named *Parallel,* which executes two different groups of child activities in parallel. As a consumer of the *Parallel* activity, you don't have to worry about starting two different paths of execution at the same time, nor do you have to worry about the details of synchronizing the completion of these two paths before moving to the next activity. These details of managing the control of flow are handled by the logic encapsulated within the *Parallel* activity.

Let us give you one more example. The purpose of a very powerful composite activity of the BAL named *Replicator* is to take a flow of one or more child activities and replicate this flow so that it can be executed multiple times with different parameters. For example, imagine that you have created a flow of activities to assign a task to a user who needs to approve a document and then to wait on that user to either approve or reject the document. However, what should you do if you need three different users to approve a document in a particular business scenario?

You can add the flow of approval-related activities within the *Replicator* activity and configure it to execute the flow three different times. You can even use the property sheet to switch the behavior of this replication by changing the *ExecutionType* property back and forth between *Sequence* and *Parallel*. This is a good example of how composite activities can encapsulate complicated control-of-flow structures to make your life easier when writing business logic.

The WF programming model defines another important concept known as a *WF program*. You can think of as a WF program as a composite activity that defines a complete and executable workflow using a composition of child activities. The concept of the WF program is essential to the integration between WF and Visual Studio 2010. That's because Visual Studio 2010 provides a visual workflow designer that allows you to design and implement a WF program by dragging activities from the toolbar to a design surface. This is true regardless of whether you are building WF programs for a SharePoint environment or a non-SharePoint environment.

SharePoint Foundation extends WF by introducing the concept of a *workflow template*. At the heart of each SharePoint workflow template is a single WF program that you design and implement using the standard workflow designer in Visual Studio 2010. The key value of the workflow template is to integrate WF programs into the SharePoint environment so that they can be installed, configured, and parameterized for use.

A workflow template built with Visual Studio 2010 requires a WF program that is compiled into an assembly dynamic-link library (DLL) and installed in the GAC. While the SharePoint developer tools in Visual Studio 2010 are able to provide transparent support for GAC installation, you should observe that this is one of the primary reasons that workflow templates cannot be used in sandboxed solutions.

Before a workflow template can be used in a SharePoint environment, it must be activated within the scope of a site collection. Activating a workflow template requires a site collection–scoped feature that includes a declarative *Workflow* element. The Collaborative Application Markup Language (CAML) definition for a *Workflow* element must include attributes for a name and an ID based on the globally unique identifier (GUID). It must also include attributes to reference the class name and assembly name of the WF program itself.

```
<Workflow
    Name="Product Approval Workflow Template"
    Description="Use to approve and reject Wingtip product proposals"
    Id="b06c5f7d-7b06-46b0-a07d-ccb2504153f5"
    CodeBesideClass="[namespace-qualified class name of WF program]"
    CodeBesideAssembly="[full 4-part name of assembly which contains the WF program]" >
  <Categories/>
  <MetaData/>
</Workflow>
```

SharePoint Foundation does not support the creation of workflow instances directly from a workflow template. Instead, you must create an intermediate layer known as a workflow association. A *workflow association* is a named set of parameterization data that is used to bind a workflow template to a specific list, document library, Content Type, or site.

Once the feature that contains the *Workflow* element for a workflow template has been activated within the current site collection, a privileged user, such as the site or list owner, can create a new workflow association on a target object such as a list or document library. This can be done by clicking the Workflow Settings link on the List Settings page to navigate to a standard application page named AddWrkfl.aspx that is used to create a workflow association.

The primary function of a workflow association is to hold parameterization data for a workflow template that is used to initialize workflow instances. Keep in mind that for one particular list or document library in a SharePoint site, you can create two different workflow associations from the same workflow template and parameterize them in different ways.

When you create a SharePoint project with a custom workflow template, the SharePoint Developer Tools provide the convenience of automating the creation of the workflow association for testing purposes. When you configure a workflow template with this option, the SharePoint Developer Tools automatically create a new workflow association for you whenever you run the Deploy command. This is very handy because it eliminates the need for a developer to create a workflow association manually when it's time to test and debug a workflow template in a SharePoint project.

Creating a New Workflow Template in a SharePoint Project

To create a custom workflow template, you must create a new SharePoint project. You can create a new SharePoint project using the Sequential Workflow project template or the State Machine Workflow project template supplied by the SharePoint Developer Tools. Alternatively, you can create a new SharePoint project using the Empty SharePoint Project template and then create add workflow templates by creating new project items using the project item templates named Sequential Workflow and State Machine Workflow, as shown in Figure 11-16. Just make sure you configure a new SharePoint project as a farm solution if you plan to add workflow templates.

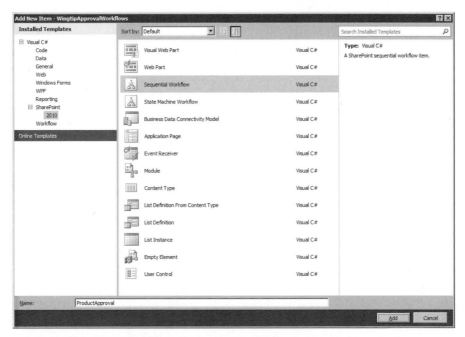

FIGURE 11-16 You can add workflow templates by creating new project items based on the project item templates named Sequential Workflow and State Machine Workflow.

Whenever you add a new workflow template to a SharePoint project, the SharePoint Customization Wizard presents a dialog in which you must select whether to configure the new workflow template for use on lists or on sites. There is a second dialog that allows you to configure Visual Studio 2010 to create a workflow association for testing purposes each time you run the build command. In many cases, you can simply reference a list or a document library that will be used in testing and debugging. Note that you cannot configure Visual Studio 2010 to create an association for you unless the target test site already has a task list and a workflow history list.

Remember that a workflow template must be enabled by activating a feature that is scoped at the site collection level. If you add a workflow template to a SharePoint project that does not already have a site collection–scoped feature, the SharePoint Developer Tools automatically add a new feature with a name such as *Feature1*. It is recommended that you change the name of this feature to something more appropriate. For example, you should rename this feature to *MainSite* to indicate that it activates at the site collection level.

Now let's discuss how you decide between creating a new workflow templates using the Sequential Workflow project item template as opposed to the State Machine Workflow project item template. First, a sequential workflow template is easier to work with because it can be modeled in the form of a flowchart. The flowchart is usually designed with several paths of execution to model a business process. When developing a sequential workflow template, you can use composite activities such as *While*, *IfElse*, and *Replicator* to design the control of flow and achieve the conditional branching required.

In some real-world scenarios, certain types of business processes are difficult to model using a flowchart or a sequential workflow template. This can be the case when a business process has many possible paths of execution that jump forward or backward in an ad hoc fashion. If you create a state machine workflow template, you have the ability to model the different states that a business process goes through on its way to completion, which provides greater flexibility.

However, there is an important issue surrounding state machine workflows that should discourage you from using them: WF support for state machine workflows has been discontinued in .NET Framework 4.0. While you can develop state machine workflow templates in Visual Studio 2010 and use them in SharePoint 2010, they are very likely to cause compatibility problems with future versions of SharePoint. Therefore, we recommend that you avoid creating state machine workflow templates and stick with creating sequential workflow templates instead.

This chapter is accompanied by a sample SharePoint project named WingtipApprovalWorkflows. We created this project using the Empty SharePoint Project template and we then added a workflow template by creating a new project item named *ProductApproval* using the Sequential Workflow project item template. Once you have created a workflow template project item, such as *ProductApproval*, you can begin to design and implement its WF program in workflow designer provided by Visual Studio 2010, as shown in Figure 11-17.

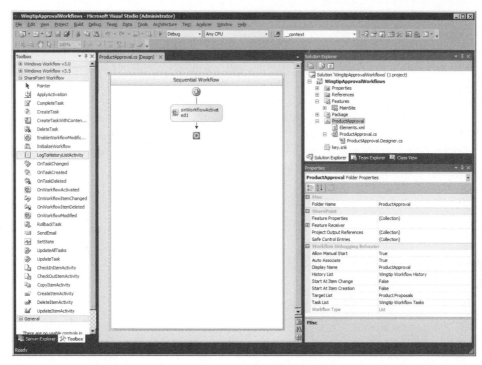

FIGURE 11-17 The designer for Visual Studio workflows did not change in Visual Studio 2010.

When developing workflow templates, you are required to work with WF program files, such as ProductApproval.cs, in both Designer view and Code view. When you are working in Designer view, the workflow designer of Visual Studio 2010 provides you with the convenience of dragging activities from the Visual Studio Toolbox to the design surface of ProductApproval.cs, which is how you compose the flow of activities for your WF program. Designer view also makes it possible to modify an activity by selecting it and then modifying its properties using a standard property sheet.

Let's begin working on the WF program of the ProductApproval workflow template. You should start by double-clicking the source file named ProductApproval.cs within the Visual Studio Project Explorer, which opens the WF program in Designer view. The next thing you must do is become comfortable switching ProductApproval.cs back and forth between Designer view and Code view, which is something you will do on a regular basis as you develop WF programs with the workflow designer.

If you right-click the window of the workflow designer, you see context menu items that allow you to toggle back and forth between Designer view and Code view. When in Designer view, there is a context menu item titled View Code. When in Code view, there is a context menu item titled View Designer. Practice moving back and forth between these two views.

You should observe that the context menu in the workflow designer window provides several other important options, as shown in Figure 11-18. A Generate Handlers menu item is used to create event handlers for the WF program and child activities quickly. Other menu items make it possible to navigate between the main SequentialWorkflow view and two other views, Cancel Handler and Fault Handler.

FIGURE 11-18 Right-clicking the workflow designer window provides several important context menu items.

When you create a new workflow template such as ProductApproval, you notice that its WF program contains an existing activity named *onWorkflowActivated1* that has been created using the *OnWorkflowActivated* activity type. This is an important requirement for any WF program targeting SharePoint Foundation or SharePoint Server 2010. More specifically, the first activity within the WF program running in a SharePoint environment must be created using the *OnWorkflowActivated* activity type. For this reason, you should never remove the activity instance named *onWorkflowActivated1*, nor should you add any other activities in front of it.

Before we make any modifications to ProductApproval.cs, let's switch over to Code view and examine the code that is provided as a starting point. The code you see should be roughly the equivalent of the following.

```
// using statements omitted for clarity
namespace WingtipApprovalWorkflows.ProductApproval {
  public sealed partial class ProductApproval : SequentialWorkflowActivity {
    public ProductApproval() {
      InitializeComponent();
    }

    public Guid workflowId = default(System.Guid);
    public SPWorkflowActivationProperties workflowProperties =
        new SPWorkflowActivationProperties();
  }
}
```

The *ProductApproval* class is defined as a partial class because the other half of the class definition exists within a source file named ProductApproval.designer.cs. You can also see that the preprovided constructor for the *ProductApproval* class calls a method from ProductApproval.designer.cs named *InitializeComponent*. The *InitializeComponent* method contains the code created by the code generator of the workflow designer that creates and initializes the activities added to the WF program while in Designer view.

We now turn our attention to the two public fields that have already been defined in the *ProductApproval* class: *workflowId* and *workflowProperties*. These fields need to be initialized by the *OnWorkflowActivated* activity whenever a new workflow instance is created from the WF program. As it turns out, the *Sequential Workflow* project item template used to create this project item has already added what is needed to initialize the *workflowProperties* field.

Initialization of the *workflowProperties* field is accomplished through data binding. The *onWorkflowActivated1* activity contains a data-binding–enabled property named *WorkflowProperties*. While in Designer view, select *onWorkflowActivated1* and inspect the property named *WorkflowProperties* in the Visual Studio property sheet. You should be able to verify that the value of this property is preconfigured with the following property value, which constitutes a data-binding expression that is evaluated at run time.

```
Activity=ProductApproval , Path=workflowProperties
```

Data binding is an important concept in WF development. The entire idea behind data binding within a WF program is to facilitate the declarative flow of data across activities. In this case, the *WorkflowProperties* property of the *onWorkflowActivated1* activity is data-bound to the *workflowProperties* field of the class for the WF program named ProductApproval. When the WF runtime creates the activity instance named *onWorkflowActivated1*, this child activity initializes the new workflow instance. After *onWorkflowActivated1* completes its work, the *workflowProperties* field in *ProductApproval* references a fully initialized object created from the *SPWorkflowActivationProperties* class, which can then be used in any event handler to retrieve information about the current workflow instance.

Now let's add a second activity to *ProductApproval* that writes a message into the workflow history table. Navigate to Designer view. In the Toolbox, locate the activity type *LogToHistory ListActivity*. Drag this activity type to the designer surface to create a new activity instance immediately after *onWorkflowActivated1*. After you create this activity, select it and examine its properties in the Visual Studio property sheet.

The new activity is named *logToHistoryListActivity1*. You can leave the name of this activity as-is or change it to something more descriptive, such as *logActivated*. You should also note that two other properties are visible within the property sheet, which are named *HistoryDescription* and *HistoryOutcome*. Whenever an activity of type *LogToHistoryListActivity* writes an entry into the workflow history table, it writes the values of these two properties so that users can see them.

While it is possible to assign static values for the *HistoryDescription* and *HistoryOutcome* properties directly inside the property sheet, it is more flexible if you create two new string fields inside the *ProductApproval* class and then data-bind them to the *HistoryDescription* and *HistoryOutcome* properties. Start by adding two fields to the *ProductApproval* class named *HistoryDescription* and *HistoryOutcome*.

```
public sealed partial class ProductApproval : SequentialWorkflowActivity {
  // other members removed for clarity
  public String HistoryDescription;
  public String HistoryOutcome;
}
```

Once you add these two public string fields to the *ProductApproval* class, you can bind them to any data-binding–enabled properties of child activities so long as these properties are based on the *string* type. Switch *ProductApproval.cs* back into Designer view and select the activity that you created from the *LogToHistoryListActivity* activity type. You can now data-bind the *HistoryDescription* and *HistoryOutcome* properties from this activity to the two fields that you just added to the *ProductApproval* class.

To configure data binding for a property, click the button with the ellipse to the right of its name, which causes the workflow designer to invoke a special dialog that makes it possible to data-bind property values to public fields or public properties exposed by another activity. Once you have data-bound the *HistoryDescription* and *HistoryOutcome* properties to the two fields in *ProductApproval*, your property sheet should look like the one shown in Figure 11-19.

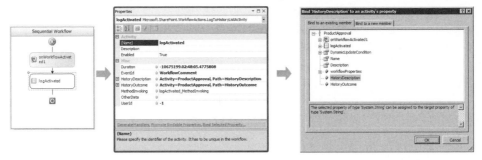

FIGURE 11-19 The properties of activities can be bound to fields within the WF program.

As you have just seen, the dialog shown on the far right of Figure 11-19 makes it possible to data-bind an activity property to an existing field or property such as the *HistoryDescription* field defined within the class for the WF program. You should also note that there is a tab in this dialog called Bind To A New Member, which provides the means to create new public fields or properties quickly inside the workflow program class. When you create a new public field or property by using this dialog, it is data-bound to the current activity property automatically. Once you become comfortable with this dialog, you will likely prefer using this technique as opposed to adding public fields and properties manually to the workflow class.

Once you successfully add the *LogToHistoryListActivity* activity and data-bind its properties, it's time to add another event handler. Right-click the *LogToHistoryListActivity* activity and click *Generate Handlers*. This creates an event handler that fires just before the *LogToHistoryListActivity* activity writes its entry into the workflow history table. Therefore, you can write code in this event handler to assign a value to each of the two fields before data binding takes place. Write the event handler using the following code.

```
private void logActivated_MethodInvoking(object sender, EventArgs e) {
  // Generate message using information of current item
  SPListItem item = workflowProperties.Item;

  // determine whether workflow is running on a standard item or a document
  if (item.File == null) {
    HistoryDescription = "Workflow started on item " + item.Title;
  }
  else {
    HistoryDescription = "Workflow started on document " + item.File.Name;
  }
  HistoryOutcome = "Workflow activation complete";
}
```

The previous example demonstrates a few important things about writing code within the event handler for a WF program targeting SharePoint Foundation. First, you see that it is very simple to program against the item or the document on which the workflow is running because the *workflowProperties* field exposes an *Item* property that, in turn, exposes a *File* property. The code in this example checks to see whether the *File* property is *null* to determine whether the workflow instance started on a standard list item or on a document. Note that if the workflow instance had been created on a site as opposed to a list, the *Item* field would be *null* as well.

Note that the WF programs run under the security context of the SHAREPOINT\SYSTEM account. If you want to log history list activity under the name of the current user, you must assign a value to the *UserId* property of the *LogToHistoryListActivity* with a value other than –1. For example, you can log the history list entries by using the account name of the user that initiated the current workflow instance by binding the *UserId* property of the *LogToHistoryListActivity* to *workflowProperties.OriginatorUser.ID*.

The second important observation about this example is that the event handler assigns values to fields that are data-bound to properties within the *LogToHistoryListActivity* activity. The timing is important here because the *LogToHistoryListActivity* activity does its work of evaluating its data-bound expressions and writing its entry into the workflow history after the event handler fires. This is the opposite of the timing with the *onWorkflowActivated* activity, which fires its event handler after completing its work of initializing the new workflow instance and assigning values back to the *workflowProperties* field in the *ProductApproval* class as a result of a data-bound property setting.

In the previous simple example, you saw the declarative data flow controlled through data-binding that worked in both directions. The first example shows how data-binding the *WorkflowProperties* property of the *onWorkflowActivated* activity enables the flow of data from a child activity to the top-level activity named *ProductApproval*. The second example shows you how to assign values to fields within *ProductApproval* that flow to a child activity.

At this point, the workflow template named *ProductApproval* has enough functionality that we can test our work. If you have configured the project item for the workflow template to create a workflow association on a document library in a test site automatically, you should be able to run the project's *Deploy* command and begin testing. You should be able to test your workflow template by initiating a workflow instance on a document within that document library where the workflow association has been created.

Deploying a Workflow Template to a Production Environment

It is convenient that Visual Studio 2010 is able to create the workflow association allowing you to test your work automatically. However, we must emphasize that this convenience does not carry over to the production environment. Therefore, you should consider whether you need to extend your SharePoint project to automate creating the required workflow association.

Let's start by reviewing the *Workflow* element that was created by the SharePoint Developer Tools and is used to activate the ProductApproval workflow template within the scope of a site collection.

```
<Workflow
    Name="Product Approval Workflow Template"
    Description="Use to approve and reject Wingtip product proposals "
    Id="b06c5f7d-7b06-46b0-a07d-ccb2504153f5"
    CodeBesideClass="WingtipApprovalWorkflows.ProductApproval.ProductApproval"
    CodeBesideAssembly="$assemblyname$">
  <Categories/>
  <MetaData>
    <AssociationCategories>List</AssociationCategories>
    <StatusPageUrl>_layouts/WrkStat.aspx</StatusPageUrl>
  </MetaData>
</Workflow>
```

This *Workflow* element has attributes for the workflow template's name, description, and ID. The SharePoint Developer Tools automatically add the attributes required to reference the class name and assembly name of the WF program associated with this workflow template properly. Within the *MetaData* element, the SharePoint Developer Tools has also added an *AssociationCategories* element to indicate that the workflow template can be used to create workflow associations on list and document libraries as opposed to sites.

In addition to activating workflow template, the *MainSite* feature of the SharePoint project named WingtipProposalWorkflow has been configured to create a document library called Product Proposals and to create a workflow association on this document library. The Product Proposals document library is created using a standard *ListInstance* element.

```
<ListInstance
  Title="Product Proposals"
  OnQuickLaunch="TRUE"
  TemplateType="101"
  FeatureId="00bfea71-e717-4e80-aa17-d0c71b360101"
  Url="ProductProposals" />
```

After creating this document library, the WingtipProposalWorkflow project creates a workflow association allowing users to initiate workflow instances to begin the approval process. However, before creating a new workflow association, you must ensure that the target site collection already has a task list and a workflow history list. The WingtipProposalWorkflow project creates these two required workflow lists using two more *ListInstance* elements.

```
<ListInstance
  Title="Wingtip Workflow Tasks"
  OnQuickLaunch="FALSE"
  TemplateType="107"
  FeatureId="00bfea71-a83e-497e-9ba0-7a5c597d0107"
  Url="Lists/WingtipWorkflowTasks" />
```

```
<ListInstance
  Title="Wingtip Workflow History"
  OnQuickLaunch="FALSE"
  TemplateType="140"
  FeatureId="00BFEA71-4EA5-48D4-A4AD-305CF7030140"
  Url="Lists/WingtipWorkflowHistory"
  Hidden="TRUE" >
```

Now that you have seen how the WingtipProposalWorkflow project creates a target document library, a task list, and a workflow history list, it's time to discuss how to create the workflow association. The WingtipProposalWorkflow project automates the creation of the required workflow association by adding the following code to the feature receiver for the *MainSite* feature.

```
public override void FeatureActivated(SPFeatureReceiverProperties properties) {
  SPSite siteCollection = (SPSite)properties.Feature.Parent;
  SPWeb site = siteCollection.RootWeb;

  // obtain references to lists
  SPList targetList = site.Lists["Product Proposals"];
  SPList taskList = site.Lists["Wingtip Workflow Tasks"];
  SPList workflowHistoryList = site.Lists["Wingtip Workflow History"];

  // obtain reference to workflow template
  Guid WorkflowTemplateId = new Guid("b06c5f7d-7b06-46b0-a07d-ccb2504153f5");
  SPWorkflowTemplate WorkflowTemplate = site.WorkflowTemplates[WorkflowTemplateId];

  // create user-friendly name for workflow association
  string WorkflowAssociationName = "Wingtip Product Approval";

  // create workflow association
  SPWorkflowAssociation WorkflowAssociation =
    SPWorkflowAssociation.CreateListAssociation(
                          WorkflowTemplate,
                          WorkflowAssociationName,
                          taskList,
                          workflowHistoryList);

  // configure workflow association
  WorkflowAssociation.Description = "Used to begin the product proposal approval process";
  WorkflowAssociation.AllowManual = true;
  WorkflowAssociation.AutoStartCreate = false;
  WorkflowAssociation.AutoStartChange = false;
  // add new workflow association to WorkflowAssociations collection on target list
  targetList.WorkflowAssociations.Add(WorkflowAssociation);
}
```

Creating and Waiting on Tasks

SharePoint Foundation adds a human dimension on top of the WF for task-driven activities. However, to take advantage of this dimension, you must learn how to develop WF programs that create SharePoint workflow tasks associated with workflow instances. It is equally important for you to learn how to put a workflow instance to sleep in a way that allows it to wake up and resume its execution when a user updates one of the tasks associated with it.

When you need to create a task that is associated with a workflow instance, you should never do it by calling the *Items.Add* method on an *SPList object,* as you would when creating new list items in other SharePoint development scenarios. Instead, you must go through the SharePoint Foundation Workflow Services application programming interface (API) so that each new task is created with a subscription that associates a new task with a workflow instance by wiring up event handlers that react to users who modify or delete the task.

Fortunately, it is not necessary for you to program against the SharePoint Foundation Workflow Services API directly. Instead, you can create WF programs using activities based on activity types such as *CreateTask, OnTaskCreated, UpdateTask, OnTaskChanged*, and *CompleteTask*. These activity types contain the code that encapsulates the necessary calls into the SharePoint Foundation Workflow Services API. When you use these activity types, you can create a WF program that creates a task and then puts the current workflow instance to sleep. Later, when the task is updated by a user, an event handler that has been registered by the SharePoint Foundation Workflow Services API fires and brings the workflow instance back to life to continue its execution.

It is important that you begin to distinguish between method activities and event activities. The activities created from method activity types, such as *CreateTask, UpdateTask, CompleteTask*, and *DeleteTask*, are represented with blue shapes in the workflow designer, whereas activities created from event activity types, such as *OnTaskCreated, OnTaskChanged*, and *OnTaskDeleted*, are represented with green shapes.

A *method activity* performs an action, such as creating or updating a task. An *event activity* runs in response to the occurrence of an action. Event activities are particularly important in creating SharePoint workflow templates because they can provide the blocking behavior required when a workflow instance needs to wait for some external event before continuing with its execution.

Let's continue working with the workflow template named ProductApproval. We are going to extend ProductApproval to create and wait for a task, and we begin by adding two new activities. First, we create a new activity by using the *CreateTask* method activity type. Next, we create a second new activity by using the *OnTaskCreated* event activity type. After these two activities are created, the Designer view window of ProductApproval.cs should look like Figure 11-20.

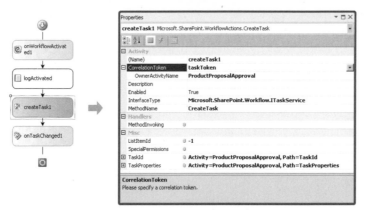

FIGURE 11-20 Task-based activities, such as *CreateTask* and *OnTaskChanged*, require a *CorrelationToken*, as well as an identifying GUID for their *TaskId* property.

When several different method activities and event activities within a WF program work on the same task, it's important for all these activities to be able to identify this task. The SharePoint workflow infrastructure relies on *correlators* to accomplish this. A correlator involves the use of both a GUID and a *correlation token*. The following text explains what is required to properly set up the correlator that allows several different activities to work on the same task at the same time.

We begin by creating a new correlation token for the task. Navigate to the property sheet for the *CreateTask* activity and look at the *CorrelationToken* property. The value for this property is initially empty, yet it needs to be assigned a valid value before the *CreateTask* activity can function correctly. If you look at the drop-down list for this property value, you see an existing *CorrelationToken* value of *workflowToken* that you can select. However, you don't want to select *workflowToken* because it identifies the workflow instance rather than the task that is being created. Instead, you must create a new *CorrelationToken* object.

It's actually fairly simple to create the new *CorrelationToken* object for the new task being created. Simply place your cursor in the property sheet and type a new string value for the *CorrelationToken*, such as *taskToken*, and then hit the Enter key. The code generator of the workflow designer responds by adding the code into ProductApproval.designer.cs to create a new *CorrelationToken* object named *taskToken*. The code generator also does the work to initialize the *taskToken* object and bind it to the *CorrelationToken* property of the *CreateTask* activity.

Note that after you create a *CorrelationToken* object and assign it to the *CorrelationToken* property of the *CreateTask* activity, you must still assign its *OwnerActivityName* property value as shown in Figure 11-20. The *OwnerActivityName* property value can point back to the parent activity, which in this case is the top-level WF program itself, named ProductApproval.

Once you create the *CorrelationToken* named *taskToken* within the property sheet for the *CreateTask* activity, you can use it as the *CorrelationToken* property value for other task-related activities within the same WF program. For example, you can select the other activity named *OnTaskCreated* and, from its property sheet, assign *taskToken* to its *CorrelationToken* property by selecting it from the drop-down menu.

After creating the correlation token for the task, the next thing you must do is add two new fields to the *ProductApproval* class that will be data-bound to properties of the *CreateTask* activity. The first field is used to track a new GUID that passes to the *CreateTask* activity so that it can initialize its correlation token properly. The second field should be defined by using the *SPWorkflowTaskProperties* class. You use this field to pass a reference to the *CreateTask* activity that points to an *SPWorkflowTaskProperties* object that holds the initial values for the task to be created.

```
public Guid TaskId = default(System.Guid);
public SPWorkflowTaskProperties TaskProperties = new SPWorkflowTaskProperties();
```

Next, you must create an event handler for the *CreateTask* activity. Note that *CreateTask* is a method activity, which means that its event handler fires before it calls the SharePoint Foundation Workflow Services API to perform its work. This gives you a chance to initialize fields within the WF program that can then be passed to the *CreateTask* activity through data-binding.

Switch back to Designer view, right-click the *CreateTask* activity, and click Generate Handlers. This generates an event handler with a name such as *createTask1_MethodInvoking*. Add the following code to this event handler to initialize the *TaskId* field with a new GUID and initialize the *SPWorkflowTaskProperties* object referenced by the *TaskProperties* field.

```
private void createTask1_MethodInvoking(object sender, EventArgs e) {
  // generate new GUID used to initialize task correlation token
  TaskId = Guid.NewGuid();
  // assign initial properties prior to task creation
  TaskProperties.Title = "Review " + workflowProperties.Item.File.Name;
  TaskProperties.Description = "Please review then approve or reject this proposal.";
  TaskProperties.AssignedTo = @"WINGTIP\Administrator";
  TaskProperties.PercentComplete = 0;
  TaskProperties.StartDate = DateTime.Today;
  TaskProperties.DueDate = DateTime.Today.AddDays(3);
}
```

As you can see, this code is simply initializing the data that the *CreateTask* activity uses to perform its work when it calls the SharePoint Foundation Workflow Services API. The final step is to data-bind the *TaskId* and *TaskProperties* fields to properties in the *CreateTask* activity. Navigate back to Designer view and select the *CreateTask* activity. Proceed to the property sheet and configure data binding so that the *TaskId* property of the *CreateTask* activity is initialized with the *TaskId* field in ProductApproval. Configure data binding so that the *TaskProperties* property of the *CreateTask* activity is initialized with the *TaskProperties* field.

You should now be through working with the *CreateTask* activity. Select the *OnTaskChanged* event activity and look at its property sheet. If you haven't already done so, assign the *CorrelationToken* object named *TaskToken* to its *CorrelationToken* property. Next, data-bind the *TaskId* property of the *OnTaskCreated* activity to the *TaskId* field.

One subtle yet important point must be understood concerning how method activities and event activities work. SharePoint Foundation batches all modifications made by a sequence of method activities into a single transaction and writes them all to the content database at once. This means that the work for a method activity is not committed when the activity finishes its work. If you don't understand when the transaction for one or more method activities is committed, you might get into trouble.

For example, what would happen if you added a *Code* activity between the *CreateTask* and *OnTaskChanged* activities? This *Code* activity would not be able to see the just-created task in a committed state because SharePoint Foundation has not yet written the task to the content database. SharePoint Foundation does not write the task to the content database until the workflow instance is put to sleep by encountering an event activity, such as *OnTaskChanged*.

Now that you have created a task, it's time to employ the *OnTaskChanged* activity to put the workflow instance to sleep. Whenever the WF program executes an *OnTaskChanged* activity, it puts the current workflow instance to sleep and registers an event handler to wake it up and resume execution whenever it is changed. In a real-world scenario, you would likely examine the *TaskStatus* field of the current task inside a loop created with a *While* activity to determine whether it has been updated to a value of *Completed*. If the *TaskStatus* field has been updated to a value of *Completed*, the workflow instance can complete its life cycle. If the *TaskStatus* field is not updated with a value of *Completed*, the workflow instance should remain in the loop of the *While* activity and put the workflow instance back to sleep by re-executing the *OnTaskChanged* activity.

Note that a *While* activity can contain only a single child activity. In situations in which you want a sequence of several child activities inside a *While* activity, you must use a slightly different approach. You can add an activity by using the *Sequence* activity type as a child activity to the *While* activity. You can then add multiple child activities to the *Sequence* activity so that you can have several child activities execute inside the scope of a *While* activity.

To see a working example, you can examine the final version of the workflow template named ProductApproval. This workflow template has a WF program that demonstrates creating a task with the *CreateTask* activity and then using an *OnTaskChanged* activity inside a *While* activity to inspect the task after it is saved. You typically will be required to manage the execution of WF programs that create tasks in this manner by using control-of-flow activities such as the *While* activity.

Understanding Workflow Input Forms

When you design a workflow template, you can create four different types of input forms, including an association form, an initiation form, a modification form, and a task edit form. Note that these forms are optional when you create a workflow template. You can add one or more of these form types to a workflow template and omit the others. You can also supply all four types of workflow input forms if you have a scenario that calls for it.

A custom *workflow association form* allows the developer to prompt the user for parameterization data when a new workflow association is created. A workflow association form is presented to the user as a final step when creating a workflow association. Note that the workflow association form can also be used by those who want to make modifications to parameterization data within an existing workflow association.

A custom *workflow initiation form* allows the developer to prompt the user for parameterization data when a new workflow instance is created from a workflow association. Note that workflow initiation forms can be used only when the workflow association allows users to start the workflow instance manually. When a workflow association is configured to start workflows automatically, it is not possible to prompt the user with a workflow initiation form.

Once a workflow instance has been started, there might be a need for the user to change some of its properties on the fly, such as who should approve the item or document in question. The *workflow modification form* is intended for this purpose. A developer can add a link to the Workflow Status page, making it possible for the user to navigate to the modification form for a particular workflow instance. Using the modification form, the developer can allow the user to perform whatever types of modifications make sense.

As you know, each workflow association is configured with a task list that makes it possible for workflow instances to create tasks and assign them to the users. SharePoint Foundation supplies a special Content Type named *WorkflowTask* with an ID of 0x010801. When you design a WF program to create tasks, you can choose the standard *WorkflowTask* Content Type or create your own custom Content Type. If you do the latter, you must create it so that it inherits from the standard *WorkflowTask* Content Type.

One advantage to creating a custom Content Type for workflow tasks is that you can add extra fields beyond those defined in the standard *WorkflowTask* Content Type. A second advantage is that you can create a custom *Task Edit Form*. This allows you to take over the user experience when a user needs to edit a task. For example, you can supply a task edit form containing only the necessary controls, such as the Approve button and the Reject button.

You can use one of two different approaches to develop workflow input forms for a workflow template. Your first option is to create workflow input forms by using custom application pages. Your other option is to create workflow input forms using Microsoft InfoPath 2010. How do you choose between them, then?

There are several benefits to using InfoPath forms when developing workflow templates. First, the integration of InfoPath forms into a SharePoint workflow template reduces the amount of code that you need to supply. Second, InfoPath forms provide a level of integration with Microsoft Office applications, such as Microsoft Word, Microsoft Excel, Microsoft PowerPoint, and Microsoft Outlook. While InfoPath forms can be displayed to the user through the browser, they can also be hosted directly from within the Office application, providing a more seamless user experience.

One important drawback to consider is that creating workflow input forms using InfoPath Forms picks up a dependency on SharePoint Server 2010. Therefore, workflow templates that use InfoPath Forms cannot be used within farms running only SharePoint Foundation. Another point is that creating workflow input forms using custom application pages is directly supported by the SharePoint Developer Tools, while creating workflow input forms using InfoPath forms is not. If you want to research further how to add workflow input forms using InfoPath, you should refer to the documentation entitled "InfoPath Forms for Workflows," which can be found online at *http://msdn.microsoft.com/en-us/library/ms573938.aspx*.

We will conclude this chapter by discussing how to creating workflow input forms using custom application pages. As you will see, the SharePoint Developer Tools provides convenient project item templates that you can use to create new association forms and initiation forms. However, the SharePoint Developer Tools do not provide a project item template for creating custom task edit forms. Therefore, we will have to do more work to add a standard application page and configure it to behave as a task edit form.

Creating Workflow Input Forms

The SharePoint Developer Tools provide dedicated SharePoint project item templates for creating a *Workflow Association Form* and a *Workflow Initiation Form,* as shown in Figure 11-21. If you want to add one of these types of workflow input forms, you should right-click the project item for the target workflow template and select the Add Item menu.

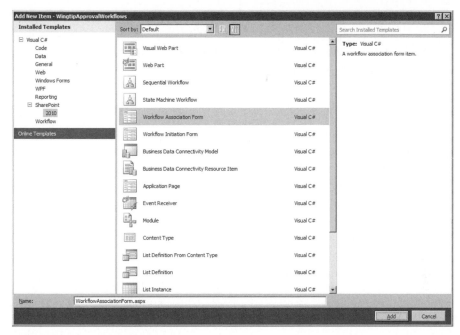

FIGURE 11-21 The SharePoint Developer Tools provides project item templates for creating workflow association forms and workflow initiation forms.

When you add a new association form or a new initiation form, the SharePoint Developer Tools puts a new custom application page into the root folder of the project item for the target workflow template. The custom application pages that are created for association forms and initiation forms already have a good deal of code behind them to assist you in managing these forms. When you add one of these workflow input forms to a workflow template, the SharePoint Developer Tools also provide the convenience of updating the *Workflow* element with the following elements.

```
<Workflow
  <!-- other attributes omitted for clarity -->
  AssociationUrl=
    "_layouts/WingtipApprovalWorkflows/ProductApproval/WorkflowAssociationForm.aspx"
  InstantiationUrl=
    "_layouts/WingtipApprovalWorkflows/ProductApproval/WorkflowInitiation.aspx" >

  <!-- Categories and MetaData elements omitted for clarity -->

</Workflow>
```

The *AssociationUrl* and *InstantiationUrl* attributes have been configured to reference the application pages for these workflow input forms. Let's now discuss some of the important details about working with a workflow association form.

An important observation is that when you configure a workflow template with a custom association form, you then take on the responsibility of supplying the code to create the new workflow association. Your application page must also supply the code to create a new task list, a new history list, or both, depending on what the user requests. Fortunately, most of the required code is supplied for you behind the application page that the SharePoint Developer Tools create when you add a new workflow association form. However, it is a good idea to examine the code that has been supplied so that you know what is happening.

Take a moment and consider the primary purpose of a custom association form. It is used to prompt users for extra parameterization data whenever they create a new workflow association. In the case of the ProductApproval workflow template, the association form is used to obtain default values for the approver, the approval scope (internal versus external), and instructions to the approver. When a user enters data into this association form and clicks OK, your code must serialize the user input values into a string that is saved as *association data*. The association data are then used by the initiation form each time a user starts a new workflow instance from the workflow association.

Open the application page named WorkflowAssociationForm.aspx and inspect the contents. You should notice that this source file does not contain any code. Instead, it simply contains input controls, two command buttons, and layout details. The actual code for the association form has been added to the code-behind class in WorkflowAssociationForm.aspx.cs.

The other important aspect of implementing an association form is how to manage user input values. The values that a user enters into the form's input controls must be serialized as a string and then saved to the *AssociationData* property of the *SPWorkflowAssociation* object. When a user chooses to modify an existing workflow association, the current value of the *AssociationData* property must be deserialized and then used to populate the form's input controls during initialization.

When the SharePoint Developer Tools generate the code-behind class for a workflow association form, they add two methods with empty implementations named *PopulateFormFields* and *GetAssociationData*. Here is what these methods look like after they have been created.

```
private void PopulateFormFields(SPWorkflowAssociation existingAssociation) {
  // Optionally, add code here to pre-populate your form fields.
}

// This method is called when the user clicks the button to associate the workflow.
private string GetAssociationData() {
  // TODO: Return a string that contains the association data that will
  // be passed to the workflow. Typically, this is in XML format.
  return string.Empty;
}
```

When you create a workflow association form, it is your job to implement *PopulateFormFields* and *GetAssociationData* to move input data back and forth between the form's input controls and a serialized string that is saved back to the *AssociationData* property prior to creating or updating the workflow association.

Note that the examples used in the ProductApproval workflow template that involve serializing workflow data use a schema-generated class named *ProductApprovalWorkflowData*. This class can be used with the *XmlSerializer* class to create strongly typed .NET Framework objects that can be converted back and forth with XML documents that adhere to the following format:

```
<ProductApprovalWorkflowData>
  <Approver>WINGTIP\WendyW</Approver>
  <ApprovalScope>Internal</ApprovalScope>
  <Instructions>Please review this proposal as soon as possible</Instructions>
</ProductApprovalWorkflowData>
```

The following implementation of the *GetAssociationData* method demonstrates reading user input values from the association form and serializing them to an XML document that is returned as a string value.

```
private string GetAssociationData() {
  // create ProductApprovalWorkflowData object
  ProductApprovalWorkflowData wfData = new ProductApprovalWorkflowData();
  // read Approver value from PeopleEditor control
  PickerEntity ApproverEntity = (PickerEntity)pickerApprover.Entities[0];
  wfData.Approver = ApproverEntity.Key;
  // read approval scope from radio buttons
  if (radInternalApproval.Checked) {
    wfData.ApprovalScope = "Internal";
  }
  else {
    wfData.ApprovalScope = "External";
  }
  // read instructions from textbox
  wfData.Instructions = txtInstructions.Text;
  // serialize ProductApprovalWorkflowData object and return XML as string
  using (MemoryStream stream = new MemoryStream()) {
    XmlSerializer serializer = new XmlSerializer(typeof(ProductApprovalWorkflowData));
    serializer.Serialize(stream, wfData);
    stream.Position = 0;
    byte[] bytes = new byte[stream.Length];
    stream.Read(bytes, 0, bytes.Length);
    string WorkflowData = Encoding.UTF8.GetString(bytes);
    return WorkflowData;
  }
}
```

Now let's discuss the workflow initiation form. Remember that workflow initiation forms can be used only with workflow associations that allow the user to start workflow instances manually through the Workflow.aspx page. You cannot present the user with an initiation form in scenarios in which you have configured a workflow association to start new workflow instances automatically whenever a new item is added to a list or a new document is uploaded to a document library. These types of scenarios do not provide an opportunity to present the user with a custom initiation form.

If you examine the content of the application page named WorkflowInitiationForm.aspx, you can observe that the input control tags and page layout are almost identical to WorkflowAssociationForm.aspx. This makes sense because the association form is used to obtain default values for all workflow instances, and the initiation form then gives users the opportunity to see these default values and, if they wish, change them when starting a particular workflow instance.

The code-behind class for the workflow initiation form contains a great deal of code that has been generated by the SharePoint Developer Tools. As in the case of implementing the workflow association form, you simply need to supply additional code to serialize and deserialize form data to and from an XML file format.

Now it's time to consider how the two workflow input forms you have seen so far interact with the WF program. You should realize that all the code behind the association and initiation forms execute before the WF program starts running. The WF program is not called into action until the user clicks the Start Workflow button on the initiation form. At that point, the WF program executes, beginning with the *OnWorkflowActivated* activity. You can add an event handler to the *OnWorkflowActivated* activity and implement it to retrieve the initiation data, deserialize it, and store it in fields defined within the WF program.

```
public class ProductApproval : SequentialWorkflowActivity {

  // fields to store initiation data from initiation form
  public string Approver = default(string);
  public string ApprovalScope = default(string);
  public string ApproverInstructions = default(string);

  private void onWorkflowActivated1_Invoked(...) {
    // deserialize initiation data;
    string InitiationData = workflowProperties.InitiationData;
    XmlSerializer serializer =
                new XmlSerializer(typeof(ProductApprovalWorkflowData));
    XmlTextReader reader =
                new XmlTextReader(new StringReader(InitiationData));
    ProductApprovalWorkflowData FormData =
          (ProductApprovalWorkflowData)serializer.Deserialize(reader);
```

```
    // assign form data values to workflow fields
    Approver = FormData.Approver;
    ApprovalScope = FormData.ApprovalScope;
    ApproverInstructions = FormData.Instructions;
  }
}
```

Up to now, you have seen how workflow data is moved between the workflow association form, the workflow initiation form, and the WF program itself. You should also observe that the workflow data has been assigned to public fields in the WF program. This ensures that the workflow data is always available throughout the lifetime of a workflow instance even after it has been saved and retrieved from the content database.

We would like to conclude this chapter with a quick discussion of adding a custom task edit form. Unfortunately, the SharePoint Developer Tools provide no dedicated project item template to create a custom task edit form. This means that adding a custom task edit farm requires more work and a greater understanding of how things work behind the scenes.

Even though it requires more work, you should still create a custom task edit form whenever you are creating a workflow template that creates tasks. If you don't, you force your users to interact with the standard task edit form of SharePoint Foundation, which does not provide a satisfactory user experience. A custom task edit form, on the other hand, can include extra command buttons, such as Approve and Reject, and direct the user's attention to the data and input values that are important to complete the business task at hand. This can make things more intuitive for users who are working with workflows to automate a business process, such as document approval.

You have seen that you add a workflow association form or a workflow initiation form by adding an attribute to the *Workflow* element that references an application page. However, there is no attribute that can be used to reference an application page for a task edit form. That's because you do not integrate a task edit form in the same fashion as the other types of workflow input forms. Instead, you must create a custom Content Type that inherits from the standard Workflow Task Content Type.

When you create a custom Content Type for a custom workflow task, you can define it to use its own custom edit form, which is the approach that we have used in our sample project. The *Workflow* element contains a *TaskListContentTypeId* attribute configured with the ID Content Type, which identifies a custom Content Type named *ProductApprovalTask* that inherits from the *WorkflowTask* Content Type.

```
<Workflow
  <!-- other attributes omitted for clarity -->
  TaskListContentTypeId="0x010801004dfe25afd26d47e0af00eb9e8b041888" >

</Workflow>
```

Implementing a custom task edit form begins with creating a custom Content Type that inherits from the Workflow Task Content Type that is part of SharePoint Foundation. As you recall, we covered the creation of a CAML definition for a custom Content Type that replaces the edit form in Chapter 8, "Templates and Type Definitions." The custom Content Type named *ProductApprovalTask* has been created for the ProductApproval workflow template.

The SharePoint Developer Tools do not allow you to create a Content Type that inherits from *WorkflowTask* when you use the SharePoint Customization Wizard. Therefore, you need to edit the elements.xml file for the Content Type manually after you create it. The Content Type ID for the standard workflow task Content Type is 0x010801. Therefore, any Content Type that derives from this must use a value of *0x010801* as the first part of its Content Type ID. You can also see that this custom Content Type definition adds two extra fields named *Instructions* and *Comments*. These fields are used to store extra data in the tasks created to assist in the product approval process.

```xml
<ContentType
  ID="0x0108004dfe25afd26d47e0af00eb9e8b041888"
  Name="Product Approval Task"
  Group="WingtipContent Types"
  Description="Used to approve or reject Wingtip product proposal"
  Inherits="TRUE" >
  <FieldRefs>
    <FieldRef ID="{e241f186-9b94-415c-9f66-255ce7f86235}" Name="Notes"
              DisplayName="Instructions"/>
    <FieldRef ID="{9da97a8a-1da5-4a77-98d3-4bc10456e700}" Name="Comments"
              DisplayName="Comments"/>
  </FieldRefs>
  <XmlDocuments>
    <XmlDocument
      NamespaceURI="http://schemas.microsoft.com/sharepoint/v3/contenttype/forms/url">
      <FormUrls xmlns="http://schemas.microsoft.com/sharepoint/v3/contenttype/forms/url">
        <Edit>_layouts/WingtipApprovalWorkflows/ProductApproval/TaskEditForm.aspx</Edit>
      </FormUrls>
    </XmlDocument>
  </XmlDocuments>
</ContentType>
```

In addition to creating the Content Type, which is required to load the custom task edit form, you must create an application page and add code behind it to produce the behavior that you need. If you examine the code-behind class for the task edit form in TaskEditForm.aspx.cs, you will be able to see how all the pieces fit together.

Conclusion

This chapter focused on the new world of workflow in SharePoint 2010. The single biggest change from SharePoint 2007 is the new capabilities of SharePoint Designer for building reusable workflows. This change is significant enough to make SharePoint Designer 2010 the recommended tool for building most workflows. The chapter reviewed the major constructs and capabilities of SharePoint Designer 2010 for building workflows and explained how to use them to automate a business process.

The chapter also covered potential scenarios where using SharePoint Designer 2010 alone will not be suitable. You learned that you have the option of using Visual Studio 2010 to develop custom actions to extend the custom workflows created with SharePoint Designer 2010 further. You also learned how to get started developing custom workflow templates. As you read through the second half of the chapter, it should have become clear that developing workflow templates is challenging and requires far greater knowledge of WF and SharePoint workflow internals. Therefore, you should use this option only if you cannot use SharePoint Designer 2010 to achieve your desired outcome.

Chapter 12
SharePoint Security

Security is an important consideration when designing and implementing a business solution with Microsoft SharePoint. You don't want users who haven't been granted the proper permissions to be able to view or edit sensitive pages, items, or documents. At the same time, you need to ensure that users with the proper permissions can access what they need. Although SharePoint goes a long way toward providing out-of-the-box security features that allow site owners to configure access rights within a site collection, a SharePoint developer should know how SharePoint security works behind the scenes, as well as how to extend the SharePoint security model with custom code.

Authentication, Authorization, and Identities

Authentication is the process of determining the identity of a user. The most common mechanism for authenticating users is to use Microsoft Windows accounts stored in Active Directory Domain Services (AD DS). This authentication first happens when a user logs on to the computer and results in an identity for the user on the network known as a *security principal*. This security principal is subsequently associated with any threads that the user initiates through applications on the desktop. If a user is authenticated against a Windows account, you can use the *System.Security* namespace in an application to retrieve the identity and the user's logon name.

```
WindowsIdentity identity = WindowsIdentity.GetCurrent;
string WindowsLogin = identity.Name;
```

ASP.NET websites can use AD DS for authentication as well as other repositories through Forms-Based Authentication (FBA). Authentication in these applications is performed by Internet Information Services (IIS) when the user accesses a page. The *System.Web.HttpContext.User* object provides an *IPrincipal* interface that abstracts away the dependency on the repository used for authentication. The following code shows how to retrieve the identity of the current user and her logon name.

```
IPrincipal aspUser = HttpContext.Current.User;
string aspUserName = aspUser.Identity.Name;
```

Claims authentication, another authentication mechanism, can be used with AD DS or with other repositories in a manner similar to FBA. The difference between FBA and claims authentication is that claims authentication is performed using a Security Token Service (STS) instead of IIS. The value of using an STS is that it separates authentication from the application, thus supporting federation between organizations that are not in the same domain.

Claims authentication is covered in more detail later in the chapter, but we introduce it here to enable a broader discussion of authentication and authorization.

IPrincipal interfaces obtained from ASP.NET Web applications that utilize claims authentication may be cast to a *Microsoft.IdentityModel.Claims.IClaimsIdentity* interface. Using the *IClaimsIdentity* interface, you may retrieve the name of the current user as shown in the following code.

```
IClaimsIdentity claimsUser = (IClaimsIdentity)Page.User.Identity;
string claimsUserName =  claimsUser.Name;
```

SharePoint does not perform any authentication on its own. Instead, SharePoint relies on IIS and STS to perform authentication. When SharePoint is configured to use *Classic Mode*, IIS and the operating system of the Web server authenticates the user against a Windows user account. When SharePoint is configured to use *Claims Mode*, an STS authenticates the user against either AD DS or some other repository such as Microsoft SQL Server. Because SharePoint is an ASP.NET application, you will always be able to obtain an *IPrincipal* interface for the current user. If SharePoint is operating in Claims Mode, then you may also cast this interface to the *IClaimsIdentity* interface.

Once a user is authenticated and her identity is known, the user needs to be authorized to access resources. *Authorization* is the process of determining what resources are available to an authenticated user. Authorization is typically performed by the application itself, which maintains some form of access control list (ACL) for each securable resource in the application. The ACL associates some aspect of the authenticated user (such as account name) with permissions defined for a securable resource. Windows applications use the *WindowsPrincipal* object to create an identity and perform authorization.

```
WindowsIdentity identity = WindowsIdentity.GetCurrent;
WindowsPrincipal principal = new WindowsPrincipal(identity);
if( principal.IsInRole(@"WINGTIP\EMPLOYEES") ){
  // Authorized!
}
```

The ASP.NET *User* object also provides a way to check to see if a user belongs to a particular role using the *IsInRole* method. For Windows users, the *IsInRole* method lets you see whether the current user is a member of an AD DS group. If you are using FBA accounts along with an ASP.NET role provider, you can also use the *IsInRole* method to check whether the FBA user has been added to a specific ASP.NET role, as shown in the following code.

```
IPrincipal aspUser = HttpContext.Current.User;
if(aspUser.IsInRole("Site Administrators") {
  // Authorized!
}
```

When an STS authenticates a user, it can also issue additional claims that become part of the user's identity. Issued claims may be accessed through the *ClaimCollection* class. Each claim in the collection is represented by a *Claim* object, which has properties such as *ClaimType* and *Value*. *ClaimType* can be thought of as the collection key that retrieves a claim value. Knowing this, authorization can be performed by checking for the existence of a claim, as shown in the following code.

```
IClaimsIdentity claimsId = (IClaimsIdentity)Page.User.Identity;
if(claimsId.Claims.Exists(C=>C.ClaimType.Equals("http://wingtip/groups")
                        && C.Value.Equals("Employees"))){
  //Authorized!
}
```

Although SharePoint does not perform authentication, it does manage user identities and perform authorization. The authorization objects in SharePoint abstract away the authentication mechanism so that the same approach works regardless of how authentication was performed. This simplifies security coding within your SharePoint solutions.

After authentication, SharePoint maintains a *user security token,* which identifies the authentication mechanism and a list of groups, membership roles for the user, or both. SharePoint is able to read the groups and membership roles of the current user very efficiently at run time by examining this token. The structure of this token varies depending on whether the user is authenticated in Classic Mode or Claims Mode.

When code runs within a custom SharePoint component, such as a Web Part or application page, it's important that you distinguish between the SharePoint security context and the Windows security context. The SharePoint components that you write often must access external resources. Access to these external resources is controlled not by SharePoint, but rather by the application that owns the external resource, such as the Windows operating system itself. This means that you must be aware of the current Windows security context, as well as the SharePoint security context. The standard web.config file for SharePoint Web applications has the following entry.

```
<identity impersonate="true" />
```

By setting the *impersonate* attribute to *true,* SharePoint instructs the ASP.NET run time to process all requests under the Windows security context of the current user. When you write code for a Web Part or application page that attempts to access an external resource, such as a file system resource, database call, or Web service call, it runs under the impersonated Windows identity of the user initiating the request. This enables the Windows authorization subsystem to determine whether it should grant or deny access.

Understanding the Windows security context is fairly straightforward when you are using Classic Mode because the identity of the user is synchronized to the same user account as the identity of the SharePoint security context. However, things aren't so obvious when you are using Claims Mode. Because claims authentication can use other repositories besides AD DS, the Windows security context may take on the identity of the IUSR_*MACHINENAME* account, or, more generically, whichever account is specified in the Authentication Methods dialog of IIS. This can be problematic when accessing external resources because the IUSR_ MACHINENAME account typically will not have rights to external resources. In such cases, you may have to use the Secure Store Service (SSS), which is covered in Chapter 13, "Business Connectivity Services."

User Information List

SharePoint stores and maintains a *user information profile* for authenticated users at the site collection level. The user information profile can be seen and updated by selecting the My Settings menu item command from the Welcome menu in the upper-right section of the home page for a site. There is only one user information profile per user that extends across all the sites for a site collection. User profile information is maintained in a hidden list known as the *User Information List*. You can view this list by browsing to the Uniform Resource Locator (URL) *http://[sitecollection]/_catalogs/users/simple.aspx*. Here, you will find basic information, such as logon names and display names for the users.

Because the User Information List is just a standard SharePoint list, it may be accessed using the *SPList* object. Of course, you must have the appropriate permissions to access the list because it is a securable object that can be seen only by site collection administrators. The following code shows how to access the list and retrieve user information.

```
using (SPSite siteCollection = new SPSite("http://intranet.wingtip.com"))
{
  using (SPWeb topLevelSite = siteCollection.RootWeb)
  {
  foreach (SPListItem user in topLevelSite.Lists["User Information List"].Items) {
    _ID = user["ID"].ToString();
    _ContentType = user["ContentType"].ToString();
    _User = user["Title"] != null ? user["Title"].ToString() : "null";
    _Account = user["Name"] != null ? user["Name"].ToString() : "null";
    _ImnName = user["ImnName"] != null ? user["ImnName"].ToString() : "null";
    _EMail = user["EMail"] != null ? user["EMail"].ToString() : "null";
    _SipAddress = user["SipAddress"] != null ? user["SipAddress"].ToString() : "null";
    _IsSiteAdmin = user["IsSiteAdmin"] != null ? user["IsSiteAdmin"].ToString() : "null";
  }
}
}
```

The User Information List maintains only a subset of information about users. If you are using SharePoint Server and have the User Profile Service application configured to import profiles, then this information will be used to fill in the User Information List. Two timer jobs, *User Profile to SharePoint Full Synchronization* and *User Profile to SharePoint Quick Synchronization,* run to copy information from the user profiles to the User Information List. User profiles are updated either through synchronization with an external repository like AD DS or when the user manually enters information into the profile through the My Site interface.

You may access the information in the user profiles programmatically through the *Microsoft .Office.Server.UserProfiles.UserProfileManager* object. This object allows you to manage profiles and the data within them. The following code shows how to retrieve a profile.

```
using (SPSite site = new SPSite("http://intranet.wingtip.com"))
{
  SPServiceContext ctx = SPServiceContext.GetContext(site);
  UserProfileManager upm = new UserProfileManager(ctx);
  UserProfile profile = upm.GetUserProfile("WINGTIP\\Administrator");
  Console.WriteLine(profile[PropertyConstants.WorkEmail].Value);
  Console.WriteLine(profile[PropertyConstants.FirstName].Value);
  Console.WriteLine(profile[PropertyConstants.PreferredName].Value);
  Console.WriteLine(profile[PropertyConstants.LastName].Value);
}
```

Users and Groups

There are two types of security principals within SharePoint: *users* and *groups*. The SharePoint object model defines the *SPPrincipal* class, which provides the base functionality for assigning permissions to a principal. The SharePoint object model subsequently defines two classes that derive from *SPPrincipal: SPUser* and *SPGroup*. These two classes extend this base class with their own unique methods and properties for working with users or groups.

The request of an authenticated user runs under the context of an *SPUser* object and carries a security token. When you create an object reference to an *SPSite,* SharePoint creates an instance of the *SPUserToken* and the *SPUser.* This always happens in the context of the site collection, and it is the user who creates the instance reference that SharePoint uses for authorization. As code attempts to access resources, SharePoint checks this user's security token against ACLs to determine whether it should grant or deny access.

SharePoint objects may either use their own ACL or inherit the ACL of a parent object. By default, most items within the SharePoint object model inherit the parent's ACL. For example, a newly created document library inherits the ACL of its parent site; and a newly created document automatically inherits the ACL of its parent document library. However, it's also possible to configure any document with its unique ACL to give it an access control policy that differs from other documents within the same document library. This can be done through either the user interface or custom code. To return the parent object containing the ACL used by any securable object in SharePoint, call its *FirstUniqueAncestorSecurableObject* property.

It is important to note that SharePoint manages users and groups and enforces authorization at the scope of the site collection. Rights assigned to a user in one site collection never affect what the user can do in another site collection. It is by design that SharePoint treats each site collection as its own independent item with respect to authorization and access control.

The SharePoint object model tracks user identities by using the *SPUser* class. If you want to access the *SPUser* object for the current user, you use the *CurrentUser* property of the *SPWeb* object associated with the current site. The following simple example shows you how to access some of the properties available through the *SPUser* class.

```
SPUser currentUser = SPContext.Current.Web.CurrentUser;
string userName = currentUser.Name;
string userLogin = currentUser.LoginName;
string userEmail = currentUser.Email;
```

The current user is always the user who was authenticated when the *SPSite* site collection object was created. If your code is running in the SharePoint website context, this is the authenticated user. If your code is running in the context of a console application, the current user is the user whose Windows principal was used to create the initial *SPSite* reference. You cannot switch the security context of the site collection or its objects after it is created; it is always the user principal who first accessed the site collection that is the current user. We will look at the elevation of privilege, delegation, and impersonation later in this chapter to further illustrate this point.

Assigning permissions directly to users is usually not a scalable and maintainable solution, especially across large enterprises with many users and sites. Along with complicating user maintenance, as ACLs grow larger, they can decrease the performance of SharePoint significantly. This is not an issue unique to SharePoint; it is the same issue solved by AD DS users and groups for any other application. SharePoint solves the problem in the same way—by defining groups.

SharePoint supports the creation of groups within a site collection to ease the configuration of authorization and access control. Groups are never created in the context of the site—they are always created in the context of the site collection and *assigned* to a site. For example, assume that we have a site located at /wingtip/sales, and that the /wingtip/sales site reference is the current context returned from *SPContext.Current.Web*. Given this environment, *SPWeb.Groups* would return the group collection of the sales site. This would be a subset of the groups available in the site collection, which is available through the *SPWeb.SiteGroups* property. For example, the following code would return the groups Team Site Members, Team Site Owners, and Team Site Visitors.

```
using (SPSite siteCollection = new SPSite("http://localhost/wingtip/sales/"))
{
  using(SPWeb site = siteCollection.OpenWeb)
  {

    foreach(SPGroup group in site.Groups)
    {
      Console.WriteLine(group.Name);
    }
  }
}
```

Groups cannot be added to a site directly—they must be added to the site collection. If you try to add a group to the site's Groups collection, you get an exception stating, "You cannot add a group directly to the Groups collection. You can add a group to the SiteGroups collection." This situation occurs because *SPGroup* is always *created* at the Site Collection level and *assigned* to the site. The following code is valid and adds the WingtipSecurityGroup to the site collection groups.

```
// Adds a new group to the site collection groups
site.SiteGroups.Add("WingtipSecurityGroup",site.CurrentUser,
site.CurrentUser,"A group to manage Wingtip Security");
```

However, this still does not associate the group with our site, nor would it be useful within the site without any permissions. To add the group to the site, create a new *SPRoleAssignment* by associating an *SPRoleDefinition* with the *SPGroup*, and then add that role assignment to the site, as in the following code sample.

```
SPGroup secGroup = site.SiteGroups["WingtipSecurityGroup"];
SPRoleAssignment roleAssignment = new SPRoleAssignment(secGroup);
SPRoleDefinition roleDefinition = site.RoleDefinitions["Full Control"];
roleAssignment.RoleDefinitionBindings.Add(roleDefinition);
site.RoleAssignments.Add(roleAssignment);
```

As with *Groups* and *SiteGroups,* multiple collections can be used to access site users. Table 12-1 lists user-related properties of the *SPWeb* site object and when to use them.

TABLE 12-1 *SPWeb* **User Properties**

Property	Description
AllUsers	Used to access any user who has accessed the site as a member of a domain group that is a site member, or any user who is explicitly a member of the site. For example, the user Terry Adams (WINGTIP\terrya) may be a member of the WINGTIP\sales group. If WINGTIP\sales has access to the Sales site and Terry has visited the site (as a member of the WINGTIP\sales group), he would gain access through the AllUsers collection. Because it is the largest collection of users available (being a combination of the SiteUsers, Users, and group memberships), you generally use the AllUsers collection when you want to access a user.
CurrentUser	Returns the current user who created the reference to the SPSite site collection. This is generally the user accessing the SharePoint website.
SiteUsers	Used to access the collection of users in the site collection. This is a subset of the AllUsers collection.
Users	The smallest collection of users, containing only the users explicitly added to a SharePoint site.

Application Pool Identities

The application pool identity plays a large role in SharePoint applications. Besides running the Web application, this account is used as the Windows account that connects to the SharePoint Content and Configuration databases, and it is the Windows account used when running code in the *SPSecurity.RunWithElevatedPrivileges* method. When you create a new Web application through the SharePoint Central Administration application, you should create it to run inside a new or existing application pool, separate from the Central Administration application pool. Moreover, application pools for Web applications that are accessible to users should be configured with a domain account that is not as privileged as the user account for the Central Administration application pool. For example, there is no reason why SharePoint code running within any application pool other than the Central Administration application pool would ever need to create a new content database or configure database security permissions.

Consider what happens when you create a new Web application through the SharePoint Central Administration application. When you do this, you get to determine whether SharePoint creates a new application pool for this Web application or uses an existing application pool. If you tell SharePoint to create a new application pool, you must supply the name and password of a valid Windows user account. When SharePoint creates the new content database, it grants this user account the *dbowner* role for that content database. SharePoint also grants the database roles *public* and *SharePoint_Content_Application_Pools* to this user account in the configuration database. You should note that user accounts that provide application pool identities must also be added to two local groups named IIS_WPG and SharePoint_WPG, so that they have the proper permissions to access SharePoint system files and specific locations within the Windows Registry and IIS Metabase.

SHAREPOINT\SYSTEM Account

The SHAREPOINT\SYSTEM account is an identity to which SharePoint maps internally when code is running under the identity of the hosting application pool. The SHAREPOINT\SYSTEM account is not recognized by Windows because it exists only within the content of the SharePoint runtime environment. This enables SharePoint to use a statically named account for system-related activity regardless of which Windows user account has been configured for the hosting application pool.

For example, if you switch the application pool from WINGTIP\SP_WorkerProcess1 to WINGTIP\SP_WorkerProcess2, code running as system code still acts and is audited as the SHAREPOINT\SYSTEM account. However, it is also important to remember that SHAREPOINT\SYSTEM is not recognized by the Windows security subsystem. Therefore, code in SharePoint running as system code is recognized by any resource outside of SharePoint under the identity of the hosting application pool when it attempts to access external resources, such as the local file system or a SQL Server database.

Escalation of Privilege

The *SPSecurity* class provides a static method named *RunWithElevatedPrivileges,* which enables code to execute as system code running under the identity of SHAREPOINT\SYSTEM. This allows code to run in an escalated security context to perform actions as the system. This method should be used with care and should not expose direct access to system resources; rather, it should be used when you need to perform actions on behalf of the system. The method is simple. You can either create a delegate to a public void method or simply write code within an inline delegate. The signature looks like the following:

```
SPSecurity.RunWithElevatedPrivileges(delegate
{
  // Code runs as the SHAREPOINT\SYSTEM user
});
```

Code within the delegate runs under the SHAREPOINT\SYSTEM security principal. As covered in the section entitled "Application Pool Identities," earlier in this chapter, this account uses the application pool identity when passing credentials to external resources, but it uses the system account internally. To modify SharePoint content under the system credentials, you need to create a new *SPSite* site collection that generates a new security context for objects referenced from the site, as in the following example. You cannot switch the security context of the *SPSite* once it has been created, but must instead create a new *SPSite* reference to switch user contexts. The following code uses the system credentials to add a list item using the profile data of the current Web user.

```
SPSecurity.RunWithElevatedPrivileges(
  delegate {
    using (SPSite site = new SPSite(web.Site.ID)) {
      using (SPWeb web2 = site.OpenWeb) {
        SPList theList = web2.Lists["visitors"];
        SPListItem record = theList.Items.Add();
        record["User"] = SPContext.Current.Web.CurrentUser;
        record.Update();
      }
    }
  }
);
```

Code running with the escalated privilege should use a new *SPSite* object for code running as the system and use the *SPContext.Current* property to access the actual calling user's identity. The *ElevatedPrivilegeWebPart* shown in Listing 12-1 demonstrates the importance of the *SPSite* site collection object in generating a security context.

LISTING 12-1 The Elevated Privilege Web Part demonstrates the security context of the *SPSite* object

```
using System;
using System.Web.UI.WebControls.WebParts;
using Microsoft.SharePoint;
using System.Security.Principal;
using System.Security;
using System.Security.Permissions;

namespace WingtipSecurity {

  [PermissionSet(SecurityAction.Demand)]
  public sealed class ElevatedPrivilegesWebPart : WebPart {

    protected override void RenderContents(System.Web.UI.HtmlTextWriter writer) {
      base.RenderContents(writer);
      SPWeb site = SPContext.Current.Web;
      // Impersonates SHAREPOINT\SYSTEM:
      SPSecurity.RunWithElevatedPrivileges(delegate {
        // The windows user is SHAREPOINT\SYSTEM:
        writer.Write("Elevated privilege Windows user: {0}<br/>",
          WindowsIdentity.GetCurrent.Name);
        // The site context is still the calling user's:
        writer.Write("site context user: {0}<br/>",
          site.CurrentUser.Name);
        // Open a new site security context using SHAREPOINT\SYSTEM:
        using (SPSite siteCollection = new SPSite(site.Site.ID)) {
          using (SPWeb site2 = siteCollection.OpenWeb()) {
            // The new site context is now SHAREPOINT\SYSTEM:
            writer.Write("New site context user: {0}<br/>",
              site2.CurrentUser.Name);
          }
        }
      });
    }
  }
}
```

Elevated privilege is useful for either writing to restricted-permission lists or using the application pool credentials to access Windows authentication–secured Web services. Listing 12-2 demonstrates the use of the system account to track visitors by writing to a restricted permission list. Regardless of the site privileges of the user, the system enters a visitor record in the Visitor list with the calling user's identity profile while using the system account security principal for authorization.

LISTING 12-2 The Visitor Tracker Web Part demonstrates the RunWithElevatedPrivileges security method

```csharp
using System;
using System.Collections.Generic;
using System.Text;
using System.Web.UI.WebControls.WebParts;
using Microsoft.SharePoint;
using System.Security.Permissions;

namespace LitwareSecurity {

  [PermissionSet(SecurityAction.Demand)]
  public sealed class VisitorTrackerWebPart : WebPart {

    [PermissionSet(SecurityAction.Demand)]
    protected sealed override void OnLoad(EventArgs e) {
      base.OnLoad(e);
      SPWeb site = SPContext.Current.Web;
      SPUser user = site.CurrentUser;
      const string listName = @"visitors";
      SPList visitorList = null;
      foreach (SPList alist in site.Lists) {
        if (alist.Title.Equals(listName,
          StringComparison.InvariantCultureIgnoreCase)) {
          visitorList = alist;
          break;
        }
      }
      if (visitorList == null) {
        // Uses the SHAREPOINT\SYSTEM credentials
        SPSecurity.RunWithElevatedPrivileges(
          delegate {
            using (SPSite siteCollection =
              new SPSite(this.Page.Request.Url.ToString)) {
                using (SPWeb systemSite = siteCollection.OpenWeb) {
                  systemSite.AllowUnsafeUpdates = true;
                  Guid listID = systemSite.Lists.Add(listName,
                    "Site Visitors", SPListTemplateType.GenericList);
                visitorList = systemSite.Lists[listID];
                visitorList.Fields.Add("User", SPFieldType.User, true);
                visitorList.WriteSecurity = 4;
                visitorList.Update();
                systemSite.Update();
              }
            }
          });

      }
```

```
        // Uses the SHAREPOINT\SYSTEM credentials
        SPSecurity.RunWithElevatedPrivileges(delegate {
          using (SPSite siteCollection =
            new SPSite(this.Page.Request.Url.ToString)) {
              using (SPWeb systemSite = siteCollection.OpenWeb) {
                SPList theList = systemSite.Lists[listName];
                SPListItem record = theList.Items.Add;
                record["User"] = user;
                record["Title"] = string.Format("{0} {1} {2}", user.Name,
                DateTime.Now.ToShortDateString(), DateTime.Now.ToShortTimeString());
                record.Update();
              }
            }
        });
      }
    }
}
```

Delegating User Credentials

Within application code running in the SharePoint Web application, the code runs under
the credentials of the application pool while impersonating the calling user. This condition
enables SharePoint to secure objects, including sites, lists, and list items, by using the calling user's identity. Identity is configured automatically through the web.config setting
`<identity impersonate="true" />`. This is true for both the Web application and Web
service endpoints. When calling Web services, you can use this identity to authenticate to
remote endpoints by setting the credentials to the Default Credentials. Note that to pass
credentials to back-end services, the SharePoint server must be set up with the rights to
delegate credentials in AD DS. For Web service requests to the same box, delegation is not
required. The following code example uses the credentials of the current user to authenticate
a Web request against a Web data source.

```
WebRequest xmlReq = WebRequest.CreateDefault(xmlUri);
xmlReq.Credentials = CredentialCache.DefaultCredentials;
```

In addition to the current user's credentials, you can access the application pool identity by
using the *SPSecurity* method *RunWithEscalatedPrivileges*.

```
SPSecurity.RunWithElevatedPrivileges(delegate {
  WebRequest xmlReq = WebRequest.CreateDefault(xmlUri);
  // Uses the app pool credentials:
  xmlReq.Credentials = CredentialCache.DefaultCredentials;
});
```

User Impersonation with the User Token

Two primary ways exist to create SPSite as a security context. One is to use the current Windows or claims identity, which is the default method whether you are accessing the site from the SharePoint Web application or an administrative console. This is also the method used with the SPSecurity.RunWithElevatedPrivileges delegate—the current principal, which happens to be SHAREPOINT\SYSTEM, is used to create the site security context.

The other way to create *SPSite* is by using an *SPUserToken* object. The *SPUserToken* is the token created upon authentication. It references the principal of the user from the identity store with its groups and roles. In the case of a Windows identity, this token is used to query AD DS for the *TokenGroups* property. These tokens time out after 24 hours, making them a good candidate for system code that needs to impersonate users in the case of workflow actions or post-processing of list data that happens slightly after the original action (not days later). This token timeout value can be set by using the Windows PowerShell console. Using the user token in the constructor of *SPSite* enables the code to make changes to the SharePoint object model just as if the actual user were making the changes.

You can request the token for any user in the system by using the *UserToken* property of the *SPUser* class. If the current user is not the user requested, SharePoint builds the token independently from the user's Security ID and group membership. You can then pass this token to the *SPSite* constructor to create a new impersonated security context.

For example, consider an event receiver attached to a custom list that will fire when new items are created. Each time a new item is created, the code will create an announcement with the credentials of the user in a separate Announcements list. To create the item under the impersonated security context, simply obtain a user token from the *SPUser* profile that created the object and pass that into the *SPSite* constructor. When the item is inserted into the Announcements list, it will be as if the impersonated user created the item, even though the event receiver is running under the identity of SHAREPOINT\SYSTEM.

```
public override void ItemAdded(SPItemEventProperties properties) {
  DisableEventFiring();
  string CompanyName = properties.ListItem["Company"].ToString();
  properties.ListItem["Company"] = FormatStringValue(CompanyName);
  properties.ListItem.Update();

  SPUserToken token =
    properties.OpenWeb.AllUsers[properties.UserLoginName].UserToken;

  using( SPSite site = new SPSite(properties.SiteId, token) )
  {
      using(SPWeb web = site.OpenWeb(properties.WebUrl))
```

```
    {
        SPListItem announcement = web.Lists["Announcements"].Items.Add();
        announcement["Title"] = properties.ListItem["Company"].ToString();
        announcement["Body"] = "A new company was added!";
        announcement.Update();
    }
}
```

Within this code sample, we are using the *AllUsers* property of the site. Users are available through a reference to the site (the *SPWeb* class). Three user collections are available within the site, and choosing which one to use may be confusing. See Table 12-1, earlier in this chapter, for a description of the options and guidance on when to use each one.

Securing Objects with SharePoint

The *SPWeb, SPList,* and *SPListItem* classes in SharePoint inherit from the abstract class *SPSecurableObject,* which encapsulates the functionality necessary to secure them from unauthorized access. Table 12-2 lists the members of the *SPSecurableObject* class.

TABLE 12-2 *SPSecurableObject* **Members**

Member	Description
BreakRoleInheritance	Creates a unique role that does not inherit from the parent object
CheckPermissions	Checks to see if the current user has a given set of permissions
DoesUserHavePermissions	Indicates if a user has a specified set of permissions
GetUserEffectivePermissionInfo	Returns detailed information about the permissions for a specified user in the current context
GetUserEffectivePermissions	Gets the effective permissions for a specified user in the current context
ResetRoleInheritance	Removes unique permissions and inherits from the parent
AllRolesForCurrentUser	Returns the roles for the current user
EffectiveBasePermissions	Gets the effective permissions for a specified user in the current object
FirstUniqueAncestorSecurableObject	Gets the object where inherited role assignments are defined
HasUniqueRoleAssignments	Indicates whether the object has unique role assignments or inherits from a parent object
ReusableAcl	Gets the access control list for the object
RoleAssignments	Gets the role assignments for the object

SPSecurableObject provides a method for checking whether permissions exist, as well as a method for demanding that the permissions exist. The first method, *DoesUserHavePermissions,* is used to query for permissions and returns a Boolean value, whereas the second method,

CheckPermissions, throws a security exception if the permission does not exist. Because this interface is common throughout the object model, it is easy to learn how to use it throughout your code. For example, to check whether the current user has permissions to view list items, you can call the *DoesUserHavePermissions* method of the *SPWeb* class, passing in the *ViewListItems* permission flag, as follows:

```
SPWeb web = SPContext.Current.Web ;
if (web.DoesUserHavePermissions(SPBasePermissions.ViewListItems){
    // Enumerate lists
}
```

The *SPList* is also an *SPSecurableObject,* which means that you can apply the same principles to checking permissions on lists. To check the user's permission to view list items within a specific list, call the list's *DoesUserHavePermissions* method as follows:

```
foreach(SPList list in web.lists){
  if (list.DoesUserHavePermissions(SPBasePermissions.ViewListItems))
    // Process the list
  }
}
```

Likewise, the same method is available in other objects, such as the *SPListItem* class, which can be used to ensure that the user has permissions to the item or document.

```
foreach(SPListItem item in list.Items){
  if (item.DoesUserHavePermissions(SPBasePermissions.ViewListItems)) {
    // Process the list item
  }
}
```

Rights and Permission Levels

Rights within SharePoint are defined by permissions within the *SPBasePermissions* enumeration. This enumeration is a flags-based enumeration in which multiple permissions can be combined to create a permission set. *SPBasePermissions* are aggregated into roles with the *SPRoleDefinitions* within the site context, in which permissions are role-based. You will most likely assign a role when assigning permissions to a security principal; when validating rights for an action on a particular object, you will check the permission itself. To assign roles to a security principal, use the *SPRoleDefinition* class. By default, each site creates the following role definitions, exposing them through the Web's *RoleDefinition* property: *Full Control, Design, Contribute, Read,* and *Limited Access.* These roles, along with their aggregated permissions, are listed in Table 12-3.

TABLE 12-3 Default SharePoint Site Roles

Site Role	SPBasePermissions
Full Control	FullMask
Design	ViewListItems, AddListItems, EditListItems, DeleteListItems, ApproveItems, OpenItems, ViewVersions, DeleteVersions, CancelCheckout, ManagePersonalViews, ManageLists, ViewFormPages, Open, ViewPages, AddAndCustomizePages, ApplyThemeAndBorder, ApplyStyleSheets, CreateSSCSite, BrowseDirectories, BrowseUserInfo, AddDelPrivateWebParts, UpdatePersonalWebParts, UseClientIntegration, UseRemoteAPIs, CreateAlerts, EditMyUserInfo
Contribute	ViewListItems, AddListItems, EditListItems, DeleteListItems, OpenItems, ViewVersions, DeleteVersions, ManagePersonalViews, ViewFormPages, Open, ViewPages, CreateSSCSite, BrowseDirectories, BrowseUserInfo, AddDelPrivateWebParts, UpdatePersonalWebParts, UseClientIntegration, UseRemoteAPIs, CreateAlerts, EditMyUserInfo
Read	ViewListItems, OpenItems, ViewVersions, ViewFormPages, Open, ViewPages, CreateSSCSite, BrowseUserInfo, UseClientIntegration, UseRemoteAPIs, CreateAlerts
Limited Access	ViewFormPages, Open, BrowseUserInfo, UseClientIntegration, UseRemoteAPIs

Permissions are stored in the ACL for each *SPSecurableObject* and cached in the binary *ReusableAcl* property. The ACL defines permissions for all users in the site collection on each object. These permissions are always accessed from the object (you will remember that object references always are accessed through the user and always contain permission information). The following code checks for permissions on the list object and, based on the AddListItems permission, decides whether to let the user add items.

```
if (list.DoesUserHavePermissions(SPBasePermissions.AddListItems)){
    // Let the user add an item
}
```

The full *SPBasePermissions* enumeration is included in Listing 12-3 for quick reference. You will see that there are both basic and advanced permissions that you can grant, not all of which are available as options in the user interface.

LISTING 12-3 The *SPBasePermissions* enumeration

```
[Flags]
public enum SPBasePermissions {
// Has no permissions on the Web site.
EmptyMask = 0,
// View items in lists and documents in document libraries.
ViewListItems = 1,
// Add items to lists, add documents to document libraries.
AddListItems = 2,
// Edit items in lists, edit documents in document libraries.
EditListItems = 4,
// Delete items from a list or documents from a document library.
DeleteListItems = 8,
```

```
// Approve a minor version of a list item or document.
ApproveItems = 16,
// View the source of documents with server-side file handlers.
OpenItems = 32,
// View past versions of a list item or document.
ViewVersions = 64,
// Delete past versions of a list item or document.
DeleteVersions = 128,
// Discard or check in a document which is checked out to another user.
CancelCheckout = 256,
// Create, change, and delete personal views of lists.
ManagePersonalViews = 512,
// Create and delete lists, add or remove columns or public views in a list.
ManageLists = 2048,
// View forms, views, and application pages. Enumerate lists.
ViewFormPages = 4096,
// Allows users to open a Web site, list, or folder.
Open = 65536,
// View pages in a Web site.
ViewPages = 131072,
// Add, change, or delete HTML pages or Web Part Pages.
AddAndCustomizePages = 262144,
// Apply a theme or borders to the entire Web site.
ApplyThemeAndBorder = 524288,
// Apply a style sheet (.CSS file) to the Web site.
ApplyStyleSheets = 1048576,
// View reports on Web site usage.
ViewUsageData = 2097152,
// Create a Web site using Self-Service Site Creation.
CreateSSCSite = 4194304,
// Create subsites such as team sites.
ManageSubwebs = 8388608,
// Create a group of users that can be used anywhere within the site collection.
CreateGroups = 16777216,
// Create and change permission levels on the Web site and users and groups.
ManagePermissions = 33554432,
// Enumerate files and folders in a Web site using Microsoft SharePoint Designer
// and Web DAV interfaces.
BrowseDirectories = 67108864,
// View information about users of the Web site.
BrowseUserInfo = 134217728,
// Add or remove personal Web Parts on a Web Part Page.
AddDelPrivateWebParts = 268435456,
// Update Web Parts to display personalized information.
UpdatePersonalWebParts = 536870912,
// Grants the ability to perform all administration tasks for the Web site as
// well as manage content.
ManageWeb = 1073741824,
UseClientIntegration = 68719476736,
// Use SOAP, Web DAV, or Microsoft SharePoint Designer interfaces.
UseRemoteAPIs = 137438953472,
// Manage alerts for all users of the Web site.
ManageAlerts = 274877906944,
```

```
// Create e-mail alerts.
CreateAlerts = 549755813888,
// Allows a user to change his or her own user information, such as adding a picture.
EditMyUserInfo = 1099511627776,
// Enumerate permissions on the Web site, list, folder, document, or list item.
EnumeratePermissions = 4611686018427387904,
// Has all permissions on the Web site.
FullMask = 9223372036854775807,
}
```

Handling Authorization Failures with *SPUtility*

You will generally secure objects, including sites and lists, by using the members of the *SPSecurableObject* class. If you need a simple check for permissions, you could also check properties of the current user, such as *IsSiteAdmin*, to ensure that the user is the site administrator. By default, the *CheckPermissions* method of the *SPSecurableObject* throws a security exception and sends an "Access Denied" message to the user; however, you may want to handle authorization failures yourself. The *SPUtility* class has several methods that are useful for handling authorization failures, including the *SPUtility.Redirect* method. The *SPUtility.Redirect* method can be used to send users to the Access Denied page by using the following syntax.

```
SPUtility.Redirect(SPUtility.AccessDeniedPage,
            SPRedirectFlags.RelativeToLayoutsPage,
            Context);
```

SPUtility also has a method that handles "Access Denied" exceptions and redirects the user to the "Access Denied" page. The *SPUtility.HandleAccessDenied* method takes an exception as a parameter and is used to handle *SecurityExceptions*.

```
try {
    // authorization code
} catch (SecurityException securityException) {
    SPUtility.HandleAccessDenied(securityException);
}
```

To check whether the user is a site administrator, you can use the *EnsureSiteAdminAccess* method of *SPUtility*. If the user is not a site administrator, SharePoint prompts for a site administrator credential. If the site administrator credential is not supplied, the user is transferred to the "Access Denied" page. Alternatively, you can also check the current user's *IsSiteAdmin* property and redirect elsewhere.

Finally, *SPUtility* has a simple method to send an HTTP 401 (Access Denied) header to the user. To send a 401 message to the user, enabling the user to either supply new credentials or end up at the "Access Denied" page, use the *SendAccessDeniedHeader* method, as in the following code.

```
try {
  // authorization code
} catch (SecurityException securityException) {
  SPUtility.SendAccessDeniedHeader(securityException);
}
```

Claims-Based Security

Although Windows authentication is still the most widely used mechanism for authenticating users, it presents several challenges to developers and IT professionals. As users increasingly need to cross system and network boundaries, new standards are emerging to simplify authentication and identity management. These standards are embodied in claims authentication.

Each of the classic authentication mechanisms, such as NTLM, Kerberos, and FBA, has limitations that directly affect the design and implementation of SharePoint solutions. Furthermore, these limitations have a larger impact on the maintenance and operation of SharePoint sites in general. Specifically, classic authentication mechanisms present the following challenges, which are explained in more detail in the following sections:

- Multiple user repositories often exist within the enterprise.

- Individual applications must run queries directly against a user repository for authentication.

- Identity exists only within a given network, and delegation of identity is not widely supported across systems.

Within any organization, custom ASP.NET Web applications, services, and SharePoint extranets often use forms-based authentication and have their own SQL Server database acting as a user repository. As a result, multiple user repositories can exist throughout an organization, which severely limits the interoperability of these systems. Furthermore, user maintenance can be extremely challenging because users must be added and removed from multiple repositories when staff changes.

In response to the challenges of multiple user repositories, many organizations have implemented AD DS as a single user repository. AD DS improves user management, but it still presents several limitations. These limitations involve the efficiency of querying AD DS and the management of identity between systems.

If AD DS is set up as the single user repository in an organization, then every application must query AD DS directly to authenticate users. Hopefully, these queries are efficient, but it would be easy for developers to write custom code inadvertently against the AD DS application programming interface (API) that causes performance problems for other applications. In addition, significant code rewrites may be necessary if directories from other organizations come into play, such as through a merger or acquisition.

Beyond simply querying for authentication, it can be difficult to manage user identity across systems and networks. It is quite common, for example, to see SharePoint use Windows authentication for users inside the firewall, but FBA for users outside the firewall. This is problematic because each authentication mechanism results in a separate identity. So if an employee logs on from home using FBA, he or she will not have the same identity as when logging in from work using Windows authentication.

Several workarounds exist today to solve various identity problems. Organizations can use a virtual private network (VPN) to allow users at home to access SharePoint using their Windows credentials. Organizations can also set up a Microsoft Internet Security and Acceleration (ISA) server that provides a forms-based logon while creating a true Windows identity. Third-party solutions, such as Citrix, can also be used to give remote users access to the network. These workarounds, however, fall short of a comprehensive solution to identity management across systems and networks. The answer to these problems lies in the implementation of claims authentication.

Claims authentication was introduced in the Microsoft .NET Framework 3.5 SP1 and is newly supported in SharePoint 2010. It is not a replacement for Windows authentication or FBA; rather, it is an authentication mechanism that can be used to federate identities across system and network boundaries. When a new Web application is created through Central Administration that uses Claims Mode authentication, the resulting IIS website is configured to be claims-aware. Claims-aware websites can still use classic repositories such as AD DS or SQL Server, but the user is also issued another claims token as part of the authentication process.

Claims authentication overcomes the current limitations of multiple repositories and centralized repositories by taking the task of authentication out of the application altogether. Under a claims authentication model, applications no longer need to worry about querying a user repository. Instead, the user arrives at the application with authentication already completed.

A common metaphor for claims authentication involves the issuing of a license and the purchase of alcohol. In this metaphor, a person (the user) wants to purchase alcohol from a store (the application). To purchase alcohol in the United States, the person must be 21 years old (the claim). At the point of purchase, the user presents a license (the token) to the clerk, who verifies the person's age and sells the alcohol to him or her.

The key to understanding this metaphor is recognizing that the license was issued not by the store, but by the state. The authentication authority is completely independent of the application that uses the token to allow access. Of course, the entire transaction hinges upon the fact that the store trusts the state to issue a valid license with a correct birth date. Furthermore, the license can be used for authentication in multiple scenarios, like cashing a check or boarding a plane.

There are several advantages to this authentication model over the current models. First, a single authentication authority can be used across multiple applications. Second, applications do not have to query a repository. Third, the authentication authority can span systems and networks. Fourth, new authentication scenarios are supported that are simply not possible with current models.

Consider the following metaphor to understand how new scenarios are enabled by claims authentication. Instead of purchasing alcohol at a store, imagine that the person wants to gain access to a club that sells alcohol. In this case, the person presents the license to the bouncer, who trusts the license and its claim that the person is 21. In response, the bouncer stamps the person's hand upon entry, so now the person can simply show the hand stamp to the bartender when ordering a drink.

The key to understanding this metaphor is that the hand stamp now represents a new claim added to the user upon authentication. The point here is that the central authority cannot know all the claims that every application wants to retain about a user. So the claims model allows for new claims to be added to the user after authentication. In subsequent resource requests, the application can simply look for the presence of the new claim and grant or deny access.

Claims Architecture

Microsoft's claims authentication architecture is based on the Windows Identity Foundation (WIF). WIF is a set of managed classes available in .NET Framework 3.5 SP1. WIF provides the foundation for creating STS. An STS authenticates a user and issues the claims token that will be used to gain access to resources that trust the STS. WIF can also be used to create claims-aware sites and services.

At the enterprise level, an organization can implement Active Directory Federation Services (AD FS) 2.0. AD FS 2.0 can issue tokens and establish trust with other organizations and systems. Organizations that share trusts can share identities across network boundaries. AD FS also supports existing authentication mechanisms, so a move to claims authentication does not stop existing applications from functioning.

The claims-aware capabilities in SharePoint 2010 are built on WIF. SharePoint can use tokens issued by an STS to grant access to SharePoint resources. In addition, SharePoint has its own STS that can add claims to a token. This is the SharePoint version of the hand stamp token discussed earlier. Figure 12-1 shows the authentication process used with claims.

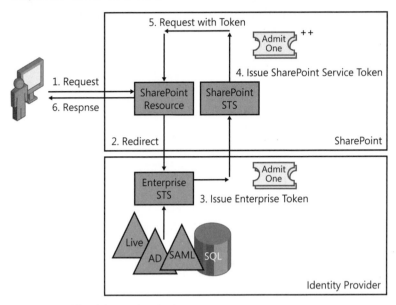

FIGURE 12-1 The claims authentication process

Authentication begins when the user makes a request to access a resource inside SharePoint. If the request does not already contain an appropriate token, SharePoint responds by redirecting the user to authenticate with the appropriate identity provider. Authentication could be done via a forms-based logon screen, a Live ID logon, or Windows authentication could authenticate the user, as described earlier in the chapter. In any case, successful authentication results in the identity provider's issuing a token to the user with a given set of claims. Once this token is issued, a service request is made to the SharePoint STS, which responds by adding claims to the token. The token is then used to access the requested resource and the response is sent to the user. Future requests for resources can simply use the previously issued token. The issued token is implemented as a persistent, encrypted cookie named "FedAuth." After authenticating to a claims-aware SharePoint site, you will see this cookie in the Temporary Internet Files on the client.

User Claims

A user claim is represented by the *Microsoft.IdentityModel.Claims.Claim* object. This object defines critical properties that specify the issuer of the claim, the type of claim, the value type of the claim, and the value of the claim. Claims are essentially key-value pairs, with the key represented by the *ClaimType* property and the value represented by the *Value* property. A claim can hold any key-value pair, such as "Group"/"Employees," "Age/21OrOlder," and "ShowSize/10." The set of claims is completely arbitrary and based on the needs of an application. The data type of the claim is further defined by the *ValueType* property. Along with the key and value, the claim contains information about the issuing authorities in the

OriginalIssuer and *Issuer* properties. To understand claims better, it is helpful to display the claims of the current user. The following code shows how to access the claim types and values (known as the *claim set*) for the current user.

```
IClaimsIdentity claimsId = (IClaimsIdentity)Page.User.Identity;
writer.Write("<p>The current User is " + claimsId.Name, string.Empty + "</p>");

foreach (Claim claim in claimsId.Claims)
{
  writer.Write("<p>ClaimType" + claim.ClaimType + ": ClaimValue" +claim.Value);
}
```

This code can be implemented in a Web Part that can be dropped on a SharePoint page. Table 12-4 shows a typical output from such a Web Part, listing the claim types and values associated with a user accessing a site using Claims Mode against AD DS. Notice that claim types typically take the form of a Uniform Resource Indicator (URI), although that is not strictly necessary, and the values vary widely.

TABLE 12-4 A Typical Claim Set

Claim Type	Claim Value
http://schemas.xmlsoap.org/ws/2005/05/identity/claims/ nameidentifier	wingtip\administrator
http://schemas.microsoft.com/ws/2008/06/identity/ claims/primarysid	S-1-5-21-2203137830-3923341303-2641441098-500
http://schemas.microsoft.com/ws/2008/06/identity/ claims/primarygroupsid	S-1-5-21-2203137830-3923341303-2641441098-513
http://schemas.xmlsoap.org/ws/2005/05/identity/claims/ upn	Administrator@WINGTIP.COM
http://schemas.microsoft.com/sharepoint/2009/08/claims/ userlogonname	WINGTIP\Administrator
http://schemas.microsoft.com/sharepoint/2009/08/claims/ userid	0#.w|wingtip\administrator
http://schemas.xmlsoap.org/ws/2005/05/identity/claims/ name	0#.w|wingtip\administrator
http://schemas.microsoft.com/sharepoint/2009/08/claims/ identityprovider	windows
http://sharepoint.microsoft.com/claims/2009/08/ isauthenticated	True
http://schemas.microsoft.com/sharepoint/2009/08/claims/ farmid	ee728f21-2434-40e7-901b-902eefef055f

Claim Type	Claim Value
http://sharepoint.microsoft.com/claims/2009/08/tokenreference	0#.w|wingtip\administrator,1293167056 94895186,Ur+PFx6YkGYfZpBA+5WQr5F HshEIP/v4VL4nG86AmmUj4NTks6Cntl-LiXdTBMosQlo8cxQSFTNXWpAlPUBHJ/ UuxdFmKGiow25/seO0Ly7Abo/k7t3bOM 5uTi29BfRViu5uyl+naD1VHe7xN4+RPdgq DJkU7g+mkFfFafvf2doKXQTmMFT4X1wl zALenvSy0OmF+jMg5x+9homMLGVz52/ MqV2BTYY5Eko94+rJd1DwIKMzAdu/ dqNJJd6ZXlt2Wm3ACsnlJvjxDV+ mfnt9AomSk4x0F18F6hOSykqr+ LAYYw1pEN0n90HQgAzUUK4F/ INQglhhbOIF6/zWnNJ25tw==,https:// extranet.wingtip.com/_windows/default. aspx?ReturnUrl=/_layouts/Authenticate. aspx?Source=%252F&Source=/
http://schemas.microsoft.com/ws/2008/06/identity/claims/groupsid	S-1-5-21-2203137830-3923341303-2641441098-513
http://schemas.microsoft.com/ws/2008/06/identity/claims/groupsid	S-1-5-21-2203137830-3923341303-2641441098-512
http://schemas.microsoft.com/ws/2008/06/identity/claims/groupsid	S-1-1-0
http://schemas.microsoft.com/ws/2008/06/identity/claims/groupsid	S-1-5-11
http://schemas.microsoft.com/ws/2008/06/identity/claims/authenticationmethod	http://schemas.microsoft.com/ws/2008/06/identity/authenticationmethod/windows
http://schemas.microsoft.com/ws/2008/06/identity/claims/authenticationinstant	2010-10-15T16:42:49.429Z

Several of the claims in Table 12-4 are worthy of further examination. First, take note of the claims *http://schemas.microsoft.com/sharepoint/2009/08/claims/userlogonname, http://schemas.microsoft.com/sharepoint/2009/08/claims/userid,* and *http://schemas.xmlsoap.org/ws/2005/05/identity/claims/name.* The "userlogonname" looks familiar because it represents the Windows account that was used to authenticate the user and subsequently issue the token. Remember that the STS authenticates against a repository before the user is granted access to SharePoint. Once the user authenticates, however, SharePoint can add additional claims to the token. In this case, the "userid" and "name" claims were added, among others. These claims are used to create the *SPUser* object. Note, however, that the value for these claims seems very strange. In the table, we see it as "0#.w\|wingtip\administrator." In fact, if you programmatically access *SPUser.LoginName,* you will see it has exactly the same value. What's going on?

Under claims authentication, the *SPUser.LoginName* is a claim. Also, remember that a claim is an object with multiple properties, such as *ClaimType, ValueType, OriginalIssuer,* and *Value*. The problem is that the *Claim* object must be stored in the *LoginName* property, but the property does not accept a *Claim* object. The solution is to encode the *Claim* and store it in the property. So what you see in the *LoginName* property is an encoded claim representing the identity of the current user.

The SharePoint object model provides several classes for working with claims. The *Microsoft .SharePoint.Administration.SPClaim* class is a SharePoint-specific class for creating and encoding claims. The constructor accepts four strings: claim type, value type, value, and issuer. The *ToEncodedString* method will encode the claim so that it can be compared to the *LoginName* of an *SPUser*. Alternately, an encoded claim may be decoded into an *SPClaim* object by using the *DecodeClaim* method of the *SPClaimProviderManager*. This is useful for taking the value of the *SPUser.LoginName* property and creating a *SPClaim* object.

In addition to the user identity, also note that the SharePoint security token is encoded as a claim value in the claim token. You can also see the references to membership in AD DS groups, as well as a specific claim indicating that the user was authenticated successfully.

For developers who are used to maintaining the security repository within the application, claims-based security can be disorienting initially. This is because much of the information necessary to perform authorization is maintained in the claims token, which is available only for the current user; you cannot access tokens for users who are not returned through *SPContext.Current.Web.CurrentUser*. Furthermore, you cannot query the user repository directly for information about users. Remember that the whole point of claims authentication is to remove authentication from the application. If you want information about other users, then you must retrieve it through the profiles or the *AllUsers, SiteUsers,* or *Users* collection.

Custom Claims Providers

When discussing the claims authentication process, we noted that applications may add other claims to a token following the initial authentication. We then showed the claim set for a typical token showing additional SharePoint claims. When making your own SharePoint solutions, you may also want to add more claims to the token that are specific to your needs. This can be accomplished by creating a custom claims provider. Custom claims providers are registered with SharePoint and called after a user successfully logs on to SharePoint, allowing you to add claims to the token. In addition, custom claims providers can be used to provide name resolution in the People Picker.

As an example of a custom claims provider, we are going to create a provider that will augment the user's claim set with information about the audiences to which they belong. Having this information in the claim set will allow custom applications to make decisions based on audience membership. For the sample, the additional claims will look something like the following.

```
Claim Type: http://www.microsoft.com/identity/claims/audience
Claim Value: All site users
```

In addition to augmenting the claim set, the custom claim provider will also allow the People Picker to resolve audiences. This will allow the claim to be used as the basis for securing objects in SharePoint. Figure 12-2 shows how the provider allows you to search for audience claims and use them to secure objects just as you would with a standard SharePoint group.

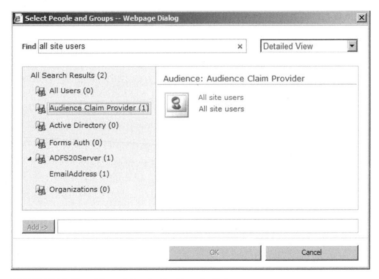

FIGURE 12-2 Resolving claims in the People Picker

A custom claims provider is created using a class that inherits from the abstract class *Microsoft.SharePoint.Administration.Claims.SPClaimProvider.* The class interface has several methods that must be implemented to get the provider working. You may create a provider that supports claims augmentation, name resolution, or both. You designate what features you support through the *SupportsEntityInformation, SupportsHierarchy, SupportsResolve,* and *SupportsSearch* methods. Returning *true* from *SupportsEntityInformation* means that your provider will augment claims. Returning *true* from *SupportsHierarchy, SupportsResolve,* and *SupportsSearch* means that your provider will define a new node in the People Picker, resolve claims, and search for claims based on wildcards, respectively.

Claims augmentation is implemented through the *FillClaimsForEntity, FillClaimTypes,* and *FillClaimValueTypes* methods. The *FillClaimTypes* and *FillClaimValueTypes* methods specify the claim types and value types that your provider will use. The following code shows the implementation for the sample.

```
protected override void FillClaimTypes(List<string> claimTypes) {
    if (claimTypes == null)
        throw new ArgumentException("claimTypes");
    claimTypes.Add(RoleClaimType);
}

protected override void FillClaimValueTypes(List<string> claimValueTypes) {
    if (claimValueTypes == null)
        throw new ArgumentException("claimValueTypes");
    claimValueTypes.Add(ValueType);
}
private static string RoleClaimType {
    get { return "http://www.microsoft.com/identity/claims/audience"; }
}

private static string ValueType {
    get { return Microsoft.IdentityModel.Claims.ClaimValueTypes.String; }
}
```

The *FillClaimsForEntity* method is called by SharePoint after an authenticated user is granted access. This method creates a new claim for each of the audiences and adds it to the claim set. All these claims will be added to the user's claims token. If the only thing you need is claims augmentation, you are finished at this point.

```
protected override void FillClaimsForEntity(System.Uri context,
                                            SPClaim entity,
                                            List<SPClaim> claims)
{
    if (entity == null)
        throw new ArgumentNullException("entity");
    if (claims == null)
        throw new ArgumentNullException("claims");
    //Add audience claims
    using (SPSite ca = new SPSite(CentralAdminUrl))
    {
        SPServiceContext ctx = SPServiceContext.GetContext(ca);
        AudienceManager mgr = new AudienceManager(ctx);

        foreach (Audience audience in mgr.Audiences)
        {
            if (audience.IsMember(entity.Value))
                claims.Add(CreateClaim(RoleClaimType, audience.AudienceName, ValueType));
        }
    }
}
```

If you want to have the provider also support the People Picker, then you must implement *FillSchema, FillHierarchy,* and *FillResolve. FillSchema* is used by the People Picker to control the display of the entity. *FillHierarchy* is used to add nodes to the People Picker. *FillResolve* is used to search for claims and resolve them. The *FillSchema* method specifies the schema of the claim provider so that it may be properly displayed, as in the following code.

```
protected override void FillSchema(SPProviderSchema schema)
{
    schema.AddSchemaElement(new SPSchemaElement(
        "Audience", "Audience", SPSchemaElementType.Both));
}
```

The *FillHierarchy* method creates a new node in the People Picker. In this sample, we are not creating any new nodes. We are simply using the root node for the provider, which we get for free. The *FillResolve* method has two overloads. One is used when a term is entered into the keyword box, and the other is used in the advanced search interface shown previously in Figure 12-2.

```
protected override void FillResolve(System.Uri context, string[] entityTypes,
                                    SPClaim resolveInput, List<PickerEntity> resolved)
{
    if (resolveInput.ClaimType == (RoleClaimType))
        resolved.Add(CreatePickerEntityForAudience(resolveInput.Value));
}
protected override void FillResolve(System.Uri context,
                                    string[] entityTypes, string resolveInput,
                                    List<PickerEntity> resolved)
{
    List<string> audiences = new List<string>;
    using (SPSite ca = new SPSite(CentralAdminUrl))
    {
        SPServiceContext ctx = SPServiceContext.GetContext(ca);
        AudienceManager mgr = new AudienceManager(ctx);

        foreach (Audience audience in mgr.Audiences)
        {
            if (audience.AudienceName.StartsWith(resolveInput,
                StringComparison.CurrentCultureIgnoreCase))
                audiences.Add(audience.AudienceName);
        }
    }

    foreach (string audienceName in audiences)
        resolved.Add(CreatePickerEntityForAudience(audienceName));
}
```

The key to implementing the *FillResolve* method is to add *Microsoft.SharePoint.WebControls .PickerEntity* objects to the generic list named *resolved. PickerEntity* objects added to this collection will appear in the People Picker interface. The following code shows a helper function for creating the appropriate *PickerEntity* object.

```
private PickerEntity CreatePickerEntityForAudience(string audience)
{
    PickerEntity entity = CreatePickerEntity;
    entity.Claim = CreateClaim(RoleClaimType, audience, ValueType);
    entity.Description = ProviderDisplayName + ":" + audience;
    entity.DisplayText = audience;
    entity.EntityType = SPClaimEntityTypes.FormsRole;
    entity.IsResolved = true;
    entity.EntityGroupName = "Audience";
    entity.EntityData["Audience"] = audience;
    return entity;
}
```

The *FillSearch* method allows users to enter a partial text string and return matching claims in the People Picker. The string is sent in as the *searchPattern* parameter, and the method adds matching claims to the *searchTree*. The following code shows the implementation for the sample.

```
protected override void FillSearch(System.Uri context, string[] entityTypes,
            string searchPattern, string hierarchyNodeID, int maxCount,
            SPProviderHierarchyTree searchTree)
{
    if (EntityTypesContain(entityTypes, SPClaimEntityTypes.FormsRole))
    {
        List<string> audiences = new List<string>;
        using (SPSite ca = new SPSite(CentralAdminUrl))
        {
            SPServiceContext ctx = SPServiceContext.GetContext(ca);
            AudienceManager mgr = new AudienceManager(ctx);

            foreach (Audience audience in mgr.Audiences)
            {
                if (audience.AudienceName.StartsWith(searchPattern,
                    StringComparison.CurrentCultureIgnoreCase))
                    audiences.Add(audience.AudienceName);
            }
        }

        foreach (string audienceName in audiences)
            searchTree.AddEntity(CreatePickerEntityForAudience(audienceName));
    }
}
```

To deploy and register the new claim provider with SharePoint, you must create a feature receiver. Unfortunately, the feature receiver created by the SharePoint developer tools in Visual Studio 2010 will not work with custom claims providers. Instead, you must create a separate class that inherits from *Microsoft.SharePoint.Administration.Claims. SPClaimProviderFeatureReceiver*. The thing to note here is how the *FeatureActivated* method calls the *ExecBaseFeatureActivated* method. This maneuver is necessary because there is a bug that will prevent the code from working properly if not wrapped in this way. The following code shows the implementation.

```
public class ProviderFeatureReceiver : SPClaimProviderFeatureReceiver
{
    private void ExecBaseFeatureActivated(SPFeatureReceiverProperties properties)
    { base.FeatureActivated(properties); }

    public override void FeatureActivated(SPFeatureReceiverProperties properties)
    { ExecBaseFeatureActivated(properties); }

    public override string ClaimProviderAssembly
    { get { return typeof(Provider).Assembly.FullName; } }

    public override string ClaimProviderDescription
    { get { return "Audience Claim Provider"; } }

    public override string ClaimProviderDisplayName
    { get { return "Audience Claim Provider"; } }

    public override string ClaimProviderType
    { get { return typeof(Provider).FullName; } }
}
```

Because the feature receiver was created by hand, you must also update the Feature.xml file by hand. The changes in the Feature.xml file just reflect the assembly and class that implement the receiver. The following code shows the Feature.xml file for the sample.

```
<Feature
    xmlns="http://schemas.microsoft.com/sharepoint/"
    ReceiverAssembly="AudienceClaims, [full assembly name]"
    ReceiverClass="AudienceClaims.ProviderFeatureReceiver"
    Id="9c87272e-28fd-473b-ae56-bd1c069a8814"
    Scope="Farm"
    Title="Audience Claims Provider">
</Feature>
```

Once the receiver is complete, the feature may be built, packaged, and deployed. When using a custom claims provider, it is useful to use a Web part to show the user's claim set as well. In this way, you can verify that the provider is working correctly. In addition, you can debug the provider by attaching to the W3wp.exe process in Visual Studio.

Conclusion

Security is a major part of any application. In SharePoint 2010, security becomes more complex because of the introduction of claims authentication. SharePoint developers should work to master security at all levels, from the operating system through the application layer. Doing so will save a lot of time when developing and deploying solutions.

Chapter 13
Business Connectivity Services

While Microsoft SharePoint Server 2010 provides a platform with significant capabilities, there will always be other systems in the organization that maintain critical business data. Systems such as customer relationship management (CRM) and enterprise resource planning (ERP) have special roles that are not replaced easily by Microsoft SharePoint. As a result, strategies must be adopted to provide interoperability between SharePoint and these systems.

In the absence of a strategy for integrating systems with SharePoint, many organizations duplicate information in SharePoint lists. Customer contact information, for example, may exist in a CRM system and also be entered into a contact list in SharePoint. Worse still, the data may be duplicated many times in different team sites by different groups. This kind of duplication leads to significant data maintenance issues because updates must be performed in many lists.

Along with these existing systems, custom applications, databases, and Web services are common within organizations. When a separate database is required, developers have historically created ASP.NET applications or custom Web Parts that act as front ends for the database to have the data appear in the SharePoint environment. However, these types of solutions generally offer little integration with SharePoint capabilities; they are largely limited to presenting data within a SharePoint Web page.

Business Connectivity Services (BCS) changes all the rules for integrating systems, databases, and Web services with SharePoint. Beyond simply bringing data into SharePoint for display, BCS allows for capabilities that simply can't exist in an ASP.NET application or custom Web Part without a significant investment. These capabilities include enterprise search, External Data columns, user profile integration, client synchronization, offline support, and Microsoft Word integration.

We should point out at the beginning of this chapter that BCS is a large subsystem within the SharePoint 2010 product. It is simply impossible to cover the entire depth of it in a single chapter.

See Also One of our authors, Scot Hillier, has written an entire book on the subject called Professional Business Connectivity Services in SharePoint 2010 *(Wrox Press, 2011), which would be a great next step for readers who want more coverage.*

Introducing Business Connectivity Services

BCS is a term for a set of technologies that integrates system data with SharePoint 2010 and Microsoft Office 2010. When discussing BCS, several new terms are introduced that will be used throughout the chapter. These terms all start with the word "External" to signify their association with BCS. The terms are listed below for reference.

- **External System**   Any data source with which BCS can connect

- **External Content Type (ECT)**   The definition of the fields and operations for connecting with an External System

- **External Data**   The data exchanged with an External System

- **External List**   A list in SharePoint based on External Data

- **External Data Column**   A column in a standard list or library whose source is External Data

- **External Data Web Part**   Any of several out-of-the-box Web Parts that can display External Data

BCS can be thought of as the evolutions of the SharePoint Server 2007 Business Data Catalog (BDC), so if you have previous experience with the BDC, you will recognize several of the components in BCS. Previous experience is not necessary, however, to implement BCS solutions successfully. Figure 13-1 shows a block diagram of the major components in BCS.

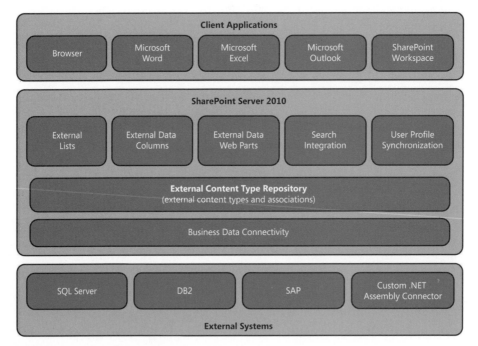

FIGURE 13-1 Major BCS components

BCS uses the term "External System" to refer to any application that is outside SharePoint. These External Systems can include third-party software, custom applications, databases, Web services, and even cloud computing solutions. The Business Data Connectivity (BDC) layer contains the plumbing, BDC Runtime application programming interface (API), and connectivity functionality necessary to communicate with External Systems. Out of the box, the BDC layer provides connectors for databases and Web services, but you can create your own connectors for any system.

The operations performed on the External Data and the schema for the returned data set is defined by an External Content Type (ECT). ECTs define fields, operations, and filters to be used with the External Data and are the heart of the BCS infrastructure. As an example, consider a manufacturing database that contains product information. An ECT named Product can be created that defines *ProductID*, *ProductName*, and *ProductDescription* fields. Furthermore, it might define operations for retrieving data based on a keyword query or exact product identifier. Defining ECTs is one of the primary activities involved in creating a BCS solution and may be performed in either Microsoft SharePoint Designer 2010 (SPD) or Microsoft Visual Studio 2010 (VS2010). ECTs are stored in a metadata catalog, which is part of the BDC Service Application and is available throughout the SharePoint farm.

While you can create many custom solutions using code, the easiest way to create a solution in BCS is through an External List. An External List is a list that is based on an ECT definition and displays External Data. Conceptually, External Lists use ECTs the same way that standard SharePoint lists use standard Content Types. External Lists can be created in the browser or through SPD without writing any code and are accessible through the *SPList* object in the server object model—the same mechanism as any regular *SPList*.

Along with External Lists, ECTs may also be used in other ways through SharePoint. SharePoint ships with a set of Web Parts called *External Data Web Parts* that can display data from External Systems based on an ECT. ECTs can also be used to create lookup fields in standard SharePoint lists. ECTs can be used to enhance the information in a user's profile by drawing on human resource systems such as PeopleSoft. Finally, ECTs can be used to facilitate searching External Systems and displaying results in SharePoint.

In Office 2010, the BCS Client layer provides the ability to display External Data in Office clients. The SharePoint Workspace (SPW) can display data from both external and standard lists together. Microsoft Outlook can display data using standard forms, such as contact lists or calendar items. Microsoft Word can use External Data to support document creation. Microsoft InfoPath is also available to customize the display and edit forms for External Data. In addition, clients running Office 2010 support access to External Data in an offline mode using a cache system that updates the External System when the client reconnects.

Creating Simple BCS Solutions

The BCS infrastructure is complex and covers a variety of authentication, authorization, and operation scenarios. The beauty of BCS, however, is that you can also create simple solutions with no code. SPD provides a set of tools you can use to create ECTs against External Systems and surface them as External Lists. In fact, the easiest way to understand the fundamentals of BCS is to create a simple solution. The classic solution is to create an ECT based on data found in the AdventureWorks database. As a sample, we'll create a solution using the Resellers table, which is partially shown in Figure 13-2.

	ResellerKey	Phone	ResellerName	ProductLine	AddressLine1	
1	1	245-555-0173	A Bike Store	Road	2251 Elliot Avenue	
2	2	170-555-0127	Progressive Sports	Mountain	3207 S Grady Way	
3	3	279-555-0130	Advanced Bike Components	Road	12345 Sterling Avenue	
4	4	710-555-0173	Modular Cycle Systems	Road	800 Interchange Blvd.	
5	5	828-555-0186	Metropolitan Sports Supply	Road	482505 Warm Springs Blvd.	
6	6	244-555-0112	Aerobic Exercise Company	Road	39933 Mission Oaks Blvd	
7	7	192-555-0173	Associated Bikes	Mountain	5420 West 22500 South	
8	8	872-555-0171	Exemplary Cycles	Touring	79945 Corporate Center Drive	
9	9	488-555-0130	Tandem Bicycle Store	Mountain	3333 Micro Drive	
10	10	150-555-0127	Rural Cycle Emporium	Mountain	6388 Lake City Way	
11	11	926-555-0159	Sharp Bikes	Mountain	52560 Free Street	
12	12	112-555-0191	Bikes and Motorbikes	Road	22580 Free Street	

FIGURE 13-2 Reseller data in AdventureWorks

Creating External Content Types

BCS solutions always begin by defining External Content Types for the schema and operations. These definitions are nearly always created using SPD. SPD provides all the basic tooling necessary to create ECTs and External Lists. In addition, ECTs can be exported from SPD so that they can be migrated from a development environment to a quality assurance (QA) environment and then to a production environment. To begin creating an ECT, you open a SharePoint site in SPD and click the External Content Types object under the list of Site Objects, as shown in Figure 13-3. This produces a list of all the existing ECTs in the farm.

FIGURE 13-3 Displaying the available ECTs

Once you have a view of the available ECTs, you may define a new one by clicking the New External Content Type button on the Ribbon. The basic ECT information consists of a Name, Display Name, Namespace, and Version. You may also select from a list of various Office Types, which determines what form will be used to render the information when it is displayed in Outlook. Figure 13-4 shows the basic ECT information for the walkthrough with the Contact Office Type selected.

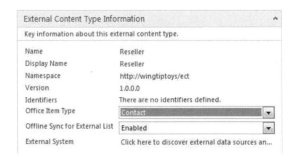

FIGURE 13-4 Basic ECT information

Once the basic ECT information is defined, you will define connection information for the External System. Clicking the Operations Design View button on the Ribbon presents a form for defining the connection information, as shown in Figure 13-5. From this form, clicking Add Connection allows you to select from three types of connections: WCF, SQL, and .NET Type. Selecting WCF allows you to connect to a Web service, SQL allows you to connect to a database, and .NET Type allows you to use a custom .NET Assembly Connector (which is covered in the section entitled "Creating .NET Assembly Connectors" later in this chapter).

When connecting to the External System, BCS supports a number of authentication mechanisms. You can connect as the current user, the SHAREPOINT\SYSTEM account, transform credentials to another account, or even use claims-based access. In this walkthrough, we connect as the current user, which will work fine if the database is on the same server as SharePoint. In more realistic environments, other authentication schemes must be used, and they are covered later in this chapter.

FIGURE 13-5 Specifying connection information

Once the data source connection is made, SPD can create operations for the ECT. When using a SQL connection, SPD can infer a significant amount of information about the data source and the operations, so it is easier to create the entire set of create, read, update, and delete (CRUD) operations. In fact, all you have to do is right-click the table in the connection and select Create All Operations from the context menu, which will start the Operation Wizard to collect the small amount of information required to complete the operation definitions. Figure 13-6 shows the context menu in SPD.

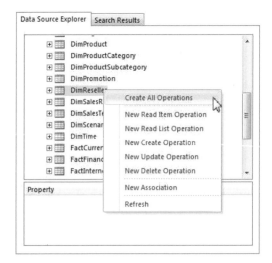

FIGURE 13-6 Creating ECT operations

The Operation Wizard starts whenever SPD needs additional information to complete the operation definition. The information required typically includes a mapping of fields between the ECT and Outlook, identification of the primary key for the ECT, and the definition of filters to throttle the size of returned result sets. SPD displays errors and warnings throughout the wizard to guide you in correctly defining the operations.

After the operations are defined, the ECT should be saved. Saving the ECT writes the definition to the metadata catalog, where it becomes available to the entire farm. After the ECT is saved, it will appear in the list of External Content Types in SPD. From the list of External Content Types, you may also export the ECT definition as an Extensible Markup Language (XML) file. This XML file can subsequently be imported through the Business Data Connectivity service interface in Central Administration.

Creating External Lists

Once the ECT is created, it can be used as the basis for an External List. External Lists can be created directly in SPD or in the browser using the Create menu in SharePoint. For this walk-through, a new External List was created directly from the summary page in SPD. Figure 13-7 shows the dialog for defining the list name and associating operations.

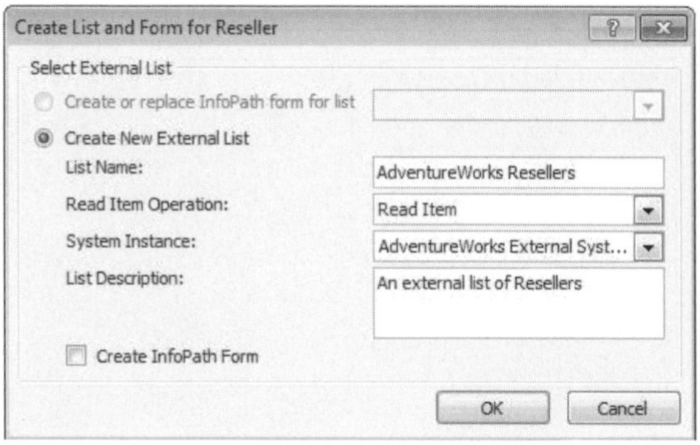

FIGURE 13-7 Creating an External List from SPD

Once the new External List is created, it may be viewed in the browser. Because all the CRUD operations were created, the resulting list supports editing, adding, and deleting items. Figure 13-8 shows the new list in SharePoint Server 2010. Note how the appearance of the External List closely resembles a standard SharePoint list. The Ribbon is functional, as well as the edit-control block (ECB) associated with individual items. Any changes to items in the list will be reflected immediately in the External System.

	ResellerKey	GeographyKey	ResellerAlternateKey	Phone	BusinessType	ResellerName
☐	1	637	AW00000001	245-555-0173	Value Added Reseller	A Bike Store
View Item		635	AW00000002	170-555-0127	Specialty Bike Shop	Progressive Sports
Edit Item		584	AW00000003	279-555-0130	Warehouse	Advanced Bike Components
Delete Item						
	4	572	AW00000004	710-555-0173	Value Added Reseller	Modular Cycle Systems
	5	322	AW00000005	828-555-0186	Specialty Bike Shop	Metropolitan Sports Supply
	6	303	AW00000006	244-555-0112	Warehouse	Aerobic Exercise Company
	7	599	AW00000007	192-555-0173	Value Added Reseller	Associated Bikes

FIGURE 13-8 The External List

Just like "regular" lists, External Lists may be taken offline through both the SFW and Outlook. For this walkthrough, the ECT was defined as a contact item in Outlook. This means that Outlook will use the standard contact list to display the data when the Connect To Outlook button on the List tab of the Ribbon is clicked. When an External List is synchronized with Outlook, BCS delivers a Visual Studio Tools for Office (VSTO) package to the client for accessing the External System. Figure 13-9 shows the External System data in Outlook.

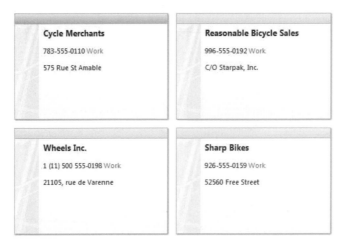

FIGURE 13-9 External data in Outlook

Clicking the Sync To SharePoint Workspace button on the List tab on the Ribbon in SharePoint will take the list offline as well. In a fashion similar to Outlook, a VSTO package will install, and then the list will be available in the SFW. Figure 13-10 shows the list in the SFW.

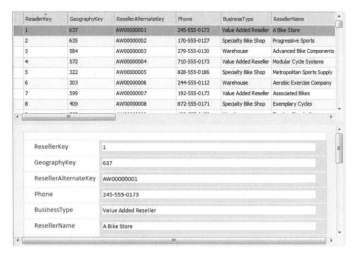

FIGURE 13-10 External data in SFW

Understanding External List Limitations

While External Lists appear similar visually to standard SharePoint lists and are supported by a *SPList* object, they do have significant limitations that must be considered in any design. These limitations include lack of workflow support and several standard list features. The following lists some of the major limitations of External Lists.

- **Approval**   Approval of items is not supported.

- **Attachments**   Attachments are not supported directly, but must be implemented using a StreamAccessor operation in a custom solution.

- **Check-in/Check-out**   Check-in and checkout of items are not supported.

- **Content Types**   Using standard site content types in External Lists is not supported.

- **Drafts**   Drafts of items are not supported.

- **ECB**   Send-To operations are not supported.

- **Events**   List event handlers are not supported.

- **Ribbon**   Datasheet View is not supported.

- **SPLINQ**   Querying through LINQ to SharePoint is not supported.

- **Templates**   Document templates are not supported.

- **Versioning**   Versioning of items is not supported.

- **Workflow**   Starting workflows from items is not supported, but workflows can read or write to External Lists through the SPList object.

- **Validation**   Validation formulas are not supported.

Despite these limitations, BCS solutions provide a powerful authentication and resource infrastructure that allows you to integrate External Data with SharePoint in a way that provides good performance and security. External Lists are not intended to be a substitute for an External System or a SharePoint list. Instead, you should think of External Lists as miniature versions of the External Systems that they represent. Through this perspective, you can see that they are intended to bring commonly used data directly to information workers without requiring a separate logon to an External System. Also, don't forget the additional capabilities that External Lists provide, such as offline access and search support.

The standard *SPList* object may be used in code running against the *Microsoft.SharePoint* namespace to access the items in External Lists, but there are a few special requirements. When code accesses the items in an External List, the unique identifier for an item is found in the *BdcIdentity* field and not the standard ID of the item. In addition, to access the list items, you must enumerate the *SPListItem* collection. Other than those restrictions, accessing the items in the list is straightforward. The following code shows how to access the items in an External List.

```
SPWeb site = SPContext.Current.Web;
SPList externalList = site.Lists[ListName];

writer.Write("<table border=\"0\">");
writer.Write("<tr>");
foreach(SPField field in externalList.Fields) {
  if (field.Title != null) {
    writer.Write("<td align=\"center\">");
    writer.Write(field.Title);
    writer.Write("</td>");
  }
}
writer.Write("</tr>");

foreach (SPListItem item in externalList.Items) {
  writer.Write("<tr>");
  foreach (SPField field in item.Fields) {
    if (field.Title != null) {
      writer.Write("<td>");
      writer.Write(item[field.Title].ToString);
      writer.Write("</td>");
    }
  }
  writer.Write("</tr>");
}

writer.Write("</table>");
```

Understanding BCS Architecture

BCS architecture consists of components on both the server and client. These components support connectivity, ECT definition, operations, and data management. The design of BCS provides for a symmetry between client and server so that clients can have equivalent functionality when offline. Figure 13-11 shows a block diagram of the BCS architecture.

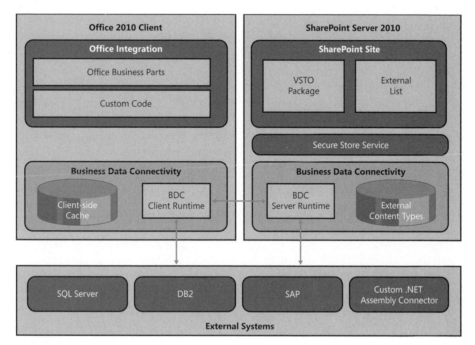

FIGURE 13-11 The BCS architecture

Understanding Connectors

BCS communicates with External Systems using connectors. Connectors contain the functionality necessary to communicate with databases, Web services, and other systems. The walkthrough presented earlier used the SQL connector to access a Microsoft SQL Server database, but BCS also supports a WCF connector for accessing Web services. The SQL and WCF connectors provide a lot of the functionality you will need for basic BCS solutions, but in more advanced cases, you may need to create a connector. When you create your own connector, you can create either a Custom connector or a .NET Assembly Connector.

You can build a Custom connector for connecting to systems other than databases and Web services. These connectors are built specifically for a certain type of system. For example, you could build a Custom connector for Microsoft Exchange Server. While Custom connectors can be created in Visual Studio 2010, there is no tooling support. This means that Custom connectors must be built up from a standard class library project. In most cases, Custom connectors will be created by third parties to target a specific system; the details of this process are beyond the scope of this chapter.

A .NET Assembly Connector is a project that you create in Visual Studio 2010 that contains the ECT definition and associated business logic for accessing a specific External System. The .NET Assembly Connector differs from the Custom connector because it targets a specific instance of a system, as opposed to all instances of a specific system type. In other words, you can use a .NET Assembly Connector to access a specific folder in Exchange Server while a custom connector could be used to access any folder in Exchange Server.

Developers are much more likely to create .NET Assembly Connectors than Custom connectors because they have tooling support in Visual Studio 2010. The .NET Assembly Connector is useful for implementing operations that are not supported by the SPD tooling, such as accessing document streams. .NET Assembly Connectors also support aggregating data from multiple sources into a single ECT and applying business rules to data before it is made available in SharePoint.

Understanding Business Data Connectivity

The Business Data Connectivity layer provides the plumbing and run-time components of BCS. These components are essentially the components that made up the Business Data Catalog in the Microsoft Office SharePoint Server (MOSS) 2007. In SharePoint 2010, Microsoft kept the "BDC" acronym for these components, but changed its definition from Business Data Catalog to Business Data Connectivity.

In SharePoint 2010, both the server and the client have BDC components to support the symmetry of operations on the client and the server. You can use a similar approach to creating BCS solutions whether you are focused on the server, client, or both. On the server, the BDC components consist of the ECT catalog and the BDC Server Runtime. On the client, the BDC components consist of a metadata cache and the BDC Client Runtime. The metadata cache can be thought of as the client-side metadata catalog, while the run-time components have symmetrical functionality to support operations against the External Systems.

Managing the BDC Service

When you create ECTs in SPD and save them, they are stored in the metadata catalog, which is a database accessed through the BDC service application. The BDC service application wraps the BDC and makes it available as a farm service so that ECTs can be used throughout the farm. Figure 13-12 shows the basic architecture of the BDC service application.

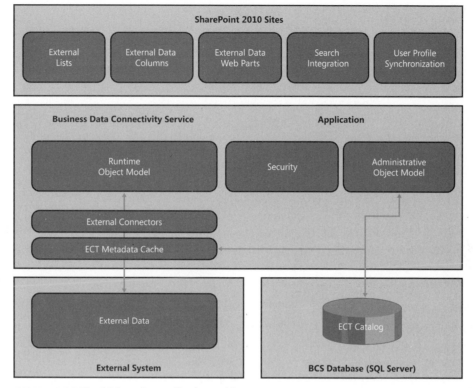

FIGURE 13-12 The BDC service application architecture

The BDC Service application wraps the BDC plumbing and makes BDC functionality available as a service. When External Systems are accessed through connectors, the returned data is made available by the BDC service application to support External Lists, searching, Web Parts, and so on. The metadata cache is maintained in the BDC service so that ECT data is accessed easily without having to read it from the database. This metadata cache is updated every minute by a timer job so that the latest changes are available. Note that External Data itself is never cached by the server—only the ECT metadata.

Along with caching metadata to improve performance, BCS implements limits on the number of connections that can be made to an External System. In addition, the BDC service application also implements five different throttle settings to limit the connections made and data returned from External Systems. Table 13-1 lists the throttle settings for the BDC service application.

TABLE 13-1 BDC Service Application Throttles

Type	Description	Scope	Default	Maximum
Connections	Total number of connections allowed to External Systems	Global	100	500
Items	Number of rows returned from a database query	Database	2000	25,000
Timeout	Database connection timeout	Database	60 sec	600 sec
Size	Size of returned data	WCF	3 MB	150 MB
Timeout	Web service connection timeout	WCF	60 sec	600 sec

Throttle values can be viewed and changed using Windows PowerShell commands. Before you can change them, however, you must get a reference to the BDC service application. The following Windows PowerShell code shows how to return a reference to the BDC service application named Business Data Connectivity.

```
$bdc = Get-SPServiceApplicationProxy | Where {$_ -match "Business Data Connectivity"}
```

Once you have a reference to the BDC service application, you can use the *Get-SPBusiness DataCatalogThrottleConfig* cmdlet and the *Set-SPBusinessDataCatalogThrottleConfig* cmdlet to view and change throttle settings. Each of these cmdlets requires you to specify the throttle that you are viewing or changing. The following code shows how to view the current throttle settings using Windows PowerShell.

```
Get-SPBusinessDataCatalogThrottleConfig -ThrottleType Connections -Scope Global
                                        -ServiceApplicationProxy $bdc
Get-SPBusinessDataCatalogThrottleConfig -ThrottleType Items -Scope Database
                                        -ServiceApplicationProxy $bdc
Get-SPBusinessDataCatalogThrottleConfig -ThrottleType Timeout -Scope Database
                                        -ServiceApplicationProxy $bdc
Get-SPBusinessDataCatalogThrottleConfig -ThrottleType Size -Scope Wcf
                                        -ServiceApplicationProxy $bdc
Get-SPBusinessDataCatalogThrottleConfig -ThrottleType Timeout -Scope Wcf
                                        -ServiceApplicationProxy $bdc
```

When changing throttle settings, you must specify the new value in the *Set-SPBusinessData CatalogThrottleConfig* cmdlet. New throttle settings take effect immediately. As a sample, the following code shows how to change the number of items that can be returned from a database.

```
$bdc = Get-SPServiceApplicationProxy | Where {$_ -match "Business Data Connectivity"}
$throttle = Get-SPBusinessDataCatalogThrottleConfig -ThrottleType Items -Scope Database
                                        -ServiceApplicationProxy $bdc
Set-SPBusinessDataCatalogThrottleConfig -Maximum 3000 -Default 1000 -Identity $throttle
```

Along with viewing or editing throttle values, you can disable them. However, disabling throttles is not something that should be done lightly. Disabling throttles can result in poor BCS performance and may affect the performance of the SharePoint farm as a whole. The following code shows how to disable the connection limit throttle.

```
$bdc = Get-SPServiceApplicationProxy | Where {$_ -match "Business Data Connectivity"}
$throttle = Get-SPBusinessDataCatalogThrottleConfig -ThrottleType Connections
            -Scope Global -ServiceApplicationProxy $bdc
Set-SPBusinessDataCatalogThrottleConfig -Enforced $false -Identity $throttle
```

The BDC service application is part of the service application framework in SharePoint. As such, it functions like any of the other shared services in SharePoint. The management interface for the BDC service application is accessible through the Central Administration home page by selecting Application Management, Manage Service Applications. Figure 13-13 shows the BDC service application in Central Administration.

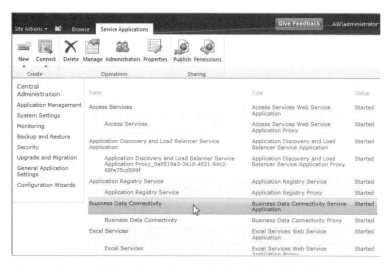

FIGURE 13-13 The BDC service application in Central Administration

From the Service Applications page, you can click the Properties button on the Ribbon and see the basic service properties for the BDC service application. In the Properties dialog, you will see the name of the database used for the ECT repository. This database is set up when the BDC service application is first created during farm installation and configuration. As with all services, you can also set administrative and connection permissions for the service so that it can be used by other servers in the SharePoint farm.

Clicking the Manage button on the Service Applications page will allow you to manage the ECTs in the repository. Here, you will see the ECTs that you have defined in SPD, along with information about the associated models and External Systems. Models may be imported and exported from this page, so you may export models from SPD in a development environment and import them into the BDC service application in QA or production environments.

Managing the BDC service application also allows you to set permissions for the various objects in your model. Users must have permissions to access the ECT and its operations before they will see data in SharePoint. This permission is separate from the actual permissions required to access an External System. There are four different rights available for an ECT: Edit, Execute, Selectable in In Clients, and Set Permissions. The Edit right grants the ability to edit models, data sources, and External Content Types. The Execute right grants the ability to perform CRUD operations. The Selectable in In Clients right grants the ability to create new External Lists, use the External Data Web Parts, and pick External Content Types from the various pickers that appear in SharePoint. The Set Permissions right grants the ability to set permissions in the BDC service.

Understanding the BDC Server Runtime

The BDC Server Runtime consists of the run-time object model, the administration object model, and the security infrastructure. The run-time object model provides access to ECTs and their associated operations, while the administration object model provides objects for managing the ECTs and their associated models. The security infrastructure facilitates authentication and authorization for ECT operations and External System access.

Understanding the Client Cache

BCS uses a client cache to store information from the ECT repository so that Office client applications can access External Systems directly. The client cache is a SQL Server Compact Edition (SQLCE) database that is installed as part of the Office 2010 installation. A synchronization process called BCSSync.exe runs on the client to synchronize the cache with model information in the BDC layer. When operations are performed on data within the Office clients, the operations are queued inside the client cache and synchronized with the External System when it is available. The synchronization process will also attempt to update data in the cache at various intervals from the External System depending on the user settings and availability of the External System. Conflicts between the cache and the External System are flagged for the user so that they may be resolved. When clients access External Systems, they always use the information in the cache to access the External System directly. There is never any case where the client application accesses the External System through the server-side components.

Understanding the BDC Client Runtime

The BDC Client Runtime, which is also called the Office Integration Runtime (OIR), is the client-side component that compliments the BDC Server Runtime. Like the server-side component, the BDC Client Runtime is responsible for the plumbing and functionality necessary to execute operations against an External System and bind the data to clients like Outlook. The BDC Client Runtime is installed on the client as part of the Office 2010 installation process just like the cache. This means that all Office 2010 client installations will support BCS functionality.

Introducing the Secure Store Service

The Secure Store Service (SSS) is a service application that provides for the storage, mapping, and retrieval of credential information. It is used in authentication scenarios where the user account is either not available or not supported by the External System. To store credential sets for an External System, a new *Target Application* must be created in SSS. The Target Application acts as a container for credential sets mapped to an External System. The Target Application settings page contains a name for the application and a setting to specify whether each individual user will have a separate set of mapped credentials or whether every user will map to a single common set of credentials. Figure 13-14 shows application settings mapping a single set of credentials to an Active Directory Domain Services (AD DS) group.

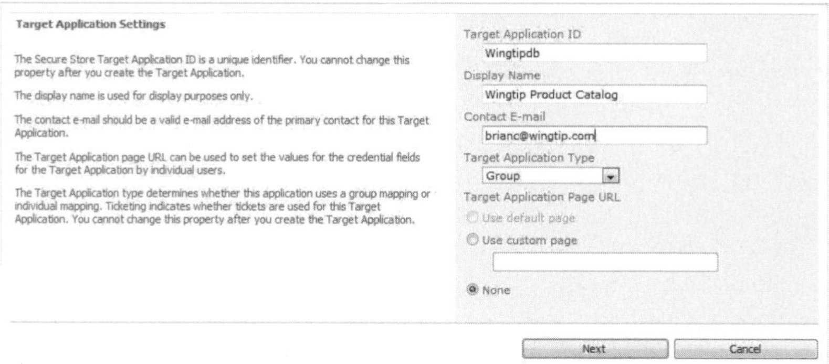

FIGURE 13-14 Creating a new Target Application in SSS

After the Target Application is defined, credential fields are defined to specify what credentials are required to access the External System. In most cases, the Target Application will save a Windows user name and password, but you could also map credentials for non-Windows authentication schemes. SSS also supports ideas such as personal identification numbers (PINs) for credentials. Figure 13-15 shows the field definition form for a Target Application.

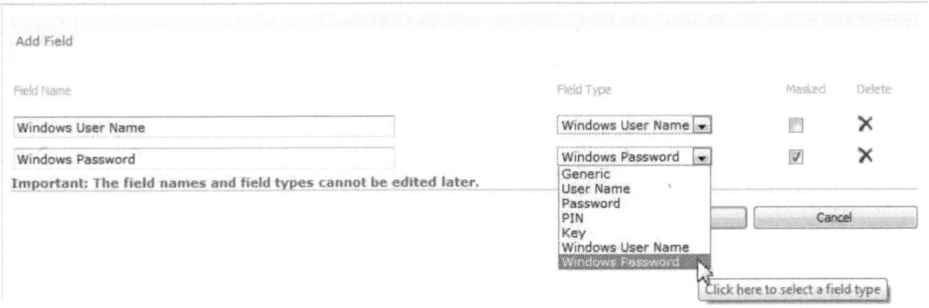

FIGURE 13-15 Defining credential fields

Once the application and credential fields are defined, you must enter the actual credential information for a given user. For each user or group that will access the External System, a set of credentials is stored in SSS. If a user should attempt to access the system without proper credentials in SSS, then that person will be directed to a logon page so the credentials can be entered and stored just-in-time. Once the credentials are mapped, you may specify the name of the Target Application in SPD during ECT creation. When specified in this way, BCS will use the SSS credentials to access the External System. Figure 13-16 shows a dialog for setting the credentials used in a group mapping. In this case, all users are utilizing a single account.

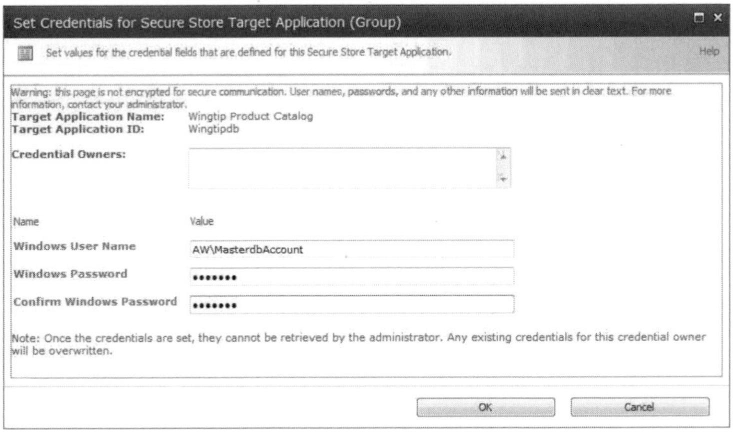

FIGURE 13-16 Mapping group credentials to a single account

The credentials stored in SSS are accessible through a set of objects designed to support your custom solutions. Using these objects, you can create solutions, such as Web Parts, that use SSS credentials to gain access to External Systems. The *Microsoft.Office.SecureStoreService* assembly contains the main classes necessary to work with SSS. In addition, the *Microsoft. BusinessData* assembly contains supporting classes for working with BCS.

The general approach to retrieving SSS credentials in code involves getting a reference to the SSS service application through the *ISecureStoreProvider* class. The *GetCredentials* method may then be called with the name of the Target Application to return the credentials.

Listing 13-1 shows how a Web Part can use this approach to build a connection string for an External System.

LISTING 13-1 Accessing the SSS programmatically

```
protected override void OnPreRender(EventArgs e) {
  string username = string.Empty;
  string password = string.Empty;

  try {
    ISecureStoreProvider p = SecureStoreProviderFactory.Create();
    using (SecureStoreCredentialCollection creds =
              p.GetCredentials(ApplicationId)) {

      // enumerate through all credentials
      foreach (SecureStoreCredential c in creds) {
        switch (c.CredentialType) {
          case SecureStoreCredentialType.UserName:
            username = ConvertToString(c.Credential);
            break;

          case SecureStoreCredentialType.Password:
            password = ConvertToString(c.Credential);
            break;

          case SecureStoreCredentialType.WindowsUserName:
            username = ConvertToString(c.Credential);
            break;

          case SecureStoreCredentialType.WindowsPassword:
            password = ConvertToString(c.Credential);
            break;
        }
      }
    }

    SqlConnectionStringBuilder cBuilder = new SqlConnectionStringBuilder();
    cBuilder.DataSource = ServerName;
    cBuilder.InitialCatalog = DatabaseName;
    cBuilder.UserID = username;
    cBuilder.Password = password;

    messages.Text = cBuilder.ConnectionString;

  }
  catch (Exception x) {
    messages.Text = x.Message;
  }
}

private String ConvertToString(SecureString s) {
  IntPtr b = Marshal.SecureStringToBSTR(s);
  try { return Marshal.PtrToStringBSTR(b); }
  finally { Marshal.FreeBSTR(b); }
}
```

Understanding Package Deployment

When a user elects to synchronize an External List with Outlook or the SFW, BCS creates a VSTO Click-Once deployment package that contains all the elements necessary to work with the list on the client. The package is created by BCS just-in-time and stored under the list in a folder named *ClientSolution*. After the package is created, the deployment is started automatically.

The package contains the BCS model defining the External System, ECTs, operations, and security information that is necessary to access and modify data. The package also contains subscription information, which tells the client cache what data to manage and how it should be refreshed. Finally, the package contains pre- and post-deployment steps that should be taken, such as creating custom forms in the client application to display the data.

Once deployed, the add-in can use Office Business Parts on the client to help render data. Office Business Parts are Windows form controls that display a single item or list of items in a task pane to simplify the rendering process so that custom task panes do not have to be created for the client.

Understanding Authentication Scenarios

When connecting to back-end systems, BCS must deal with several different authentication scenarios. In the simplest case, BCS may be passing Windows credentials from the user through to the External System. However, most real-world applications have more complex requirements, such as proprietary authentication mechanisms, tokens, or claims. For BCS solutions to be secure, they must deal with these situations adequately.

Configuring Authentication Models

BCS supports two authentication models: *Trusted Subsystem* and *Impersonation and Delegation*. In the Trusted Subsystem model, BCS uses a single account to access the External System regardless of the user identity. Under Impersonation and Delegation, BCS attempts to impersonate the user and access the External System. The *AuthenticationMode* element in the BDC Metadata Model determines how authentication is performed and has several different options.

Understanding Passthrough Authentication

Passthrough authentication is used in the Impersonation and Delegation authentication model. Setting the value of the *AuthenticationMode* element to *Passthrough* causes BCS to use the credentials of the current user to access the External System. You can set up

Passthrough authentication by selecting the Connect With User's Identity option when creating a connection to an External System in SPD. The following code shows a portion of a BCD Metadata Model connecting to the AdventureWorks database using *Passthrough* authentication.

```
<LobSystemInstances>
  <LobSystemInstance Name="Adventureworks Data Warehouse">
    <Properties>
      <Property Name="AuthenticationMode" Type="System.String">
        PassThrough
      </Property>
      <Property Name="DatabaseAccessProvider" Type="System.String">
        SqlServer
      </Property>
      <Property Name="RdbConnection Data Source" Type="System.String">
        AWSQL
      </Property>
      <Property Name="RdbConnection Initial Catalog"
               Type="System.String">AdventureworksDW</Property>
      <Property Name="RdbConnection Integrated Security" Type="System.String">
        SSPI
      </Property>
      <Property Name="RdbConnection Pooling" Type="System.String">true</Property>
    </Properties>
  </LobSystemInstance>
</LobSystemInstances>
```

While *Passthrough* authentication is easy to implement, it is unlikely to be useful in many situations because of a particular limitation in Windows authentication known as the *double-hop* issue. Windows authentication takes two forms: NTLM and Kerberos. NTLM is the classic challenge-response protocol used to authenticate users. Kerberos is an advanced ticket-based protocol that is much more secure. NTLM authentication is often compared to a carnival where you must pay for each ride separately. Kerberos, on the other hand, is often compared to a theme park where you pay for one ticket and then have access to all the rides. While Kerberos authentication is considered to be a best practice for BCS, many organizations still run under NTLM authentication.

The double-hop issue describes a scenario under NTLM authentication where the Web server attempts to impersonate a user through a series of "hops" involving multiple servers. As a simple example, consider the walkthrough that was presented at the beginning of the chapter using *Passthrough* authentication.

When a user makes a request to view an External List, SharePoint will attempt to impersonate the user. This impersonation is done at the ASP.NET level, independent of BCS. However, when BCS subsequently attempts to access the data source, it will be prevented from continuing to impersonate the user, and the account identity will change to that of the system account. At this point, the original user identity is lost and access to the data source will be denied.

The double-hop issue is not a bug; it was a built-in feature of NTLM. The limitation is designed to prevent viruses from accessing network resources should credentials be compromised. Kerberos does not suffer from this limitation because its ticketing-based protocol is more secure than challenge-response. So changing the network authentication mechanism from NTLM to Kerberos will solve this problem. Otherwise, you must use a different BCS authentication mechanism to access External Systems.

Understanding *RevertToSelf*

RevertToSelf is used in the Trusted Subsystem model of authentication. Setting the value of the *AuthenticationMode* element to *RevertToSelf* causes BCS to use the credentials of the application pool to access the External System. The following code shows a BDC Metadata Model using *RevertToSelf* authentication.

```
<LobSystemInstances>
  <LobSystemInstance Name="Adventureworks Data Warehouse">
    <Properties>
      <Property Name="AuthenticationMode" Type="System.String">
        RevertToSelf
      </Property>
      <Property Name="DatabaseAccessProvider" Type="System.String">
        SqlServer
      </Property>
      <Property Name="RdbConnection Data Source" Type="System.String">
        AWSQL
      </Property>
      <Property Name="RdbConnection Initial Catalog"
               Type="System.String">AdventureworksDW</Property>
      <Property Name="RdbConnection Integrated Security" Type="System.String">
        SSPI
      </Property>
      <Property Name="RdbConnection Pooling" Type="System.String">true</Property>
      <Property Name="ShowInSearchUI" Type="System.String"></Property>
    </Properties>
  </LobSystemInstance>
</LobSystemInstances>
```

Configuring *RevertToSelf* is accomplished by editing the connection information for the External System after it is defined. In the SharePoint Designer, on the Summary View for the ECT, the connection information may be edited by clicking the hyperlink for the External System. Figure 13-17 shows the Connection Properties dialog. *RevertToSelf* is specified by selecting the BDC Identity option under Authentication Mode.

FIGURE 13-17 Using the BDC identity to access an External System

Using *RevertToSelf* authentication eliminates the double-hop issue because BCS is no longer attempting to impersonate the user all the way to the External System. The drawback to this approach, however, is that all access is accomplished using the same account. As a result, no auditing of individual activities against the External System is possible.

In addition to the limitations imposed by *RevertToSelf* authentication, it is important to understand that the application pool identity is a powerful one whose credentials must be protected. Along with being the account under which the Web application runs, the application pool identity is used to access the content database, as mentioned earlier. Furthermore, the application pool identity is the account under which code runs when the *SPSecurity.RunWith ElevatedPrivileges* method is called in SharePoint, which essentially allows code to perform any action in a SharePoint farm. For this reason, *RevertToSelf* is disabled by default and must be enabled explicitly using the following Windows PowerShell script.

```
$bdc = Get-SPServiceApplication
 | where {$_ -match "Business Data Connectivity Service"}
$bdc.RevertToSelfAllowed = $true
$bdc.Update;
```

Understanding Secure Store Options

SSS is a flexible credential management service that supports both the Trusted Subsystem and Impersonation and Delegation authentication models. If you map all user credentials to a single group account in SSS, then you can support the Trusted Subsystem authentication model. If you map user credentials to a unique set of credentials per user, then SSS is supporting the Impersonation and Delegation authentication model. SSS is a far superior choice to either *Passthrough* or *RevertToSelf* because you can configure access to External Systems such that auditing is still possible while still overcoming double-hop issues. SSS is capable of managing three different types of credentials: Windows, SQL, and user name/password. These three credential types, *WindowsCredentials*, *RdbCredentials*, and *Credentials,* correspond to three different settings for the *AuthenticationMode* element.

Setting the *AuthenticationMode* element to *WindowsCredentials* is used with External Systems that support Windows authentication. Setting the *AuthenticationMode* to *RdbCredentials* is used with External System that supports SQL authentication, such as SQL Server. Setting the *AuthenticationMode* to *Credentials* is used with External Systems that support simple user name/password authentication. The *WindowsCredentials* and *RdbCredentials* are used by selecting the Impersonate Windows Identity or Impersonate Custom Identity option, respectively, in the Connection Properties dialog. The *Credentials* setting is used exclusively with Web services that do not support Windows authentication.

In addition to the primary SSS application, BCS also supports a secondary SSS application that can be used for application-level authentication. This functionality exists to support special situations in which the External System requires credentials to be passed to the system as part of each operation. The credentials held in the secondary application can be configured as a filter to restrict the results returned from the External Systems. Filters are discussed in the section entitled "Defining Filters" later in this chapter.

Accessing Claims-Based Systems

Claims authentication is a new form of authentication available in SharePoint 2010; it is covered in detail in Chapter 12, "SharePoint Security." Claims authentication overcomes the current limitations of multiple user repositories and centralized user repositories by moving the task of authentication out of the application altogether. Under a claims authentication model, applications no longer need to worry about querying a user repository. Instead, the user arrives at the application with authentication already completed.

Because SharePoint 2010 supports claims authentication, BCS can also use claims to authenticate against External Systems. To implement claims authentication, the External System must support claims and trust the claims provider used with SharePoint. Currently, there are few systems that support claims authentication, but the number will increase over time. A likely scenario today involves a custom Windows Communication Foundation (WCF) service that implements claims authentication.

To implement claims authentication, the *AuthenticationMode* should be set to *Passthrough*. None of the other configuration really makes sense because claims authentication is based on delegating the user's identity. For the most part, claims-based authentication happens automatically, provided that the External System accepts the token offered by BCS. In the case where SharePoint is operating in a "claims aware" mode, but the External System is not, the correct approach is to use SSS to transform credentials.

Accessing Token-Based Systems

Today, many Web-based applications use a token-based authentication system. These systems typically have a logon mechanism that is separate from the applications that they support. For example, Window Live has a logon system that uses a Windows Live ID that is used for many applications including HotMail, SkyDrive, and Live Mesh. Regardless of the application, however, users always use the same logon screen to authenticate and receive a token that is trusted by the applications.

BCS can support authentication against token-based systems, but it requires the creation of a custom SSS provider designed to work with the particular token system in use. In addition, a custom handler must be created to redirect users to the appropriate logon page for the system. The SharePoint software development kit (SDK) contains more information on this approach, which is beyond the scope of this chapter.

Managing Client Authentication

BCS clients are designed to have symmetry with the server-side functionality so that they can operate offline. The Application Model created in SPD is synchronized with clients when External Lists are accessed through Office clients and later using subscription information. Some authentication settings, however, will not work correctly from the client because they don't make sense. For example, when you set the client *AuthenticationMode* to *RevertToSelf*, BCS is supposed to use the application pool account when accessing the External System. However, clients have no mechanism to use this account because they always access the External Systems directly. Additional problems can occur when a Trusted Subsystem authentication model maps to group credentials in SSS. In this case, BCS will prompt the user to enter credentials for the group, but the user is unlikely to know these credentials.

Passthrough is the mode that makes the most sense for clients. When you set the client *AuthenticationMode* to *Passthrough*, the client will always try to connect to the External System using the Windows credentials of the current user. This means that the External System must support Windows authentication and the current user must have rights to perform the requested operations.

Client credentials are stored not in SSS, but in the Credential Manager. The Credential Manager is a password store system that supports single sign-on (SSO) to a variety of systems, including websites and remote computers. Credential Manager is part of the client operating system, so you can open it within Windows and view and manage your credentials. If authentication should fail from the client, BCS automatically deletes the credentials from the Credential Manager store and prompts you to enter them again.

Creating External Content Types

Defining External Content Types is the primary activity necessary to implement BCS solutions. The definition of an ECT includes all the information schema, data operations, relationships, filters, actions, and security descriptors necessary to bring External System data into SharePoint. All this information is defined inside a BDC Metadata Model, which is an XML file stored in the ECT repository. While SPD does a good job giving you visual tools to create the model, there are times when you will want to modify the XML directly. Therefore, you should understand the basic structure of the XML model. Listing 13-2 shows part of the basic XML structure with an emphasis on the ECT definition represented by the *Entity* element.

LISTING 13-2 Partial XML model

```xml
<?xml version="1.0" encoding="utf-16" standalone="yes"?>
<Model>
  <LobSystems>
    <LobSystem Type="Database" Name="Wingtip Products">
      <LobSystemInstances>
        <LobSystemInstance Name="Wingtipdb">
        </LobSystemInstance>
      </LobSystemInstances>
      <Entities>
        <Entity Namespace="http://www.wingtip.com"
                Version="1.1.0.0"
                EstimatedInstanceCount="10000"
                Name="Product"
                DefaultDisplayName="Product">
        </Entity>
      </Entities>
    </LobSystem>
  </LobSystems>
</Model>
```

Creating Operations

BCS supports a wide variety of operations designed to facilitate accessing systems and performing CRUD functions. Generally, you will be concerned with basic reading and writing to External Systems using *Finder* (Read List), *SpecificFinder* (Read Item), *Creator* (Create), *Updater* (Update), and *Deleter* (Delete) methods. These methods are also supported in SPD through menus in the Operations Design view. Methods that are not supported by SPD offer additional functionality and control, but they must be created by manually editing the BDC Metadata Model or creating a .NET Assembly Connector. Manually editing the XML model requires that you export the model, edit it, and import the new model. Table 13-2 lists all the supported BCS operations.

TABLE 13-2 Supported BCS Operations

Name	Description
Finder	Returns multiple records from an External System based on a wildcard
SpecificFinder	Returns a single record from an External System based on a primary key
IdEnumerator	Returns all primary keys from an External System to support search indexing
Scalar	Returns a scalar value from an External System
AccessChecker	Checks to see what rights are allowed for a user
Creator	Creates a new record in an External System
Updater	Updates an existing record in an External System
Deleter	Deletes a record in an External System
ChangedIdEnumerator	Returns primary keys for records that have changed to support incremental search indexing
DeletedIdEnumerator	Returns primary keys for records that have been deleted to support incremental search indexing
AssociationNavigator	Navigates from one entity to a related entity
Associator	Associates an entity with another entity
Disassociator	Disassociated one entity from another
GenericInvoker	Used to perform operations not supported by any of the defined operations
StreamAccessor	Supports accessing BLOB data from an External System
BinarySecurityDescriptorAccessor	Returns a security descriptor
BulkSpecificFinder	Returns a set of records from the External System in a batch based on a set of primary keys
BulkAssociatedIdEnumerator	Returns a set of primary keys representing records associated with an entity
BulkAssociationNavigator	Supports navigation from one entity to many related entities
BulkIdEnumerator	Returns all primary keys in a batch from an External System to support search indexing

Finder methods are used to return a result set from the External System and are one of two required operations for External Lists. You can create a *Finder* method in SPD by selecting to create a *New Read List* operation. Listing 13-3 shows the definition of a *Finder* method.

LISTING 13-3 A *Finder* method

```xml
<Method Name="Read List" DefaultDisplayName="Product Read List">
  <Properties>
    <Property Type="System.Data.CommandType, [assembly name for System.Data]"
              Name="RdbCommandType">Text</Property>
    <Property Name="RdbCommandText" Type="System.String">
      SELECT TOP(@ProductID) [ProductID] , [ProductName]
      FROM [dbo].[Products] ORDER BY [ProductID]
    </Property>
    <Property Name="BackEndObjectType"
              Type="System.String">SqlServerTable</Property>
    <Property Name="BackEndObject" Type="System.String">Products</Property>
    <Property Name="Schema" Type="System.String">dbo</Property>
  </Properties>
  <Parameters>
    <Parameter Direction="In" Name="@ProductID">
      <TypeDescriptor TypeName="System.Int64" AssociatedFilter="Filter"
                      Name="ProductID">
        <DefaultValues>
          <DefaultValue MethodInstanceName="Read List"
                        Type="System.Int64">100</DefaultValue>
        </DefaultValues>
      </TypeDescriptor>
    </Parameter>
    <Parameter Direction="Return" Name="Read List">
      <TypeDescriptor
          TypeName="System.Data.IDataReader, [assembly name for System.Data]"
          IsCollection="true" Name="Read List">
        <TypeDescriptors>
          <TypeDescriptor
            TypeName="System.Data.IDataRecord, [assembly name for System.Data]"
            Name="Read ListElement">
            <TypeDescriptors>
              <TypeDescriptor TypeName="System.Int32" ReadOnly="true"
                              IdentifierName="ProductID" Name="ProductID" />
              <TypeDescriptor TypeName="System.String" Name="ProductName">
                <Properties>
                  <Property Name="Size" Type="System.Int32">50</Property>
                  <Property Name="RequiredInForms"
                            Type="System.Boolean">true</Property>
                  <Property Name="ShowInPicker"
                            Type="System.Boolean">true</Property>
                </Properties>
                ...
    </Parameter>
  </Parameters>
```

```
<MethodInstances>
  <MethodInstance Type="Finder" ReturnParameterName="Read List" Default="true"
                  Name="Read List" DefaultDisplayName="Product Read List">
    <Properties>
      <Property Name="UseClientCachingForSearch" Type="System.String"></Property>
      <Property Name="RootFinder" Type="System.String"></Property>
      <Property Name="LastModifiedTimeStampField"
                Type="System.String">LastUpdate</Property>
    </Properties>
  </MethodInstance>
</MethodInstances>
</Method>
```

In the definition for the *Finder* method, SPD automatically generates a SQL query to retrieve items for display in the list if the External System is a database. This is done when the methods are created in the wizard. If you want, you can use stored procedures or views instead of dynamic SQL. Also, note how the return parameters are defined so that BCS understands the data returned from the External System. In particular, note the use of the *TypeDescriptor* element. *TypeDescriptor* is used to map data types in the External System to .NET data types in BCS.

You can create multiple *Finder* methods, but one will always be designated as the default. The default *Finder* method forms the basis of the default view of an External List and provides support for indexing the External System so it can be searched. SPD automatically adds a *RootFinder* property to the default *Finder* method. This property is used when indexing the External System to specify the records in the External System that should be indexed. In addition, the method can designate a timestamp field to support incremental crawls. Designating a field as a timestamp is done in the Return Parameters section of the Operation Wizard and appears in the BDC Metadata Model as a *LastModifiedTimeStamp* property.

SpecificFinder methods are used to return a single item from the External System and are also required to support External Lists. *Creator*, *Updater*, and *Deleter* methods are optional for External Lists. All the methods have similar XML structures in the BDC Metadata Model. You can examine these structures easily by creating models and exporting them from SPD.

Creating Relationships

BCS supports the definition of relationships between entities, which allows you to display relationships and navigate between entities within SharePoint. Within the SharePoint Designer, one-to-many, self-referential, and reverse associations are supported by the tooling. The most common type of association in BCS solutions is the one-to-many association, whereby a parent entity instance is related to many child entity instances. Self-referential associations are just like one-to-many relationships, except that a self-referential relationship uses the same ECT as both the parent and the child. Reverse associations return a single parent entity instance for a child entity instance. Reverse associations are not supported for tables and views, but they are supported for stored procedures and Web services because the reverse association is not inherent in the database schema. It must be programmed explicitly through a stored procedure or Web service.

To create a relationship, you select New Association from the context menu in the Operations Design view. This will start a wizard to help you define the new association. The wizard will ask you to select another ECT with which to make the association. If the ECTs are based on related tables in a database, then SPD will infer the relationship using the foreign key. If not, then you will have to specify the relationship manually by associating fields from the parent to child ECT. Listing 13-4 shows a relationship between a *Product* entity and a *Category*.

LISTING 13-4 An entity relationship

```
<Method IsStatic="false" Name="CategoryAssociation">
  <Properties>
    ...
  </Properties>
  <Parameters>
    <Parameter Direction="In" Name="@CategoryId">
      <TypeDescriptor ... />
    </Parameter>
    <Parameter Direction="Return" Name="CategoryAssociation">
      <TypeDescriptor ...>
        <TypeDescriptors>
          ...
        </TypeDescriptors>
      </TypeDescriptor>
    </Parameter>
  </Parameters>
  <MethodInstances>
    <Association Name="CategoryAssociation" Type="AssociationNavigator"
      ReturnParameterName="CategoryAssociation"
      DefaultDisplayName="Category Association">
      <Properties>
        <Property Name="ForeignFieldMappings" Type="System.String">
        ... ForeignFieldMapping ForeignIdentifierName="CategoryId" ...
        </Property>
      </Properties>
      <SourceEntity Namespace="http://www.wingtip.com" Name="Category" />
      <DestinationEntity Namespace="http://www.wingtip.com" Name="Product" />
    </Association>
  </MethodInstances>
</Method>
```

Defining Filters

When creating *Finder* and *SpecificFinder* methods, you quite often want to limit the information that is returned from the External System. You may want to limit the returned data simply to prevent a large amount of data from being requested, support conditional queries, paging, or wildcards. The Application Model supports all these types of filters. Filters can also be thought of as input parameters to an ECT operation. Generally, their values are set by the calling client before the operation is invoked. The wizards in SPD will help you define the most common filters when you are creating ECTs. Table 13-3 lists all the filters supported in BCS.

TABLE 13-3 Supported BCS Filters

Filter	Description
ActivityId	A globally unique identifier (GUID) representing the correlation Id of the current operation
Batching	Information about the current batch operation for filtering
BatchingTermination	Information about the current terminating batch operation for filtering
Comparison	Filters the records returned based on a value compared to a specific field
Input	Can be used by the operation as an input value when the operation is called.
InputOutput	Can be used by the operation as both an input and output value when the operation is called.
LastId	Identifies the Id of the last item in an operation
Limit	Limits the total number of records returned to a fixed amount. Not compatible with the *PageNumber* filter.
Output	Can be used by the operation as an output value when the operation is called.
PageNumber	Limits the records returned using paging. Not compatible with the *Limit* filter.
Password	The password for the current operation
SsoTicket	The ticket for use when authenticating
Timestamp	Filters the records returned based on a specified *DateTime* field
UserContext	Context information about the current user
UserCulture	The current user culture
Username	The current user name
UserProfile	Profile information about the current user for filtering returned results
Wildcard	Filters the records returned based on *Starts With* or *Contains* values

Whenever you are creating *Finder* and *SpecificFinder* methods, you should define a *Limit* filter for the operation. This filter ensures that large result sets are not returned to an External List and are critical for maintaining BCS performance. While BCS does implement throttling at the system level, the ECT should implement its own tighter limits to ensure query performance is maintained.

Defining filters in SPD is done in the Operation Wizard on the Filter Parameters Configuration page. On this page, you may click Add Filter Parameter to add a new filter. After adding a new filter, you must then click the Filter hyperlink to open the Filter Configuration dialog. Figure 13-18 shows the Filter Configuration dialog within the Operation Wizard.

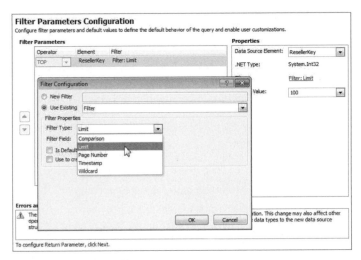

FIGURE 13-18 Defining filters

Using ECTs in SharePoint 2010

Once you have created ECTs, they may be used in a variety of ways. External lists are the simplest way to use them. Beyond creating the list, you may also enhance the list with custom forms, actions, and profiles. SharePoint can also use ECTs to display data in Web Parts, support enhancements to other lists, and as a source for custom solutions.

Creating Custom Forms

Although External Lists have several limitations, they also have many of the same capabilities as a standard list. When created from SPD, for example, you may also select to create an InfoPath form for editing items by clicking the Create Lists And Form button. Creating an InfoPath form allows you to customize the appearance of the form, as well as add validation logic.

Once you have created the InfoPath form, it may be edited by clicking the Design Forms In InfoPath button, which is available on the List Settings tab. Clicking this button will open the form in InfoPath, where you will have complete control over the appearance and functionality of the form. Figure 13-19 shows a simple item edit form that has been modified in InfoPath.

Phone	
Business Name	
Address	
Annual Sales	
Year Opened	

FIGURE 13-19 An External List form in InfoPath

In addition to creating InfoPath forms, you may also create new ASPX forms for External Lists. The default forms created for the External List use the List Form Web Part (LFWP). The LFWP executes Collaborative Application Markup Language (CAML) queries against the External List to display items. Unfortunately, the LFWP does not support modifying its presentation; therefore, a new form must be created instead.

Clicking the New button above the form list in SPD opens the Create New List Form dialog. This dialog is used to create new, edit, and display forms that are based on the Data Form Web Part (DFWP). The DFWP uses Extensible Stylesheet Language for Transformations (XSLT) to transform list data into a display. Modifying this XSLT can change the presentation of list data easily.

Using External Data Columns

Along with using an ECT as the basis for a list, you can use an ECT as the source for a column in another list. This capability is known as an External Data Column. When you create an External Data Column for a list, you select the ECT to use as the basis for the column. You may then select one or more of the fields available in the ECT to display alongside the column you are creating. These additional fields are known as *projected fields* because they project data from the ECT into the parent list. Figure 13-20 shows an external column definition.

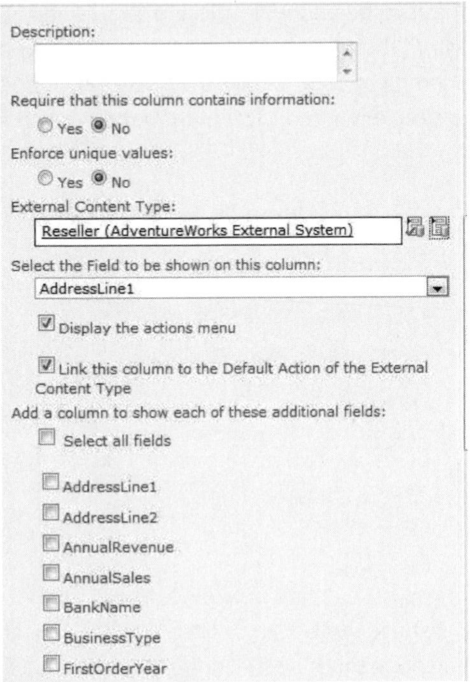

FIGURE 13-20 Defining an external column

External Data Web Parts

Another way you can use ECTs is through a set of Web Parts that ship with SharePoint Server 2010 known as External Data Web Parts (also called Business Data Web Parts). External Data Web Parts are designed specifically to display ECT data and relationships. The available parts include the Business Data List, Business Data Related List, and Business Data Item. These Web Parts display a list based on an ECT, a list based on an ECT association, or a single item, respectively.

The Business Data List part allows you to select an ECT, and then it displays a list of data based on a *Finder* method that you specify. In many ways, this Web Part is like an External List. You can, for example, modify the view by selecting which columns to display. If you have filters defined for the *Finder* method, these can be used to turn simple queries against the list to change the view. Finally, you can change the appearance of the list by altering the XSLT contained within the Web Part. This XSLT is used to transform the data returned for display in the Web Part.

The Business Data Related List is meant to be used in conjunction with the Business Data List to show data based on an association between two ECTs. After selecting an ECT for both the Business Data and Business Data Related lists, you can use the Web Part menu to connect the two lists. Once connected, the Business Data List Web Part acts as a filter against the Business Data Related List Web Part. This gives users a simple way to filter the list view by clicking items in the related list.

The Business Data Item Web Part is used to display a single record based on an ECT. This Web Part is configured by first selecting the ECT and then selecting the particular record to display. This Web Part is especially useful when combined with the Business Data Item Builder Web Part, which builds a business item from query string parameters in the page Uniform Resource Locator (URL). This combination of the Business Data Item Builder Web Part and Business Data Item Web Part is used by BCS to create a profile page for an ECT. Profile pages are discussed in the next section. Figure 13-21 shows the Business Data List, Business Data Related List, and Business Data Item Builder Web Parts on a page.

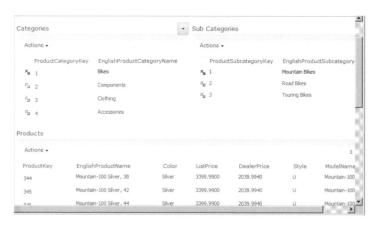

FIGURE 13-21 Business Data Web Parts

Creating a Profile Page

When SharePoint surfaces ECT data in lists and Web Parts, it does not necessarily show all the available fields and associations. For example, when an ECT is used as the source for an external column, only a single field is required for display. When users see partial ECT data, however, they are quite often interested in being able to see the data behind it. This is where profile pages enter the picture. A *profile page* is a dedicated page that shows all the ECT data for a specific record. This way, users can jump from partial ECT data to a complete view of the record.

The Business Data Item Builder and Business Data Item Web Parts are deployed onto a dedicated profile page. The profile page is typically accessed through an action. An action is defined as a hyperlink containing query string parameters that can be used by the Business Data Item Builder Web Part to construct the profile page. Actions are often surfaced as a drop-down menu associated with the displayed ECT data. Figure 13-22 shows a profile page.

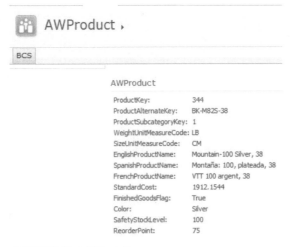

FIGURE 13-22 A BCS profile page

Before you can create profile pages, they must be enabled through the BDC service application. On the Edit tab for the BDC service application, you can click the Configure button in the Profile Pages group. In the Properties dialog that opens, you must specify a SharePoint site where the profile pages can be created. After that, you can simply select ECTs and click the Create/Upgrade button to make profile pages for the ECTs that you select. You can also make profile pages in SPD when you are designing your ECT.

Searching External Systems

ECTs created with SPD already support indexing by SharePoint Search with no additional work. However, External Systems will be indexed only if you explicitly set up a content source that includes the ECT. Content sources can be created within the Search service application, where you will have the option to create a content source associated with an External System.

When you select to create a new content source from an ECT, you will be presented with a drop-down list of the available BDC service applications. When you choose a BDC service application, you will then have the option to index all External Systems associated with the selected service or to pick particular systems. Figure 13-23 shows the content source creation options.

External Data Source

A Line of Business Data content source crawls external data sources defined in an Application Model in a Business Data Catalog Service Application.

Select whether to crawl all external data sources in the Business Data Catalog Service Application, or include only selected external data sources.

Crawl Rule: To create a crawl rule for an external data source, use the following pattern:
bdc3://*ExternalDataSourceName*

Select the Business Data Catalog Service Application:

Business Data Connectivity

○ Crawl all external data sources in this Business Data Catalog Service Application

● Crawl selected external data source
  ☐ Adventureworks Data Warehouse
  ☐ AWDW
  ☐ Dining Guide
  ☐ ImagesLobSystemInstance
  ☐ MiniDMS
  ☐ ShowClaimsService

FIGURE 13-23 Defining a content source

After a content source is created and crawled, it may be used in the standard ways. This means that you may simply go to the Search Center, type a keyword, and return records from the External System. These results include a hyperlink to the profile page so that users can see the full details of the returned records. You may also set up search scopes and use them to search only the External System data.

Supplementing User Profiles

The User Profile service application is used to synchronize data from AD DS to the profile database maintained by SharePoint. The profile database contains rich information about users that can be displayed in sites. The User Profile service application maps AD DS fields to fields in the user's profile. On a scheduled basis, this information is imported from AD DS.

In much the same way that you can add search connections to External Systems through ECTs, you can add profile synchronization connections. Adding a new synchronization connection allows you to use data from External Systems to supplement the data in the profile system. This is often useful in organizations that maintain a Human Resources (HR) system but do not have rich data in their AD DS system. In such cases, ECTs are designed against the HR system and mapped to fields in the profile database. Figure 13-24 shows a new connection being created in the User Profile service application.

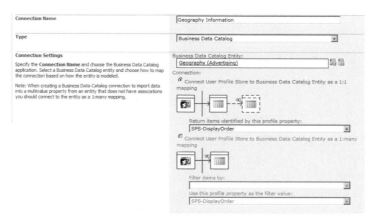

FIGURE 13-24 Connecting BCS with user profiles

Using ECTs in Office 2010

Along with using ECTs on the SharePoint server, they can be used in Office 2010 clients. With little effort, ECTs can be surfaced as lists in the SharePoint Workspace (SFW), items in Outlook, or metadata columns in Word. Furthermore, Office clients can sync with SharePoint to allow External Lists to be managed offline.

Using the SharePoint Workspace

SPW is an Office 2010 client designed to be the main application for managing SharePoint data offline. Using SPW, users can select to synchronize sites, lists, and libraries between their client and the SharePoint server. SPW was formerly known as Groove and still supports all the peer-to-peer capabilities of that product.

SPW has a simple interface that allows for synchronization to be initiated either through the browser or the SPW client. In the browser, users can synchronize a single list or an entire site. Clicking the Sync To SharePoint Workspace button on the List tab causes SPW to synchronize a list. Clicking the same button on the Site Actions menu causes SPW to synchronize an entire site. The SPW client contains a Launchbar that is accessible from an icon in the tray. The Launchbar lists the available sites and allows you to specify new sites to synchronize by providing a URL. Figure 13-25 shows the Launchbar.

FIGURE 13-25 The SPW Launchbar

SPW also contains a Workspace Window that can be opened to show all the available lists and libraries on a site. In the walkthrough earlier in the chapter, the Workspace Window was used to view an External List. You can use the Workspace Window to work with both lists and library documents, make changes, and synchronize them with the server. When documents are added to the workspace, SPW will upload them to the server if it is online. If the server is offline, then documents are queued for upload in the Upload Center. The Upload Center presents the status of document upload and is accessible through an icon in the tray. Figure 13-26 shows the Upload Center.

FIGURE 13-26 The Upload Center

You can manage the synchronization permissions through the SharePoint site. Site Collection administrators can use the standard permission settings to control who has access to the site. An additional option on the Site Settings page allows the administrator to set whether a particular site is available for offline use.

Understanding Outlook Integration

While SPW is a powerful client for managing SharePoint sites, many users prefer to have data available to them in Outlook as well. Lists may be synchronized with Outlook by clicking the Connect To Outlook button on the List tab. Just like SPW, Outlook allows users to work with data offline and then synchronize it with SharePoint later.

When synchronizing External Lists, ECTs can use Outlook forms by explicitly declaring that they should be displayed as an appointment, contact, task, or post when they are designed in SPD. Selecting to display an ECT as a particular type of Office item requires that External System fields be mapped to Outlook fields in the SPD wizard. Generally, the SPD wizard will prompt for the correct mapping through messages. This mapping ensures that the data is displayed correctly inside Outlook.

When you synchronize lists to Outlook, a VSTO solution is installed for working with the items. While the synchronization behavior works out of the box, you could choose to enhance the overall solution with your own VSTO solutions, which could be a full-blown custom VSTO solution created in Outlook or a special declarative solution unique to BCS. Creating these advanced custom VSTO solutions is beyond the scope of this chapter.

Using Word Quick Parts

When you choose to create an external column for a document library, this column will show in Word in the Document Information Panel (DIP) at the top of the document. The DIP is designed to present metadata information so that it can be filled in during the document creation process, as opposed to prompting for metadata values when the document is saved.

In conjunction with viewing the metadata values in the DIP, document templates can also use Quick Parts. Quick Parts in Word allow you to insert fields into the document template that are bound to the metadata fields of the document. When a user fills in the field as part of the document creation process, the metadata values are set automatically. Adding Quick Parts to a document is done by selecting the appropriate metadata field from the Quick Parts list, which appears on the Insert tab in Word.

While Quick Parts work well with all manner of document metadata, they work especially well with ECTs. This is because the Quick Parts will surface a picker dialog for metadata that is based on an ECT. This makes it easy for users to select valid values for the metadata while improving the document creation experience. Figure 13-27 shows a document with a Quick Part based on an ECT. In the image, you can see the Quick Part field, the picker dialog, and the Quick Part list on the Insert tab.

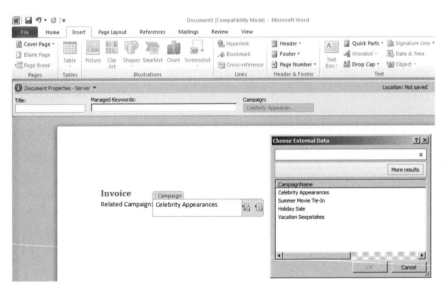

FIGURE 13-27 Quick Parts in a document

Creating Custom BCS Solutions

While BCS offers significant functionality without writing any code at all, there are advanced scenarios in which you will want to write custom code. To support custom solutions, BCS has a complete set of object models for manipulating External Data and managing ECT metadata. These models can be used on both the client and the server and have a high degree of symmetry between the two programming models. Along with coding against the client and server model, you can create your own External System connectors called .NET Assembly Connectors. These connectors are one of the most common BCS customizations because they give you a significant amount of control over the business logic applied to External Data.

Using the BDC Runtime Object Models

The BDC Server Runtime and BDC Client Runtime are the object models used for manipulating External Data. Using the object models, you can perform full CRUD operations on External Data through custom code. This is the programming interface used by External Lists and Outlook, which means you can create custom Web Parts, pages, and add-ins for SharePoint and Office clients.

Using the object models requires you to set references in Visual Studio 2010 to the appropriate assemblies where the programming interface is defined. Selecting the correct assemblies is first a matter of deciding whether you are creating a server-side customization or a client-side customization. For server-side customizations, you will need to set references to the assemblies *Microsoft.BusinessData.dll* and *Microsoft.SharePoint.dll*. For client-side customizations, you will need to set references to *Microsoft.BusinessData.dll* and *Microsoft.Office.BusinessApplications.Runtime.dll*.

After you set references to the appropriate assemblies, the first challenge is to connect to the appropriate catalog. If you are on the server, then you will connect to the metadata catalog associated with the BDC service application. If you are on the client, then you will connect to the client cache.

Connecting to the metadata catalog on the server can be done with or without a SharePoint context, but the code will be different. In any case, you must get a reference to *BdcService ApplicationProxy,* which can then be used to connect with the metadata catalog, which is represented by the *DatabaseBackedMetadataCatalog* object. If your code is running with a SharePoint context, then the following code will connect to the metadata catalog.

```
BdcServiceApplicationProxy p =
    (BdcServiceApplicationProxy)SPServiceContext.Current.GetDefaultProxy(
    typeof(BdcServiceApplicationProxy));
DatabaseBackedMetadataCatalog catalog = sap.GetDatabaseBackedMetadataCatalog;
```

If your code is running outside a SharePoint context, then you will need additional code to connect with *BdcServiceApplicationProxy*. The following code shows how to create a LINQ query to return the application proxy.

```
SPFarm farm = SPFarm.Local;
SPServiceProxyCollection spc = farm.ServiceProxies;
BdcServiceApplicationProxy sap =
(BdcServiceApplicationProxy)((from sp in spc
                             where sp.TypeName.Equals("Business Data Connectivity")
                             select sp).First.ApplicationProxies.First);
DatabaseBackedMetadataCatalog catalog = sap.GetDatabaseBackedMetadataCatalog;
```

In addition to using the *BdcServiceApplicationProxy* object to establish context, you may use the *Microsoft.SharePoint.BusinessData.SharedService.BdcService* class. The *BdcService* class is an abstraction of the BDC Service Application, which is useful for determining whether or not a BDC Service Application is available in the farm. The following code shows how to connect to the metadata catalog.

```
BdcService service = SPFarm.Local.Services.GetValue<BdcService>;
  if (service == null)
    throw new Exception("No BDC Service Application found.");
DatabaseBackedMetadataCatalog catalog =
  service.GetDatabaseBackedMetadataCatalog(SPServiceContext.GetContext(site));
```

If your code is running on the client, then you will connect to the client cache instead of the metadata catalog. The client cache is represented by the *RemoteSharedFileBacked MetadataCatalog* object. The following code shows how to make the connection.

```
RemoteSharedFileBackedMetadataCatalog catalog = new RemoteSharedFileBackedMetadataCatalog;
```

Once you make a connection to the appropriate catalog, you can read or write to the entities that it contains. These changes will be reflected in the External System, as well as any External Lists based on the ECT. Listing 13-5 shows how to retrieve an entity and print the values of its fields using a *Finder* method.

LISTING 13-5 Retrieving an entity

```
IEntity ect = catalog.GetEntity("http://www.wingtip.com/products", "Product");
ILobSystem lob = ect.GetLobSystem;
ILobSystemInstance lobi = lob.GetLobSystemInstances["Wingtipdb"];
IFilterCollection filter = ect.GetDefaultFinderFilters;
IEntityInstanceEnumerator ects = ect.FindFiltered(filter, lobi);
while (ects.MoveNext) {
  Console.WriteLine(ects.Current["ProductName"].ToString);
}
```

If the *Finder* method defines filters (such as a limit, wildcard, or page filter), then these values must be provided in the call to the *FindFiltered* method. An *IFilterCollection* instance can be returned by calling the *GetFilters* method of the *IMethodInstance*. The values for the filters may then be set. The following code shows how to get the filter collection and set values.

```
IMethodInstance mi =
  ect.GetMethodInstance(FinderMethodInstanceName, MethodInstanceType.Finder);

IFilterCollection filters = mi.GetFilters;
(filters[0] as LimitFilter).Value = 10;
(filters[1] as PageNumberFilter).Value = 2;
(filters[3] as WildcardFilter).Value = "Bike";
(filters[4] as ComparisonFilter).Value = "CN123720";
```

Calling *SpecificFinder* is done through the *FindSpecific* method. When calling the *FindSpecific* method, you will always provide an *Identity* object, which represents the identifier for the desired entity instance. Simply create a new *Identity* object using the appropriate value and pass the object as an argument. *Identity* objects can be created with any data type, but be aware that *String* values are case-sensitive when used as *Identifiers*. The following code shows how to call the *FindSpecific* method.

```
//Connect to BDC Service Application
BdcService service = SPFarm.Local.Services.GetValue<BdcService>;

if (service != null) {
//Get Metadata elements
  DatabaseBackedMetadataCatalog catalog =
    service.GetDatabaseBackedMetadataCatalog(SPServiceContext.Current);
  IEntity ect = catalog.GetEntity(EntityNamespace, EntityName);
  ILobSystem lob = ect.GetLobSystem;
  ILobSystemInstance lobi =
    lob.GetLobSystemInstances[LobSystemInstanceName];
}

//Execute SpecificFinder
int id = 5;
IMethodInstance mi = ect.GetMethodInstance(SpecificFinderMethodInstanceName,
                                MethodInstanceType.SpecificFinder);
IEntityInstance item =
    ect.FindSpecific(new Identity(id), SpecificFinderMethodInstanceName, lobi, true);
```

To invoke an *Updater* method, you first use the *FindSpecific* method to return the entity to update. The field values of the return entity may then be modified, and those modifications are committed through the *Update* method of the *IEntityInstance* interface. To invoke a *Deleter* method, you first use the *FindSpecific* method to return the entity instance to delete. The entity instance may then be deleted using the *Delete* method of the *IEntityInstance* interface.

Along with reading or updating entities, you can create new ones. As with other operations, these changes will flow all the way back to the External System. Of course, if you are writing to the client cache, the changes will be made only when the client is online. Listing 13-6 shows how to add a new record to an External System through the ECT.

LISTING 13-6 Creating an entity

```
IView v = ect.GetCreatorView("Create");
IFieldValueDictionary dict = v.GetDefaultValues;
dict["ProductName"] = "New Toy";
dict["LastUpdate"] = DateTime.Today;
Identity id = ect.Create(dict, lobi);
```

Using the Administration Object Model

Along with the Runtime Object Model, BCS has an Administration Object Model. The Administration Object Model allows you to manipulate the metadata for an Application Model. To work with the Administration Object Model, you must set references to *Microsoft .BusinessData.dll* and *Microsoft.SharePoint*.

As with the Runtime Object Model, you must first connect to the appropriate catalog before you can manipulate the data. In the case of the Administration Object Model, you must connect to the *AdministrationMetadataCatalog* object. Connecting to this catalog requires a reference to *BdcServiceApplicationProxy*, just as it did with the Runtime Object Model. Listing 13-7 shows how to connect to the catalog if your code is running outside a SharePoint context. Inside the context, you can use the *SPServiceContext* object as discussed previously.

LISTING 13-7 Connecting to the catalog outside SharePoint

```
SPFarm farm = SPFarm.Local;
SPServiceProxyCollection spc = farm.ServiceProxies;
BdcServiceApplicationProxy sap =
  (BdcServiceApplicationProxy)
    ((from sp in spc
      where sp.TypeName.Equals("Business Data Connectivity")
      select sp).First.ApplicationProxies.First);

AdministrationMetadataCatalog catalog = sap.GetAdministrationMetadataCatalog;
```

The Administration Object Model provides a set of objects that allow you to manipulate the Application Model XML. The names of the objects correspond closely with the names of the elements in the Application Model. Listing 13-8 shows a complete example of creating a simple Application Model from code and saving it into the metadata catalog.

LISTING 13-8 Creating an Application Model

```
Model model = Model.Create("MiniCRM", true, catalog);
LobSystem lob =
  model.OwnedReferencedLobSystems.Create("Customer", true, SystemType.Database);
LobSystemInstance lobi = lob.LobSystemInstances.Create("MiniCRM", true);

lobi.Properties.Add("AuthenticationMode", "PassThrough");
lobi.Properties.Add("DatabaseAccessProvider", "SqlServer");
lobi.Properties.Add("RdbConnection Data Source", "CONTOSOSERVER");
lobi.Properties.Add("RdbConnection Initial Catalog", "MiniCRM.Names");
lobi.Properties.Add("RdbConnection Integrated Security", "SSPI");
lobi.Properties.Add("RdbConnection Pooling", "true");

Entity ect = Entity.Create("Customer", "MiniCRM", true,
                           new Version("1.0.0.0"), 10000,
                           CacheUsage.Default, lob, model, catalog);

ect.Identifiers.Create("CustomerId", true, "System.Int32");

Method specificFinder =
  ect.Methods.Create("GetCustomer", true, false, "GetCustomer");

specificFinder.Properties.Add("RdbCommandText",
    "SELECT [CustomerId] ,[FullName] " +
    "FROM MiniCRM.Names " +
    "WHERE [CustomerId] = @CustomerId");

specificFinder.Properties.Add("RdbCommandType", "Text");

Parameter idParam =
  specificFinder.Parameters.Create("@CustomerId", true, DirectionType.In);

idParam.CreateRootTypeDescriptor(
    "CustomerId", true, "System.Int32", "CustomerId",
    new IdentifierReference("CustomerId",
        new EntityReference("MiniCRM", "Customer", catalog), catalog),
    null, TypeDescriptorFlags.None, null, catalog);

Parameter custParam =
  specificFinder.Parameters.Create("Customer", true, DirectionType.Return);

TypeDescriptor returnRootCollectionTypeDescriptor =
    custParam.CreateRootTypeDescriptor(
        "Customers", true,
        "System.Data.IDataReader, [full assembly name for System.Data]",
        "Customers", null, null, TypeDescriptorFlags.IsCollection, null, catalog);

TypeDescriptor returnRootElementTypeDescriptor =
    returnRootCollectionTypeDescriptor.ChildTypeDescriptors.Create(
        "Customer", true,
        "System.Data.IDataRecord, [full assembly name for System.Data]",
        "Customer", null, null, TypeDescriptorFlags.None, null);
```

```
returnRootElementTypeDescriptor.ChildTypeDescriptors.Create(
        "CustomerId", true, "System.Int32", "CustomerId",
        new IdentifierReference("CustomerId",
            new EntityReference("MiniCRM", "Customer", catalog), catalog),
        null, TypeDescriptorFlags.None, null);

returnRootElementTypeDescriptor.ChildTypeDescriptors.Create(
        "FirstName", true, "System.String", "FullName",
        null, null, TypeDescriptorFlags.None, null);

specificFinder.MethodInstances.Create("GetCustomer", true,
                                    returnRootElementTypeDescriptor,
                                    MethodInstanceType.SpecificFinder, true);

Method finder = ect.Methods.Create("GetCustomers", true, false, "GetCustomers");

finder.Properties.Add("RdbCommandText",
                    "SELECT [CustomerId] , [FullName]FROM MiniCRM.Names");
finder.Properties.Add("RdbCommandType", "Text");

Parameter custsParam = finder.Parameters.Create("Customer", true,
                                            DirectionType.Return);

TypeDescriptor returnRootCollectionTypeDescriptor2 =
    custsParam.CreateRootTypeDescriptor(
        "Customers", true,
        "System.Data.IDataReader, [full assembly name for System.Data]",
        "Customers", null, null, TypeDescriptorFlags.IsCollection, null, catalog);

TypeDescriptor returnRootElementTypeDescriptor2 =
    returnRootCollectionTypeDescriptor2.ChildTypeDescriptors.Create(
        "Customer", true,
        "System.Data.IDataRecord, [full assembly name for System.Data]",
        "Customer", null, null, TypeDescriptorFlags.None, null);

returnRootElementTypeDescriptor2.ChildTypeDescriptors.Create(
        "CustomerId", true, "System.Int32", "CustomerId",
        new IdentifierReference("CustomerId",
            new EntityReference("MiniCRM", "Customer", catalog), catalog),
        null, TypeDescriptorFlags.None, null);

returnRootElementTypeDescriptor2.ChildTypeDescriptors.Create(
        "FirstName", true, "System.String", "FullName",
        null, null, TypeDescriptorFlags.None, null);

finder.MethodInstances.Create("GetCustomers", true,
                            returnRootCollectionTypeDescriptor2,
                            MethodInstanceType.Finder, true);


ect.Activate();
```

Creating .NET Assembly Connectors

A .NET Assembly Connector associates a custom assembly with an ECT so that you can control precisely how information is accessed, processed, and returned from External Systems. Creating a .NET Assembly Connector is done using Visual Studio 2010 and starts by selecting the Business Data Connectivity Model project in the SharePoint 2010 group.

The new project template provides a simple entity definition to use as the starting point for your ECT. The starting entity is visible immediately on the design surface in the project. The design surface displays the identifier field and the methods for the entity. When the project is first created, the entity has an identifier field named *Identitfier1* and methods named *ReadList* and *ReadItem*. The identifier is essentially the primary key for the entity. The *ReadList* and *ReadItem* methods represent the *Finder* and *SpecificFinder* methods for the entity. Figure 13-28 shows the starting entity.

FIGURE 13-28 The starting entity in Visual Studio

One of the first tasks to perform in the project is to define any additional methods you need for the entity. Right-clicking the entity and selecting New Method will create a new method definition. When the new method definition is created, the Method Details pane will open so that you may define the method further.

Methods in BCS are actually prototypes, which must be implemented through a Method Instance. In the Method Details pane, you may define the Method Instance type to use. Visual Studio supports all the available method types described earlier in this chapter.

Along with the entity on the design surface, the template project provides two classes: *Entity1* and *Entity1Service*. The *Entity1* class contains the definitions for all the fields in the entity, while the *Entity1Service* class contains the implementation for the Method Instances.

The project template defines a simple entity with two fields: *Identifier1* and *Message*. *Identifier1* is the primary key for the entity, and *Message* is a field that contains a text message. There is nothing special about these fields or methods—the project template simply creates them as an example to get you started. In fact, the project is complete as soon as it is created. You can run it directly from Visual Studio and create a new External List. So, the project template functions as a starting point for your project as well as a sample application.

As a more practical example, this section will present a walkthrough that creates a .NET Assembly Connector that returns data from an XML file. The XML file has product data that will be the basis for an External List. Listing 13-9 shows the data.

LISTING 13-9 Example data

```xml
<?xml version="1.0" encoding="utf-8" ?>
<Products>
  <Product ID="1" Manufacturer="Microsoft" Name="XBox-360" />
  <Product ID="2" Manufacturer="Seagate" Name="Harddrive" />
  <Product ID="3" Manufacturer="Dell" Name="Laptop" />
  <Product ID="4" Manufacturer="Microsoft" Name="Zune" />
</Products>
```

For this walkthrough, a new Business Data Connectivity Model project was created and the existing entity was modified. The entity was renamed to *Product,* and the model was updated to have an identifier named *ID*. The method definitions were also updated to return additional fields for *Name* and *Manufacturer*. The complete model can be seen using the BDC Model Explorer, which is part of the project. Figure 13-29 shows the complete model for the Product entity.

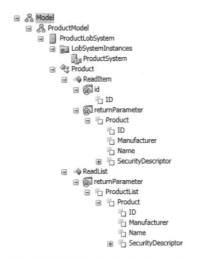

FIGURE 13-29 The Product BCS model

After the model entity is modified, the entity class itself must be updated to reflect the actual fields to be returned from the External System. In this example, *ID, Name*, and *Manufacturer* fields had to be added, while the *Message* field was removed. The following code shows the final definition for the *Product* class.

```
public partial class Product
{
    public string ID { get; set; }
    public string Manufacturer { get; set; }
    public string Name { get; set; }
}
```

Once the entity definition is complete, the method implementations must be coded. Each method in the entity corresponds to a method in code. For the example, this means coding a *ReadList* and *ReadItem* method. Listing 13-10 shows the implementation for the methods.

LISTING 13-10 Implementing *ReadList* and *ReadItem*

```
public static Product ReadItem(string id) {
  try {
    XDocument d =
      XDocument.Load(SPUtility.GetGenericSetupPath("/") +
                    "TEMPLATE\\LAYOUTS\\ProductConnector\\ProductData.xml");

    var q = from c in d.Descendants("Product")
            where c.Attribute("ID").Value.Equals(id)
            select new {
              ID = c.Attribute("ID").Value,
              Name = c.Attribute("Name").Value,
              Manufacturer = c.Attribute("Manufacturer").Value
            };

    Product product = new Product{
    ID = q.First.ID,
    Name = q.First.Name,
    Manufacturer = q.First.Manufacturer,

    return product;
  }
  catch (Exception x) {
    PortalLog.LogString("Product Model (Read Item): {0}", x.Message);
    return null;
  }
}

public static IEnumerable<Product> ReadList {
  try {
    XDocument d =
      XDocument.Load(SPUtility.GetGenericSetupPath("/") +
                    "TEMPLATE\\LAYOUTS\\ProductConnector\\ProductData.xml");

    var q = from c in d.Descendants("Product")
            select new {
              ID = c.Attribute("ID").Value,
              Name = c.Attribute("Name").Value,
              Manufacturer = c.Attribute("Manufacturer").Value
            };
```

```
    List<Product> products = new List<Product>;

    foreach (var p in q) {
      products.Add(new Product { ID = p.ID,
                                 Name = p.Name,
                                 Manufacturer = p.Manufacturer });

    }

    return products;

  }
  catch (Exception x)  {
    PortalLog.LogString("Product Model (ReadList): {0}", x.Message);
    return null;
  }
}
```

Because the data source is an XML chunk, it was simple to implement an *XDocument* instance to load the XML. LINQ queries were then used against the XML chunk to return the desired data. After the methods are implemented, the .NET Assembly Connector is complete. The project may be deployed directly to SharePoint, and an External List can be created against the Product ECT.

The key thing to note about the .NET Assembly Connector is that it gives complete control over the method implementations. This means you can implement additional business rules or security functions easily when retrieving data from External Systems.

Conclusion

Business Connectivity Services (BCS) is a powerful mechanism for connecting SharePoint to External Data. BCS solutions can be imagined to span a spectrum from simple no-code solutions to full-code solutions using run-time object models and .NET Assembly Connectors. SharePoint developers should think of these BCS components as a primary mechanism for creating solutions that require data from an external source.

Chapter 14
Enterprise Content Management

Microsoft Office SharePoint Server (MOSS) 2007 represented Microsoft's first entry into Enterprise Content Management (ECM). In SharePoint Server 2010 (SPS2010), Microsoft has changed and improved their ECM offering dramatically by simplifying how users participate in ECM solutions, as well as extending the capabilities of the platform.

This chapter will first explain Microsoft's approach to ECM in SPS2010 and will then explore the different components that fall under the ECM label: document management, records management, and Web content management. As with most areas of the SharePoint platform, many of these capabilities are extensible, and therefore some customization scenarios are provided.

ECM in SharePoint Server 2010

It helps to have an understanding of Microsoft's approach to ECM before exploring what SPS2010 has to offer. Many leaning analysts firms, including Gartner Group and Forrester, have shown over the years that the majority of ECM deployments do not succeed or meet their full potential. This is a disturbing fact, considering that ECM deployments are expensive and demand significant resources in terms of equipment, personnel, and time. The precise reasons for this troubling fact are not known. However, it can usually be attributed to two things: lack of user adoption and participation and the inability of records managers to find content and effectively manage the solution.

With SPS2010, Microsoft is taking a different approach to ECM than other competing solutions in the market. Typically, users have to submit their content to an ECM implementation for recordkeeping or to comply with established policies. SPS2010 is different in that it brings the ECM capabilities to the users where they do most of their content creation and collaboration: right inside the Microsoft SharePoint sites. This addresses the challenge around user adoption and participation. Users are more likely to participate when they can easily check documents in and out, mark them as records, or assign tags where they are used to working and collaborating on the content. For records managers, SPS2010 includes capabilities simplifying eDiscovery (finding content), auditing, and setting up holds for content involved in litigation.

"Featurization" of ECM Capabilities for Wide Use

The previous version of SharePoint, MOSS 2007, had a very different approach to ECM than what is in SPS2010. Microsoft provided site templates that served the purpose of managing documents and records. It was in these two templates, the Document Center and the Records Center, where users found ECM capabilities like the ability to mark content as a record or to establish holds.

In SPS2010, these capabilities, along with many new ones, have been refactored into SharePoint Features, enabling site collection and site owners to add these capabilities to sites based on any template. For instance, pages within a wiki site or posts within a blog site can now be designated as a record.

In SPS2010, the following ECM-supporting capabilities have been packaged as SharePoint Features available on any SharePoint site:

- Content Organizer
- Document ID Service
- Document Sets
- Holds and eDiscovery
- In-Place Records Management
- Metadata Navigation and Filtering
- Ratings

ECM Site Templates

SharePoint ships out of the box with two site templates addressing ECM: the Document Center and the Records Center. The Document Center site template is designed to serve as a central place for users to collaborate or store a large number of documents. It has been pre-configured with specific features that address document management capabilities. Users can elect to have a central Document Center implementation that stores a large number of documents for the organization, or they can create smaller instances for specific purposes within existing site collections using the site template. Some of the capabilities that it offers include the following:

- Unique Document IDs
- Multi-stage content retention policies and file plans
- Location-based metadata defaults
- Metadata-driven navigation and filtering

The Records Center template, like the Document Center template, also has been configured with specific features. Users can submit documents to the Record Center, which uses the Content Organizer to determine, based on the metadata of the document, where the document should be stored and marked as a record. It also contains a *Drop Off Library*, which serves as a *catch-all* for content that does not match a rule and needs to be processed by a librarian or records manager. Like the Document Center, the Records Center site template can be used to create a single instance that everyone in the organization uses, allowing corporate librarians and records managers to define one set of policies and retention schedules, or it can be used to create smaller, team-based Records Center implementations for distinct policies and retention schedules.

Document Management

SPS2010 includes many capabilities and features that enable organizations to implement very flexible and robust document management solutions. This section will explore some of the most common document management capabilities and how a developer can implement and interact with them.

Large Lists

One new capability is providing a sort of self-health aspect to document libraries (and lists) that contain a large quantity of data. When lists contain a lot of content, SharePoint has to work very hard to retrieve and render datasets from queries that exceed 5,000 items. This can put an unnecessary burden on the system, affecting all the users on the site. SharePoint 2010 addresses this with the concept of *large lists*. The primary purpose behind large lists is to protect the server from being overtaxed, thereby improving the health and reliability of the environment for all users.

When a list contains more than 5,000 items, it is flagged automatically as a large list, a value that can be configured in Central Administration. This tells SharePoint to stop processing queries and report an exception if the result set grows beyond this threshold. Site collection and farm administrators have a higher threshold of 20,000 items that applies to their queries, a value that can be configured in Central Administration. When queries exceed these limits, users should refine their queries or list view filters to limit the scope of the results.

Administrators using Windows PowerShell can configure some of the large list throttling. A *service window* can be created where throttling is disabled, providing a period for developers to run their expensive queries. This is done by setting the start hour, start minute, and the duration (in hours) of how long the window is open, as shown in Listing 14-1.

LISTING 14-1 Enabling a large list query service window

```
# create a service window of 3 hours from 11 PM until 2 AM for expensive queries
PS C:\> $webApp = Get-SPWebApplication http://intranet.wingtip.com
PS C:\> $webApp.DailyStartUnthrottledPriviledgedOperationHour = 23
PS C:\> $webApp.DailyStartUnthrottledPriviledgedOperationMinute = 0
PS C:\> $webApp.DailyUnthrottledPriviledgedOperationsDuration = 3
PS C:\> $webApp.Update()
```

Administrators can configure the default throttling limits as well, using the following properties:

- *SPWebApplication.MaxItemsPerThrottledOperation* (default 5,000)

- *SPWebApplication.MaxItemsPerThrottledOperationOverride* (default 20,000)

- *SPWebApplication.MaxItemsPerThrottledOperationWarningLevel* (default 3,000)

Developers can also override the throttling in their queries using a new property on the *SPQuery* and *SPSiteDataQuery* objects called *QueryThrottleMode*. This property can be set to one of three values:

- **SPQueryThrottleOption.Default**   Throttling is enabled for all users except for local administrators. Throttling includes the number of items and number of Lookup, Person/Group, and Workflow Status fields in the query.

- **SPQueryThrottleOption.Override**   Throttling is disabled for the administrator. For all other users, if they are granted Full Read or Full Control (a Web application security policy setting), the limits are not applied to the number of items returned, but they are applied to the number of Lookup, Person/Group, and Workflow Status fields in the query. For all other users, SPQueryThrottleOption.Default applies.

- **SPQueryThrottleOption.Strict**   Throttling applies to the number of items and number of Lookup, Person/Group, and Workflow Status fields in the query, as well as the number of items in the query, regardless of the user's permissions or Web application security policy settings.

The ability to override the self-protection capabilities in SharePoint may seem counterintuitive, because it could support bad coding practices. However, like the powerful *SPSecurity .RunWithElevatedPrivliedges()* method, it provides an important capability that cannot be met any other way. Used sparingly as part of a well-thought-out application design and highlighted in code reviews, it should not present a problem. It is important to note, however, that administrators have the final say in this matter—they can block this override capability by setting a property on the Web application, as shown in Listing 14-2.

LISTING 14-2 Disabling code-based query overrides

```
PS C:\> $webApp = Get-SPWebApplication http://intranet.wingtip.com
PS C:\> $webApp.AllowOMCodeOverrideThrottleSettings = $false
PS C:\> $webApp.Update()
```

Check-in/Checkout

One of the most common and basic document management capabilities is check-in and checkout. When an item is checked out, no other user can make changes to it until it is checked in. One major improvement in SharePoint 2010 is the ability to check in and check out multiple documents at one time. This addresses the tedious task of checking in multiple documents manually after uploading them to a document library, as shown in Figure 14-1.

FIGURE 14-1 Checking in multiple documents

Checking a file in or checking it out programmatically is fairly straightforward. After checking the status of the file, developers can check it in by calling the *CheckIn()* method and (if they want) specifying the checking type, as shown in Listing 14-3.

LISTING 14-3 Checking in all checked-out documents in a library

```
using (SPSite siteCollection = new SPSite("http://intranet.wingtip.com")) {

  SPWeb site = siteCollection.RootWeb;
  SPList list = site.Lists["Shared Documents"];

  foreach (SPListItem item in list.Items) {
    if (item.Level == SPFileLevel.Checkout)
      item.File.CheckIn("Checking file in.", SPCheckinType.MajorCheckIn);
  }
}
```

Document Sets

SharePoint document libraries allow users to create and interact with individual files. These individual files can be the target of workflows and event receivers, support versioning, or have unique permissions applied to them. In many cases, however, a single document does not represent a complete work product. A work product may consist of multiple documents, such as an invoice with supporting timesheets, travel receipts, a statement of work, and other resources.

Folders can be used to group documents; however, folders cannot be versioned or be the target of an event receiver or workflow.

SPS2010 introduces a new capability called a document set, which enables users to create a single work product that contains multiple work items. A document set has all the same characteristics of an individual document, and all items within the document set retain their individual capabilities as well. A document set is based on a specific content type called *Document Set,* which adds the following other characteristics to a typical folder:

- **Allowed Content Types**   The types of content that are permitted within the document set.

- **Shared Fields**   Common columns that exist on the document set and child content types. When the value is changed in the document set, SharePoint automatically updates the metadata on all documents in the document set with the new value.

- **Welcome Page**   SharePoint implements documents sets as a Web Part Page when users view them with a browser. The Welcome page displays specified fields from the document set's content type, as well as the individual files that make up the document set.

- **Default Content**   When users create a new instance of the document set, it can provision new content that is associated with one of the allowed content types automatically.

When interacting with a document set, the SharePoint interface adds a new contextual tab group that provides additional functionality that you do not normally have in a document library, as shown in Figure 14-2.

Wingtip Sales Conference

City	Las Vegas
State/Province	NV
Start Date	11/1/2010
End Date	11/5/2010 5:00 PM

View All Properties
Edit Properties

☐ Type	Name	Modified	☐ Modified By
📄	ExpenseReport ☆ NEW	10/19/2010 7:32 AM	WINGTIP\administrator
📄	GSA Schedule Session Notes ☆ NEW	10/19/2010 7:32 AM	WINGTIP\administrator
📄	Internaional Business Session Notes ☆ NEW	10/19/2010 7:32 AM	WINGTIP\administrator
📄	Widget Product Compete Session Notes ☆ NEW	10/19/2010 7:32 AM	WINGTIP\administrator

FIGURE 14-2 Trip report document set

Creating a new document set with the browser is simple. First, create the content types (which must be derived from the Document content type) that will be allowed within the document set. Then create a new content type that derives from the Document Set content type and configure its settings. The Document Set content type is added to the site's Content Type Gallery by activating the Document Set feature. Once a document set has been created, it can then be added to a document library in the same way that regular content types are added.

Creating Document Sets Declaratively

Creating document sets through the browser is simple, but it is not a very reusable approach. Another approach is to create them declaratively with SharePoint features, packaged in SharePoint solution packages (*.wsp) and deployed where and when needed, thus addressing both the portability and reusability issues.

The SharePoint developer tools in Microsoft Visual Studio 2010 do not contain a project template or project item template for creating custom document sets, so it must be done by hand. Because a document set is a special kind of a content type, the process for creating a document set is identical to creating a content type except that it has a few extra steps.

Before creating the document set, create all the site columns and content types that will be used within the document set. These should be provisioned before creating the document set.

When defining the document set content type, ensure that it inherits from the Document Set content type (ID = 0x0120D520). The definition should also identify itself as a document set, enabling certain client capabilities like the Document Set contextual tab group and customizations to the ECB menu. This is done by adding *ProgId="SharePoint.DocumentSet"* to the *<ContentType />* element, as shown in Listing 14-4.

LISTING 14-4 Declaring a new Document Set content type

```
<ContentType ID="0x0120D52000e0130de6901740a69cff09cb2906dbc8"
             Name="Invoice Document Set"
             Group="Wingtip Content Types"
             ProgId="SharePoint.DocumentSet">
```

It is also good practice to tell SharePoint where the folder for the content type should be created and what to name it. This will be useful when specifying the default content that should be provisioned in new instances of the document set.

```
<Folder TargetName="_cts/Invoice Document Set" />
```

Next, add the site columns to the document set content type. Some of these fields will be used on the document set's Welcome page, and some will be synchronized with the matching fields on the documents that make up the document set, as shown in Listing 14-5.

LISTING 14-5 Specifying the fields in a document set

```
<FieldRefs>
  <FieldRef ID="{8553196d-ec8d-4564-9861-3dbe931050c8}" DisplayName="Invoice Name"
            Description="Enter in the format of [CUSTOMER]-[INVOICE NUMBER]." />
  <FieldRef ID="{038D1503-4629-40f6-ADAF-B47D1AB2D4FE}" Name="Company"
            DisplayName="Company" Required="TRUE" />
  <FieldRef ID="{83729202-DCA7-4BF8-A75B-56DDDE53189C}" Name="InvoiceNumber"
            DisplayName="Invoice Number" Required="TRUE" />
  <FieldRef ID="{0BFAF66B-BB9A-4876-AAFA-4D5223352745}" Name="InvoiceAmount"
            DisplayName="Invoice Amount" Required="TRUE" />
  <FieldRef ID="{06F6AF4F-F1AD-491B-B83C-6BC47739731A}" Name="InvoiceDate"
            DisplayName="Date Invoice Received" Required="TRUE" />
  <FieldRef ID="{885F61BF-F61C-42DE-89D9-4AA7E562CBBF}" Name="InvoicePaymentTerms"
            DisplayName="Payment Terms" Required="TRUE" />
  <FieldRef ID="{444F753B-D35C-4E93-845A-3EDA63214C30}" Name="InvoicePaidStatus"
            DisplayName="Paid Status" Required="TRUE" />
</FieldRefs>
```

The rest of the content type definition is specific to creating a document set. SharePoint sets the document set specific characteristics via the *<XmlDocuments />* section of the content type. First, add all the content types that are allowed in the document set, referencing them by their *ContentTypeId*, as shown in Listing 14-6.

LISTING 14-6 Specifying the allowed content types in the document set

```
<XmlDocument NamespaceURI="http://schemas.microsoft.com/office/
                          documentsets/allowedcontenttypes">

  <act:AllowedContentTypes xmlns:act="http://schemas.microsoft.com/office/
                                      documentsets/allowedcontenttypes"
                           LastModified="1/1/2010 08:00:00 AM">

    <!-- Document -->
    <AllowedContentType id="0x0101" />

    <!-- Invoice -->
    <AllowedContentType id="0x01010079156360b718448b8cd89ea90a9db922" />

    <!-- Receipt -->
    <AllowedContentType id="0x0101002bc80a9a6946417891f8d100cebace6a" />

    <!-- Timesheet -->
    <AllowedContentType id="0x01010100202388ebe7f24afb8c44263ea755cfc1" />

  </act:AllowedContentTypes>
</XmlDocument>
```

There is one column in the invoice document set that should be kept in sync with all other content types in the collection: Invoice Number. Designate this as a shared field, referencing the ID of the Site Column definition, as shown in Listing 14-7.

LISTING 14-7 Specifying the shared fields in the document set

```
<XmlDocument
   NamespaceURI="http://schemas.microsoft.com/office/documentsets/sharedfields">

  <sf:SharedFields
     xmlns:sf="http://schemas.microsoft.com/office/documentsets/sharedfields"
     LastModified="1/1/2010 08:00:00 AM">

    <!-- Invoice Number -->
    <SharedField id="83729202-DCA7-4BF8-A75B-56DDDE53189C" />

  </sf:SharedFields>
</XmlDocument>
```

Next, specify the fields in the document set content type that should be displayed on the Welcome page when users view an invoice instance, again referencing the ID of the Site Column definition, as shown in Listing 14-8.

LISTING 14-8 Specifying the Welcome page fields in the document set

```
<XmlDocument NamespaceURI="http://schemas.microsoft.com/office/
                          documentsets/welcomepagefields">

  <wpFields:WelcomePageFields xmlns:wpFields="http://schemas.microsoft.com/office/
                                             documentsets/welcomepagefields"
                              LastModified="1/1/2010 08:00:00 AM">

    <!-- Invoice Number -->
    <WelcomePageField id="83729202-DCA7-4BF8-A75B-56DDDE53189C" />

    <!-- Invoice Amount -->
    <WelcomePageFIeld id="0BFAF66B-BB9A-4876-AAFA-4D5223352745" />

    <!-- Date Invoice Received -->
    <WelcomePageField id="06F6AF4F-F1AD-491B-B83C-6BC47739731A" />

    <!-- Payment Terms -->
    <WelcomePageField id="885F61BF-F61C-42DE-89D9-4AA7E562CBBF" />

    <!-- Paid Status -->
    <WelcomePageField id="444F753B-D35C-4E93-845A-3EDA63214C30" />

  </wpFields:WelcomePageFields>
</XmlDocument>
```

When users create new instances of the document set, it should contain a blank timesheet attached to the Timesheet content type. First, configure the document set so that it provisions the default content, as shown in Listing 14-9.

LISTING 14-9 Specifying document set default content

```
<XmlDocument NamespaceURI="http://schemas.microsoft.com/office/documentsets/
defaultdocuments">

  <dd:DefaultDocuments
    xmlns:dd="http://schemas.microsoft.com/office/
                 documentsets/defaultdocuments"
    AddSetName="TRUE"
    LastModified="1/1/2010 08:00:00 AM">

    <DefaultDocument name="WingtipTimesheet.xsn"
                     idContentType="0x01010100202388ebe7f24afb8c44263ea755cfc1" />

  </dd:DefaultDocuments>
</XmlDocument>
```

Next, the timesheet template needs to be provisioned into the SharePoint site in the document set's location specified earlier. Add a new Module project item in the Visual Studio 2010 project that contains a Microsoft InfoPath timesheet file and provision it to the folder of the document set, which was specified previously with the *<Folder TargetName />* element, as shown in Listing 14-10.

LISTING 14-10 Provisioning document set default content

```
<Module Name="InvoiceDocSet_DefaultContent">
  <File Path="InvoiceDocSet_DefaultContent\WingtipTimesheet.xsn"
        Url="_cts/Invoice Document Set/WingtipTimesheet.xsn" />
</Module>
```

At this point, the document set is complete. An optional step is to create a custom Welcome page that users will be taken to when they view the document set. When showing the document set, SharePoint looks for a file named DocSetHomePage.aspx in the document set's folder. If it exists, it will be used as the Welcome page for that document set. If it doesn't exist, a generic Welcome page will be shown instead.

In the case of the invoice document set, the Welcome page should display a message about how much the company can save if the invoice is paid during the discount period and how many days remain until the invoice is past due. To create a custom Welcome page, create a copy of the default Welcome page that is provisioned by the Document Set Feature found in {SharePoint Root}\TEMPLATE\FEATURES\DocumentSet and provision it using a Module SharePoint project item, as shown in Listing 14-11.

LISTING 14-11 Provisioning the document set Welcome page

```
<Module Name="InvoiceDocSet_WelcomePage" RootWebOnly="TRUE">

  <File Path="InvoiceDocSet_WelcomePage\DocSetHomePage.aspx"
        Url="_cts/Invoice Document Set/DocSetHomePage.aspx">

    <AllUsersWebPart WebPartOrder="0" WebPartZoneID="WebPartZone_TopLeft">
      <!-- WebPart element omitted for clarity -->
    </AllUsersWebPart>

    <AllUsersWebPart WebPartOrder="0" WebPartZoneID="WebPartZone_CenterMain">
      <!-- WebPart element omitted for clarity -->
    </AllUsersWebPart>

    <AllUsersWebPart WebPartOrder="0" WebPartZoneID="WebPartZone_Top">
      <!-- WebPart element omitted for clarity -->
    </AllUsersWebPart>

  </File>
</Module>
```

The three *<AllUsersWebPart />* elements provision an Image Web Part with the default document set image, a Document Set Contents Web Part that shows the contents of the Web Part, and the Document Set Properties Web Part that shows all the Welcome page properties. The easiest way to get these values is to copy them from the element manifest in the out-of-the-box *DocumentSet* feature.

At this point, the Visual Studio 2010 project should look similar to Figure 14-3.

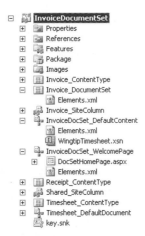

- **InvoiceDocumentSet**
  - Properties
  - References
  - Features
  - Package
  - Images
  - Invoice_ContentType
  - Invoice_DocumentSet
    - Elements.xml
  - Invoice_SiteColumn
  - InvoiceDocSet_DefaultContent
    - Elements.xml
    - WingtipTimesheet.xsn
  - InvoiceDocSet_WelcomePage
    - DocSetHomePage.aspx
    - Elements.xml
  - Receipt_ContentType
  - Shared_SiteColumn
  - Timesheet_ContentType
  - Timesheet_DefaultDocument
  - key.snk

FIGURE 14-3 An invoice document set in the Visual Studio 2010 project

Package, deploy, and activate the Feature that provisions the invoice document set Feature and add it to a document library. Test everything by creating a new instance of the document set to see the results. Figure 14-4 shows an invoice for work performed with payment terms of 2% 10 NET 30, meaning that if it is paid within 10 days of receipt, the payee can take an automatic 10% discount.

Corporate Office Renovation

Renovations to the Wingtip home office.

Invoice Number	2845
Invoice Amount	$34,912.00
Date Invoice Received	10/15/2010
Payment Terms	2% 10 NET 30
Paid Status	UNPAID

Save 2% ($698.24) if paid within 6 days!

View All Properties
Edit Properties

Type	Name	Modified	Modified By
	Corporate Office Renovation - WingtipTimesheet NEW	10/19/2010 7:40 AM	WINGTIP\administrator

FIGURE 14-4 An invoice document set

Document IDs

When users create or add a document to a document library, they can share it with their colleagues by sending them a Uniform Resource Locator (URL) that points to the document. This is a great way to reference the document at a later date. If the document is moved or renamed, though, it will now have a completely different URL, making the old one useless.

SPS2010 addresses this common challenge by introducing a new capability called *Document IDs*. When the Document ID Service feature is activated on a site collection, all documents and document sets within that site collection are automatically assigned a site collection scope unique ID—a string value that stays with the document regardless of what happens to it *within that site collection*. Any existing documents already in the site collection when the feature is activated will be assigned document IDs in a deferred batch process implemented by the Document ID Assignment Job timer job.

Regardless of whether a document is renamed or moved within a site collection, users will always be able to find it using the unique document ID. SPS2010 has a special application page, DocIdRedir.aspx, which accepts the document ID as a query string value and will redirect the requester to the document within the site collection. In addition, the Document ID Service feature adds a new *Find by Document ID* Web Part to the Web Part Search category that allows users to enter the unique ID to be routed to the document.

Document IDs are generated by a document ID provider. When the Document ID Service is activated, it adds a new site column to the document and document set content types to store the ID. When a user requests a document using a document ID, by default, SharePoint first tries to find the document using the out-of-the-box search capability. If it cannot find the document, it falls back on the document ID provider to give it the opportunity to find the document.

Creating Custom Document ID Providers

Developers can create custom document ID providers when they want to override either the default document ID string pattern or how documents are found. This is done by first creating a provider and then registering it with a site collection.

To create a new document ID provider, create a new class that inherits from the *Microsoft .Office.DocumentManagement.DocumentIdProvider* class. This class has four members that should be overridden:

- **GenerateDocumentId()**   This method is responsible for creating the unique document ID string. Overriding this allows the developer to change how new document IDs are generated. It is the responsibility of the developer to ensure that the generated ID is unique across the site collection. Also note that, if desired, this method could be used to generate an ID that is unique at a scope higher than site collection, such as Web applications or even the whole farm.

- **GetDocumentUrlsById()** This method accepts a document ID string and returns a list of URLs for the corresponding document. It can return multiple values because developers can copy documents programmatically from one location to another and specify that the document ID be retained on the copied instance.

- **GetSampleDocumentIdText()** This method generates a sample document ID string that is displayed in the Find by Document ID Web Part, giving users a hint as to what the ID looks like.

- **DoCustomSearchBeforeDefaultSearch** This Boolean property tells SharePoint if it should default to using the SharePoint search feature or the document ID provider to find the URL of the document ID string.

The following code listing demonstrates a custom document ID provider that uses the first part of the hosting Web Application, site collection, site, list, and list item's ID as the document ID string, as shown in Listing 14-12.

LISTING 14-12 A custom document ID provider

```
public class MoreUniqueDocumentIDProvider : DocumentIdProvider {
  private const string DOCID_FORMAT = "{0}-{1}-{2}-{3}-{4}";

  public override bool DoCustomSearchBeforeDefaultSearch {
    get { return false; }
  }

  public override string GenerateDocumentId(SPListItem listItem) {
    string listItemID = listItem.ID.ToString();
    string listID = listItem.ParentList.ID.ToString().Substring(0, 4);
    string siteID = listItem.Web.ID.ToString().Substring(0, 4);
    string siteCollectionID = listItem.Web.Site.ID.ToString().Substring(0, 4);
    string webAppID =
          listItem.Web.Site.WebApplication.Id.ToString().Substring(0, 4);
    return string.Format(DOCID_FORMAT, webAppID, siteCollectionID,
                      siteID, listID, listItemID);
  }

  public override string[] GetDocumentUrlsById(SPSite hostingSiteCollection,
                                        string documentId) {
    List<string> possibleURLs = new List<string>();
    string[] brokenDownDocID = documentId.Split("-".ToCharArray()[0]);

    // find the Web application
    SPWebService webService = hostingSiteCollection.WebApplication.WebService;
    foreach (SPWebApplication webAppplication in webService.WebApplications) {
      if (webAppplication.Id.ToString().StartsWith(brokenDownDocID[0])) {
        // find the SPSite (if multiple, won't matter as it will go to next one...)
        foreach (SPSite siteCollection in webAppplication.Sites) {
          if (siteCollection.ID.ToString().StartsWith(brokenDownDocID[1])) {
            // find the SPWeb (if multiple, won't matter as it will go to next one...)
```

```
                foreach (SPWeb site in siteCollection.AllWebs) {
                   if (site.ID.ToString().StartsWith(brokenDownDocID[2])) {
                      foreach (SPList list in site.Lists) {
                          if (list.ID.ToString().StartsWith(brokenDownDocID[3])) {
                          // find the item in the list
                          SPListItem targetItem = list.GetItemById(
                                                      Int32.Parse(brokenDownDocID[4]));

                          if (targetItem != null)
                              possibleURLs.Add(String.Format("{0}//{1}",
                                                      site.Url,
                                                      targetItem.Url));

                      }
                   }
                }
                site.Dispose();
             }
          }
          siteCollection.Dispose();
       }
     }
   }
   return possibleURLs.ToArray();
}

public override string GetSampleDocumentIdText(Microsoft.SharePoint.SPSite site) {
   return string.Format(DOCID_FORMAT,
      "55DA526F", "FD9D4836", "FD0910DC", "15B4AD8A", "ABDC1A45");
}
}
```

After creating the document ID provider, it needs to be registered with a site collection. This can be done using the Feature receiver of a site collection scoped feature. Use the *Microsoft .Office.DocumentManagement.DocumentId* class to set the provider for a specified site collection, as shown in Listing 14-13.

LISTING 14-13 Registering custom document ID providers

```
public override void FeatureActivated(SPFeatureReceiverProperties properties) {
   SPSite siteCollection = properties.Feature.Parent as SPSite;
   MoreUniqueDocumentIDProvider docIDProvider = new MoreUniqueDocumentIDProvider();
   DocumentId.SetProvider(siteCollection, docIDProvider);
}

public override void FeatureDeactivating(SPFeatureReceiverProperties properties) {
   SPSite siteCollection = properties.Feature.Parent as SPSite;
   hMicrosoft.Office.DocumentManagement.DocumentId.SerDefaultProvider();
}
```

Records Management

In the 2007 release, SharePoint located all records management capabilities and features within the Records Center site template. In SPS2010, Microsoft has changed their approach to records management by converting many of the records management–specific capabilities into SharePoint features that can be activated on a site based upon any template. This provides additional flexibility to organizations in that they can still elect to have a single dedicated Records Center for the whole organization, or, by using these capabilities in other site templates, multiple smaller implementations throughout the organization. Some of the records management features include:

- Content Organizer

- Holds and eDiscovery

- In-Place Records Management

Declaring Records

The SharePoint feature In-Place Records Management enables users to declare records in a document library alongside other collaborative content. While it can be configured to allow for users to declare (and undeclare) records manually, this is something that should be undertaken as part of the business process. Document libraries can be configured to declare files as records automatically when they are added. Microsoft SharePoint Designer 2010 and Visual Studio 2010 provide actions and activities for use in SharePoint workflows to declare and undeclare an item as a record, as shown in Figure 14-5.

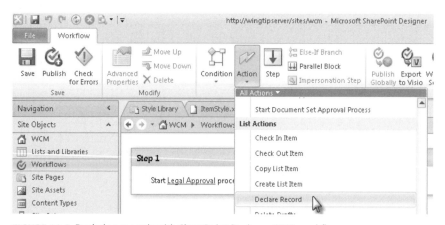

FIGURE 14-5 Declaring records with SharePoint Designer 2010 workflows

Under certain conditions, developers may need to declare a file as a record programmatically, such as within an event receiver when certain metadata properties are found. Declaring and undeclaring a record programmatically involves a single line of code, as shown in Listing 14-14.

LISTING 14-14 Declaring and undeclaring files as records programmatically

```
// using Microsoft.Office.RecordsManagement.RecordsRepository;

SPListItem targetDocument = GetDocument();

// Declare file as record
Records.DeclareItemAsRecord(targetDocument);

// Undeclare file as record
Records.UndeclareItemAsRecord(targetDocument);
```

Content Organizer

Similar to the Document ID Service, the new Content Organizer is designed to assist in the management of large libraries. Many times, users are not sure into which document library or folder they should put a document. In the case of a large, central Document Center or Records Center implementation, users know that they need to submit the document, but they have no idea where to put it within that implementation. The Content Organizer assists with this task by looking at new content, checking the document's metadata against some predefined and prioritized rules, and, if a matching rule is found, saving the content to the document library and folder specified in the rule. It can even manage large libraries by automatically creating new folders if the content in the target folder grows beyond a specified threshold.

Once the site-scoped Content Organizer feature is activated, two new links are added to the Site Administration section in the Site Settings page. One provides the settings for customizations, such as whether a Drop Off Library is required, a folder size should be managed automatically, or content can be routed to a subsite.

The other link provides access to the rules used by the Content Organizer. All rules are stored in the RoutingRules list and are based on the Rule content type, which is new in SPS2010. When a user creates or uploads a new document to the site, the Submit Document dialog displays a message that the content will be moved according to the defined rules, as shown in Figure 14-6.

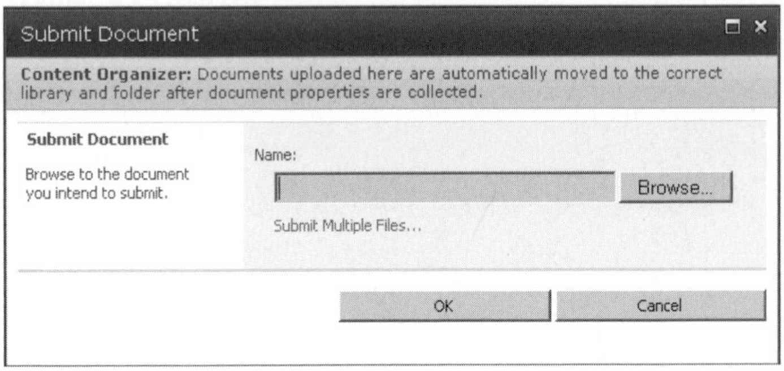

FIGURE 14-6 Uploading documents when the Content Organizer is activated

Web Content Management

Web Content Management (WCM) is the collection of capabilities and features used to facilitate a content-managed site on the SharePoint platform. WCM existed in SharePoint 2007 but was based on many of the capabilities in the now-discontinued Microsoft Content Management Server 2002.

With WCM in SPS2010, customers can create Publishing sites that are designed to have few content contributors but a large number of content consumers. This differs from a traditional SharePoint collaboration experience, in which there are many contributors interacting with many consumers.

A Publishing site is a SharePoint site that has the Publishing features activated. This is an important distinction because the Publishing features add a considerable amount of infra-structure to a site collection upon which they are activated.

SPS2010 WCM can be used in a various scenarios, such as the primary corporate Internet-facing .com site, a company intranet site, a partner extranet site, or even as a divisional portal. Each implementation can use different capabilities in SPS2010 WCM.

Page Rendering Process

The process of rendering requested pages in Publishing sites differs from traditional collabo-ration sites in SharePoint. This is because the content pages within a Publishing site are not real pages. Instead, they are simply items in a SharePoint list: the Pages library. Each item in this list contains some important information:

- **Page Name**   The page's file name as it will be listed in the URL, such as homepage.aspx
- **Page Layout**   The name of the page layout, an .aspx file, that defines how the content on the page should be rendered

- **Scheduling Details**   A collection of fields that specifies when the page should be published or expired, once it has been approved for publication

- **Content Fields**   The collection of image, text, and rich text fields that contain the content on the page

A requested page is rendered using various components. The URL tells SharePoint where it will find the page, specifically which site collection, site, library, and list item. It uses the file name requested to find the specific file in the Pages library. In turn, this list item tells SharePoint which page rendering, a special *.aspx page called a "page layout," to use in rendering the page. ASP.NET loads the page layout, which contains master page content placeholders and a reference to the site's master page. These two files are merged.

Dynamic content areas in the page—those areas where content owners can manage the content—are implemented using two types of controls: field controls and Web Part Zones. The contents of field controls are stored with the page item itself in the Pages list and are mapped to one of the content fields defined on the page. Web Part Zones can contain Web Parts, the contents of which are stored separately inside the content database. The page rendering process gets the Web Parts and their data for a specific zone in the requested page from the ASP.NET Personalization store, which has been incorporated into the site collection's content database.

The distinction of where content is stored (either in the page item using field controls or in the ASP.NET Personalization store using Web Parts) is important because it affects the versioning of a page. When a page is modified, by default the list item is versioned. This versions the content referenced by field controls, but not Web Parts because the data in the Web Part is not saved with the page, as shown in Figure 14-7.

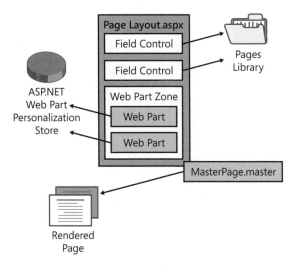

FIGURE 14-7 SharePoint Server 2010 Web content management page rendering

Creating New Page Types

When creating new pages in SPS2010 content, authors can pick from various types of pages and different rendering options. Each of the page types are implemented using content types that are derived from the Page content type. The Page content type contains the minimum required information for the page, such as the file name, page layout to use, a thumbnail image of the page to display in content rollup scenarios, content owner contact details, and the scheduling information, as shown in Figure 14-8.

FIGURE 14-8 Page types and rendering options

Once the new content type for the page type has been created, a site designer or developer can create one or more rendering options for the content authors to choose from. This is done by creating a page layout, associating it with the new page type's content type, and saving it to the Master Page Gallery. Designers and developers add field controls and Web Part Zones to the page layout to implement the rendering of the page.

Site designers and developers can use SharePoint Designer 2010 to create new page layouts using a what-you-see-is-what-you-get (WYSIWYG) rich experience and to associate the page layout with a specific page type in a wizard-like fashion.

Developers can also use Visual Studio 2010 to create page types and page layouts using features and solution packages (*.wsp) allowing for more code reuse and testing in moving the solution between environments (that is, development, testing, staging, and production). The SharePoint Developer Tools do not include specific project item templates for doing this, but it can be achieved using the content type and module item templates.

First, create a new content type using the Content Type project item that inherits from the Page content type. Create any necessary site columns that will be used in the content type, as well as the content type itself, as shown in Listing 14-15.

LISTING 14-15 Creating a page type (content type) declaratively

```xml
<?xml version="1.0" encoding="utf-8"?>
<Elements xmlns="http://schemas.microsoft.com/sharepoint/">

  <!-- new site column based off the "single line of text" field type -->
  <Field SourceID="http://schemas.microsoft.com/sharepoint/v3"
         ID="{0D499375-D734-43DB-A2EE-343B490B9CB0}"
         Name="PRByLine" DisplayName="Press Release ByLine" Group="Wingtip"
         Type="Text" Required="FALSE" Sealed="FALSE" Hidden="FALSE" />

  <!-- new site column based off the "publishing html" field type -->
  <Field SourceID="http://schemas.microsoft.com/sharepoint/v3"
         ID="{0C50E0BF-A35C-4A38-B784-AFA60BBADC00}"
         Name="PRBody" DisplayName="Press Release Body" Group="Wingtip"
         Type="HTML" Required="FALSE" Sealed="FALSE" Hidden="FALSE" />

  <!-- Parent ContentType: Page
    (0x010100C568DB52D9D0A14D9B2FDCC96666E9F2007948130EC3DB064584E219954237AF39)
  -->
  <ContentType ID="0x010100C568DB52D9D0A14D9B2FDCC96666E9F2007948130EC3DB064
                   584E219954237AF39008d9a0288b03e457abc84303bcdaa9cd7"
               Name="Press Release" Description="Wingtip Press Release"
               Group="Wingtip" Inherits="TRUE" Version="0">
    <FieldRefs>
      <FieldRef ID="{0D499375-D734-43DB-A2EE-343B490B9CB0}" Name="PRByLine" />
      <FieldRef ID="{0C50E0BF-A35C-4A38-B784-AFA60BBADC00}" Name="PRBody" />
    </FieldRefs>
  </ContentType>
</Elements>
```

To add the page layout, add a Module project item to the project. Remove the default sample .txt file and add a new file named PressRelease.aspx. Add the following markup to the new file, creating a basic rendering for the press release content type, as shown in Listing 14-16.

LISTING 14-16 Creating a press release page layout

```aspx
<%@ Page language="C#"
    Inherits="Microsoft.SharePoint.Publishing.PublishingLayoutPage,
             Microsoft.SharePoint.Publishing, [full assembly name]" %>

<%@ Register Assembly="Microsoft.SharePoint, [full assembly name]"
            Namespace="Microsoft.SharePoint.WebControls"
            TagPrefix="SharePointWebControls" %>

<%@ Register Assembly="Microsoft.SharePoint.Publishing, [full assembly name]"
            Namespace="Microsoft.SharePoint.Publishing.WebControls"
            TagPrefix="PublishingWebControls" %>
```

```
<asp:Content runat="server" contentplaceholderid="PlaceHolderPageTitle">
  <SharePointWebControls:FieldValue id="PageTitle"
                                    FieldName="Title"
                                    runat="server"/>
</asp:Content>


<asp:Content runat="server" contentplaceholderid="PlaceHolderPageTitleInTitleArea">
  <SharePointWebControls:TextField ID="TitleField"
                                   FieldName="Title"
                                   runat="server" />
</asp:Content>

<asp:Content runat="server" contentplaceholderid="PlaceHolderMain">
  <SharePointWebControls:TextField ID=" PRByLineField"
                                   FieldName="PRByLine"
                                   runat="server"/>
  <br />
  <PublishingWebControls:RichHtmlField ID="RichHtmlField1"
                                       FieldName="PRBody"
                                       runat="server"/>
</asp:Content>
```

Adding this file to the project item will update the feature's elements.xml file automatically to reference the *.aspx page. The target of where the file will be provisioned needs to be updated, and a few properties need to be set using the *<File URL="" />* attribute. In addition, the module needs to be configured to provision the file as content in the library by setting the *<File Type="" />* attribute to *GhostableInLibrary*. The property references are used to specify the values of certain metadata fields in the Master Page Gallery, as shown in Listing 14-17.

LISTING 14-17 Provisioning the page layout

```
<Elements xmlns="http://schemas.microsoft.com/sharepoint/">

  <Module Name="PressReleaseLayout" RootWebOnly="TRUE"
          Path="PressReleaseLayout" Url="_catalogs/masterpage" >

    <File Url="PressRelease.aspx" Type="GhostableInLibrary">

      <Property
        Name="PublishingAssociatedContentType"
        Value=";#Press Release;#0x010100C568DB52D9D0A14D9B2FDCC96666E9F2007948130
                EC3DB064584E219954237AF39008d9a0288b03e457abc84303bcdaa9cd7;#" />

      <Property
        Name="ContentType"
        Value="$Resources:cmscore,contenttype_pagelayout_name;" />
```

```
    <Property
      Name="Title"
      Value="Wingtip Press Release" />

  </File>
 </Module>
</Elements>
```

The listing includes three important properties:

- **ContentType**   This is the ID of the page layout content type. The value in the listing is what should be used for all page layouts because it is what SharePoint will be looking for.

- **PublishingAssocatedContentType**   This value tells SharePoint which content type this rendering is associated with. It contains two delimited values separated with ;#. The first value is the name of the content type. The second value is the content type's unique ID.

- **Title**   This is the name of the page layout.

Finally, build and deploy the project and activate the site collection scoped feature to create the site columns and content type, and provision the new page layout. Now, when creating a new page, the Press Release page type with a single rendering should appear in the list of available options, as shown in Figure 14-9.

FIGURE 14-9 Creating custom page types

Content Aggregation with the Content Query Web Part

A very common task in a managed content site is to aggregate content from various places in a site collection to a single page. In these scenarios, Publishing sites can take advantage of the Content Query Web Part (CQWP) that is included in SPS2010 WCM. This is the preferred method of aggregating content in a Publishing site because it has been highly optimized. It uses the same underlying components that are used to create and render the Publishing site navigation, including advanced caching techniques.

The CQWP is a very flexible Web Part that allows content authors to select content from across a site collection applying filtering and different grouping options. The CQWP takes the results from the query and converts them to Extensible Markup Language (XML). It then takes this XML result set and applies an Extensible Stylesheet Language for Transformations (XSLT) template that contains the presentation option selected by the content owner to generate the Hypertext Markup Language (HTML) used to render the results.

Creating Custom CQWP Styles

While Microsoft includes various rendering options for the CQWP, a common task is to create a custom rendering for specific implementations. This involves creating a custom XSLT template and registering it with the CQWP.

A challenge with creating CQWP rendering templates is that the result set could have heterogeneous types of content returned, each with different column names. When the XSLT needs to reference a column, it has no way of determining whether a particular result in the XML contains an element for that particular column. To address this challenge, Microsoft created slots in the CQWP style templates. A *slot* is simply a variable declared in the XSLT file. When the style is selected in the browser's Web Part tool pane, it displays all available slots. The page content author can then provide a semicolon-delimited list of fields to attempt to insert into the slot. If there is no content or field for a particular search result, it proceeds to the next one. This not only makes the XSLT much simpler, but it also makes it easier for the content author to control which columns take precedence.

You can create a custom presentation option by modifying the existing XSLT file used by the CQWP. Open the ItemStyle.xsl file in SharePoint Designer 2010 found in the Style Library's XSL Style Sheets subfolder. Find a template that is the closest match for the desired rendering, create a copy, and rename it. Listing 14-18 demonstrates taking the default Image on Left rendering and renaming it to InsideSharePoint2010.

LISTING 14-18 Provisioning the page layout

```xml
<xsl:template name="InsideSharePoint2010"
              match="Row[@Style='InsideSharePoint2010']"
              mode="itemstyle">

  <xsl:variable name="SafeLinkUrl">
    <xsl:call-template name="OuterTemplate.GetSafeLink">
        <xsl:with-param name="UrlColumnName" select="'LinkUrl'"/>
    </xsl:call-template>
  </xsl:variable>

  <div class="item">
    ...
  </div>

</xsl:template>
```

Next, create a new variable by referring to an attribute in the XML named *CustomSlot,* which will be passed to the template:

```
<div class="item">
  <xsl:value-of select="@CustomSlot" />
  ...
</div>
```

Save all changes, check in the XSLT file, and add a CQWP to a page. Open the tool window, and, in the Content Query – Presentation – Styles section, set Item Style to InsideSharePoint2010, and then apply the changes to see the new slot appear, as shown in Figure 14-10.

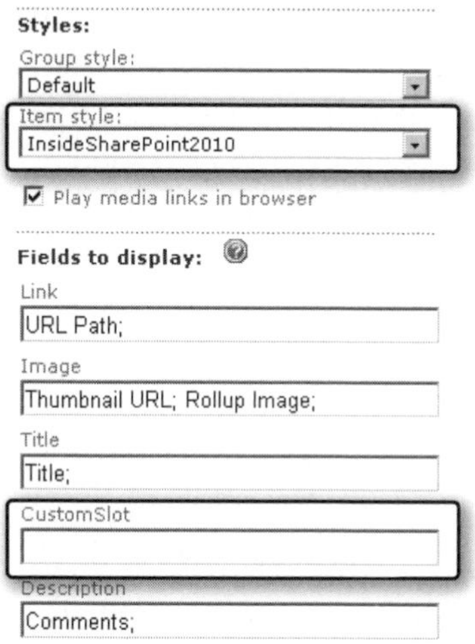

FIGURE 14-10 Creating custom CQWP slots

To inject content into this slot, add one or more column names from the result set separated by semicolons.

Managed Metadata

Users will find metadata throughout SharePoint quickly in any place where content can be created. In SharePoint, this has traditionally been tied to lists and document libraries, allowing users to add fields to items to provide a more detailed description of the content.

SPS2010 takes metadata much further, in that it provides additional capabilities to create reusable enterprise taxonomies and folksonomies. Taxonomies are hierarchical sets of terms, or tags, usually centrally defined. Folksonomies are similar to taxonomies in that they are a collection of terms, but they have no organization or hierarchical structure. Metadata is used in many more places throughout SharePoint, such as refining search results, filtering and navigating content within SharePoint lists and document libraries using the new Metadata Navigation Settings list, and enabling users to tag pages in social solutions.

Management and syndication of metadata is facilitated with the new Managed Metadata Service (MMS). The MMS allows users to create and manage taxonomies and folksonomies. SPS2010 supports both taxonomies and folksonomies. Taxonomies can be defined either as global or local. Global taxonomies are available to all site collections in Web applications associated with the MMS. Local taxonomies are defined and managed at the site collection level and are not shared across site collections.

Administrators serving the role as librarians, information architects, or records managers use the Term Store Management Tool to manage taxonomies and folksonomies. Start the Term Store Management Tool by selecting the MMS instance in Central Administration on the Manage Service Applications page and clicking the Manage button on the Ribbon. Each MMS implementation has a single term store that contains one or more groups of term sets. Groups are used very much like site column or content type groups, in that they make it easier to find relevant term sets.

Term Sets

Term sets are hierarchical collections of terms. Each term set can be configured to have an open or closed submission policy. An open submission policy allows anyone to insert terms into the term set, while a closed submission policy is the exact opposite—only a defined group can insert terms into the term set.

Each term in the term set has various characteristics:

- **Default Label**   The label used for the term set when it is selected and displayed in the user interface.

- **Description**   A brief description of what the term is used for.

- **Available for Tagging**   A flag indicating if the term can be used to tag content. Some terms are used for grouping child terms and should not be used with tagging solutions. For example, in a term set used to define age groups, the various age groups may be given names such as Toddler, Adolescent, Teen, Young Adult, Adult, and Elderly. These should not be used in tagging, but they can be used to find the appropriate age group tag.

- **Language**   Each term can be translated to multiple languages (depending on the language packs installed in the SharePoint farm). Users tagging content with the tag named *mountain bicycle* in English would see the tag as *bicicleta de montaña* in Spanish, assuming that the Spanish language pack was installed on the server and their browser was set to a local of es-es.

- **Synonyms** Some terms may be different depending on the users and the context. Users can tag content using the default label or any listed synonym and have the same term from the term set associated with the content. For instance, the term *New York City* may have synonyms JFK, LGA, and EWR for the three airports in and around New York.

The MMS also manages the process of renaming terms and updating the content tagged with those terms. When a term is updated, the Taxonomy Update Scheduler timer job looks at all changes and updates the content with any changes applied to the terms. By default, this process runs once an hour.

Creating Term Sets Programmatically

Creating terms using the browser is very straightforward using the Term Store Management Tool. In addition, administrators can import existing taxonomies using this tool. The import process requires a *.csv file formatted a specific way. For details on this format, see the following page on Microsoft TechNet at *http://technet.microsoft.com/en-us/library/ee424396.aspx*.

The out-of-the-box taxonomy import process is somewhat limiting, in that it does not provide a way to include multiple language translations for a tag or synonym. It also will not merge terms into an existing taxonomy. SPS2010 includes a robust application programming interface (API) that developers can use to create and manage taxonomies. The API is found in the *Microsoft.SharePoint.Taxonomy.dll* assembly. The first step in working with the MMS is to create a *TaxonomySession* object. This object's constructor accepts an instance of a site collection called *SPSite*. This will serve as the entry point to the available term stores (MMS instances). The next step is to get a reference to a term store using the *TaxonomySession.TermStores* collection. This collection contains references to all the MMS instances with which the current site collection's hosting Web application is associated. Each term store has a collection of groups accessible in the *TermStore.Groups* collection. Finally, each group has a collection of term sets called *Group.TermSets*. Each term set contains a collection of terms called *TermSet.Terms*.

Creating a new term set programmatically is an option available to developers who need a customized import process, such as merging terms into an existing term set, importing from another system, or adding translations or synonyms. Microsoft has made it very easy to create new groups and term sets within an MMS instance. Listing 14-19 demonstrates getting a reference to an existing term store and creating a new group and term set.

LISTING 14-19 Working with the MMS programmatically

```
using (SPSite siteCollection = new SPSite("http://intranet.wingtip.com")) {

    // get reference to the taxonomy term store
    TaxonomySession taxonomySession = new TaxonomySession(siteCollection);

    // get reference to first term store
    TermStore termStore = taxonomySession.TermStores["Wingtip Corporate Metadata"];
    string termGroupName = "Locations";
    Group termGroup =
        termStore.Groups.Where(x => x.Name == termGroupName).Count() > 0 ?
                                         termStore.Groups[termGroupName] :
                                         termStore.CreateGroup(termGroupName);

    string termSetName = "United States Geography";
    TermSet termSet =
        termGroup.TermSets.Where(x => x.Name == termSetName).Count() > 0 ?
                                         termGroup.TermSets[termSetName] :
                                         termGroup.CreateTermSet(termSetName);
    termStore.CommitAll();
}
```

Creating new terms and labels is just as straightforward:

```
Term newTerm = termSet.CreateTerm("term name", 1033);
newTerm.CreateLabel("term synonym", 1033, false);
Term newTerm2 = newTerm.CreateTerm("term 2 name", 1033);
```

Similar to updating SharePoint sites or list items, all changes must be committed back to SharePoint using the *TermStore.CommitAll()* method.

Creating Managed Metadata Columns

Metadata can be used in many ways throughout SPS2010. One way is with a new field type that can create columns in lists, libraries, and content types called Managed Metadata. New columns based on Managed Metadata require a few characteristics unique to the field type to be set at creation time:

- **Term Set**   The term set that the field is associated with that users will use to select terms. This can be in any available term store; that is, a global term store (aka an MMS instance) with which the hosting Web application is associated or a local term set managed at the site collection level.

- **Display Format**   Specifies if just the term should be displayed (that is, Mountain Bicycle) or if the entire lineage to the term should be displayed (that is, Products\Toys\ Bicycles\Mountain Bicycle).

- **Allow Fill-in**   If the term set is open, this will allow users to insert their own terms into the hierarchy. If the term set is closed, this option is disabled.

Setting these values through the browser interface is straightforward using the new column wizard-like interface. When creating columns through code or declaratively, developers need to specify the MMS instance as well, something that was not required when creating it through the browser because it could be determined automatically based on the term set selected.

To create a new Managed Metadata column programmatically, first get a reference to the four necessary taxonomy objects, as shown in Listing 14-20.

LISTING 14-20 Connecting to the MMS instance and term set

```
using (SPSite siteCollection = new SPSite("http://intranet.wingtip.com")){
  TaxonomySession taxonomySession = new TaxonomySession(siteCollection);
  TermStore termStore = taxonomySession.TermStores[0];
  Group termGroup = termStore.Groups["Locations"];
  TermSet termSet = termGroup.TermSets["United States Geography"];
}
```

Next, create the column using the field type *TaxonomyFieldType* and set the MMS instance (indicated by the *TaxonomyField.SspId* property) and the term set ID, as shown in Listing 14-21.

LISTING 14-21 Creating Managed Metadata columns programmatically

```
TaxonomyField taxonomyField =
  list.Fields.CreateNewField("TaxonomyFieldType", "Location Tag") as TaxonomyField;

taxonomyField.SspId = termStore.Id;
taxonomyField.TermSetId = termSet.Id;
taxonomyField.AllowMultipleValues = true;

list.Fields.Add(taxonomyField);
list.Update();
```

Finding Terms and Writing to Metadata Columns

The most common things that developers will need to do when working with metadata in SPS2010 is finding terms in the term store and writing to Managed Metadata columns. Finding terms in a term set or MMS instance can be done using the *GetTerms()* method. This method is found on the *TaxonomySession, TermSet,* and *Term* objects. It has multiple overload options that provide different filtering criteria made up of different combinations of the following potential parameters:

- **TermLabel**   The string to find for the term. This string can be the default label or one of the synonyms.

- **LCID**   The culture ID of the label to look up.

- **DefaultLabelOnly**   Determines if SharePoint should perform the lookup against only the default labels, or if it should include synonyms.

- **StringMatchOption**   Determines if an exact match should be performed, or if the *TermLabel* parameter should be treated as the start string in the search.

- **ResultCollectionSize**   The maximum number of terms that should be returned in the search.

- **TrimUnavailable**   Determines if tags that have the *IsAvailableForTagging* property set to true should be returned in the results or excluded.

The *GetTerms()* method returns a collection of terms in a *TermCollection* object. Listing 14-22 looks for all terms that match a specific state.

LISTING 14-22 Finding terms in a term set

```
TaxonomySession taxonomySession = new TaxonomySession(SPContext.Current.Site);
TermStore termStore = taxonomySession.TermStores["Wingtip Corporate Metadata"];
Group termGroup = termStore.Groups["Locations"];
TermSet termSet = termGroup.TermSets["United States Geography"];
TermCollection terms = termSet.GetTerms("FL", true));
```

Once terms have been found and acquired, the next step is to write them to a Managed Metadata column. Writing to columns based on the *Managed Metadata* field type is a little different from writing to columns of other types. First, get a reference to the column in the list, and then call the *SetFieldValue()* method to update the value of a specific list item, as shown in Listing 14-23.

LISTING 14-23 Setting the value of a Managed Metadata column

```
List<Term> selectedTerms = new List<Term>();
selectedTerms.AddRange(terms.ToList());
TaxonomyField locationTags = listItem.Fields["Location Tag"] as TaxonomyField;
locationTags.SetFieldValue(listItem, selectedTerms);
listItem.Update();
```

Extending LINQ Entity Models to Support Managed Metadata Columns

The new support in SharePoint 2010 for LINQ-based queries provides developers a much more productive way to read and write data in SharePoint lists. In-depth coverage of the LINQ integration and support in SharePoint 2010 is featured in Chapter 9, "Accessing Data in Lists."

To use LINQ, developers must first create an entity model using the command-line tool SPMetal.exe. This tool creates the entity model based on the lists in the target site, but it includes only columns that are based on field types that are included with SharePoint Foundation 2010 (SPF2010). This means that Managed Metadata columns are not included in the LINQ entity models.

Microsoft does provide a way for developers to extend the generated model by augmenting it with columns that were excluded. This is done by creating a partial class that mirrors the signature of the generated object, except that it also implements the *ICustomMapping* interface. This interface defines three methods that SharePoint will use to map data to and from the database from the custom field and also do conflict resolution.

Consider a list named *Contact List With Automatic Tags,* which is created using the Contacts list template. After creating this list, a new *Location Tag* column, based on the Managed Metadata column, is created. After running *SPMetal.exe*, when working with objects in that list via the new entity model, notice that the Location Tag column is missing, as shown in Figure 14-11.

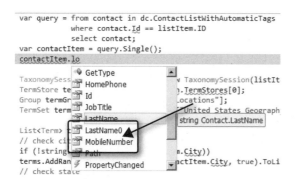

```
var query = from contact in dc.ContactListWithAutomaticTags
            where contact.Id == listItem.ID
            select contact;
var contactItem = query.Single();
contactItem.lo
```

FIGURE 14-11 LINQ entity model missing Managed Metadata columns

Now, create a new partial class that matches the prototype from the generated class exactly, and then add the interface *ICustomMapping*:

```
public partial class ContactListWithAutomaticTagsContact : Contact, ICustomMapping
```

Next, create the new column object in the class. This is what will be used by developers working with the model, as shown in Listing 14-24.

LISTING 14-24 Adding a Managed Metadata column to extended LINQ models

```
private TaxonomyField _taxonomyFields;
public TaxonomyField LocationTag {
  get { return _taxonomyFields; }
  set {
    if (value != _taxonomyFields) {
      this.OnPropertyChanging("LocationTag", _taxonomyFields);
      _taxonomyFields = value;
      this.OnPropertyChanged("LocationTag");
    }
  }
}
```

Now, implement the three required methods defined by the interface. These methods tell the LINQ to SharePoint provider how to get the data from the database and put it into the *LocationTag* property, do the opposite in taking the object and writing it back to the database, and perform any conflict resolution, as shown in Listing 14-25.

LISTING 14-25 *ICustomMapping* interface implementation

```
[CustomMapping(Columns = new string[] { "Location_x0020_Tag" })]
public void MapFrom(object listItem) {
  SPListItem item = listItem as SPListItem;
  this.LocationTag = item["Location_x0020_Tag"] as TaxonomyField;
}

public void MapTo(object listItem) {
  SPListItem item = listItem as SPListItem;
  item["Location_x0020_Tag"] = this.LocationTag;
}

public void Resolve(RefreshMode mode,
                    object originalListItem,
                    object databaseListItem) {

  SPListItem originalItem = originalListItem as SPListItem;
  SPListItem databaseItem = databaseListItem as SPListItem;
  TaxonomyField originalValue = originalItem["Location_x0020_Tag"] as TaxonomyField;
  TaxonomyField databaseValue = databaseItem["Location_x0020_Tag"] as TaxonomyField;

  switch (mode) {
    case RefreshMode.OverwriteCurrentValues:
      this.LocationTag = databaseValue;
      break;
    case RefreshMode.KeepCurrentValues:
      databaseItem["Location_x0020_Tag"] = this.LocationTag;
      break;
```

```
    case RefreshMode.KeepChanges:
      if (this.LocationTag != originalValue)
        databaseItem["Location_x0020_Tag"] = this.LocationTag;
      else if (this.LocationTag == originalValue && this.LocationTag != databaseValue)
        this.LocationTag = databaseValue;
      break;
  }
}
```

Finally, compile the project to see the new column appear in the entity model. Now it can be used like other properties in LINQ queries, as shown in Figure 14-12.

FIGURE 14-12 LINQ entity model with Managed Metadata columns

Because the customizations to the model are in a separate code file, facilitated by the fact that *SPMetal.exe* generates entity models using partial classes, the model can be refreshed in the future without affecting the customizations.

Enterprise Content Types

The term store is not the only capability that the MMS has to offer. Another feature is that it can syndicate content types from one site collection across multiple site collections so long as those site collections are hosted in Web applications linked to the MMS instance. This simplifies content type management because one site collection can be used to create and manage all enterprise content types for the organization and let the MMS syndicate them to other site collections that are used to manage content.

Set up the syndication process by first going to a single site collection and activating the Content Type Syndication Hub site collection scoped feature. Next, configure the MMS instance to use that site collection as the hub for all content types. This is set by going into Central Administration/Application Management/Manage Service Applications, selecting the MMS instance, and clicking the Properties button on the Ribbon. At the bottom of the dialog, enter the URL of the site collection and then click OK.

Once the syndication has been set up, the content type settings page in the hub site collection now includes the Manage Publishing for This Content Type link. This page enables users to publish, unpublish, or republish the content type to all site collections consuming the syndicated content types.

When a content type is syndicated, all its characteristics are syndicated. The syndication process involves creating a new content type in the subscribing site collections. When the content type is created in the subscribing site collections, it is marked as read-only. This blocks users from customizing the content type, ensuring that future publish and republish actions will succeed. However, users can customize the content type by creating a new content type that inherits from the syndicated one and use the local, non-syndicated one.

Conclusion

This chapter covered some of the new and improved capabilities in SPS2010 that can be used to implement ECM solutions. Microsoft's approach of bringing ECM capabilities to where users do most of their work should improve user participation. True to the SharePoint platform, developers can extend and customize many capabilities, such as document sets, the Document ID Service, and Managed Metadata.

Chapter 15
SharePoint Search

Of all the components available in Microsoft SharePoint Server 2010, Enterprise Search has the highest profile and the greatest impact on users. Searching has become a normal part of everyday life. Users utilize Web-based search engines like Bing and Google for both personal and professional needs. Concepts such as keyword searching, advanced searching, and search links are familiar to everyone. In fact, Enterprise Search has become a primary entry point into Microsoft SharePoint—the first place someone goes when trying to find information. If the search engine returns strong results, then users will be satisfied with SharePoint. On the other hand, poor search results can lead to negative opinions of SharePoint overall. Because Enterprise Search plays such a significant role in the success of SharePoint Server 2010, it is important to deploy, configure, and customize it correctly.

Contributing to the complexity of Enterprise Search is the fact that Microsoft includes five different search offerings under the SharePoint 2010 umbrella. The offerings include Microsoft SharePoint Foundation 2010 Search, Microsoft Search Server Express, Microsoft Search Server 2010, Microsoft SharePoint Server 2010, and FAST Search Server 2010 for SharePoint. Each of these offerings is intended for use in different situations, provides different levels of functionality, and has different licensing requirements.

SharePoint Foundation 2010 Search is the search engine that ships with SharePoint Foundation. This search engine works only on a single site collection at a time and cannot index external data sources. This engine is intended for team or departmental installations of SharePoint that do not require Enterprise Search.

Search Server Express is an Enterprise Search product that is freely downloadable. This engine can index external sources and supports search federation. It is intended for organizations that want an Enterprise Search capability but do not require significant scalability.

Search Server 2010 is an Enterprise Search engine that can scale across multiple servers and tens of millions of items. This product is the upgraded version of Search Server Express. It is intended for organizations that need a scalable search engine but are not using SharePoint Server 2010.

SharePoint Server 2010 includes all the capabilities of Search Server 2010, along with the integration of people search, taxonomy, and social networking. This is the Enterprise Search engine that is built into SharePoint Server, and it is the one that most readers will be using. Therefore, this chapter will focus on the overall search architecture and customizations that can be created by developers using SharePoint Server 2010.

FAST Search Server 2010 for SharePoint is the most powerful of all the search offerings. FAST provides scalability beyond any of the other offerings and supports additional customizations and configurations. While a discussion of FAST is beyond the scope of this book, many of the customizations presented in this chapter will also work with the FAST engine.

Introducing Search-Based Applications

Traditionally, search engines have been used to return results for a specific user request as a list ranked by relevance. The results might provide some basic information, such as the title of a document or the date of a Web page along with a description, but users typically have had to follow links to see if the item was of interest. More recently, however, this paradigm is being replaced with the concept of a *search-based application*. A search-based application is a custom application that is written around a search engine.

The value of a search-based application is that it presents search results in an appropriate form and allows the user to operate on the results directly. A good example of a search-based application is the Bing video search. Figure 15-1 shows the results of searching for the term "SharePoint." You can see that the search results are returned as videos that may be played directly from the page, thus making it significantly easier to locate items of interest.

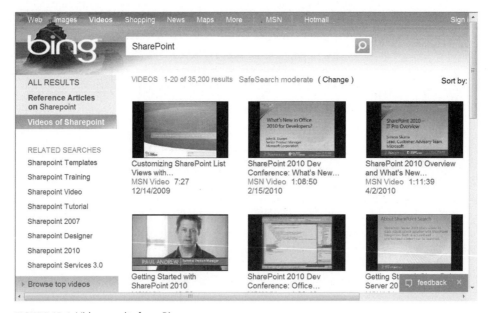

FIGURE 15-1 Video results from Bing

Although the default search results page in SharePoint still displays items in a simple list, you will find that the customization opportunities tend to support the creation of search-based applications. These customizations include the ability to influence the search results' sort and ranking, change the way search results appear on the page, and create completely custom solutions against the search object model.

The concept of search-based applications is important to keep in mind as you work through this chapter. Instead of simply returning items from a search, give consideration to how the results appear and what operations can be performed. Then think about how the customizations presented in this chapter come into play.

As a quick example of a search-based application in SharePoint, consider the management of tasks for users. Task lists can be created in any site within SharePoint, so it is often the case that someone is assigned tasks in multiple sites. In many cases, users might not even know they have been assigned a particular task. Setting alerts on all the lists is unmanageable because the notifications become a form of internal spam. Thus, users are sometimes left unable to effectively manage their tasks.

In the past, developers have often created "rollups" to solve this problem. Rollup solutions go out to all sites looking for tasks and then display them in a single master list to the user. The problem with this, however, is that it can be very CPU-intensive if done incorrectly. A search-based solution is a better idea.

Instead of a single master list of tasks, imagine that a user goes to a specialized Search Center that runs a query to return all the task items for the current user sorted by due date. In addition, the user can see the key information for each task, such as title, due date, and priority. The user could also operate on the task directly in the search results by changing its status or editing the description. This is a search-based solution that is truly useful to a user. Keep this idea in mind as you learn more about SharePoint Server search.

Understanding Search Architecture

The search architecture for Microsoft SharePoint Server 2010 is complex. It includes components for crawling and indexing content, administration, and search query execution. Figure 15-2 shows a block diagram of the search architecture.

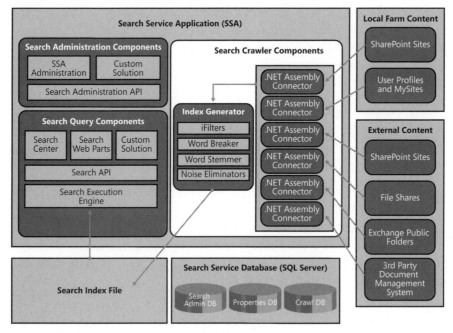

FIGURE 15-2 SharePoint Server 2010 search architecture

Understanding the Search Service Application

In the center of the search architecture is the Search Service Application (SSA). The SSA is one of the many shared services available in SharePoint Server. This means that you may create and share instances of the SSA across farms just like any other service application. From the Central Administration website, you may access the SSA by selecting Manage Service Applications. From the list of service applications, you may select the SSA, set its properties, designate administrators, and enter the administration pages. Figure 15-3 shows the SSA in the list of service applications.

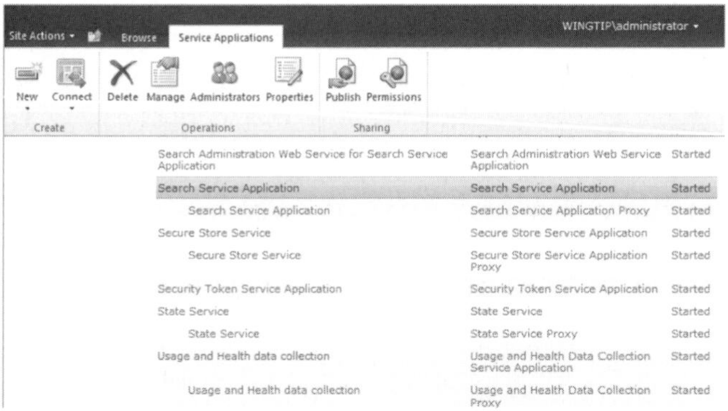

FIGURE 15-3 Managing the SSA

Within the SSA are three databases: the Search Service database, the Managed Properties database, and the Crawl database. The Search Service database maintains configuration data for the SSA. The Managed Properties database contains the definitions for Managed Properties that are defined and mapped to crawled properties. The Crawl database contains configuration information related to content sources to be crawled. The SSA also maintains the index file that is built during the crawl and provides support for Federated Search connectors. Each of these components supports search administration, which is accessed by clicking the Manage button for the SSA.

Understanding the Indexing Process

The indexing process is responsible for building the index file. The index file contains properties from content sources, along with access control information that ensures search results display only content for which the user has rights. The process of building the index file involves crawling the designated content sources.

A content source is a repository that you want to search. Content sources can be SharePoint sites, websites, external file systems, Exchange Server public folders, Business Connectivity Services (BCS) External Systems, or other custom repositories. The Index Engine gains access to these repositories through .NET Assembly Connectors and access to the contents of individual items through IFilters.

Chapter 13, "Business Connectivity Services," presented the fundamentals of .NET Assembly Connectors, which are used by BCS to connect with External Systems. The indexing process uses these same components to connect with content sources. In previous versions of SharePoint, Protocol Handlers were the primary means of connecting with content sources, but they were difficult to create in managed code. In SharePoint 2010, Protocol Handlers are still supported, but .NET Assembly Connectors should be created whenever a custom repository is used as a content source.

Just as in previous versions of SharePoint, IFilters are used to allow the indexing process to access the contents of an item. For example, IFilters allow the indexing process to access the body of Microsoft Office documents so that a full-text search can be performed. While SharePoint 2010 ships with IFilters for Office documents, you may need to install additional IFilters for other types, such as Portable Document Format (PDF) documents. Generally, IFilters are available from the appropriate manufacturer, such as Adobe, and require a simple installation on the server where the indexing process runs.

Understanding the Query Process

Once the index file is created, it may be used to support query execution. Query execution begins when a user navigates to the Search Center and enters a query. The query in the Search Center may take the form of a simple keyword or an advanced search with multiple values against multiple Managed Properties.

When the user issues a search, the query is sent to the search engine. Within the search engine, the query processor accepts the query and also retrieves any required information from the Managed Properties database. Information from the Managed Properties database is required any time a query is issued against a specific Managed Property, such as *Title*. The combination of the user query and Managed Property information is then sent to the query server, which executes the query and returns the results. The results are returned as Extensible Markup Language (XML) to the Search Center where they are formatted using Extensible Stylesheet Language for Transformations (XSLT).

Along with performing a query on its own index, SharePoint can send the query out to other federated search locations. Federated search locations are connections to other search services that independently run the query and return the results separately to the Search Center for display. Communication with federated locations is based on the Open Search protocol, so any search service that supports Open Search can be used as a federated location.

Introducing Search Web Parts

The primary way in which users interact with the search engine is through a set of search Web Parts that ship with SharePoint. These search Web Parts may be used independently, but they are most often used as part of an Enterprise Search site created through a site template. The Enterprise Search template contains Web Parts for issuing queries and returning results. Table 15-1 lists the Web Parts and their purposes.

TABLE 15-1 Search Web Parts

Web Part	Description
Advanced Search Box	Allows users to create detailed searches against Managed Properties
Federated Results	Displays results from a federated search location
People Refinement Panel	Presents facets that can be used to refine a people search
People Search Box	Allows users to search for people using a keyword
People Search Core Results	Displays the primary result set from a people search
Refinement Panel	Presents facets that can be used to refine a search
Related Queries	Presents queries related to the user's query
Search Action Links	Displays links for Really Simple Syndication (RSS), alerts, and Windows Explorer

Web Part	Description
Search Best Bets	Presents best-bets results
Search Box	Allows users to enter keyword query searches
Search Core Results	Displays the primary result set from a query
Search Paging	Allows a user to page through search results
Search Statistics	Presents statistics such as the time taken to execute the query
Search Summary	Provides a summary display of the executed query
Top Federated Results	Displays top results from a federated location

Each of the Web Parts listed in Table 15-1 is configurable in various ways that are useful when creating search solutions. Furthermore, you can inherit from many of the Web Parts to create your own custom versions. You'll learn more about customizing these Web Parts later in the chapter.

Introducing the Search Object Models

SharePoint Server 2010 contains two object models to support search. One object model is an administration application programming interface (API) that can be used to perform administrative operations on the SSA. The other is a search object model that can be used to create custom search solutions that execute keyword query and full-text query searches. Object models are covered in the section entitled "Working with Keyword Query Syntax" later in the chapter.

Creating Ranking Models

When users execute queries, they expect to have the most relevant items appear near the top when the results are displayed. The ranking engine is responsible for assigning a ranking score to each returned item based upon a number of factors defined in a *ranking model*. The ranking model contains the rules that will be applied to the search results and determine ranking. SharePoint Server 2010 ships with several ranking models that are applied when you search different contexts, such as documents or people. You can list all the ranking models available in your environment with the following Windows PowerShell command.

```
Get-SPEnterpriseSearchServiceApplication | Get-SPEnterpriseSearchRankingModel | Format-List
```

When you list the ranking models, you will notice that one of them is designated as the default model. This is the model that is used in SharePoint searches out of the box. You'll also notice that there are several models to support people search and social networking.

The parameters used by the ranking model can be either *query-independent* or *query-dependent*. Query-independent parameters are computed at crawl time because they are static and will not change regardless of the query that is run. Query-dependent parameters are computed when the search is executed because they are affected by the search that the user runs. This distinction is important because a ranking model will not be able to gain access to query-independent information if the query is formed in such a way that it fails to access the static information. This can happen when a user forms a query strictly against a Managed Property. In this case, the Managed Property database is accessed, and there is no need for a full search of the index. So for efficiency, the static data is skipped. However, this can give strange results if the ranking model is highly dependent on query-independent factors.

One of the main query-independent parameters that you can affect is the proximity of an item to an authoritative page. An *authoritative page* is a way of specifying which pages in SharePoint are the most important. Authoritative pages are designated through the search administration interface in Central Administration. When designating authoritative pages, you may specify a page as being either most authoritative, second-level authoritative, third-level authoritative, or non-authoritative. The ranking of an item within search results will be higher based on its click distance from an authoritative page, with different multipliers being used for the various levels. Non-authoritative pages will be pushed to the bottom of the search results.

In previous versions of SharePoint, authoritative pages were the primary way to influence the relevancy of items in search. SharePoint Server 2010, however, supports the concept of a custom ranking model. A custom ranking model allows you to specify query-independent and query-dependent factors that should be used when ranking search results. This gives you a powerful way to influence the display of results within your search-based applications.

Before proceeding to discuss the creation of custom ranking models, it is important to consider the difference between ranking results and sorting results. As discussed previously, ranking results should involve both query-independent and query-dependent factors that influence the order in which results are displayed. Sorting, on the other hand, is always completely static. For example, ranking documents by searching the body for keywords is dynamic and depends on the keyword. Sorting the same documents by creation date will not change no matter what keywords are used in the search. The point is that you should never use a custom ranking model when what you want is a fixed sort.

A custom ranking model is best used in situations where the default ranking model is not returning documents of interest close enough to the top and the introduction of an authoritative page does not solve the problem. This means that you will likely create few custom ranking models, but they can be very useful when necessary. Fixed sorts, on the other hand, can be accomplished using the query object model.

Creating a Custom Ranking Model

In SharePoint 2010, not all the internal ranking model capabilities are available to your custom ranking models, but there is enough power to have a significant impact on the search results. Custom ranking models are created as XML files that specify the query-independent and query-dependent factors to use when ranking search results. Listing 15-1 shows a sample custom ranking model that gives extra weight to the title of an item and Microsoft Word documents. Such a model might be used if an organization's most important documents are typically in Word format, and the title of the document contains key information.

LISTING 15-1 A sample custom ranking model

```xml
<?xml version='1.0'?>
<rankingModel
    name='NewRankingModel'
    id='11111111-65CD-4a1b-9A63-F7ECB4B6BB5E'
    description = 'Sample ranking model'
    xmlns='http://schemas.microsoft.com/office/2009/rankingModel'>
    <queryDependentFeatures>
        <queryDependentFeature
          name='Body' pid='1' weight='10.0000000000'
          lengthNormalization='2.8898552470'/>
        <queryDependentFeature
          name='Title' pid='2' weight='100.0000000000'
          lengthNormalization='0.9574077587'/>
        <queryDependentFeature
          name='Author' pid='3' weight='0.1000000000'
          lengthNormalization='1.0131509886'/>
        <queryDependentFeature
          name='AnchorText' pid='10' weight='0.1000000000'
          lengthNormalization='2.6713762088' />
        <queryDependentFeature
          name='DisplayName' pid='56' weight='0.1000000000'
          lengthNormalization='0.9713508040'/>
        <queryDependentFeature
          name='ExtractedTitle' pid='302' weight='0.1000000000'
          lengthNormalization='1.0095022768'/>
        <queryDependentFeature
          name='QueryLogClickedText' pid='100' weight='0.1000000000'
          lengthNormalization='1.6000001537'/>
    </queryDependentFeatures>
    <queryIndependentFeatures>
        <queryIndependentFeature
          name='DistanceFromAuthority' pid='96' default='5' weight='0.1000000000'>
            <transformInvRational  k='0.1359244473'/>
        </queryIndependentFeature>
        <queryIndependentFeature
          name='URLdepth' pid='303' default='3' weight='0.1000000000'>
            <transformLinear max='1000'/>
        </queryIndependentFeature>
```

```
      <queryIndependentFeature
        name='DocumentPopularity' pid='306' default='0' weight='0.1000000000'>
          <transformRational k='1.2170868558'/>
      </queryIndependentFeature>
      <queryIndependentFeature
        name='DocumentUnpopularity' pid='307' default='0' weight='0.1000000000'>
          <transformRational k='0.7333557072'/>
      </queryIndependentFeature>
      <categoryFeature name='FileType' pid='98' default='0'>
          <category name='Html' value='0' weight='0.1000000000'/>
          <category name='Doc' value='1' weight='100.0000000000'/>
          <category name='Ppt' value='2' weight='0.1000000000'/>
          <category name='Xls' value='3' weight='0.1000000000'/>
          <category name='Xml' value='4' weight='0.1000000000'/>
          <category name='Txt' value='5' weight='0.0000000000'/>
          <category name='ListItems' value='6' weight='0.1000000000'/>
          <category name='Message' value='7' weight='0.1000000000'/>
      </categoryFeature>
      <languageFeature name='Language' pid='5' default='1' weight='10.0000000000'/>
    </queryIndependentFeatures>
  </rankingModel>
```

Custom ranking models begin with the *rankingModel* element. The only required attribute for this element is the *id* attribute, which is a globally unique identifier (GUID) that identifies the model. The other attributes are optional and are used largely for readability. In addition, the namespace must be called *http://schemas.microsoft.com/office/2009/rankingModel*. The child elements of the *rankingModel* are a set of *queryDependentFeatures* and *query IndependentFeatures*, which specify the factors that will be used for dynamic and static ranking, respectively.

The *queryDependentFeature* element has *name, pid, weight*, and *lengthNormalization* attributes. The *queryIndependentFeature* element has *name, pid, default*, and *weight* attributes. The *name* attribute is optional and is used primarily for readability. The *pid* is the property identifier for the Managed Property that is being referenced. The *weight* is a relative attribute that determines the effect that the factor will have on the ranking. The *lengthNormalization* attribute is a number used to account for differences in the lengths of various properties. The *default* attribute is the value to be used when an actual value cannot be determined.

The *categoryFeature* and *languageFeature* elements are children of the *queryIndependent Feature*. The *categoryFeature* element allows you to specify a set of possible values for a Managed Property and give different weights to each one. The *languageFeature* element gives extra weight to an item if it is in the default language. Finally, the *transformRational, transformInvRational*, and *transformLinear* elements associate additional functions with the model that transform the weighting values.

Working with Managed Property Identifiers

Managed Property identifiers are critical to the creation of custom ranking models because both the *queryDependentFeatures* and the *queryIndependentFeatures* can use Managed Properties. When creating custom ranking models, you can choose which Managed Properties you want to include in the model, whether their effect is static or dynamic, and the weight of their impact. To do this, however, you must know the identifier for the Managed Property. You can use the following Windows PowerShell script to list all the Managed Properties and their identifiers.

```
Get-SPEnterpriseSearchServiceApplication | Get-SPEnterpriseSearchMetadataManagedProperty
```

SharePoint Server comes with many Managed Properties already defined, but when you are creating search-based applications, you will quite often need to create your own Managed Properties. Managed Properties are created through the search administration interface in the Central Administration site. Essentially, Managed Properties are properties that refer to one or more crawled properties. Managed Properties allow you to group together several different crawled properties that might refer to the same thing and represent them as a single Managed Property. For example, the Managed Property *Title* refers to the crawled properties *Mail:5*, *People:PreferredName*, *Basic:displaytitle*, and *ows_Title*. This grouping not only makes it easier to work with several crawled properties at once, it also provides a more readable name.

Determining Weight Values

When creating a custom ranking model, you must set the weights that will be used for each one of the Managed Properties. The weights you apply can be any value, and they are relative to all the other weights in the ranking model. You can also set default values for *queryIndependentFeatures* if an item does not have the specified Managed Property.

All this means that you can disregard certain properties by setting them to zero or greatly enhance them with a large number relative to the other weighting values. It is important to remember, however, that using very large or very small numbers can overwhelm your model and essentially turn it into a sorting algorithm instead of a ranking model.

Understanding Length Normalization

Of all the pieces in the custom ranking model, perhaps none is as mysterious as the *length-Normalization* attribute. Length normalization is the process of accounting for the length of a string when keywords are found in it. This is necessary because longer strings have a better chance of containing a keyword, but that does not necessarily mean they are more relevant.

While the *lengthNormalization* attribute is required, it can be difficult to know what value to use. As a general guide, examine Listing 15-1 earlier in this chapter and you will see that long strings like *Body* have a number greater than 1, while shorter strings like *Title* have a value less than 1.

Introducing Transforms

Transforms apply functions to *queryIndependentFeatures*. These functions use an additional factor as an input to the transformation function. A complete description of the effects of each transformation is beyond the scope of this chapter. Generally, these transforms will not be necessary for simple ranking models.

Using a Custom Ranking Model

Once you have created a custom ranking model, you can use it with SharePoint Server. The process of using the custom ranking model involves several steps. First, you must enable any associated Managed Properties for use with the model. Second, you must install the ranking model. Third, you must reference the new model in either a custom solution or existing Web Part. Creating custom solutions is covered later in the chapter. For now, this section will focus on using the custom ranking model with existing search Web Parts.

When you create a custom ranking model, you will quite often be creating new Managed Properties for use in the weighting strategy. Previously, you saw how to get the identifier for a Managed Property so that it could be referenced in the ranking model. However, Managed Properties are not enabled for use as query-independent parameters by default. You must allow it explicitly. So if your model uses a Managed Property as a query-independent feature, you must set the *EnabledForQueryIndependentRank* property to *True*. You can set the property using the following Windows PowerShell code, substituting the name of the specific Managed Property for *PropertyName* in this example.

```
$p = Get-SPEnterpriseSearchServiceApplication |
    Get-SPEnterpriseSearchMetadataManagedProperty -Identity {PropertyName}

$p.EnabledForQueryIndependentRank = $true

$p.Update
```

The next step is to install the custom ranking model. Installing the custom ranking model is accomplished using the Windows PowerShell cmdlet *New-SPEnterpriseSearchRankingModel*. This cmdlet takes as a parameter the complete ranking model as a *string*. Therefore, you have to crunch your ranking model into a single piece of text by removing all the line breaks and white space so it can be passed as a parameter. Once this is done, the following Windows PowerShell script will install the new ranking model.

```
Get-SPEnterpriseSearchServiceApplication |
  New-SPEnterpriseSearchRankingModel -RankingModelXML {Crunched Ranking Model}
```

The final step in the process is to reference the custom ranking model in the Search Core Results Web Part. The Search Core Results Web Part displays the primary result set from a search and uses the default ranking model out of the box. However, it has a *DefaultRankingModelID* property that may be changed to reference the *Id* of any custom ranking model, such as the required *id* attribute shown earlier in Listing 15-1.

To change the *DefaultRankingModelID* property, you must navigate to a search results page and place that page in edit mode. Once in edit mode, the Search Core Results Web Part may be exported as an XML file. After exporting the Web Part, you can open it in an editor and search for the *DefaultRankingModelID* property, which will be empty. When the property is empty, the default ranking model is used. Simply change this value by hand and save it. You may then return to the search page and import the new file as an instance of the Search Core Results Web Part. Deleting the original Web Part from the page completes the process. Now when you search, the new ranking model will be used. The following code shows how the property appears in XML after editing.

```
<property name="DefaultRankingModelID" type="string">
  0D4CB5B6-2FA3-4D7F-AF79-EF0DE64F242C
</property>
```

Customizing Search Centers

The Enterprise Search Center site template is available from the Create dialog for creating new Search Centers. Search Centers are publishing sites that have a Pages library, a Site Pages library, and a Site Assets library. While Search Centers support one-click page creation, most of the time you will add content to the site using one of the four page layouts associated with the Pages library and described in Table 15-2.

TABLE 15-2 Search Center Page Layouts

Page Layout	Description
Search Box	This is the page layout that is used as an initial search page. It contains the Search Box Web Part.
Search Results	This is the page used to show search results and initiate subsequent searches. This page contains several Web Parts for displaying and manipulating search results.
Advanced Search	This is the page layout that is used to display the Advanced Search Web Part, which allows for selecting multiple search parameters.
People Search Results	This is the page layout used to show search results for the People tab in the Search Center. This page contains several Web Parts for displaying and manipulating search results.

The Search Center uses a significantly different interface than any of the other site templates in SharePoint. This is because the Search Center is based on an interface that uses a single tab for each search scope. The page layouts are all designed to support the tab interface, and the site template uses the *minimal.master* master page to remove the Quick Launch and the Ribbon. Figure 15-4 shows a typical Search Center.

FIGURE 15-4 A Search Center

Adding New Tabs

By default, the Search Center has an All Sites tab and a People tab, which correspond to search scopes. What's interesting—but also potentially confusing—about the Search Center template is that it actually has two sets of tabs. One set is used to render initial tabs before a search is executed, and the other is used to render tabs that appear in the search results. However, both sets of tabs are given the same name to make it appear as though only a single set of tabs exists. The Tabs In Search Pages list contains the first set of tabs, and the Tabs In Search Results list contains the second set of tabs. When you create search-based applications, you will quite often deploy them as new tabs within the Search Center based on custom search scopes. This means that adding a new tab is a multistep process involving the creating of a search scope, page layouts, and tabs.

Creating a search scope is accomplished through the Search Service Application. Within the SSA, you will find a Scopes link, where you may define a new search scope based on Web address, property, or content source. Once defined in the SSA, you can make the scope available to a site collection. This process starts in the Site Collection by browsing to Site Settings, Site Collection Administration, and Search Settings, and then enabling custom scopes, which requires you to enter the Uniform Resource Locator (URL) of the new Search Center. After that, you can go to Site Settings, Site Collection Administration, and Search Scopes, and then decide whether to use the new scope in the Scopes drop-down list.

Once the scope is defined and available, you may go to the Search Center to define search and search results pages. The best way to add the required pages is simply to select View All Site Content from the Site Actions menu in the Search Center. From the All Site Content page, click the Pages library link. Within the Pages library, click the Documents tab and finally the New Document button on the Ribbon, which will present the Create page.

On the Create page, you will see the four different page layouts available for the Search Center. For a typical search-based application, you will create a Search Box page and a Search Results page. The exact names of the pages don't matter as long as you keep track of them. Typically, however, these pages are named *Scope*Search.aspx and *Scope*Results.aspx, with "Scope" replaced in the page name with the actual name of the scope.

Once the pages are created, you can create the associated tabs. Again, the best way to do this is on the All Site Content page. In the Tabs In Search list, create a new tab using the same name as the scope and associate the search page. In the Tabs In Search Results list, create a new tab using the same name as the scope and associate the results page. At this point, you should be able to see the new tab in the Search Center. Creating the tabs and pages is not enough, however, to duplicate the functionality of the other tabs in the Search Center. To have the new scope fully implemented, changes must be made to several Web Parts.

First, a change must be made to the Search box Web Part on both the search and results page. This can be done by simply putting the appropriate page in edit mode and selecting to edit the Search Box Web Part. Under the Miscellaneous category, locate the Target Search Results Page URL and change it to be the name of the results page created earlier. In addition, a change must be made to the Search Core Results Web Part on the results page. In this Web Part, under the Location Properties category, you must enter the name of the scope in the *Scope* property. After these changes are complete, publish both the search and results pages. The new scope is now available to the Search Center.

Customizing Search Core Results

The Search Core Results Web Part is central to all search-based applications. You have already seen that altering the *DefaultRankingModelID* or the *Scope* property can have a significant impact on the displayed search results. You can also customize which columns to display in the search results and the format of the display. Finally, you can create a custom Web Part that inherits directly from the Search Core Results Web Part to gain access to the query pipeline.

Working with Displayed Results

The columns that appear in the search results are specified by the *Fetched Properties* property, located under the Display Properties category of the Web Part. This property contains an XML chunk that defines which properties should appear in the search results. Listing 15-2 shows the default XML contained in the *Fetched Properties* property.

LISTING 15-2 The *Fetched Properties* property

```
<root xmlns:xsi="http://www.w3.org/2001/XMLSchema-instance">
  <Columns>
    <Column Name="WorkId"/>
    <Column Name="Rank"/>
    <Column Name="Title"/>
    <Column Name="Author"/>
    <Column Name="Size"/>
    <Column Name="Path"/>
    <Column Name="Description"/>
    <Column Name="Write"/>
    <Column Name="SiteName"/>
    <Column Name="CollapsingStatus"/>
    <Column Name="HitHighlightedSummary"/>
    <Column Name="HitHighlightedProperties"/>
    <Column Name="ContentClass"/>
    <Column Name="IsDocument"/>
    <Column Name="PictureThumbnailURL"/>
    <Column Name="ServerRedirectedURL"/>
  </Columns>
</root>
```

You can customize the *Fetched Properties* XML to return different columns. Simply add or remove *Column* elements from the XML. Note that the column *Name* must refer to an existing Managed Property. In addition, adding the column to the *Fetched Properties* XML will not actually cause the column to be displayed in the search results. For this to happen, you must also modify the XSLT used to render the search results.

Search results are returned to the Search Core Results Web Part as XML. This XML is transformed into the display seen in the Search Center by applying the XSLT contained under the Display Properties of the Search Core Results Web Part properties. While you have complete access to this XSLT and can customize it significantly, SharePoint provides no graphical environment for understanding how changes to the XSLT will affect the display of the search results. Fortunately, we can use a combination of SharePoint Designer (SPD) and Microsoft Visual Studio to create and analyze the XSLT.

To begin modifying the XSLT, you must first get a copy of the raw XML sent to the Search Core Results Web Part prior to transformation. The simplest way to do this is to replace the XSLT with a *null* transformation. Doing so will cause the search results to appear as XML. Be sure that you have created all required Metadata Properties and updated the *Fetched Columns* before generating the raw XML. Listing 15-3 shows the *null*-transformation XSLT to use.

LISTING 15-3 Generating raw XML in the search results

```
<?xml version="1.0" encoding="utf-8"?>
<xsl:stylesheet xmlns:xsl="http://www.w3.org/1999/XSL/Transform" version="1.0">
  <xsl:output method="xml" version="1.0" encoding="utf-8" indent="yes"/>
  <xsl:template match="/">
    <xmp>
      <xsl:copy-of select="*"/>
    </xmp>
  </xsl:template>
</xsl:stylesheet>
```

After you have a copy of the raw XML generated by the search, you can use it as a basis for creating the desired XSLT. The simplest way to create XSLT is by using SPD. This is because the Data View Web Part accepts an XML file as a data source and will generate XSLT as you use SPD to customize the display.

Start by opening SPD to any site. You will not be keeping any of the pages you create for this exercise, so the exact location of the pages is irrelevant. Once inside SPD, click on the Data Sources object, and then select to add a new XML File Connection from the New group on the Ribbon. Add the raw XML file that you generated from the search results.

Next, add a Web Part page to the site and place it in edit mode. From the edit menu, insert a Data View Web Part based on the raw XML file. Once the Data View Web Part is on the page, you can use the Add/Remove Columns dialog to decide what columns to display. In addition, you can go directly to the source view to make edits to the generated XSLT, which is contained between the *XSL* tags in the document. Once you have the search results appearing as you want them, simply copy the XSLT out of SPD and into the Search Core Results Web Part.

Working with the Query Pipeline

When users enter a search query, it is passed to the Search Core Results Web Part for execution. Within the Search Core Results Web Part, the *QueryManager* coordinates the execution of the query and returns the results as XML. This XML is then transformed using the provided XSLT, and the Search Core Results Web Part renders the search results in the Search Center.

In previous versions of SharePoint, the search Web Parts were sealed so that developers had no access to *QueryManager*. In SharePoint Server 2010, however, developers can inherit from search Web Parts and thus gain access to the query pipeline. This means that developers can manipulate the query before it is executed and manipulate the results after the query is run.

To gain access to the query pipeline, developers inherit from the Search Core Results Web Part. In Visual Studio 2010, a reference must be set to the *Microsoft.Office.Server.Search.dll* assembly. The Search Core Results Web Part is contained within the Microsoft.*Office.Server. Search.WebControls* namespace, and the *QueryManager* object is contained within the *Microsoft.Office.Server.Search.Query* namespace.

Access to the *QueryManager* object is obtained by overriding the *GetXPathNavigator* method. The *QueryManager* object gives direct access to the submitted query through the *UserQuery* property. Any manipulation of the query text occurs before the query is executed. This gives you the opportunity to implement search customizations that were not possible in earlier versions of SharePoint. For example, Listing 15-4 shows a complete Web Part that manipulates the submitted query by adding an *AssignedTo* qualifier to the current query. The effect of this change is that the search results will contain only items that are assigned to the current user. To use the custom Web Part, you would simply replace the Core Search Results Web Part on the search results page.

LISTING 15-4 Manipulating the query text in a custom Web Part

```
using System;
using System.ComponentModel;
using System.Web.UI;
using System.Web.UI.WebControls;
using System.Web.UI.WebControls.WebParts;
using Microsoft.SharePoint;
using Microsoft.SharePoint.WebControls;
using Microsoft.Office.Server.Search.Query;
using Microsoft.Office.Server.Search.WebControls;
using System.Xml.XPath;

namespace CustomSearchParts.AssignedToMeResults {

  public class AssignedToMeResults : CoreResultsWebPart {
    protected override XPathNavigator GetXPathNavigator(string viewPath) {

      // get reference to Query Manager
      QueryManager queryManager =
        SharedQueryManager.GetInstance(this.Page).QueryManager;

      // Modify User Query
      queryManager.UserQuery +=
        " AssignedTo:" + SPContext.Current.Web.CurrentUser.LoginName +
        " AssignedTo:" + SPContext.Current.Web.CurrentUser.Name;

      return base.GetXPathNavigator(viewPath);
    }
  }
}
```

In addition to gaining access to the *QueryManager*, developers can access the federated search locations associated with the SSA. Accessing the collection of federated locations opens up additional search customizations through the *Location* object. For example, Listing 15-5 shows a complete Web Part that exposes a *RankingModelId* property. Earlier in the chapter, the *DefaultRankingModelId* property was altered by exporting and importing the Search Core Results Web Part. By creating a custom Web Part, you can expose the property directly in the Web Part.

LISTING 15-5 Modifying properties on federated search locations

```
using System;
using System.ComponentModel;
using System.Web.UI;
using System.Web.UI.WebControls;
using System.Web.UI.WebControls.WebParts;
using Microsoft.SharePoint;
using Microsoft.SharePoint.WebControls;
using Microsoft.Office.Server.Search.Query;
using Microsoft.Office.Server.Search.WebControls;
using System.Xml.XPath;

namespace CustomSearchParts.RankingModelIdResults {
  public class RankingModelIdResults : CoreResultsWebPart {

    //Use default ranking model to start
    private string rankingModelId = "8f6fd0bc-06f9-43cf-bbab-08c377e083f4";

    [ Personalizable(PersonalizationScope.Shared),
      WebBrowsable(true),
      WebDescription("The ID of the Ranking Model to use"),
      WebDisplayName("Ranking Model ID"),
      Category("Configuration") ]
    public string RankingModelID {
      get { return rankingModelId; }
      set { rankingModelId = value; }
    }

    protected override XPathNavigator GetXPathNavigator(string viewPath) {
      try {
        QueryManager queryManager =
          SharedQueryManager.GetInstance(this.Page).QueryManager;
        foreach (LocationList locList in queryManager) {
          foreach (Location loc in locList)
            try { loc.RankingModelID = RankingModelID; }
            catch { }
        }
      }
      catch { }

      return base.GetXPathNavigator(viewPath);
    }
  }
}
```

Working with Keyword Query Syntax

While users are generally familiar with typing a keyword into the search box to initiate a search, they are not often familiar with the special keyword query syntax supported by SharePoint. Keyword query syntax allows users to enter keywords, phrases, and Managed Property names to create sophisticated searches. In addition, keyword query syntax supports operations and wildcards.

The simplest form of keyword query is to enter a single term, without spaces or punctuation (for example, Training). This form will cause SharePoint to search both the index and the Metadata Properties, returning all matching results. A more sophisticated search would involve multiple keywords, but these must be enclosed in quotations (for example, "Training Materials").

Required and excluded terms may be added to the query using plus (+) and minus (-) signs. For example, the following query returns results for the term "business" except when it is used in the phrase "Business Connectivity Services" or "Business Intelligence."

```
business - "Business Connectivity Services" -"Business Intelligence"
```

Operators may also be used with keywords. This includes Boolean operators, wildcards, and arithmetic. Boolean operations are done using the *AND* and *OR* operators. Wildcards are supported via an asterisk (*). The following examples show a query with a Boolean operator.

```
"Business Connectivity Services" OR "Business Intelligence"
```

Managed Properties may also be used as filters for keyword queries. This allows you to create queries that use the full power of the keyword query syntax against specific fields. Table 15-3 shows several keyword queries along with an explanation.

TABLE 15-3 Keyword Query Samples

Query	Description
`Lastname:A*`	Returns people whose last name starts with *A*
`AverageRating>0`	Returns items whose average rating is greater than zero
`Training +isDocument:1`	Returns documents that are related to training
`Training +Author:"Scot Hillier"`	Returns items authored by Scot Hillier
`Client AND Server`	Returns items containing both "Client" and "Server"

Along with using keyword query syntax in Search Center, developers may also create custom search Web Parts based on keyword queries. The *KeywordQuery* class contains the functionality necessary to issue keyword queries programmatically. The *KeywordQuery* class contains several properties for preparing the query and an *Execute* method to run the query. The query results are returned as a *ResultTableCollection*, which contains a collection of *IDataReader* objects. Listing 15-6 shows the basic code for using the class.

LISTING 15-6 Using the KeywordQuery class

```
SearchServiceApplicationProxy proxy =
    (SearchServiceApplicationProxy)SearchServiceApplicationProxy.GetProxy(
                    SPServiceContext.GetContext(SPContext.Current.Site));

KeywordQuery keywordQuery = new KeywordQuery(proxy);
keywordQuery.ResultsProvider = SearchProvider.Default;
keywordQuery.ResultTypes = ResultType.RelevantResults;
keywordQuery.EnableStemming = false;
keywordQuery.TrimDuplicates = true;
keywordQuery.QueryText = query;
ResultTableCollection results = keywordQuery.Execute;
ResultTable result = results[ResultType.RelevantResults];

DataTable table = new DataTable;
table.Load(result, LoadOption.OverwriteChanges);
myGrid.DataSource = table;
myGrid.DataBind;
```

To use the *KeywordQuery* class, you must create an instance that references the SSA proxy. Once the class is created, then you can set the *QueryText* property with keyword query syntax. Additional properties, such as *TrimDuplicates* and *EnableStemming,* allow finer control over the query. When the results are returned, you may process them manually or bind them directly to a control.

Working with SQL Full-Text Search

Along with keyword queries, you may also create solutions that use Enterprise SQL Search Query syntax. Enterprise SQL Search Query syntax is a full query language that gives you significant control over the executed query. The following code shows a query that returns the documents that were added to the SharePoint portal within the past week.

```
SELECT url, title, author
FROM Scope
WHERE "scope" = 'All Sites'
AND isDocument=1
AND write >DATEADD(Day,-7,GetGMTDate)
```

You can see that the Enterprise SQL Search Query syntax is straightforward. The *SELECT* part is used to designate the columns to return from the query. The *FROM* part always contains the *Scope* statement, refined by the *WHERE* part, which specifies the exact scope to search. The *WHERE* part also contains the filters to apply. The *WHERE* part supports arithmetic operators, Boolean operators, and more specific full-text predicates, such as *FREETEXT* and *CONTAINS. FREETEXT* matches the meanings of phrases against fields, while *CONTAINS* does a straight match against the text in a field.

The *FullTextSqlQuery* class is used to create and issue queries based on the Enterprise SQL Search Query syntax. Using the *FullTextQuery* class is similar to using the *KeywordQuery* class. The query is set in the *QueryText* property, and additional properties are available to refine the search. Like the *KeywordQuery* class, the *FullTextQuery* class returns results as a *ResultTableCollection*. Listing 15-7 shows the code to use the *FullTextQuery* class.

LISTING 15-7 Using the FullTextSqlQuery class

```
SearchServiceApplicationProxy proxy =
  (SearchServiceApplicationProxy)SearchServiceApplicationProxy.GetProxy(
SPServiceContext.GetContext(SPContext.Current.Site));
FullTextSqlQuery queryObject = new FullTextSqlQuery(proxy);
queryObject.ResultsProvider = SearchProvider.Default;
queryObject.ResultTypes = ResultType.RelevantResults;
queryObject.EnableStemming = true;
queryObject.TrimDuplicates = true;
queryObject.QueryText = queryString;
ResultTableCollection results = queryObject.Execute;
```

Creating .NET Assembly Connectors for Search

As mentioned earlier in the chapter, .NET Assembly Connectors replace Protocol Handlers as the mechanism that the indexing engine uses to access various repositories. You can create a .NET Assembly Connector to index any external system, including databases, proprietary document managements systems, and custom applications. So long as you have access to an API for the external system, you can create a .NET Assembly Connector to support indexing and searching that system. Because .NET Assembly Connector fundamentals were covered in Chapter 13, this chapter will focus only on the requirements for enabling search.

Search-Enabling a Model

Whenever any External Content Type (ECT) is created in BCS, there is an XML model that gets created behind the scenes. This model defines the external system, entities, relationships, methods, and user access rights for the ECT. The same is true when a .NET Assembly Connector is created. The primary difference is that the external system is defined as an association between a .NET assembly and the ECT.

When you use SPD to create ECTs, the model is generated for you so that you never have to deal with XML directly. When you use Visual Studio 2010 to create a .NET Assembly Connector, you also have design tools that hide the XML, but you often have to edit the XML model manually to get the exact capabilities you need. In Visual Studio, the XML model is contained in a file with a *.bdcm* extension. When this file is opened, it appears in three windows. First, a design surface is available for creating entities. Second, a detail section is available for method definitions. Third, the BDC Explorer is available for browsing the model. Figure 15-5 shows the three windows of information for the model described in Chapter 13. This model used a .NET Assembly Connector to connect with product information.

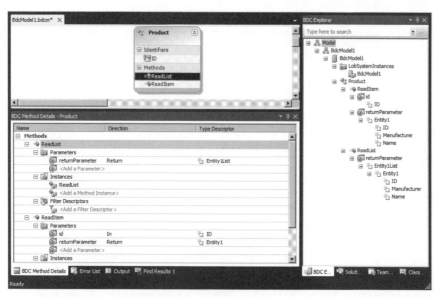

FIGURE 15-5 Viewing a .NET Assembly Connector

You may view the XML for the model directly by right-clicking the *.bdcm* file in the Solution Explorer and selecting Open With from the context menu. When the Open With dialog appears, select to open the file with the XML Editor. If you study the XML model alongside the BDC Explorer, you will begin to see that the BDC Explorer contains a node for each key element in the model. This concept is important because you typically will be adding information to model elements when you prepare a .NET Assembly Connector to support search.

To search-enable an existing model, you must make two changes. The first change is to designate which method to call during the indexing process. The second change allows the model to appear as a content source in search. Both changes are simple edits to the XML.

Chapter 13 discussed BCS operations in detail. In particular, *Finder* methods were defined as methods that return many records from an external system. Essentially, a *Finder* method defines a view of an external system. When search crawls an external system, it needs to know which of the available *Finder* methods represents the entire population of records to index. This finder method is known as the *RootFinder* method.

In your .NET Assembly Connector, you designate the *RootFinder* by first selecting the method instance in the Method Details pane. When you select it, the Properties window in Visual Studio 2010 will show details for the method. From this window, you can open the Custom Properties collection. In the Property Editor window, you can enter the *RootFinder* designation with a *Type* of *System.String* and a *Value* of *x*. Figure 15-6 shows the modifications being made to the sample from Chapter 13.

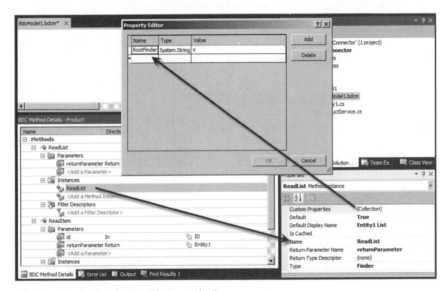

FIGURE 15-6 Setting the *RootFinder* method

After setting *RootFinder*, you can open the model XML in Visual Studio and see how the new information was added to the model. The following code shows the resulting XML.

```
<MethodInstances>
  <MethodInstance Type="Finder"
    ReturnParameterName="returnParameter"
    Default="true" Name="ReadList"
    DefaultDisplayName="Entity1 List">
    <Properties>
        <Property Name="RootFinder" Type="System.String">x</Property>
    </Properties>
  </MethodInstance>
</MethodInstances>
```

Once *RootFinder* is defined, you must make a change to allow the .NET Assembly Connector to appear as a content source in search. This is accomplished by applying the *ShowInSearchUI* property to the model. This property is applied by selecting the *LobSystemInstance* for your project under the *LobSystemInstances* folder in the model explorer. You may then create the property, again setting its value to *x*, using the same technique as for *RootFinder*. Figure 15-7 shows the modifications.

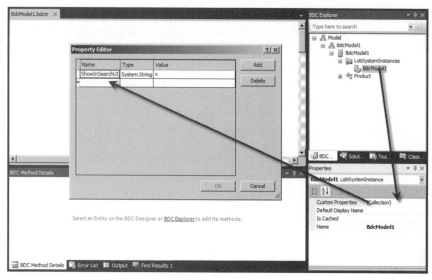

FIGURE 15-7 Applying the *ShowInSearchUI* property

After applying the *ShowInSearchUI* property to the model, it is a good idea to examine the XML and verify the change. The following code shows the modified model for the sample in Chapter 14, "Enterprise Content Management."

```
<LobSystemInstances>
  <LobSystemInstance Name="BdcModel1" >
    <Properties>
      <Property Name="ShowInSearchUI" Type="System.String">x</Property>
    </Properties>
  </LobSystemInstance>
</LobSystemInstances>
```

Once you have completed the two modifications, the model is search-enabled. You may deploy the feature and immediately select it as a search content source. It is worth noting that when you create models using SPD, the *RootFinder* and *ShowInSearchUI* properties are added automatically.

Implementing Security in Search Results

While search-enabling a BCS model is fairly simple, this process provides no security checking against search queries. This means that when a search is run against the external system, all matching results will be returned regardless of whether the current user is supposed to see them. In most production applications, you will want to implement an access control list (ACL) that specifies rights for the records returned when searching with a .NET Assembly Connector. This is accomplished by adding a special method to the model called a *BinarySecurityDescriptorAccessor* method.

The process to implement security begins by adding a new method to the model. In Visual Studio, you can right-click the entity in the design surface and select Add New Method from the context menu. You can then give it a name such as *ReadSecurityDescriptor*. Once created, the method will appear in the Method Details pane.

Now in the Method Details pane, you must create a new method instance beneath the new method. Once the new method instance is created, you can change its *Type* in the Properties window to *BinarySecurityDescriptorAccessor*.

The new method instance will require input and output parameters. Typically, the input parameters are the identifier for an item and the user name of the current user. The output parameter must be a *byte* array that holds the security descriptor. The following code shows the XML for the new method.

```xml
<Method Name="ReadSecurityDescriptor">
  <Parameters>
    <Parameter Name="id" Direction="In">
      <TypeDescriptor Name="ID" TypeName="System.String" IdentifierName="ID" />
    </Parameter>
    <Parameter Name="acl" Direction="Return">
      <TypeDescriptor Name="SecurityDescriptor"
        TypeName="System.Byte[]" IsCollection="true" >
        <TypeDescriptors>
          <TypeDescriptor Name="SecurityDescriptorByte" TypeName="System.Byte"/>
        </TypeDescriptors>
      </TypeDescriptor>
    </Parameter>
  </Parameters>
  <MethodInstances>
    <MethodInstance Name="ReadSecurityDescriptorInstance"
      Type="BinarySecurityDescriptorAccessor" ReturnParameterName="acl"/>
  </MethodInstances>
</Method>
```

When you create the new method definition, Visual Studio will automatically generate a method stub in code that accepts the input parameters and returns a byte array. Your job is to write code for this method that creates an ACL for the item.

When the *BinarySecurityDescriptorAccessor* method is called during the indexing process, *username* will be the account performing the search crawl. This is fine because this account will simply be designated as the owner account for the ACL. In the method, you may add other permissions for users based on whatever criteria you need. For example, the code in Listing 15-8 grants access to all users.

LISTING 15-8 Creating a security ACL

```
public static byte[] ReadSecurityDescriptor(string id, string username) {
  try {
    //Grant everyone access
    NTAccount workerAcc = new NTAccount(
    username.Split('\\')[0], username.Split('\\')[1]);
    SecurityIdentifier workerSid =
        (SecurityIdentifier)workerAcc.Translate(typeof(SecurityIdentifier));
    SecurityIdentifier everyone =
        new SecurityIdentifier(WellKnownSidType.WorldSid, null);
    CommonSecurityDescriptor csd = new CommonSecurityDescriptor(
        false, false, ControlFlags.None, workerSid, null, null, null);
    csd.SetDiscretionaryAclProtection(true, false);
    csd.DiscretionaryAcl.AddAccess(
    AccessControlType.Allow, everyone, unchecked((int)0xffffffffL),
    InheritanceFlags.None, PropagationFlags.None);
    byte[] secDes = new byte[csd.BinaryLength];
    csd.GetBinaryForm(secDes, 0);
    return secDes;
  }
  catch (Exception x)  {
    PortalLog.LogString("Product Model (ReadSecurityDescriptor): {0}", x.Message);
    return null;
  }
}
```

After creating the *BinarySecurityDescriptorAccessor* method, a property must be added to the *Product* entity to hold the ACL. In the sample, this property is named *SecurityDescriptor*. The model must then be updated to relate the *BinarySecurityDescriptorAccessor* method to the *SecurityDescriptor* property. The following code shows how to relate the entity and the method instance.

```
<MethodInstances>

  <MethodInstance Name="ReadSecurityDescriptorInstance"
                  Type="BinarySecurityDescriptorAccessor"
                  ReturnParameterName="acl">
    <Properties>
      <Property Name="WindowsSecurityDescriptorField" Type="System.String">
        SecurityDescriptor
      </Property>
    </Properties>
  </MethodInstance>

<MethodInstances>
```

Crawling the .NET Assembly Connector

When your .NET Assembly Connector is complete, you should be able to select it as a content source and initiate a full crawl. When you crawl the solution for the first time, it's a good idea to attach Visual Studio to the crawl process (mssdmn.exe) and watch how the crawl progresses. Set breakpoints in the *Finder*, *SpecificFinder*, and *BinarySecurityDescriptorAccessor* methods. Also, be sure that you have granted access in the BCS service to the account that will perform the crawling.

When the crawl is initiated, you should see the *Finder* method called first. You'll then see the *SpecificFinder* called for each individual item returned from the *Finder* method. Along the way, the security descriptor should be built for each item. After the crawl completes, check the crawl log for errors. Now you can run a search against the crawled data. SharePoint should use the security descriptors that you constructed to limit access to items as appropriate.

Conclusion

This chapter focused on all the components necessary to create search-based applications in SharePoint 2010. When designing your solutions, you should give consideration to creating solutions that use search, either through keyword queries, full-text queries, or .NET Assembly Connectors, and present results to users so that they can be understood and acted upon. Keep in mind that search-based solutions include much more than just running queries and displaying results.

Index

Symbols

$ (dollar sign)
   ASP.NET syntax, 294
$filter command, 390
$ object shortcut, 387
$ operator, 387
$skip command, 390
$SPUrl expression, 164
$top command, 390
.ascx files, 178
.aspx pages, 147
.bdcm extension, 591
_controltemplates directory, 122,
   179
({}) curly braces
   GUIDs, 295
.dwp extension, 190
-eq Windows PowerShell comparison operator, 26
-ge Windows PowerShell comparison operator, 26
-gt Windows PowerShell comparison operator, 26
_layouts directory, 122, 155
-le Windows PowerShell comparison
   operator, 26
-like Windows PowerShell comparison operator, 26
-lt Windows PowerShell comparison
   operator, 26
~masterurl/default.master, 136
.NET 3.5, 5
.NET Assembly Connectors, 496,
   525, 531–534, 573
.NET Assembly Connectors for
   search, 590–596
   crawling the .NET Assembly
      Connector, 596
   implementing security in search
      results, 593–595
   search-enabling a
      model, 590–593
.NET Framework, 36
   asynchronous programming, 220
   JavaScript client object
      model, 378
.NET objects, 29
.NET serialization, 287
-ne Windows PowerShell comparison operator, 26

-notlike Windows PowerShell comparison operator, 26
(pound sign)
   parameter value, 312
~sitecollection token, 156
:: (two colons) operator, 29
.webpart extension, 190
.webpart file, 200
.xml file, 200

A

AccessChecker method, 511
access rights, 16
accordions, 388
ACL (access control list), 456
   rights, 593
Action element, 420, 423
action function, 419
actions, 403
   custom, 419–426
   workflow, 397
activate scope, 314
activating
   features, 61, 80
activation dependencies, 53, 303
   about, 52
ActivationDependency
   element, 303
activation scope, 314
Active Directory Domain Services, 6
Activities property, 428
Activity class, 421
ActivityExecutionContext
   parameter, 422
ActivityExecutionStatus
   enumeration, 423
ActivityId filter, 515
adding
   application pages, 151
   CAML elements to elements.
      xml, 156
   Content controls, 159
   CSS rules, 184
   elements, 182
   event handlers, 155
   event receivers to brand child
      sites, 165
   Feature Receivers, 76
   feature receivers to apply brand-
      ing attributes, 162
   features, 75

fields to a list using site
   columns, 239
files to document libraries, 346
HTML meta tags, 184
with LINQ to SharePoint, 342–344
SharePoint project items, 78–82
user controls to pages, 181
AddLookup method, 233
Add method, 127, 140, 227, 249,
   266, 346
Add New Item dialog, 79
Add-PSSnapin, 31
AD DS (Active Directory Domain
   Services), 455
   claims architecture, 475
   implementing, 473
   synchronizing data, 521
AD DS group
   SSS, 501
AddStyleAttribute method, 171
AddWrkfl.aspx, 430
administrating sandbox
   solutions, 108–116
   Central Administration
      tools, 108–111
   using Site Collection tools, 115
   using Windows PowerShell, 114
AdministrationMetadataCatalog
   object, 528
Administraton Object
   Model, 528–530
AdminTasks server template, 326
ADO.NET code
   reading and writing from Share-
      Point databases, 8
ADO.NET Data Services. See WCF
   Data Services
Advanced Search, 581
Advanced Search Box, 574
AfterProperties collection
   property, 272
Agenda server template, 326
AJAX
   JavaScipt client object model, 382
AJAX list controls, 384
alerts, 571
All Items view, 235
AllowMultipleControls
   attribute, 184
AllowPartiallyTrustedCallers
   attribute, 92

K

Kerberos, 505
KeywordQuery class, 588
keywords
    query syntax, 588
    var keyword, 334

L

lambda expressions, 333
language
    term sets, 560
languageFeature element, 578
LastId filter, 515
LastModifiedTimeStamp
    property, 513
LAYOUTS directory, 102, 105
LayoutsPageBase class, 152, 157
layouts.sitemap file, 158, 159
LCID parameter, 563
length normalization
    ranking models, 579
lengthNormalization attribute, 578,
    579, 580
Leq element, 323
-le Windows PowerShell comparison
    operator, 26
L (Extensible Markup Language)
    Application Model XML, 528
LFWP (List Form Web Part), 517
libraries
    BAL, 427
    check-in/checkout
        documents, 539
    creating and interacting with indi-
        vidual files, 540
    document libraries, 248–258,
        344–351, 346, 459
    Document Library, 226
    Drop Off Library, 537
    Form Library, 226
    In-Place Records
        Management, 550
    lists and content types, 395
    Managed client object
        model, 366
    MicrosoftAjax.js script library, 383
    Pages library, 581
    Picture Library, 226
    SharePoint Foundation Activity
        Library, 427
    Silverlight.js library, 377
    Style Library, 162–166
    Web Part Gallery, 189
    wiki page libraries, 18
    Wiki Page Library, 226
library object model
    about, 344–347

life cycle events, 383
-like Windows PowerShell compari-
    son operator, 26
Limited Access site role, 470
Limit filter, 515
Link content type, 241
LinkFilenameNoMenu field, 248
Links List, 226
Links server template, 325
LinkTitle field, 230
LinkTitleNoMenu field, 231
LinkTitleNoMenu site column, 236
LinkTitle site column, 236
LINQ, 329–335, 335–344, 564
    about, 330
    adding, deleting and updating to
        SharePoint, 342–344
    generating entities with
        SPMetal, 335–340
    JOIN operation, 235
    language elements, 331–335
    Managed Metadata columns, 565
    queries, 351
    querying to SharePoint, 340
    returning collections, 357
LINQ queries, 358, 365, 526
list
    libraries and content types, 395
    Tabs In Search Pages list, 582
List Actions, 404
ListAdded event handler, 261
List attribute, 193
ListCreationInformation object, 364
ListData.svc, 389
List Definition From Content Type
    project item template, 298
List Definition project item
    template, 298
list definitions, 98, 292–303
    creating content type
        definitions, 296
    creating list definitions, 298–302
    creating site column
        definitions, 294
    feature activation
        dependencies, 302–303
List element, 339
ListInstance CAML element, 99
ListInstance element, 95, 226, 249,
    302, 439
ListInstance element type, 47
ListInstance items, 92
List instances, 98
ListItem, 355
ListItemCreationInformation
    object, 364
ListItem property, 273
list items
    creating, 364

displaying in Silverlight, 375
ListPrintingUtility, 100
list relationships, 233
lists, 225–247, 319–352. *See
    also* document library
    AJAX list control, 384
    Business Data Related List, 519
    content types, 241–247
    creating, 364
    creating and customizing, 18
    document libraries, 344–351
    document management, 537
    external lists, 491–494
    fields and field types, 229–235
    LINQ, 329–335, 335–344
    object model, 319
    querying lists with
        CAML, 321–329
    site columns, 236–240
    synchronizing in Outlook, 523
    Tabs In Search Results list, 582
    views, 235
Lists collection, 227
Lists element, 311
List Settings page, 19
ListSiteMapPath controls, 159
Lists property, 319, 324
List<string> collection, 111
ListTemplate CAML element, 99
ListTemplateCatalog server
    template, 326
ListTemplate element, 299
ListTemplate element type, 48
ListTemplateId attribute, 265
list templates, 225
ListTemplates element, 310
ListUrl attribute, 265
List View Threshold, 327
list workflows, 401
LoadControl method, 199
loading
    libraries, 377
    operations, 356–358
    pages in JavaScipt client object
        model and running code
        on, 382
Load method, 356
LoadQuery method, 356
logon credentials, 362
Log property, 337
LogToHistoryListActivity activity
    type, 436
lookup fields, 233
Lookup field type, 230
looping support, 418
Lt element, 323
-lt Windows PowerShell comparison
    operator, 26

About the Authors

Ted Pattison

Ted Pattison is an author, instructor, and co-founder of Critical Path Training (*www.CriticalPathTraining.com*), a company dedicated to education on SharePoint technologies. For the last five years, Ted has worked with Microsoft's Developer Platform Evangelism group research-ing and authoring SharePoint training material for early adopters. Ted started working with SharePoint 2010 in August of 2008 and since that time has led a series of training classes in which he has already taught hundreds of professional developers how to get started building custom business solutions using the SharePoint 2010 platform.

You can visit Ted's blog at *http://blog.tedpattison.net*.

Andrew Connell

Andrew Connell is an author, instructor, and co-founder of Critical Path Training, a SharePoint education–focused company. He has a background in content management solutions and Web development that spans back to his time as a student at the University of Florida in the late 1990s managing class sites. He has consistently focused on the challenges facing business today to maintain a current and dynamic online presence without having to rely constantly on Web developers or have a pro-ficiency in Web technologies.

Andrew is a six-time recipient of Microsoft's Most Valuable Professional (MVP) award (2005–2010) for Microsoft Content Management Server (MCMS) & Microsoft SharePoint Server. He has authored and contributed to numerous MCMS and SharePoint books over the years, in-cluding his book *Professional SharePoint 2007 Web Content Management Development*. He is also the author of numerous articles on the Microsoft Developer Network (MSDN).

Andrew has spoken on the subject of SharePoint development and WCM at conferences such as TechEd, SharePoint Connections, VSLive, SharePoint Best Practice Conference, SharePoint Evolutions Conference, Microsoft's TechReady Conference, Office Developer Conference, and Microsoft SharePoint Conference in the United States, Australia, England, Spain, and the Netherlands.

You can find Andrew on his blog (*http://www.andrewconnell.com/blog*) or follow him on Twitter *@andrewconnell*.

Scot Hillier

Scot Hillier is an independent consultant and Microsoft SharePoint Most Valuable Professional (MVP) focused on creating solutions for information workers with SharePoint, Office, and related .NET technologies. He is the author/coauthor of 15 books and DVDs on Microsoft technologies, including *Professional Business Connectivity Services*.

Scot splits his time between consulting on SharePoint projects, speaking at SharePoint events like Tech Ed, and delivering training for SharePoint Developers. Scot is a former U.S. Navy submarine officer and graduate of the Virginia Military Institute.

Scot can be reached at *scot@shillier.com*.

David Mann

David Mann is a co-founder of Aptillon (*www.aptillon.com*), a leading SharePoint-focused consulting company, a part-time trainer for Critical Path Training, and a four-time SharePoint MVP. As a developer, software architect, author, and trainer, he has focused on Microsoft's Information Worker and Collaboration stack, working with portal, collaboration, and content management technologies for over 14 years.

Dave is the founder of the Tri-State SharePoint User Group, focused on developer, administrator, and end-user topics covering SharePoint and the entire Office System. He is the author of *Workflow in the 2007 Microsoft Office System* and has written whitepapers for MSDN and articles for magazines and online sites. He presents regularly at SharePoint and Office user groups and code camps and has presented or moderated sessions at major conferences, including Tech Ed, Microsoft's SharePoint Conference, the Microsoft Office Developer's Conference, and the SharePoint Best Practices Conference. Dave has also done MSDN webcasts on topics related to SharePoint development.